POSTERS

IDENTIFICATION
AND PRICE GUIDE

With best wishes —

Tony Fusco

IDENTIFICATION AND PRICE GUIDE

2ND EDITION

TONY FUSCO

The **CONFIDENT COLLECTOR**™

AVON BOOKS ◆ NEW YORK

Important Notice: All of the information, including valuations, in this book has been compiled from the most reliable sources, and every effort has been made to eliminate errors and questionable data. Nevertheless, the possibility of error always exists in a work of such scope. The publisher and the author will not be held responsible for losses which may occur in the purchase, sale, or other transaction of property because of information contained herein. Readers who feel they have discovered errors are invited to *write* the author in care of Avon Books so that the errors may be corrected in subsequent editions.

THE CONFIDENT COLLECTOR: POSTERS IDENTIFICATION AND PRICE GUIDE (2nd edition) is an original publication of Avon Books. This edition has never before appeared in book form.

AVON BOOKS
A division of
The Hearst Corporation
1350 Avenue of the Americas
New York, New York 10019

Copyright © 1994 by Tony Fusco
Inside cover author photo by Robert Four
The Confident Collector and its logo are trademarked properties of Avon Books.
Interior design by Robin Arzt
Published by arrangement with the author
Library of Congress Catalog Card Number: 93-42431
ISBN: 0-380-77010-5

Library of Congress Cataloging in Publication Data:

Fusco, Tony.
    The confident collector posters identification and price guide /
Tony Fusco.
        p.   cm.
    Includes bibliographical references and index.
    1. Posters—Collectors and collecting—Catalogs.   I. Title.
    NC1810.F86   1994   93-42431
    741.6'74'075—dc20   CIP

First Avon Books Trade Printing: May 1994

AVON TRADEMARK REG. U.S. PAT. OFF. AND IN OTHER COUNTRIES, MARCA REGISTRADA. HECHO EN U.S.A.

Printed in the U.S.A.
ARC 10 9 8 7 6 5 4 3 2 1

❦ CONTENTS ❦

❦ ACKNOWLEDGMENTS ❦

We have pooled the information you will find in this volume from scores of expert resources across the United States and Europe in an attempt to present as comprehensive an overview of the poster field today as the pages of this guide will allow. As far as we know, this guide is unique in the world of poster collecting, and even more so because of the many individuals who contributed their time and energy to make it happen. We want to acknowledge those who have provided that help.

First we would like to thank those individuals who agreed to contribute chapters and articles for this volume, in the order in which they appear: Kathryn Myatt Carey, conservator, Medford, Massachusetts; Richard Rudnitsky, Vintage European and American Posters, Miami, Florida; Linda Tarasuk, La Belle Epoque, New York, New York; Bernice Jackson, Bernice Jackson Fine Arts, Concord, Massachusetts; Frank Fox, professor of history specializing in Eastern Europe, Merion Station, Pennsylvania; John Heller, Heller & Heller/Posters at Work, New Rochelle, New York; George Dembo, The Poster Master, Chatham, New Jersey; Mary Ellen Meehan, Meehan Military Posters, New York, New York; Harvey Abrams, olympic historian, Harvey Abrams Books, State College, Pennsylvania; Ken Trombly, P.C., dealer and specialist in magic posters, Washington, D.C.; and Mark Wilson, private collector specializing in cartoon posters, Castle Rock, Washington.

On a subject-by-subject basis, we would also like to thank the following individuals who contributed their time, materials, collecting information, advice, and photographs. Many are new colleagues, and many of these same individuals assisted with the first edition of this guide, and their information continues to be useful in building the body of resource and reference material available to us.

French and Belgian Posters: Nicolas Bailly, Bailly Fine Arts, New York, New York; Barbara Kaplan, Circa 1900, Morganville, New Jersey; Jacques Athias, Club of American Collectors of Fine Arts, New York, New York; Steve Harris, Sarah Stocking, and Dennis Lewis, Harris Gallery, Berkeley, California; Lucy Broido, Lucy Broido Graphics, Bryn Mawr, Pennsylvania; Laura Gold, Park South Gallery, New York, New York; Steven D. Little, Pasquale Iannetti Art Galleries, San Francisco, California; Susan Reinhold and Robert Brown, Reinhold Brown Gallery, New York; Stephen Ganeles, Stephen Ganeles Antique Posters & Prints, New York, New York; Thomas Boss, Thomas G. Boss

Fine Books, Boston, Massachusetts; and Benno Bordiga, William R. Davis Fine Arts, New York, New York.

Italian Posters: Bernice Jackson, Bernice Jackson Fine Arts, Concord, Massachusetts; and Kate Hendrickson, Chicago, Illinois.

Swiss Posters: Eric Kellenberger, The Kellenberger Collection, Blonay, Switzerland; and Bernice Jackson, Bernice Jackson Fine Arts, Concord, Massachusetts.

English Posters: David Gartler, Poster Plus, Chicago, Illinois; Richard Barclay, Barclay-Samson, Ltd., London, England; John Cumming, Bloomsbury Book Auctions, London, England; Jacques Athias, Club of American Collectors of Fine Arts, New York, New York; and the Cooper Hewitt Museum, New York, New York.

Dutch Posters: Stephen Ganeles, Stephen Ganeles Antique Posters & Prints, New York, New York; Bernice Jackson, Bernice Jackson Fine Arts, Concord, Massachusetts; James Lapides, private collector, New Haven, Connecticut; and Piet Van Sabben, Van Sabben Poster Auctions, Bennebroekerlaan, Holland.

Polish Posters: Frank Fox, Merion Station, Pennsylvania; Judy Sullivan, Eastern European Art Company, Carbondale, Colorado; and Al Hoch, private collector, Lexington, Massachusetts.

American Turn-of-the-Century Posters: Gail Chisholm, Chisholm Gallery, New York, New York; Joseph Goddu, Hirschl & Adler Galleries, New York, New York; and Thomas Boss, Thomas G. Boss Fine Books, Boston, Massachusetts.

Mather Work Incentive Posters: John Heller, Heller & Heller/Posters at Work, New Rochelle, New York.

The Posters of Ben Shahn: George Dembo, The Poster Master, Chatham, New Jersey.

The Posters of David Lance Goines: Sean Thackrey and Sally Robertson, Thackrey & Robertson, San Francisco, California; and Thomas Boss, Thomas G. Boss Fine Books, Boston, Massachusetts.

Mobil Oil Posters: Arthur Bernberg, Great Expectations, Inc.; and Seymour Chwast, The Pushpin Group, New York, New York.

World War Posters: Mary Ellen Meehan, Meehan Military Posters, New York, New York; and David Gartler, Poster Plus, Chicago, Illinois.

Travel and Transportation Posters: Steve Harris, Sarah Stocking, and Dennis Lewis, Harris Gallery, Berkeley, California; Nancy Steinbock

Posters and Prints, Albany, New York; Bernice Jackson, Bernice Jackson Fine Arts, Concord, Massachusetts; Mike Slemmer, private collector, Cambridge, Massachusetts; Al Hoch, private collector, Lexington, Massachusetts; and John and Valerie Mickey, private collectors, Vancouver, Canada.

Olympic Posters: Harvey Abrams, Harvey Abrams Books, State College, Pennsylvania.

Magic Posters: Ken Trombly, P.C., Washington, D.C.; and Caroline Birenbaum, Swann Galleries, New York, New York.

Cinema Posters: Michael Schwartz, Camden House Auctioneers, Beverly Hills, California; Ron Davis and Joe Burtis, Hollywood Poster Art, Hackensack, New Jersey; Walter and Roger Reed, Illustration House, New York, New York; Bill Miller, Odyssey Auctions, Corona, California; Jim Valk, Cinema City, Muskegon, Michigan; Dwight Cleveland, Chicago, Illinois; and Morris Everett, The Last Moving Picture Company, Cleveland, Ohio, and Hollywood California.

Cartoon Posters: Mark Wilson, Castle Rock, Washington.

We are sure that you will note the wide-ranging participation of numerous auction houses throughout this volume. We want to extend our thanks to several individuals, some of whom are also mentioned above, who worked with us to provide background information, photographs, and prices realized on the full range of poster-collecting areas you find represented here.

Our special thanks to Cynthia Stern and Pamela Tapp at Butterfield & Butterfield, San Francisco and Los Angeles, California; Nancy McClelland, Roberta Maneker, and Susan Britman, of Christie's and Christie's East, New York, New York; Richard Barclay of Christie's London, England; Maron Matz Hindman, of Leslie Hindman Auctioneers, Chicago, Illinois; R. Neil and Elaine Reynolds, Poster Mail Auction, Waterford, Virginia; Phelps Fullerton, formerly of Rivo Olivers, Kennebunk, Maine; Piet Van Sabben, Van Sabben Poster Auctions, Bennebroekerlaan, Holland; and an extremely special big, big thanks to Caroline Birenbaum of Swann Galleries, New York, New York.

The poster field is lucky to have attracted many talented writers and scholars who have devoted years and even lifetimes to studying and writing about the field. We are indebted to writers such as Richard Allen, Victor Arwas, Lucy Broido, Robert K. Brown and Susan Reinhold, Joseph Darracott, Bevis Hillier, David Keihl, Eric Kellenberger, Patricia Franz Kery, Jack Rennert, Alain Weill, Stuart

Wrede, and many others who have made significant contributions to the body of information available today on posters.

We also wish to thank many private collectors who allowed us to photograph their poster collections, and our assistant, Todd Bachmann, for his enormous help on this volume. Last but not least we wish to express our thanks to our friends, editor Dorothy Harris and assistant editor Karen Shapiro, for their great support on several collecting guide projects over the years, and to Lisa Considine, associate editor at Avon Books, for always being there to help.

When we wrote the first edition of this guide, we told those who might be interested that our goal was not to just create a price guide, but to foster a network of collectors, dealers, auction houses, museums, and resources interested in the world of posters. In this, our second edition, we hope that we have strengthened that network even further. Now we invite you to join the network by taking advantage of the hundreds of resources we have assembled here.

—Tony Fusco and Robert Four

PART ONE

An Introduction to the Field

❦ CHAPTER 1 ❦
The World of Posters

From the late 1800s until after the turn of the century, Europe and America were in a frenzy over a new form of advertising, which was also a new form of art: the illustrated color advertising poster. Gone were drab streets and boring broadsides. The boulevards of Paris, the tiny streets of Belgium and Holland, the otherwise solemn squares of London, and the shop windows of the United States proliferated with colorful images—a veritable public poster parade—created by some of the most talented artists of the times.

Today, as more and more posters become "antiques," reaching the one-hundred-year-old mark, the popularity of posters is at an all-time high. The market for posters today is sophisticated, increasingly complex, and more global.

The first all-poster auction was held in this country in 1979. Since that time, the collecting field has expanded widely to include the creative output of numerous countries and several subject specializations. Even posters of relatively recent origin have seen dramatic increases in attention, scholarship, and prices, especially as the recognition of graphic design in general has grown.

THE FIRST POSTER COLLECTORS

In the late 1800s, the illustrated or "pictorial" poster was quickly seized upon by collectors and enthusiasts. Luckily for us, some of these zealous early collectors crept through the night to sponge off posters from the walls of buildings and secrete them away. Poster shows and exhibitions abounded, drawing thousands of visitors. Poster collecting clubs, societies, and publications sprang up all over Europe and the United States.

It was not long before poster artists and publishers realized they could overprint a commercial edition and make it available for sale through print dealers, such as Editions Sagot on Rue Chateaudun in Paris. Early French artists such as Mucha, Berthon, and others issued decorative lithographic panels, which were essentially paper posters without type, which people could display in their homes.

During the 1890s, Sagot offered posters such as Toulouse-Lautrec's *La Revue Blanche* for 5 francs, and *Jane Avril* for 10 francs. Sagot also commissioned well-known artists, such as Paul Cesar Helleu, to create posters for his gallery. For his publications, Sagot commissioned works such as George De Feure's captivating poster for *Almanach de Paris* (see French poster Price Listings).

We've not found anyone who can totally explain why such a riotous collecting spree should have descended upon the lowly poster, a "poor cousin" of the fine arts. However, more than likely it was a combination of several factors.

Cities were burgeoning with the rise of a new merchant class that sought art for their homes. Posters were large decorative works that cost relatively little. In addition, illustrated advertising posters were a new notion and had stirred public interest. Each new poster was eagerly anticipated and written about.

Numerous publications and periodicals fanned the fires of the poster fad. As early as 1886, publishers were issuing illustrated catalogs and books of posters. Starting in 1896, under the direction of Jules Chéret, the Parisian printer Chaix started reproducing the best posters of Europe and America in miniature lithographic plates for collectors. Called *Les Maîtres de L'Affiche*, or "Masters of the Poster," each monthly issue contained four posters. In all, by 1900, 256 plates had been issued. (See the section on *Les Maîtres de l'Affiche* in the chapter on French and Belgian Posters.) Other publications and miniature poster issues for col-

English monthly magazine, *The Poster*. Courtesy of Poster Mail Auction Company.

lectors included *Les Affiches Illustrées* and the biweeklies *La Plume* and *L'Estampe et L'Affiche.*

In other countries, the poster craze was just as strong. In London a monthly magazine called *The Poster* kept collectors up-to-date with the latest news.

In Germany, *Das Plakat*, or "The Poster," included numerous finely printed tipped-in miniature posters from 1913 to 1921.

In the United States, collectors turned to the pages of *The Chap Book*, printed in Chicago from 1894 to 1897; William Bradley's *Bradley: His Book*, printed in Springfield, Massachusetts, from 1896 to 1897; *The Poster*, printed in Chicago from 1910 to 1930, and others. (See Bibliography for a full listing of Historical References.)

Whatever the reason for the phenomenal rise in the popularity of the poster by World War I the poster craze was all but extinguished. Poster collecting did flourish again between the two World Wars, but only briefly.

THE POSTER REVIVAL

During the 1960s in both Europe and the United States, there was a renewed interest in the decorative styles of the period between the turn of the century and the 1930s that focused primarily on Art Nouveau and Art Deco. Interest was heightened by important museum exhibitions of these decorative styles, including those featuring the works of Aubrey Beardsley, Alphonse Mucha, Cassandre, and others.

Evidence of this resurgence of interest can be seen in the impact early posters had on the designs of San Francisco rock posters of the late 1960s. One San Francisco publisher even took the name "Tea Lautrec Litho." Pop artists such as Andy Warhol, who was a notable collector of Art Deco, aided the popularization of commercial imagery.

Posters once again became popular collectibles, and the greatest artists could still be found in abundance at relatively low prices. For example, a 1966 Sotheby auction realized a price of 580 pounds, or about $1,000, for Toulouse-Lautrec's *Divan Japonais*, and a record price of 2,100 pounds, or about $3,800, for *Jane Avril*—both posters would easily bring over $30,000 today.

More articles and books about posters began to appear, written by the leading writers on the Art Deco and Art Nouveau styles. This group included Bevis Hillier and Victor Arwas. Poster exhibitions were mounted at museums, and more collectors became aware of their growing value.

By the end of the 1970s, the poster medium had firmly reestablished itself as a collecting field. In 1979 the auction house of Phillips in New York held the first all-poster auction in this country, with resounding success. Mucha's *La Dame aux Camelias* brought $16,500, and Toulouse-Lautrec's *Divan Japonais* brought $19,000 in a negotiated sale four days later. A rare poster by Charles Rennie Mackintosh produced for the Glasgow Institute of Art also brought $19,000 at an auction in France the same year.

Much of the market's attention in the late 1970s and early 1980s focused on the work of French artists such as Toulouse-Lautrec, Alphonse Mucha, Jules Chéret, and A. M. Cassandre. Today, while French posters remain perhaps the most popular, the posters of numerous other countries have taken their rightful place in the market and in private and institutional collections.

Unfortunately, a soft economy, overspeculation at early auctions, and the discovery that some posters were not as rare as originally thought all led to a "correction" in prices. Consequently the poster market cooled off from 1982 to 1985, with some prices declining quite rapidly. However, the poster had achieved the status of a firmly established collectible.

TODAY'S POSTER MARKET

Throughout the last half of the 1980s, the poster market rose steadily, pulled along, like most other art and collecting fields, by a booming economy. Many new price records were set. In 1989 a new record for a poster at auction was established at Poster Auctions International in New York for Toulouse-Lautrec's often-illustrated *Moulin Rouge* poster: $200,000 plus a 10 percent buyer's premium of $20,000.

Some of the upsurge in prices had to do with the greatly increased participation of foreign buyers in American art markets. When the recession hit, the poster market was not immune, and some prices dropped as much as 20 to 25 percent. Yet, even with this overall setback, posters still break records at auction, and more people seem willing to pay higher prices than ever before.

In specific areas, such as cinema posters, prices have actually increased even during the recession, though other factors are at work in that field. (See the chapter on Cinema Posters for more information on the current market.) The fiftieth anniversary of World War II has also caused price increases for related pieces.

For the most part the base of support for prices, the foundation for the poster market, is more stable and stronger than ever. Because the market is so broad, most poster prices have remained stable.

Recognition of their value has taken posters out of general antique and ephemera shows and put them into fine print and art fairs. However, visually striking posters are still within the reach of average collectors.

As the market has grown, it has also broadened tremendously. Scholarship and museum shows afford new discoveries every year. More books have been written on posters than on any other form of advertising, and several new volumes appear annually.

Long-undervalued areas have turned into specializations—turn-of-the-century American, Dutch, avant-garde and constructivist, Swiss, German, Italian, Hungarian, Russian, Polish, Danish— with collecting bases that can be expected to continue to grow through the next decade. Collecting by subject—war, travel, circus, magic, cinema, and other areas—has also become more specialized. In each chapter of this book we try to provide general market information on the specific field under review.

Today, growing numbers of "average" Americans appreciate and seek to own art, and for many the poster has become the art form of choice. By delving more deeply into the incredibly wide field of poster art, one is sure to be attracted to an artist, country, or subject. The investment of time and money will certainly reward the astute collector with both an appreciation of great art and, at least over the long term, an appreciation in value.

Contemporary poster publishers and patrons today, such as Lincoln Center, the School of Visual Arts in New York, and the Mobil Corporation's "Mobil Masterpiece Theatre" television productions, are creating outstanding, collectible posters by commissioning leading artists. Individual contemporary poster artists such as David Lance Goines are also highly popular with collectors. In other countries, contemporary artists are also receiving well-deserved recognition for their contributions to the world of posters.

The poster-collecting field never stays the same for very long. Posters of different subjects, artists, eras, and schools of design will come and go out of fashion. "New" artists will be discovered, and new records will be set.

For the future of poster collecting, one thing is certain: The poster market is now a fully established and increasingly well-respected collecting field and, as such, now faces new horizons and challenges for both dealers and collectors.

In compiling the information for this volume, we set out to overview the poster-collecting field as it is today, and to provide a reference for now and the future. In terms of the poster market, it's a snapshot of a moving target.

❦ CHAPTER 2 ❦
How to Use This Book

NOTE: This book is a market survey, not a bible. Our goals are to report on the market, to offer an overview and some specialized insights into poster collecting, and to provide a variety of resources. Our hope is that you come away with a broader knowledge and appreciation of posters, and get a sense of the market. Put this book to use by exploring the field that suits your interest and your pocketbook: Go to museums and shows, visit dealers, buy reference books and auction catalogs, and experience the market firsthand.

IF YOU CAN'T FIND IT HERE

We've introduced each section with an essay, often by a leading authority in the field, to give you a better sense of the scope of each area of poster collecting. Unfortunately, we could not mention all of the talented artists, graphic designers, printers, and others whose contributions have had an impact on poster history. In other words, if a particular artist or poster you are looking for is not included here, it does not necessarily mean that category or designer is not worth collecting.

We concentrated on those posters and artists a collector is most likely to find on the market today. The scarcity of posters by certain artists, such as posters of the Vienna Secession, has removed them almost entirely from the trading arena, making market information about them less accessible. Besides the countries we were able to cover individually in this volume, others, such as Japan, Scandinavian countries, Germany, Spain, Russia, and South America, have produced and continue to produce interesting poster designs. Note that some artists from these countries are included in subjects such as World War and Travel and Transportation.

TO FIND A PARTICULAR ARTIST

If you are looking for information on a particular artist, and know his or her nationality or the country or countries in which the artist worked or lived, look in the chapters on those countries first. However, you should also note that the artist you are looking for may also be included under one or more of the subject chapters. For example, Theophile Steinlen is included both in the chapter on French Posters and in the chapter on World War posters. Check the Index to find other mentions of a specific artist.

ABOUT THE RESOURCE GUIDE

For collectors with particular interests, or those who just want to learn more about posters, we created the extensive Resource Guide at the back of this volume.

The Resource Guide gives you the names, addresses, and phone numbers of auction houses, dealers, museums, conservators, periodicals, and other individuals we've consulted in putting this book together. There is also a bibliography that will help you find other books and periodicals of interest to you.

One great advantage to poster collectors is that the field is so thoroughly chronicled. Advertising posters have been written about almost from the day they were created. Turn-of-the-century magazines and publications informed early collectors of new issues and new artists in the field, and these publications serve today as the earliest written histories of the poster. In addition, dozens of books have been written on specific artists, countries, and artistic movements, providing the avid collector with important resources.

If you would like to find out more about any aspect of posters, the Resource Guide can help. In addition, the dealers who are listed in this volume are always willing to answer questions and guide you to other sources of information that will enhance your knowledge of posters.

❧ CHAPTER 3 ❧
Important Notes on the Price Listings

NOTE: We advise you to read this chapter closely. It includes important information on how the prices in this book were established, and other things to watch for in determining values for buying and selling posters.

As is often true of any collectible, the market value of many posters depends on what the buyer is willing to pay. We know more than one avid poster collector who will pay high prices for posters he or she really needs for a collection.

To a beginning collector some of the prices given in the following pages may seem high. The poster market today is firmly established, so prices have a broad base of support. The best and often the highest-priced posters are frequently bought by serious collectors, museums, and dealers who work with an international clientele. In the context of prices for paintings, even the highest prices for posters can appear modest.

Even with the overall setback to prices in the late 1980s and early 1990s, some posters still break records at auction, and more people seem willing to pay higher prices than ever before. However, many visually striking posters are still within the reach of average collectors.

In each category, we have offered a sampling of prices, not necessarily an exhaustive list. If you do not find the exact poster you are looking for here, the prices given can still be used for comparison. Also, reputable dealers and auction houses will always be willing to quote what they feel a particular poster is worth. If you feel that you have acquired a particularly valuable piece or collection, you may want to pay for a professional appraisal, whether or not you are planning to sell. An appraisal of value can also help you plan for insurance and estate purposes.

HOW POSTERS ARE DESCRIBED AND LISTED

Each listing gives as much of the following information as was available to us.

- Name, nationality, and life dates of the artist
- Title of the poster
- Year or approximate year when the poster was created
- The printing medium used (lithograph, photo-offset, silk screen, etc.), and the printing company
- Description and additional background on the poster or artist
- Condition or other information that may affect collectible value (see notes on condition below)
- Any notes on the collectibility of the poster—whether it represents a good, very good, or outstanding example of a particular genre, subject, or artist (see also A Key to Collectible Value)
- Mounting information—whether the poster is mounted on linen, Japan paper, Chartex, or some other backing; when no indication is given, the poster is assumed to be "plain paper"
- Size, width preceding height
- Retail price range or auction price realized

For a description of poster printing techniques and for definitions of terms commonly used in the poster field, please refer to the chapter entitled Poster Printing and Terminology.

CONDITION KEY

For the price listings, we have combined two "condition keys" that you will see used by dealers and auction houses. In this book you will see the words "mint," "very good," etc., describing the posters. In dealer or auction catalogs you will sometimes see condition described as A, B, C, etc.

Below are the definitions of these terms:

MINT	A+	Flawless; no repairs; new.
FINE	A	Fresh colors and no paper loss; only extremely minor or unobtrusive repairs or tears; folds not apparent.
VERY GOOD	A− B+	Fresh colors overall; minor or slight paper loss, but expertly repaired and not on image or critical area; very light staining, dirt, fold, tear, etc., but not on image or critical area.
GOOD	B B−	Good colors and lines overall; some paper loss, but not on image or critical area; some light staining; high-quality restoration, but

not immediately evident, or only one or two noticeable repairs; folds somewhat apparent.

FAIR   C   Image clear, but colors and lines somewhat faded; some paper loss or noticeable repairs in image area; light staining, dirt, or folds more pronounced.

POOR   D   Image not intact, or colors and lines faded or marred beyond appreciation of artist's intent; overly pronounced light staining; overly visible or poorly executed repairs; dirt or folds obvious.

HOW GIVEN PRICES WERE ESTABLISHED

The purpose of this book is not to *set* prices on posters, but to *report* actual prices in the market. The vast majority of price listings in this book were observed by us, or reported to us primarily by collectors, dealers, or auction houses during 1992 and 1993. We also anonymously gathered information about pricing at dealer shops, exhibitions, and antique shows.

Price Ranges

When a price range is given after a description, it represents a retail "asking price" reported to us by one or more dealers. However, retail prices can vary greatly depending on the condition of the poster, the dealer from whom you are buying, whether or not the poster has been restored, and many other factors. (See A Key To Collectible Value for more information on poster values.) The price ranges in this volume are offered as a guide only.

Auction Prices

When the price given for a poster is followed by the indication (Auc. # ___), it means that this price was reported to us by one of the auction houses listed in the Resource Guide. The twenty-five indexed auctions represented in this volume are individually listed at the front of the Resource Guide, giving the auction house, date of the sale, whether the reported prices did or did not include the buyer's premium, and the percentage of the buyer's premium for that particular auction. For foreign auctions, exchange rates are also given.

Multiple Prices

Where more than one auction or retail price was available, or where both an auction price and a retail price are known, the description will be followed by more than one price indication. In some instances you'll see that the auction price exceeded the retail price at which the poster is generally available on the market. In still other cases, two prices may reflect values for posters that represent the same image but are different sizes or in different conditions. Our hope is that your understanding of pricing will be enhanced by these comparisons.

OTHER MARKET FACTORS

Whether your intention is to buy or sell posters, the following are some other things you should note.

Prices in Market Can Change Rapidly

Some areas cool off, other trends pop up. There have been some rapid price changes, both up and down, in poster prices in the last few years.

Important discoveries, new books and scholarly research, exhibitions, auctions, and other factors can send prices up or down almost overnight. It might be discovered that fewer—or many more—examples of a particular work exist. A rash of fakes can send prices tumbling as collectors become wary of a particular field. Important anniversaries, such as the fiftieth anniversary of World War II, bring renewed awareness of certain fields.

In the late 1980s there was a rapid upswing in prices for all art, partially due to the greatly increased participation of foreign buyers in American art markets. When the recession hit, the poster market was not immune, and some prices dropped as much as 20 to 25 percent. One major exception is cinema posters, which have increased in value more rapidly during the recession than they did prior to it, though other factors are at work in that field. (See the chapter on Cinema Posters for more information.) However, for the most part prices held steady during the recession.

The best advice we can offer is to use this book as a starting point, then go out into the market and discover what is happening in your area of interest today.

Prices for Posters Have Not "Nationalized"

That is, poster prices are not consistent across the country, and there can be great variations in the retail price of a given poster depending on where and from whom it is bought. Generally speaking, New York and California tend to have the highest retail prices for posters, with the following major metropolitan areas not far behind: Chicago, Washington, D.C., Philadelphia, Denver, Boston, Miami, Atlanta.

The poster market is becoming increasingly "self-conscious." Information on the "going price" and on prices realized at auction is more readily available than ever before. There are still bargains to be found in out-of-the-way shops, smaller towns, and through dealers who do not specialize in posters.

Selling To or Buying From a Dealer

The prices in this guide do not necessarily represent the price at which a particular dealer will buy or sell a poster. If you are looking to sell your poster to a dealer, do not expect to get the retail price range represented here. Dealers can't pay retail prices because they are in the business of "brokering" posters, and need to mark up the price to make a profit.

In buying from a dealer, be aware that you are in part paying for the dealer's costs above and beyond the purchase cost—and this can impact the retail price. The dealer must pay for the costs of carrying inventory, overhead, salaries, rent, shipping, and more. Dealers may have also incurred the time and expense of restoration and cleaning, or of research and documentation.

In addition, high-quality material is getting more and more difficult and expensive for dealers to obtain, and many report having to spend increased amounts of time at auctions and elsewhere, including travel to distant parts of the globe. As with any service, the price you will pay reflects these "service" costs as well.

Many collectors prefer to let the dealers do this legwork, and also rely on the dealers' expertise, with the reassurance that reputable dealers will stand behind what they sell.

Buying or Selling at Auction

More individual collectors are attending auctions, and auction house personnel are happy to advise them. However, many collectors still do not understand the auction process.

First, realize that each auction is a unique event that will never be re-created. The price realized depends largely on who is bidding. If there are two individuals in the room who desperately want the same poster for their collections, you can bet the price will soar. If there is just one person in the room who wants a certain poster, he or she will perhaps get it at a price much lower than retail. However, many auction houses have "reserves," a minimum price they guarantee the consignor.

When the bid runs very high at an auction, it is more likely to be a collector than a dealer who is willing to go the distance. A dealer who pays the highest possible price for a poster may not be able to sell it at a profit. When it is a dealer who places the highest bid, chances are that he or she has been authorized in advance by a collector to do so.

Auction prices listed in a guide such as this are generally lower than retail because dealers acquire inventory at auctions for resale. So don't expect to purchase a poster from a dealer at auction price listed here. Remember, too, that the auctions prices included here do not necessarily represent the best or most important work of a given artist, or the best condition in which a poster might be found.

Prices realized also depend on how the auction is promoted. For example, one dealer complained that a major poster auction had not been advertised broadly enough, and that those most likely to buy the posters offered were not in attendance. Of course, this was great news for those who were in the auction, but for those who consigned the posters, the results were disappointing.

Remember, too, that almost all posters at auction are sold "as is." That means it is your responsibility to completely inspect the poster you intend to buy, judging its condition, authenticity, and importance. You are responsible for having it restored, repaired, or cleaned. If you are confident about your ability in these areas, you can still acquire some real bargains at auction.

While you can be fairly confident about the catalog descriptions given by major auction houses, even they say that the descriptions are "their opinion," in an effort to limit their liability.

Less experienced auctioneers and out-of-the-way auctions miscatalog posters all the time. One recent catalog advertised an "original French lithograph" that appeared to be the famous, rare three-sheet *Moulin Rouge* by Toulouse-Lautrec, which holds the record for a poster sold at auction of $220,000. The ad, we weren't surprised to learn, was misleading, as the piece was a copy done in the 1920s. The poster world has numerous fakes, forgeries, and reproductions, and many smaller auctioneers unknowingly fall into the same traps as collectors.

❦ CHAPTER 4 ❦
A Key To Collectible Value

What's the difference between a $2,000 Chéret and a $7,000 Chéret? Why did Lautrec's *Moulin Rouge* sell for a record-breaking $220,000 at auction? How big an effect will condition have on a poster's value? How are poster values different in specific fields such as magic, circus, war, or cinema posters?

In many of the price listings we have included notes about the collectibility of a poster— whether it represents a "good," "very good," or "outstanding" example of an artist's work or a particular genre. By comparing some of these indications, we hope you will gain a sense of relative values, as well as a sense of the broad price range for an artist or subject.

However, many factors come into play when determining the value of a poster, and this chapter outlines some of the key factors that can affect its collectibility.

ARTISTIC ACHIEVEMENT

In almost all categories of posters, work by recognized artists and graphic designers will always have a higher value than those by lesser-known or anonymous designers.

Artists such as Toulouse-Lautrec, Alphonse Mucha, A. M. Cassandre, Edward Penfield, Jan Toroop, Ludwig Holhwein, Adolfo Hohenstein, Otto Baumberger, Pierre Bonnard, Privat Livemont, and numerous others are widely recognized as masters and innovators whose work stands head and shoulders above the work of their contemporaries.

Most designers of this stature were considered important contributors to the world of posters during their lifetimes, and produced a significant body of work with consistently high quality to earn that reputation. Some, like Bonnard and Toulouse-Lautrec, had strong reputations as painters, and actually created very few posters.

Remember, however, that an "unknown" artist today can become a celebrated "rediscovered" artist tomorrow. While Cassandre is recognized today, his reputation was reestablished with the resurgence of interest in Art Deco. The past twenty years have brought to light numerous designers from different countries and schools of design whose important contributions were previously unrecognized, so use your instincts.

The value of a recognized artist's name doesn't apply in fields such as magic, circus and cinema posters, where the artist is almost never known. While artistic quality has some impact, in these areas the subject is usually vastly more important in establishing value.

ORIGINALITY/AUTHENTICATION

We're not referring to "creativity" here, but to a different concept of originality: A poster for a Toulouse-Lautrec exhibition at the Boston Museum of Fine Arts is not a Toulouse-Lautrec poster. To have real value in the poster world, the poster must be an *original* design by the artist, intended for use as a poster, and must indeed be an example from the original edition.

This may seem obvious to some people, but it is completely misunderstood by others—even those who would never confuse a Renoir painting with a poster for a Renoir exhibition.

To be fair, this concept can be particularly confusing when one is talking about the posters of artists such as Pablo Picasso, Joan Miró, Marc Chagall, and other modern painters. There are literally hundreds of different posters for Picasso exhibitions, but only about fifty were actually created by Picasso specifically as posters. The rest use a reproduction of one of his paintings or drawings to advertise an exhibition, and have very little collectible value. Because of this, it sometimes takes considerable research to authenticate what is and what is not an original poster design by a modern artist.

Very few posters, except more contemporary ones, were ever handsigned by the artist. A hand signature by an artist such as Picasso can add considerable value to a poster, even one that is not an original poster design.

Usually you will hear a signature referred to as being "on the stone," "in the block," or "in the matrix," meaning that the artist signed the lithographic stone, the plate, or other art medium before the poster was printed. The listings in this book, unless otherwise noted, assume that the poster is signed in this manner. Some artists used monograms or marks to identify their work. For example, the Swiss artist Otto Baumberger signed his posters with a single "B."

One of Baumberger's lithographic posters, for Baumann hats, was later reprinted by photo-offset means, and the "B" was respectfully removed before reprinting. This is also a rare instance in which the reprint actually has some collecting value. Note, however, that the vast majority of original lithographic posters were never originally reprinted because usually the stone was polished down to be used to print another poster. Later photo-offset reproductions of these have little or no value to collectors.

RARITY

This is basically the principle of supply and demand: A rarely seen poster will attract more interest, and may therefore sell for a considerably higher price, especially at auction. A rare proof of a poster before the text was applied can also bring a high price in many instances. A rare variation in design or text can also prompt a high bid from a collector.

The Dutch artist Jan Toroop's poster for the play *Pandorra* can sell for as much as $35,000, not only because it is a stunning design by an important artist, but because only a handful are known to have survived. War posters from Nazi Germany and Fascist Italy can command high prices today because most were destroyed when the Allies invaded, and they are now sought after as important historical documents. Posters from the Russian Revolution are even scarcer and more highly prized.

The Toulouse-Lautrec *Moulin Rouge* that broke auction records at $220,000 in 1989 at Poster Auctions International in New York was a rare full three-sheet poster, and some estimate that as few as ten of these full-size posters exist. The same poster without the top sheet, which is only slightly easier to come by, is valued at only about one half of that amount.

In the vast majority of cases involving early posters (most often called "vintage" posters) produced before World War II, nobody really knows how many of each poster were originally printed, let alone how many were saved, and in what condition. What is known, however, is that photo-offset printing after World War II allowed posters to be printed in much greater quantities than before.

Generally, the rarity and the age of a poster go hand in hand. Older posters were produced in fewer quantities, fewer survived, and more of those that did survive are now "off the market" in museums and private collections.

Rarity alone, however, is not enough to make a poster valuable. For example, if you have an artistically and historically unimportant poster by an unknown artist, even though it is the only one that survived, don't expect much demand for it.

CONDITION

Condition, especially for serious collectors, is an important part of the value of any poster, and greatly influences how much they are willing to pay for it. (See the Condition Key in the preceding chapter as well as the article by Kathryn Myatt Carey on Conservation and Care of Posters.)

For *truly* rare posters, collectors may be willing to lower their standards a bit where condition is concerned. But even for many recognized posters, condition can make a difference of thousands of dollars in price. This is especially true of posters that appear with some regularity on the market, because collectors know that if they can wait a bit, the same poster, in better condition will surface.

For example, Cassandre's *Normandie* poster, when found in "A" condition, can sell as high as $8,000 or more, but one in "C" condition might bring only $4,000 or less.

SUBJECT

Several poster-collecting fields place a greater emphasis on subject than on other keys to value. In the world of magic posters, for example, Houdini posters generally command higher prices than posters featuring any other magician. In the field of circus posters, certain circuses are more sought after than others. Of cinema posters, certain Hollywood stars are much more popular than others, and classic titles such as *King Kong* or *Metropolis* command top dollar.

If you collect war posters, you know that recruiting posters are rarer and generally more sought after than bond posters. Poster subjects that somehow capture our imagination and become classics always lead their fields. For example, many World War I posters can still be bought for under $300, but James Montgomery Flagg's classic Uncle Sam "I Want You" poster can sell for more than $2,000.

The subject matter can also have an impact on value. For example, Jules Chéret's poster for the American dancer Loie Fuller at the Folies Bergère can bring thousands of dollars more than his poster for cough drops.

Very broadly speaking, posters for well-known performers, artistic events, and important exhibitions sell better than product posters.

PRINTING PROCESSES

The earliest illustrated posters were printed by stone or zinc lithography, a recognized artistic medium. They will always have greater desirability than later photographic offset-printed posters, although other factors described above can make some offset posters soar at auctions. In addition lithographic posters were printed in far fewer numbers than modern photo-offset printing allows. (For more detailed information on printing techniques, see the chapter entitled Poster Printing and Terminology.)

MOULIN ROUGE HAD IT ALL

Why did Toulouse-Lautrec's *Moulin Rouge* break all auction records for posters? Following the key above, it was an outstanding example in the body of work of an important artist; it was extremely rare, particularly because it included the top sheet; it was in very good condition; it was a historically important entertainment subject; and it was a stone lithograph. The poster, quite simply, had it all.

❧ CHAPTER 5 ❧
Poster Printing and Terminology

PRINTING TECHNIQUES

By the late 1700s printers in Europe were looking for new and better ways of printing illustrations, especially in books. Intaglio printings are those made from an incised plate, such as etchings and engravings. This method had virtually replaced relief printing, or printing from raised surfaces, such as in a woodcut.

It was discovered that one could engrave on wood, if the engraving was done across the end grain. Wood engravings, often seen in early newspapers such as *Harper's Weekly*, became very popular, as did steel engravings. In the earliest posted bills, sometimes called *broadsides*, such as "Wanted" posters or early political posters, a small wood or steel engraving was often used to illustrate the poster.

However, engravings weren't efficient, because the text of a book was still printed in relief and the illustrations had to be printed separately from the text. Raised metal type would remain the primary form of text printing until after World War II.

Then, in 1798 a German named Alloys Senefelder created the printing method known as lithography from the word *lithos*, or stone. This printing method, and later methods, such as offset printing, are called *planographic*. That is, the ink is carried on a flat surface rather than on raised edges or in incised lines.

It was not until the mid 1800s, however, that the lithographic process was perfected. Jules Chéret further refined the lithographic printing technique and mastered the process of color lithography, leading to an explosion of illustrated lithographically printed posters. That's why today Chéret is referred to alternately as "The Father of Modern Color Lithography" and "The Father of the Modern Illustrated Poster." (See the chapter on French Posters for more about Chéret's work with lithography.)

In early lithographic posters, the artist or an assistant would draw an image directly onto a slab of limestone, using a grease crayon. Ink is then applied. The ink floats on the surface of the grease and is not absorbed by the stone. The ink is then transferred to the paper. This printing method proved itself versatile and could produce multiple printed effects.

Grease pens and crayons were effective for creating lines and details, and for achieving the tones and effects of chalk drawing. When larger strokes were required, a brush was used to achieve painterly effects by covering larger areas of the stone with grease. Spatter technique, in which ink is sprayed randomly onto the greased limestone by scraping a blade across a brush full of ink, was used in stunning ways by poster artists such as Henri de Toulouse-Lautrec.

Lithography offered printers the ability to do somewhat larger runs than previous printing methods. The image did not wear down as was the case with relief and intaglio illustrations. Lithography, and the many variations on it, would become the first viable large-scale commercial printing method.

However, many people still do not realize what a cumbersome, exacting process stone lithography is. It had major drawbacks. In France the limestone most commonly used was imported Bavarian limestone, which was heavy, fragile, and expensive. The stones themselves were huge. In addition, a separate stone was used for each different color of the poster — sometimes as many as nine or ten stones were used to create the colorful translucent effects today's collector treasures.

After the ink was applied to the stone, the paper was laid on the stone, a metal backing was laid on top, and the entire stone passed on runners under a wooden bar called a scraper, which applied pressure to lift the ink from the stone to the paper. The process had to be repeated for each color, and each color had to be registered correctly! No wonder stone lithographic posters from Chéret, Mucha, Lautrec, and others are so highly valued.

When the printing run was completed, very often the stones were ground down to erase the first image and then used again to produce another poster. Once the printer completed the initial printing of a lithographic poster, only rarely would another print be made.

Because of the problems associated with limestone lithography, commercial printers started using roughened zinc plates instead, and for a while during the 1800s these prints were called *zincographs*. Today they are most often called *lithographs*, and sometimes *chromolithographs*. A lithograph and a chromolithograph are produced by essentially the same process; however, chromolithograph is a somewhat pejorative term that refers to more commercially produced work.

Lithographs are distinctive in the evenness with which the ink is applied to the paper. Under a magnifying glass one can see that the colors of a lithographic poster are evenly distributed, and this is one method of identifying a poster as a lithograph. Note that in some cases, various screens were used to give a lithograph texture, so the use of a screen alone does not mean a poster isn't a lithograph.

Before the turn of the century, printers experimented with other kinds of printing processes, including transfer lithographs, where the image is not drawn on the stone but transferred from some other medium to the stone; and *collotypes*, a delicate, commercially inviable process that was used until very recently to faithfully reproduce works of art in finely printed editions.

In most cases it is very difficult, even for a specialist, to distinguish between the kinds of printing described here, and today all of them are often referred to as "lithographs." Innovative printing methods were not adopted universally. Artists had individual preferences, and some continued to render their posters through relief methods, such as a woodcut or a linoleum cut, also called a *linocut*. Posters designed in this manner are printed on a letterpress. For example, Robert Bonfils's poster for the 1925 Paris Exposition was a woodcut. (See the photo in the price listings at the end of the chapter on French Posters.) Swiss artists of the Basel School headed by Armin Hofmann also used relief processes to create posters in the 1950s and 1960s. Some fine artists, such as Picasso, continued to use lithography to create posters in the decades after World War II.

In the 1940s and 1950s, silk-screening became a popular artistic medium for creating fine prints. In the silk-screen method, each color of ink is forced through a fine screen onto the paper. The early forerunner of the silk screen was the stencil, and some posters, notably Dutch typographic posters from the De Stijl design movement, were stenciled. A *serigraph* is a similar, though more mechanized and commercially viable, form of silk-screening, allowing for larger and faster runs. It is used today to create both posters and "art prints."

Until World War II, however, lithography was the most widely used method of poster printing. However, the use of photography in the printing process did dramatically change the way in which posters were created and printed.

Photography in printing was being experimented with as early as 1850, and the first negatives weren't film, but hand-drawn glass negatives. After the turn of the century, pioneering poster artists, notably in Holland and Switzerland, experimented with *photomontage* posters. Their creations are posters that are collages of photos and hand-drawn illustration. The Swiss ski posters of Herbert Matter are excellent examples of the eye-catching effects of early photomontage posters. (See the chapter on Swiss Posters for more information on early photomontage posters.)

In the poster field one will sometimes hear photomontage posters refered to as *photolithographic* posters, although photolithography actually has a broader meaning. A photolithograph is any image that has been created photochemically. Virtually all photolithography is printed using photographic negatives on offset presses. It is the process most commonly used by commercial printers today.

In offset printing, the plate never touches the paper. Rather, a rubber roller picks up the ink from the plate, which has been photochemically etched, and then runs it over the paper, "offsetting" the image to the page. Offset printing allowed for higher speeds, bigger runs, and easier registration.

The vast majority of French train posters before World War II were lithographs printed in runs of as many as 5,000 to 10,000. After World War II, when France began to heavily promote itself to tourist markets around the world, offset posters became the norm, with print run as high as 60,000.

While the value of any poster has to do with numerous factors (see the section A Key to Collectible Values), posters that are hand-drawn and printed by stone or zinc lithography will always be more valuable than those reproduced by photographic means. Not only are they rarer because they are older, less available, and usually printed in much smaller quantities, but there is also an artistic value involved. Lithographic posters are original works of art drawn by the artist or rendered by the hand of a lithographic draftsman directly onto the stone or plate.

With a photo-offset poster, taking a photograph of the artist's original work is the first step in creating the poster. The negative of the photo is used to etch the plates from which the poster will be printed.

In order to make the plate, the negative must be screened into a series of very tiny, regular dots in neat straight lines. Look at any photograph in this book under a strong magnifying glass and you will see the dots and lines of photo-offset printing, as compared to the even application of ink on a lithograph. This is one way to tell if the Cassandre *Normandie* poster your mother gave you is a lithograph or a later photo-offset reproduction.

In this book we use the term *lithograph* for any poster printed lithographically; *photomontage* for the combination of photographic and hand-drawn images; *relief* for woodcuts or linoleum cuts; and *photo-offset* for photographically printed posters.

Methods used in prints and poster making can be confusing. One of the best resources for approaching these questions in an academic way is the book *How to Identify Prints*, by Bamber Gascoigne (see Bibliography).

GLOSSARY OF TERMS

Aside from printing terminology, collectors, dealers, and scholars commonly use many of the following words, which you will see in catalogs and descriptions of posters. Among the most frequently used are:

ACTIVE MARKET — You'll hear dealers say, "That poster isn't available on the active market," meaning that a certain poster doesn't come up for sale or at auction very often, but might still be available privately.

BLIND STAMP — Some publishers use a blind stamp to identify their editions. The blind stamp is embossed into the paper, leaving a raised image, much like a notary public's seal.

BROADSIDE — The term broadside is used to refer to posters with only small or no illustrations. Text comprises most of the poster image. Broadsides were the advertising forerunners of illustrated posters.

BUYER'S PREMIUM — Refers to the commission, generally 10 percent, but in some cases 15 percent, of the final bid price, paid by the buyer to the auction house.

CATALOGUE RAISONNÉ — A catalogue raisonné is an attempt to definitively catalog the works of a particular artist. Research works such as these are often cited as references for posters.

CHARTEX — Chartex is a type of synthetic material that was at one time used to mount posters. Very stiff and inflexible, it is heat-sealed to the paper, and next to impossible to remove. Backing on Chartex can significantly reduce the value of a poster.

DATE STRIP — Also called a "banner," these were added to posters to announce specific performances, dates, etc. Some collectors look for date strips with magic, circus, and theater posters.

EDITION

Edition refers to the number of posters printed. In most cases, no one really knows how many were printed, let alone how many were saved. However, in some instances where the records were kept, we do have information on the edition size.

FOLIO FOLDS

Many posters are too big to store flat, and were therefore folded and stored in drawers. While it is always better to find posters in mint condition, traces of folio folds are extremely common in some very desirable posters. However, watch for folds along which there are tears, or that are obtrusive because they are stained along the fold.

FOXING

Foxing is a term used to describe rusty-colored spots on paper, caused primarily by moisture. Foxing can be reduced, if not eliminated, with proper treatment, but excessive foxing does lower the value of a poster, especially if it affects the image.

JAPAN PAPER

Japanese papers are generally delicate mulberry fiber papers used by many paper conservators for mounting posters. Posters are usually mounted on Japan paper using a wheat paste.

LAID DOWN

Sometimes used to describe a poster that has been mounted on linen or Japan paper. Be aware, however, that the term *laid down* can also mean that the poster has been glued to cardboard, a wood panel, or some other backing that is difficult and costly to remove.

LIGHT STAINING

The discoloration that occurs when a poster has been exposed to too much light, artificial or sunlight. See the chapter on Conservation and Care of Posters in this volume.

LIMITED EDITION

Generally a limited or numbered and signed edition refers to fine art prints and not to posters. However, some contemporary posters are issued in limited editions.

LINEN-MOUNTED
OR ON LINEN

This means the poster has been laid down on cloth, usually using some form of animal glue. Mounting posters on linen was long thought to be the best way to preserve them, although other methods are now generally preferred by conservators. In the earliest examples of posters mounted in this way, the linen is a very thin muslin-type cloth. Today most "linen" used to mount posters is really cotton canvas.

MARGINS

The area of blank paper around the image area of the poster. Posters that have retained their margins are generally more valuable than those that have been trimmed or cut down.

MARK OR
MONOGRAM

Some artists did not sign their posters with their names, but used a mark to identify their work. This is the case with Toulouse-Lautrec, for example. Other posters are simply "monogrammed" with the artist's initials.

MAQUETTE

Refers to the original art or sketch an artist might render before the poster is made, often either a watercolor, drawing, or some form of graphic design. The common term "mock-up" is derived from maquette.

MONOGRAPH

A book on a single artist, sometimes overviewing the artist's entire *oeuvre* or "body of work."

MOUNTED

See *Laid Down*.

ONE SHEET
TWO SHEET, ETC.

Some posters are billboard size, and are printed on several sheets of paper. One sheet, half sheet, two sheet, and other poster sizes generally are used to refer to standard posters sizes, and are explained in the chapter Cinema Posters.

ON THE STONE

Generally posters are not signed or dated in pencil as fine art prints were. Instead, an artist using the lithographic method would sign the poster directly on the lithographic stone. In printing using blocks, such as woodblocks, one might see a signature "in the block." In photolithographic or photo-offset printing, the signature will be "in the matrix."

PANEL

Panels or "decorative panels," as they are sometimes called, are poster-size lithographs on paper. They were created by several artists during the poster "craze" of the 1890s. These designs are generally without advertising text, and were meant to be used as decorations in the home.

PAPER SIGN

Generally used in reference to early American product advertising, a "poster" and a "paper sign" often differ only in that paper signs generally have frames, and were considered more permanent than posters.

PROOF

Artists often pulled "trial" posters to see how the image looked before the advertising message or text was applied. These are sometimes called "proof before letters" or "proof before text," and can be very valuable.

REGISTRATION

Sometimes small marks were used in the margins of a poster so that the printer could line up the paper correctly when printing a poster that used more than one color. In some posters you will see where the registration is off, and the color goes beyond the area it was intended for.

SECONDARY MARKET

The term secondary market is generally used to refer to all antiques, because they are not being sold directly by those who created them. In the field of graphics and works on paper, it is used to refer to works by artists no longer available directly from the artist, the artist's agent, or the original publisher.

STATE

Generally used to mean one stage in the process towards the completion of a final print or poster.

An artist may print a few proofs to see how a piece looks, make some changes, and then print a "second state," etc.

TIN SIGN
A term from product and store advertising, it means what it says. Essentially this is an advertising poster, often rendered lithographically on tin.

TO THE TRADE
Dealers who sell only to other dealers are selling "to the trade." At shows you'll hear a dealer ask another, "Do you offer a discount to the trade?" meaning a dealer discount.

❦ CHAPTER 6 ❦
Starting a Poster Collection

As in any collecting field, the more you know about posters before you decide what to buy, the better off you will be in the long run.

What you'll hear over and over from experts in the field is that the best way to start a poster collection is not to immediately make a purchase. Rather, read about posters, go and see them at museums and dealer galleries. Go to auctions that include posters—just to see them firsthand at the preview and to observe the auction process. Go window-shopping. Don't spend your hard-earned money until you have a good knowledge of the posters and the market in which you are interested.

Especially if you are a beginning collector, we encourage you to thoroughly read the chapter Important Notes on the Price Listings and the other introductory information in this volume. It is very important to give yourself this grounding in the field before you start buying.

With prices on many artists and posters reaching into the tens of thousands of dollars, you may decide to invest in today's "blue chips," or you may want to collect in a field that hasn't yet gone out of reach, depending on your budget. You will find ample information and advice on collecting and "investing" in posters in the pages of this guide.

Not all posters are expensive, although you most often read about those that break records. Many areas of poster collecting are likely to appreciate over the next decade, but can still be bought at reasonable prices.

Posters by lesser-known or anonymous European and American turn-of-the-century artists can still be very affordable. Many American and European World War I and World War II posters are still good buys. Thousands and thousands of cinema poster titles are within the reach of those with only modest amounts of money to spend. Numerous posters for travel, products, exhibitions, circuses, magicians, and other subjects are also accessible with limited funds.

As the collecting horizon moved away from its focus on French posters over the past ten years, both American posters and posters from Italy, Switzerland, Holland, Poland, and other countries have seen increased attention. Like French posters, the outstanding examples by the best artists of these countries can be very expensive. However, good and very good examples by talented poster designers can still be purchased for moderate sums.

Really the first step is to decide what kind of posters you like and what kind you would like to collect. Flip through the pages of this book and you'll see the wide range of options you have in the poster-collecting field.

Some collectors decide to concentrate on a particular artist, genre, or subject. For example, some people collect only bicycle posters, product posters, Olympic posters, magic posters, etc. Within those fields people sometimes specialize even further. Others collect a variety of different posters simply because they are attracted to particular images.

Whichever way you go, you should set standards and try to collect the very best examples you can find, both in terms of quality and condition (see Chapter 4, A Key To Collectible Value).

❦ CHAPTER 7 ❦
Fakes, Forgeries, and Reproductions

Happily, the poster field has not been fraught with as many fakes and forgeries as some other fields, such as paintings, but fakes do exist. With the prices for some posters reaching into the tens of thousands, the field is bound to encounter its share of *Mona Lisa*s.

The most common deception, whether intentional or not, is the sale of a photo-offset poster reproduction as an original lithograph. Knowing whether the poster was originally produced as a lithograph will help you spot the photo-offset fakes. Below you'll find information on how to tell the difference between the two.

The copyrights on many vintage posters, if they had them to begin with, ran out long ago. Anyone with a printing press can print and distribute for sale a vast number of poster titles by notable artists, or reproduce them on T-shirts, mugs, and other items. Popular artists whose work has been reprinted include Toulouse-Lautrec, Mucha, Cassandre, Pierre Fix-Masseau, and Ludwig Hohlwein. For example, a catalog of Poster Originals, Ltd., of New York has reproductions of Ludwig Hohlwein's poster for the delicatessen *Wilhelm Mozer*, with its bright red lobster, as well as Tom Purvis's British rail poster *East Coast by LNER*.

Many vintage movie posters were reproduced in the 1960s and 1970s by a company called Portal Publications. About a year ago I was very sorry to have to tell an excited volunteer at the thrift shop at the Cooper Hospital in Camden, New Jersey, that a poster starring Shirley Temple in *The Little Colonel* was not a valuable original, but a Portal Publication reproduction. This company received franchises from other artists and publishers in the late 1960s and 1970s to reproduce other posters, such as rock posters and certain posters by David Lance Goines. These are usually marked "Portal Publications," but an unscrupulous trader might simply clip off the publisher's mark.

The Italian Ricordi opera posters have long been favorites for reproductions, especially by Fiesta Arts Company, which used to advertise in the pages of *Ovation* magazine. Collectors should avoid these smaller-format photo-offset posters for operas by Puccini, Verdi, and others, which feature productions of *Rigoletto*, *Turandot*, *Madama Butterfly*, and

32

so forth. The size of the reproductions, usually about 14 x 20 inches, should be enough to alert an astute collector, as the originals were sometimes larger than 40 x 80 inches.

In the pages of the art gallery and frame supply trade magazine *Art Business News*, editions of new posters are constantly being announced. Mostly these are contemporary posters, but unfortunately, some are reproductions of original vintage material. We've recently seen a 1915 *Indian Motorcycle* reproduction poster announced by the company Gilmore Red Lion of California, "which specializes in racing posters from the past"; and a reproduction of a vintage *Vermouth Bianco* poster from Michel Beja publishers in New York.

A publisher named Claude Lockwood in Dundee, Michigan, sent us information on his photo-offset reproductions of famous war posters, such as Christy's *If You Want to Fight, Join the Marines*, Leyendecker's *U.S.A. Bonds*, and even Flagg's famous *I Want You* poster.

While the intent of these publishers is not to deceive the public, but to make a profit, the real problem occurs when the poster leaves the manufacturer's hands and winds up at a flea market or antique show where either the seller or the buyer doesn't know any better.

Fortunately, the stone or zinc plate lithographic process is a difficult and expensive one to re-create, so the reprinted posters are usually produced using modern photo-offset means. Under a strong magnifying glass a lithograph will generally have an evenness in its colored areas. Lines in lithographs often look like they have been drawn by crayon, and spatter areas look like spattered paint. Most "vintage" posters produced before World War II are lithographs, though some countries adopted photo-offset printing earlier.

In the more modern photo-offset process, a photograph is taken of the original art and turned into a negative. The negatives are used to photochemically etch the plate from which the poster will be printed. To make the etching possible, the negative must be turned into a series of very tiny, regular dots in neat straight lines. These can't often be seen with the naked eye, but are readily apparent under a jeweler's lens or a very strong magnifying glass. Look closely at any of the photographs in this book and you will see the dots and lines (called a dot matrix) of photo-offset printing. (See the chapter Poster Printing and Terminology for more information on printing processes.)

A few posters, such as Albert Bergevin's *Avranches* poster, Paul Colin's *Bal Tabarin*, and Maurice Dufrène's *Rayon des Soieries* opera poster, were targets for lithographic counterfeiting in the mid-1980s. These attempts to defraud are so well executed that only subtle differences in color tipped off the poster community. Word about these kinds of forgeries tends to travel quickly through the trade, and reputable dealers will avoid any questionable poster.

A few other lithographic reproductions have also been reported to us. In the 1920s and 1930s the New York Graphic Arts Society reprinted several posters by Toulouse-Lautrec and others. Sometimes these are marked with the name of the company on the back, and sometimes the margin is stamped "Copyright S.M.A." The *Divan Japonais* reproduction is very close in size to the original. Since the poster had to be rerendered to be printed as a lithograph, happily some of the details of the printing are sloppy enough to identify it as a fake. During the revival of popularity of the poster in the late 1960s, the French printer Mourlot also reproduced lithographic copies of posters by Alphonse Mucha.

In 1987 the Wheatley Press in Los Angeles published a stunning book on American Works Progress Administration posters by Christopher DeNoon entitled *Posters of the WPA* (see Bibliography). Unfortunately, a few years later, the same press began selling reproductions of many of the fascinating posters found in the pages of that book. The publisher proudly announced its reproductions in ads that ran in magazines such as *Metropolis*.

These reproductions were issued as serigraphs, a cousin of the silkscreen printing process, which is difficult if not impossible to differentiate from a lithograph. The publisher's ad proudly announced that the reproductions were printed in the "original size and number of colors." I have already seen one of these at an antique show being offered as the original poster. Fortunately for the collector, they can be distinguished from the originals. Instead of thin poster paper, the publisher chose a heavy 100 percent rag archival paper—the kind of quality paper never used for "throwaway" advertising.

Learning as much as you can about the originals will help you avoid fakes. While the world of posters is quite broad, detailed descriptions of hundreds and hundreds of posters now exist in books and auction catalogs. One of the first questions a dealer may ask when someone calls to find out if his or her Toulouse-Lautrec is real is "What size is it?" If the *Moulin Rouge* poster in the caller's possession is much smaller than the original, it is probably one of the many reproductions of his work that have been printed over the years.

However, note that some early small "reproductions" of posters have collecting value, such as the early lithographic editions of *Les Maîtres de L'Affiche* from 1896 to 1900, *Das Plakat, L'Estampe Moderne*, and others. (See the information on *Les Maîtres de l'Affiche* in the chapter on French and Belgian Posters.)

WHAT IS BEING DONE ABOUT FAKES?

Professionals concerned about the reputation of the antiques business have been taking the problem of fakes and forgeries into their own hands in recent years. Dealers exchange information about fakes they encounter regularly. Members of the Professional Show Managers Association (PSMA) are trying to find new ways to identify and keep reproductions out of shows. One show manager, Irene Stella, even created a traveling exhibition to educate the public about fakes.

If you feel you have identified a fake or forgery at a show, or have been the victim of a deception, you should report it to the show management. If they brush you off, or seem not to care, it's best not to attend that show again.

Connie Swaim, editor of *Antique Week*, has crusaded against fakes for some time by frequently publishing articles about fakes in many different collecting fields. Other antique and art trade publications are increasingly publishing articles along the same lines. Personally, we would like to see all antique and fine art publications refuse to accept advertising from publishers and manufacturers of reproductions.

The recently formed American Antique Association (AAA) has made the war on fakes the launching pad for their organization. Their goal is to change the federal laws and require all reproductions to be clearly and indelibly marked as such. They have established a hot line for reporting fakes: (800) 473-7816. Information on their newsletter and membership is available by calling (319) 386-7866.

While these efforts will not stop deception in its tracks, and may not focus specifically on posters, all collecting fields stand to benefit from their efforts. Such efforts reflect well on the professionalism and ethics of the antiques profession.

A RULE OF THUMB

One simple rule of thumb to follow is this: If you are offered an "original" poster at a price that seems too good to be true, such as a Mucha for only a few hundred dollars, it probably is. Vintage posters have had tremendous exposure in recent years, and it is doubtful that any antiques dealer or someone in the trade would be unaware of their great value.

If you find a poster at a flea market or a garage sale, where the seller may truly not be aware of the value, you should take the risk of purchasing what you believe to be an original only if: (a) the price is what you would pay for a reproduction and (b) you truly like the poster. You may have made a find, but if you didn't, you may have to live with your mistake for a very long time!

In each chapter of this book and in specific listings, we have noted any known fakes or forgeries to provide information to help you determine the originality of a poster. Learning about fakes and forgeries will help you become a "confident collector" and avoid the traps into which beginning collectors sometimes stumble.

❦ CHAPTER 8 ❦
Conservation and Care of Posters

BY KATHRYN MYATT CAREY

Kathryn Myatt Carey is a professional associate of the American Institute for Conservation (AIC), specializing in the conservation of works of art on paper, and providing a full range of conservation services. You can contact her at 24 Emery Street, Medford, Massachusetts 02155, (617) 396-9495.

In 1891 Henri de Toulouse-Lautrec was photographed with Charles Zidler, director of the Moulin Rouge cabaret in Paris. In the photo, Zidler proudly points to a poster, *Bal du Moulin Rouge*, designed in 1889 by Jules Chéret. The poster had been mounted on wood to flatten it for display, but at the time the photo was taken, the wood had split, tearing the poster horizontally. It is almost certain that neither Toulouse-Lautrec nor Zidler gave the slightest thought to repairing this wonderfully designed work of art. It had successfully advertised the open ball at Moulin Rouge: It had served its purpose, and would probably be discarded. *(For a fine example of this poster, see color center insert.)*

Now that many posters have attained the status and high prices of fine art, poster dealers and collectors are more concerned than ever with proper conservation. Ideally you should look for posters that are in fine to mint condition, and avoid posters with tears in the image, faded colors, excessive dirt, or stains. However, vintage posters have been treated as "throwaway" advertising for almost one hundred years, so it is not surprising that many of the posters on the market, both restored and unrestored, are in less than fine condition.

It is important for you as a collector to know something about the conservation and care of posters to ensure that your collection will maintain its beauty and grow in value. Also, knowing just a little about common problems will help you know what to look for to make decisions about poster purchases more wisely.

POSTER COMPOSITION

Posters are paper, and all paper collectibles are susceptible to damage and deterioration from chemical, environmental, and physical sources. Damage may also be accelerated by fluctuating heat and humidity.

Poster paper is made from ground wood pulp containing about 29 percent lignin, 44 percent cellulose, 27 percent other carbohydrate materials, and 1 percent extractives. The presence of lignin in wood pulp paper accelerates the breakdown of the cellular chain structure when exposed to light. Lignin is chemically unstable, and breaks down to produce acidic components that attack the cellulose. When this happens, the poster will "yellow" and can become brittle. You may also hear this breakdown called "light staining" or "time staining." Newspapers are made from inexpensive wood pulp paper, and you can easily detect this yellowing after leaving a newspaper in the sun for just a few hours.

As the printing process became more sophisticated, posters were more commonly printed on coated or "glossy" papers, to facilitate print clarity. For the most part, however, coated papers are still wood pulp paper, and are susceptible to the same problems as vintage posters, although the effects may take longer to appear.

Poster paper readily absorbs moisture from the atmosphere, forming sulfuric acid, which also breaks down the paper's cellular structure. Acid may also leach into the paper from old mats and backings, causing what is commonly called *mat burn*.

Other common problems with posters include superficial dirt, old tape and hinges, inadequate or destructive backings, breaks and tears along folds, damage caused by insects and mold, stains, paper losses, and loss of the medium.

Medium is defined as the actual instrument or material used by the artist to execute a work of art: watercolor, oil, graphite, etc. Most vintage posters are lithographs, printed using a special ink on lithographic stones or on zinc plates. More recent posters are produced by photo-offset lithography. This method "offsets" the image from a photographic negative onto a rubber roller that runs the ink across the page. Other posters were created as linoleum cuts (also called linocuts), woodcuts, or silk screens.

As with paper, the medium is sensitive so its environment and will be affected by exposure to light, humidity, pollution, or heat. Some media have a chemical sensitivity to changes in pH or can be affected by oxidation or reduction reactions.

Common problems include color changes or fading, especially fading of red pigments. A vintage poster whose colors have faded may have been overexposed to light. When you're looking to buy, seek out posters with rich, even coloration.

Silk screens and other prints made with stencils have a soft, matte surface that is extremely vulnerable to scratching or burnishing. Silk-screen ink has also been known to react negatively with Plexiglas.

As advertising, posters, by nature, were designed to be disposable. They do not have the advantage of being executed on high-quality paper and are not printed with the most stable media. They present the collector and conservator with a set of complicated and somewhat difficult conservation problems as the paper is always fragile and acidic.

In the hands of a specialist, most posters can be cleaned by immersion in water. However, lithographic inks are sensitive to solvents and can be slightly soluble in water. The inks used in woodcuts and linocuts have a tendency to bleed. Never wet a poster in the hope of cleaning surface dirt or stains. This should be done only by a professional.

DAMAGE CAUSED BY MAN

Man is the greatest source of potential damage to poster art. Improper handling, storage, and framing can cause harm to the paper as well as alteration of the medium. Poor handling can cause abrasions, skinning, creases, folds, tears, distortion, smudging, flaking, or medium loss.

In the late nineteenth century, framers, restorers, and dealers developed the process of *paper marouflage,* or mounting posters and other oversize artworks on cloth linings. This was often done as a means of making posters easier to handle. While this practice has continued to the present day, mounting posters on linen or cotton canvas can result in many problems.

The use of incorrect mounting materials or methods may cause uneven attachment, discoloration, or wrinkling. Lined pieces are rolled to facilitate storage and shipping, but rolling can cause compression or cracking of the paper and medium. When there is humidity in the air, the cloth will contract while the paper will expand, producing mechanical stresses, shearing, and loss of adhesion. Adhesives used in the mounting process can be another source of strain.

In addition to these problems, mounting on cloth also presents aesthetic questions. The paper can lose its tone, texture, and flexibility, or the imprint of the cloth may show on the paper surface.

As the problems associated with linen mounting have become more apparent in recent years, the practice of mounting posters directly on linen has diminished somewhat, although you'll still find posters in the marketplace mounted in this manner. In many cases such backing can be removed by a conservator without damaging the paper, depending on the type of adhesive used.

All in all, however, it is best to buy posters that are unmounted. If mounting is needed to strengthen a weak or brittle paper, posters should be mounted on Japan paper using only a reversible wheat paste starch.

Another common and damaging practice is the use of self-adhesive tape. Scotch or masking tapes should never be applied to posters to fix a problem. Tapes such as these are usually applied to an already weakened area, and only serve to cause even more serious damage later. They will stain the paper and may require the use of strong solvents for removal. Heat-set tissue has also been used to laminate posters to cloth or board backings. It is also very damaging to the poster and is almost impossible to remove.

CONSERVATION TREATMENT OF POSTERS

Conservation is defined as examination (determining the nature or properties of materials and the causes of their deterioration and alteration), restoration (correcting deterioration and alterations), and preservation (preventing, stopping, or retarding deterioration).

A qualified conservator can provide sound, ethical preservation services for posters, define present and potential problems, provide treatment where necessary, and advise on appropriate conditions for storage and exhibition. All conservation treatment decisions should be made by the owner using the expert advice of the conservator.

Conservators are concerned with a number of factors in preserving a poster: structural stability, counteracting chemical and physical deterioration, and performing conservation treatment based on an evaluation of the aesthetic, historic, and scientific characteristics of the object.

Chemical conservation treatments include: alkalization and neutralization to reduce the acidity of the paper and buffer it to slow down future acid accumulations from the air; washing to remove dirt and reduce stains; and other processes including solvent treatments, enzyme usage, sizing replacement, fumigation, and humidification. These treatments are designed to ensure the longevity of the piece.

In addition, consolidation, backing removal, mending, filling of losses, drying, and flattening can be used to strengthen weakened paper. Filling losses should be done with a matching piece of paper, and tears can be repaired with Japan paper and wheat paste starch. Never trim a poster, and if your poster already has a piece torn away, save the piece as it will be vital in the restoration process.

Replacement of pigment, sometimes called *inpainting*, should always be done in moderation. Inpainting can usually be seen by raking the poster over a light; you should avoid purchasing posters that have excessive amounts of inpainting.

ENVIRONMENTAL RISKS

Extensive research had indicated that the lower the temperature at which paper is stored, the longer it will last. With every 10-degree decrease in temperature, the life of paper is approximately doubled. The ideal environment for storage of works of art on paper is a constant temperature of 55 degrees Fahrenheit and a relative humidity level of 50 percent.

As we noted earlier, paper is susceptible to deterioration due to moisture, oxidation, and photochemical reactions, and each of these processes is accelerated by heat and humidity. Fungi or mold spores, always present in the air, will also grow in high humidity and at high temperature.

Light reacts photochemically on ingredients and impurities in the paper. The products of these reactions then react with the cellulose, breaking molecular bonds and weakening the materials. Exposure to sunlight or light with high ultraviolet content can bleach some colors completely. After prolonged exposure to light, paper becomes more vulnerable to other forms of deterioration, causing it to become brittle and acidic, and lose strength. Infrared light actually changes the chemical bonds in the cellulose. This disintegration continues even if the poster is placed in darkness after exposure.

Posters should be stored in a darkroom. Safe levels of illumination for viewing are no higher than 25 lux. Notice how low the lights are in museums. Never use a gallery lamp on posters, as this can cause "hot spots" where the color fades.

MATTING, FRAMING, AND STORAGE

For display, posters should be matted and framed. The mat should be museum-quality, 100 percent acid-free, all-rag mat board. The mat prevents direct contact between the poster and the glass or Plexiglas. The poster should never be taped to the mat, and even so-called library tape, which is commercially available, can cause damage.

Rather, the poster should be "hinged" to hang behind the mat, using hinges made of Japan paper attached with wheat paste starch. The hinges are weaker than the poster paper, so if a framed poster falls off the wall, the hinges will tear rather than the poster paper.

Posters should never be displayed where they will be in direct sunlight or fluorescent light, and it is best to use a protective ultraviolet filtering glass or Plexiglass, sometimes referred to as "UV-coated." Plexiglas should not be used for display of any silk-screened poster.

If posters are to be stored, they should be kept flat in acid-free folders or encapsulated in 3-millimeter Melinex Mylar. For storage of valuable posters, a climate-controlled vault or room is well worth the time and effort invested in its design and construction. The vault should be kept at a constant temperature of 55 degrees Fahrenheit and a relative humidity level of 50 percent rh. It should be clean, dark, free of insects, and have a free circulation of filtered air.

While no one expects even an avid poster collector to become a trained paper conservator—and your home is probably not designed as a museum with light, temperature, and humidity controls—knowing the standards you should follow can at least help you take every measure possible to protect your posters and increase their longevity and value.

Remember the poster by Jules Chéret we mentioned at the beginning of this chapter that was torn and mounted on wood? Today, in fine condition, that poster is worth as much as $6,000 on the market . . . and that should be reason enough for caring properly for your collection.

❧ CHAPTER 9 ❧
Beauty Is in the Eyes of the Collector

BY RICHARD RUDNITSKY

Richard Rudnitsky is a collector and dealer of vintage posters in the Miami Beach Art Deco district and Long Island, New York. His collection ranges from fine turn-of-the-century posters to pieces from the 1950s. You can contact him at Vintage European and American Posters, 345 Ocean Drive #1019, Miami Beach, Florida 33139, (305) 673-8145, or at (516) 931-2787.

PICASSO WAS RIGHT ON THE MONEY

"By all means buy with your head," advised the great Picasso. "But do not forget to enjoy with your heart."

Picasso was a poster artist in his own right. And when it comes to looking at posters as an investment, his insight is right on the money in more ways than one. In my experience, the best way, if not the *only* way, to invest is first and foremost with your heart. If an image is beautiful and you love it, it probably has a good speculative value. It will inevitably be worth more as time passes.

Here's why: Posters have an intrinsic value. They salvage our history from time's ravages. They serve as a chronicle not only of early advertising, but of technology, style, and humor. They are rare. They are beautiful. They are also diminishing in supply.

In the world of vintage posters, one thing remains constant: There are no new vintage posters. Eventually every last attic will have been combed in search of that elusive find. Soon there will be nothing left to be discovered. It will be a sad day for linen backers, and a happier day for auctioneers. If you make the right acquisitions, prices can only go one way. But what is the right work to buy?

IF YOU LOVE IT . . .

I have one criterion for what I sell. I only sell posters I love. If I don't love an image, I cannot sell it. My hands won't reach for a poster that doesn't please me. I cannot fool anyone with a plastic smile. The calculated words "Isn't it just marvelous?" will not part my lips unless the poster *is* marvelous. Then I probably won't have to say that because clients will see it with their own eyes.

Collectors are always concerned with what a specific poster will be worth in the future. I tell them I don't know. It is simple enough to determine what it is worth now: Look in this book! But what about a piece that is not cataloged? Is it a good buy? Start by looking at it. Do you find it beautiful? My guess is that if you think so, someone else would too. Trust your eyes. Trust your heart. If you do, you're probably on your way to making a wise investment that you will certainly enjoy.

BEAUTY FOR A SOU

The first poster collectors had the right idea long before any poster was considered vintage, and ages before anyone might have thought a single poster would one day be sold for five digits. For a sou, a penny, a poster could be had. They were valuable to the first collectors because they were seductive, beautiful lithography. That's why they survived two world wars and countless paper shortages over the course of this century. They were beautiful. Whether they were "worth something" was hardly an issue. People loved beauty. People appreciated fine workmanship. Happily, we can still love and appreciate their beauty today.

JUST ONE LOOK IS ALL IT TOOK

Perhaps the best testament to following your heart is the story of how I got into poster dealing. I was living in Spain in the early 1980s. I had a portable computer that, by today's computer standards, would now be considered antediluvian. I was heading back to the United States.

A friend of mine was desperate for a computer. The European prices were more than double American prices. He suggested I part with mine and get a new one back in the States. The problem was that he didn't have much money. He asked me if I would consider a swap.

"For what?" I asked skeptically.

"For some old posters," he said, joking, but not joking. "You have to see them, they're beautiful."

He really didn't know how good his posters were, and I didn't know what I was getting into. I agreed to have a look. We went down to his wine cellar. Through dust and spiderwebs, he dug up a crumpled old folder his French father had left there long before anyone liked Ike. Just one look was all it took. From the first time I saw them—there were nine posters—I knew we had a deal.

Courtesy of Vintage
European and
American Posters.

They depicted a glorious world now gone—wine, early aviation, a sultry cabaret singer. I was entertained and moved by their beauty. I was intrigued and felt that they had to be worth something.

One poster from that collection, depicted here, is a Dutch insurance poster ca. 1908. The Dutch copy across the bottom of the poster says "Two Paths of Life—*Verzekerd* (Insured) and *Onverzekerd* (Uninsured)." The insured are happy couples marching arm in arm up to heaven while the uninsured are broken loners limping down to hell.

Posters were never meant to be subtle. They are often, as this one is, absolutely charming! I loved it and traded my computer for the Dutch poster along with the eight others.

The names of the artists didn't mean much to me then, but they do now. Among them were Cappiello, Pal, Cassandre, and Chéret! The poster god had smiled on me that day. From that day on, I was hooked.

Back then, I told my friend that the posters were among the most beautiful artwork I had ever seen.

"Of course they are," he said, with his Catalan nonchalance. "Richard, don't you realize that throughout history the best artists have always been commercial artists? Do you think all the artists of the Middle Ages were religious fanatics? It was the only place they could make a buck. Same here."

I never worried if I was getting my money's worth. I did, of course, and then some.

My friend was content with the computer, and I was excited about the posters. After we were done, I asked him which of us, in his opinion, was getting a better deal. "That is a gamble we'll both have to take," he said.

You bet it is.

❧ CHAPTER 10 ❧
Posters in Interior Design

BY LINDA TARASUK

Linda Tarasuk is co-owner of La Belle Epoque Vintage Posters, specializing in fine lithographic posters from the Art Nouveau and Art Deco periods. You can contact her at La Belle Epoque, 282 Columbus Avenue, New York, New York 10023, (212) 362-1770.

Posters make a grand statement when used in an interior setting, be it residential or commercial. Their size, energy, and color make them fun to work with, while still being extremely affordable. *(For a stunning example of posters used in interior design, see the color insert, photo 1.)*

Today, more people than ever are discovering the art of integrating fine posters into the decor of their homes and offices. If you are wondering how posters might work in your living spaces, here are a few ideas to get you started.

A poster can be used as a focal point in a room, and through its subject, it can tell a story appropriate either to the room itself or to the people who live or work there.

For example, the poster can depict the profession of the owner, such as medicine, entertainment, manufacturing, law—you name it. Many people enjoy having posters that reflect their hobbies and other interests, such as golf, tennis, bicycling, or cars. Poster topics are enormously varied. A poster might also be integrated into the feeling or purpose of the room; for example, a food- or drink-related poster is wonderful for the kitchen or dining area.

Fine examples of vintage posters exist in a wide variety of design styles—realistic, romantic, modern, cubist—styles that will complement any decor. For example, an Art Nouveau poster with its soft lines looks wonderful with traditional furnishings. However, it can also be used to soften a more contemporary or modern environment, just as a poster with clean angular Art Deco lines might set off accents of a more traditional home.

46

When in search of posters for home or work environment, start by looking at a wide variety of posters. This will give you a better sense of what interests you, both in terms of subject and in terms of style, and you will begin to visualize how posters might work in your decor. At first you might feel a bit intimidated choosing and using posters in interior design, but once you get used to working with them and see what they can do for an interior, you'll be hooked!

One of the best things about using posters in interior design is the way in which they can be used in very different spaces. For example, in spaces that are too narrow for a piece of furniture, a poster adds a new visual dimension.

Using a poster in a small, enclosed room or area actually makes it appear larger. Most people think that a small wall needs something small. Actually, a larger piece looks much better.

Consider the impact of color when using posters in interior design. The lively, exuberant colors of a vintage poster might be the splash of color needed to breathe life into a monotone room. Conversely, a very colorful room may benefit from a quieter, two-color poster that complements the background.

Even a very busy room can benefit from a poster that carries the same theme and colors. A room with a lovely floral print in pinks, greens, and yellows is the perfect setting for a colorful floral poster by Alphonse Mucha, such as his *Bières de la Meuse*. You can use posters either to blend or to contrast color-wise.

A poster can also introduce an entirely new color into the environment in a totally unexpected way. I've had several customers come into the gallery saying they don't want a poster with red in it, only to fall in love with a poster with bright red-orange lettering. I usually tell them to take it home to see what happens. Inevitably they report that the red lettering has added to the room.

Posters are also unique conversation pieces from a bygone era, imparting a sense of history to a room. As advertising art, they are documents of another time, and were meant to be displayed and appreciated—not put away in a drawer or closet. They can transport you and your guests to a different time and place. Just looking at a turn-of-the-century poster leads you to imagine what life was like, and to feel the *joie de vivre* they portray.

Over the past ten years, an increasing number of commercial and business spaces have also started using posters in interior design. Large lobbies, open wall spaces, waiting areas, and other commercial interiors benefit greatly from the use of posters. Corporate facilities, restaurants, clothing stores, theaters, and other locations are wonderful back-grounds for vintage posters.

When you begin to explore the world of posters, you'll find it's no exaggeration to say that there is something for everyone. There is practically no area of life, work, leisure, entertainment, or business that is not captured in fine poster art.

PART TWO

European Posters

❧ CHAPTER 11 ❧
French and Belgian Posters

FRANCE—"THE CRADLE OF THE MODERN POSTER"

If there were something called the Tomb of the Unknown Designer, Parisians would certainly claim to be the keepers of the flame. Much French energy has been expended over the past one hundred years to convince the rest of the world that France is the absolute center of the designed environment. In some cases, the French have a legitimate claim to hegemony, and the early poster is one such case. Paris was the "Cradle of the Modern Poster."

That is not to say that all of the outstanding artists from the beginnings of poster design were French—far from it. Paris was the magnet for talented designers from Switzerland, Belgium, Italy, Czechoslovakia, Holland, and elsewhere. However, outstanding artists living in Paris are automatically part of French national heritage.

So it was with Swiss artist and posterist Eugene Grasset (1845–1917), who would become the major theoretician of the Art Nouveau movement. When Grasset immigrated to Paris from Lausanne, Switzerland, in 1871, the field of illustrated posters was still in its infancy. Jules Chéret (1836–1933) was just experimenting with color lithography. Three years earlier, the French fine artist Edouard Manet had created the first illustrated advertising poster. His design for the poster *Champfleury Les Chats*, which advertises a book, was a black-and-white lithograph pasted to a larger sheet of colored paper.

It wasn't until 1881 that a new bill-posting law was passed that created official posting places, which protected posters from vandalism. In a very French manner, the government set about creating a format for standard sizes based on two existing posters, the *Colombier* (24 x 32½ inches) and the *Grand Aigle* (27½ x 43¾ inches). In a manner typical of French people faced with a government regulation, these sizes were not always adhered to, and many posters were printed in several different dimensions, reduced in size for collectors' portfolios, or scaled to fit into publications and newspapers.

The importance of the 1881 law was that merchants and businessmen who occupied positions of power in Paris were free to commission advertising posters to their hearts' content, and talented artists were attracted to the newly sanctioned medium by droves.

Posters came forth in an explosion, and artists' reputations were made seemingly overnight. The first poster exhibition was held in Paris in 1884, with posters pasted from floor to ceiling of the gallery, much as they would appear on the street hoardings. The first ten years of such postings were dominated by the work of Jules Chéret, who had his first one-man exhibition in Paris in 1890. By then, his color lithographic techniques were legendary, and the cities of France were overrun with posters.

JULES CHÉRET (1836–1932) AND THE ART OF COLOR LITHOGRAPHY

Jules Chéret is called alternately "the father of color lithography" and "the father of the modern illustrated poster." He devoted his career to the development of color lithography as an inspired art, integrated with the modern phenomenon of advertising — opening the way for a younger generation of artists, including Lautrec, Steinlen, and Mucha to produce spectacular works in the medium. (For a description of the lithographic process, see the chapter Poster Printing and Terminology.)

Influenced both by artists of the day and by eighteenth-century roco-co painters, Chéret's posters capture the essence of an era and style in the arts called *La Belle Epoque,* or "the Beautiful Epoch."

The Belle Epoque style was forwarded by numerous fine artists who finally succeeded in establishing the fine art print as a genre to be respected on a par with oil paintings. Artists such as James Tissot (1836–1902), Edgar Chahine (1874–1947), Manuel Robbe (1872–1936), and Paul Cesar Helleu (1859–1927) concentrated on the image of an elegant and sophisticated woman who represented all that was civil and good about life in a time of peace. Helleu created at least one poster for the famous Parisian print and poster dealer Sagot. Robbe also was commissioned to design posters.

Born in Paris in 1836, Chéret was the son of a typographer, and was apprenticed to a lithographer at age thirteen. He spent many years working for various printers, attended l'Ecole Nationale de Dessin, and spent his Sundays sketching and studying paintings in the Louvre. In his twenties Chéret made two trips to London to seek work, and on the second trip was hired by the French perfume maker Eugene Rimmel, who became the artist's benefactor. In 1866 Rimmel advanced Chéret the funds to return to Paris and set up his own printworks with the massive presses needed to produce large color stone lithographs.

Chéret set out to completely transform the dull advertising broadsides that papered walls and kiosks along the streets of Paris, enlarging them to bold dimensions replete with bright color and eye-catching imagery. His success brought acclaim among clients, critics, collectors, artists, and people in the streets.

He was awarded a silver medal at the 1878 International Exposition and the gold medal in 1889. By 1890 he was made a chevalier of the Legion d'Honneur, commended for creating a new art industry through the application of art to commercial and industrial printing. In 1900, after creating more than a thousand posters, he retired to Nice and devoted himself to painting until blindness made work impossible. The Louvre organized a retrospective exhibition of his work in 1912, and in 1928 the Musée Chéret was founded in Nice. He died in 1932 at age ninety-six.

Chéret at his most fanciful created parades of colorful personages, which often included a Pierrot, masked dancers, marionettes, and coquettes. His idealized woman, an allegorical beauty who often seems to be almost floating on air, had a pretty countenance that became so recognizable that she has come to be called "Chérette." This celebratory population of characters promoted performers, masked balls, music halls, operas, skating rinks, novels, aperitifs, medicinal bitters, bicycles, lamp oil, and even cough drops.

He is still the most popular of French poster artists because of his talent, his ground-breaking lithography, and his prolific production. His posters are everywhere on the market, and range in price from under $1,000 to $8,000 and sometimes more, with most of them bringing $2,000 to $5,000. Thoroughly chronicled, his work is the subject of a well-known *catalogue raisonné* or a systematic complete listing of his work by Lucy Broido (see Bibliography).

ARTISTS INFLUENCED BY CHÉRET

It is indeed hard to find a French artist of the time who was not influenced in some way by Chéret, either in terms of artistic style or lithographic technique. Chéret's printworks ultimately merged with another company to create Imprimerie Chaix, where he remained a partner and the artistic director. Chaix was responsible for a huge outpouring of posters for an incredibly large number of clients, and the numerous artists commissioned to produce works were perhaps the most strongly influenced by him.

In addition Chaix in many ways set the tone for the whole world of poster collecting, with its serial publication of *Les Maîtres de L'Affiche*, or

"The Masters of the Poster," over 250 plates that represented, in miniature, some of the best posters from numerous countries. (See special section on *Les Maîtres de L'Affiche* in this chapter.)

Among the many artists influenced by Chéret who are today collected and recognized as poster artists in their own right are: Alfred Choubrac (1853–1902), who created some four hundred posters; Henri Gray (aka Henri Boulanger, 1858–1924), who created some stunning designs, notably *Petrole Stella*; René Pean (1864–1940); the travel posterist Misti (aka Ferdinand Mifliez, 1865–1923); and Georges Meunier (1869–1934), who was employed as a staff artist by Chaix, and whose posters are gaining increased recognition in today's market.

Two other artists influenced by Chéret deserve special mention: Jules-Alexandre Grün (1886–1934) and Pal (aka Jean de Paléologue, 1860–1942).

Grün left his distinctive mark on the French poster world by the turn of the century, designing for many famous singers of the café concert. His highly original and comic designs for such posters as *La Pepinière — Oh! la la! Mon Empereur!*, ca. 1900, have long been overshadowed by his towering contemporaries.

Grün's women are not the diaphanously clad winsome lasses of Chéret, but rather buxom, fun-loving Parisiennes who laugh the night away at the Bal Tabarin and other cabarets. While the market has taken note of his work in the last five years, many of his posters are still undervalued, and relatively affordable for an early artist of his quality.

Jean de Paléologue, who signed his work "PAL," has emerged strongly in the market in the last few years, but also remains relatively undervalued. He was born a Rumanian prince, but abandoned his homeland for London in the 1880s, where he did illustrations for magazines, including a few sought-after caricatures for the satirical society publication *Vanity Fair*.

He moved to Paris in 1893, and from that time until about 1900, he produced a large number of outstanding posters. Though no doubt influenced by Chéret, his posters were mainly printed by Chéret's competitors. His works range from stunning effects of light and color for the performer *Loie Fuller at the Folies Bergère*, to clowns advertising brandy. He designed for a variety of subjects, including bicycles, butter, resorts, publications, and opera.

His elegantly dressed women are more voluptuous than Chéret's, and more alluring than Grün's, and his sense of color is outstanding. In 1900 he moved to the United States, where he worked again as an illustrator. He created a few rarely seen posters for the American magazine *Truth*, and finally retired to Miami.

THE PAINTER-POSTERISTS

In the early 1890s, several fine artists were attracted to poster design. Several who were best known for painting rather than printmaking made significant contributions to the field. Pierre Bonnard (1867–1947) and Edouard Vuillard (1868–1940), two of the so-called Nabis painters, both produced posters that are today highly sought after, with prices in the $5,000 to $10,000 range. In 1897 Bonnard created the first poster for the influential journal *L'Estampe et L'Affiche*, which chronicled the print and poster world.

In the year 1890, as the story goes, a friend came to compliment Bonnard on a poster he had seen in the street, and asked to meet Bonnard's printer, Ancourt. The friend thought that he, too, might turn his painting skills to poster commissions. Bonnard was more than happy to introduce his printer to his aristocratic friend: Henri de Toulouse-Lautrec (1864–1901).

Toulouse-Lautrec's artistry towers above the world of the French poster in the 1890s. While he created only thirty or so, they are considered the highest expression of the art form and command the highest prices on today's market, ranging all the way up to the current record price of $220,000 for *Le Moulin Rouge*, which, in fact, was his first poster, created in 1891.

Much myth surrounds the life of this diminutive giant, whose legs atrophied as the result of childhood accidents. His imagery is full of dynamic movement and irreverent portraits of the chanteuses of Monmartre. He was influenced by Japanese design styles, and admired Gaugin, van Gogh, and Edgar Degas. He perfected his illustrative style by working for many periodicals, such as *Paris Illustré*, *Le Rire*, and *Courrier Français*, among others. He became a master of the lithographic technique called "spatter," in which ink is sprayed on the lithographic stone by drawing a blade over the brush.

Ironically, perhaps because of the singularity of his talent, Toulouse-Lautrec did not have a large impact on other French poster artists, unless one counts one or two very rare posters by Jacques Villon (1875–1963) and the effect he may have had on Theophile-Alexandre Steinlen (1859–1923).

Steinlen followed in the footsteps of his countryman Grasset, immigrating to Paris from Switzerland in 1872. His social realist style sets him apart from the gaiety that was the Paris of the bourgeoisie and bistros, and marks him as one of the most original posterists of the period. A Socialist, he also worked as an illustrator for the publications *Gil Blas Illustré*, *L'Echo de Paris*, and *L'Assiette au Beurre*. He had a distinct love for cats, and depicted them frequently in his posters. He is also one of the most widely recognized French World War I poster artists (see the chapter on World War Posters).

Steinlen has a strong and growing following in the poster market today, especially as an appreciation of history's more sobering realities seems to be on the rise. Prices for his posters already range from a few thousand dollars to more than $15,000, and the years ahead will definitely see continued appreciation of his artistic talents.

ALPHONSE MUCHA (1860–1939) AND THE EMERGENCE OF ART NOUVEAU

A new movement in the decorative arts, Art Nouveau, began to have an impact on the world of posters in the 1890s. It was led by Eugene Grasset, whose posters reflect his taste for the Gothic, and who played a role not unlike that of William Morris in the English Arts and Crafts movement. While his theories had perhaps a stronger impact than his posters, he influenced many other artists.

The Art Nouveau style is characterized by its sinuous, free-flowing lines, drawn mostly from nature. Women with long, tendril like hair, dragonflies, and vinelike plants were all popular Art Nouveau motifs, not only in graphics, but in furniture, glass, and other decorative arts.

When one thinks of Art Nouveau posters in France, one is most likely to think of the artist who seems to epitomize the style: Alphonse Mucha (1860–1939). Born in Czechoslovakia and trained at the Munich Fine Arts Academy, he came to Paris, where he studied at the Académie Julian until 1889.

He worked exclusively for the printing firm F. Champenois in Paris. From the time he created his first poster in 1894, his influence spread beyond the borders of France to other countries, including Italy, the United States, Belgium, and Germany, where Art Nouveau was called Jugendstil after the periodical *Jugend*, which promoted the new style.

His posters for Sarah Bernhardt are among the most sought after of all French posters. Mucha designed all of the posters for her plays from 1894 to 1903, as well as sets and costumes for her productions. Today, Mucha's posters and his decorative panels are highly prized and highly valued, with many commanding over $10,000.

Other artists recognized for their posters in the Art Nouveau style are Italian-born Manuel Orazi (1860–1934), who designed stunning posters for performers and for *La Maison Moderne*, one of the leading Art Nouveau shops founded in 1899; and the Dutch immigrant Georges de Feure (aka Georges van Suilters, 1868–1943), whose poster for the *Almanach de Paris* is well-known and whose work continues to gain popularity.

Yet another Art Nouveau artist, Paul Berthon (1872–1909), who studied under Grasset, deserves special mention. His soft, pastel color palette and almost mystic imagery distinguish his work. Berthon is also known for decorative lithographs and panels without text, as well as for his advertising posters. These often appear together at auctions and at dealers' shops. The best reference to his work and that of his teacher is *Berthon & Grasset*, by Victor Arwas (see Bibliography).

Art Nouveau was the predominant style in the decorative arts for about twenty years, roughly from 1890 to 1910. The style really peaked near the turn of the century, and slowly ebbed during the following decade. It flourished more in Europe than in America, though some American poster artists, such as Louis Rhead and Will Bradley, made notable contributions.

The term Art Nouveau is said to have originated with a shop called Maison de l'Art Nouveau, owned by Siegfried Bing. Bing exhibited leading artists, including Bonnard, Vuillard, and Aubrey Beardsley. Rene Lalique created many of his best Art Nouveau jewelry designs for Bing's store.

At the end, the Art Nouveau style became so obsessed with the excesses of ornamentation that it became further and further detached from the integration of art and life it claimed to seek. Design movements centered outside of France and in opposition to Art Nouveau were poised to have a dramatic impact on graphic design and all the decorative arts. Their influence would be felt particularly after World War I.

SOME SUBJECT AREAS FOR COLLECTING EARLY FRENCH POSTERS

Le Salon des Cent

By the mid-1890s, the poster was firmly established as an important advertising medium and artistic vehicle. In 1890 the United States had its first exhibition of French posters at the Grolier Club in New York. In 1894 the Salon des Cent was established in Paris, organized by Léon Deschamps, editor of the literary artistic review *La Plume*. Monthly exhibitions featured one artist or several, but no more than a hundred items were shown at a time, and thus the name.

Among others, Deschamps commissioned Eugene Grasset (1841–1917), Frimin Bouisset (1859–1925), Frederick Cazals (1865–1941), Fernand Fau (1858–1917), Arsène Herbinier (1869–?), Pierre Bonnard (1867–1947), Andrew Kay Womrath (1869– ?), George de Feure, and even one (honored) American, Louis Rhead (1857–1927).

The artists from this series bringing the highest prices today are Alphonse Mucha, who designed two annual posters, and Toulouse-Lautrec, who created a poster for the Salon's "International Poster Exhibition" in 1896.

Posters in the Salon des Cent series represent some of the finest poster artists of the day, and have become a popular collecting "motif" for some.

French Opera Posters

In 1976 author Lucy Broido drew attention to the wide range of French posters created for opera, operettas, and musical ballets, and created another "motif" for collecting that continues today (see Bibliography).

From the late 1860s until about 1930, the music publishing firms Heugel & Company and G. Hartman commissioned dozens of posters for opera, operettas, and ballets by musicians such as Louis Varney, Jules Massenet, and Richard Strauss.

Many well-known artists from the Belle Epoque through the Art Deco period were commissioned to create opera posters, including Eugene Grasset, PAL, Steinlen, Henri Gray, René Pean, Alfred Choubrac, Emile Bertrand, Georges Dola (1872–1950), Manuel Orazi (1860–1934), Georges Rochegrosse (1859–1938), and Maurice Dufrène (1876–1955), who headed the boutique La Maîtrise at the department store Galleries Lafayette.

Rather surprisingly, many of these posters remain very affordable to the beginning collector, and are often found at antique and poster shows. The earlier opera and operetta posters are generally smaller than many French posters, but are highly decorative full-color lithographs. Happily, many of them can still be purchased for a few hundred dollars, and only a few sought-after ones sell for more than $1,000.

Les Maîtres de l'Affiche

In 1896 Imprimerie Chaix, which had absorbed Chéret's own printing company, began to issue posters in miniature for collectors under Chéret's direction. Called *Les Maîtres de L'Affiche*, or "Masters of the Poster," they were issued in monthly portfolios of four posters each, with a total of 256 plates issued until 1900. It is said that Chéret himself closely supervised the lithographic rendering of the posters into miniatures.

Les Maîtres was only one of several publications that sprung up to supply to the recently established poster-collecting market. (See the section on The First Poster Collectors in Chapter 1, The World of Posters.) Today, as then, these miniatures are a way for collectors to appreciate and create a truly international collection.

Each month a subscriber to the series would receive four plates in an issue that cost about 2½ francs. Chéret, ever the self-promoter, made sure that the first plate in each issue was one of his own designs, though he chose the best European and American posterists to complete the issues. The full sheet of each poster carries the embossed blind stamp of the publisher in the margin.

Today, while some plates sell for under $100, many of those by leading artists can sell for several hundred. However, when compared to the several-thousand-dollar value of the original, large version of the same image, they are still a bargain. Individual plates have been appearing with increasing frequency at auctions, and the complete collection, bound into five volumes with covers designed by Paul Berthon (1872–1909), has brought over $16,000 at auction.

As a guide to identifying the plates, a collector should be armed with the Dover paperback *Masters of the Poster 1896–1900*, a softcover book featuring full-page color reproductions of all 256 plates in the series. We have included a special pricing section for *Les Maîtres* at the end of the price listings following this chapter.

DESIGN INFLUENCES FROM OTHER COUNTRIES

Before the turn of the century, design movements outside of France were growing up in opposition to Art Nouveau, which, proponents of these movements felt, was altogether too leisurely and ornate a style for the changing world. By 1910 the Art Nouveau style had essentially been replaced in France, but the emergence of a new dominant style was not complete until after World War I when the Art Deco style evolved from a host of influences.

The Glasgow School and the Arts and Crafts Movement

Charles Rennie Mackintosh's Glasgow School and the Arts and Crafts Movement in England were among the first to strive for a more functional style of design in the decorative arts. The Arts and Crafts movement in both England and the United States fought against the use of ornamentation for its own sake. Arts and Crafts posterists began to design with simplified shapes and flat colors. (See the chapters on English Posters and American Turn-of-the-Century Posters.)

The Vienna Secession

In Vienna, architect Otto Wagner insisted on a return to straight lines and geometric forms, and Adolf Loos attacked what he called the "delirium of Art Nouveau." In 1897 Architect Josef Hoffmann and some of his students founded the Vienna Secession, a movement that was committed to functional and geometric designs.

Posters of the Viennese Secession, some of which are very scarce, have doubled and tripled in price since the 1986 Museum of Modern Art exhibition "Vienna 1900." They appear very rarely on the market, and many can bring tens of thousands of dollars. Noted artists include Gustav Klimt (1862–1918), Egon Schiele (1890–1919), Koloman Moser (1868– 1918), Berthold Löffler (1874–1960), and others.

German Design and the Bauhaus

German posterists such as Ludwig Hohlwein (1874–1949) developed a simplified, more geometric style shortly after the turn of the century, which was more directly influenced by Vienna and the Arts and Crafts movement than the posters in France. The German Bauhaus, founded in 1919, did as much to revolutionize typography as architecture. Often elongated and condensed, the new typography lent itself to the sense of speed that characterized modern design and modern life. Many of the new typefaces were sans serif, adding to their sleekness. Popular new styles included Paul Renner's "Futura" (1928), Koch's "Kabel" (1927), Eric Gill's "Gill Sans" (1928), and others still widely used today.

Many of the founders and teachers of this design school came to the United States in the 1930s, fleeing Nazi Germany. The Bauhaus relocated to Chicago in 1937, and had a strong impact on American graphic design.

These and other design influences, such as the Futurists in Italy and the Dutch De Stijl design movement, would slowly but surely have an impact on changing the face of graphic design in France.

FRENCH POSTERS FROM 1900 TO WORLD WAR I

After the turn of the century, and until the outbreak of World War I, French poster art declined somewhat. Lautrec died in 1901, and Paul Berthon in 1909. Other posterists from the 1890s went on to new professions. In 1904 Alphonse Mucha left France, making several trips to the United States and finally returning to Czechoslovakia in 1912, where he devoted himself to painting and creating official designs for Czech bank notes and other government commissions.

One outstanding posterist did emerge in the period from 1900 to the outbreak of World War I: an Italian immigrant, Leonetto Cappiello (1875–1942). Though he continued to receive commissions from Italian clients, Cappiello arrived in Paris in 1898, and by the year 1900 was already well-known for his "French" posters.

Cappiello's posters are notable for their direct impact: bold, striking color combinations; plain, often black, backgrounds that serve to emphasize the central illustration and product name; and humorous, eye-catching images of people and animals, often in close-up.

Where earlier poster artists often sought to paint an entire scene or an elaborate cast of characters, Cappiello was an ad man's dream—a designer who understood the value of sheer visual impact in delivering a sales message. No wonder he was so often commissioned by manufacturers of an array of products, including cars, beverages, cigarettes, corsets, perfumes, soaps, household products, and chocolate. Less frequently he would also be commissioned by cabaret performers and the Folies Bergère.

Before World War I, most of Cappiello's posters were printed by the firm Vercasson. After World War I, Cappiello would continue to produce posters with unmistakable talent, usually printed by Devambez. It is now estimated that Cappiello created nearly one thousand poster designs, not only for French clients, but for advertisers in Italy, Belgium, Spain, England, and other countries.

His posters are receiving increased exposure and attracting new collectors. Many of his posters already sell in the $2,000 to $5,000 range; however, some very good ones are still available for less than that. He will undoubtedly appear frequently on the market in the years ahead.

By the time France entered World War I, a new design style, today called Art Deco, was already emerging. However, the full flowering of the new style would be retarded until after the war, as artists put their talents at the service of their patriotic duties (see the chapter World War Posters).

FRENCH ART DECO

The French design style that was emerging at the time, now called Art Deco, was more simplified than Art Nouveau, but still reflected a spirit of opulence in its use of exotic woods and materials in furnishings and decorations. It was strongly influenced by the lavish sets and costumes of Sergei Diaghilev's *Ballets Russes*, which arrived in Paris in 1909. French Art Deco had its roots in the world of fashion, and its influence expanded when the fashion designers became *ensembliers*, or "interior designers."

The most outspoken French advocate of a more modern style, architect Le Corbusier, had been influenced by the German Werkbund exhibition in Paris in 1910. However, his more angular modern style, characterized by the use of materials such as tubular steel, was more Germanic than French. It was, in fact, this Germanic style that would have the greatest impact on American Art Deco.

The early French Art Deco artists, however, were able to keep the new style at bay until after the famous 1925 Paris *Exposition des Arts Décoratifs et Industriels Modernes*. Their desire to ignore the modernists was evident when a 10-foot-high fence was constructed to hide Corbusier's pavilion at the Exposition. They would have nothing to do with a display where furniture was called "household equipment."

The world was changing around them, however. The pressures of urbanization, a growing demand for industrialized production, and economic imperatives would force the adoption of the new style almost universally before the 1929 Wall Street crash. The grand French Art Deco style would survive into the 1930s only through commissions for ocean liners and public buildings.

Graphic design also changed to fit the times. Advertising became a critical vehicle to attract wider markets to a host of new manufactured goods being offered. Modern posters had to feature images and print strong enough to be read from passing cars. They captured atttention with typography, the central image of the product, bold lines and colors, short messages, and interesting angles and perspectives. Important "advertising agencies," such as Cassandre's Alliance Graphique, were founded by poster artists.

It has been argued that posters were, in fact, the vanguard of the new design movement. In many instances the advertising poster was the general public's first exposure to new design ideas.

Happily, fine art printing techniques such as lithography still dominated poster production, offering artists an appropriate medium for expressing their talents while serving commercial interests. Even the photomontage posters of the period were primarily the execution of an artist's, rather than a camera's, vision. After World War II, however, the photographic image would overcome the illustrated image, almost completely displacing the fine artist from the world of commercial advertising.

Highly sought-after posters of the Art Deco period include works by artists such as Jean Carlu (b. 1900), Paul Colin (1892–1985), Daniel DeLosques (1880–1915), Jean-Gabriel Domergue (1889–1961), Jean Dupas (1882–1964), Charles Gesmar (1900–1928), Georges Lepape (1887–1917), and Charles Loupot (1892–1962).

Some of the best posters of this period were created for performers and cabarets. Well-known stage performers such as Josephine Baker, Mistinguett, Alice Soulie, Spinelly, Marguerite Valmond, and others commissioned new posters frequently. Gesmar, who designed about fifty posters in his short lifetime, created almost half of them for Mistinguett!

Paul Colin's posters for Josephine Baker's *Revue Nègre* at the Music Hall des Champs Elysée did as much to promote a new form of poster design as black American jazz. All posters for Josephine Baker skyrocketed in the past few years, and the rare *La Revue Nègre* was reportedly sold a few years ago by a dealer for $45,000. Colin also created posters by Loie Fuller, the Casino de Paris, Tabarin, and other performers and theaters. He went on to have a very productive career, creating fine poster designs into the 1950s.

Georges Lepape is best known for his fashion illustrations for *Vogue*, but was also commissioned to create several posters. Charles Loupot and Robert Bonfils (1882–1972) both created posters for the 1925 Paris *Exposition des Arts Décoratifs et Industriels Modernes*, which are highly sought after for both their design and historic importance.

Jean Carlu was inspired by the cubists, and created stunning Art Deco designs. He later devoted his graphic skills to the World War II effort, creating effective wartime Art Deco posters. He continued to design posters in the decades after the war, and many of these posters from the 1950s, 1960s, and even 1970s are today finding a place in the market.

Jean Dupas developed an original style that is immediately recognizable, particularly in his posters for the *Salon des Artistes Décorateurs*, the influential circle of artists who controlled the world of French design until the 1925 Exposition. Dupas's most sought-after posters, however, were created for the London Underground (see the chapter on English Posters).

By far the most collected and overall highest-priced artist of the Art Deco period is A. M. Cassandre (1901–1968), who created an entirely new style of advertising design, reflective of the later trends of Art Deco, and more "modern" than France had seen until that time.

Cassandre's first poster appeared in 1923 and set the tone for a whole new style. He influenced an entire generation of graphic designers, both in France and abroad. An important exhibition of his work was held in this country in 1936 at the Museum of Modern Art in New York, and his influence consequently spread in America. However, it was not until 1951 that the Musée des Arts Decoratifs in Paris held a retrospective of his work.

Many posters by Cassandre, especially his posters for the French state railways or *Chemins de Fer* and for ocean liners such as *La Normandie*, easily sell in the range of $8,000 to $20,000 and often more. His bold avant-garde style quickly became the standard of French Art Deco design, replacing the early fashion influence with architectural and structural design elements.

Recent years have seen record-breaking prices for some Cassandre posters as a well-heeled circle of collectors in both the United States and Japan have vied for the rarest example.

Another French posterist, Pierre Fix-Masseau (1869–1937), had been a sculptor, but became a poster artist between the two world wars. The influence of Cassandre is evident in his poster *Exactitude*, promoting the French railways.

Another artist with a distinctive style whose work is, happily, more affordable is Francis Bernard. Bernard was employed for thirty years as the art director for the Salon des Arts Ménagers, or the "Salon of Household Arts," an annual Parisian "home show." His posters, which presaged the post–World War II style of the 1940s and 1950s, can still be purchased for under $1,000.

Bernard Villemot (1911–1989) has gained attention in recent years for his simple yet effective designs for Bally shoes and other commercial clients. Villemot posters have become very popular in the last few years since his death, and appear on the market with increasing frequency. Prices can vary greatly, so it is best to shop around.

As French posters evolved from the Art Nouveau to the Art Deco period, there was a widening gulf between "artists' posters" and those by graphic designers created for commercial advertisers. While today we recognize the enormous talents of Cassandre, he was, in fact, not a painter, and did not gain recognition in the world of fine art in his lifetime, in spite of the museum exhibitions already mentioned.

THE MODERN MASTERS

French and French-based artists such as Pablo Picasso (1881–1973), Marc Chagall (1887–1985), Joan Miró (1893–1983), Georges Braque (1882–1963), Raoul Dufy (1877–1953), Fernand Leger (1881–1955), and Henri Matisse (1869–1954) created several fine artists' posters, mainly for their own exhibitions.

However, be aware that few were actually designed by the artists originally and specifically as posters. More often, a gallery or a museum simply reproduced one of the artist's paintings on a poster to announce an exhibition. The latter have very little value and won't appreciate much over time. For example, there are hundreds of Picasso exhibition posters, but only about fifty of them are considered "original" posters, designed specifically by him as posters.

Posters by these artists are most commonly found in editions published by Galerie Maeght. Before 1964, most were printed by the lithographer Atelier Mourlot, where many of these artists also created their fine prints. After that time, most were printed by Maeght's own company, Arte. Maeght has reprinted many of these later posters, and so they have remained inexpensive and not very collectible.

Without a reference book it is almost impossible in many cases to know the difference between an "original" poster and one that simply reproduces another work of art. *Catalogue raisonnés* on individual artists can be used to determine if a work was originally designed as a poster, or if it was first created as a painting, print, or drawing. The best single source is the book *Les Affiches Originales des Maîtres de L'Ecole de Paris* (The Original Posters of the Masters of the French School), compiled by Fernand Mourlot in 1959. Out of print, it can still be bought through rare book dealers. At $250–$300, it is well worth the price if you are serious about collecting these artists.

Though still affordable, the original posters by these artists have appreciated over the years, and will probably continue to do so. However, in many cases you can still purchase an original Picasso or Miró poster for $500 to $1,000.

If the poster is signed by hand by the artist, as opposed to being signed on the lithographic stone, the price can easily triple or quadruple. Even nonoriginal posters that are hand-signed easily bring hundreds of dollars, and some nonoriginal, unsigned Picasso posters can sell in the $200–$400 range, depending on the importance of the exhibition.

Also note that because these posters are relatively recent, there is no reason to settle for less than excellent condition. Be aware, too, that lithographs, linocuts, silk screens, and other fine art printing techniques will always have more value than posters that are photo-offset-printed. (See the chapter on Poster Printing and Terminology for more information.)

Some of the original posters to look for are Picasso's Vallauris posters for his ceramics exhibitions, which he designed and printed between 1948 and 1964. Depending on how early the poster is and whether or not it is hand-signed, it can sell for a few hundred dollars to $5,000 and more.

Other Picasso posters worth owning are *Galerie 65–Cannes*, 1956; *Galerie Leiris: Peintres 1955–56;* the two ceramic exhibition posters for *La Maison de la Pensée Française*, 1958; the exhibition of his original posters in 1959 held at the same place; the 1959 Galerie Leiris poster *Los Meines;* and *Côte d'Azur*, 1952.

Joan Miró also created several posters that are increasingly in demand. Among the more valuable are *Oeuvres Récentes — Galerie Maeght*, 1956; *Galerie Matarasso*, 1957; *Le Lézard aux Plumes*, 1975; and *La Caixa*, 1979.

(*Author's note:* Special thanks to Bob Brown and Susan Reinhold of Reinhold Brown Gallery, New York, who provided the basis of this section on Modern Masters, excerpted from the first edition of this guide.)

BELGIAN POSTERS

Before 1890, few notable illustrated posters had been produced in Belgium. However, tied to France both culturally and commercially, Belgium soon discovered the talents of Chéret, who exhibited in

Brussels in 1890. Posters in Belgium followed the same stylistic development from Art Nouveau to Art Deco as French posters. Because many Belgian artists have French names, they are often mistakenly identified as French posterists.

The art world in Belgium was flourishing in the 1890s, and most of the artists belonged to one of several "circles" or artists' societies. One of the most influential of these circles was called "The Twenty." This group would later change their name to *La Libre Esthetique* (The Free Esthetic). In 1894 they started a magazine under the same name, which promoted posters as a new art form.

Other publications and other circles were springing up as well, including *Pour L'Art* (For Art, 1891), *Le Sillon* (The Furrow, 1893), and *l'Art Idealiste* (Idealistic Art, 1896). Posters for these publications are among the most sought-after Belgian posters today. Many leading artists, including Theodore Van Rysselberghe (1862–1926) and Fernand Toussaint (1873–1956), created works for these publications.

Toussaint was a painter, and created only a few posters. In this way, his work is comparable to that of Henri de Toulouse-Lautrec in France. His first poster for *Le Sillon*, created in 1895, has a finely executed painterly feel and Art Nouveau hand lettering. It can sell for more than $20,000. His 1897 poster for *Café Jacqmotte* is a strikingly colorful work, and also sells in the same price range.

From this cultural and literary arena, Belgian posters would soon spread to other more commercial fields, as merchants began commissioning artists to execute posters.

If Toussaint was the Belgian Lautrec, Privat Livemont (1861–1936) is often considered the Belgian Alphonse Mucha. In fact, the two artists developed their art, their reputations, and their own personal styles almost simultaneously.

Livemont studied in Paris, where he painted architectural decorations and stage designs. He was a prolific posterist. Although he began his first poster work in 1896, by 1900 he had created more than thirty posters, some for French clients. For the most part, Livemont used the female form (most often in profile), elaborate ornamentation, and a variety of color combinations to attract the viewer's eye. Like Chéret and other leading posterists, Livemont drew his designs directly on the lithographic stone himself. He often used the talented firms of J.-L. Goffart in Brussels or Van Leer in Amsterdam for printing his posters. Like Mucha, he also created decorative panels, printed like his poster images, but with little or no advertising text, for use as decorations in the home.

Livemont's work is very popular today, and he has a strong following of collectors. Many of his posters sell in the range of $3,000 to $8,000, but can sell for as much as $10,000 and higher. He created posters for numerous products, resorts, and manufacturers, including the liqueur *Bitter Oriental, Cacao Van Houten,* colognes, corsets, and perfumes.

Henri Meunier (1873–1922) was another outstanding Belgian Art Nouveau artist. He participated in the Sillon exhibitions beginning in 1898, and developed a reputation for his posters featuring concerts and cultural events. One of his most striking and desirable posters is from 1897 for *Rajah* coffee. It depicts an exotic-looking woman sipping her coffee against a plain background where the steam makes lazy Art Nouveau swirls in the air. The colors reinforce the overall feeling with flat shades of tan, flesh, brown, and accents of green and red, all applied in a manner reminiscent of Japanese prints.

Belgium is a country whose culture is really half-Flemish and half-French. The Flemish, until relatively recently, have primarily comprised the working classes, whereas the French generally belonged to the more highly educated and urban merchant classes. The proximity of Holland had an impact on artists whose roots were in Flanders or Zeeland.

The most outstanding Flemish artist of the early period was Hendrick Cassiers (1858–1944). His best-known works promote shipping companies such as the Ostende-Dover Line, which crossed the English Channel, the Red Star Line (which became the Holland America Line), and the America Line. Other well-known works feature beach resorts and other subjects. His scenes often include Flemish peasants in their traditional costumes, such as Flemish workers smoking pipes and wearing fishing gear, standing on the shore watching the steamers arrive.

Other Belgian artists of this early period to look for are: Emile Berchmans (1867–1947), Gisbert Combaz (1869–1941), Adolphe Crespin (1859–1944), Auguste Donnay (1862–1921), James Ensor (1860–1949), George Lemmen (1865–1916), Victor Mignot (1872–1944), Armand Rassenfosse (1862–1934) Felicien Rops (1833–1898), and Henry van de Velde (1863–1957).

After World War I, Belgian posters, like the French, changed to fit a faster and more complex world where advertising was designed in a different manner. However, Belgium was slow to make the changes, and did not even have a pavilion at the 1925 Paris *Exposition des Arts Décoratifs et Industriels Modernes.*

The best "Belgian" posterist of the new era, and the leading exponent of the Art Deco style in Belgian posters, would come from Switzerland. His name was Léo Marfurt (1894–1977). After moving to Belgium in 1927, he created an advertising agency, Les Creations Publicitaires, which he ran until 1957. Like Cassandre's agency in France, Marfurt's agency created posters for many clients, products, and services, including Belga Cigarettes, Chrysler and Minerva automobiles, the English LNER (London and North Eastern Railway), resorts, and a host of others.

In addition to Marfurt, some good poster designs of the period came from Francis Delamare, who also founded an advertising agency; Auguste Mambour (1896–1968); Milo Martinet; Lucien de Roeck (b. 1915); and others, including the country's leading surrealist painter, Rene Magritte (1898–1967).

From the 1930s until now, many of the best Belgian posters are for travel, fairs, and festivals. The Art Deco style continued to be used in Belgium through the 1950s, and posters from this period are now increasingly seen at shows. In addition, as the Flemish population has increasingly entered the middle classes and the political and economic mainstream, posters in Flemish are more common.

TO LEARN MORE ABOUT FRENCH AND BELGIAN POSTERS

French posters are the most frequently seen at any poster exhibition or sale, and Belgian posters are often found alongside them. For collectors with serious interest in French posters, we suggest that you visit one of the dealers we recognized for their assistance with this chapter in the Acknowledgments or those listed in the Resource Guide.

Several museums have fine collections of French posters, including the Art Institute of Chicago, the Baltimore Museum of Art, the Museum of Modern Art in New York, and the Zimmerle Art Museum at Rutgers University in New Brunswick, New Jersey, which also has a comprehensive collection of Belgian posters from 1890 to 1910.

More has been written about French posters and French poster artists than the posters of any other country. At the end of this guide we list numerous current and historical references for learning more about the French posters. In 1970, during the resurgence of interest in Art Nouveau, a touring exhibition of works by Belgian artists entitled *La Belle Epoque* traveled to ten museums in the United States, featuring many of the early artists noted in this chapter. The catalog, by Yolande Oostens-Wittamer, serves as an excellent guide to early Belgian poster art (see Bibliography.)

FRENCH AND BELGIAN POSTERS—PRICE LISTINGS

NOTE: See the chapter Important Notes on the Price Listings for more information on prices given. Unless otherwise noted as Belgian, posters and artists are French. Also note that many French and Belgian artists also have listings in other chapters such as World War Posters, Travel and Transportation Posters, etc.

❦ ANONYMOUS

Antibes, Côte D'Azur, ca. 1920. Lithograph. A young lady with her parasol and dog looks out at the coastline. Very good condition, on linen, 30 x 42 inches.
$1,125 (Auc. #17)

Bruxelles/Foire Internationale, 1950. Photo-offset. Belgian Art Deco image of the Brussels Grand Palais. In deep blue, gray, light blue, and orange. Good condition, linen-mounted, 24 x 39 inches. $200–$250

Familial Radio, ca. 1930. Lithograph. A young boy sitting in front of a radio highlighted by a warm glow. Good condition, on linen, 32 x 47 inches. $500–550

Kina-Lillet, ca. 1895. Lithograph. Printed by Herold & Compagnie. Fine condition, on linen, 38½ x 54 inches. $150 (Auc. #18)

Liqueur de St. Barbe, ca. 1905. Lithograph. A devilish figure sneaks out a window after stealing a bottle of liqueur. Fine condition, 45 x 60 inches. $650–750

Le Lion, Bougie Bollingkx, ca. 1900. Lithograph. Belgian poster printed by Lithographie Internationale. Fine condition, 19 x 28 inches. $525 (Auc. #18)

Roger & Gallet/Jean Marie Marina, Eau de Cologne. Lithograph. Printed by Fiedler. Fine condition, 35 x 50 inches. $250 (Auc. #18)

Terminus Absinthe. Lithograph. Printed by Affiches Camis, Paris. Sarah Bernhardt and an ornately costumed figure. Good condition, 38 x 49 inches.
$440 (Auc. #19)

Triple Sec Allary. Lithograph. Printed by F. Javanuad, Angouleme. A gentleman holds his glass out to the viewer. Very good condition, 45 x 60½ inches.
$495 (Auc. #19)

Veuve Amiot, ca. 1925. Lithograph. Printed by Gaillard. Fine condition, on linen, 47½ x 62½ inches. $200 (Auc. #18)

❦ ERIC AES

Enrade, au Théâtre du Vieux Colombier, 1927. Lithograph. Film poster. Very good condition, 32 x 47 inches. $475 (Auc. #17)

❦ GUY ARNOUX

Les Vins de Bourgogne, ca. 1925. Lithograph. A soldier, dressed in a long blue coat and black boots, enjoys a glass of wine. Fine condition, 32 x 47 inches.
$400–$450

❦ H. AVELOT

Frédérique, 1927. Lithograph. Printed by Chachoin, Paris. A dancer in spotlights has her body all twisted. Fine condition, on linen, 32 x 47 inches. $225 (Auc. #18)

❦ EMILE BEAUSSIER (1874–?)

Théâtre de Lyon/Les Chanteurs de Nurenberg. Lithograph. Theater announcement for a performance of Wagner. Very good condition, 39½ x 81½ inches. $522 (Auc. #19)

❦ ALBERT BERGEVIN (1887–1974)

Avranches, ca. 1925. Lithograph. Young woman with parasol and binoculars looks out on Mont St. Michel. *Note:* Lithographic forgeries of this poster have appeared in recent years. Buyer beware! Fine condition, 23⅝ x 31⅝ inches.
$1,800–$2,000

❦ ANDRE BERMOND

Vals Casino. Lithograph. Blue-suited man takes a drink. Very good condition, 24½ x 39½ inches. $165 (Auc. #19)

❦ FRANCIS BERNARD (1900–?)

> NOTE: Bernard served as the art director for the Salon des Arts Ménagers for over thirty years and designed numerous posters for this annual "Home Show."

Arts Ménagers/VIIe Salon, 1930. Lithograph. White stylized figure holds a red broom. Very good condition, 46½ x 62 inches. $715 (Auc. #19)

Arts Ménagers/Grand Palais/24 Fevrier-20 Mars, ca. 1935. Comical figure carries a painter's canvas in the form of a house. In blue, yellow, orange, red, and green on a black field. Very good condition, 47 x 63 inches. $400–$500

Bal Des Petits Lits Blanc, 1919, by Francis Bernard. Courtesy of Swann Gallery, Inc.

Arts Ménagers/XIXe Salon, 1942. Lithograph. Huge head peaks into a house through the open roof. In yellow, red, blue, black, and pink on a brown field. Fine condition, smaller version, 14 x 22 inches. $150–$250

Bal des Petits Lits Blanc, 1919. Lithograph. Printed by Paul Martial. For the Bal-Opera. Strong design with a female head in profile with a male frontal. A very good example of the artist's work. Good condition, 45 x 60 inches. $1,210 (Auc. #19)

❧ **PAUL BERTHON (1872–1909)**

> NOTE: *Berthon is known for decorative panels without text as well as for his advertising posters, and these often appear together at auctions and at dealers' shops. The best reference to his work is the book* Berthon & Grasset, *by Victor Arwas. See Bibliography.*

Almanach d'Alsace et de Lorraine, 1896. Lithograph. Printed by Chaix. For the Alsacian publication. A peasant girl in traditional costume. A very good example of Berthon's style. Fine condition, 14½ x 22⅛ inches. $2,000–$2,200

Les Boules de Neige, 1900. Lithograph. A decorative panel showing a woman picking Guelder roses. Good condition, 21⅛ x 15⅜ inches. $575 (Auc. #11)

Concert Mystique, 1901. Lithograph. One of five decorative panels of medieval musical instruments. Printed on cream wove paper in an edition of about 200, second state. 18 x 13½ inches. $1,200–$1,300

From the author's collection. Photo by Robert Four.

Les Eglantines, 1900. Lithograph. A decorative panel, usually paired with *Les Boules de Neige,* above, showing a woman picking wild roses. Signed in pencil, numbered 53/110. Good condition, 21¼ x 15¼ inches. $500–$700

Leçons de Violon, 1898. Lithograph. Printed by Chaix. Advertising violin lessons. Good condition, smaller format, 10½ x 7⅞ inches. $546 (Auc. #11)

As above, signed in pencil, without text. Good condition, 21⅜ x 15⅞ inches. $805 (Auc. #11)

Le Livre de Magda, 1898. Lithograph. Gold-haired woman with doves, advertising the book of poems by Armand Silvestre. Good condition, 15 x 22⅜ inches. $747 (Auc. #11)

As above, fine condition, 15¼ x 22½ inches. $1,980 (Auc. #19)

La Princesse au Crapaud, 1899. Lithograph. Printed by Chaix. A decorative panel depicting a princess about to kiss a toad. Rarely seen. Good condition, on linen, 17½ x 22¾ inches. $1,495 (Auc. # 11)

Queen Wilhelmena, 1901. Lithograph. Published by Ulman Company. This was a commemorative print, edited in several sizes, showing the young queen in profile, with windmills in the distance. A good example, but commonly found. Good condition, 12⅞ x 14½ inches. $302 (Auc. #10)

As above, fine condition, 14 x 15 inches. $357 (Auc. #19)

Revue d'Art Dramatique, 1897. Lithograph. Printed by Bourgerie & Compagnie. Advertising the art journal. Good condition, 13¾ x 21½ inches. $862 (Auc. #11)

Sainte Marie des Fleurs, 1898. Lithograph. Printed by Bourgerie & Compagnie. Designed to advertise a novel. Rarer version, without text. Good condition, 13¹¹⁄₁₆ x 21¼ inches. $920 (Auc. #11)

Courtesy of
Swann
Galleries, Inc.

Sarah Bernhardt, 1901. Lithograph. A portrait of the famous actress, and one of the best-known images by Berthon. Without text. Good condition, on linen, 14¼ x 20 inches. $1,092 (Auc. # 11)

❦ EMILE BERTRAND

Cendrillon, 1899. (Ref: Broido, *French Opera Posters* #35.) Lithograph. Printed by Devambez. For an opera with music by Jules Massenet (1842–1912). Stunning Art Nouveau design for the *conte de fees* or "fairy tale" of Cinderella. Mint condition, 24 x 31 inches. $750–$950

❦ PAUL BONET

La Reliure Originale Xeme-XXeme Siècle, 1947. Lithograph. To advertise a bookbinding exhibition. Black lettering, green ornaments and gold stars on cream. Fine condition, 17 x 22 inches. $250–$300

❦ ROBERT BONFILS (1886–1972)

Exposition Internationale des Arts Décoratifs, 1925. Woodcut. Printed letterpress by Imprimerie de Vaugirard, Paris. Depicting a woman and a gazelle in Art Deco style. The official poster for the 1925 Exposition from which the term "Art Deco" is drawn. Very good condition, 15¼ x 23½ inches. $2,500–$3,000

From the author's
collection. Photo by
Robert Four.

Courtesy of
Bailly Gallery.

❦ PIERRE BONNARD (1867–1947)

L'Estampe et l'Affiche, 1897. Lithograph. For the influential print collectors' publication. Abstracted image of older woman putting on glasses to watch a younger one go by, carrying a large portfolio out of which prints are falling. Very good condition, 24 x 31 inches. $5,500–$6,500

La Revue Blanche, 1894. Lithograph. Printed by Ancourt, Paris. Abstracted image of a small boy and a woman in a ruffled cape and large hat holding a copy of the magazine. Fine condition, 24¼ x 31¼ inches. $9,000–$10,000

❦ LOUIS BOUAT

Source Verdier: Limonade "Cevenole." Lithograph. Gold-haired woman holds up a bottle. Very good condition, 47 x 62½ inches. $247 (Auc. #19)

❦ CAMILLE BOUCHET

Cognac Jacquet, ca. 1905. Lithograph. Luxuriant peacock posed beside bottle of cognac. Very good condition, on linen, 47 x 63 inches. $450–$550

❦ FIRMIN BOUISSET (1859–1925)

Chocolat Menier, 1892. Lithograph. Printed by Affiches Camis. A little girl writes the name "Chocolat Menier" on a wall with a crayon. This poster was printed with several variations in text and in different languages. Fine condition, on linen, 34 x 50 inches. $1,300–$1,600

Les Specialités, *Maggi, Profitens à tout ménage.* Lithograph. Printed by Affiches Camis. Young girl in red dress holds a blackboard with prices. Tan background. Very good condition, on linen, 38¾ x 50⅞ inches. $1,000–$1,100

❦ ROGER BRODERS (1883–1953)

Marseille, ca. 1929. Lithograph. For the French railways. The port shows a line of steamships in Art Deco style. *Note:* See additional listings for this artist under Travel and Transportation. Fine condition, on linen, 25 x 39½ inches.

$1,775 (Auc. #18)

❦ LEONETTO CAPPIELLO (1875–1942)

> NOTE: Cappiello's posters have increased dramatically in popularity in the last five years, and today seem to be everywhere on the market. While he executed some sought-after posters for clients in his native Italy (see Italian Posters), he worked mostly in France. In all, he designed almost 1,000 posters. Most of his posters from 1900 to 1916 were printed by Vercasson, and from World War I until 1937, primarily by Devambez.

Bally/Lyon, 1933. Lithograph. Printed by Damour Editions. A later poster by the artist. Fine condition, on linen, 47 x 62 inches.

$325 (Auc. #18)

Benedictine, ca. 1920. Lithograph. With a lantern and champagne, a man looks out at the cityscape at night. Very good condition, on linen, 50 x 77 inches.

$450 (Auc. #17)

Cachou Lajaunie: Indispensable aux Fumeurs, 1900. Lithograph. Printed by Vercasson. Woman smiling, holding a cigarette and the breath freshener advertised. Good condition, 37 x 51½ inches.

$825 (Auc. #19)

Cachou Lajaunie, 1920. Lithograph. Printed by Devambez. The artist's second poster for the same product. Flamboyant female in a feathered dress exhaling smoke. Fine condition, 39 x 59 inches.

$1,320 (Auc. #19)

Corset Le Furet, 1901. Lithograph. Printed by Vercasson. A very good example of an early Cappiello poster. Fine condition, 40 x 55 inches.

$2,500–$2,700

Courtesy of
Harris Gallery.

Je Ne Fume Que Le Nil, Papier à Cigarettes. Lithograph. Elephant with red and orange cape. A fairly easily found poster on the market today. Very good condition, large horizontal, 63 x 47 inches. $500–$650

Nitrolian/Sec Aussitôt Peint, 1929. Lithograph. Printed by Devambez. Man painting stairs with the paint that is "dry as soon as painted," as the outline of a woman in white descends. A good example of the artist's work, though relatively easy to find. Very good condition, 47 x 62 inches. $935 (Auc. #19)

Poeles Manquette, 1925. Lithograph. Printed by Devambez. Very good condition, on linen, 50 x 76 inches. $725 (Auc. #17)

Pur Champagne/Damery-Epernay, 1902. Lithograph. Printed by Vercasson. Woman with a red-feathered hat pours champagne. Fine condition, on linen, 39⅛ x 54⅜ inches. $3,200–$3,400

Job/Papier à Cigarettes, 1912. Lithograph. Printed by Vercasson. Corpulent, turbaned man dressed all in white enjoys a cigarette. Very good condition, 46 x 62½ inches. $1,210 (Auc. #19)

Maurin Quina, 1906. Lithograph. Printed by Vercasson. Bright green devil with red mouth. Very good condition, 46 x 62¼ inches. $495 (Auc. #19)

Montre Élection, 1922. Lithograph. Printed by Vercasson. For the watchmaker. An excellent example of the artist's style. This example framed, in fine condition, 30 x 46 inches. $3,100–$3,200

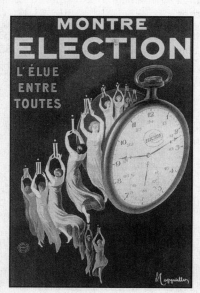

Courtesy of
Harris Gallery.

Mossant, 1938. Lithograph for Mossant hats. Three men's arms with hats in hand as they doff them in a greeting. Very good condition, 47 x 62 inches.

$880 (Auc. #19)

SFER—20 Radiola, 1925. Lithograph. Printed by Les Nouvelles Affiches Capiello Devambez. A woman enjoys listening to radio programs from all over the world. An outstanding example of Cappiello's style. Fine condition, 21⅝ x 30½ inches. *See color insert, photo 2.* $4,200–$4,400

Le Thermogène-Engendre la Chaleur, 1909. Lithograph. Printed by Vercasson. Fire- breathing man to promote a heating pad. This poster had multiple printings and is therefore fairly common. Good condition, 47 x 62½ inches

$495 (Auc. #19)

Valdespino, 1906. Lithograph. Printed by Vercasson. A smiling mask is surrounded by grapes on the vine. Fine condition, on linen, 38 x 53 inches. $650 (Auc. #18)

Veuve Amiot: Grands Vins Mousseux, 1922. Lithograph. Published by Les Nouvelles Affiches Cappiello. Figure of a king in red, yellow, and black. Good condition, 44 x 60 inches. $1,760 (Auc. #10)

As above, very good condition, 47½ x 63 inches. $550 (Auc. #19)

✤ CARDAILBAC

Papier Photographiques Martin, 1897. Lithograph. Woman in a detailed dress in a Gothic setting. Good condition, 39½ x 51 inches. $1,100 (Auc. #19)

✤ JEAN GEORGES CARLU (b. 1900)

> NOTE: See also the chapter on World War Posters for additional listings of posters by Carlu.

Aquarium de Monaco, 1926. Lithograph. Outstanding design, close-up of a stylized fish and eel against a black background. A very good example of Carlu's work. Fine condition, on linen, 28½ x 40 inches. $4,000–$5,000

Exposition Internationale Paris, 1937. Lithograph. Multicolored flags form the background for a face in profile. This poster was printed in several sizes, and is relatively easy to find in the market. Very good condition, larger version, 40 x 59 inches. $550 (Auc. #19)

As above, fine condition, 24 x 39 inches. $500–$600

Grandes Fêtes de Paris, 1934. Lithograph. Printed by Cassandre's firm, Alliance Graphique, Paris. Outstanding design of monocled gentleman and woman with beret in profile, similar to Carlu's famous cover for the April 1931 *Vanity Fair* magazine. An outstanding example. Fine condition, impressive in size, 62½ x 46 inches. $15,000–$20,000

🌿 A. M. CASSANDRE (1901–1968)

> NOTE: For additional posters by Cassandre, see the chapters on Dutch
> Posters and Travel and Transportation Posters.

Bonal/Ouvre L'Appetit, 1935. Lithograph. Printed by L. Danel, Paris. Stylized man drinking Bonal while a huge key "unlocks his appetite." Later version, background yellow and orange, with two lines of copy under the word "Bonal." Fine condition, on linen, 47⅛ x 62⅞ inches. $1,800–$2,200

As above, first version, 1933, background shades of brown and only one line of text. $3,500–$4,000

Cesar, 1935. Lithograph. Cigar advertisement showing just the hand comfortably holding the cigar. Very good condition, on Japan paper, 35 x 50 inches.
$4,150 (Auc. #18)

Challenge Round de La Coupe Davis, 1932. Lithograph. Published by Alliance Graphique. The tennis ball files right at the viewer. The same image was also used for a poster announcing the "Grande Quinzaine Internationale de Lawn Tennis" in May and June of the same year. Fine condition, on linen, 45 x 62 inches.
$8,000– $10,000

Dubonnet, 1932. Lithograph. Stylized image of a gentleman pouring from a bottle. On linen, 48 x 66½ inches. $1,650 (Auc. #13)

As above, 1935. Fine condition, smaller version, on linen, 14 x 10 inches.
$1,200 (Auc. #18)

As above, ca. 1952. Photo-offset. Fine condition, on linen, 48½ x 67 inches.
$2,075 (Auc. #17)

Ecosse, Par Les Trains de Luxe, 1928. Lithograph. For British Railways/LMS. A composite of the forms of castle stones and the amorphous forms of nature. Very good condition, on linen, 25 x 40 inches. $2,525 (Auc. #18)

Italia, 1936. Lithograph. Printed by Coen, Milan. For the Italian tourist office. Collage of sports equipment against a beautiful Italian landscape. This poster is found in several languages, with and without subtexts. Fine condition, 24½ x 39¼ inches. $2,000–$2,500

As above, but depicting an outline of Madonna and child against Roman ruins.
$1,500–$2,000

Fêtes de Paris, 1935. Lithograph. Bust of a woman against images of Parisian monuments. Very good, on Japan paper, 47½ x 63 inches. $900 (Auc. #17)

Normandie/New York Via Le Havre et Southampton, 1935. Lithograph. Published by Alliance Graphique. Rare version of this poster with "New York" in bold white letters. On linen, 28 x 43 inches, *See color insert, photo 6.*
$11,550 (Auc. #13)

From the collection of
Mike Slemmer. Photo
by Robert Four.

❧ HENRI CASSIERS (BELGIAN, 1858–1944)

> NOTE: Cassiers's most sought-after posters are for the Red Star Line ocean liners.

Gournay S/Marne, 1927. Lithograph. Printed by Chachoin, Paris. Travel poster depicting a corpulent man carrying his fishing equipment. Very good condition, 39 x 58 inches. $247 (Auc. #19)

❧ JEAN DOMINIQUE VAN CAULAERT (1897–1979)

Mistinguett, 1937. Lithograph. Printed by Atelier Girbal, Paris. The actress appears in rags carrying umbrella, for the show *Ca c'est Parisien* at the Theatre Mogador. Good condition, 46 x 61¼ inches. $440 (Auc. #19)

❧ FREDERIC AUGUSTE CAZALS (1865–1941)

7me Exposition du Salon des Cent, 1894. Lithograph. For the annual salon. Two gentlemen examine the works of art. Fine condition, on linen, 15½ x 24 inches. $1,475 (Auc. #18)

As above, fine condition, on linen. $3,500–$4,500

❧ CHANCEL

Le Tzarewitch. Lithograph. Printed by Leroy & Herve-Baille. For the operetta. Two figures, one in red, on blue and white background. Very good condition, 31 x 47½ inches. $660 (Auc. #19)

🍂 JULES CHÉRET (1836–1932)

> *NOTE: Chéret designed more than 1,000 posters, many of which are still available at affordable prices. The reference numbers following the titles below refer to* The Posters of Jules Chéret: A Catalogue Raisonné, Second Edition, *by Lucy Broido. Also, several listings in this chapter refer to Lucy Broido's book* French Opera Posters. *See Bibliography.*

Alcazar d'Été/Lidia, 1895 (Broido #174). Lithograph. Printed by Chaix. For the café concert Alcazar d'Été. A very good example of the artist's work. Fine condition, on linen, 34 x 48⅜ inches. $3,500–$4,000

Arlette Dorgère, 1904 (Broido #221). Lithograph. Printed by Chaix. For the performer. A full-length portrait of the chanteuse in a long red robe and wide-brimmed hat. Fine condition, two sheets, on linen, 35 x 96½ inches.
$3,500–$3,800

L'Auréole du Midi, 1893. (Broido #975). Lithograph. Printed by Chaix. For the lamp oil. This example printed with black and red stones only. Good condition, 32½ x 49¼ inches. $805 (Auc. #12)

Bal du Moulin Rouge, 1889 (Broido #316). Lithograph. Printed by Chaix. For the legendary Montmartre showplace. An outstanding example of Chéret's work and an important document of the era. Fine condition, on linen, 34¼ x 47¼ inches. *See color insert, photo 5.* $3,000–$4,000

Courtesy of Butterfield & Butterfield.

Courtesy of Park South Gallery.

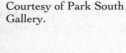

Benzo Moteur, 1900 (Broido #1031). Lithograph. Printed by Chaix. For gasoline. A woman in her car looks back at a couple driving behind her. Very good condition, on linen, 33 x 47 inches. $1,275 (Auc. #18)

As above, fine condition, on linen. $2,500–$2,700

La Bodinière, 1900 (Broido #275). Lithograph. Printed by Chaix. Very good condition, on Japan paper, 33½ x 47½ inches. $475 (Auc. #17)

La Closerie des Genets, 1890 (Broido #667). Lithograph. Printed by Chaix. For the serialized novel published in *Le Radical*. Very good condition, 34 x 47 inches. $440 (Auc. #19)

Cosmydor Savon, 1891 (Broido #937). Lithograph. Printed by Chaix for Cosmydor soap. Good condition, linen-mounted, 48 x 34½ inches. $1,200–$1,300

Eldorado, 1984 (Broido #218). Lithograph. Printed by Chaix. The smaller version of this well-known poster for the music hall Eldorado, published as a supplement to the newspaper *Le Courier Français*. In fine condition, 15 x 21½ inches. $1,300–$1,600

Le Figaro, 1895 (Broido #570). Lithograph. Printed by Chaix. One of several posters designed by Chéret for this political periodical. Very good condition, on linen, 24 x 32½ inches. $450 (Auc. #18)

Folies-Bergère/L'Arc en Ciel, 1893 (Broido #123). Lithograph. Printed by Chaix. Four artists from the ballet-pantomime under a rainbow. Fine condition, a very good example of the artist's mastery of color lithography, on linen, 32 x 47½ inches. $2,200–$2,600

Folies Bergère/La Loie Fuller, 1893 (Broido #125). Lithograph. Printed by Chaix. For the Paris debut of the celebrated American dancer who invented a new choreography of floating movement, diaphanous costumes, and multicolored, projected electric lights, inspiring works by many artists and sculptors, including one of Chéret's finest posters. Fine condition, linen-mounted, 33⅜ x 48¼ inches. $5,000–$7,000

Halle aux Chapeaux, 1892 (Broido #830). Lithograph. Printed by Chaix. Depicting a little girl and her mother trying on hats. Good condition, linen-mounted, 33¾ x 48⅜ inches. $1,800–$2,300

Montagnes Russes, 1888 (Broido #342). Lithograph. Printed by Chaix. For the Parisian amusement hall. Very good condition, on linen, 33 x 46 inches. $624 (Auc. #17)

Musée Grévin, Théâtre Des Fantoches, 1900 (Broido #471). Lithograph. Printed by Chaix. Without text, retailed through the bookseller Sagot. Depicting a variety of colorful entertainers in lively colors. Fine condition, 34⅜ x 48⅞ inches. $2,000–$2,400

As above, but with text for "Les Fantoches de John Hewelt." In this case, the image with text is rarer than without. $3,500–$4,000

Palais de Glace, 1894 (Broido #365). Lithograph. Printed by Chaix. For the famous ice- skating rink on the Champs Elysées. The smaller version, published as a supplement to the newspaper *Le Courier Français*. Fine condition, 13 x 21 inches.

$900–$1,100

As above, fine condition, 34½ x 47 inches. $3,500–$4,000

Pippermint, 1899 (Broido #883). Lithograph. Printed by Chaix. For the liqueur. Lady in mint green dress against red background pours out a glass. Very good condition, 35 x 48½ inches. $1,045 (Auc. #19)

Quinquina Dubonnet, 1895 (Broido #873). Lithograph. Printed by Chaix. Lady in a green dress holds a bottle of the aperitif in one hand, a snifter in the other. A good example of a Chéret beverage poster. Fine condition, on linen, 33⅝ x 45¾ inches. $1,800–$2,200

Saxoléine, 1900 (Broido #957). Lithograph. Printed by Chaix. Woman in a green dress, red background and blue lettering. One of several posters by Chéret for Saxoléine lamp oil. Fine condition, 34 x 48 inches. $1,800–$2,000

Scaramouche, 1891 (Broido #238). Lithograph. Printed by Chaix. For the performances at the Nouveau Théâtre. Multicolored clown performers. Very good condition, 34 x 48½ inches. $715 (Auc. #19)

From the author's collection.
Photo by Robert Four.

From a private
collection.

Skating-Rink, Grandes Bailes de Mascaras, ca 1876 (Broido #351). Lithograph. Printed by *Imprimerie* Chéret. In Spanish for distribution outside France. A parade of costumed people. Very good condition, 26 x 30½ inches.

$300 (Auc. #17)

La Terre/par E. Zola, 1889 (Broido #620). Lithograph. Printed by Chaix. For the novel by Emile Zola, depicting an old farmer and broken-down farm equipment. Very good condition, long vertical format, on linen, 34 x 92 inches.

$450 (Auc. #17)

Viviane, 1886. (Ref: Broido, *French Opera Posters* #43). Lithograph. Printed by Chaix. For the ballet at the Eden-Théâtre. Bright yellow ballerina on blue, green, and orange background. Fine condition, 21½ x 29½ inches. $495 (Auc. #19)

❦ ALFRED CHOUBRAC (1853–1902)

Esclarmonde, 1889 (Ref: Broido, *French Opera Posters* #37). Lithograph. Printed by F. Appel. For the opera with music by Jules Massenet. Detailed royal image in red, blue, and green with red lettering. Fine condition, 32 x 46½ inches.

$220 (Auc. #19)

❦ PAUL COLIN (1892–1985)

Arts Ménagers/16ᵉ Salon, 1936. Lithograph. Printed by Bedos, Paris. For the annual Home Show. Four men of different professions working around a house. In very good condition, on linen, 44½ x 61 inches. $1,000–$1,400

Cie. Gle. Transatlantique/Atlantique-Pacifique-Mediterranée, ca. 1937. Lithograph. Signed in plate. Stylized steamship, with French flag as backdrop, 15¾ x 23½ inches. $1,093 (Auc. #15)

Haut de Cagnes/Ou la Joie de Vivre, 1971. Photo-offset. Printed by Bedos, Paris. For the artisans of the area. In yellow, red, and black. Fine condition, 31 x 46½ inches. $550–$650

Liqueur Izarra, ca. 1948. Photo-offset. Stylized figures dancing around a large bottle of the Basque liqueur. Fine condition, on linen, 31 x 47 inches. $1,500–$1,800

Marguerite Valmond, 1928. Lithograph. Printed by Chachoin, Paris. Wonderfully soft portrait of the French singer. Very good condition, linen-mounted, 47 x 63 inches. $1,000–$1,200

Tabarin, 1928. Lithograph. Printed by Chachoin. An excellent example of the artist's Art Deco design, juxtaposing the three different images of the same female figure. Very good condition, on linen, 15 x 24 inches. $2,500–$3,500

❦ GISBERT COMBAZ (BELGIAN, 1869–1941)

La Libre Esthetique, 1899. Lithograph. Printed by J. L. Goffart. For the annual salon at the Brussels Musée Moderne. Elaborate Art Nouveau design of a fruit tree and a rising sun with patterned rays. Fine condition, 14½ x 26½ inches.

$1,800–$2,000

❦ ADOLPHE CRESPIN (BELGIAN, 1859–1944)

Paul Hankar Architecte, 1894. Lithograph. Printed by Ad. Merlens, Brussels. A bearded and bespectacled architect leans over his drafting board. Considered Crespin's finest poster, with elaborate patterned borders including triangles and rulers. Fine condition, 15½ x 21¼ inches. $6,000–$8,000

❦ ADOLPHE CRESPIN (BELGIAN, 1859–1944) AND EDOUARD DUYCK (BELGIAN, 1856–1987)

Alcazar Royal, 1896. Lithograph. Printed by Couweloos, Brussels. Three fashionable ladies in yellow, orange, and blue, for the Brussels nightclub. Very good condition, 23 x 35 inches. $467 (Auc. #19)

Nieuport Bains, 1895. Lithograph. Printed by Merlens, Brussels. A soldier with horn and drum for a concert of military music. Very good condition, 23½ x 39¼ inches. $330 (Auc. #19)

❦ ANDRE DAUDÉ (1897–1979)

Pianos Daudé, ca. 1925. Lithograph. Printed by Pag, Paris. Stylized view of pianist from overhead. Very good condition, on linen, 46 x 61 inches. $825 (Auc. #18)
As above, fine condition, 46½ x 62½ inches. $1,320 (Auc. #19)

❦ FRANCIS DELAMARE (BELGIAN)

Repos Ste. Elisabeth, 1920. Lithograph. Printed by Vromant & Compagnie, Brussels. Two women take their "cure" under a beach umbrella. Vibrant colors in an Art Deco style. Fine condition, 24 x 33½ inches. $357 (Auc. #19)

Poster by Andre Daudé. Courtesy of Swann Galleries, Inc.

❦ **DELVAL**

Fap'anis—Celui des Connoisseurs, ca. 1930. Lithograph. Printed by Publicite Wall, Paris. Woman in bright orange skirt waves a feather fan, with image repeated in the bottle. Very good condition, 63 x 47 inches. $247 (Auc. #19)

As above, fine condition, on linen. $500–$700

❦ **HENRY JULIEN DETOUCHE (1854–1913)**

22e Exposition des Cent, 1896. Lithograph. A seated lady imitates swans with her hands and arms. Fine condition, 18 x 25 inches. $900 (Auc. #18)

❦ **GEORGES DOLA (1872–1950)**

La Chauve Souris (Die Fledermaus), 1904 (Ref: Broido, *French Opera Posters* #47). Lithograph. For the Strauss operetta at the Theatre des Varietes. A very good example of a French operetta poster. Fine condition, on linen, 23¼ x 31½ inches. $700– $900

Le Pays du Sourire, 1940. Lithograph. Printed by Max Eschig. For the operetta with music by Franz Lehar. A couple surrounded by Chinese motifs. Fine condition, 30½ x 46 inches. $660 (Auc. #19)

❦ **JEAN-GABRIEL DOMERGUE (1889–1962)**

Alice Soulie, 1926. Lithograph. Printed by Chachoin. Entertainer covers her bare breasts with ostrich feathers. Fine condition, on linen, 47 x 63 inches.
          $575 (Auc. #18)

As above, good condition, 46½ x 62½ inches. $660 (Auc. #19)

As above, on linen, fine condition. $1,000–$1,200

Colette Mars/Disques Columbia, ca. 1950. Lithograph. Printed by Hubert Baille & Company. Fine condition, on linen, 31 x 46½ inches. $525 (Auc. #17)

Diane Belli, 1923. Lithograph. The flirtatious female dancer kicks her leg out. Very good condition, on Japan paper, 46 x 62 inches. $1,650 (Auc. #17)

L'Hiver À Monte Carlo, 1937. Lithograph. Printed by Lucien Serre. High-style couple enjoys the off-season. A very good example of the artist's work. Fine condition, on linen, 24 x 39 inches. $2,000–$2,500

Renee Ludger, 1925. Lithograph. Close-up of the performer with a jaded look. Very good condition, on Japan paper, 37½ x 47½ inches. $600 (Auc. #17)

❦ **KEES VAN DONGEN (1877–1968)**

Bal à L'Opera, ca. 1920. Lithograph. Couple closely dances amidst crowds. Very good condition, on Japan paper, 43½ x 63½ inches. $1,782 (Auc. #18)

🌿 RODGERS DUNCAN

Joyce-Paris, 1988. Photo-offset. Printed by Affiches du Marval, Paris. Fashion poster, woman in stripes with oversize hat and gloves. Fine condition, 48 x 62 inches. $440 (Auc. #19)

🌿 MAURICE DUFRÈNE (1876–1955)

Rayon des Soieries, 1930 (Ref: Broido, *French Opera Posters* #17). Lithograph. Printed by Chaix, for an operetta set in the silk department of a department store. Stylized woman with arm outstretched, draped with bolts of silk. Note: Lithographic forgeries of this poster appeared on the market a few years ago. In the original, only one fold of silk is green; the forgery has more than one. Fine condition, on linen, 31 x 47 inches. $1,200–$1,400

🌿 JEAN DUPAS (1882–1964)

> NOTE: Dupas also designed several highly-prized posters for London Transport and other English clients. See additional listings in the chapter on English Posters.

Arnold Constable, 1928. Lithograph. For the English department store. Depicting elegant ladies dressed in the latest fashions, with doves hovering above. Fine condition, 36½ x 54 inches. $2,500–$3,000

Bordeaux, 1937. Lithograph. Published by the municipality of Bordeaux. Depicting a stylized seminude woman between two pillars representing various scenes and products of Bordeaux. Fine condition, 27⅝ x 43 inches. $4,620 (Auc. #13)

XVeme Salon des Artistes Décorateurs, 1924. Lithograph. For the annual Salon that led up to the 1925 Exposition. Two women, one in profile, one full face. A very good example of the artist's style, relatively easy to find. Fine condition, on linen, 15 x 23¼ inches. $2,500–$3,000

🌿 LEON DUPIN

Rita, 1933. Lithograph. Printed by Joseph Charles, Paris. Cartoon-like character carries two huge cookies. Fine condition, 39 x 35 inches. $467 (Auc. #19)

🌿 ERTÉ—aka ROMAIN DE TIRTOFF (1892–1990)

Alcazar De Paris, 1970. Photo-offset. Printed by St. Martin. Woman in clown outfit dances admist balloons and confetti. Fine condition, 30½ x 46 inches. $900–$1,200

Folies Bergère/Folies En Folie, ca 1970. Photo-offset. Printed by St. Martin. Dancer in orange with black studded boots and gloves. Very good condition, 46 x 61½ inches. $440 (Auc. #19)

❦ GEORGES DE FEURE—aka GEORGES VAN SLUITERS (1868–1943)

Le Diablotin, 1894. Lithograph. Printed by J. Weiner. For the periodical. A fashionably dressed woman, with a devil in the background. Fine condition, on linen, 23 x 31 inches. $1,600–$1,800

Paris Almanach, 1894. Lithograph. Printed by Bourgerie & Compagnie, Paris. For the periodical published by Sagot. A desirable example of the artist's style, albeit still relatively easy to find on the market. Very good condition, 24½ x 31½ inches. $3,000–$4,000

❦ PIERRE FIX-MASSEAU (b. 1905)

> NOTE: For listings by this artist, see the chapter on Travel and Transportation.

❦ L. GADOUD

Vins Camp Romains, 1935. Lithograph. Printed by Affiches Camis, Paris. Three shades of red sihouettes of Roman soldiers, on a black background. Very good condition, 47 x 63 inches. $880 (Auc. #19)

As above, on linen, fine condition. $1,000–$1,100

❦ RAYMOND GID (b. 1905)

Bally, 1976. Photo-offset. Contour-style sketch of human body reaching to the footwear. Fine condition, on linen, 46 x 62 inches. $750 (Auc. #18)

Posters by Georges de Feure. From a private collection.

❦ CHARLES GESMAR (1900–1928)

Mistinguett, 1925. Lithograph. Featuring a close-up of the chanteuse with mammoth jewels on her fingers. *Note:* It is estimated that Gesmar designed more than twenty posters for Mistinguett. Very good condition, on linen, 44 x 63 inches.
$2,000–$2,200

Mistinguett/Casino de Paris, 1922. Lithograph. Depicting the performer sitting on a three-legged stool, with a parakeet perched on her bejeweled fingers. Very good condition, on linen, 30 x 47 inches. $2,500–$3,000

❦ EUGENE GRASSET (1845–1917)

Grafton Gallery Exhibition, 1893. Lithograph. A decorative panel with no text. A flowing, lovely Art Nouveau woman amidst trees and flowers. Pastel colors. Very good condition, 19 x 26½ inches. $800–$1,100

Marque Georges Richard/Cycles & Automobiles, 1899. Lithograph. Printed by Vaugirard. Woman in orange holds the handle of a bicycle. Very good condition, 58 x 43 inches. $1,980 (Auc. #19)

Salon des Cent, 1894. Lithograph. Woman with a notebook examines flowers. Good condition, 14⅝ x 23 inches. $660 (Auc. #10)
As above, fine condition, on linen, 15½ x 23½ inches. $1,125 (Auc. #18)

Tinta L. Marquet, 1892. Lithograph. Printed by G. de Malherbe. For writing ink. A woman gazes up from the letter she is writing. A very good example of the artist's work. Fine condition, 33 x 45 inches. $1,900–$2,250

❦ HENRI GRAY—aka HENRI BOULANGER (1858–1924)

Petrole Stella, 1897. Lithograph. Printed by Courmont Freres. Stunning design for lamp oil. three nude women with butterfly wings soar in the air above the rays of a rising sun. One of Gray's best designs, albeit still widely available. Fine condition, 39 x 51 inches. $2,500–$3,500

Mam'zelle Boyscout, 1905 (Ref: Broido, *French Opera Posters* #29). Lithograph. Printed by Delancey & Fil. For the operetta at the Theatre de la Renaissance. Female dressed in a Boy Scout uniform gives a salute. Very good condition, 26½ x 35 inches. $302 (Auc. #19)

Le Treport, 1897. Lithograph. For the French railways. Advertising the beach resort and casino. Another version of this poster shows the woman's legs bare. In fine condition, on linen, 25 x 40 inches. $800–$900

❦ JULES-ALEXANDRE GRÜN (1886–1934)

Bal Tabarin, 1904. Lithograph. Printed by Chaix. A gentleman, his revealingly dressed companion, and their black coachman off to the nightclub. A second, less

Poster by Henri Gray. From the collection of Al Hoch. Photo by Robert Four.

Poster by Jules-Alexandre Grün. Courtesy of William Doyle Galleries.

desirable version shows the third person as a white male companion. A very good example of the artist's work. Fine condition, on linen, 34½ x 48 inches.
$2,800–$3,200

Hotel Du Pacha Noir. Lithograph. Printed by Chaix. A stock poster for the night spot with an inset panel blank. Very good condition, 34½ x 49½ inches.
$900–$1,000

La Pepinière/Oh! la la! Mon Empereur!, ca. 1900. Lithograph. Printed by Charles Verneau. For a musical review, depicting a Montmartre woman admiring a cloaked gentleman. A good example of the artist's style. Fine condition, on linen, 35 x 48½ inches.
$1,300–$1,500

Scala C'est d'un Raid, 1902. Lithograph. Printed by Bourgerie, Paris, Woman in revealing dress with flower clenched in her teeth. Grün designed several posters for the Scala nightclub. Very good condition, linen-mounted, 34 x 48 inches.
$1,500–$1,800

✣ ALBERT GUILLAUME (1873–1942)

Tous Disent Je ne Fume que le Nil. Lithograph. Printed by Affiches Camis. Six men of different backgrounds, each enjoying a cigarette. Very good condition, 49 x 79 inches.
$605 (Auc. #19)

❧ PAUL CESAR HELLEU (1859–1927)

Ed. Sagot, 1897. Lithograph. In shades of sepia, advertising Sagot, the largest print and poster dealer in Paris at the time. A beautiful image, still relatively easy to find. Very good condition, 29 x 41½ inches. $495 (Auc. #19)

As above, fine condition. $600–$800

❧ ARSENE HERBINIER (1869–?)

Salon des Cent, 38ᵉᵐᵉ Exposition D'Ensemble, 1899. Lithograph. Woman shown surrounded by intertwining flowering plants. Very good condition, 18½ x 25½ inches. $1,125 (Auc. #18)

❧ HENRI-GABRIEL IBELS (1867–1936)

J. Mevisto, 1892. Lithograph. Ibel's full-length image of the singer Mevisto as a Pierrot. Very good condition, 25 x 71 inches. $900–$1,100

❧ LOUIS ICART (1887–1951)

Monte-Carlo. Lithograph. Two women sitting back to back on a large beach ball, advertising the joys of Monte Carlo in the summer. Bright blues, yellows, blacks, and whites. One of very few posters by Icart. Fine condition, 30¼ x 44½ inches. $1,800–$2,200

❧ CHARLES KIFFER (b. 1902)

> NOTE: *Kiffer designed several posters for the performer Maurice Chevalier from the 1930s through the early 1960s.*

Maurice Chevalier/Casino de Paris, 1937. Lithograph. Two showgirls and a dancing Chevalier superimposed on a larger profile of the singer. Fine condition, 47 x 63 inches. $2,500–$3,500

❧ MARCEL LEBRUN

Cristille. Lithograph. Woman in a mountain landscape gazes at a bottle of liqueur. Very good condition, 37¼ x 54½ inches. $247 (Auc. #19)

❧ MAURICE LELOIR (1853–1940)

Cigale, 1904 (Ref: Broido, *French Opera Posters* #37). Lithograph. Printed by Devambez. For a ballet with music by Jules Massenet. Generous Cigale, having given away all her wordly goods, begs to be let in from the cold. Fine condition, 22 x 36 inches. $450–$550

❦ HENRI LE MONNIER

Cordial-Medoc. Lithograph. Yellow heart-shaped figure holds a bottle and glass. Fine condition, 32 x 30 inches. $192 (Auc. #19)

Valmya, 1937. Lithograph. Woman in striped dress holds a glass of wine. Very good condition, 47 x 61½ inches. $247 (Auc. #19)

As shown above, on linen, fine condition. $450–$550

❦ GEORGES LEPAPE (1887–1971)

Spinelly, 1914. Lithograph. Famous image of the singer, smiling behind her lace fan, an Art Deco classic. Very good condition, on linen, 33 x 45 inches. $1,600–$2,000

❦ PRIVAT LIVEMONT (BELGIAN, 1861–1936)

Absinthe Robette, 1896. Lithograph. Printed by J. L. Goffart. Woman in pale yellow shawl holds up a glass of absinthe. Printed in an edition of 500. Ten years later, in 1906, Belgian law forbade the sale or use of absinthe. Good condition, 29¾ x 41⁵⁄₁₆ inches. $1,840 (Auc. #11)

As above, fine condition, 32 x 43 inches. $3,300 (Auc. #19)

As above, fine condition, 32 x 43 inches. $3,500–$4,000

Poster by Privat Livemont. Courtesy of Butterfield & Butterfield.

Poster by Henri Le Monnier. Courtesy of Stephen Ganeles Antique Posters and Prints.

Ameublement, ca. 1900. Lithograph. Red-haired female in profile. Small format, horizontal, with blank area for text. Fine condition, 10 x 4¾ inches.

$412 (Auc. #19)

Bitter Oriental, 1897. Lithograph. Printed by J. L. Goffart. For a liqueur. In ocher, red, blue, and black. Fine condition, on linen, 32½ x 43½ inches. $3,000–$3,200

Michiels Frères, 1902. Lithograph. Printed by Affiches Privat Livemont, Brussels. For the landscape nursery. Beautiful image of a woman and her daughter, without text. Good condition, 16 x 29⅛ inches. $3,450 (Auc. #11)

Rajah, 1899. Lithograph. Printed in Amsterdam. For the tea company. Striking Art Nouveau design, with steam rising from the teacup to form the product name. Fine condition, on linen, 17 x 29¾ inches. $3,500–$4,500

🦳 DANIEL DE LOSQUES—aka DAVID THOROUDE (1880–1915)

Mistinguett. Lithograph. Printed by Cachoin, Paris. Woman in red dress on green and blue background. Good condition, 41½ x 75½ inches.$330 (Auc. #19)

As above, woman in blue dress on green background. Very good condition, 42½ x 75½ inches. $330 (Auc. #19)

🦳 CHARLES LOUPOT (1892–1962)

> NOTE: Loupot's poster career started in Switzerland. See the price listings following the Swiss chapter for more examples of his work.

Exposition Internationale des Arts Décoratifs—Paris 1925. Lithograph. Factories whose smoke makes flowers in the sky. A very collectible poster from the 1925 Exposition. Very good condition, on linen, 15 x 23 inches.

$1,800–$2,000

🦳 J. MAJORELLE (BELGIAN)

Marrakech, 1926. Lithograph. Travel poster. Good condition, on linen, 31 x 42½ inches. $575 (Auc. #15)

🦳 MARC-LUC

Prochainement Ouverture, 1925. Lithograph. Printed by Daude Freres, Paris. Two women in scarlet, black, and yellow on their way to shop at the new department store. Good condition, 47½ x 63½ inches. $660 (Auc. #19)

🦳 LÉO MARFURT (BELGIAN, 1894–1977)

Bruxelles Exposition Universelle, 1935. Lithograph. Using Belgian national colors— black, red, and aqua—as backdrop for Atlas carrying the world. Good condition, 46 x 62 inches. $1,000–$1,500

❧ GEORGE MEUNIER (1869–1942)

Lox, 1895. Lithograph. Printed by Chaix, Paris. For the "tonic-aperitif." Meunier was influenced by Chéret. Fine condition, on linen, 33⅜ x 47¾ inches.
$1,800–$2,200

À La Place Clichy, 1897. Lithograph. Printed by Chaix. Advertising toys and gifts, with a jester and a woman on a rocking horse. Very good condition, 34½ x 49 inches.
$800–$1,200

❧ HENRY MEUNIER (BELGIAN, 1869–1942)

Ameublements, 1897. Lithograph. Printed by Renette, Brussels. For a furniture company. Good condition, 22¼ x 13½ inches.
$700–$800

Rajah, 1897. Lithograph. Printed by J. E. Goosens, Brussels. For Rajah coffee. An exotic-looking woman drinks while the steam rises in Art Nouveau swirls. In browns, tan, flesh, red, and green. Very good condition, on linen, horizontal, 30 x 24 inches.
$2,000–$2,500

Waux Hall, 1897. Lithograph. Printed by J. E. Goussens, Brussels. Green-gowned woman stands in forest setting, with blank panel for announcing next attraction. Very good condition, 23½ x 34½ inches.
$800–$900

❧ MORNAS

Nuits de Théâtre/Danse, 1953. Lithograph. Printed by Ateliers Brugiers, Nimes. Figure in red dancing against stylized partner in stripes behind. In a post-Art Deco style. Fine condition, 15 x 23 inches.
$522 (Auc. #19)

❧ ALPHONSE MUCHA (1860–1939)

NOTE: Mucha's posters were exclusively printed by F. Champenois, Paris, where he was a staff artist. Reference numbers noted on the listings below refer to Alphonse Mucha: The Complete Posters and Panels, by Jack Rennert and Alan Weill (see Bibliography).

Chocolat Masson, 1897 (Ref: Rennert/Weill 37, V.I.). Lithograph. Four sheets, each with a three-month calendar at the bottom. Fine condition, each 6 x 17½ inches.
$4,450 (Auc. #18)

Été, 1896 (Ref: Rennert/Weill 18). Lithograph. Decorative panel showing summer personified as a woman resting at a pond's edge. Good condition, on linen, 22 x 41 inches.
$2,975 (Auc. #17)

F. Champenois, 1898 (Ref: Rennert/Weill 18). Lithograph. For Mucha's printer, Champenois. Good condition, on Japan paper, 23 x 29 inches. $5,650 (Auc. #17)

Flirt, 1900 (Ref: Rennert/Weill 72). Lithograph. For Lefevre-Utile Biscuits. Gentleman and lady flirt in a flower garden. Good condition, on linen, 10 x 23⅜ inches. $2,475 (Auc. #10)

As above, fine condition, 11 x 24 inches. $2,640 (Auc. #19)

Lefevre-Utile/Sarah Bernhardt, 1904 (Ref: Rennert/Weill 86). Lithograph. Very good condition, on linen, 20 x 27 inches. $3,575 (Auc. #17)

Lorenzaccio, 1896 (Ref: Rennert/Weill 20). Lithograph. For Sarah Bernhardt at the Theatre de la Renaissance. Good condition, on linen, 15 x 39 inches. $3,564 (Auc. #17)

Job, 1898 (Ref: Rennert/Weill 51). Lithograph. Well-known poster for cigarette paper. Good condition, on linen, 37¼ x 55½ inches. $4,400 (Auc. #10)

La Plume, 1896 (Ref: Rennert/Weill 19 V.I.). Lithograph. For the literary magazine. A woman in profile against the signs of the zodiac. Good condition, on linen, 19 x 25½ inches. $6,675 (Auc. #18)

Salon des Cent, 1896 (Ref: Rennert/Weill 12). Lithograph. Printed by Champenois. For the annual artists' Salon. An outstanding example of the artist's work. Fine condition, 17 x 25 inches. $15,000–$16,000

Courtesy of Butterfield & Butterfield.

La Samaritaine, 1897 (Ref: Rennert/Weill 24). Lithograph. Sarah Bernhardt as Photina leans on a water vase. 22½ x 68½ inches. *See color insert, photo 4.*

$7,475 (Auc. #14)

❧ PH. H. NOYEZ

Limonade Brault, 1938. Lithograph. Printed by Joel Bellon. Six mermaids swim around a bubbly glass of lemon beverage. Fine condition, 46 x 63 inches.

$880 (Auc. #19)

❧ OKLEY

Casino de Paris, 1950. Photo-offset. Printed by Ets. St. Martin, Paris. Dancers on stage do high kicks. Fine condition, 39 x 57 inches. $550 (Auc. #19)

❧ OLSKY

Chapeaux Mossant, 1928. Lithograph. Gentleman in shadows holds out a fedora. Very good condition, on linen, 47 x 63 inches. $1,925 (Auc. #18)

❧ MANUEL ORAZI (1860–1934)

Palais de la Danse, 1900. Lithograph. Printed by Bourgerie. Greek goddess of dance in pastel colors, advertising the dance palace at the Paris Exposition Universelle of 1900. Very good condition, framed, 23 x 63 inches. $3,000–$3,500

❧ ORSI (1889–1947)

La Revue Nègre, 1925. Lithograph. Cabaret theater poster featuring black dancers. Very good condition, on Japan paper, 48 x 63 inches.$9,650 (Auc. #18)

❧ PAL—aka JEAN DE PALÉOLOGUE (1860–1942)

Enghien les Bains, 1899. Lithograph. Dance hall performer is shown with her fan doing a kick step. Very good condition, on linen, two sheets, 43 x 84 inches.

$1,275 (Auc. #17)

La Française, ca. 1898. Lithograph. Printed by Chardin. Very good condition, on linen, 45 x 62 inches. $300 (Auc. #17)

Les Fétards, 1897 (Ref: Broido, *French Opera Posters* #44). Lithograph. Printed by E. Delancy, Paris. For the operetta with music by Victor Roger (1854–1903), at the Theatre du Palais Royal. A voluptuous woman dancing in a revealing pink dress. Good condition, 23 x 30¾ inches. $500–$700

La Loie Fuller, 1897. Lithograph. Printed by F. Hermet, Paris. PAL executed several posters for this performer. In stunning colors, and a very good example of the artist's work. Fine condition, 37¼ x 51½ inches. $2,800–$3,000

La Loïe Fuller, 1897, by PAL. Courtesy of Park South Gallery.

Loterie, 1900. Lithograph. Printed by Chardin, Paris. Woman with masks around her waist holds a wheel with wings. Very good condition, 40 x 60 inches.

$605 (Auc. #19)

Phebus, ca. 1898. Lithograph. Printed by Paul Dupont, Paris. A very good example of the artist's work. Fine condition, 42½ x 57⅜ inches. *See color insert, photo 3.*

$3,400–$3,600

Rayon d'Or, ca. 1895. Lithograph. Printed by Paul Dupont, Paris. A nude woman with diaphanous wings hangs from a shining star created by this gas lamp. A good example of the artist's work. In fine condition, 30 x 45 inches. $1,400–$1,600

Théâtre des Bouffes, ca. 1900. Lithograph. Printed by Paul Dupont, Paris. Male and female dancers performing. Very good condition, 42½ x 59 inches.

$357 (Auc. #19)

Visitez Le Palais-Royal, ca. 1898. Lithograph. Woman bedecked in jewelry and elaborate headdress advertises the shops at Palais Royal. Fine condition, on linen, 43 x 54 inches. $1,950–$2,250

❧ RENÉ PEAN (1864–1940)

Le Fiancé de Thylda, Théâtre Cluny (Ref: Broido, *French Opera Posters* #51). Lithograph. For the Louis Varney operetta at the Theatre Cluny, 22½ x 32 inches.

$400 (Auc. #16)

As above, on linen, fine condition. $500–$600

Au Trois Quartiers, ca. 1900. Lithograph. Printed by Chaix. For a sale of toys and gifts. A Christmas angel bestows gifts on small children. Fine condition, on linen, 43 x 63 inches. $1,100–$1,300

❦ PABLO PICASSO (1881–1973)

> *NOTE: Many posters for Picasso exhibitions exist that simply reproduce a painting by the artist. Collectible posters are those designed by the artist specifically for use as a poster.*

Le Cubisme/Musée National D'Art Moderne, 1953. Lithograph. After Picasso. Reproducing a painting by Picasso for a museum show. Mint condition, 20 x 30 inches. $75–$125

Exposition Poteries, Fleurs, Parfums, Vallauris A.M., 1948. Lithograph. Designed by the artist, signed on the stone, for the 1948 exposition of his pottery. Fine condition, 15¾ x 23½ inches. $700–$900

Galerie 65/Cannes/14 Aout-30 Septembre, 1956. Lithograph. Designed by the artist, published by Mourlot. In fine condition, 19 x 27½ inches. $1,400–$1,600

March Against Death—March on Washington, November 13–15, 1969. One of the artist's last original posters, designed for a demonstration against the Vietnam War. Fine condition, 15 x 23 inches. $385 (Auc. #22)

❦ MANUEL ROBBE (1872–1936)

L'Eclatante, 1895. Lithograph. Printed by Bourgerie, Paris. For the oil lamp. In red, green, yellow, and gray. Good condition, two sheets, 37 x 51 inches. $1,800–$2,000

❦ ROBYS

Kina-Lillet, 1937. Lithograph. Printed by Affiches Stentor, Paris. White-gowned woman with red and gold grapes. Fine condition, 51 x 77½ inches. $605 (Auc. #19)

Premier Fils, 1936. Lithograph. Printed by L. Marboeuf, Paris. Woman in orange flanked by a jockey and three horses. Very good condition, 51½ x 78½ inches. $385 (Auc. #19)

❦ GEORGES ROCHEGROSSE (1859–1938)

> *NOTE: The most sought-after posters by Rochegrosse were for the Automobile Club of France, and can sell for over $3,000.*

Don Quichotte, 1910 (Ref: Broido, *French Opera Posters* #41). Lithograph. Printed by Ed. Delanchy, Paris. For the operetta by Jules Massenet. Don Quixote on horseback in mountain valley. Fine condition, 27 x 35 inches. $500–$600

Louise, 1900 (Ref: Broido, *French Opera Posters* #22). Lithograph. Printed by Ed. Delanchy. For the operetta by Gustave Charpentier. Romantic couple embraces above the town. Very good condition, 24½ x 35 inches. $275 (Auc. #19)

🌿 J. ROSETTI

La Raphaëlle Liqueur Bonal, 1908. A biplane lassos the bottle from the waiter's tray. Very good condition, 47 x 63 inches. $357 (Auc. #19)

As above, on linen, fine condition. $550–$650

🌿 ROUGEMONT

Mistinguett. Lithograph. Printed by Richier Laugier, Paris. The performer in a striking, colorful costume, smoking a cigar. Very good condition, 46 x 62½ inches.
$3,080 (Auc. #19)

🌿 THEODORE VAN RYSSELBERGHE (BELGIAN, 1862–1926)

La Libre Esthetique, 1897. Lithograph. Printed by Vve. Monnom, Bruxelles. Belle Epoque-style woman reads the arts publication. Very good condition, 26½ x 36¾ inches. $3,500–$4,000

🌿 THEOPHILE-ALEXANDRE STEINLEN (1859–1923)

> NOTE: Steinlen's social realist style lent itself to the masterful posters he created for World War I. See the chapter on World War Posters for additional listings.

Affiches Charles Verneau, also called **La Rue**, 1896. Lithograph. Printed by Charles Verneau. The street life of Monmartre. A rare and outstanding example of the artist's work. Good condition, six sheets, 117½ x 92½ inches.
$14,850 (Auc. #17)

Poster by J. Rosetti. Courtesy of Stephen Ganeles Antique Posters and Prints.

A La Bodinière/Exposition Steinlen, 1894. Lithograph. Printed by Charles Verneau, Paris. For the artist's own painting exhibition. Cats were a favorite subject of the artist. Fine condition, on linen, horizontal, 30½ x 23½ inches.
$4,500–$5,000

Exposition de Peintures/Th.-A. Steinlen, 1903. Lithograph. Printed by Ch. Wall, Paris. A worker gazes desparingly over an industrial area. A good example of the artist's work. Very good condition, on linen, 37½ x 54 inches.
$2,000–$2,500

Jean Borlin, 1920. Lithograph. Printed by Chachoin. For the Swedish performer/ dancer. Very good condition, on linen, 62 x 91 inches. $1,950 (Auc. #17)

Jenny Hasselquist, 1920. Lithograph. Printed by Chachoin. For the Swedish dancer. Designed as a pair with the poster above for Jean Borlin. Very good condition, on linen, 64 x 89½ inches. $2,375 (Auc. #17)

Lait pur Sterilisé de la Vingeanne, 1894. Lithograph. Printed by Charles Verneau, Paris. Charming image of little girl drinking her milk while three cats look on hungrily. A very good example of the artist's work. Good condition, on linen, 39 x 55 inches. $7,000–$8,000

Le Journal/La Traité des Blanches, 1899. Lithograph. Advertising a novel on white slavery by Dubut de Laforest. The first edition of this poster, confiscated by the police, showed a woman's bare breast. This example, second edition, larger version, 50 x 64 inches. $6,500–$7,000

From a private collection.

Courtesy of Butterfield &
Butterfield.

Le Locataire, 1913. Lithograph. For the publication of a tenants' federation. Fine condition, 48 x 61 inches. $2,200–$2,400

Le Petit Sou, 1900. Lithograph. Printed by Charles Verneau, Paris. For the socialist newspaper. Marianne in broken shackles leading the workers to the Bastille. Very good condition, center panel only, no text, 39 x 53 inches. $605 (Auc. #19)

Le Rêve, 1890 (Ref: Broido, *French Opera Posters* #28). Lithograph. Printed by Gillot, Paris. For the operetta ballet. Designed with Japanese motifs. In rich grays, green, ocher, and orange. Fine condition, 24½ x 35 inches. $605 (Auc. #19)

🌿 TAMAGNO (1851–?)

Demandez un Marra, ca. 1895. Lithograph. Printed by La Lithographie Parisienne. A couple at leisure sip their drinks. Fine condition, 39½ x 55 inches.
$475 (Auc. #17)

As above, fine condition, 38½ x 54½ inches. $990 (Auc. #19)

Terrot & Compagnie. Lithograph. By La Lithographie Parisienne. Man and woman biking in the mountains. In blue, green, brown, and red. Mint condition, 38½ x 54 inches. $1,300–$1,600

🌿 HENRI DE TOULOUSE-LAUTREC (1864–1901)

> NOTE: *Toulouse-Lautrec created only some thirty posters, but many versions exist, including those with/without text. Reference numbers in the listings refer to Wolfgang Wittrock's* Toulouse Lautrec: The Complete Prints. *London: Sotheby's Publications, 1985.*

Babylone d'Allemagne, 1894 (Wittrock P12). Lithograph. Printed by Chaix, Paris. For the book by Victor Joze. Very good condition, on linen, 33½ x 47 inches.
$32,000–$43,000

The Chap Book, 1896 (Wittrock P18). Lithograph. Printed by Chaix, Paris. Commissioned by Stone & Kimball, the Chicago publisher of the *Chap Book*. Illustrating "The Irish and American Bar" in Paris. A very good example of Lautrec's work. Fine condition, 23¾ x 16⅛ inches. $35,000–$45,000

Confetti, 1893 (Wittrock P13). Lithograph. Printed by Bella & deMalherbe, London and Paris. For the English paper manufacturers J. & E. Bella. Fine condition, on linen, 16½ x 22½ inches. $30,000–$43,000

Divan Japonais, 1893 (Wittrock P11). Lithograph. Printed by Edw. Ancourt, Paris. The well-known image of Jane Avril watching the show at the Parisian cabaret named for its Jananese decor. A very good example of the artist's work. Fine condition, 23¾ x 31¼ inches. $38,000–$47,000

Eldorado/Aristide Bruant Dans Son Cabaret, 1892 (Wittrock P5). Lithograph. Printed by Edw. Ancourt, Paris. For the performer Aristide Bruant (1851–1923). Fine condition, on linen, 38½ x 55½ inches. $30,000–$40,000

Jane Avril, 1893 (Wittrock P6B). Lithograph. Printed by Chaix, Paris. The performer dancing onstage, framed by a design proceeding from the neck of a cello. An excellent example of the artist's work. Very good condition, 36½ x 49½ inches. $40,000– $45,000

Moulin Rouge, 1891 (Wittrock P1B). Lithograph. Printed by Ch. Levy. Lautrec's first poster became his most famous, conveying an entire era marked by the famous Montmartre night spot. The most sought-after of all Lautrec's works. Fine condition, the rare three-sheet poster, 48½ x 77½ inches. $250,000–$300,000

La Revue Blanche, 1895 (Wittrock P16). Lithograph. Printed by Edw. Ancourt, Paris. For the Parisian periodical published 1891–1903. Depicts a well-dressed Parisienne with muff and plumed hat ice-skating. One of Lautrec's best-known posters, and a good example of his work. Fine condition, 35½ x 49 inches. $14,500 (Auc. #16)

As above, on linen, fine condition. $25,000–$35,000

Salon Des Cent/Exposition Internationale d'Affiches, 1895 (Wittrock P20). Lithograph. Printed by Bourgerie, Paris. For the annual Salon. Woman in a deck chair. Fine condition, on linen, 16¼ x 28¼ inches. $27,000–$34,000

Courtesy of Leslie Hindman Auctioneers.

🐚 FERNAND TOUSSAINT (BELGIAN, 1873–1956)

Le Sillon, 1895. Lithograph. Printed by O. de Rycker. In pale blue, pink, yellow, and black. A young winged girl personifies Glory, standing in a field holding a shaft of wheat and a sickle. One of the most sought-after Belgian posters. Very good condition, 32⅛ x 42⅛ inches. $15,000–$20,000

🐚 SUZANNE VALADON

L'Aide Amicale Aux Artistes, 1927. Lithograph. Printed by l'A.A.A.A., Paris. Studio model painting the banner for the ball to benefit artists. Very good condition, 30 x 47½ inches. $825 (Auc. #19)

🐚 R. DE VALERIO

Cherry Maurice Chevalier, ca. 1935. Lithograph. Printed by Devambez, Paris. For the cherry liqueur named after the great entertainer. In very good condition, 46½ x 62 inches. $522 (Auc. #19)

🐚 MARIE VASSILIEFF

Ball Bullier, 1924. Lithograph. Printed by Risacher, Paris. An outstanding angular design. Fine condition, this example framed, 33 x 48½ inches. $2,200 (Auc. #19)

Courtesy of Swann
Galleries, Inc.

❦ BERNARD VILLEMONT (1911–1989)

NOTE: Villemont posters have become very popular in the last few years since his death, and appear on the market with increasing frequency. Prices can vary greatly, so it is best to shop around.

Bally, 1974. Photo-offset. Printed by IPA, Paris. Two nude female figures sitting back to back. Fine condition, 46 x 60½ inches. $440 (Auc. #19)

Bally, 1982. Photo-offset. Printed by IPA, Paris. A woman sitting cross-legged. Fine condition, this example framed, 45½ x 62 inches. $412 (Auc. #19)

Bally 1989. Photo-offset. Printed by A. Karcher, Paris. A lady in a polka-dot dress kicks her leg back to show her shoe. Fine condition, on linen, 36 x 50 inches.
$375 (Auc. #17)

As above, excellent condition, framed, 47 x 69 inches. $412 (Auc. #19)

Negrita. Le Rhum, 1980. Photo-offset. Printed by Imp. Bedos & Compagnie, Paris. Fine condition, two sheets, horizontal, overall size 88 x 56½ inches.
$880 (Auc. #19)

Perrier, 1980. Photo-offset. Printed by Lalande-Courbet, Paris. Two intertwined figures with the legend "fou de soif?" ("crazy from thirst?"). Fine condition, 47 x 68 inches. $467 (Auc. #19)

❦ RENÉ VINCENT (1879–1936)

NOTE: Among Vincent's most sought-after posters are those he designed for Peugeot and other auto makers.

Michelin, ca. 1905. Lithograph. "Bib," the Michelin man, laughs as a man pulls a tire from his tire body to repair a flat. Very good condition, 23¾ x 28 inches.
$380 (Auc. #24)

Poster by Bernard Villemont. Courtesy of Swann Galleries, Inc.

Porto Ramos-Pinto. Lithograph. Printed by Vercasson, Paris. Man and woman kissing a glass held by a cupid. Fine condition, 14½ x 20¼ inches. $275 (Auc. #19)

As above, mint condition. $400–$500

❦ EDOUARD VUILLARD (1868–1940)

Album d'Estampe Originales, 1899. Lithograph. Designed as the cover for a proposed collection of prints to be published by Roger Mars and Andre Marty, which was never published. Very good condition, 18⅛ x 25 inches. $3,000–$4,000

❦ WELY

Les Demoiselles Des St. Cyriens, 1898. Lithograph. Printed by Ed. Delancy, Paris. For the Theatre Cluny. Woman in pink dress about to play badminton. Fine condition, 23½ x 31 inches. $440 (Auc. #19)

❦ ADOLPHE WILLETTE (1857–1926)

Exposition Internationale, 1893. Lithograph. Printed by Charles Verneau, Paris. A woman driving a chariot pulled by angels. Fine condition, 38 x 54 inches.

$440 (Auc. #19)

❦ ANDREW KAY WOMRATH (1869–?)

XXVe Exposition Salon des Cent, 1897. Lithograph. A man examines pottery while a woman glances at prints. Fine condition, 16 x 22 inches. $950 (Auc. #18)

❦ ZIG—aka LOUIS GAUDIN (d. 1936)

Mistinguett/Casino de Paris, 1931. Lithograph. Printed by Central Publicité, Paris. The stylized performer holds a hug feather fan and rides bareback on a team of horses. Zig designed most of Mistinguett's posters after the death of Gesmar. Fine condition, long, vertical format, on linen, 30 x 90 inches. $2,800–$3,300

LES MAÎTRES DE L'AFFICHE—PRICE LISTINGS
(LISTED ALPHABETICALLY BY ARTIST)

> NOTE: These posters are miniature versions of the original posters. The date following the title is the original date for the poster, not the republication date in Les Maîtres. This series of posters was printed on 11¼-x-15½ inch sheets, with the embossed blind stamp of the publisher. The size given is the image size. See preceding chapter for more information.

❦ THE BEGGARSTAFFS aka

WILLIAM NICHOLSON (ENGLISH, 1872–1949) AND

JAMES PRIDE (ENGLISH, 1866–1941)

Harper's Magazine, 1895. Lithograph. Plate 16 from *Les Maîtres* 1896. Fine condition, 8¾ x 10 inches. $250–$300

❧ PIERRE BONNARD (FRENCH, 1867–1947)

La Revue Blanche, 1894. Lithograph. Plate 38 from Les *Maîtres*. Good condition, 9⅛ x 11⅜ inches. $230 (Auc. #11)

❧ WILLIAM CARQUEVILLE (AMERICAN, 1871–1946)

Lippincott's/May, 1895. Lithograph. Plate 44 from *Les Maîtres*. A young woman picks yellow flowers. Fine condition, 7½ x 11¾ inches. $150–$200

❧ JULES CHÉRET (FRENCH, 1836–1932)

> NOTE: Chéret was the artistic director at Imprimerie Chaix, the publisher of
> Les Maîtres de L'Affiche, and ensured that his work was well represented.
> Of the 256 plates in the series, 67, slightly more than one fourth, were his.

Le Punch Grassot, 1895. Lithograph. Plate 5 from *Les Maîtres*. Good condition, 9⅛ x 12¾ inches. $300–$350

Les Pays des Fées, 1889. Plate 181 from *Les Maîtres*. Advertising "The Country of the Fairies" at the 1889 Universal Exposition. Good condition, 9 x 12⅝ inches. $425–$450

❧ GEORGE DE FEURE (FRENCH, aka GEORGES VAN SLUITERS, 1868–1943)

Journal des Ventes, 1897. Lithograph. Plate 146 from *Les Maîtres*. Good condition, 7⅞ x 11⅞ inches. $287 (Auc. #11)

❧ OTTO FISCHER (GERMAN, 1870–1947)

Kunst-Anstalt Feur Moderne Plakate/Wilhelm Hoffmann Dresden, 1896. Lithograph. Plate 127 from *Les Maîtres*. For the Wilhelm Hoffmann poster-printing works. Fine condition, 7¾ x 12 inches. $350–$400

❧ EUGENE GRASSET (SWISS, NATURALIZED FRENCH, 1845–1917)

Sarah Bernhardt/Jeanne D'arc, 1893. Lithograph. Plate 174 from *Les Maîtres*. Striking image of Sarah Bernhardt as Joan of Arc leading the troops. Fine condition, 8⅞ x 13⅝ inches. $250–$300

Century Magazine/Life of Napoleon, 1894. Lithograph. Plate 126 from *Les Maîtres*. For the American magazine. Fine condition, 8 x 12¼ inches. $250–$300

Photo by Otto Fischer. From the author's collection. Photo by Robert Four.

Poster by Eugene Grasset. Courtesy of Thomas G. Boss Fine Books.

🔥 DUDLEY HARDY (ENGLISH, 1866–1922)

A Gaiety Girl. Lithograph. Plate 4 from *Les Maîtres*. For the musical comedy. Good condition, 6½ x 10⅛ inches. $150–$200

🔥 FRANK HAZENPLUG (AMERICAN, 1873–AFTER 1908)

Living Posters, 1897. Lithograph. Plate 87 from *Les Maîtres*. Fine condition, 9 x 12¾ inches. $150–$175

🔥 FRED HYLAND (ENGLISH, ACTIVE IN THE 1890S)

Harper's Magazine, 1896. Lithograph. Plate 120 from *Les Maîtres*. Good condition, 7⅞ x 12⅛ inches. $300–$500

🔥 PRIVAT LIVEMONT (BELGIAN, 1861–1936)

Cabourg, 1896. Lithograph. Plate 88 from *Les Maîtres*. Very good condition, horizontal, 11¼ x 7½ inches. $650–$700

🔥 HENRI MEUNIER (BELGIAN, 1869–1942)

Rajah, 1897. Lithograph. Plate 156 from *Les Maîtres*. Good condition, 10⅛ x 7¾ inches. $880 (Auc. #10)

❦ **ALBERT GEORGE MORROW (ENGLISH, 1863–1927)**

The New Woman, by Sydney Grundy, 1894. Lithograph. Plate 79 from *Les Maîtres.* For the London Comedy Theatre production. Fine condition, 10 x 13¼ inches. $125– $150

❦ **ALPHONSE MUCHA (FRENCH, 1860–1939)**

La Samaritaine. Lithograph. Plate 166 from *Les Maîtres.* For the play starring Sarah Bernhardt. Very good condition, 5⅜ x 14¾ inches. $862 (Auc. #11)

❦ **EDWARD PENFIELD (AMERICAN, 1866–1925)**

Harper's March, 1895. Lithograph. Plate 20 from *Les Maîtres.* A woman and a hare in pursuit of a *Harper's* blown away by the wind. Fine condition, 7¼ x 10 inches. $200–$250

Harper's May, 1896. Lithograph. Plate 115 from *Les Maîtres.* A young woman holds two smug cats. Fine condition, 7¾ x 11½ inches. $200–$300

❦ **ETHEL REED (AMERICAN, 1874–AFTER 1898)**

Miss Traumerei, 1895. Lithograph. Plate 99 from *Les Maîtres.* Woman seated at a piano. Fine condition, 8⅝ x 14 inches. $275–$325

The Quest of the Golden Girl, 1896. Lithograph. Plate 128 from *Les Maîtres.* For the novel by Richard La Galienne. Fine condition, 7¾ x 12 inches. $225–$250

❦ **FRITZ REHM (GERMAN, 1871–1928)**

Cigaretten Laferme Dresden, 1897. Lithograph. Plate 124 from *Les Maîtres.* Good condition, 7¾ x 12 inches. $300–$400

❦ **THEOPHILE ALEXANDRE STEINLEN (FRENCH, 1859–1923)**

Helle, 1896. Lithograph. Plate 34 from *Les Maîtres.* For the opera at the National Academy of Music. Very good condition, 8¾ x 11¼ inches. $287 (Auc. #11)

Lait Pur Sterilisé, 1894. Lithograph. Plate 95 from *Les Maîtres.* One of Steinlen's best-known images, of a little girl sipping milk while her cats watch hungrily. Very good condition, 9 x 12½ inches. $300–$350

❦ **HENRI DE TOULOUSE-LAUTREC (FRENCH, 1864–1901)**

NOTE: *Henri de Toulouse-Lautrec is represented by five plates in* Les Maîtres, *which are among the most sought-after and highest-priced from the series.*

La Chaine Simpson, 1896. Lithograph. Plate 238 from *Les Maîtres.* Blue-clad cyclists in a race. Fine condition, horizontal, 12½ x 9½ inches. $412 (Auc. #19)

La Revue Blanche, 1895. Lithograph. Plate 82 from *Les Maîtres*. Very good condition, 9⅛ x 12½ inches. $977 (Auc. #11)

❦ CHARLES H. WOODBURY (AMERICAN, 1864–1940)

The July Century, 1895. Lithograph. Plate 32 from *Les Maîtres*. Brightly lit Japanese lanterns with the heads of a crowd silhouetted in the background. Fine condition, 8¼ x 13½ inches. $250–$300

Society of Painters in Water Color of Holland, 1895. Lithograph. Plate 112 from *Les Maîtres*. For the first annual exhibition in the United States. Fine condition, 7⅞ x 11 inches. $200–$250

Courtesy of
Thomas G. Boss
Fine Books.

❧ CHAPTER 12 ❧
Italian Posters

BY BERNICE JACKSON

Bernice Jackson is a fine arts consultant, offering a wide range of posters, and specializing in posters of several countries, including Italy, Holland, Switzerland, Russia, and others. You can contact her at P.O. Box 1188, Concord, Massachusetts 01742, (508) 369–9088.

Italian vintage posters from 1890 to World War II offer collectors a breathtaking diversity of artists, styles, and subjects. From the earliest Art Nouveau posters for automobiles, products, and opera, to the Art Deco period with its angularity and bold colors in posters for travel, fashion, and industry, to the historically important and striking images of the Fascist regime, Italian posters are capturing a wider audience than ever before.

THE ITALIAN POSTER AND THE HOUSE OF RICORDI

Lithographic posters were produced as early as the 1860s. However, it was in the 1880s and 1890s that illustrated pictorial posters really came into prominence in Italy, in large measure due to the firm of Ricordi.

This music publisher and printer, founded by Giovanni Ricordi (1785–1853), was brought to the forefront by his grandson Giulio Ricordi (1840–1912), when he began to publish the operatic works of Verdi and Puccini. Ricordi started an in-house graphic arts department in 1874, which soon became its own company under the name *Officine Grafiche Ricordi*.

In the mid-1880s, as Paris saw a prolific production of posters from artists such as Jules Chéret and Alphonse Mucha, Italy found its first champion in Adolfo Hohenstein. His 1895 poster for the opera *La Bohème*, published by Ricordi, was the beginning of a long line of posters designed in the Art Nouveau style. In Italy, Art Nouveau was called

109

"Stile Liberty," due to the popularity of Art Nouveau decorative arts from the London shop of A. L. Liberty.

Many of the early, great pictorial lithographic posters were for the opera. The grand scale and spectacle of opera easily lent itself to poster designs of heroic scope and magnificence. Godlike creatures, demons, and figures drawn from mythology abound, bathed in heavenly light with colors reminiscent of earlier Italian artistic masterpieces, which surrounded the artists of Rome.

However, everyday products—newspapers, cigarettes, cars, fertilizer, gas lamps—were also sold by muscular messengers of the gods or angelic spirits in long, flowing robes. Posters of this early period are often called "monumental," also because of their multiple-sheet size.

The year 1895 also marked the *Instituto Italiano d'Arte Graphica* guild's founding of the review *Emporium*, which promoted the Liberty movement in Italy. The review was launched at the first Venice Biennale, which was the first art exhibition in Italy to give posters a prominent role. Ricordi's exhibition at the Biennale, established it as the leading printer for lithographic posters, and won it numerous clients.

By 1900, several great poster talents had emerged, the majority of whom worked under Hohenstein at Ricordi: Leopoldo Metlicovitz, Giovanni Mataloni, Achille Mauzan, Marcello Dudovich, Aleardo Villa, and Franz Laskoff. Even the great poster artist Leonetto Cappiello, who had immigrated to France, accepted commissions for Ricordi clients.

E. & A. MELE DEPARTMENT STORE

One of Ricordi's most important clients, apart from opera, was the department store E. & A. Mele of Naples. This store became one of the great Italian poster patrons, much the same way the PKZ department store did in Switzerland.

Emiddi and Alfredo Mele's store operated from 1896 to about 1915. Ricordi designed and printed their posters for almost two decades, commissioning artists such as Metilcovitz, Aleardo Terzi, Dudovich, Achille Beltrame, Gian Emilio Malerba, Franz Laskoff, Cappiello, and others.

Italy, like many countries, was experiencing the rise of an urban bourgeoisie, and Mele posters projected images of affluent, well-dressed, and well-mannered gentlemen and ladies. Like its French and American counterparts, the department store of E. & A. Mele not only sold, but came to almost dictate fashion in clothing and decorative arts. These posters are highly collectible today and have received renewed attention in recent years.

The settings for the posters are as important as the fashion in achieving the effect Mele sought: a gentleman with his valet, a fashionable lady entering her coach, a villa balcony overflowing with flowers, a salon with distinctively styled furniture. Each of these conveyed a way of life to which Mele customers aspired—a way of life that would be shattered by World War I.

EARLY ITALIAN POSTER ARTISTS

Adolfo Hohenstein (1854–1928) is often called the "Father of the Italian Poster," though he was born in Russia of German parents. While he was influenced by Mucha, the boldness of his style set him apart. His posters captured the imagination for their realistic figures, palette of rich colors, and stunning effects of light and shadow.

After the poster for Puccini's *La Bohème* in 1895, he went on to design other great opera posters for Mascagni's *Iris* (1898), Puccini's *Tosca* (1899), and *Madama Butterfly* (1904). His talent and inventiveness were evident from the start. For the *Corriere della Sera*, an evening newspaper, he depicted Hermes, the messenger of the gods, perched on a streetlamp, shouting to passersby in the streets.

He created numerous other designs, including product posters for Monowatt Bulbs, Cintura Calliano, and Bitter Campari. Hohenstein became the artistic director at Ricordi in 1889, where he influenced an entire generation of Italian graphic design. He received commissions from Belgium and France, and left Italy for Germany in 1906.

Leopoldo Metlicovitz (1868–1944), the most prolific posterist of this early period, developed a mastery of color printing techniques, which earned him the position of technical director at Ricordi shortly after he joined the firm in 1891. His poster *Fleurs de Mousse* (1898), for a French perfume company, is captivating. He also designed works for the opera, including posters for *Iris* (1899) and *Madama Butterfly* (1904).

His early posters often used elaborate Art Nouveau border designs that framed the central image. Later, his style changed, and he often used allegorical figures or muscular athletes to portray heroic themes. His prizewinning design for the 1906 *International Exposition*, which marked the opening of a locomotive tunnel, is a dramatic portrayal of Mercury riding the engine. His poster for the *Turin International Exposition* (1911) shows two athletes planting the flag. In another poster for *Mostra del Ciclo e dell'Automobile* (1907), a winged allegorical figure is seen flying beside the moving car.

Other rare posters by Metlicovitz include his 1908 poster for *Superator* gas heaters, the Italian Riviera resort of *Spezia* (1907), and

Compagnia d'Opere Comiche (1910) with its technically superb play of light and shadow on the gown and hair of the central figure.

His posters display his abilities to blend colors, maximize the effects of light, and ultimately create both highly decorative and very effective advertising. His versatility brought him commissions to design posters for the full range of Ricordi clients, including manufacturers of various products, automobiles, liqueurs and wine, expositions, and more. He is the most widely represented early Italian poster artist on the market today.

Giovanni Mataloni (dates unknown) is credited with having designed the first commercial Italian poster of note in 1895, for *Brevetto Auer* gaslight fixtures. Both Hohenstein and Metlicovitz were influenced by this lesser-known Art Nouveau artist, whose posters are extremely rare in today's market. Mataloni came to Ricordi in 1890, and designed posters for such clients as the Sicilian daily newspaper *L'Ora* (1909).

Achille Mauzan (1883–1952) was born in France, but settled in Turin in about 1909. At the time, Turin was the center of a thriving silent film industry. Reportedly, Mauzan designed close to fifteen hundred posters for films in the span of just a few years, though few appear on the market today. This incredibly prolific production is due to the fact that silent movies of the day were short features, and often many films were produced in the course of one week. Mauzan accommodated the large output of posters by using only four colors, which sped up the production process. He joined Ricordi in 1912, designing many of its posters for film clients.

After World War I, Mauzan continued to design posters, often using humorous effects and caricatures to promote a range of products. He was commissioned by leading advertising agencies such as Maga and Cosmos, and finally established and operated his own poster company in Buenos Aires, Argentina, from 1927 to 1932. His work was then, and is today, recognized as the best poster design of the period based in South America.

Marcello Dudovich (1878–1962) is one of the most widely recognized and collected Italian posterists, perhaps because his prolific career spanned several decades. He joined Ricordi in 1897, working under Metlicovitz, but left to work for the printer Edmondo Chappius in Bologna from 1899 to 1905. He returned to Ricordi in 1906, and was often called upon to design posters for the department store E. & A. Mele.

A famous and highly sought-after Dudovich poster from this period is *Marca Zenit* (1911), which simply and effectively shows a man's hat, gloves, and cane poised on a chair. His posters for Mele and other clients feature elegantly dressed men and women in a somewhat stylized manner that established him as a leading fashion illustrator.

In 1911 he again left Ricordi, this time for a position in Munich on the staff of the avant-garde review *Simplicissimus*, where he stayed until the outbreak of World War I. He then returned to Ricordi again, working with the film industry in Turin along with Mauzan.

After the war, Dudovich stayed in Milan, and finally founded the Star agency, which he led from 1921 to 1950. One of his most important clients was the Rinascente department store in Milan, for whom he created more than one hundred posters in vivid colors and a stronger Art Deco style. His agency also produced posters for travel, products, and automobiles such as Fiat. Though his career spanned both the Art Nouveau and Art Deco periods, his posters are relatively rare on the market, and many bring high prices.

Aleardo Villa (1865–1906) joined Ricordi in 1895, and produced numerous designs for Mele from 1898 to about 1905. Villa also designed early posters for Benz automobiles, Fernet Brioschi, and other Ricordi clients. A talented poster artist, his work was cut short by his untimely death in 1906.

Franz Laskoff (1869–1921) was born Francois Laskowski in Poland. He produced only about twenty known designs for posters, and was influenced by the simple, direct graphics of the English posterists, the Beggarstaffs. Laskoff used flat tones of color and somewhat geometric forms that set his posters apart from the prevalent Art Nouveau. One of his best-known posters, for Mele (1902), is an elegant gentleman seated in a cane chair on his yacht, smoking a pipe, while the crescent moon glimmers on the water. He also produced posters promoting wine, paint, bicycles, and other products, as well as posters for French clients.

Leonetto Cappiello (1875–1942), though Italian by birth, made his career for the most part in France. While he was commissioned occasionally by Italian clients, even fewer of his Italian posters were printed in Italy. The most notable ones were produced by Ricordi for Mele. Cappiello is thought by many to be the greatest posterist between World War I and II, and was certainly one of the most prolific.

Other Italian artists of the pre–World War I period worth looking for include: Achille Beltrame (1871–1945), Leonardo Bistolfi (1859–1933), Gino Finetti (1887–1955), Riccardo Galli (1869–1944), Pipein Gamba (1868–1954), Gian Emilio Malerba (1880–1926), Plinio Nomellini (1866–1943), Enrico Sacchetti (1877–1967), and Aleardo Terzi (1870–1943).

THE EMERGENCE OF MODERN GRAPHIC DESIGN

Italy was slower than some countries to accept stylistic changes in graphic design after World War I. Some prominent artists of the prewar period continued their work without much innovation. Others, such as Metlicovitz, somewhat adopted the new styles, but produced posters far less distinguished than their early work. Of those already mentioned, Dudovich made the most successful transition to a more modern style.

The advertising agency Maga also produced a large number of posters in the 1920s, under the direction of Giuseppe Maganoli. Maganoli commissioned artists such as Nizzoli and Terzi, but many of its posters are simply signed "Maga" and not by the artist. Maga also employed the young Severo Pozzati before he left to study design with A. M. Cassandre in France.

One of the first avant-garde posterists was Federico Seneca (1891–1976), who started producing posters in the early 1920s for the Perugina Company's Buitoni products. His stylized, faceless figures and modernist lines were not adopted by other artists until several years later.

In 1929 Edouardo Perisco became the art director for the new review *Campo Grafica*, and began publishing the work of the Bauhaus and the French post-Cubist school. His influence was felt on a younger generation of Italian artists, including Chiattone, Erberto Carboni, Murani, and futurists such as Fortunato Depero.

During this time, Antonio Boggeri's graphic design workshops became a focal point for avant-garde artists such as Xanti Schawinsky, Marcello Nizzoli, Carboni, Ricas, Murani, Muratore, and Franco Grignani. Later, Max Huber came from Switzerland, bringing the influences of modern abstract Swiss design. Boggeri's studio found a few forward-thinking clients who were ready to modernize their advertising.

Xanti Schawinsky (b. 1904), who had studied at the Bauhaus, designed graphically strong posters for *Princeps* (1934), *Illy* coffee, *Spestre* seltzer (1935), and other products.

Erberto Carboni (1889–1984), who was inspired by A. M. Cassandre, designed for *Mostra Nazionale d'Agrumicultura* and for Shell Oil. Cassandre was himself commissioned by Motta, and he went on to design travel posters such as *Italia* (1935), and product posters for other Italian firms.

FASCISM AND POSTER ART

While a few Italian poster artists in the 1920s experimented with new graphic idioms, it was not until the 1930s that modern design began to take hold. When it did, it also coincided with the rise of official Fascist art, which was responsible for both some of the best and some of the least graphically interesting posters of the period.

Some of those that are graphically less appealing looked back to the "glories" of classical Rome. These posters are tinged with a pompous attitude or illustrated with the stuff of Roman legends such as Romulus and Remus.

However, a few Fascist poster artists created outstanding modernist designs commissioned by the state. One of the best was Franco Chelini (1916–after 1960). His 1942 poster for a state-sponsored regatta depicts a crew team so stylized as to almost be abstract. The same year he designed a poster for Labor, showing a hammer forging a sword. Both of these are titled as the year "XXI" for 1942, because Mussolini changed the calendar, starting "Year I" in 1922 to mark his rise to power.

Gino Boccasile (1901–1952), who had produced travel and product posters, such as his striking Art Deco designs for Bantam hats starting in 1935, went on to produce some of the most horrifying Fascist anti-American posters in World War II, which are rare collectors' items for war poster buffs.

Fascist Italian posters are, of course, extremely rare, as many were destroyed by the Italians themselves upon the arrival of the Allied powers.

THE IMPACT OF FUTURISM

Where the posters of the 1920s and the 1930s in Italy excel, they draw their strength from the German Bauhaus, as well as from the small but influential Italian "futurist" movement, which began in 1909 and continued through the 1920s.

Futurism peaked in Italy about the same time that Cubism was taking center stage in France. The same year (1909) that the Ballets Russes arrived in Paris, a futurist poem published in a Parisian newspaper proclaimed, "Speed is our god, the new cannon of beauty."

One year later, in 1910, the futurists published the *Manifesto of Futurist Painters*, to help disseminate their work. Parisians were shocked at the violent nature of much of the art. Among leading futurist artists were Umberto Boccioni, Giacomo Balla, Gine Severini, and Martinetti. They succeeded at depicting speed and movement in their work through the use of multiple-imaging, oblique angles, and shading.

Favorite overall themes, besides speed, were power and energy—both industrial and natural. Paintings depicted cars and railroad trains at full throttle, and industrial motifs were juxtaposed next to natural ones. Nature itself made the canvas quiver in the forms of storms, lightning bolts, volcanoes, tidal waves, and rearing horses. By the beginning of World War I, the influence of futurism was apparent in many applied arts, but it wasn't until the 1930s that its impact would be felt on the graphic style of its native country.

Fortunato Depero (1892–1960) was one of the leading theorists of the new wave of the futurist movement, publishing the manifesto

Depero Futurista in 1927. He created stunning posters for the *Societa nationale gazometri,* for Cirio food products, and for futurist theater productions.

OTHER MODERN ERA PATRONS AND ARTISTS

One important poster patron was Olivetti Corporation, headed by Adriano Olivetti, who understood the need to advertise modern products to consumers with a graphic style that was up-to-date. Marcello Nizzoli (1887–1969) joined Olivetti in 1938, designing many posters for the company. He was also often commissioned for automobile posters.

Campari also recognized the need to update its image with the buying public, and commissioned posters from artists such as Nizzoli, Depero, and Plinio Codognato (1878–1940).

Motta, the Milan bakery, commissioned Severo Pozzati (1895–1983), who signed his posters "Sepo." Pozzati had become well-known in France, where he had worked since about 1920, but was virtually unknown in his native Italy. He designed posters for *Lavol* (1932), *Noveltex* collars (1928), and other products.

Automobile and auto racing were important poster patrons, continuing a tradition of great poster art, which had started with Metlicovitz. Fiat commissioned artists such as Giuseppe Riccobaldi (1887–?), who designed three posters for the car company. Other artists known for their automotive posters are Franz Lenhart (1898–1992), Franco Codognato (b. 1911), the son of Plinio Codognato, and Aldo Mazza (1880–1964).

Araca (dates unknown) designed several cubist posters in the 1930s, including *Sniafiocco, Il Cotone Nazionale* (1935), for the cotton industry.

Other notable Italian artists of the modern period include Galileo Chini (1873–1956); Paulo Garetto (b. 1903), who made his career largely in the United States before returning to Italy in 1942; Franco Grignani (b. 1908); Giovanni Guerrini (b. 1887); Giorgio Muggiani (1887–1938); Enrico Prampolini (1894–1955); and Mario Sironi (1885–1961).

THE SCARCITY OF ITALIAN POSTERS

Until recent years Italian posters were largely ignored in a market dominated by French design.

This neglect of Italian poster art has a historical precedent: As Italian poster production was established somewhat later than in other countries, Italian posters did not draw the attention of the early poster collectors and societies.

The voluminous survey *Les Affiches Etrangeres Illustrées* (Illustrated Foreign Posters), published in 1897, made little mention of Italian posters, while even Japanese posters had their own chapter. In *Les Maîtres de L'Affiche* (The Masters of the Poster), published 1896–1900, only Hohenstein, Mataloni, and a lesser artist, G. Buono, were represented.

Even though there was large-scale production of posters in Italy in the years before World War I, relatively little was saved, perhaps reflecting a cultural bias against advertising art. In France, poster collecting was a phenomenon, and there were numerous clubs, expositions, publications, and galleries that promoted posters and poster collecting. In Italy almost no activity of this kind existed.

The rise of Fascism in Italy, which in its turn created some outstanding graphic design, posed a threat to earlier posters that reflected bourgeois values. It is believed that thousands upon thousands of earlier posters were destroyed when the Fascist regime took over printing companies. Likewise, when the Allies liberated Italy, many Italian citizens destroyed any Fascist art in their possession.

All of these factors contribute to the scarcity of Italian posters on the market today, and to rising prices for the best examples of each period in Italian poster design.

ITALIAN POSTERS—PRICE LISTINGS

NOTE: See the chapter Important Notes on Price Listings for more information on prices given. Also note that some Italian poster artists also have listings under other chapters such as World War Posters and Travel and Transportation.

❦ ANONYMOUS

A. P. I. Voghera. Lithograph. Woman in pink and green holding multicolored candy. Very good condition, 13½ x 19¼ inches. $385 (Auc. #19)

Ferrovia Elettrica Stresa-Mottavone, ca. 1908. Lithograph. Printed by Richter, Naples. Trolley makes its way up from a lake setting. Good condition, 26½ x 39 inches. $660 (Auc. #19)

As above, fine condition. $900–$1,200

Liquore del Reno, ca. 1930. Lithograph. Woman in blue and yellow sitting at a café. Fine condition, 13½ x 21 inches. $605 (Auc. #19)

Lugano/Grand Palace Hotel. Lithograph. Beautiful lake setting. Very good condition, horizontal, 39½ x 27½ inches. $825 (Auc. #19)

Roma, ca. 1950. Photo-offset. Published by Enit. Depicting the Roman Coliseum. Very good condition, 26 x 39 inches. $250–$300

❦ ARACA (DATES UNKNOWN)

Sniafiocco/Il Cottone Nazionale, 1935. Lithograph. A geometricized blue finger spinning yarn against a black background. Fine condition, on linen, 54¾ x 76½ inches. $1,500–$1,800

❦ GINO BOCCASILE (1901–1952)

Bantam, 1935. Lithograph. Gentleman with a green hat. Fine condition, small format, 9¼ x 13½ inches. $357 (Auc. #19)

Cappello Bantam, 1938. Lithograph. The letter B becomes the body of a man tipping his hat. Clever, stylized typographic poster. Very good condition, 39 x 53 inches. $1,320 (Auc. #19)

As above, mint condition. $1,500–$1,800

India, ca. 1935. Lithograph. Travel poster showing man in turban sitting in an arcade looking at the minarets. Very good condition, 26 x 38½ inches.

$605 (Auc. #19)

Lloyd Triestino/Africa, ca. 1935. Photo-offset. Travel poster showing two stylized African women crossing a bridge. Very good condition, 24½ x 38 inches. $700–$800

Lloyd Triestino/Australia, ca. 1935. Photo-offset. Travel poster showing a huge sheep. Very good condition, 24½ x 38 inches. $250–$300

❦ LEONETTO CAPPIELLO (1875–1942, WORKED MAINLY IN FRANCE)

E. & A. Mele/Novita per Signora/Napoli, 1902. Lithograph. Printed by Ricordi. A woman trying on a yellow dress in front of a mirror. A very good example of the artist and the client. Fine condition, two sheets, on linen, 59⅛ x 81⅜ inches. $7,000–$7,500

❦ FRANCO CHELINI (1916–AFTER 1960)

Prelittoriali Del Lavoro XXI, 1942. Lithograph. Fascist poster for labor. Showing a hammer forging a sword. The "XXI" stands for 1942, because Mussolini changed the calendar, starting it as "Year I" in 1922 to mark the era of his rise to power. An important, stunning poster. Fine condition, 18⅝ x 27⅜ inches. *See color insert, photo 9.* $4,500–$4,800

❧ DILULLO (DATES UNKNOWN)

A. P. I. Voghera. Lithograph. Lady in green plays with a young child. Very good condition, 27½ x 39¼ inches. $247 (Auc. #19)

❧ MARCELLO DUDOVICH (1878–1962)

Distillerie Del L'Aurum/Pineta Di Pescara, ca. 1935. Lithograph. Woman in white holding an Aurum liquor bottle. Good condition, on linen, 39½ x 55 inches.

$3,000–$3,500

E. & A. Mele/Ultime Novita per Signora, 1907. Lithograph. Printed by Ricordi. A long, monumental poster featuring two elegant women, the one in the foreground wearing a very long fur over her shoulders. Fine condition, on linen, 41½ x 87 inches. $15,000–$17,000

Lloyd Triestino/India/Express Service to Bombay, ca. 1930. Lithograph. Travel poster showing an elephant with guards. Fine condition, 24¾ x 38 inches.

$1,200–$1,500

Marca Zenit/Borsalino, 1911. Lithograph. Printed by Ricordi. This award-winning poster depicts a golden-yellow room, and a chair on which a man's hat and gloves rest next to his walking stick. An outstanding example of the artist's early work. Fine condition, on linen, 40½ x 56⅜ inches. $10,000–$12,000

As above, but a rare larger size, 56⅜ x 81½ inches. $20,000–$25,000

Courtesy of Bernice
Jackson Fine Arts.

Courtesy of Bernice
Jackson Fine Arts.

Rinascente/Apertura Di Stagione, 1949. Lithograph. For the department store. Depicting a striding woman in a plaid skirt and shawl. Fine condition, on linen, 39¼ x 55 inches. **$5,000–$5,500**

Rinascente/Esposizione Rhodia Albene, 1936. Lithograph. For the department store. Two women against a dark blue background, one wearing a colorful plaid dress, the other a polka-dot dress. A very good example of the artist's Art Deco style. Very good condition, on linen, 54¾ x 77⅛ inches. **$6,500–$7,000**

❧ E.B. (MONOGRAM)

Anisetta de Giorgi. Lithograph. Women in red and man in black toast. Very good condition, 15½ x 20¼ inches. **$385 (Auc. #19)**

❧ EMKA (DATES UNKNOWN)

Baicoli/A. Colussi, 1949. Lithograph. A vignette with a couple in eighteenth-century dress. Very good condition, 27½ x 39 inches. **$192 (Auc. #19)**

As above, mint condition. **$250–$275**

Focaccia Veneziana/A. Colussi, 1932. Lithograph. Cake with a winged lion above. Very good condition, 27½ x 39 inches. **$247 (Auc. #19)**

❧ FARKAS (DATES UNKNOWN)

Modiano, 1932. Lithograph. Silhouette of hand holding cigarette and matchbox. Very good condition, on linen, 27½ x 39 inches. **$600 (Auc. #18)**

❧ ORIO GALLI (DATES UNKNOWN)

Caffe Moretto, 1970. Lithograph. Lettering in the configuration of a coffeepot. Very good condition, 35½ x 50½ inches. $357 (Auc. #19)

❧ PAULO GARRETTO (b. 1903, WORKED EXTENSIVELY IN UNITED STATES)

Lord, 1950. Lithograph. Display of a white hat on a stylized head. Fine condition, 9¼ x 12¼ inches. $302 (Auc. #19)

Olimpic, 1937. Lithograph. Stylized figure leaping across a hat. Fine condition, 9¼ x 13 inches. $385 (Auc. #19)

❧ ANTONIO HOFER

Settimana Dell'Alto Aidge XI, 1933. Lithograph. Fascist poster for an agricultural exposition. The "XI" stands for 1933, in Mussoini's calendar, which started it as "Year I" in 1922 to mark the era of his rise to power. Fine condition, on linen, 27½ x 39⅜ inches. $2,500–$2,700

❧ ADOLFO HOHENSTEIN (1854–1928)

Chiozza E Turchi, 1899. Lithograph. Printed by E. Chappius. Fine condition, 11 x 20 inches. $1,350 (Auc. #17)

Iris, 1898. Lithograph. Printed by Ricordi. For the opera by Mascagni. Depicting the scene where Iris is covered by veils. Huge blossoming irises in the foreground. An excellent example of the artist's work. Fine condition, on linen, monumental in size, 37¾ x 108¾ inches. $12,000–$14,000

Poster by Antonio Hofer.
Courtesy of Bernice
Jackson Fine Arts.

Monte Carlo/Tir aux Pigeons, 1900. Lithograph. Printed by Ricordi. Text in French. Gentleman with a shotgun in the foreground, dressed in rose-colored suit. In very good condition, 32½ x 43 inches. $4,000–$5,500

❧ FRANZ LASKOFF (1869–1918)

E. & A. Mele/Novita per Uomo, 1900. Lithograph. Printed by Ricordi. Depicting a well-dressed man on his yacht. A very good example of the artist's talent with flat color fields. Very good condition, on linen, 59 x 81 inches. $7,500–$8,500

❧ FRANZ LENHART (1898–1992)

Campionati del Mondo de Sci, Febbraio, 1941. Lithograph. Skier shown from below as he descends onto the slopes. Very good condition, on linen, 39½ x 55 inches. $1,125 (Auc. #17)

Internationales Tanzturnier, 1926. Lithograph. A couple performs the tango. Very good condition, 29 x 39½ inches. $475 (Auc. #17)

Modiano, 1935. Lithograph. Sophisticated woman wearing a fashionable hat, smoking a Modiano cigarette. Striking Art Deco style in green and black. An outstanding example of the artist's work. Fine condition, 39½ x 55 inches. $3,000–$4,000

❧ GIOVANNI MATALONI (DATES UNKNOWN)

Brevette Auer, 1985. Lithograph. Printed by Instituto Cartografico. Cited as one of the first successful commercial posters in Italy, with highly decorative Art Nouveau borders, the lamplight forming a halo around the woman's head. Fine condition, on linen, 39 x 58 inches. $2,500–$3,500

Incandescenza/Lampada a Petrolio, 1896. Lithograph. A nude woman holding a lantern. Very good condition, 36 x 57 inches. $2,500–$3,000

❧ ACHILLE MAUZAN (1883–1952)

> NOTE: Mauzan lived in Buenos Aires, Argentina, from 1926 to 1932, and opened an advertising agency there, producing some of the best Art Deco-period posters to come out of South America.

Bonomelli/Vermouth Bianco, ca. 1925. Lithograph. Published by the Maga agency. Depicts a woman holding a glass in one hand and a bunch of grapes in the other. Fine condition, 36 x 49 inches. $1,000–$1,200

Divano-Letto Novaresi, ca. 1925–1930. Lithograph. A woman in a bathrobe gives a huge yawn. Fine condition, 35 x 56 inches. $500–$600

Impermeabili/Moretti, ca. 1930. Lithograph. Published by Maga agency. For the raincoat manufacturer. Fine condition, 55 x 80 inches. $275 (Auc. #17)

❧ LEOPOLDO METLICOVITZ (1868–1944)

Compagnia D'Opere Comiche e D'Operette, 1910. Lithograph. Printed by Ricordi. The singer's green gown and gardenia corsage are bathed in light. A very good example of the artist's style. Fine condition, on linen, 39⅞ x 56⅞ inches. *See color insert, photo 8.* $11,000–$12,000

E. & A. Mele/Mode Novita, 1908. Lithograph. Printed by Ricordi. A colorfully rich poster. Fasionable woman seated on a couch with her husband behind her. Fine condition, 53½ x 81½ inches. $6,000–$8,000

Fleurs de Mousse, 1898. Lithograph. Printed by Ricordi. For the French perfume maker. A young nude woman holds the vial of perfume, and is surrounded by blossoms and butterflies. A well-known poster by the artist. Fine condition, on linen, 31½ x 42¾ inches. $5,000–$6,000

Impermeabili/Moretti ca. 1930. Lithograph. Printed by Ricordi. Man in trench coat stands on top of an umbrella in the pouring rain. Still relatively easy to find on the market, but a very good poster from the artist's later period. Very good condition, 38 x 54 inches. $495 (Auc. #19)

As above, very good condition. $550–$650

Courtesy of Bernice
Jackson Fine Arts.

Madama Butterfly, 1904. Lithograph. Printed by Ricordi. For the opera by Puccini. Dressed in traditional costume, Madame Butterfly gazes out the window at birds in their nest. Without text, as it is most commonly found. Fine condition, on linen, 39¾ x 57½ inches. $13,000–$14,000

Spezia, 1907. Lithograph. Printed by Ricordi. For the resort on the Italian Riviera. A red-haired goddess rises from the sea as the ocean liner *Roma* approaches. Without the bottom sheet of text. A very good example of the artist's early work. Fine condition, on linen, 41 x 59 inches. $6,500–$6,800

As above, with the bottom sheet of text. $9,500–$10,000

Superator, 1908. Lithograph. Printed by Ricordi. For the gas heater. A fashionably dressed young couple warm themselves. A very good example of the artist's work. Fine condition, on linen, 41 x 56½ inches. $7,300–$7,600

🍃 MARCELLO NIZZOLLI (1887–1969)

FN/Fabrique Nationale, ca. 1925. Lithograph. Published by Publivox. Woman puts on lipstick as she rides behind silhouetted motorcycle driver. A strong Art Deco graphic. Fine condition, on linen, 33 x 48 inches. $6,000–$8,000

🍃 PLINIO NOMELLINI (1866–1943)

Oli Sasso, 1908. Lithograph. Printed by Ricordi. For the olive oil maker. Striking Art Nouveau image of a woman in an olive tree. A very good example of the artist's work. Fine condition, on linen, 55¾ x 77¼ inches. $9,000–$10,000

Courtesy of Bernice
Jackson Fine Arts.

Courtesy of Bernice
Jackson Fine Arts.

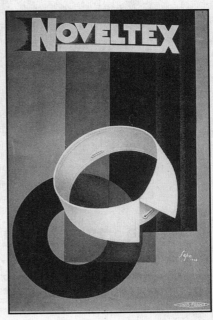

Courtesy of Bernice
Jackson Fine Arts.

❦ A. POMI (DATES UNKNOWN)

Luxardo, 1938. Lithograph. Two Luxardo bottles in a spotlight. Fine condition, 39 x 55 inches. $700–$900

❦ XANTI SCHAWINSKY (b. 1904)

Princeps, S.A. Cervoitalia, 1934. Lithograph. Published by Studio Boggeri. Classical bust is shown tipping a fedora. Fine condition, on linen, 39½ x 55½ inches. $1,800–$2,200

❦ SEPO (aka SEVERO POZZATI, 1895–1983)

Noveltex, 1928. Lithograph. A strong geometric design advertising collars for men. A fine example of the artist's style. Very good condition, on linen, 36⅝ x 56½ inches. $3,300–$3,500

❦ ALEARDO VILLA (1865–1906)

E. & A. Mele/Massimo Buon Mercato, ca. 1900. Lithograph. Printed by
Ricordi. Depicting two fashionable women surrounded by flowers on a balcony.
Fine condition, on linen, 59 x 81 inches. $14,000–$15,000

❦ CHAPTER 13 ❦
Swiss Posters

THE EARLY SWISS POSTER

At the turn of the century, the lithographic pictorial advertising poster was flourishing in France, but had only just begun to make its appearance in Switzerland. While it was not until after 1910 that Switzerland would see an explosion of poster design and use, early pioneers of the Swiss poster were establishing the foundations of what would become a strong and well-supported national tradition of excellence in poster design.

One reason the Swiss were late to adopt the poster was the absence of any bill-posting system for outdoor advertising, although a standard size, 35⅝ inch wide x 50⅜ inches high, was widely adopted in Europe as early as 1903.

Then, in 1910, the *Allgemeine Plakatgesellschaft* (the General Poster Company) was created in Geneva for the sole purpose of displaying posters, and began doing so on panels in such a way as to not impinge on the natural environment. In 1914 the tidy Swiss uniformly adopted the standard size, and by 1925 the posting system had been expanded to include the entire country. This company still holds the concession for poster display through contracts with about two thousand communes, and posts about two million posters a year.

The earliest poster designers were painters who turned their talents to this new commercial art form. One of the first outstanding poster artists in Switzerland was Emile Cardinaux (1877–1936).

Cardinaux's first major client was the Swiss Federal Railways, and in 1903 he began to create lithographic travel posters in six colors, chiefly for display in train stations. That year he had spent some time in Paris, and had learned to lithograph in Munich, drawing his posters directly on the lithographic stone. Cardinaux's outstanding use of color in his travel and winter sports posters for Davos, Saint Moritz, the Jungfrau Bahn, and other destinations makes him one of the most sought-after early Swiss poster artists today.

J. E. WOLFENSBERGER AND
THE ART OF LITHOGRAPHY

In 1904 Cardinaux was introduced to the Zurich printer Johann Edwin Wolfensberger (1873–1944). Wolfensberger taught numerous artists the craft of lithography, and served as a liaison between artists and clients.

The quality of work from "Wolfsberg," the trade name used, ensured its place as the most influential printer in the history of the Swiss poster. Wolfensberger opened his printworks in about 1900, and his work was carried on by his son Jakob Edwin Wolfensberger (1901–1971), and by a third generation of the family who runs the business today.

Not all artists drew directly on the lithographic stone themselves. Sometimes the artist's painting was rendered on the stone by a lithographic draftsman.

The best lithographic stones in Switzerland usually came from the Solnhofer limestone quarry between Munich and Nuremberg. These massive stones, which weighed as much as 2,500 pounds, were sometimes set up on easels to facilitate painting. Since each color used in the poster required its own stone—sometimes as many as twelve—a single poster could occupy the entire work of a print studio for two or three weeks. The process was difficult, costly, and full of unforeseen hazards, but the result was an intensity of color capable of sublime transparencies and nuances impossible to achieve in other media.

Offset printing, using a zinc plate, arrived from America at the turn of the century, and by 1910 there were already ten offset presses operating in Switzerland. By the 1950s, no stone lithography presses existed, and by the end of the 1970s, most of the letterpress print shops, used to print linocut and typographic posters, had gone out of business as well.

THE "OBJECT POSTER" EMERGES

By far the most towering figure in Swiss poster design during the first half of the century is Otto Baumberger (1889–1961). Like many of the early Swiss artists, Baumberger considered himself a painter, and by 1917 had already lithographed some forty-five posters. During his long career he created some 250 posters in a diversity of styles.

Baumberger was to be recognized as the leading artist of a new style of posters that featured the product itself in close-up. This type of poster, called *sachplakat* in German, literally "object poster," was created in 1910 by the German artist Lucian Bernhard (1883–1972).

Niklaus Stoecklin (1896–1982), a Basel painter who began producing posters in the early 1920s, is also considered a master of the object poster. Stoecklin studied with Burkhard Mangold, and produced some seventy-five posters in his lifetime.

Other artists noted for object poster designs include Peter Birkhauser (1911–1976), Carl Bockli (1889–1970), Donald Brun (b. 1909), Hans Erni (b. 1909), Charles Kuhn (b. 1903), and Herbert Leupin (b. 1916).

In this style of poster, sometimes called "objective realism," the realistically painted product takes center stage in the design, with little or no other design aside from the name of the product in a bold typographic style.

This marked a total departure from product advertising of the Belle Epoque era where the product might barely be visible amidst a scene full of well-dressed men and beautiful women with flowing tresses. Perhaps object posters emerged to fit a faster, industrialized world. Whatever the reason, they remained popular in Switzerland until about 1960.

Baumberger started the object poster revolution in Switzerland in 1919, with his realist chef d'oeuvre *Baumann* for the hat manufacturer, depicting a huge top hat with the name "Baumann" across the bottom, the address, and nothing more.

Four years later, in 1923, he startled the public again with an extreme close-up of a man's coat revealing the label "PKZ," for the men's clothing store. This poster was so realistically drawn that Baumberger later reported that designers in other countries asked for the photo negative so they could produce copies. Of course, no negative existed — the work was lithograph, painted on a lithograpic stone, and the stone, as usual, had been ground down after printing to be reused for another poster.

Like many of the German designers affiliated with the Bauhaus, in the 1930s, Lucian Bernhard, the innovator of the object poster, fled Nazi Germany for New York, where he had a profound effect on graphic design and typography in the United States.

OTHER NOTABLE EARLY SWISS POSTERISTS

Otto Morach (1877–1973) distinguished himself as a travel poster artist. Travel posters of this early period reflected the great natural beauty of Switzerland with its mountains and lakes that are vacationers' playgrounds in both winter and summer. Morach belonged to a radical group of Swiss painters that included the Dadaists Arp and Piciaba, and created posters in an idiom previously unknown in poster art in Switzerland, but one that was eventually widely accepted.

Another notable early poster artist was Burkhard Mangold (1873–1950), whose highly individual style is colorfully elegant. His talent is reflected in the forty or so posters he created before 1910, and throughout his career into the 1930s.

Other early poster artists include Robert Hardemeyer (1876–1919), today considered a pioneer of Swiss poster art, who died prematurely in a flu epidemic; Ferdinand Hodler (1853–1918), who designed the poster for the 19th Exhibition of the Vienna Secession in 1904; Cuno Amiet (1868–1961), who was designing posters as early as 1902; Augusto Giacometti (1877–1947), known for travel and exposition posters in the 1920s and 1930s; Alfred Heinrich Pellegrini (1881–1958), who produced notable posters for sports and theatrical events; and Maurice Barraud (1889–1954), known for his posters depicting beautiful women. (He created about thirty lithographic posters between 1915 and 1945.)

Other painters who each produced a few posters include Hans Berger, Karl Bickel, Alexander Brugger, Wilhelm F. Burger, Otto Ernst, Francois Gos, Paul Kammuller, Hugo Laubi, Ernst Linck, Carl Roesch, Carl Scherer, Rudolf Urech, and Otto Wyler.

FOREIGN INFLUENCES AND THE SWISS ABROAD

It was almost inevitable, given Switzerland's geographic location and politically neutral stance, that design influences from France, Italy, Germany, Austria, and other countries would be strongly reflected in the development of the Swiss poster. Likewise, Swiss artists have had a formidable impact on graphic design in other countries.

Before 1910, Swiss poster artists tended to leave Switzerland to pursue their careers in Paris. Two of the most important of these are Eugene Grasset (1845–1917), who moved to Paris from Lausanne in 1871 and became the leading theorist of the Art Nouveau movement, and Theophile-Alexandre Steinlen (1859–1923), also from Lausanne. Other notable Swiss-born artists and designers who immigrated to France include Felix Vallotton (1865–1925), Charles Edouard Jeanneret, better known as Le Corbusier (1887–1965), and Jean Tinguely (b. 1925).

Notable foreign artists who designed posters for Swiss clients include French artists A. M. Cassandre (1901–1968) and Charles Loupot (1892–1962), whose poster career was launched in Switzerland with several notable designs in the teens and 1920s; German artists Ludwig Hohlwein (1874–1949) and Carl Moos (1879–1959), who relocated permanently to Switzerland in 1915; and Italian artist Leonetto Cappiello (1875–1942), who actually lived and worked mainly in France.

Several Swiss artists also studied lithography, design, and typography in Germany. They include Mangold, Baumberger, Gardinaux, Morach, and Stoecklin, who studied in Munich; and Donald Brun, Max Bill, Fritz Buhler, Hans Erni, and others who studied in Berlin.

These crosscurrents in the world of design before World War II have also traced in fields such as fine arts, architecture, and decorative arts, and reflect the fact that international communications, transportation, and publishing were making the world smaller every day.

Many Swiss artists returned from abroad to their neutral homeland during the 1930s, such as Fritz Buhler and Herbert Leupin from Paris, Donald Brun from Berlin, and Theo Ballmer from the Bauhaus. Many of these "repatriates" settled in Basel, a thriving hub of graphic design, where their influence would increasingly be felt in the 1940s and 1950s.

After World War II, as we note later, Swiss graphic designers made a lasting impression on American graphic design as principal designers for American corporations and as teachers at such schools as Yale University, Rhode Island School of Design, and Philadelphia School of Art.

SWISS POSTER PATRONS

The most important early patron of poster art in Switzerland was the PKZ department store. Today, the posters PKZ commissioned from several notable artists are the most collectible and often the highest-priced of all Swiss posters.

PKZ commissioned foreign artists such as Ludwig Hohlwein and Charles Loupot, but their Swiss artist roster reads like a history of the Swiss poster: Emile Cardinaux, Burkhard Mangold, Niklaus Stoecklin, Martin Peikert, Karl Bickel, Herbert Leupin, Hans Falk, Hugo Laubi, Otto Morach, Herbert Matter, Charles Kuhn, and several others.

Other commercial advertisers who helped foster Swiss poster design through their commissions include Bally shoes, Steinfels soap, Binaca toothpaste, Eptinger, Bell hams, Remington typewriters, Kaller's (a competitor of PKZ), Raga cigarettes, Gaba lozenges, and Suchard chocolate.

The poster in Switzerland has enjoyed a long tradition of both public and government patronage. Exhibitions of poster art were mounted at the Museum of Applied Arts in Zurich as early as 1911, and retrospective poster exhibitions are a common occurrence in Switzerland today.

Since 1941 the Swiss government has annually awarded prizes for the best posters. Chosen by a jury appointed by the Swiss federal government for outstanding artistic and printing achievement, the winners (usually about twenty-four are chosen) are prominently displayed in all of the larger cities and towns in Switzerland. This governmental patronage has had the effect of both increasing the public's appreciation of poster art and encouraging talented individuals to pursue careers in graphic design.

THE RISE OF THE GRAPHIC DESIGNER

In 1918 Ernst Keller (1891–1968) became the first teacher of "graphic design" at the School of Arts and Crafts in Zurich, and a champion of the status of graphic design vis-à-vis painting. He created nearly one hundred posters, mostly reproduced in letterpress from his own linocuts.

The early poster painters had little to do with lettering, and the integration of text into early posters sometimes leaves something to be desired. In the 1920s and 1930s, as graphic designers replaced painters as the creators of posters, typography became a more integrated and vital feature of the poster.

The Swiss Werkbund, which had been founded on the German model in 1913, preferred typographic posters without any other ornamentation. This school of design was given new life as many designers in Germany immigrated to Switzerland after Hitler's rise to power in 1933, including such outstanding figures as Max Bill (b. 1908) and Jan Tschichold (1902–1974). After World War II, the typographic poster in the 1950s and 1960s would rise to a new level of excellence with a second wave of artists led by Armin Hofmann (b. 1920) and Emil Ruder (1914–1970) in Basel, and Josef Müller-Brockman (b. 1914) in Zurich.

Notable graphic artists who created posters during this period include Eric de Coulon (1888–1956), who designed outstanding travel posters and who also evolved a style of poster that relied on monumental letters that framed the central object; Johann "Hans" Handschin (1899–1948), who trained as an architect and developed a specialty with airbrush technique; Johann Arnhold (1891–1955); Emil Huber (1883–1943); André Simon (1899–1959); and Willi Tanner (b. 1907), among others. Later graphic designers who distinguished themselves in the travel poster field include Walter Herdeg (b. 1908) and Carlo Vivarelli (b. 1919).

THE FIRST PHOTO POSTERS

Unlike other countries, Switzerland's neutrality during World War I allowed the arts to continue to develop in an unbroken continuum.

Poster art was influenced by a wide range of fine arts painting styles, including cubism, expressionism, and surrealism. Within Switzerland itself, the most influential fine arts movement was the Dada movement, developed as a literary movement during the war in Zurich in 1916, and which lasted for only a short time, until 1923.

The founder of the movement was the Swiss poet Tristan Tzara, but its influence rapidly spread to artists like Piciaba, Max Ernst, Marcel Duchamp, and Kurt Schwitters, among others. The Dada visual aesthetic involved radical combinations of imagery and shifts in perspective, in many ways not unlike surrealism.

As the Dadaists began to experiment with photography, it undoubtedly had a strong impact on graphic designer Herbert Matter (1907–1984), who had also studied in Paris with painter Fernand Leger. Matter was the first to produce a series of photomontage posters in the 1930s, which combine both photography and hand illustration.

Baumberger and Stoecklin had already anticipated the advent of the photographic poster with their hyperrealistic object posters designed to communicate clear and direct information. However, the color photo poster reached its apogee in around 1935 with Matter's sensational photomontages, about ten of which appeared in the years 1934–1936.

In 1952 Matter's influence extended to a younger generation of American graphic artists when he became a professor of photography at the Yale University School of Art in New Haven, where a retrospective exhibition of his work was mounted in 1978. His work is included in the collection of the Guggenheim Museum.

THE MODERN SWISS POSTER

After World War II, a new graphic design style emerged in Switzerland that would have an impact far beyond its borders. This avant-garde style, based on abstract constructivist and minimalist tendencies coupled with a strong reliance on typography, has become known as the International Typographic Style.

The beginnings of this style were already in place in the 1930s, as we have seen, when German artists such as Max Bill and Jan Tschichold immigrated to Switzerland. Tschichold brought with him a strong background in the graphic arts from his experience with the Bauhaus and Russian constructivists including El Lissitsky.

In the 1950s and 1960s, two important schools of graphic design developed in Switzerland, one centered in Zurich under the leadership of Josef Müller-Brockman, and the other in Basel under the leadership of Armin Hofmann and Emil Ruder. Both of these schools had an impact on graphic design in the United States that continues until today.

Müller-Brockman, who studied with Ernst Keller, became a professor at the School of Applied Art in Zurich in 1957, after two decades of successful graphic design for private and government clients. A year later he founded and became coeditor of the international magazine for graphic design *Neue Grafik*. Since that time he has lectured widely on an international basis as well as authoring several books on graphic design.

Müller-Brockman's posters reflect his lifelong fascination with constructivism and geometry. His affinity for classical music led him to create some of the most innovative concert posters, which are musical themselves in their use of basic forms and colors and in their rythmic-dynamic composition. In other posters for client products, Müller-Brockman uses photography and photographic effects to maximum impact. Since the 1960s, his work has been widely shown in this country at the American Institute of Graphic Arts, New York, private galleries, and the Art Center College of Design in Pasadena, California.

Armin Hofmann began teaching at the Basel School of Design in 1946. Extending his influence to the United States, he has lectured and taught at Philadelphia College of the Arts, Harvard University, Rhode Island School of Design, and Yale University, where he is a faculty member in the department of graphic design. His work is included in the collection of the Museum of Modern Art in New York City.

The style of poster Hofmann pioneered with Emil Ruder has had an impact on an entire generation of designers. The Basel School believed that graphic design for advertising should have both immediate commercial impact and an enduring aesthetic quality that makes a contribution to the advancement of the art form. In his posters, the simplest and most universal elements are used to create an abstract structure as the vehicle for communication. This is in marked contrast to today's dominant forms of advertising, where often a "visual gimmick" or device is used to draw the attention of the viewer, such as a seminude woman holding a bottle of beer.

In 1986 Yale University mounted a retrospective exhibition entitled "The Basel School of Design and Its Philosophy: The Armin Hofmann Years, 1946–1986," which featured work by six teachers and forty students of the Basel School.

In a lecture he delivered on the opening of that exhibition, Hofmann stated "A primary objective of my work with black-and-white posters is to counteract the trivialization of color as it exists today on billboards and in advertising . . . Such literal translations hinder constructive thinking, absorption in the subject matter, and poignancy of recollection; they are ultimately counterproductive, producing no afterimages to exist in memory."

Emil Ruder began teaching at the school in 1942, where he headed typography classes. He became the director of the school in 1965, and held that position until his death in 1970.

Two other important poster artists and teachers at the Basel School are Robert Buchler (b. 1914), who retired from the school in 1965, and Wolfgang Weingart (b. 1941), who joined the faculty in 1968 and has lectured extensively in the United States. Weingart's "collagist" designs are strikingly complex, yet reflect the formal reliance on geometry achieved by older members of the school.

Another Swiss artist who has had an impact on American graphic design is Erik Nitsche (b. 1908), who moved to the United States in 1934 and became art director for General Dynamics Corporation in 1955. Nitsche created twenty-nine posters for General Dynamics, printed in four different series from 1955 to 1960, including the 1955 and 1958 "Atoms for Peace" series and the 1958 "Exploring the Universe" series, which are becoming increasingly well-known among collectors of modern graphic design.

SWISS POSTERS—PRICE LISTINGS

Note: See the chapter Important Notes on Price Listings for more information on prices given. Also note that some Swiss artists have listings in other chapters such as Travel and Transportation.

❦ ANONYMOUS

Bon Genie, 1950. Photo-offset. A woman in casual attire lounging near a swimming pool. In yellow, blue, and white. Fine condition, 35 x 50 inches. $450–$500

Kandersteg, ca. 1940. Lithograph. Fine condition, 25 x 40 inches.
$250 (Auc. #18)

Zoologischer Garten, Basle, ca. 1935. Lithograph. A large polar bear looks at the viewer. Fine condition, 35½ x 50 inches. $450 (Auc. #17)

Jardin Zoologique Bale, ca. 1938. Lithograph. Printed by Wasserman. Close-up of a seal. Fine condition, 35½ x 50½ inches. $225 (Auc. #18)

As above, close-up of a polar bear. $750 (Auc. #18)

Urania, Zurich Bier und Speise Restaurant, ca. 1950. Photo-offset. Printed by J. C. Muller, Zurich. Waitress comes around to the customers. Very good condition, 35 x 50 inches. $165 (Auc. #19)

❦ CUNO AMIET (1868–1961)

Bahnhof Buffet, Basel, 1921. Lithograph. Portly gentleman appreciates his sip of wine. Very good condition, 35½ x 50 inches. $675 (Auc. #17)

❧ JOHANN ARNHOLD (1891–?)

PKZ, 1927. Lithograph. Printed by Wolsberg, Zurich. A handsomely dressed gentleman in a suit and overcoat. Printed in deep, rich colors. Fine condition, on linen, 36 x 51 inches. $5,000–$6,500

❧ NANCY BAUCH

9ᵉ *Festival Internationale du Film de Comedie,* 1989. Photo-offset. For the Vevey film festival. Mint condition, 36 x 50 inches. $150–$250

❧ OTTO BAUMBERGER (1889–1961)

> NOTE: *Baumberger's long career spanned many decades and styles, and many of his posters are highly sought after in the market. Often his posters are only signed with a "B." See also Travel and Transportation Posters.*

Baumann, 1922. Lithograph. Printed by Mentor Verlag, Zurich. Close-up of the Baumann top hat, the address, and little more. Second edition (first edition in 1919 with a different address). Well-known design, famous as the first Swiss "object poster." An outstanding example. In fine condition, 36 x 50 inches. (Be aware that there is yet another, later photo-offset version of this poster, printed in 1950 by Bollmann, Zurich, without the "B" in the upper left-hand corner, which is much less valuable.) $2,500–$3,500

Poster by Johann Arnhold.
Courtesy of Bernice Jackson
Fine Arts.

Poster by Otto Baumberger.
Courtesy of Kellenberger Collection.

Doelker, 1920. Lithograph. Printed by Wolfsberg, Zurich. Elegantly dressed couples in the Doelker department store in Zurich. Fine condition, 36 x 50 inches.
$1,000–$1,500

Hotel St. Gothard, 1917. Lithograph. A lobster dinner with wine and fruit. Fine condition, 35½ x 50 inches. $600 (Auc. #18)
As above, fine condition, 35½ x 50 inches. $1,200–$1,400

Neue Zurcher Zeitung, 1928. Lithograph. Printed by Wolfsberg, Zurich. For the Zurich newspaper. Silhouetted profiles against newspapers. Very good condition, 36½ x 50½ inches. $1,045 (Auc. #19)

PKZ, 1923. Lithograph. Printed by Wolfsberg, Zurich. Extremely finely executed close-up of a coat with the PKZ label, so exact that many wrongly assume it to be a photograph. An important example of Swiss lithographic poster art. Fine condition, 35 x 50 inches. *See color insert, photo 11.* $5,000–$7,000

❦ PAUL BENDER

riri, 1950. Photo-offset. Depicting unzipped portion of a partially closed zipper, arranged as a design element. In red and gray. Fine condition, 35 x 50 inches.
$500–$600

❦ EDOUARDO GARCIA BENITO (SPANISH, 1891–?)

Candée Snow-Boots Cautchoucs, 1929. Lithograph. Striking Art Deco design of woman walking her dog in the rain, wearing her Candée rubber boots. An outstanding example, in fine condition, 36 x 50 inches. $2,400–$3,000

❦ KARL BICKEL (1886–1982)

PKZ-So Kleidet, 1928. Lithograph. Printed by Wolfsberg, Zurich. Smartly dressed gentleman enjoys the scent of flowers. A very good example of PKZ poster. Very good condition, 35 x 50½ inches. $4,840 (Auc. #19)

❦ CARLO BISCARETTI

Anisetta Evangelista, 1925. Lithograph. Depicting a monkey drinking the anisette liquor. Fine condition, 40 x 56 inches. $300–$500

❦ PAUL BRUHWILER (b. 1939)

Raymond Chandler/Film Noir, 1979. Photo-offset. A stunning poster with a mysterious pair of eyes looking out from under the brim of a hat, peering over the words. In black and gray. Very good condition, 35 x 50 inches. $900–$1,000

Poster by Karl Bickel.
Courtesy of Swann
Galleries, Inc.

Poster by Donald Brun. Courtesy
of Kellenberger Collection.

❦ DONALD BRUN (b. 1909)

Flandor, Dessert-Creme Pudding, ca. 1945. Lithograph. Comical character carries a huge pudding. Fine condition, 36 x 50 inches. $400–$600

❦ ROBERT BUCHLER (b. 1914)

Typographie, 1960. Letterpress in one color. For an exhibition at the Gewerbemuseum, Basel. Fine condition, 35½ x 50¼ inches. $300–$400

❦ EMIL CARDINAUX (1877–1936)

> NOTE: Cardinaux is recognized as the best early Swiss travel posterist. His striking colors and painterly style were well executed lithographically, most often by the firm Wolfsberg.

Jungfrau-Bahn, 1910. Lithograph. Printed by Wolfsberg, Zurich. Mountain climbers are shown making their way through the peaks. Fine condition, 28 x 40 inches. $1,125 (Auc. #17)

Jungfrau-Bahn, 1911. Lithograph. Printed by Wolfsberg, Zurich. Two men and a woman reach the top of a mountain peak. Very good, on Japan paper, 35½ x 48 inches. $1,925 (Auc. #18)

Palace Hotel/St. Moritz, 1918. Lithograph. Printed by Gebr. Fretz, Zurich. Perhaps Cardinaux's best-known poster, depicting fashionable tourists enjoying ice-skating. Fine condition, on linen, 35 x 50 inches. $4,500–$5,500

🍂 TH. DELECHAIX

Exposition, Société des Amis des Arts, 1902. Lithograph. Mythological scene with child playing music. Fiine condition, 27 x 39½ inches. $750 (Auc. #17)

🍂 EDOUARD ELZINGRE (1880–1966)

Montreaux-Berner Oberland, ca. 1930. Lithograph. Printed by Sonor. Fine condition, 25 x 40 inches. $350 (Auc. #18)

🍂 HANS ERNI (b. 1909)

Knie (Circus), 1988. Photo-offset. A very good abstract design in a contemporary poster. Earlier posters by Erni can sell at higher prices. Mint condition, 36 x 50 inches. $200–$300

🍂 OTTO ERNST (1884–1967)

Engelberg, ca. 1920. Lithograph. A luge is shown speeding around a turn. Fine condition, on Japan paper, 24½ x 40 inches. $725 (Auc. #17)

🍂 HANS FALK (b. 1918)

PKZ, 1944. Lithograph. A gentleman lifts up an overcoat to show the PKZ label inside. Very good, on linen, 36 x 50½ inches. $450 (Auc. #18)

Poster by Hans Erni. Courtesy of Kellenberger Collection.

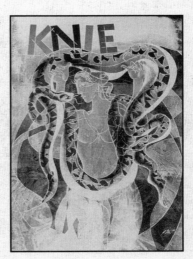

❦ NOEL FONTANET (1898–1982)

Restaurant du Nord, Genève, ca. 1927. Lithograph. Waiter superimposed on chef marches out with the meal. Fine condition, 36 x 50½ inches. $975 (Auc. #18)

❦ K. DOMINIC GEISSBÜHLER (b. 1932)

John Cage Europeras 1 & 2, 1991. Photo-offset. A complex abstract design for the contemporary operas. Mint condition, 36 x 50 inches. $200–$300

❦ GYLSSLER

Strawinsky Fest, 1968. Photo-offset. Design and all information for the Stravinsky festival in a huge S on a black background. Fine condition, 36 x 50 inches. $300–$400

❦ HANS HANDSCHIN (1899–1948)

> NOTE: Handschin created several stunning product and retail posters in an Art Deco style.

Elco Papiers, 1940. Lithograph. Showing a stylized woman gazing intently at an envelope she holds in her hand. In red, black and white. Very good condition, on linen, 35 x 50 inches. $750–$900

❦ ROBERT HARDMEYER (1876–1919)

Ovignac Senglet, ca. 1910. Lithograph. Attributed to this early Swiss artist. Fine condition, 72 x 51 inches. $800–$1,200

Courtesy of Kellenberger Collection.

🌿 ARMIN HOFMANN (b. 1920)

J. Brahms/Ein Deutsches Requiem, 1986. Photo-offset. Printed in two colors. A more recent example of the artist's work. Mint condition, 35½ x 50¼ inches.
$650–$750

Kunsthalle Basel/Jacques Lipschitz, 1958. Letterpress-printed two-color linocut. Fine condition, 35½ x 50¼ inches. $800–$900

Kunsthalle Basel/Leger/Calder, 1957. Letterpress-printed two-color linocut. Mint condition, 35½ x 50¼ inches. $900–$1,000

La Suisse A L'Epoque Romaine, 1957. Letterpress-printed three-color linocut. A good example of an early poster by Hofmann. Fine condition, 35 x 50 inches.
$1,000–$1,100

Theater Bav Von Der Antike, 1958. Letterpress-printed black-and-white linocut. A classic example of Hofmann's style. Mint condition, 35 x 50 inches.
$1,300–$1,500

🌿 WERNER JEKER (b. 1944)

7e Festival International du Film de Comedie, 1987. Silk screen. An abstract design for the Vevey festival. Mint condition, 36 x 50 inches. $200–$300

Vogue, 1984. Silk screen. For the exhibition of photography in Lausanne. Mint condition, 36 x 50 inches. $200–$300

Poster by Armin Hoffman. Courtesy of Bernice Jackson Fine Arts.

Poster by Werner Jeker. Courtesy of Kellenberger Collection.

Courtesy of Bernice
Jackson Fine Arts.

🦪 ERNST KELLER (1891–1968)

Jemoli gut und billig, 1957. Lithograph. A very good example of Keller's typo-graphical abstract style. This poster was printed with text in black and three different backgrounds of orange, tan, or green. Fine condition, 35 x 50 inches.
$1,400–$1,500

Pferd Und Mensch, 1956. Lithograph. Printed by City-Druck AG. Very good condition, on linen, 35½ x 50 inches. $675 (Auc. #17)

🦪 CHARLES KUHN (b. 1903)

Taxamater, Selnau, 1928. Lithograph. Stylized taxi automobile is shown. Fine condition, on linen, 35½ x 50 inches. $725 (Auc. #17)

🦪 CLAUDE KUHN-KLIEN (b. 1948)

Naturhistoriches Musuem Bern, ca. 1985. Silk screen. A humorous juxtaposition of a toucan's beak and a rhino's horn. Mint condition, 36 x 50 inches.
$200–$300

🦪 HERBERT LEUPIN (b. 1916)

AGFA, 1956. Lithograph, for the film manufacturer. Good condition, 35½ x 50 inches. $1,500 (Auc. #18)

Eptinger, 1940. Lithograph. Depicting a prosperous-looking gentleman holding a glass up as if to make a toast, in front of him a table with a bottle of Eptinger. In yellow, orange, and brown. Fine condition, 35 x 50 inches. $600–$750

Knie (Circus), 1956. Photo-offset. A clown balances the letters of the work "Knie" on his knee. Fine condition, 36 x 50 inches, or smaller variation.

$400–$600

Steinfels, 1942. Poster of a huge clothespin surrounding a box of Steinfels detergent. In white, brown, and green. A very good example of a Leupin "object poster." Fine condition, 35 x 50 inches. $900–$1,100

❦ CHARLES LOUPOT (1892–1962)

> *NOTE: Loupot's early career was launched in Switzerland, and the posters of this period are most sought after. Later he worked in his native France (see chapter on French Posters).*

Cigarettes Mekka, 1919. Lithograph. Elegant woman in a flowing red dress enjoys her exotic brand of cigarettes. A rare early work and outstanding example. Fine condition, 35½ x 51 inches. *See color insert, photo 10.* $15,000–$20,000

Poster by Herbert Leupin. Courtesy of Kellenberger Collection.

Courtesy of
Kellenberger
Collection.

Fourrures Canton, 20 Rue du Bourg (after Loupot), ca. 1950, Lithograph. Stylized woman in a flowing white fur coat and muff. Note that the rare original design dates to ca. 1920, with the company address as 24 Rue du Bourg. Fine condition, 36 x 50 inches.　　　　　　　　　　　**$1,775 (Auc. #17)**
$2,000–$3,000

SATO/Cigarettes Eqyptiennes, 1919. Lithograph. Printed by Sauberlin & Pfeiffer, Vevey. Exotic woman sits on a cushion and enjoys a cigarette. An outstanding early design by Loupot. Fine condition, on linen, 35 x 50 inches.
$10,000–$11,000

Seident-Grieder Zurich, 1918. Lithograph. Woman shows off her fashionable coat. Very good condition, on Japan paper, 351/2 x 51 inches.　**$5,050 (Auc. #18)**

🌿 BURKHARD MANGOLD (1873–1950)

Ausstellung Orient Teppiche, 1913. Lithograph. Customers are shown Oriental carpets. Fine condition, 27½ x 39 inches.　　　**$1,200 (Auc. #18)**

Brautausstattungen, Zuber Buhler & Co., 1912. Lithograph. A seated woman is shown sewing linens. Very good condition, 37 x 53½ inches.　**$1,200 (Auc. #18)**

🌿 HERBERT MATTER (1907–1984)

> NOTE: Matter was a pioneer of the photomontage poster and recognized for this travel posters. See additional listings under Travel and Transportation.

PKZ, 1928. Lithograph. Printed by Wolfsberg, Zurich. Classic Art Deco poster for the men's clothing store depicting a valet showing men's coats. An excellent example of the artist's early style. Very good condition, 35 x 50 inches.

$8,000–$10,000

❦ CARL MOOS (1879–1959)

Pontresina, ca. 1910. Lithograph. In black and white. Skier flies through the air over a mogul. Fine condition, on Japan paper, 25 x 40 inches. $825 (Auc. #17)

As above, two mountain climbers look down into the mountain valley. Fine condition, on Japan paper, 25 x 40 inches. $600 (Auc. #17)

❦ OTTO MORACH (1896–1953)

Davos, 1927. Lithograph.Printed by Wolfsberg, Zurich. Stylized view of the town at the end of a road below a series of bridges. Fine condition, on linen, 35 x 50½ inches. $2,500–$3,000

PKZ/Jedermann, 1928. Lithograph. Printed by Wolfsberg, Zurich. Two identical, stylized businessmen, one in blue and one in crimson, read newspapers. Very good condition, on linen, 36 x 50 inches. $2,500–$3,500

❦ JOSEF MÜLLER-BROCKMAN (b. 1914)

Akari, 1975. Photo-offset. For the Japanese lamp manufacturer. With two circles of multicolored light on a black background. Mint condition, 35 x 50 inches.

$600–$650

Courtesy of Bernice
Jackson Fine Arts.

Juni-Festwochen/Zurich, 1959. Letterpress-printed linocut. In three colors for a music concert. A very good example of the artist's geometric style. Mint condition, 35 x 50 inches. $1,100–$1,200

Musica Viva, 1960. Photo-offset. For a Zurich concert hall. Müller-Brockman's Musica Viva posters are among his most sought-after designs. Mint condition, 35 x 50 inches. $1,200–$1,500

❦ ERIK NITSCHE (b. 1908)

Atoms for Peace, 1955. Lithograph. Printed by Marsens, Lausanne. For General Dynamics. One of twenty-nine posters in three series, the first of which was printed lithographically. Mint condition, 35 x 50 inches. $700–$750

❦ MARTIN PEIKERT (1901–1975)

Globus, 1925. Lithograph. Gentleman dressed in formal wear with cane and gloves. Very good condition, on linen, 36 x 50 inches. $675 (Auc. #18)

❦ PERCIVAL PERNET (1890–1977)

Grand-Prix, 1948. Lithograph. Speedboats are shown racing around a buoy. Fine condition, 25 x 39 inches. $975 (Auc. #17)

❦ RIBES

Charlie Chaplin, 1989. Photo-offset. For the 100th anniversary festival at Vevey. Mint condition, 20 x 28 inches. $100–$150

Poster by Erik Nitsche.
Courtesy of Bernice
Jackson Fine Arts.

✹ A. BENOIS DI STETTO

Grindelwald, 1937. Lithograph. Printed by Kummrly & Frey. Fine condition, on Japan paper, 27½ x 39½ inches. $275 (Auc. #17)

✹ NICKLAUS STOECLKIN (1896–1982)

Autocars Postaux, 1925. Lithographs. Printed by Wolfsberg, Zurich. The incredible winding roads and steep cliffs of the Alps shown are to encourage you to take a bus trip. Gorgeous color. A rare early example of the artist's work. Very good condition, on linen, 35 x 50 inches. $5,500–$7,000

Bell, 1952. Photo-offset. Close-up of a Christmas ham, decorated with a bow and mistletoe. In black, pink, and brown. Stoecklin is well-known for his captivating product posters. Very good condition, 35 x 50 inches. $500–$550

Bi-Oro, Anti-Solaire, 1941. Lithograph. Sunglasses and lotion are paired together. Very good condition, 35½ x 50 inches. $450 (Auc. #17)

Binaca, 1941. Lithograph. Poster depicting a hand clad in armor holding a tube of Binaca toothpaste. In black, red, and gray. Fine condition, 35 x 50 inches.
$600–$700

✹ WOLFGANG WEINGART (b. 1941)

Kunst Gewerbe Museum/Zürich, 1980. Photo-offset. A fine example of the artist's complex abstract designs. Fine condition, linen-mounted, 35 x 50 inches.
$550–$600

Courtesy of Bernice
Jackson Fine Arts.

CHAPTER 14

English Posters

In England, early pictorial posters were overlooked by the staid business community, and typographic broadsides cluttered the walls of buildings. Although Fred Walker had created a stunning pictorial woodcut poster for *The Woman in White* at the Olympic Theatre in 1871, it was not until Aubrey Beardsley's (1872–1898) poster for *Avenue Theatre* in 1894 that the advertising poster gained any recognition as either an artistic or commercial medium.

Beardsley, who died at the young age of twenty-five, created as few as five or six posters. Most examples are today held by museums. His graphic design style influenced an entire generation of English and American artists, including the American Will Bradley (1868–1962). Beardsley's work rarely appears on the market, and when available, often sells in the range of $2,000 and more.

After Beardsley's controversial launch of the poster in English life, other artists began to make their mark. Dudley Hardy (1867-1922) executed several posters for music halls, Savoy Theatre performances, and Gilbert and Sullivan's D'Oyly Carte Opera Company, and is perhaps best-known for his 1894 poster *A Gaiety Girl*, for the London play.

Another artist, John Hassal (1868–1948), designed for many publishers and literary magazines, and his work is also worth seeking out. David Allen & Sons, the leading lithographic firm of the time, also employed other artists, primarily for theatrical entertainment posters.

Early English poster artists James Pryde (1869–1941) and William Nicholson (1872–1949) worked together under the name "the Beggarstaff Brothers." They established a simplified style, using flat color fields that avoided outlining the image.

While some producers and manufacturers did employ the Beggarstaffs' talents, such as Kassama Corn Flour, Beefeater, and Rowntree's Cocoa, in all they only produced about a dozen posters. However, their work was recognized early on by other graphic designers, and six of their posters were included in *Les Maîtres de l'Affiche*, the "Masters of the Poster" series published by Jules Chéret (see chapter on

French Posters). Their ground-breaking design affected English poster art for many years, and influenced German artists as well as American artists like Edward Penfield.

The Beggarstaffs' posters do surface from time to time on the auction market, and are generally valued from $20,000 to $25,000 and more due to their design significance.

THE ARTS AND CRAFTS MOVEMENT AND THE GLASGOW SCHOOL

There is no doubt that the English and American Arts and Crafts movement, with its sparse, moralistic tone and its opposition to extravagance, contributed to the popularity of the Beggarstaff style.

Today, while the Arts and Crafts collecting field still is primarily focused on Stickley and other furniture, pottery, and on decorative arts such as copper and mica lamps, several Arts and Crafts auctions have broadened to include graphics.

A much smaller but equally significant design movement in terms of its long-term impact was Scotland's Glasgow School. Its leading artist Charles Rennie Mackintosh's (1868–1928) style combines the design complexities of Art Nouveau with the functional, geometric shapes of the Arts and Crafts style.

His few designs for posters, and those of his colleagues Margaret MacDonald and Herbert and Francis McNair, are extremely rare. When they appear on the market, which is rarely, they bring prices equal to the highest prices ever paid for posters.

The Glasgow School had an effect on the design of the Viennese Secessionists and the artists of the Wiener Werkstatte. In fact, one of the leading artists of the Viennese Secession, Josef Hoffmann (1870–1956), eventually married Mackintosh's sister. (See additional information about posters of the Vienna Secession under Design Influences in the chapter on French Posters.)

ENGLISH POSTER PATRONS

World War I helped advance the acceptance of posters in England as a means of public communication, and several of England's best artists from the period are also represented in the chapter on World War Posters. However, the movement to popularize posters in England started before World War I, thanks to a handful of important poster patrons.

With French posters, one seems most often to talk about the artists, each of whom may have worked for several clients. With English posters, one more often hears the name of the clients who hired the artists: London Transport, Shell Oil Company, and British Railways. Although some collectors of English posters specialize by artist, more often they specialize in collecting the advertiser. (See information and price listings for British Railway posters in the chapter on Travel and Transportation Posters.)

Many of the same outstanding artists worked for more than one of the clients above: Edward McKnight Kauffer (1890–1954), an American by birth; Austin Cooper (1890–1964), who immigrated to England from Canada; Charles Pears (1873–1958); Frank Newbould (1887-1950); Tom Purvis (1888–1959); Norman Wilkinson (1882–?); Fred Taylor (1875–1963); J. S. Anderson; John Armstrong; Paul Nash; and several others whose names are becoming better-known today.

Shell Oil Company posters, most of which were produced with the slogan "You Can Be Sure of Shell," were commissioned from E. McKnight Kauffer and other leading artists, and executed in a wide variety of styles from cubist avant-garde to painterly landscapes. These, along with British Railway posters, are increasingly seen at poster auctions and shows.

The Shell Oil poster-collecting field got an added boost in 1992 with the publication of *The Shell Poster Book*, with an introduction by David Bernstein. The book reproduces ninety-two full-page, full-color posters created for the company and shows the wide range or artists and styles that comprised this important and long-term advertising campaign.

The large, horizontal formats of the British Railway posters of the 1920s and 1930s, most often 50 x 40 inches (sometimes called a "quad royal"), and those of the Shell series, most often 45 x 30 inches, have made them favorites for decorating large spaces, both residential and commercial. Along with London Transport posters, they represent the best English graphic design from the period between the two world wars.

SPECIAL FOCUS: LONDON TRANSPORT POSTERS

As early as 1908, London Transport became the first important English poster patron to recognize the value of poster advertising. They began to commission artists to create visually attractive posters, and today it is one of the longest-running advertising concepts in history, not to mention its lasting impact on graphic design.

Under the direction of Frank Pick, London Transport, which operates the city's bus and underground lines, drew on the talents of the best English graphic artists. Pick also remodeled the subway stations, making them more attractive and uniform. He also instituted the use of modern sans serif type styles in advertising. The Baynard Press and the

Curwen Press, leading lithographers, were called upon frequently to execute the works, but several other presses were used as well.

As Londoners increasingly used automobiles in their beautiful but congested capital, the goal of London Transport advertising, admirable then as now for environmental reasons, was to increase the use of public transportation.

The posters also served to advertise London's many museums and attractions to residents and tourists alike — all reachable by public transport. Rather than show the means of transportation, the posters displayed the destinations in enticing ways: the beauty of Kew Gardens, the countryside near London, concert halls, shopping areas, etc.

Frank Pick headed the advertising for London Transport for almost thirty years, during which time he commissioned dozens of leading graphic artists, including several mentioned above: McKnight Kauffer, Frank Brangwyn (1867-1956), Austin Cooper, E. A. Cox, Paul Nash, Frank Newbould, Charles Pears, Gerald Spencer Pryse (1881–1956), Graham Sutherland, Fred Taylor, Horace Taylor, and numerous others. He also commissioned outstanding artists from other countries, including avant-garde artists Moholy-Nagy and Man Ray, and French artists André Marty (1882–1974) and Jean Dupas (1882–1964).

The posters created by avant-garde artists Laszlo Moholy-Nagy (Hungarian, 1895–1946) and the surrealist artist/photographer Man Ray (American, 1890–1976) are very rare, and have not appeared on the market in many years. These would fetch very high prices if found.

Jean Dupas's posters for London Transport are today as highly sought after as those of E. McKnight Kauffer, and in some cases bring even higher prices.

For example, the Club of American Collectors of Fine Arts, Inc., in New York City recently offered two very rare Dupas posters for sale in the range of $19,000: *Thence to Hyde Park* and *Beside the Silver Thames*, both designed in 1930. Larger than the standard format for London Underground posters (approximately 25 x 40 inches, sometimes called a "double royal"), these were created in the horizontal "quad royal" size of approximately 50 x 40 inches.

In these as in all his posters, Dupas presents highly stylized, very fashionable people in idealized and extravagant settings. His figures appear statuesque, in an almost literal sense, which may be due to his training as a sculptor.

Edward McKnight Kauffer, who moved to England from the United States in 1914, is recognized as the most outstanding "English" graphic designer. His work is stunning, simple, and boldly avant-garde. Happily, he was also a prolific graphic designer and received numerous commissions, so his work is widely available on the market today. However, as he is widely recognized as England's most important posterist, prices for his work range from near $1,000 to $10,000.

McKnight Kauffer received his first commission for London Transport in 1915, and went on to create several outstanding posters for this client, including his *London Museum* in 1922, depicting the flames of the Great Fire of London, and his 1930 *Power, the Nerve Center of the London Underground*, depicting a man's fist protruding from a factory and train wheel, emanating zigzag lightning bolts. This poster is truly one of England's most avant-garde designs. Like Cassandre in France, McKnight Kauffer influenced an entire generation of graphic designers, setting the tone and the pace for a new form of advertising in England.

From November 1989 through April 1990, the Cooper Hewitt Museum in New York, which is the Smithsonian Institution's National Museum of Design, presented an exhibition of E. McKnight Kauffer posters and graphics from their permanent collection of more than 1,225 works by the artist.

A few poster dealers, such as Chicago's David Gartler of Poster Plus, have developed a specialization in London Underground posters. In October 1992 Poster Plus held an exhibition of more than 150 London Transport posters from a private collection. Prices ranged from $400 to $4,000, and most were the standard English double royal size of 25 x 40 inches.

Courtesy of Cooper-Hewitt Museum.

Few records of edition sizes exist for most collectible posters; however, because London Underground posters were printed for a specific client, there are records of the edition size on some examples. While we may know that many were printed in editions of 1,000 to 1,500, few were saved after they served their original purpose.

After World War II and until today, London Transport has continued its tradition of commissioning some of the country's best artists to create images for their posters. Several very good reference books have been published on London Transport and London Underground posters for those who wish to learn more about these outstanding posters (see Bibliography).

ENGLISH POSTERS—PRICE LISTINGS

NOTE: See the chapter Important Notes on the Price Listings for more information on prices given. Also note that many English artists also have listings under other chapters such as Travel and Transportation for posters created for British Railways.

❦ J. S. ANDERSON

Motorists Prefer Shell, 1935. Lithograph. Depicting a streamlined motorcar as the background, with pistons and tubes in the foreground. One of the finest designs in the series. Very good condition, horizontal, 45 x 30 inches.

$2,250 (Auc. #20)

As above, on linen, fine condition. $4,500–$5,000

❦ JOHN ARMSTRONG (1893–1973)

Artists Prefer Shell, ca. 1935. Lithograph. Unusual poster from the series, depicting a conch shell, artist's palette, and Greek goblet. Very good condition, linen-mounted, 45 x 29½ inches. $1,600–$1,900

❦ JOHN BAINBRIDGE (1918–1978)

Royal London, Buckingham Palace, 1953. Lithograph. For London Underground. Stylized view of a guard outside the palace. Fine condition, on linen, 24½ x 39½ inches. $275 (Auc. #17)

❦ DORA BATTY

From Town To Open Country/30 Minutes, 1925. Lithograph. For London Transport. Printed in an edition of 1,000. A good example of London Transport posters. Fine condition, 25 x 40 inches. $2,000–$2,250

Poster by Dora Batty.
Courtesy of Poster Plus.

Poster by Aubrey Beardsley.
Courtesy of Thomas G. Boss
Fine Books.

❦ EDWARD BAWDEN

Kew Gardens, 1936. Lithograph. Printed by Curwen Press. For London Transport. Very good condition, 25 x 40 inches. $625 (Auc. #20)

You Can Be Sure of Shell/Walton Castle, 1936. Lithograph. In the Shell series "To Visit Britain's Landmarks." This series is more "touristic" and less avant-garde graphically, but still has several good examples of the Shell series. Very good condition, horizontal 45 x 30 inches. $575 (Auc. #20)

❦ AUBREY BEARDSLEY (1872–1898)

Publisher/Children' s Books, 1894. Lithograph. For a London publisher. One side of the poster lists current books, the other side has a plumed woman sitting in a chair. The same figure was later used for *The Yellow Book* by the publisher Copeland & Day in Boston. Good condition, on linen, 19½ x 29¾ inches. $2,000–$2,200

The Savoy, 1896. Lithograph. A thoughtful, exotically dressed man on a tilted stool contemplating the announcement. Fine condition, small size, 7½ x 9¾ inches. $850– $900

❦ R. ANNING BELL

The Studio, ca. 1900. Lithograph. Salome presenting the head of John the Baptist to Herodias. Good condition, 10 x 14 inches. $300–$350

❦ FRANK BRANGWYN (1867–1956)

Pollard's the House of the Craftsmen, ca. 1925. Lithograph. Interior view of the craftsmen at work. Very good condition, 38 x 57 inches. $825 (Auc. #17)

❦ TOM ECKERSLEY AND ERIC LOMBERS

Scientists Prefer Shell, 1936. Lithograph. Depicting test tubes on a tabletop and deep space beyond. Very good condition, horizontal, 45 x 30 inches.
$975 (Auc. #20)

Winter Shell Until Next May, 1937. Lithograph. A great image of the Scottie. Very good condition, horizontal, 45 x 30 inches. $775 (Auc. #20)

❦ CLIFFORD AND ROSEMARY ELLIS

Travels in Space on Your Doorstep, 1937. Lithograph. Printed by Curwen Press. For London Transport. Very good condition, 25 x 40 inches.
$525 (Auc. #20)

❦ JOHN COPLEY

For London Music, ca. 1935. Lithograph. For London Transport. Fine condition, 25 x 40 inches. $800–$900

Poster by Tom Eckersley and Eric Lombers. Courtesy of Bloomsbury Book Auctions.

Poster by Jim Copley. Courtesy
of Poster Plus.

Poster by Jean Dupas.
Courtesy of Club of American
Collectors of Fine Arts, Inc.

🌿 E. A. COX

London's Country, 1924. Lithograph. For London Transport. Printed in an edition of 1,500. Fine condition, 25 x 40 inches. $800–$900

🌿 JEAN DUPAS (FRENCH, 1882–1964)

Camden Town, Chalk Farm or Regents Park, 1933. Lithograph. For London
Transport. Depicting an entire family riding an elephant at the zoo. Very good
condition, 28 x 43½ inches. *See color insert, photo 7.* $3,300 (Auc. #013)

***Richmond Station for the River/Regatta-Time's Pleasant Thrice Pleasant in
Laughing July***, 1933. Lithograph. For London Transport. A very good example
of a Dupas poster for London Transport. Very good condition, 23 x 38½ inches.
                                                                  $5,600–$5,800

***Thence To Hyde Park, Where Much Good Company and Many Fine
Ladies***, 1930. Lithograph. For London Transport. An elaborate large scene of
stylized people enjoying the park, a woman on horseback, and the surrounding
greenery. An outstanding example of Dupas's work. Fine condition, 39½ x 49
inches. $19,000– $20,000

Where Is This Bower Beside the River Thames, 1930. Lithograph. For London Transport. As above, stylized figures, many reclining, sailboats, and leafy trees in a distinctive Dupas style. An outstanding example. Fine condition, 39½ x 49 inches.
$19,000–$20,000

❧ ABRAM GAMES (b. 1914)

Starlight Special, 1958. Lithograph. Printed by Baynard Press. For the London Underground. Fine condition, 25 x 40 inches. $300 (Auc. #18)

❧ EDWARD MCKNIGHT KAUFFER (1890–1945)

Actors Prefer Shell, 1935. Lithograph. Strikingly abstract, an actor holds up a square mask in front of his face. Very good condition, horizontal, 45 x 30 inches.
$2,825 (Auc. #20)

Aeroshell Lubricating Oil, 1932. Lithograph. A racing car against a dark blue field, subtitled *The Aristocrat of Lubricants*. Very good condition, perhaps the best example of the Shell Oil series, linen-mounted, horizontal, 45 x 30 inches.
$9,000–$11,000

BP Ethyl Anti-Knock Controls Horse Power, ca. 1935. Photomontage. With a statue of a horse in an angular design. Very good condition, horizontal, 45 x 30 inches. $1,800 (Auc. #20)

Explorers Prefer Shell, 1935. Lithograph. Very good condition, horizontal, 45 x 30 inches. $2,225 (Auc. #20)

Power, the Nerve Center of the London Underground, 1930. Lithograph. A factory and a train wheel from which a man's fist protrudes, emanating zigzag lightning bolts. An excellent example of the artist's style and perhaps the most sought after London Underground poster. Good condition, linen-mounted, 25 x 40 inches. $7,000–$9,000

Spring in the Village, 1936. Photomontage. Printed by the Baynard Press. For London Transport. Very good condition, 25 x 40 inches. $725 (Auc. #20)

Spring on the Hillside, 1936. Photomontage. Printed by the Baynard Press. For London Transport. Very good condition, 25 x 40 inches. $425 (Auc. #20)

The Wallace Collection, 1925. Lithograph. Printed by the Baynard Press. For London Transport. Very good condition, on linen, 25 x 40 inches.
$450 (Auc. #18)

❧ CHARLES RENNIE MACKINTOSH (1868–1928)

Glasgow Institute of the Fine Arts, 1895. Lithograph. Excellent example of Mackintosh's style. Extremely rare. Very good condition, on linen, 33½ x 89½ inches. $92,075 (Auc. #17)

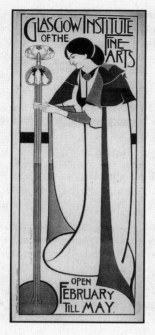

Poster by Charles Rennie
Mackintosh. Courtesy of
Christie's London.

Poster by Roy Meldrum.
Courtesy of Poster Plus.

❦ ROY MELDRUM

Something Different at Every Turn, 1933. Lithograph. For London Transport.
Printed in an edition of 3,000. Fine condition, 25 x 40 inches. $800–$900

❦ M. MILES

For the Zoo, 1933. Lithograph. For London Transport. Good condition, 25 x 40
inches. $475 (Auc. #20)

❦ CHRISTOPHER R. W. NEVINSON

Take the Motor-Bus for Picnicking, 1921. Lithograph. For London Transport,
encouraging Londoners to travel to the end of the line for rural enjoyment.
Printed in an edition of 1,000. Fine condition, 25 x 40 inches. $800–$900

❦ OZ (MONOGRAM)

Zoo/Regents Park, Camden Town, St. Johns Wood, ca. 1935. Lithograph. For
London Transport. A striking design. Fine condition, 25 x 40 inches. $600–$700

❦ CHARLES PEARS (1873–1958)

The Student Travels Underground, 1930. Lithograph. For London Transport, advertising reduced rates for students. Fine condition, 25 x 40 inches.

$900–$1,000

❦ CHARLES SHAW (1872–1974)

Smokers Prefer Shell, 1936. Lithograph. Very good condition, 45 x 30 inches.

$725 (Auc. #20)

❦ WALTER SPRADBERRY

At London's Service/Beefield Farningham, 1934. Lithograph. For London Transport. Printed in an edition of 2,000. Fine condition, 25 x 40 inches.

$800–$900

❦ GRAHAM SUTHERLAND

Doctors Prefer Shell, 1934. Lithograph. Depicting a tabletop with doctor's bag, stethoscope, etc. Very good condition, 45 x 30 inches. $1,275 (Auc. #20)

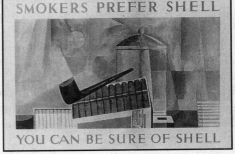

Poster by Oz. Courtesy of Poster Plus.

Poster by Charles Shaw. Courtesy of Bloomsbury Book Auctions.

CHAPTER 15 ❦
Dutch Posters

Over the last five years, the field of Dutch poster collecting has expanded considerably, welcoming a range of new collectors both in the United States and abroad. While many examples of Dutch arts are recognized, appreciated, and collected throughout the world, from Rembrandt oils to Dutch ceramics, Dutch posters have remained relatively unknown until recently.

One pivotal event in raising the level of awareness of Dutch poster design was an exhibition that toured nine museums in the United States. Entitled "The Modern Dutch Poster: the First Fifty Years," it was curated by Stephen Prokopoff, director of the Krannert Art Museum at the University of Illinois; it toured nine U.S. museums from November 1986 through January 1989, closing at the Cooper-Hewitt in New York.

The exhibition was organized by the Print and Publicity Foundation of Amsterdam with assistance from poster dealer Bernice Jackson of Massachusetts, who served as the Foundation's U.S. representative. It primarily featured selections from two Dutch collectors, Werner Löwenhardt and Martijn Le Coultre. The accompanying book *The Modern Dutch Poster* provides an excellent overview of the richness and diversity of Dutch poster art (see Bibliography).

Since that time there has been a major increase of interest in Dutch poster art. New developments that have added fuel to the fire include the establishment of Van Sabben Poster Auctions in Holland by Piet Van Sabben, and the launch of an international magazine devoted to posters called *Affiche*, also based in Holland (see resource guide).

True to its historic role as a European crossroads and international marketplace, Holland was influenced by numerous design movements that had an impact on poster design.

Dutch posters from the 1890s to the turn of the century not only reflect the French Belle Epoque and Art Nouveau style, but also evidence influences from the Arts and Crafts movement in England, the Vienna Secession, and early German poster design. Though all of these tendencies are evident, even early on there is a decidedly different look to Dutch posters, especially in terms of decorative and ornamental details.

Important artists from this early period, some of whom went on to have very long and important careers in poster design, include Jan Ros (1875–1952), Jan Toorop (1858–1928), Johan Thorn Prikker (1868-1932), J. G. van Caspel (1870–1928), Jacques Zon (1872–1932), Wilhelm Pothast (1877–1916), Georg Reuter (1875–1966), Albert Hahn (1877–1918), Chris LeBeau (1878-1945), C. A. Lion Cachet (1864–1945), R. N. Roland Holst (1868-1938), and Jac. Jongert (1883–1942).

Jan Toorop is one of the most sought after early poster artists, especially for his Art Nouveau-inspired posters such as *Delftsche Slaolie* (Delft Salad Oil), ca. 1895, and for later, cubist/futurist-inspired works such as his 1919 *Pandorra*, for a play by Arthur van Schendel. Only a handful of examples of this rare work are known to exist, and it can bring as much as $35,000, the top price for a Dutch poster.

R. N. Roland Holst's unmistakable style and a natural flair for the dramatic contribute to his rank among early Dutch poster designers. His posters for theatrical and musical productions such as *Lucifer* (1910) and *Faust* (1918) command high prices.

Jacob (Jac.) Jogert is also highly regarded, both for his early ornamental style, evident in such posters as *Internationale Gastoonstelling* (International Gas Exhibition, 1912), and for later, strikingly modernist or painterly works, such as *Van Nelle's Tabak* (1920).

After the turn of the century, avant-garde design movements from several countries had an increased impact in Holland, including cubism and the Italian futurist movement. Although Dutch poster art had its own character, a unique national style had not yet really taken hold.

Then, in 1917, a small group of Dutch artists and designers, including the well-known painter Piet Modrian, founded the magazine *De Stijl*, or "the Style." This design movement emphasized geometric abstraction of form, straight lines, and primary colors.

Carried into the world of poster design, these concepts were embodied in posters that used little illustration, but relied on the vertical, horizontal, or angular arrangement of typographical and geometric elements for their impact, perhaps reflective of Holland's long history of book design and typographic production. The movement was marked by a Calvinist attitude, and saw itself as purifying design by removing excessive decoration and ornamentation.

De Stijl designers whose posters are sought after today include Piet Zwart (1885–1977), H. Th. Wijdeveld (1885–1987), Antoon Kurvers (1889–1940), J. J. Hellendoorn (1878- 1959), Sybold van Ravesteyn (1889–1983), and several others. The De Stijl movement also had an impact on other designers who had previously worked in other styles, and on poster design in general. While many De Stijl-inspired posters are still affordable, prices for others have soared past the $10,000 mark.

The impact of the Art Deco movement as it was evolving in France was strongly felt in Holland, especially in product and travel poster design. Modern movements from other countries seeped into French design starting in about 1909, and were transformed into the design style that dominated the 1920s and 1930s in commercial advertising and decorative arts, now called Art Deco.

The French artist A. M. Cassandre had a considerable impact in Holland, and was commissioned by several Dutch enterprises to create posters that can bring very high prices today. Notable artists working in an Art Deco style in the Netherlands include Wim ten Broek (b. 1905), who created posters for Holland-America Line ocean liners; Agnes Canta (1888-1964); Jan Wijga (1902–1978), for KLM (Royal Dutch Airlines); and Johann von Stein (1896–1965), for Lloyd Lines.

Photomontage posters, created by blending photography and illustration, also had their early champions in Holland in the early 1930s, about the same time Herbert Matter was experimenting with the form in Switzerland. Notable photomontage artists include Willem Gispen (1890–1981), Meijer Bleekrode (1896–1943), Louis Frank (b. 1907), and Wim Brusse (1910–1978).

As in many countries, poster patrons played an important role in the development of Dutch poster design by commissioning artists to execute works. Important poster patrons in Holland included Delft Salad Oil, KLM (Royal Dutch Airlines), ocean line companies, and annual fairs such as Jaarbeurs Utrecht.

Many distinguished artists created posters for this annual industries fair in Utrecht, such as C. A. Lion Cachet, Agnes Canta, Jac. Jongert, Louis Raemaekers (1865–1956), Meomie Schwartz (1876–1942), and Henri Verstijnen (1882–1947). Henri Pieck (1895–1972) created posters for the Utrecht fair that are graphically stunning views of industrial buildings in an Art Deco style. A contemporary Dutch artist whose work is gaining increased recognition is Otto Treumann (b. 1919), who also contributed some notable designs for the Utrecht fair.

COLLECTING DUTCH POSTERS

Collectors are now discovering the wide-ranging scope of Dutch poster design, which also includes cinema, theater, musical events, and product advertising, as well as social, civic, and political issues and causes.

Dutch posters are generally smaller than their French counterparts, probably because they were often meant to be displayed in commonly tiny streets and shop windows rather than on grand boulevards. Early Dutch posters were lithographed in smaller editions than the posters of many other countries, making them less available and more subject to price increases as demand for them grows. Dutch poster artists are gaining recognition, and their names are becoming familiar ones in the collecting field.

There are a host of artists worth collecting, some well-known and many lesser-known. While some of the best have captured the imagination of the collecting world and are already fetching high prices, many outstanding examples of Dutch poster art representing products, fairs, travel, exhibits, and other areas are still available in the $500 to $1,000 retail range.

DUTCH POSTERS—PRICE LISTINGS

NOTE: See the chapter Important Notes on the Price Listings for more information on prices given. Several Dutch artists are also included in chapters such as Travel and Transportation. The reference numbers following the titles of some listings refer to plates in the book The Modern Dutch Poster, *created as the catalog of the touring museum exhibition, which closed at the Cooper Hewitt in 1989 (see Bibliography).*

✤ ANONYMOUS

Architectuur en Kunstnyverheid, 1927. Lithograph. Strong De Stijl typographic style, with letters against a central column of contrasting color. In cream, red, and blue. Fine condition, 23 x 39½ inches. $800–$900

V.A.A. Diploma, ca. 1930. Lithograph. A strong De Stijl typographic style, with lettering between two stripes of red and black. Fine condition, 21½ x 35 inches. $400–$450

✤ BRIAN

Erste Luchtverkeer Tentoonstelling Amsterdam/E.A.T.A., 1919. Lithograph. Printed by Kotting, Amsterdam. For the first air show in Holland. Depicting a giant airman surrounded by flying biplanes. Very good condition, 31 x 43 inches. $1,000–$1,200

✤ WIM BRUSSE (b. 1910)

Sterk Door Werk/Niet Wachten/Nu opdrachten, ca. 1948. Photomontage. Printed by Kunstdruk Luii & Co., Amsterdam. For work safety. Good condition, backed on cardboard, 24 x 40 inches. $850 (Auc. #25)

✹ H. P. BERLAGE (1856–1934)

Norlandische TramwegMij, 1893 (MDP #2). Lithograph. Printed by Roeloffzen & Hubner, Amsterdam. For the "North Holland Tramline." A very good early design. Good condition, 22½ x 40½ inches. $2,250 (Auc. #24)

✹ JOHANN BRIEDE (1885–?)

Tentoonstelling/Gemeentelyk Financieel Gebeid, 1916. Lithograph. In shades of brown for a financial services congress, in a De Stijl typographic style with elaborate borders. Very good condition, 28 x 42 inches. $1,200–$1,400

✹ WIM TEN BROEK (b. 1905)

> NOTE: Wim ten Broek is known for his outstanding ocean liner posters and was influenced by A. M. Cassandre. See also Travel and Transportation.

New York Were Idtentoonstelling Excursies per Holland-Amerika Lijn, 1938. Lithograph. Printed by Joh. Enschede and Son, Haarlem. For excursions to the New York World's Fair. American and Dutch flags fly over liner and skyline of New York and Trylon and Perisphere. Very good condition, 30 x 38½ inches.
$1,200 (Auc. #25)

✹ C. A. LION-CACHET (1864–1945)

Delftsche Slaolie (Delft Salad Oil), ca. 1900. Lithograph. Featuring a bottle of the salad oil on a decorative background. Very good condition, small format, 12½ x 22½ inches. $500 (Auc. #25)

✹ AGNES CANTA (1888-1964)

Jaarbeurs Utrecht 3–12 Sept, 1935. A huge bell rings out an invitation to the Utrecht Fair. Mint condition, 29 x 39 inches. $750–$850

✹ JOHANN GEORG VAN CASPEL (1870–1928)

Patee-Rijwielen, 1897. Lithograph. In van Caspel's naive Belle Epoque style. For a bicycle dealer, showing a man changing tires. A very good design. Very good condition, 21 x 30 inches. $2,100 (Auc. #24)

Hinde-Rywielen, 1896 (MDP #9). Lithograph. Printed by Steendruk v/h Amand, **Amsterdam. For Hinde Bicycles**. An outstanding design in fresh pastel colors, and a sought-after poster. Good condition, horizontal, 42½ x 31½ inches.
$8,775 (Auc. #24)

Posters by Johann Georg
van Caspel. Courtesy of Van
Sabben Poster Auctions.

Poster by A. M. Cassandre.
Courtesy of Van Sabben
Poster Auctions.

❦ A. M. CASSANDRE (FRENCH, 1901–1968)

NOTE: The great French posterist A. M. Cassandre's advertising agency, Alliance Graphique, served several Dutch clients. His style had a strong impact on Dutch graphic design in the 1920s and 1930s, and his Dutch posters are highly sought after.

Automobiel & Motorrijweil Tentoonstelling/Amsterdam, 1929. Lithograph. Printed by Nijgh & van Ditmar, Rotterdam. For the automobile show. A complex design of superimposed imagery. Very good condition, $32\frac{1}{2} \times 45\frac{1}{2}$ inches.
$7,675 (Auc. #25)

Statendam/Holland America Line, 1928. Lithograph. Printed by Nijgh & van Ditmar, Rotterdam. For the ocean liner company. A stunning design of the smokestacks, printed with a brown border. (*Note:* At this same auction, the original gouache design for this poster sold for $34,825. See photo under Travel and Transportation.) Very good condition, $25\frac{1}{2} \times 35$ inches. $5,575 (Auc. #25)

Van Nelle/Pakjes Koffie, 1931. Lithograph. Printed by Nijgh & van Ditmar, Rotterdam. For packaged coffee. A geometric design proceeding from a huge coffee bean. Rare. Very good condition, horizontal, 64 × 48 inches.
$9,400 (Auc. #25)

❦ JOAN COLLETTE (1889–1958)

Stemt de Katholieke Lyst, ca. 1920. Lithograph. Encouraging citizens to "Vote the Catholic List." A stylized knight with his shield. Very good condition, 28 x 42 inches. $800–$900

❦ AART VAN DOBBENBURGH (1899–1989)

De Drinker/Blauwe Week Commissie, 1935 (MDP #98). Lithograph. In black and white. Printed for the "Blue Week Committee" against alcoholism, depicting a man slumped over a table with his drink in hand. Very good condition, 31 x 43½ inches. $600–$750

Openuchttheater Zandvoort, 1933. Lithograph. For a production of *Salome*. A haunting image of a woman being embraced by a skeleton in a clown's outfit. Very good condition, 22 x 32½ inches. $900–$1,000

Voor Ket Kind, 1941. Lithograph. Printed by Senefelder, Amsterdam. In black and white. Depicting an old woman's hands caressing a young girl's face for a fund "For the Children." Very good condition, 23½ x 38 inches. $550–$600

❦ EPPO DOEVE (1907–1984)

Amsterdam Diamanstad, 1949. Photo-offset. Showing a diamond worker at work on a cutting wheel. Very good condition, 31 x 43 inches. $700–$800

Heineken's/Het meest getapt, ca. 1948. Photo-offset. Printed by Kunstdruk Luii & Co., Amsterdam. Showing an elderly waiter presenting a glass of Holland's most famous beer. In very good condition, 32 x 44 inches. $700 (Auc. #25)

❦ ARJEN GALEMA (1886–1974)

KLM Royal Dutch Airlines, ca. 1930 (MDP #89). Photo-offset. Printed by Kunstdruk Luii & Co., Amsterdam. Early KLM poster shows airliner flying past a ghostly Dutch galleon. Very good condition, 25¾ x 39½ inches.
$1,475 (Auc. #25)

❦ ALBERT HAHN, SR. (1877–1918)

Colonial Exhibition, 1914. Lithograph. Printed by Ellerman, Harms & Co., Amsterdam. An ornate image of a young woman from Java, text in English. Very good condition, 42 x 31 inches. $1,800–$2,200

❦ J. J. HELLENDOORN (1878-1959)

Tentoonstelling Arti et Industriae, ca. 1923 (MDP #65). Letterpress-printed typographic poster, red on white, for an art & industry exhibition. A very good example of the Dutch De Stijl movement. In very good condition, 23½ x 35¼ inches. $3,075 (Auc. #24)

❦ HENDRICUS A. HENRIET (1903–1945)

Bosch Plan, 1936. Lithograph. For an exhibition, depicting sailboats, a horseback rider, and a line of men planting trees. Very good condition, 28 x 41 inches.
$750–$850

❦ ADRIANN VAN'T HOFF (1893–1939)

Rotterdam-Zuidamerika Lyn, ca. 1928. Lithograph. Printed by Boudier, Den Haag. A stylized view of the bow of the ocean liner, with waves and gulls flying alongside. The influence of Cassandre is unmistakable. Very good condition, 28½ x 41 inches.
$1,600–$1,800

❦ PIETER HOFMAN (1885–1965)

Genealogisch/Heraldische/Tentoonstelling, 1933. Lithograph. For an exhibition of genealogy and heraldry. Outstanding lettering and a herald of a lion posed with a sword. Very good condition, 25 x 35 inches.
$850–$950

❦ JOACHIM VAN HOUWENINGE (1898-?)

Teltoonstelling Haagsche Schetsclub, 1930. Lithograph. Printed by S. Lankhout, Den Haag. For an exhibition of the Hague Sketch Club. Spare design of a hand holding a paintbrush, fixing its subject. Very good condition, 25 x 35 inches.
$1,000–$1,200

❦ RAOUL HYNCKES (1893–1973)

Eerstdaags Faust/Ned. Opera, ca. 1920. Lithograph. Printed by Kunstdruk Luii & Co., Amsterdam. For the production of Faust. A very good example of the artist's style. Very good condition, 31½ x 43 inches.
$2,525 (Auc. #25)

Zomerfeesten Amsterdam, 1932 (MDP #95). Photo-offset. Printed in black, gray, and brown. For the "Summer Festival." An abstracted collage of beverage, art, and other images. Very good condition, 25 x 34½ inches.
$1,200–$1,300

❦ JACOB (JAC.) JONGERT (1883–1942)

Internationale Gastentoonstelling Amsterdam, 1912 (MDP #27). Lithograph. For an international gas exhibition in the Paleis Voor Volksvlijt. Male nude holds a boy in an ornate background. A very good example of Jongert's early style. Very good condition, 29½ x 59 inches.
$3,080 (Auc. #19)

As above, very good condition.
$6,000–$6,500

Elfde Jaarbeurs Utrecht, 1924. Lithograph. Printed in yellow, red, and blue. An example of a more Art Deco style by the artist. Very good condition, 26½ x 40 inches.
$575 (Auc. #25)

Poster by Jacob Jongert.
Courtesy of Stephen Ganeles
Antique Posters and Prints.

Poster by Anton Kurvers.
Courtesy of Stephen Ganeles
Antique Posters and Prints.

Oud/Apricot Brandy, ca. 1920 (MDP #52). Lithograph. Printed by Immig and Son. In rich blues, blacks, and brown. An outstanding design, in a painterly manner. Mint condition, 30½ x 39½ inches. $7,500–$8,000

Van Nelle's Tabak, 1920 (MDP #51). Lithograph. Printed by Immig and Son. An outstanding design, in a painterly manner. Good condition, 25½ x 39 inches.
$3,500 (Auc. #25)
As above, fine condition. $7,500–$8,000

🌿 ALBERT KLIJN (1895–?)

Regata/Reclame-en Grafische Arbeid, 1919. Lithograph. Printed by Kotting, Amsterdam. In beige, brown, and sienna. For an exhibition or graphic work. Very good condition, 31 x 43 inches. $1,600–$1,700

🌿 WILLEM KLIJN (1892–1961)

Regata Feest Park, 1919. Lithograph. Printed by Kotting, Amsterdam. For an amusement park. A colorful design featuring two jesters. Very good condition, 31½ x 43 inches. $900–$1,000

❧ ANTON KURVERS (1889–1940)

PBNA, 1920. Lithograph. In black, red, and green. For the *Politechnical Bureau Nederland Arnhem*. Very good condition, 24 x 47 inches.　　　　$1,500–$1,600

❧ CHRIS LEBEAU (1878-1945)

De Magier (The Wizard), ca. 1914 (MDP #38). Lithograph. Printed by S. Lankhout, Dan Haag. In black and white. A stunning design, and a very sought-after poster.　　　　$15,000–$16,000

❧ BART ANTHONY VAN DE LECK (1876–1958)

Batavier-Lijn, 1914 (MDP #35). Lithograph. Printed by Geuze, Dordrecht. For the liner that sailed from Rotterdam to London, depicting a full side view of the ship. An important early Dutch poster. Very good condition, horizontal, 43½ x 29½ inches.　　　　$21,600 (Auc. #24)

❧ LOUIS DE LEEUW (1875–1931)

Volksfeest Arnhem, 1919. Lithograph. For the People's Festival in Arnhem, depicting a man marching with a flag to another's drumming. A comic and merry poster. Very good condition, 30½ x 43 inches.　　　　$450–$500

❧ HUIB LUNS (1881–1942)

Tentoonstelling/Kind/Kunst/School/Rotterdam, ca. 1915. For an exhibition of children's art. Very good condition, 20 x 41½ inches.　　　　$650 (Auc. #24)

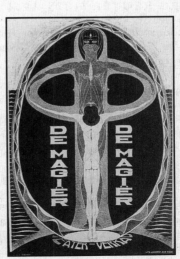

Poster by Chris Lebeau.
Courtesy of Stephen Ganeles
Antique Posters and Prints.

Lustrumfeesten Utrecht, 1921. Lithograph. Printed by Van Geelen. For the Utrecht festival. Very good condition, 28 x 29 inches. $425 (Auc. #24)

Pour L'Art Exposition, ca. 1920. Lithograph. In beige and brown. Text in French for an exhibition at the Musée Moderne. A dramatic example of the artist's work. Very good condition, 19½ x 36½ inches. $1,100–$1,200

🍂 MURATTI

Jaarbeurs Utrecht, 1931. Lithograph. Showing the searchlights over the city to announce the fair. Very good condition, 29½ x 40 inches. $625 (Auc. #25)

🍂 HENRI PIECK (1895–1972)

Jaarbeurs Utrecht, ca. 1933. Lithograph. Printed by DeMass, Rotterdam. An outstanding design for the annual industries fair, featuring Art Deco stylized factories. Very good condition, 29½ x 40 inches. $1,200–$1,300

Jaarbeurs Utrecht, 1934. Lithograph. A futuristic-looking Mercury beams his light on the city of Utrecht for the annual industries fair. Very good condition, 34 x 47 inches. $1,080 (Auc. #24)

🍂 LOUIS RAEMAEKERS (1865–1956)

Jaarbeurs Utrecht, 1928. Lithograph. Striking image of Mercury reaching up to the sky against a gray and red striped background. Very good condition, 26 x 43 inches. $1,100–$1,200

🍂 GEORG REUTER (1875–1966)

Bijbeltentoonstelling/Museum Fodor Amsterdam, 1937. Lithograph. Printed by Senefelder. For a Bible exhibition. Ornate poster with deep blues and golds. Very good condition, 23½ x 35 inches. $1,100–$1,200

🍂 JAN RINKE (1863–1922)

Delftsche Slaolie (Delft Salad Oil), ca. 1900. Lithograph. Executed in an Arts and Crafts style. A woman in apron and bonnet stands at the window. In browns and beige. Good condition, 19 x 30 inches. $1,125 (Auc. #24)

🍂 CORNELIUS ROL (1877–1963)

Entos/Amsterdam, 1913 (MDP #31). Lithograph. Printed by Ellerman, Harms and Company. For the first Dutch maritime exhibition. An elaborate design in reds and blue, featuring a sailing vessel. Very good condition, 25½ x 41¼ inches. $1,600–$1,800

🔥 RICHARD (R. N.) ROLAND-HOLST (1868–1938)

Electra, 1920. Lithograph. Printed by Tresling, Amsterdam. For the play. In sepia, brown, and black. Depicting Electra gazing down in misery. A good example of the artist's style. Very good condition, 27 x 39 inches. $2,125 (Auc. #25)

Eere-Tentoonstelling Bosboom, 1917. Lithograph. Printed by Tresling, Amsterdam. For an exhibition. In sepia and brown. Very good condition, backed on thick paper, 29½ x 39 inches. $1,400 (Auc. #25)

Lucifer, 1910 (MDP #25). Lithograph. Printed by Tresling, Amsterdam. A dramatic theatrical poster of a man hanging above the fires of hell. In sepia, rust, and black. Roland Holst designed the decor and costumes for the play as well as the poster. One of the best examples of the artist's work. Very good condition, 29 x 48½ inches. $14,000–$16,000

Wagner, 1932. Lithograph. To celebrate a festival in honor of the fiftieth anniversary of the composer's death. Very good condition, 33 x 47 inches.
          $1,200–$1,400

🔥 JOHANNES ROS (1875–1952)

Tentoonstelling Opvoeding van de Jeugd, 1919. Lithograph. Printed by S. Lankhout, Den Haag. For an exhibition for partents on raising children. A complex Art Nouveau design in muted greens and maroons. A very good example of the artist's work. In fine condition, 28 x 32½ inches. $1,800–$2,200

Poster by R. N. Roland-Holst. Courtesy of Bernice Jackson Fine Arts.

❧ MEOMIE SCHWARTZ (1876–1942)

Jaarbeurs Utrecht, 1924. Lithograph. Printed by Kotting, Amsterdam. Colorful design for the tenth annual fair, showing an ocean liner on the bottom half. Very good condition, 32 x 44 inches. $775 (Auc. #25)

❧ N. SICKENGA

Inklaren, ca. 1930. Lithograph. In blue and red. Depicting cubist stylized delivery men picking up packages. Very good condition, 24 x 40 inches. $700–$800

Nacht Treinen, ca. 1935. Lithograph. In yellow, brown, and black. Advertising the "Night Trains." A very good example of the artist's style. Very good condition, 24 x 40 inches. $850–$950

❧ JOOP SJOLLEMA (1900–1990)

Chaliapine/Boris Godounov, 1931 (MDP #97). Lithograph . Printed by L. van Leer, Amsterdam. For the Wagner Society of Amsterdam. A stunning design, especially in the geometric framing of the tragic image and the use of gold ink. One of the best posters by this artist. Very good condition, horizontal, 48 x 36 inches. *See color insert, photo 12.* $9,000–$11,000

De Hollandsche Aquarellisten Kring/Sted. Museum Amsterdam, ca. 1935. Lithograph. Printed by Dieperink, Amsterdam. For an exhibition of watercolorists. Very good condition, 23½ x 33 inches. $700–$800

Poster by N. Sickenga. Courtesy of Stephen Ganeles Antique Posters and Prints.

Courtesy of Bernice
Jackson Fine Arts.

Ichnaton, 1926. Lithograph. In black and brown. Printed for a student celebration at the University of Utrecht. A very good example of the artist's stylized yet classical style. Fine condition, 32½ x 47 inches. $2,200–$2,500

Nederlandisch Musikfeest, 1935. Lithograph. Printed by van Leer, Amsterdam. Conductor raises a baton, collage of musicians in the background. Very good condition, 34 x 59 inches. $1,750 (Auc. #25)

Universiteit Utrecht/300 Jaar, 1936. Lithograph. For the three hundredth anniversary of the University of Utrecht, with the unlikely image of a jester in profile. Very good condition, 27½ x 47 inches. $1,000–$1,200

🌿 WILLY SLUITER (1873–1949)

Hilversum/Lawn Tennis, 1916. Lithograph. Printed by Senefelder, Amsterdam. For the national and Olympic tennis matches. Stylized player takes his best shot. Very good condition, 26 x 36 inches. $2,925 (Auc. #25)

Laren Tentoonstelling, 1915. Lithograph. Printed by Senefelder, Amsterdam. Depicting a stylized painter and violinist with a flirtatious woman. Good condition, 30 x 43 inches. $1,950 (Auc. #24)

As above, fine condition, on linen. $3,200–$3,600

Naar Kaulen/Nieuve Treinen, 1914. Lithograph. Printed by Senefelder, Amsterdam. A stylized man and woman with a porter about to take the "new train." Very good condition, 25½ x 34 inches. $875 (Auc. #24)

1916 Olympische Spelen/Amsterdam Stadion, 1916. Lithograph. Printed by Senefelder, Amsterdam. For the Olympic games, showing a charioteer and team of horses. In very good condition, 24 x 36 inches. $1,750 (Auc. #24)

Vereeniging tot Bevordering van Beekdende Kunsten, 1915. Lithograph. Printed by Senefelder, Amsterdam. A woman with a parasol examines art while a heavyset gentleman wipes his brow. Very good condition, this example signed and dated by the artist, 26½ x 40 inches. $1,400 (Auc. #24)

❧ JOHANNES (JAN) SLUYTERS (1881–1957)

Avond-Feest, 1915 (MDP #24). Lithograph. Printed by Senefelder, Amsterdam. For an evening party of the Association of Dutch Artists' Societies. A very good example of the artist's early painterly style, 28¼ x 45 inches. $2,250 (Auc. #25)

Charlotte Kohler, 1925. Lithograph. Printed by Senefelder, Amsterdam. For the popular Dutch singer. Very good condition, 28 x 43 inches. $650–$750

Zegepraal, 1904 (MDP #23). Lithograph. Printed by Senefelder, Amsterdam. For the novel *Victory*, by Israel Querido. An early example of the artist's painterly style. Very good condition, 26 x 45¾ inches. $6,000–$6,500

❧ JAN TH. TOOROP (1858–1928)

Arnhem, 1900. Lithograph. In an Art Nouveau style, standing woman giving her hand to a kneeling woman, both of them in long dresses. In yellow and brown. Very good condition, 32 x 40 inches. $5,500–$6,000

Delftsche Slaolie (Delft Salad Oil), ca. 1895 (MDP #5). Lithograph. Printed by S. Lankhout, Den Haag. Stunning Art Nouveau-inspired design of two women in long, flowing robes and tresses of hair that fill the image area. In pale yellow, purple, and white. Delft Salad Oil was one of the first great patrons of poster art in Holland, and this is considered the best example of the patron's commissions. Fine condition, 27 x 39 inches. $12,500–$15,000

Pandorra, 1919 (MDP #45). Lithograph. Printed by S. Lankhout & Company, Den Haag. Theater poster for the play by Arthur van Schendel. Distinctive design with cubist/futurist influences. One of the most sought after Dutch poster designs. 33 x 44 inches. $30,000–$35,000

❧ OTTO TREUMANN (b. 1919)

Jaarbeurs Utrecht, 1949. Photo-offset. A three-dimensional *U* frames the distant city for the annual fair. A very good example of the artist's style. Very good condition, 30½ x 41 inches. $700–$750

Jaarbeurs Utrecht, 1954. Photo-offset. Printed by Offsetdruk de Jong & Company, Hilversum. A drop of water above gears, on a black background. Very good condition, 33 x 46½ inches. $600 (Auc. #25)

Poster by Jan th. Toorop. From the collection of Jim Lapides. Courtesy of Bernice Jackson Fine Arts.

Poster by Otto Treumann. Courtesy of Van Sabben Poster Auctions.

🌿 HENRI VERSTIJNEN (1882–1947)

Jaarbeurs Utrecht, 1924. Rotogravure (a color photographic newsprint process). Printed by Affiche Ned. Rotogravure Mij, Leiden. For the Utrecht fair, featuring a stunning eagle perched on a rock. Very good condition, 25 x 35 inches.

$800–$900

🌿 WALTER

Kiest Rood/SDAP, ca. 1929. Lithograph. A bold pro-Communist (*rood*="red") political poster showing one hand holding a hammer, and another a bloody sword. In red and black on white. Very good condition, 22 x 31½ inches.

$1,000–$1,100

🌿 WIEGMAN

Herwonnen Lvenskracht, 1920. Lithograph. For the fight against tuberculosis, depicting a rising sun through flowering branches of the trees. Very good condition, 24 x 36 inches.

$850–$900

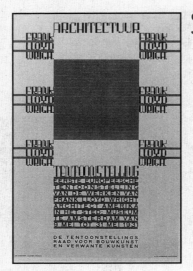

Courtesy of Bernice
Jackson Fine Arts.

🐚 H. TH. WIJDEVELD (1885–1987)

Architectuur—Frank Lloyd Wright, 1931 (MDP #67). Letterpress-printed by Joh. Enschede, Haarlem. For the first Frank Lloyd Wright exhibition in Holland. In red, white and black. Fine example of De Stijl design, and a sought-after subject matter. Very good condition, 19½ x 30½ inches. $18,500 (Auc. #24)

As above, very good condition. $15,000–$18,000

Don Karlos, 1919. Lithograph. Printed by Steendrukkerji Belderbos & Coesel, Amsterdam. For the play by Frederick von Schiller. In browns and sepias. An early poster by the artist, influenced by the style of Roland-Holst. Very good condition, 37 x 48 inches. $1,950 (Auc. #25)

🐚 JACQUES ZON (1872–1932)

Delftsche Slaolie (Delft Salad Oil), 1898 (MDP #13). Lithograph. Printed by S. Lankhout, Den Haag. A princess with her broken bottle of salad oil is saved by a knight in white armor bringing her a new bottle. Art Nouveau style, similar to the French artist Grasset. Very good condition, 27½ x 72½ inches. $850 (Auc. #25)

🐚 L. ZWIERS (1871–1953)

Decorative Ontwerpen/Stedtlijk Museum, 1917. Lithograph. Printed by Dieperink, Amsterdam. Very good condition, 21½ x 25 inches. $650 (Auc. #24)

❦ CHAPTER 16 ❦
Polish Posters

BY FRANK FOX

Frank Fox is a professor of history, specializing in Eastern Europe. His series of articles on Polish poster artists has appeared in The World & I *magazine,* The Poster Quarterly, *and other publications. Posters from his collection have been exhibited at Philadelphia's Port of History Museum and at Lincoln Center. You can write to him at: 51 Merbrook Lane, Merion, Pennsylvania 19066.*

Polish posters have been one of the best-known secrets in the field of poster collecting. Those who purchased them for the last fifteen years were fortunate to acquire one of the great bargains of the art world. Now that the reputation of the Polish poster artist is finally secure on the international market and prices are steadily rising, look for a very brisk trade in both prewar and postwar posters.

The posters, like the artists, are highly individualistic. The Polish poster artist, well educated, multifaceted in his interests, trained in architecture, painting, stage design, and illustration, conveys in his posters images allusions from the classical to the avant-garde. While the American public has been late in appreciating Polish poster art, Europeans have been aware of the skills of their colleagues in Eastern Europe for the better part of this century.

It wasn't until after 1915 that Poland adopted the poster as a commercial art form to any degree. One of the early Polish poster artists best known in the West, Tadeusz Gronowski (1894-?) was a contemporary of Cassandre and was certainly influenced by him. He pioneered a widely copied airbrush technique in the 1920s and 1930s.

From his trips to France, Gronowski brought back new graphic design styles and ideas, and the new geometry of the Art Deco period. Gronowski and other Polish graphic artists were well represented at the 1925 Paris *Exposition des Arts Décoratifs et Industriels Modernes*. He is also known for a few posters commissioned by French clients.

Another early Polish poster artist whose work is becoming better known to American collectors is Stefan Norblin (1892-?). Though he is not necessarily considered an avant- garde artist, from the mid-1920s to the early 1930s Norblin created several stunning lithographic posters for the burgeoning Polish tourist industry, mostly for the Polish state railways. Often these posters will have legends in three or four languages, as they were destined for distribution outside as well as within Poland to encourage tourism.

With rich transparency of color and striking imagery, Norblin's posters are glimpses of a broad spectrum of Polish life, from scenes of peasants in colorful traditional costumes, to posters that touted Poland's industrial advances, such as the factories in Upper Silesia *(see color insert, photo 13)* or his stylized view of *Gdynia/New Baltic Harbour.*

Other Polish artists whose names appear on travel posters of this period include Acedamski, Jarocki, Kossak, Bogdan Nowakowski, and Strychalski. The November 1928 issue of the American trade publication *Printers' Ink Monthly* devoted its cover article to these Polish travel posters, and praised the "strange minor color keys, the mysterious elusive blues . . . Critics agree that many Polish posters are art in the truest sense, ruggedly drawn and with a greater appreciation of color and display than casual study might disclose."

These Polish travel posters appear more and more infrequently on the market outside of Poland, and can command prices ranging from a few

Gdynia, by Stefan Norblin. From the collection of Al Hoch.

hundred dollars to well over $1,000 for an outstanding image by the leading artist Stefan Norblin.

Before World War II, Polish graphics reflected many different influences in Western art. Polish artists won numerous prizes at the 1937 World's Fair in Paris. However, World War II decimated the ranks of the Polish artists, and when the occupation by one invader ended, another totalitarian system took over. Yet even in the hostile environment of Communist Poland, the skills of the poster artists revived.

The prewar luminaries such as Gronowski, Tadeusz Trepkowski, Henryk Tomaszewski (b. 1914), and Erik Lipinski survived the war years to inspire and instruct a new generation of students. As one walks the grimy, cheerless streets of Warsaw, it's easy to imagine what the brightly colored posters of those students and others — Roman Cieslewicz (b. 1930), Jan Lenica (b. 1928), Jan Mlodozeniec (b. 1929), Waldemear Swierzy (b. 1931), Franciszek Starowieyski (b. 1930), and Maceij Urbaniec (b. 1925) — meant to people in Warsaw in the decades after the destructive conflict.

It says something about the respect accorded the Polish poster artists that new posters by these older men are still produced and displayed in the Polish capital, joined by an ever-growing number of younger artists. For example, Swierzy is still active in the Polish poster arena, and is recognized for his posters promoting jazz and rock concerts, cinema, and other events.

The second and third generation of Polish poster artists who have achieved prominence in more recent years include Rafal Olbinski,

Police, by Mieczyslaw Gorowski. From the Fox Collection.

Michal Klis, Andrzej Pagowski, Wieslaw Walkuski, Wiktor Sadowski, Meiczyslaw Gorowski, Eugeniusz Stankiewicz, Jan Aleksium, Jan Sawka, Jerzy Czerniawski, and Stasys Eidrigevicius.

From the late 1950s to the 1970s, the influence of Polish poster design grew as a nation hungry for visual representation of historical truths flocked to see the daring films of Andrzej Wajda. His work, and that of other film, play, and musical festival directors, stimulated interest in collecting the posters that advertised the productions. Warsaw soon became the center for international poster competition, and in 1968 the world's first museum devoted entirely to posters opened at Wilanow Palace, on the outskirts of Warsaw. As in the United States during the 1960s and early 1970s, music, art, and politics intermixed.

During the intoxicating few years of the rise of Solidarity, from the late 1970s to 1981, Polish cities were filled with more and more poster art until the entire country resembled one huge outdoor gallery. The American public was fortunate to see the best of these Polish posters in 1978, when the Smithsonian Institution and the Maryland Institute's College of Art sponsored a traveling exhibit created by Warsaw's Poster Museum. It was this intensely productive period that brought the Polish poster international recognition.

According to Jan Lenica, an acknowledged leader in Polish poster art, the essence of the Polish poster lies in its capacity to surprise the

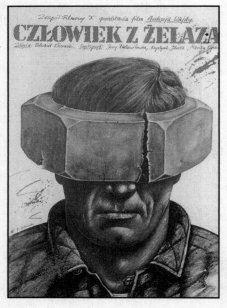

Man of Iron, by Rafal Olbinski. From the Fox Collection.

viewer. Now in his mid-sixties, Lenica resides in Paris and has been teaching in Berlin's prestigious *Hochschule*. (*For an example of Lenica's work, see his poster for* Don Giovanni *in the color insert, photo 14.*)

Lenica believes that the Polish poster is the very antithesis of decorative art, for it relies on the power of the creator's intellect, unlike the propaganda poster or a commercial poster in which the artist conveys someone else's ideas. Prizes awarded to Polish poster artists in worldwide competitions in the last decade are proof that they are among the best practitioners of the art of poster design today.

The crushing of Solidarity in 1981, and the restrictions and shortages that followed, challenged Polish poster artists once again. If poster exhibits could not travel after 1981, Polish artists did, and a number of outstanding ones immigrated to the United States. If you notice an unusual cover on a national magazine, a striking illustration on the op-ed page of a major newspaper, or a particularly eye-catching poster announcing a new Broadway play, you are very likely seeing the work of such admirable Polish poster artists as Rafal Olbinski, Jan Sawka, Andrzej Czeczot, Andrzej Dudzinski, and Junusz Kapusta.

POLISH POSTER-COLLECTING TRENDS

At poster auctions held in recent years in Poland, it has become clear that the most sought-after posters are those of the period following the establishment of an independent Polish state in 1918, particularly those images that portray the struggle with Communist Russia. As is the case with the Soviet posters of the same period, such images are rare, and the retail prices may be considerable sums. Also very desirable and hard to get due to export restrictions, both from the Russian and the Polish sides, are posters of constructivist designs. Polish posters from the 1920s, especially those by Stefan Norblin and Tadeusz Gronowski, are also popular.

Due to government regulations, no Polish posters designed before 1945 can be removed from Poland. Therefore, earlier posters are increasingly rare in American and European markets, and can command high prices.

Posters by painters who were prominent in the 1920s and 1930s are specially desirable, notably those by Theodor Axentowicz, Karol Frycz, Josef Mehoffer, and Edmund Bartlomiejczyk. The line between fine art and poster art was never as finely drawn in Poland as it had been in the United States. Today, a number of outstanding Polish poster artists, such as Jan Sawka, Rafal Olbinski, and Wiktor Sadowski, have exhibitions of their paintings in Japan, a country whose gifted artists recognize the talents of their colleagues in Eastern Europe.

I started collecting Polish posters in the early 1980s. Polish by birth, I returned in 1975, my first visit since departure in 1937. The images fascinated me, and I soon began to trust my eyes when I was told that my collection included the best of the current poster art. Four thousand posters later, after attending the 1986 Warsaw Biennale, I became a true convert to the growing movement of admirers of Polish poster art. In writing about it, I met some of the leading artists. I interviewed Gronowski and have visited such luminaries as Henryk Tomaszewski, Hubert Hilscher, Waldemar Swierzy, Jan Mlodozeniec, Franciszek Starowieyski, Andrzej Pagowski, and Wiktor Sadowski.

Less than ten years ago, one could purchase a contemporary Polish poster for the equivalent of thirty cents in the Warsaw marketplace. Today prices have increased twentyfold in Poland, and the average price of a contemporary Polish poster in the United States ranges between $30 and $100, depending on the artist and the image. Posters by well-established artists such as Starowieyski or Lenica may command higher prices. In France and Germany, where the Polish poster is held in high repute, a popular poster such as that of Wiktor Sadowski's *My Fair Lady* has sold for as much as $200.

Most contemporary Polish posters are roughly 27 x 39 inches, in either a vertical or horizontal format. The wide range of subjects, artists, and styles makes it a field in which there is something for everyone.

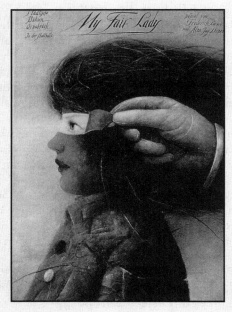

My Fair Lady, by Wiktor Sadowski. From the Fox Collection.

Depending on your tastes, you can choose pieces that feature anything from political slogans to cinema to Jimi Hendrix concerts.

However, one should exercise caution when buying posters printed in Poland. Since the artists were paid by the government for their work, they had no control over subsequent reprintings. Once when Jan Lenica visited me, he noticed that I had several copies of his famous poster of Berg's *Wozzeck*. He quickly pointed out to me the difference in colors between the original run and the subsequent editions. (Note: The image of this poster is featured on the cover of Alain Weill's massive compendium *The Poster: A Worldwide Survey and History*. See Bibliography.)

TO FIND OUT MORE ABOUT POLISH POSTERS

The most knowledgeable authority on the history of the Polish Poster is Szymon Boyko, who makes his home in Poland and lectures each summer at the Rhode Island School of Design. He has written extensively on the Polish poster, although his work, written in Polish, is not accessible to most Americans.

A short survey is available under the title *Poster Art in Poland* by Joseph S. Czestochowski. It was published as a catalog for the exhibit sponsored in 1978 by the Smithsonian Institution, the Maryland Institute College of Art, and the Polish Poster Museum. Mr. Czestochowski also published forty-six plates in full color of that exhibit in 1979 (Dover Press). This work includes short biographies of the leading Polish poster artists.

One of the best sources is a catalog that was published by the Berlin *Hochschule der Kunste* and the Polish Poster Museum in 1980. Entitled *Das Polnische Plakat* (The Polish Poster), it contains many color reproductions and biographies of Polish artists from 1892 to 1980. A good survey book on the Polish poster for English readers remains to be written; however, a full chapter is devoted to postwar Polish Posters in Alain Weill's book, *The Poster: A Worldwide Survey and History*.

In Poland, aside from the vast collection of posters at the Poster Museum in Wilanow, the best private collection is that of Krzysztof Dydo, who has a gallery in Cracow and stages frequent exhibits of contemporary Polish posters.

In the United States, some of the dealers who specialize in Polish Poster art are Martin Rosenberg in Chicago and Judy Sullivan in Carbondale, Colorado. Occasionally Meehan Military Posters in New York, and George Goodstadt's Antique Poster Collection in Ridgefield, Connecticut, will offer some unusual Polish posters.

The Mona Lisa, by Maciej
Urbaniec. From the Fox
Collection.

Among the private collections, primarily in the category of film
posters, the most extensive one is that of Richard Koszarski, a professor
at Columbia University and the curator of the Museum of the Moving
Image, in Astoria, New York. The Biennale sponsored by the Colorado
State University at Fort Collins has featured numerous Polish poster
artists. One should add that our Library of Congress, as a repository of
printed materials from the world over, has a fine collection of Polish
posters. Elena Millie, the curator of the Print Collection, is very knowledgeable about the Polish posters and has written many essays on the
subject. Among collectors who travel between Poland and the United
States seeking out new sources for buyers and sellers, one could single
out Michal Ponisz, whose specialty is unusual film posters, such as the
Polish edition of *Gone with the Wind.* These are very difficult to find and
naturally command high prices.

There is every indication that Polish posters will continue to serve as
a source of pleasure and investment for collectors in the United States
and abroad.

For many Americans, their only exposure to Polish posters has been
the delightful and often quirky images for the *Cyrk* (Circus) by such
artists as Roman Cieslewicz, Rafal Olbinski, Jan Sawka, Waldemar
Swierzy, and Maciej Urbaniec.

However, once you are drawn into the world of Polish posters, other
artists and other subjects will beckon you with vibrant colors, humor,
and multilayered meanings that are the hallmarks of the best of Polish
poster art.

PART THREE

American Posters

❦ CHAPTER 17 ❦
American Turn-of-the-Century Posters

By the mid-1800s, posters were widely used in the United States, even in billboard size. Large-format black-and-white woodcuts made their appearance on America's streets to promote a range of products and entertainments. While Jules Chéret was transforming the streets of Paris into a colorful poster gallery by the 1870s, the early forms of commercial poster advertising in the United States were drab, unartistic, and severely criticized.

Early major color lithographic printers such as Strobridge in Cincinnati, Ohio, and Courier in Buffalo, New York, were being commissioned by clients to produce advertising posters by the late 1880s. However, the first industry to truly capitalize on the advent of color lithography for posters was the circus. As early as 1891, Strobridge was creating spectacular color posters for Barnum & Bailey, including a highly prized series that features the two showmen's portraits in black-and-white lithography next to a colorful scene such as "Bronze-Hued Performing Stallions" or the bareback-riding "Native Mexican Vacqueros" (see the chapter on Circus Posters).

In the cities, the strongest reaction to the early, rather ugly hoardings came from writers for magazines and publications, which in turn became the first to commission artists to create posters. In the late 1880s magazines such as *St. Nicholas*, *The Century*, and *Harper's* commissioned artists such as Louis Rhead and Eugene Grasset to design their covers. When the magazine was printed, an additional number of covers would be printed on a heavier card stock to be used in shop windows.

The illustrated color advertising poster slowly gained exposure and acceptance. A ground-breaking poster exhibition was hosted by the Grolier Club in New York in 1890. Featuring mainly French posters, its impact on illustrators and graphic designers spurred the development of the poster as an art form.

Then, in 1893, *Harper's* hired the artist/illustrator Edward Penfield (1866–1925) to create a new poster each month, and the poster explosion rocked America. From that time until the beginning of the new cen-

tury, a host of talented artists emerged. While other product manufacturers, notably those of bicycles, began to commission many of these
same artists to create posters, no industry was as active or as dedicated
to the new commercial art form as publishing.

By the end of 1893, other publications such as *Lippincott's*, *Scribner's*,
and *The Century* were also commissioning artists to create poster designs.

For the most part, posters designed for these periodicals, as well as
for book publishers and other literary clients, tend to be smaller than
European posters, often no more than 12 x 18 inches or 15 x 20 inches.
This is due to the fact that they were designed to be posted in store windows and on news kiosks rather than on boulevards. Perhaps their size
is part of the reason they were late to gain popularity in the current
poster-collecting market, but their rediscovery is now well established;
and prices for them have increased steadily over the past ten years.

Their smaller size has had one distinct advantage: They can often be
found in very good to fine condition, as they did not necessarily need to
be folded for storage. In addition, their smaller size means they were less
likely to be mounted on linen or other backings over the years.

By the time Jules Chéret published *Les Maîtres de l'Affiche*, or "The
Masters of the Poster" series of miniature posters for collectors from
1896 to 1900, many American artists were recognized internationally for
their contributions to the field (see *Les Maîtres de l'Affiche* in the chapter
on French Posters).

Chéret included posters by Americans Will Bradley (1868–1962),
William Carqueville (1871–1946), Arthur Wesley Dow (1857–1922),
Alice R. Glenny (1858–?), Frank Hazenplug (1873–after 1908),
Maxfield Parrish (1870–1966), Edward Penfield (1866–1925), Ethel
Reed (1874–after 1898), Louis Rhead (1857–1926), M. Louis Stowell
(a student of Dow's), and Charles H. Woodbury (1864–1940). Not bad
for a country that had a relatively late start in the poster arena. In the
1890s numerous other Americans would also lend their talents to the
world of the poster.

Basically, two stylistic tendencies dominated American posters of the
day: Arts and Crafts and Art Nouveau. Some artists' work shows influences from both. Another important influence, also felt in Europe, was a
Japanese simplicity of line and color, sometimes called Japonisme.

The Art Nouveau style in America, greatly influenced by French
artists such as Eugene Grasset, found stunning expression through the
work of such artists as English-born Louis Rhead, Maxfield Parrish,
and Will Bradley. The spare Arts and Crafts style, English and
Germanic in its roots, was reflected in the work of numerous artists,
including Charles Woodbury, William Carqueville, J. J. Gould (about

1875–1935), Elisha Brown Bird, and the leading posterist, Edward Penfield.

Penfield studied at the Art Students League in New York, and was highly influenced by the solid color fields and simple images of both the English Arts and Crafts school and German posterists. Over a period of six years he produced posters of a consistent quality for Harper's, in addition to his work for other clients.

His posters often use vivid colors in striking combinations. His figures are strongly outlined, usually dominate the foreground, and tend to represent fashionable, sophisticated society types with a penchant for things British. Many good examples of his posters for *Harper's* can still be purchased for under $1,000, with outstanding examples bringing $2,000, $3,000, and more. His most expensive posters are those he created for *The Northampton Cycle Co.* (ca. 1899) and Stearns bicycles, which can bring more than $10,000 today.

Penfield's style influenced numerous other American artists, such as William Carqueville, who designed monthly posters from 1894 to 1895 for *Lippincott's*. Carqueville developed his own personal style which distinguished his employer's posters from those of *Harper's*. His designs generally incorporate only a few colors, and have stark backgrounds. His thin-waisted women are also drawn more sparingly than those of Penfield. Today, very good examples of his work can still be purchased for about $700, with the best examples just over $1,000, though that price is almost double what it was only a few years ago.

When Carqueville left *Lippincott's* he was replaced with an artist whose work is often directly compared to that of Penfield: J. J. Gould. Gould created monthly poster designs from 1895 to 1897 that so directly competed with Penfield's designs that at one point there was talk of a lawsuit. Many of Gould's designs can still be purchased for about $500, but there is a growing appreciation of his work, and some of his best posters fetch prices equal to those paid for Penfield.

The Century, which had in some ways established the practice of commissioning artists by recruiting Eugene Grasset, didn't hire a staff artist to exclusively produce posters. Instead it continued to commission posters in a range of sometimes daring artistic styles from talented artists such as Elisha Brown Bird (1867–1943), Charles Dana Gibson (1867–1944) (creator of the "Gibson girl"), Herbert Myron Lawrence (1852– 1937), Joseph Christian Leyendecker (1874–1951), Edward Henry Potthast (1857–1927), George Edmund Varian (1865–1923), George A. Williams, and Charles Woodbury. However, Maxfield Parrish and Louis Rhead are the most highly valued of the *Century* artists, with some of their posters bringing more than $3,000.

Some artists only designed a single poster for *The Century*, making their work difficult to find and sought after by genre collectors, such as Potthast's only poster, which can bring as much as $1,000 today. J. C. Leyendecker's poster for the August 1896 *Century* is also hard to find. After the turn of the century Leyendecker had commercial success with his illustration work for *Collier's* and *Saturday Evening Post*, and posters for commercial clients such as Arrow Collars and Shirts and Chesterfield cigarettes.

Parrish's poster for *Scribner's* is even more highly valued than his work for *Century*, bringing in the range of $5,000 or more. For the most part, *Scribner's* did not turn to full-image illustrated posters, but continued to use a format that included a small illustration and several lines of copy announcing the contents of each issue. While these are generally less desirable to poster collectors today, certain examples, such as those by William Glackens (1870–1938), can bring high prices.

Other artists who designed posters for *Scribner's* include Henry McCarter (1865–1943) and Howard Chandler Christy (1873–1952), who, along with Leyendecker, became one of America's more distinguished World War I posterists.

The Chicago literary journal *The Chap-Book*, published by Stone & Kimball, commissioned numerous notable artists to design posters, such as Elisha Brown Bird, Claude Fayette Bragdon (1866–1946), Frank Hazenplug (1873–after 1908), and J. C. Leyendecker. Hazenplug's poster for the publication in 1895, also called The Red Lady, sells for more than $1,500, but perhaps the single most expensive "American" poster of the period is *The Chap Book* poster designed by the great Henri de Toulouse-Lautrec (1864–1901), which can sell for as much as $45,000!

By far the best-known of all *The Chap-Book* artists is Will Bradley (1868–1962), who created seven posters for the publication.

Bradley was a self-taught artist who mastered the printing and typography trades, and designed posters for *The Inland Printer*. In 1894 he founded his own company, Wayside Press, and his own magazine, *Bradley: His Book*, both based in Springfield, Massachusetts. Bradley's posters for *The Chap-Book* command in excess of $2,000, but certain posters he created for his own publication, such as his 1896 poster known as *The Kiss*, can bring ten times that price. Like Penfield, he, too, designed a stunning bicycle poster, for *Victor Cycles*, which can also bring in the range of $20,000.

Bradley's posters are true masterpieces of both poster art and American Art Nouveau. The Art Nouveau style, which was short-lived in France, where it had all but disappeared by the turn of the century, had even less impact in the United States. Apart from the glass and lamps of Louis Comfort Tiffany, the movement had its strongest expression in this country in the world of graphic design and posters.

Louis Rhead was a master of Art Nouveau graphics. He designed posters for *The Century*, *St. Nicholas*, *Scribner's*, the newspapers *The Sun* and *The Morning Journal*, as well as for the publications of Louis Prang & Company. Boston publisher Louis Prang is best-known for his chromolithographic reproductions of famous paintings, an inexpensive art introduction course for Americans of the era, but he also produced writing papers and greeting cards and is said to have been the innovator of the Christmas card. Some of Rhead's most outstanding poster designs were created for Prang publications.

Another artist who deserves special mention, though she may have designed only two posters, is Evelyn Rumsey Cary (1855–1924). Cary was a Buffalo painter who is best remembered for the poster for the 1901 Pan American Exposition showing Niagara Falls as a watery Art Nouveau maiden, the *Maid of the Mist*. She also designed an early poster for *Woman Suffrage*, in 1905.

Other literary journals and book publishers commissioned artists to create posters. Among those now prized by collectors are Arthur Wesley Dow (1857–1922), for his poster for *Modern Art* journal; Florence Lundborg (1871–1949), who designed several posters for the San Francisco-based literary journal *The Lark*; Maurice Prendergast (1861–1929); Ethel Reed (1874–after 1898), for her posters for books published by Lamson Wolffe & Company and Copeland & Day; and John Sloan (1871–1952), for *The Echo* journal and for books.

As in other fields of collecting, as the most recognized artists' work continues to go up in price, other, lesser-known artists become more highly valued, and appear on the market more frequently.

Literally dozens of other artists designed posters for the magazines, journals, and book publishers mentioned above. Though they were perhaps not as artistically accomplished as the leading designers, their posters can still be purchased for under $100 to $200. Due to their connection to the world of publishing, these posters are found more often at book fairs and book auctions than at fine art or antique events. Because of their low prices, they can also be found at ephemera and paper fairs.

Ironically, the success and populariy of these posters seems to have had, in the end, a negative impact. By the mid-1890s, many of these publications were overprinting their posters for direct sale to collectors. As exhibitions of posters and publications such as The *Modern Poster*, *The Poster*, and *Poster Lore* proliferated, the posters began to cost more than the publications themselves. Publishers watched as poster sales increased while sales of the publication declined.

By the end of the 1890s, magazine publishers anxious to counteract the trend started to emphasize the design of the periodical cover, forcing collectors to buy the magazine if they wanted the artwork. Magazines such as *Collier's, Ladies Home Journal, Life, Truth, Vogue,* and *Saturday Evening Post* became the patrons of many illustrators and artists. Often these magazines were as large as the posters that had been so popular in the 1890s. In the book publishing world the transition was marked by the advent of the illustrated paper dust jacket.

While fine poster art in America was gaining popularity in other fields, such as magic and theatrical productions, events and expositions, and posters and tin signs for an array of products (today sometimes called "country store" advertising), it was on the decline in the publishing world. A unique era in American poster history had come to a close.

TO FIND OUT MORE ABOUT AMERICAN TURN-OF-THE-CENTURY POSTERS

Major collections of American posters exist at the Metropolitan Museum of Art in New York, the New York Public Library, the Boston Public Library Print Department, and the Santa Barbara Museum of Art. Sometimes smaller libraries and museums will also have collections of these posters. Viewing museum holdings, which are not necessarily on display, often requires an appointment (see Resource Guide).

The best available reference book is the catalog of the Metropolitan Museum of Art collection by David Kiehl, *American Art Posters of the 1890s* (see Bibliography). This book can be purchased through the museum's bookstore, and illustrates and annotates about three hundred posters by seventy different artists.

AMERICAN TURN-OF-THE-CENTURY POSTERS— PRICE LISTINGS

NOTE: See the chapter Important Notes on the Price Listings for more information on prices given. Reference numbers following the titles of some of the entries refer to David A. Kiehl's American Art Posters of the 1890s in The Metropolitan Museum of Art, including the Leonard A. Lauder Collection.

🌿 EDWIN AUSTIN ABBEY (1852–1911)

The Quest of the Holy Grail by Edwin Abbey, 1895 (Kiehl 1). Lithograph. Apparently the artist's only poster. Advertising the book published by R. H. Russell & Son. 16½ x 23 inches. $600–$800

Poster by Will H. Bradley.
The Blue Lady. Courtesy of
Swann Galleries, Inc.

Poster by Will H. Bradley.
Courtesy of Thomas G. Boss
Fine Books.

❦ WILL H. BRADLEY (1868–1962)

Bradley: His Book, Christmas, 1896. Lithograph. Signed "B" in lower right. Beautiful design of a woman before a grove of trees holding a spray of holly. Good condition, 29 x 42 inches. $2,000–$2,200

The Chap-Book, 1894, also called *The Blue Lady* (Kiehl 14). Lithograph. Woman in a deep blue forest, with red lettering. A good example of Bradley's work. Very good condition, this example framed, 12½ x 18½ inches. $1,430 (Auc. #19)

The Chap-Book/May, 1895 (Kiehl 18). Lithograph. Woman completely enveloped in a maze of flowers. Design of vertical lines throughout the image adds to the impressionist feeling. Fine condition, 13¼ x 20 inches. $2,000–$2,500

The Chap-Book/Thanksgiving, 1895 (Kiehl 23). Lithograph. Two identical women in swirling gowns holding up a platter of food. Fine condition, 13 x 19½ inches. $3,000–$4,000

Inland Printer/St. Valentine, 1895. Lithograph. A woman plays a guitar. Fine condition, on linen, 13½ x 22 inches. $1,800–$2,000

Narcoti-Cure, 1895. Color zincograph. Showing a white knight slaying the evil-looking "tobacco habit." Rare. Fine condition, 14 x 20 inches. $3,800–$4,200

❦ WILLIAM CARQUEVILLE (1871–1946)

International/February, 1897. Lithograph. For the St. Valentine's Day issue of the magazine. In black and green. Very good condition, 11¾ x 17½ inches.
$125–$150

Lippincott's/October, 1895 (Kiehl 54). Lithograph. A young woman pensively walking through blowing leaves at sunset. Good condition, 12½ x 18½ inches.
$450–$550

As above, in very good condition. $385 (Auc. #19)

As above, in mint condition. $700–$900

Lippincott's/September, 1895. Lithograph. A young woman in vacation dress, on the deck of a boat, waving good-bye. Very good condition, 12½ x 19 inches.
$600–$650

❦ EVELYN RUMSEY CARY (1855–1924)

Pan American Exposition/Buffalo 1901, 1900. Lithograph. From the painting *The Spirit of Niagara*, also called *Maid of the Mist*, by Cary, with border and lettering by Frederic F. Hellmer. Fine condition, on linen, 24½ x 47 inches. *See color insert, photo 17.* $5,000–$6,000

Poster by William Carqueville.
Courtesy of Thomas G. Boss
Fine Books.

❦ R. L. EMERSON

The Atlantic/July, 1895. Lithograph. Two galleys fighting. Done in navy blue on yellow paper. Very good condition, 11½ x 15½ inches. $100–$125

The Atlantic/September, 1895. Lithograph. A Greek goddess holding a cup. Done in brown on white paper. Good condition, 11 x 15 inches. $100–$125

❦ VESPER C. GEORGE

Bostonian/Knight Templar Number. Lithograph. Knight Templar on horseback. Vesper George had his own school of art in Boston. Good condition, 10½ x 13½ inches. $75–$100

❦ WILLIAM GLACKENS (1870–1938)

Scribner's/February. Lithograph. People gather at a newsstand that features a poster for Scribner's. Very good condition, 14½ x 22 inches. $412 (Auc. #19)

❦ JOSEPH J. GOULD, JR. (CA. 1875–CA. 1935)

Lippincott's/July, 1986. Lithograph. Woman in yellow riding a bicycle. Fine condition, 14½ x 18½ inches. $467 (Auc. #19)

Lippincott's/November, 1896. Lithograph. Men watching a football game. Very good condition, 13 x 16¼ inches. $275 (Auc. #19)
As above, in very good condition. $450–$500

Lippincott's/December. Lithograph. Woman in green and red walking through a snowstorm. Very good condition, 9 x 13½ inches. $302 (Auc. #19)

❦ ERNEST HASKEL (1876–1925)

The Sunday Journal, 1896. Lithograph. Poster for the New York newspaper shows a woman in a flowing cape and dress playing pipes. Good condition, on linen, 14 x 20 inches. $300–$350

❦ LOUISE LYONS HEUSTIS (DATES UNKNOWN)

Chiffon's Marriage by Gyp, 1895. Lithograph. A young woman daydreaming in a hammock with her novel in one hand. Good condition, 10 x 9 inches. $125–$150

❦ G. F. KERR (DATES UNKNOWN)

New York Journal/Easter. Lithograph. An angel blows a horn at sunrise. Good condition, 40 x 30 inches. $165 (Auc. #19)

Courtesy of
Chisholm Gallery.

Courtesy of Chisholm
Gallery.

❦ MAXFIELD PARRISH (1870–1966)

The Century/Midsummer Holiday Number, 1897 (Kiehl 134). Lithograph. A nude girl in a grove of trees, almost appearing to be leaning against the outline of the poster. Fine condition, 11½ x 19 inches. $2,800–$3,000

Scribner's/Fiction Number, August 1897 (Kiehl 135). Lithograph. An outstanding design of a young nude girl reading her magazine in a forest of deep blue-greens, gray, and black. Rare. Fine condition, 14¼ x 19¾ inches. $6,000–$6,500

❦ EDWARD PENFIELD (1866–1925)

Harper's/April, 1896 (Kiehl 156). Lithograph. A man holding an umbrella, and a woman in cape and hat. Very good condition, 13½ x 17⅞ inches. $650–$750

Harper's/August, 1897 (Kiehl 199) Lithograph. A woman about to sit in a beach chair, with a row of houses behind her. An excellent example of a Penfield *Harper's* poster. Fine condition, 13¼ x 18½ inches. $2,500–$2,800

Harper's/February, 1896. Lithograph. Couple in brown and yellow against a gray landscape and deep blue sky. Good condition, 11 x 19½ inches. $800–$900

From the author's
collection. Photo
by Robert Four.

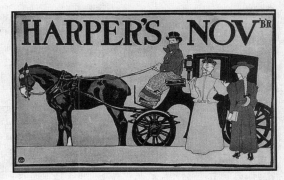

Harper's/July, 1896 (Kiehl 182). Lithograph. A woman holding an umbrella. Fine condition, on linen, 14 x 18½ inches. $1,600–$1,800

Harper's/June, 1896 (Kiehl 181). Lithograph. A woman in a rocking chair attentively reads her magazine. A very good example of a Penfield *Harper's* poster. Fine condition, 13½ x 18½ inches. *See color insert, photo 15.* $1,800–$2,200

Harper's/June, 1898 (Kiehl 211). Lithograph. A woman riding sidesaddle. Fine condition, 16 x 19¼ inches. $650–$800

Harper's/March, 1896 (Kiehl 178). Lithograph. Woman in long black gown with masks on the wall behind her. Very good condition, 10½ x 18 inches.
$440 (Auc. #19)
$1,000–$1,300

Harper's/March, 1898 (Kiehl 208). Lithograph advertising "Stirring Times in Austria Described by Mark Twain," with a portrait of Twain. Fine condition, 12½ x 15½ inches. $500–$600

Harper's/November, 1896 (Kiehl 186). Lithograph. Image of a man riding in a carriage. Fine condition, 13½ x 18 inches. $1,100 (Auc. #19)
$2,000–$2,500

Harper's/Nov'B'R, 1899. Lithograph (Kiehl 216). Two women ascending a coach. Fine condition, horizontal, 18 x 11 inches. $900–$1,200

❧ EDWARD HENRY POTTHAST (1857–1927)

The Century/July Number, 1896. Lithograph (Kiehl 229). A beautiful woman in a red dress amidst green leaves with a red bird perching. Potthast's only known poster for *The Century*. Very good condition, 14¼ x 20¼ inches. $950–$1,000

❧ ETHEL REED (1874–AFTER 1898)

Folly or Saintliness, 1895. Lithograph. Outline of a woman in orange against black background. Fine condition, 14¾ x 20¼ inches. $495 (Auc. #19)

Poster by Louis John Rhead.
Courtesy of Chisholm Gallery.

Poster by Ethel Reed.
Courtesy of Thomas G.
Boss Fine Books.

The House of Trees and Other Poems, by Ethelwyn Wetherald, 1895 (Kiehl 237). Linocut. Woman in dark green with a book sits in a park. Fine condition, 9½ x 18 inches. $412 (Auc. #19)

Jacques Damour, by Emile Zola, 1895 (Kiehl 243). Lithograph. For the novel published by Copeland & Day. An impressionist close-up of a man and woman under a streetlamp. Fine condition, 11½ x 18½ inches. $450–$600

Miss Traumerei by Albert Morris Bagby, 1895 (Kiehl 235). Lithograph. For the novel, a woman at the piano with yellow and green flowers. Fine condition, 13¾ x 22 inches. $715 (Auc. #19)
                                                                     $1,100–$1,300

❦ LOUIS JOHN RHEAD (1857–1926)

Century Magazine/Midsummer Holiday Number, 1894 (Kiehl 249). Lithograph. A woman reads her magazine seated amidst colorful flowers. A very good example of the artist's work. Fine condition, horizontal, 18⅝ x 13½ inches.
                                                                     $2,500–$3,500

Lundborg's Perfumes, 1894. Lithograph. Beautiful woman with perfumes displayed on a classical column capital. Very good condition, 11½ x 17½ inches.
$1,300–$1,500

L. Prang & Co.'s Holiday Publications, 1896 (Kiehl 251). Lithograph. Advertising the Christmas cards, books, and letter papers of the Boston publisher Louis Prang. A good example of Rhead's work. Fine condition, 15⅜ x 20¾ inches.
$1,400–$1,600

Prang's Easter Publications, 1895 (Kiehl 258). Lithograph. Close-up of a woman with an Easter lily. An outstanding example of the artist's work. Striking colors. Fine condition, 17 x 24 inches. *See color insert, photo 16.*
$4,000–$5,000

❦ CHARLES SEARLE

The American Wheelman, ca. 1898. Lithograph, In an Art Nouveau style. For the magazine devoted to bicycling. Good condition, 9½ x 12⅛ inches.
$250–$300

❦ JOHN SLOAN (1871–1951)

The Echo. For Sale Here, 1895. Lithograph. A young woman blows a horn announcing The Echo. Fine condition, 6 x 10 inches.
$2,500–$3,500

Poster by Louis John Rhead. From the author's collection. Photo by Robert Four.

Poster by John Sloan.
Courtesy of Thomas G. Boss
Fine Books.

From the author's
collection. Photo
by Robert Four.

❧ GEORGE A. WILLIAMS

Klondike/Century/March, 1897. Lithograph. For the issue featuring the 1896 Alaskan gold rush in the Klondike region. Fine condition, 12¼ x 17 inches.

$400–$500

❧ CHAPTER 18 ❧
Mather Work Incentive Posters

BY JOHN L. HELLER

John L. Heller is president of Heller & Heller/Posters at Work, specializing in American work incentive posters, particularly those produced by the Mather Company, and also offering an ever-changing and eclectic collection of American and European posters of outstanding graphic quality. You can contact him at 50 Webster Avenue, New Rochelle, New York 10801, (914) 235-0300, fax (914) 235-0314.

The word *poster* usually brings to mind bold advertising designed to sell products, places, and events. There have always been government-issued political and propaganda posters, especially in wartime. Yet, for the most part, poster designers and printers have sought commissions from private industry, theater, tourism, and other fields.

However, one of the most remarkable series of privately printed posters sold to the public did not advertise products or places. Rather, their objective was to create, modify, or change attitudes and work practices. These are the work inventive posters produced by the Mather Company of Chicago from 1923 to 1929.

Charles Mather was a member of an old printing family in Chicago. As a youth he learned the lithographer's trade. As a young man he temporarily abandoned the printing business and went to work for a large advertising company. It was a time when advertising was becoming a major force in American society and when many of the leading ad agencies of today were in their infancy.

It was also a time when advertising was thought to have a potentially utopian function. President Calvin Coolidge, in a 1926 speech to the American Association of Advertising Agencies, said, "By changing the attitude of mind, it (advertising) changes the material condition of people—advertising ministers to the spiritual side of trade."

Was Mather influenced by these concepts? Who knows? But when he returned to the printing business in the early 1920s, he was deeply imbued with their practical effects. While he was not selling anything with his posters, his sense of the function of advertising is obvious.

In the introduction to his 1926–27 catalog he states, "This series of 78 posters is a continuous internal organization advertising campaign that sells the worker your (the employer's) ideas — constructive, cost-cutting, time-saving, friction-reducing, morale-developing ideas about the job, the department, the firm, and the worker's future. The experience of Mather clients proves that the worker's 'buys' ideas when so advertised just as he buys advertised goods in a store."

Mather began producing posters he called "constructive organization posters" in 1923. But before he could produce them, he had to invent them: What he developed was unique. There was no precedent for his idea, and no model to follow. While there had been posters extolling patriotism during World War I, and posters warning of safety hazards, there had never been a continuous series devoted exclusively and relentlessly to attitudes in the workplace. The only predecessors of these posters were cards with simplistic mottos that the company printed (during slow periods to keep the staff busy), which were distributed to commercial and industrial customers.

The posters were a natural blending of Mather's talents as a lithographer, copywriter, and entrepreneur. He wrote the text for them, printed and sold them. He hired a number of Chicago illustrators to provide the graphic designs. They worked for him on a free-lance basis during the six years that these posters were published. At times these free-lancers were given assignments to produce specific images to fit the particular text Mr. Mather had written. In other instances they supplied drawings to which he fitted appropriate messages.

The Mather Company underwrote all the costs of producing these posters. No government or other public funds were involved, as they were in the production of similarly oriented WPA posters ten years later. The posters were sold either by yearly subscription to business organizations throughout the country or on an individual or multiple basis through catalogs.

The catalogs, besides showing the year's output of posters, provide fascinating insight into Mather's sales ability and personality, as well as into the concepts of business organization and worker relations that were prevalent at the time.

For example, the 1926–27 catalog index notes, "Every known destructive practice among workers is covered by at least one poster, and usually by a series from which you can choose the most suitable to meet the condition of the moment. Should the trouble prove obstinate, follow up the first poster selected with one or more others in the series. In this way, the problem will be handled from every angle—no matter what posters you select for display, morale will be improved, turnover reduced, loyalty stimulated, results and greater profits insured for your firm."

Incidentally, there are 136 destructive work practices alphabetically listed in the index. Hence, the employer was admonished that a subscription for all seventy posters produced that year could cure all his employee problems, but he did have the option of being selective and resolving only the most pressing and immediate situations.

Always the entrepreneur, Mather even sold a device to display the posters. Each poster came with two holes in the top border. His device was a flat metal plate with two prongs extending from it. It was free to subscribers and sold separately to those who only bought a few posters.

Over the six-year period in which they were published, more than 350 posters with different graphic images and written texts (Mather called them "messages") were created. Text and image were always conceived as an integral whole. Subtle or obvious, the images always represented the story set out in the messages.

Thus in the 1929 poster *Out of the Running: Success Never Waits*, a magnificent racehorse with jockey astride is seen charging ahead, no doubt a winner—until you look carefully and see the rest of the field in the background, obviously many furlongs ahead. The same graphic/text relationship is found in all of Mather's output except that it became more refined, more sophisticated, as the years passed.

The text always had the same format: a bold headline, the message in several lines, and a concluding tag line. This was obviously a holdover from his copywriting days at the ad agency. It's amazing, given the sheer number of posters produced, that the texts were never repeated. Nor, for that matter, were the graphic images. Every poster created was an original.

The only difference that occurred in the text over the years was a general tightening up of the message, a reduction in the number of lines of text and a less strident one. In the earliest posters, those of 1923, for example, the message might consist of nine or ten short lines of text. This might be fine for a newspaper or magazine ad, but not for something hung on the wall that is intended to convey a quick, sharp impression. In the 1929 series, the body of the message generally consisted of only three or four short lines. From a design perspective, the written words became far more integrated into the overall composition of the poster, as opposed to early examples in which text was set as a block of copy with little design relationship to the graphic image.

As the message matured over the years, so did the images, with the most elegant and refined produced in the final year, 1929. The posters are all 36 x 42 inches, and about seventy-five were created, about the same number as in each of the years 1923–27. Except for the horizontal 1923 series, all of the posters were vertical format.

By 1929 the illustrations had been greatly simplified in terms of drawing techniques, number of physical elements portrayed, and use of color. Perhaps the artists — Hal Depuy, Willard Frederik Elmes, Frank Beatty, Robert Beebe, and Henry Lee, Jr. — had been influenced by the earlier *sach plakats* or "object posters" produced by German artists such as Ludwig Hohlwein. Planes of bright color were now used to create the figures and objects, rather than the intricately drawn, dramatically naturalistic illustrations of the early years.

The figures were pulled forward to the picture plane, the surface of the poster, simplifying perspective and in most instances reducing the backgrounds to a wash of color, which was often textured. The earlier posters, particularly those of 1923, attempted to portray greater depth of field and consisted of elaborate backgrounds portraying idealized cityscapes (sometimes resembling the Emerald City of Oz) or views of contemporary American transportation technology.

Over the years, the number of figures in each poster was greatly reduced. Many of the 1923–25 posters contained numerous figures performing a variety of tasks. By 1929 the posters displayed only one figure, object, or animal standing alone as the main focus of the poster. This effort towards simplification and a bold single image is further evidence of the influence of German poster art.

The color palettes also evolved, becoming brighter, clearer, and the most dominant factor in the design. The number of different colors used was greatly expanded. Subtle colors were replaced with bolder, richer tones, making the posters more eye-catching. Color planes were used to delineate the figures, replacing the previous method of outlining figures with dark lines. Hence many of the later posters have a more "painterly" style as opposed to hard line illustration.

While the style and designs of the posters evolved over the years, one aspect of their production remained constant throughout: the extremely high quality of the lithography. Mather exerted complete and careful control over the entire printing process, and no doubt because of this, the posters are truly lithographic gems.

It is a shame that the series had to end as it did in 1929. By that time Mather and his artists had really "gotten it right," but with the Depression in full force, there was no work. Hence there was no need for work incentive posters — and no money for employers to buy them.

Today, either because of the recognition of their outstanding and glorious graphics or simply because of the nostalgia they evoke, more and more collectors have begun to discover these relatively unknown works of art. Dealers are displaying them at shows and in galleries. They have also appeared at poster auctions in the United States and abroad.

Because of this renewed interest and their relative scarcity, prices, while still reasonable for such outstanding graphics, have risen consistently. Ten years ago, some of the best examples of the 1929 series were being sold for $200 each. Dealers today offer them at prices ranging between $800 and $1,200. At a 1993 New York poster auction, two 1929 posters, *Strut Your Stuff* and *A Well Earned Rest*, each sold for $1,100 with buyer's premium.

Retail prices on posters from earlier years vary. The 1927 series with their exotic tapestried matting range in price between $575 and $750. The posters of 1923–25, difficult to find today, range in price between $375 and $725.

In recent years, finding mint examples of these posters has become exceedingly difficult. Many, of course, were lost or destroyed. Those remaining will most likely have small tears or minor paper losses in the borders, due to the way in which they were initially used, handled, or stored. Many can still be found in A/B condition, but because so many are found in this condition, it has a negligible impact on their value. The higher prices in each category depend mainly on the quality of the design.

If present trends are any indication, demand for the Mather posters will continue to grow over the years. With supply limited, heightened collector interest will also cause prices to rise. It is the lucky collector who bought these posters inexpensively years ago. It is the sophisticated collector who will be buying them now and in the future.

MATHER WORK INCENTIVE POSTERS— PRICE LISTINGS

❧ **1923**

Excuses Get You Nothing: Know What You're Doing Before You Do It,
1923. Lithograph. A desolate-looking worker sitting on a park bench, a Lincolnesque statue adjacent against a "blueprintlike" background of buildings and trees. Very good condition, on linen, 27½ x 41½ inches. $675–$725

Loyalty Always Inspires Confidence: A Loyal Worker Gets the Preference,
1923. Lithograph. Designed by Robert Beebe. A herculean worker levers a huge rock uphill in front of a mystical glowing cityscape. Very good condition, on linen, 27½ x 41½ inches. $675–$725

There's Only One Way to Become Manager: What Are You Doing to Win Success?, 1923. Lithograph. Designed by Robert Beebe. An obviously successful executive leaning back in his desk chair studying his papers. Very good condition, on linen, 27½ x 41½ inches. $625–$675

🌿 **1924**

All Together Pull: Pull Together When You Want to Win, 1924. Lithograph. T-shirted and shorts-clad members of a tug-of-war team all successfully pulling on a stout rope. Very good condition, on linen, 47½ x 36 inches. $725–$775

One Second Late Will Miss a Train: Unless Your Work Is Right, It's Wrong, 1924. Lithograph. A dapperly dressed man with a scowl on his face looking at his watch as his train pulls out of the station. Very good condition, on linen, 47½ x 36 inches. $725–$775

Why Are You Here? Good Workers Are Always Important, 1924. Lithograph. The boss in wing collar and vest connected by a telephone wire to a variety of workers. Very good condition, on linen, 47½ x 36 inches. $525–$625

🌿 **1925**

Dimes Are the Daddies of Dollars: No Dollars No Payroll, 1925. Lithograph. Overscaled dimes rolling away from a torn money bag. Good condition, on linen, 47½ x 36 inches. $475–$500

Courtesy of Heller and
Heller/Posters at Work.

Courtesy of Heller and
Heller/Posters at Work.

Where Am I? Start Right, You'll Finish Right, 1925. Lithograph. A startled-looking camper viewing a golden sun rising over tall pine trees. Good condition, on linen, 47½ x 36 inches.　　　　　　　　　　　　　$395–$450

❧ **1927**

Both Eyes Wide Open: Today's Effort Counts for You, 1927. Lithograph. Designed by Willard Frederik Elmes. A royal mounted policeman in red coat astride a noble steed, surrounded by a blue-green tapestry-patterned border. Good condition, on linen, 47½ x 36¼ inches.　　　　　　　$850-$975

Say It and Smile: Smiles Chase Grouches, 1927. Lithograph. Designed by Willard Frederik Elmes. A smiling pretty girl in white dress and red tie surrounded by a yellow tapestry-patterned border. Very good condition, on linen, 47½ x 36¼ inches.　　　　　　　　　　　　　$950-$1,025

❧ **1929**

Anything Overlooked? Let's All Help, 1929. Lithograph. Designed by Willard Frederik Elmes. A large red ship hull under construction surrounded by scaffolding and a chance. Fine condition, on linen, 44 x 36 inches.　　$975–$1,100

Diving for Success: Mean It and You'll Make It, 1929. Lithograph. Designed by Willard Frederik Elmes. A dark-skinned diver in orange trunks under green water with yellow fish. Fine condition, on linen, 44 x 36 inches.　　$975–$1,100

He Merely Struts: Ability Needs No Fine Feathers, 1929. Lithograph. Designed by Willard Frederik Elmes. A brilliantly colored peacock with tail feathers extended. Fine condition, on linen, 44 x 36 inches.　　$875–$950

Courtesy of Heller and
Heller/Posters at Work.

"Jumpy": Size It Up—and Keep Cool, 1929. Lithograph. A brightly colored elephant rearing up in the presence of a small mouse. Fine condition, on linen, 44 x 36 inches. $875–$950

Lazy Man's Luck: Shirkers Land No Prizes, 1929. Lithograph. A fisherman's line comes up empty. Very good condition, on linen, 44 x 36 inches. $850-$975

Out in Front: To Get Ahead, Be Ahead, 1929. Lithograph. Golden purple-sided speedboats race on a bright blue sea. Good condition, on linen, 44 x 36 inches. Sold as high as $1,100 at auction. $925–$1,025

Out of the Running: Success Never Waits, 1929. Lithograph. Designed by Frank Beatty. A galloping racehorse with jockey astride, other horses in the background many furloughs ahead. Fine condition, on linen, 44 x 36 inches. $975–$1,100

The Perfect Finish: Only Full Days Make Full Records, 1929. Lithograph. Designed by Frank Beatty. A majestic racing sailboat tacking to the finish, glorious bright colors. Fine condition, on linen, 44 x 36 inches. *See color insert, photo 18.* $975–$1,100

Ready to Spring! When We're Wrong—Let's Say So, 1929. Lithograph. Designed by Willard Frederik Elmes. A gold and brown striped tiger with claws extended, about to pounce from a green/blue/red background. Fine condition, on linen, 44 x 36 inches. $975–$1,100

Courtesy of Heller and Heller/Posters at Work.

Strut Your Stuff: Holding Back Holds You Back, 1929. Lithograph. Designed by Henry Lee, Jr. A colorfully costumed drum major marches proudly. Fine condition, on linen, 44 x 36 inches. Sold as high as $1,100 at auction. $975–$1,100

The Teamworker! For All Is for Yourself, 1929. Lithograph. A black and yellow bumblebee sitting on a stalk of orange-yellow flowers. Fine condition, on linen, 44 x 36 inches. $975–$1,100

Your Best Bet: Poor Results Is Poor Business, 1929. Lithograph. Designed by Willard Frederik Elmes. An industrial harbor scene, with tugboats, railroad train, factory building, crane, and cityscape in earth colors. Fine condition, on linen, 44 x 36 inches. $975–$1,100

❧ CHAPTER 19 ❧
The Political and Propaganda Posters of Ben Shahn (1898–1969)

BY GEORGE DEMBO

George Dembo is president of Gallery 9—The Poster Master, specializing in patriotic, political, and propaganda posters, as well as American turn-of-the-century posters. You can contact him at 215 Main Street, Chatham, New Jersey 07928, (201) 635-6505, fax (201) 635-0212.

Ben Shahn's career as a poster artist began in the 1930s, when, during the Depression, he worked for the Farm Security Agency as a photographer. While at FSA he produced his first poster, *Years of Dust,* an image of a gloomy farmer caught in the ravages of the dust storms that plagued the farm belt in the 1930s. Clearly this poster was influenced by the many dust-bowl photographs taken by Shahn and others at FSA. This poster, along with others he created from 1938 to 1948, were tough, hard-to-look-at images of men: men at work, imprisoned, and impoverished.

These pictures project unusual strength, not only in the depiction of the figures' muscularity, but also in the power of the blunt messages that accompanied the images. "ORGANIZE!" "REGISTER!" "VOTE!" "PEACE!" are strong calls to action, and Shahn's talent in combining text and image is very compelling.

Shahn's working-class origins and his commitment to liberal social and political causes had an impact on his early work. Later, in the 1950s and beyond, his poster commissions were mostly for concerts, exhibitions, and other public events, such as his poster for the Spoleto Festival of 1965, and the opening of Lincoln Center/Philharmonic Hall of 1962. The change in subject matter was accompanied by a change in style. The strong, painterly images of men gave way to linear drawings and designs that were much lighter in feeling, but certainly possessed a beauty all their own.

For the most part the posters of this later era (with a few exceptions) have not received the same kind of attention from collectors the earlier works have. Perhaps these early posters are set apart by his powerfully expressed point of view or their political content. In general, political posters of this vintage have become very collectible as the material becomes scarce. The temporal and ideological distance from the present makes the views expressed and the style of expression look "antique."

In 1942 Shahn worked for the Office of War Information (OWI) in Washington. This organization was the center of political controversy during its entire existence because of strong and verse opinions about what America's official propaganda source should be saying.

As a result the OWI Graphics Division produced far fewer posters than its World War I predecessor, the Division of Pictorial Publicity. Only two of Shahn's designs for OWI were actually printed and distributed. *This Is Nazi Brutality* and *We French Workers Warn You* are perhaps the strongest images in all Shahn's poster work, and certainly among the strongest World War II images anywhere.

By 1944 Shahn had begun to work for the labor union AFL/CIO's Political Action Committee. It was here that his most interesting and most collectible posters were produced. Of these the best-known (and also the rarest) is *For Full Employment After the War*, more commonly known as *The Welders*. Shahn designed this poster while still at OWI, but the inclusion of an African-American welder caused immediate controversy, and it was rejected by the government. The controversy continued even after it was published. Shahn's liberalism expressed in his posters often provoked reaction, which is, after all, the true purpose of a poster.

Another of his significant works is *A Good Man Is Hard to Find*, produced for the 1948 presidential election in which Shahn supported the

Courtesy of The
Poster Master.

From the author's collection. Photo by Robert Four.

candidacy of Henry Wallace against Dewey and Truman. Borrowing from a 1948 *Life* magazine photo of Truman seated at the piano with Lauren Bacall sitting atop it, Shahn drew Truman at the piano with Dewey sprawled on top. On the music rack of the piano are several sheets, one of which is titled *A Good Man Is Hard to Find*.

One of the last political posters Shahn designed was for Eugene McCarthy's 1968 bid for the presidency. A simple design combining a dove with only the words "McCarthy" at the top, and "Peace" at the bottom, create a strong and effective message.

Prices for posters by Shahn range from lows of $50–$100 for minor exhibition and concert images printed in large quantities, to $5,000 and more for his best early political works. His two war posters were printed in large editions and are readily available from dealers. They range in price from $350–$750 or so, depending on condition. Both of these posters, like so many other World War II posters, were folded as they came off the press, so in most cases, fold marks will show. There may also be wear at the fold intersections, depending on how many times the poster has been unfolded and refolded.

At the high end of Shahn's price range are his political posters of the 1940s, with *The Welders* at the top of the list. Because of its powerful image, which includes the rare figure of an African-American, and the scarcity of this poster, recent sales have been in the $4,000–$5,500 range. A close second, in some cases even running ahead of *The Welders*, is *A Good Man Is Hard to Find*. One example, in good condition, sold for $4,620 at auction in 1988.

Shahn's other strong political pieces of the 1940s range between $1,200 and $2,000, depending on the image and condition. These are also more readily available than the two mentioned above. However, they are just as collectible and in time will increase in value as have other works by Shahn as more collectors come to appreciate this outstanding American artist. To explore Shahn's work further, consult the references listed in the Bibliography.

CHAPTER 20

The Posters of David Lance Goines

David Lance Goines (b. 1945) is an artist, calligrapher, and printer of fine books who lives in Berkeley, California, where he heads the Saint Heironymous Press.

Goines is a poster maker in the traditional sense: His clients come to him with commissions for posters—to announce events or publicize a business or product by a publicly posted notice. His ability to combine the commercial concerns of the client with his own uncompromised aesthetic integrity has created a true modern revival of the medium of fine poster art.

In the interview preface to the book *Goines Posters* (Alphabet Press, 1985), Goines stated that he "consciously emulated the work of those artists whom I admire, most notably Ludwig Hohlwein, Charles Rennie Mackintosh, Hans Rudi Erdt, Albrecht Durer, Hokusai and Hisoshige."

Perhaps Goines was referring to the German artists Hohlwein's and Erdt's flat color fields and simplified design; the refined ornamentation of Mackintosh's Glascow School; Durer's attention to detail; and the delicate openness of Japanese prints. Whatever the influences may have been, Goines has developed his own unique style.

At the time of the interview, Goines generally hand-signed 326 posters in addition to the print run requested by the client: three hundred numbered 1–300, and twenty-six lettered A-Z as artist's proofs. In certain cases, fewer than three hundred were hand-signed, and those posters tend to be more expensive today. Currently, Goines signs only one hundred or fewer of each image.

It is these signed posters that have become collectible and highly valued in the poster market. Those collectors who want to be assured of receiving a hand-signed copy of each poster at the price of issue subscribe to his series through the gallery of Thackery & Robertson in San Francisco, which has exclusively represented the artist since 1972.

His most popular series of posters is for the restaurant Chez Panisse, for whom he has created more than fifteen posters, from the first in 1972 up to their twentieth anniversary in 1991. Some of his posters are so popular, they have had more than one edition. However, with very few exceptions, no editions other than the first are hand-signed.

Many of his signed posters have appreciated considerably in value as their availability has diminished. Signed copies of several of his earliest posters, from 1968 to 1973, are no longer available directly, and some have begun to appear on the secondary market. Those that are still available from this early period can range in price as high as $2,500 for a signed first edition.

With only a few exceptions, signed posters from 1976 to 1991 are available for less than $450, and with only one exception, from 1982 onward, examples of his can be purchased for less than $250. The majority of unsigned posters, though identical to the higher-priced counterparts in all other respects, can often be bought for under $100. However, a few posters are so hard to obtain that even the unsigned version can bring $500 or more.

The technical excellence with which Goines executes his posters is an inherent part of their appeal. Unlike most contemporary poster makers, who send their designs to commercial printers to be mechanically processed, Goines does all the production work himself. The only exception he makes is for posters that include gold foil stamping, which is done by a colleague at another firm.

His use of photo-offset lithography is also unique. For his color posters, instead of the usual four-color separation process of modern offset printing, which results in an overall dot pattern, Goines makes separate solid-tone plates for each color he uses, ranging in number from four to as many as twenty. The colors created in this often painstaking manner are extraordinarily subtle and complex. Goines's use of this solid-color offset lithography process is entirely personal, and involves as high a degree of craftsmanship as any of the more traditional methods of fine printmaking.

Some time ago, in response to some evidence of pirating, Goines licensed Portal Productions to reproduce a certain number of his posters. These are printed by four-color-process photo-offset, and therefore have the dot pattern on close inspection, allowing a collector to easily distinguish them from the originals (see the chapters on Poster Printing and Terminology and Fakes, Forgeries and Reproductions).

Since his first one-man exhibition in 1973 at Thackrey & Robertson gallery (then called The Poster), Goines has had numerous one-man shows, including major retrospectives at the Achenbach Foundation for Graphic Arts at the Fine Arts Museum of San Francisco in 1976–77, and the University Art Museum at the University of California, Berkeley, in 1977.

His posters have also been included in notable exhibitions such as "Images of an Era: The American Poster 1945–75." The Smithsonian Institution organized the exhibit, which opened at the Corcoran Gallery of Art in Washington, D.C., and traveled throughout the United States and Europe. Goines's work was also featured in "The Modern American Poster," an exhibition organized by the Museum of Modern Art, New York, which traveled to the National Museums of Modern Art in both Kyoto and Tokyo in 1983–84.

His posters are a part of many museum collections, including the Achenbach Foundation for the Graphic Arts, the Fine Arts Museum of San Francisco, which owns a complete set of the posters; the Metropolitan Museum of Art, New York; the Museum of Modern Art, New York; the Musée des Arts Décoratifs, Paris; the Smithsonian Institute, Washington, D.C.; and the Victoria and Albert Museum, London.

David Lance Goines is today one of America's preeminent poster artists and will undoubtedly be among those artists sought after by poster collectors in the next millennium.

Special thanks to Sean Thackrey and Sally Robertson of Thackrey & Robertson gallery for providing the basis of information for this chapter.

DAVID LANCE GOINES—PRICE LISTINGS
(IN ALPHABETICAL ORDER)

NOTE: The price listings that follow are current prices for David Lance Goines's posters that are signed by the artist, unless otherwise noted, and available through Thackrey & Robertson in San Francisco (see resource guide). The reference number refers to the artist's own cataloging of his work, with 148 posters cataloged from 1968 to 1991. Numbers 1–116 are pictured in full color in Goines Posters (Alphabet Press, 1985) (see Bibliography).

Bach, 1973 (Goines #26). For Bach concerts using medieval representations of the gospels. Five colors, first edition, 250 posters printed, hand-signed edition of 25. Mint, 18 x 24 inches. **$2,500**

As above, unsigned. **$500**

Bookshop, Santa Cruz, 1976 (Goines #59). Wine bottle and glass against an architectural background. Six colors, 2,517 posters printed, hand-signed and numbered edition of 200, with 26 artist's proofs, A-Z. Mint, 18 x 24 inches. **$150**

Bordeaux, 1987 (Goines #128). Wooden door with a lantern in front. Thirteen colors, 2,616 posters printed, hand-signed and numbered edition of 300, with 26 artist's proofs. Mint, 18 x 24 inches. $150

By Hand, 1974 (Goines #44). Advertisement for handmade clothing store. Five colors, first edition, 2,398 posters printed, hand-signed and numbered edition of 100, with 26 artist's proofs. Mint, 18 x 24 inches. $500

Chez Panisse, 1972 (Goines #14). The first of several posters for the restaurant, with a redheaded woman with feathered hat holding an aperitif. Four colors, first edition, 1,000 posters printed, hand-signed edition of 100. Mint, 15 x 24 inches. $1,500

Chez Panisse 4th Birthday, 1975 (Goines #49). A vase of Mackintosh-styled flowers. Nine colors, 834 posters printed, hand-signed and numbered edition of 100, with 26 artist's proofs A-Z. Mint, 18 x 24 inches. $1,500

Chez Panisse Sixteenth Birthday, 1987 (Goines #129). Eight colors, 1,416 posters printed, hand-signed and numbered edition of 300, with 26 artist's proofs, A-Z. Mint, 17½ x 24 inches. $150

Cody's Books, 1983 (Goines #101). Woman holding a book with olive tree behind. Eleven colors, 2,350 posters printed, hand-signed and numbered edition of 300, with 26 artist's proofs. Mint, 17½ x 24 inches. $250

A Constructed Roman Alphabet, 1979 (Goines #85). Two colors, 1,873 posters printed, hand-signed and numbered edition of 300, with 26 artist's proofs. Mint, 18 x 24 inches. $250

Domus, 1984 (Goines #109). Anniversary poster for this carpet center. Eleven colors, 2,015 posters printed, hand-signed and numbered edition of 300, with 26 artist's proofs. Mint, 18 x 24 inches. $150

Dow and Frosini, 1979 (Goines #82). Advertisement for framing with a woman entwined with floral setting. Thirteen colors, 4,305 posters printed, hand-signed and numbered edition of 300, with 26 artist's proofs. Mint, 18 x 24 inches. $100

Eastman House (Pink), 1972 (Goines #21). Poster for a film festival from the archives of the Eastman House. Four colors, 100 posters printed, hand-signed edition of 16. Mint, 18 x 24 inches. $1,500

Eat, Chez Panisse 9th Birthday, 1980 (Goines #89). Lilies and a woman's lips. Twelve colors, 1,990 posters printed, hand-signed and numbered edition of 300, with 26 artist's proofs. Mint, 16⅞ x 24 inches. $1,200

Guinness, 1973 (Goines #25). A bottle of Guinness is wedged between halves of a loaf of bread. Seven colors, 206 posters printed, hand-signed edition of 100. Mint, 18 x 24 inches. $1,500

Courtesy of
Thomas G. Boss
Fine Books.

Hubbard Keyboard Instruments, 1982 (Goines #100). Eighteenth-century couple in costume starts to dance. Thirteen colors, 3,870 posters printed, hand-signed and numbered edition of 300, with 26 artist's proofs. Mint, 18 x 24 inches.
$150

New York, 1984 (Goines #112). View of a gentleman's midsection holding his timepiece, for a special exhibition at Poster America. Nineteen colors, 2,967 posters printed, hand-signed and numbered edition of 300, with 26 artist's proofs. Mint, 16⅛ x 24 inches.
$250

Northface, 1980 (Goines #90). Beautiful scene looking up from a mountain valley as an ad for outdoor equipment. Thirteen colors, 3,330 posters printed, hand-signed and numbered edition of 300, with 26 artist's proofs. Mint, 16⅞ x 24 inches.
$400

Oakland Symphony, 1983 (Goines #103). Violin with acorns and a rainbow for strings. Twelve colors, 1,600 posters printed, hand-signed and numbered edition of 300, with 26 artist's proofs. Mint, 17½ x 24 inches.
$400

Parsifal, 1983 (Goines #102). For a film by Francis Ford Coppola based on the Wagner opera. Eight colors, 2,965 posters printed, hand-signed and numbered edition of 300, with 26 artist's proofs. Mint, 16¾ x 24 inches.
$150

The Poster, Santa Barbara, 1974 (Goines #36). Design of wings in a Frank Lloyd Wright-style. Nine colors, first edition, 482 posters printed, hand-signed edition of 100. Mint, 12¼ x 24 inches.
$600

Courtesy of
Thomas G. Boss
Fine Books.

Courtesy of
Thomas G. Boss
Fine Books.

San Francisco Symphony, 1975 (Goines #55). An ear evolves out of a conch shell. Seven colors, first edition, 634 posters printed with the type "Marathon 1976," hand-signed and numbered edition of 100, with 26 artist's proofs. Mint, 15¼ x 24 inches. **$450**

Twelve (Chez Panisse twelfth birthday), 1983 (Goines #104). Decorative coffeepot in floral setting. Twelve colors, 1,600 posters printed, hand-signed and numbered edition of 300, with 26 artist's proofs. Mint, 17½ x 24 inches. **$150**

Wings, 1980 (Goines #87). Ad for a showing of the first Academy Award Best Picture (1927–28), showing a black bird landing. Four colors, 2,754 posters printed, hand-signed and numbered edition of 300, with 26 artist's proofs. Mint, 16⅝ x 24 inches. **$100**

⚜ CHAPTER 21 ⚜
Mobil Oil Posters

In recent years, many fine poster series have been created by large corporations that commissioned leading artists. As you have probably noted in other chapters in this volume, the same process took place in many countries during past eras. Commercial poster patrons, such as PKZ department store in Switzerland, Shell Oil in England, Delft Salad Oil in Holland, E. & A. Mele department store in Italy, and numerous others have been vital to keeping the art of the poster alive over the last century.

Mobil Corporation's sponsorship of the "Mobil Masterpiece Theatre" series on PBS television, as well as other programs, gave rise to the creation of a series of outstanding lithographic poster designs. Today Mobil is recognized as one of the most important commercial patrons of the poster.

Unlike posters from other contemporary publishers, the "Mobil Masterpiece Theatre" posters are not available directly from the publisher, and many are eagerly sought after by collectors on the secondary market.

Arthur Bernberg of Graphic Expectations in Chicago, which specializes in posters of the performing arts, has assembled a large and impressive collection of these posters, produced primarily in two sizes: 30 x 46 inches and 48 x 68 inches.

Generally, the smaller posters in the series are more affordable, with most ranging in price from $50 to about $300, although some rarer outstanding designs in this size can bring as much as $500–$700. While some of the larger posters are still available for under $500, many titles range all the way up to more than $2,000 for two sought-after posters by Paul Davis.

Besides Davis, numerous other outstanding contemporary artists have created posters for Mobil, including Seymour Chwast, Ivan Chermayeff, Edward Gorey, Chuck Wilkinson, and others whose names will become increasingly familiar to poster collectors as time goes on. These artists have also left their mark by creating posters for other contemporary clients and publishers.

Paul Davis, for example, is well-known for his posters for New York theatrical productions, such as *Three Penny Opera* (1976) and *The Cherry Orchard* (1978) for Lincoln Center; and the Broadway musical *For*

Colored Girls Who Have Considered Suicide When the Rainbow is Enuff (1977).

Seymour Chwast is the founder and president of The Pushpin Group, a graphic design firm in New York that creates posters, packaging, and other commercial design for numerous clients (see resource guide). In addition to designing posters for Mobil, Chwast has created posters for the New York City Opera, *Forbes* magazine, the Cannes Film Festival, and others.

In the price listings that follow we present a small cross section of these fine posters which will appeal not only to collectors of contemporary graphic design but to those who were moved by any one of the numerous television programs that were "made possible by a grant from Mobil."

Collectors who are interested in contemporary design should look through the pages of contemporary publications such as *Communication Arts*, *Publicité*, and *Advertising Art* to familiarize themselves with the current graphic arts scene.

Today's patrons of outstanding design include opera, symphony, and ballet companies, fairs and festivals such as the Spoleto Festival in Charleston, government agencies, museums, visual design publications, the travel industry, and other large corporations.

It has been only a little over one hundred years since the advent of the illustrated advertising poster. One hundred years from now, future collectors will look back on our era as a particularly fertile time of poster production.

"MOBIL MASTERPIECE THEATRE"—PRICE LISTINGS

❦ IVAN CHERMAYEFF

> NOTE: Mr. Chermayeff graduated from Yale University. He is a partner in a very successful graphic design firm and the recipient of numerous awards for his work. He also has designed posters for the School of Visual Arts in New York City, where he has taught.

Lillie, 1979. Lithograph. Printed by Todd Edelman Budelli & Associates. A popular "Masterpiece Theatre" production shown in many encore seasons. In blues, purples, and turquoise. A good example of both the artist and the series. Mint condition, 30 x 46 inches. $225–$275

❦ SEYMOUR CHWAST (b. 1931)

> NOTE: Mr. Chwast is a founder of Pushpin Studios and a designer and illustrator of many children's books. He is the winner of many awards including AIGA gold medal.

The Charmer. Lithograph. Gentleman in his sports car is being pursued by ladies. Fine condition, 30 x 46 inches. $200–$250

Charters and Caldicott, 1986. Lithograph. Printed by Todd Edelman Budelli & Associates. In black and pink with blue accents against a white background; type in gray and mauve. A very good example of the artist's work. Fine condition, 48 x 68 inches. $1,200–$1,300

Doug Henning: Houdini Water Torture Escape. Lithograph. The magician is shown in the torture tank with miniature assistants at its side. Very good condition, 30 x 46 inches. $725–$775

I, Claudius, 1977. Lithograph. A highly recognizable poster from one of the most popular "Masterpiece Theatre" productions, done in a mosaic tile style. In green, blue, red, and gold against white background. Mint condition, 30 x 46 inches. $350–$400

Nicholas Nickleby. Lithograph. Cast of characters on a ladder situated on Nicholas Nickleby's shoulders. Fine condition, 30 x 46 inches. $250–$300

Poirot. Lithograph. A stylized illustration of Agatha Christie's famous sleuth, with his face forming the second *o* in his name. Fine condition, 30 x 46 inches. $200–$250

Song by Song. Lithograph. For the monthly musical series on great American lyricists. Dance pair sing and dance across a piano keyboard. Fine condition, 30 x 46 inches. $350–$400

Courtesy of Graphic Expectations.

Star Quality. Lithograph. Stories of Noel Coward with him seated in an armchair. Fine condition, 30 x 46 inches. $200–$250

🌿 PAUL DAVIS

> *NOTE: Mr. Davis heads his own New York design company. His illustrations can be found on posters, book and album covers, and magazines. He is the winner of many awards, and is also well- known for his Broadway posters.*

The Adventures of Sherlock Holmes, 1985. Lithograph printed by Todd Edleman Budelli & Associates. The illustration is so accurately detailed as to sometimes cause the observer to think he is looking at a color photograph. Highly desirable. Fine condition, 48 x 68 inches. $2,250–$2,500

King Lear, 1984. Lithograph. Printed by Todd Edelman Budelli & Associates. In blue, gold, and white. An excellent example of Davis's design. Fine condition, 48 x 68 inches. $2,250–$2,500

🌿 PHILIP GIPS

> *NOTE: A graduate of Yale University, Mr. Gips is the winner of many awards.*

Testament of Youth, 1980. Lithograph. In various blues, black, red, and white. Mint condition, 30 x 46 inches. $175–$200

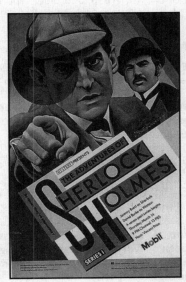

Poster by Paul
Davis. Courtesy
of Graphic
Expectations.

❦ EDWARD GOREY

> NOTE: A winner of a Tony Award for his work on the Broadway production of Dracula, Mr. Gorey is also the author of many books and has done numerous illustrations for theater and dance companies.

Dr. Jekyll and Mr. Hyde, 1981. Lithograph. A very captivating Jekyll and Hyde. In red, black, and white. A good example of the artist's unmistakable style. Mint condition, 30 x 46 inches. $300–$350

❦ BARBARA SANDLER

> NOTE: Ms. Sandler studied painting at the Art Students League in New York. She maintains a dual career as a serious painter and an illustrator.

Sergeant Cribb, 1980. Lithograph. A stunning poster in many colors from one of the most popular series featured under "Mystery! Presents." Mint condition, 30 x 46 inches. $225–$250

❦ DANIEL SCHWARTZ

> NOTE: Mr. Schwartz studied at the Art Students League and the Rhode Island School of Design. He has won the Society of Illustrators Gold Medal ten times.

A Town Like Alice, 1981. Lithograph. Printed by Todd Edelman Budelli & Associates, signed in the block. A multicolor illustration of the main characters against a field of brown, green, and blue; type is in gray. A fine example of the artist's work. Mint condition, 30 x 46 inches. $175–$200

❦ NORMAN WALKER

> NOTE: Mr. Walker, a graduate of Art Center College of Design in Los Angeles, has done illustrations for many major magazines.

Quiet as a Nun, 1982. Lithograph. Another key illustration for a popular "Mystery! Presents" series. Mainly in black, brown, and burnt orange. Fine condition, 48 x 68 inches. $750–$800

❦ CHUCK WILKINSON

> NOTE: Mr. Wilkinson is from Detroit and has won many awards for illustration.

Love for Lydia, 1979. Lithograph. This poster for "Masterpiece Theatre" 1979–80 has been a favorite in the graphic design community and among collectors. In purple, mauves, and yellows. Excellent example of the series. Fine condition, 48 x 68 inches. $875–$975

Poster by Daniel Schwartz.
Courtesy of Graphic
Expectations.

Thérèse Raquin, 1981. Lithograph. Printed by Todd Edelman Budelli &
Associates. For a multipart "Masterpiece Theatre" based on Emile Zola's novel.
Another favorite of collectors. In dark purples and mauves with copper skin
tones. Mint condition, 30 x 46 inches. $225–$275

Same as above, fine condition, 48 x 68 inches. $750–$850

PART FOUR

World War, World Travel, and World Games

❦ CHAPTER 22 ❦
World War Posters

BY MARY ELLEN MEEHAN

Mary Ellen (Mel) Meehan and her brother, Jim, own Meehan Military Posters, New York, the only poster dealership devoted solely to World War I, World War II, and Spanish Civil War posters. They publish two full-color catalogs annually, illustrating and annotating more than five hundred posters from around the world. Catalogs, $10 each postpaid. Contact Meehan Military Posters, Box 477 Gracie Station, New York, New York 10028, (212) 734-5683, fax (212) 535-4249.

SURVEY

Posters for commerce and theater were already a vibrant part of popular culture when World War I erupted in 1914. Unlike posters for products and entertainment, war posters were about survival. They roused the most basic passions and engaged the most talented artists. Great war posters magnified the power of the image while limiting the accompanying text. A high level of literacy was not required to appreciate them, intense commitment to a cause was.

All combatants in both world wars turned to posters to shape and manipulate popular opinion. Alfred Leete's 1915 recruiting poster *Britons — Lord Kitchener Wants You*, which featured a stern Lord Kitchener pointing at the viewer, was crucial to raising an entire army to replace the army decimated in the first year of the war.

Although most war posters were printed by their respective governments, private companies also contributed images as a public service. Thanks to mass production, and government and private distribution networks, war posters were everywhere, burning urgent demands for men and money into the conscience of the viewer.

American poster artists, who donated their time in World War I and worked for scale wages in World War II, were often famous magazine and advertising illustrators. Charles Dana Gibson, creator of the seduc-

229

tive Gibson girl, headed the Division of Pictorial Publicity during World War I. He enlisted his pals, the most eminent illustrators of the day, Howard Chandler Christy, James Montgomery Flagg, and Joseph Leyendecker, among others, to design war posters.

This group met on a weekly basis to divvy up poster assignments, then adjourned to Keene's Chop House or the Salmagundi Club in New York to toast one another. The fervor of these meetings is legendary. The Office of War information, responsible for many World War II poster designs, was considerably more sedate. Ben Shahn and Norman Rockwell were among the celebrated artists who produced memorable posters.

War taxed the entire society, not just the combatants. Recruiting posters are only a part of the vast array of subjects tackled by poster artists throughout both wars.

Posters helped to regulate aspects of everyday life that had not played a part in war before. War required money, increased production of war material, and food and fuel conservation. A new phase was even coined to describe this domestic battleground: the "home front."

Posters designed to sell war bonds dominate the poster production of all countries involved. These posters often featured soldiers enduring harrowing combat conditions. Unlike the soldiers, civilian viewers were asked only to invest money in interest-bearing government loans.

Industrial Production was another major subject. Powerful images reminded factory workers that they were "soldiers of production." Conservation was another important theme. The need to cut back on consumption of sugar, fats, and meat so that they could be shipped to the front inspired several sumptuous World War I images. Posters advocating home canning, victory gardens, carpooling, and lowering thermostats were popular in World War II.

Espionage posters flourished after Pearl Harbor. *A Slip of the Lip Might Sink a Ship* has become a talisman of the war. World War II posters incorporated advanced graphic design and photomontage developed in the 1930s. These stylistic and technical changes did not alter the role of the poster, which once again became an effective government tool for marshaling public and private support for the war.

COLLECTING TRENDS

The market for military posters has long been dominated by museums and collectors, and thus avoided the recent recession produced by speculators in the general art market.

Images of fine artistic merit produced during the war are startlingly appropriate to the late twentieth century. Bond brokers respond to patriotic bond posters. Production posters attract manufacturers. Companies with secrets to keep collect espionage posters. Modern scrap dealers display wartime recycling posters. The need to eat proper food is timeless; food and fuel conservation posters now decorate kitchens and dining rooms.

The appearance of excellent new books, notably Paret, Lewis, and Paret's *Persuasive Images* and Nelson's *The Posters that Won the War* (see Bibliography), has broadened the general market for military posters.

The high artistic quality of World War I posters has always attracted a strong following. The fiftieth anniversary of World War II has prompted museum exhibitions and TV specials that keep us aware of our part in the struggle we couldn't afford to lose. This exposure has further increased the demand for World War II posters. As the collecting base for both World War I and World War II posters broadens, top-quality posters are becoming markedly harder to find.

Many collectors focus on the work of specific artists. The former line between poster artist and fine artist has been all but eliminated, echoing James Montgomery Flagg's assertion, "The only difference between a fine artist and an illustrator is the latter can draw, eats three square meals a day, and can afford to pay for them."

The tendency to examine the past through posters is now especially evident in the reunited Germany. World War I German posters are among the most artistically sophisticated images, and are eagerly sought by museums and collectors.

The 1989 fall of communism has also affected the market for Russian military posters. A few much-prized czarist posters appeared on the European market recently, although they are still very rare. How a "politically incorrect" Russian poster survived over seventy years is still a mystery. World War II posters have also begun to trickle out of the former Soviet Union, illustrating in graphic, if not to say grisly, detail Soviet Russia's preeminent role in defeating Germany.

World War I posters that would command high prices and attention if they could be found include Leete's previously mentioned British recruiting poster. James Montgomery Flagg's renowned *I Want You* was based on the Leete prototype. Posters pertaining to the 1915 Turkish victory in Gallipoli are virtually impossible to find and highly sought after. Posters featuring World War I aviation of all countries are also very much in demand.

In the United States, Fred Spear's *Enlist* is one of the rarest and most expensive World War I posters. Issued in 1915 by the Boston Committee of Public Safety to draw attention to the sinking of the luxury liner *Lusitania* by a German U-boat, the poster illustrates a mother and child slowly sinking to the bottom of the sea. This powerful poster caused riots when it appeared on the streets of Boston.

Serious World War II collectors often concentrate on recruiting posters from the elite units of the world's armies. Posters featuring marines, rangers, aviators, paratroopers, submarines, and armored units are particularly prized.

Highlighted by current social issues, American reexaminations of the positions of women and blacks in society have focused new attention on posters that reflect their contributions. Posters documenting the sacrifices and successes of individual black soldiers (e.g., the Congressional Medal of Honor winner Dorie Miller) are in demand. The part played by women in winning both wars has been belatedly recognized. Their service in industry, medicine, business, conservation, and the armed services is the subject of many increasingly popular posters from both world wars.

Many war posters are collected not just for their striking images but for their conjunction with Pearl Harbor—the Blitz in Britain, the Bataan Death March, Iwo Jima, and D day are typically popular subjects.

The opening of new Holocaust museums in Washington, New York, and several other cities has focused attention on Europe's dark past and its legacy of ethnic hatred. *Der Ewige Jude* (The Eternal Jew), issued for the infamous degenerate art exhibition organized by the Nazis in 1937, recently sold for a record price. Anti-Semitic posters are very scarce.

All Nazi posters were ordered destroyed as part of the de-Nazification program imposed by the Allies at the end of World War II. The high prices realized by Nazi and anti-Semitic posters today reflect not only this scarcity but the important role of the poster in sanctioning the bigoted attitudes that led to the Holocaust.

In spite of very high prices for rare war posters, generally military posters are still very affordable, and within the reach of any beginning poster collector. There are still many super images in the $100 to $200 range, including Norman Rockwell's famous *Four Freedoms* series.

Military posters are time capsules of historical events that shaped our world. Men joined the service and risked their lives in response to posters. Citizens in Nazi-occupied countries were executed for defacing or removing German posters. It is hard to overestimate the importance of posters produced in response to war. Military posters have survived the flames of the world wars, albeit in small numbers, survived the plethora of newer images, and have taken their place in the artistic mainstream of the twentieth century.

OUTSTANDING ARTISTS: WORLD WAR I

Great Britain

Frank Brangwyn (1867–1956) was a student of the nineteenth-century artist William Morris, a pioneer of the Arts and Crafts movement. Morris wanted to restore a handmade quality to art and furniture in a world saturated with paintings that looked like photographs, and "cookie cutter" furniture produced by factories. Brangwyn followed Morris's lead, designing individualistic posters highly charged with a personal sense of outrage. He documented German atrocities with the emotional intensity of an on-the-spot sketch.

His famed *At Neuve Chapelle* (1917) shows an artillery gun crew in action (see photo in the price listings). While the actual battle of Neuve Chapelle was a minor Canadian victory, Brangwyn's detailed and sympathetic rendering presented it as a universal example of the desperation and courage of men under fire. Curiously, Brangwyn's posters, including some of his war images, were featured in a wartime issue of the German poster magazine *Das Plakat*, a signal honor for an enemy artist.

Gerald Spencer Pryse (1881–1956) studied in London and Paris, becoming adept at watercolors, lithography, and poster design. His superb military posters sprang from his own extensive experience on the battlefield. Pryse won both the Military Cross and the Croix de Guerre for bravery. The artist put a high premium on a sense of immediacy, so much so that his military posters were drawn directly on lithographic stones that he carried to the front.

The Only Road for an Englishman (1914) illustrated ordinary British soldiers marching "through darkness to light—through fighting to triumph." The idealistic concept is not glamorized; Tommies are shown marching resolutely through a sad and devastated Belgian city to their rendezvous with the enemy. The image is typical of Pryse's brilliant, richly textured posters testifying to the bleak reality of the battlefield.

France

Abel Faivre (1867–1945) was renowned as an artist and cartoonist before the war. The prolific Faivre designed posters throughout the war for all the French loan drives. One of his most evocative war loan posters, *L'Emprunt Nationale* (1918), shows a vanquished kaiser on bended knee, sword broken, and shoulders slumping under the combined weight of Allied flags massed above him. The tips of the flags burst out of the frame, the faces of the flag bearers are hidden by the swirling flags conveying a sense of unstoppable energy. Faivre shows a dramatic moment—the old order figuratively swept away before our eyes (see photo in the price listings). His originality, sense of color, and refined sense of detail are the hallmarks of a top-quality artist. Faivre, one of the quintessential French war poster artists, was reputedly a great friend of the hedonist Pierre Auguste Renoir.

Maurice Neumont (1868–1930) was an illustrator who trained with the famous Romantic painter Gerome, and was awarded the Legion d'Honneur for his artistic contributions to the war. He organized canteens in Paris for artists and their families as well as designing camouflage for the army and posters. Neumont traveled to the front, risking his life to record battlefield conditions. *On Ne Passe Pas* (They Shall Not Pass), 1918, shows the dreadful battlefield conditions that turned the sleepy country town of Verdun into a fiery hell. Neumont depicts a ragged and tattered poilu so determined to stand his ground, he seems rooted to the earth (see photo in the price listings).

Germany

Hans Rudi Erdt (1883–1918), who worked in Berlin, was one of pre-war Germany's top graphic designers, who sadly died prematurely during the influenza epidemic of 1918. His posters are distinguished by strong spare forms and swirling textural patterns. His *U-Boat Heraus* (The U-Boats Are Out), 1917, for a documentary film about U-Boat warfare, is one of the great posters of the twentieth-century. The deadly action is tightly compressed inside the letter *U*, which also doubles as a cutaway of the sub's steel hull. *U-Boat Heraus* would be one of the most expensive military posters, exceeding $10,000, if it could be found. Another dramatic Erdt design, *Helden a'd Somme* (Heroism on the Somme), 1916, commands almost as high a price. This poster was also designed for a film celebrating a costly German victory. Its rarity and stunning graphics combine to create an immediate impact *(see color insert)*.

Fitz Erler (1868–1940) was a Paris-trained artist and cofounder of the influential German Art Nouveau magazine *Die Jugend*. The German General Staff considered his posters so superior that *Helpt Uns Siegen* (Help Us Win), 1916, was also printed as a postcard distributed to soldiers to send home in demonstration of their fighting spirit. The poster/postcard shows a young soldier gazing across no-man's-land from behind barbed wire. His face expresses a level of serenity that only belief in ultimate victory can inspire (see photo in the price listings). Erler witnessed warfare firsthand and was haunted by visions of soldiers. He wrote of soldiers he had met, "You are always with me, you follow me until your real face becomes plain and you finally take shape as the man with the steel helmet before Verdun."

Ludwig Hohlwein (1874–1949) began his career as an architect and evolved into Germany's most prolific poster artist for both general advertising and military posters. His extensive career spanned both world wars. One of his best-known World War I posters, *Volkspende* (People's Charity), 1918, shows a somber German prisoner of war with a bright red heart glowing over his shoulder. The heart represents the generosity of the German people who still saw him as a hero despite his defeat (see photo in the price listings). This sympathetic treatment of the widespread human misery produced by war is a standard Hohlwein theme. His reputation as a poster artist continues to grow with dealers and auction houses in Europe and America. A major retrospective of Hohlwein posters was organized in 1985 by the prestigious Staatlische Galerie in Stuttgart.

United States

Howard Chandler Christy (1873–1952) was a student of William Merritt Chase. During the Spanish-American war he inveigled an assignment to Cuba as an artist-correspondent for several well-known magazines. In Cuba Christy hooked up with Teddy Roosevelt and his Rough Riders, and formed a lifelong friendship with the future president. Christy's illustrations of actions in Cuba, including the charge at Santiago, made him famous as a military illustrator when World War I began.

However, by 1917 Christy was more interested in the girl the soldier left behind than in the soldier himself. The artist invented the "Christy girl," his ideal woman, and incorporated her into all his war posters. Christy girls managed to be saucy, wholesome, and alluring at the same time—no mean feat in an age more puritanical than our own.

His *Gee! I Wish I Were a Man—I'd Join the Navy!* shows a winsome young woman snapping imaginary suspenders over a borrowed middy. Christy posters have wit and beauty enlivened by bravura brushwork. After the war Christy executed portraits of celebrities and produced a series of admirable murals. His most celebrated mural is *The Signing of the Constitution* (1940), in the Rotunda of the Capitol in Washington. Christy will be a subject of an important new monograph due to appear in 1994.

James Montgomery Flagg (1877–1960) studied in London, Paris, and New York. He was recognized as an artistic prodigy while still in his

teens and had early success both as an artist and an extroverted bon
vivant. He was employed by all the popular illustrated magazines, and
his penchant for publicity made him well-known to millions. It was *I
Want You for U.S. Army* (1917) that catapulted Flagg from fame to
immortality (see photo in the price listings). The image, a self-portrait of
the artist in a patriotic costume of his own design, was so successful that
Flagg stopped going to Keene's Chop House for the weekly meeting of
war poster artists, claiming he was bored with "rising toasts."

Flagg announced he made "friends and enemies lavishly." One of his
best friends was John Barrymore. Flagg's charcoal studies of
Hollywood personalities appeared in *Photoplay* until the 1950s. His
extravagant comments kept his name in the press; he would be a perfect
candidate for the talk show circuit today.

Flagg's most outlandish comments were reserved for modern artists.
He was especially contemptuous of Picasso, and almost equally scornful
of Renoir, Manet, and Cézanne. Flagg's arcane attitudes alienated the
abundantly talented artist from the postwar generation. He died in semi-
obscurity in his early eighties.

OUTSTANDING ARTISTS: WORLD WAR II

Britain

Abram Games (b. 1914) was England's premier poster designer,
known for his abstract monumental subjects, executed with finesse and
exceptionally fine integration of typography and image. He designed
well-regarded posters for Shell, London Transport, and the Post Office.
During World War II the post of "official war artist" was created for
Games. His masterpiece, *Join the ATS* (1941), was infamous during the
war as "the blond bombshell." The poster depicted a volunteer with the
Auxiliary Territorial Service in a seductive design of dramatically lit
interlocking triangles. Despite the abstraction, the figure was considered too sexy to attract the type of volunteer the ATS was seeking. After
considerable debate in Parliament, the poster was withdrawn. In order
to save scarce paper, the rejected poster was pulped and the paper recy-
cled; today it is the rarest of Games's works. Games recently sold his
own copy of this stunning poster at auction in London, where it fetched
a record price. It was Games who commented that the high quality of
wartime poster art was due to the titanic struggle's high purpose: freedom. A comprehensive exhibition of Games's posters has recently circu-
lated at museums throughout England.

Pat Keely (d. 1970) was a gifted British designer who achieved prewar fame for his series of travel posters commissioned for the London

Transport and Southern Railways. His *Wireless War* (ca. 1942) uses circular shapes dizzily bubbling from a radar tower to illustrate the achievements of British scientists in their secret war against Germany. Keely's posters are distinguished by playful shapes, a spare sci-fi quality, and a sprightly palette often at odds with the grim messages of World War II posters.

France

Jean Carlu (b. 1900) abandoned his studies as an architectural student in 1918 when he lost his right arm in an accident. Carlu then took up a successful career as a graphic designer committed to political causes. Some of his best-known posters were designed for the Agency of Graphic Propaganda for Peace. In an ironic turnaround, he came to New York in 1939 as director of the "France at War" exhibition at the French Pavilion in the World's Fair. When the Germans overran France the following spring, Carlu was marooned in New York. He found immediate employment for his talents as a poster designer for the Office of War Information in Washington.

Carlu was a passionate believer in the theory that economic might would win the war. His famed *America's Answer: Production!* (1941) shows a worker's gloved hand tightening a gear formed from the letter *O* of "production." This economical image was voted best poster of the year by the Art Director's Club in 1942. The clever integration of image and typography typifies Carlu's sophisticated graphic style (see photo in the price listings).

Paul Colin (1892–1985) produced posters for theater, dance, and cabarets, scoring a major success in 1925 with his posters for *Revue Nègre*, starring Josephine Baker. Just before the fall of France, Colin designed his striking *Silence* (1940). In this classic espionage poster, a looming spy listens in on a seemingly casual conversation between a soldier and a civilian. To illustrate the dangers of the uncertain world, Colin uses expressionistic color: The innocence of white is paired with the ominous quality of blue-black. After the war Colin produced distinguished travel posters for Air France. His posters have attracted a strong following on both sides of the Atlantic.

Italy

Gino Boccasile (1901–1952) began and ended his career as a commercial poster artist. However, during the war Boccasile used his talents to produce disturbing, often gory, posters for Mussolini's Fascist government. The most infamous Boccasile poster is untitled, but its image of a viciously caricatured black American sergeant carrying off a classical statue with a $2 price tag around its neck is still shocking. Italy had invaded Ethiopia in 1936 and had demonized its black adversaries. The Fascist habit of treating blacks as subhumans carried over into World War II. When Italy switched sides and joined the Allies in 1943, most Fascist posters were destroyed, often by Italians fearing reprisals. Consequently all Italian war posters are extremely rare. A selection of Boccasile's posters was part of a recent major exhibition at the Palazzo Permanente in Milan.

United States

Edward McKnight Kauffer (1890–1979) trained in San Francisco and Chicago. He moved to London in 1914, where he made a name for himself by producing an exceptional series of posters for London Transport and British Petroleum. He returned to the United States in 1940 when things looked particularly dicey for the embattled British, and turned his attention to war posters. His *You Can Set Their Spirit Free*, which dealt with the plight of POWs, is illustrative of his polished technical ability, which came to typify the "modern" style. Kauffer was honored with a one-man exhibition at the Museum of Modern Art in New York in 1937, and another at the Victoria and Albert Museum in London in 1955.

Norman Rockwell (1894–1978), himself an American original, is an icon among American illustrators and the father of the "magic realist" school. His covers for *The Saturday Evening Post* are classics reflecting the idealistic values and joys of everyday American life. His famous World War II posters include *The Four Freedoms* (see photos of two in the price listings) and *Let's Give Him Enough Time*. The latter is an industrial production poster showing a lone GI hunched over his outdated machine gun. Intent on the fight, he's unaware that his ammo is running out, but the viewer, who sees the action from a different perspective, is not. This potent action image was displayed in munitions factories, where workers, so far from the hazards on the front, could see for themselves the life-and-death consequences of giving their defenders enough ammo on time. A major Rockwell retrospective, organized by the Brooklyn Museum, is indicative of the rising stature of the artist who modestly called himself an illustrator.

Jes Schlaijker (b. 1897) was born in Copenhagen and became a naturalized American citizen. He enjoyed a successful career as an advertising illustrator in New York before moving to Washington, where he volunteered his services to the government. As the official United States war artist from 1942 to 1945, Schlaijker produced a magnificent set of posters honoring various branches of the army. His meticulously detailed style is comparable to Rockwell's, but while Rockwell's subjects were humble ordinary people, Schlaijker's figures have been transformed by war into monumental heroes. In Schlaijker's oeuvre, heroic allegory never slips into bombast and perfectly describes the transformation of the boy next door into valorous soldier (see photo in the price listings).

Behn Shahn (1898–1969) was born in Lithuania but moved to New York while still a boy. He is best-known for his social protest graphics of the 1930s. During the war he used his graphic skills and social conscience to alert viewers to the sad fate of people conquered by the Nazis. *This is Nazi Brutality* (1942) is one of Shahn's most celebrated works. The image shows a man abducted from the Czech village of Lidice, near Prague. It was here that a team of British-trained commandos had assassinated Reinhardt Heydrich, the head of the German SS. Shahn's depiction of the manacled Czech hostage, who wears a hood and is seen standing before a brick wall, leaves no doubt that he will be executed momentarily. All men of Lidice over fourteen were shot in reprisal for the Heydrich assassination; the women and children were deported to Germany, never to return. After the war Shahn continued to focus on images that dealt with civil rights. He was one of the most respected and honored graphic artists of the twentieth century (see also the chapter on The Political and Propaganda Posters of Ben Shahn in this volume).

Germany

Otto Anton (1895–1976) achieved fame before the war as a travel poster artist, specializing in posters for the Hamburg-Amerika shipping line. During the war he produced several striking recruiting posters for the SS. One of his most famous designs, *Waffen-SS* (1941), shows the chiseled features of a young man of the approved Aryan type standing underneath a flag bearing the SS runes. The powerful contours of the semiabstract design distinguish it from run-of-the-mill National Socialist posters (see photo in the price listings).

FORECAST FOR FUTURE COLLECTING AND MARKET TRENDS

Military posters are unquestionably among the best bargains of the poster market, which augurs for strong future growth in value. Many good posters are still available for $100 to $200, and an enormous range of posters can still be purchased for under $1,000. Outstanding posters by Howard Chandler Christy, James Montgomery Flagg (including *I Want You for U.S. Army*), and Ludwig Hohlwein are today in the $2,000 range. Magnificent and rare posters, for example, *U-Boat Heraus* by

Hans Rudi Erdt and certain posters by Hohlwein, are around $10,000, with a current top price near $15,000.

Scarce posters of interesting subjects by celebrated artists are in demand as museums take posters off the market on a permanent basis. The Smithsonian Institution in Washington is circulating an exhibition entitled "Produce for Victory—Posters of the American Home Front 1941–45." With a three-year schedule, it will be seen at various museums throughout the country until 1995, and is bound to stimulate the already burgeoning World War II market. World War I posters enjoy a traditionally solid market that is also steadily growing. While not covered here, Spanish Civil War posters have a devoted following, as they are among the most potent images ever produced.

TO FIND OUT MORE ABOUT WAR POSTERS

There are more than seventy museums at military bases in the United States, most with significant collections of World War I and World War II posters. Important collections include the U.S. Military Academy at West Point; the U.S. Naval Academy (Beverly R. Robinson Collection) in Annapolis, Maryland; the War Memorial Museum at Newport News, Virginia; and the University of Texas in Austin. Herbert Hoover was one of the first celebrated Americans to collect World War I posters on a huge scale. His collection is now a part of the Hoover Institute at Stanford University, Palo Alto, California, which has more than 45,000 military posters (see the Resource Guide for listings of some of these museums).

Significant foreign collections include the Canadian War Museum, Ottawa; the Royal Army Museum, London; the Musée de l'Armée, Paris; and the Herresgeschitche Museum, Vienna. Two Australian museums also have outstanding poster collections: the War Memorial Museum in Canberra, and the Maritime Museum in Sydney.

The Imperial War Museum in London deserves special mention. The museum, ironically established in the notorious eighteenth-century British madhouse Bedlam, won an award when it was modernized in 1991 as one of the finest museums in Europe. A great number of military posters enliven its first-class displays. Part of its huge poster collection is also cataloged in the museum's interactive computer and is readily available to museum visitors.

Numerous well-written books on war posters have been published though some are out of print, such as Walton Rawls's *Wake Up, America!—World War I and the American Poster*. A classic in the field, it is the authoritative book on World War I posters. In the World War I price listings that follow, references are made to this book, as well as to Remy Paillard's *Affiches 14–18*, which documents more than four hundred World War I posters, mainly French.

Two excellent new books appeared in 1992, both lavishly illustrated and informative: Paret, Lewis, and Paret's *Persuasive Image — Posters of War and Revolution*, and Derek Nelson's *The Posters That Won the War — The Production, Recruitment and War Bond Posters of WWII*. In the World War II price listings that follow, some references are made to the latter. Additional reference works on war posters are listed in the Bibliography.

WORLD WAR POSTERS—PRICE LISTINGS

Note: See the chapter Important Notes on the Price Listings for more information on the prices given. Also note that most World War I posters are lithographic, and most World War II posters are offset-printed. Some artists produced posters for both wars. Reference numbers following the titles of some of the entries refer to Walton Rawls's Wake Up, America—World War I and the American Poster, *Remy Paillard's* Affiches 14–18, *and Derek Nelson's* The Posters that Won the War—The Production, Recruitment and War Bond Posters of WWII.

WORLD WAR I

✺ **ANONYMOUS**

American Fund for French Wounded. Nurses shown stacking supplies from the Red Cross, Very good, linen-mounted, 33 x 39 inches. $450–$500

An Appeal To You. A British soldier stands signaling for the viewer to join in the ranks. Very good, linen-mounted, 25 x 39 inches. $200–$225

Back Him Up! A mud-spattered Canadian infantryman faces incoming explosions. Fine, linen-mounted, 25 x 39 inches. $225–$275

The Best Money Box, War Savings. A stamp booklet rests near a globe, encouraging British to save money. Mint, 20 x 25 inches. $80–$125

Bring Him Home. Triumphant Canadian veteran waits on sea wall for funds to put him on troopship home. Fine condition, linen-mounted, 25 x 36 inches.
$350–$400

Britain Needs You at Once. Saint George on his steed, killing the kaiser's wicked dragon. Very good, linen-mounted, 20 x 30 inches. $425–$475

Courtesy of Meehan Military Posters.

The Call To Duty, Join the Army, 1917. Bugler sounds the call to arms from mountaintop with flag. Fine, linen-mounted, 30 x 40 inches. $285–$350

Canada War Savings Stamps Help Pay for the War, 1919. Wounded Canadian illustrates $5 stamp. Fine, 21 x 27 inches. $85–$125

Come into the Ranks . . . You Are Wanted at the Front. Male civilians watch recruits parading alongside the Union Jack. Very good, 25 x 39 inches.
$185–$225

Engineers Blaze the Trail for Education!, 1919. Recruitment of engineers, showing them with tools and rifles, standing tall. Mint, 18 x 23 inches.
$145–$175

Faith in Canada. A treasure chest of gold is used to promote the purchasing of bonds with cash. Fine, 24 x 36 inches. $275–$325

Finish the Job!, 1918. Ship sets sail from New York harbor. Mint, 21 x 11 inches. $85–$125

Four Reasons for Buying Victory Bonds. Four images of the leaders of the Central Powers explain the need for Canadian bonds. Fine, linen-mounted, 20 x 30 inches. $250–$300

The Glad Hand To the "Big First," 1919. Issued to honor the First Division's welcome-home parade in New York City. Fine, linen-mounted, 17 x 27 inches.
$275–$325

Going, Going, GONE, 1918 (Rawls #176). A large red arrow points out job opportunities in Signal Corps's Aviation Section. Very good, linen-mounted, 30 x 38 inches. $750–$800

He Did His Duty, Are You Doing Yours? Portrait of Lord Roberts from the Boer Wars as British recruiter. Fine, 20 x 25 inches. $175–$200

He Is Getting Our Country's Signal. U.S. sailor in his whites signals to the viewer to join the fleet. Mint, 20 x 30 inches. $325–$375

Help! Your American Red Cross. Heroic nurse accompanying wounded Yank to ambulance amidst explosions. Fine, linen-mounted, 30 x 46 inches.
                                                                                                                    $185–$225

Join the Air Service (Rawls #174). Curtiss Jennys and paratrooper encircle the American Air Service's brand-new logo. Fine, linen-mounted, 20 x 30 inches.
                                                                                                            $1,500–$1,600

Join the Irish Canadian Rangers. Poster of soldier waving shamrocks. Fine, linen-mounted; 28 x 41 inches. $375–$425

Learn to Make and Test the Big Guns, 1919. Railway guns are tested at the Aberdeen Proving Grounds. Fine, 25 x 19 inches. $225–$275

Lend Your Money To the Government, 1917. Poster for the benefits of purchasing bonds shows the U.S. Treasury building. Very good, linen-mounted, 56 x 38 inches. $325–$375

Liberty Loan Wear This Button—It Is a Badge of Honor. A badge of honor is given to those who invested in Liberty Loans. Fine, 20 x 30 inches. $85–$125

A Million Boys Behind a Million Fighters. Every American Should Enroll in the Victory, Boys. Placard for enlisting youngsters to support at home. Mint, 13 x 20 inches. $75–$100

On the Job for Victory, ca. 1918 (Rawls #185). A shipyard worker stands in front of an incomplete ship hull urging fund contributions. Fine, 20 x 30 inches.
                                                                                                                    $150–$175

Our Boys Need Sox—Knit Your Bit. A knitting basket high with yarn with the Red Cross symbol behind. Mint, linen-mounted, 24 x 46 inches. $425–$475

Polish Victims Relief Fund. Image of Madonna appears to the Poles above the ruins of their homes. Fine, 20 x 30 inches. $265–$325

Re-establish Him. Canadian soldier stands at crossroads of life. Mint, 24 x 36 inches. $275–$325

Remember! The Flag of Liberty, Support It!, 1918 (Rawls #210). Young immigrant family is shown ready to pledge allegiance. Mint, linen-mounted, 20 x 30 inches. $175–$250

Ring It Again, 1918. Liberty Bell as enduring symbol to promote bonds. Fine, 20 x 30 inches. $125–$150

Rumania's Day. Rumanian decision to join the Allies. Fine, 20 x 30 inches. $185–$225

Save a Loaf a Week. Householders urged to eat less bread to save wheat for war zones. Fine, 21 x 29 inches. $90–$125

Shall We Be More Tender with Our Dollars?, 1917. U.S. sailor and soldier request the purchase of bonds with a quote from the Secretary. Fine, linen-mounted, 20 x 30 inches. $150–$175

Strike Now! An enraged doughboy uses a cowering German soldier as bayonet practice. Fine, linen-mounted, 20 x 30 inches. $225–$275

Subscribe to the 7th . . . War Loan, 1917. Double-headed imperial eagle symbolizes the union of Austria and Hungary. Fine, linen-mounted, 24 x 37 inches. $345–$400

Subscribe to the 7th War Loan, 1917. Austrian mountain trooper and plane guard the coast near Trieste. Fine, linen-mounted, 38 x 29 inches. $385–$450

They Serve France. How Can I Serve Canada? Frenchwomen are shown plowing the fields with no help at all. Fine, 24 x 35 inches. $245–$300

Today Buy That Liberty Bond, 1918. Bold and vibrant sun in red peers over the mountains. Mint, linen-mounted, 14 x 22 inches. $60–$100

245th Battalion Canadian Grenadier Guards. A recruiting poster with Canadian guns catapulting Germans over the edge. Fine, linen-mounted, 28 x 42 inches. $650–$700

Uphold Our Honor, Fight for Us. Radiant Columbia appeals for volunteers. Fine, linen-mounted, 28 x 40 inches. $475–$525

U.S. Marines, Soldiers of the Sea. Ships in the background as marines storm the shore. Fine, linen-mounted, 30 x 40 inches. $575–$625

U.S. Marines Want You. Marine with commanding presence to persuade recruits. Fine, 20 x 30 inches. $175–$200

V Invest. Bold blue V on a red background encourages purchasing of bonds. Mint, linen-mounted, 20 x 30 inches. $115–$150

What Can You Do? Join Our Red Cross, ca. 1915. Red Cross nurse helps a wounded soldier and refugee family. Fine, 28 x 42 inches. $150–$175

YOU Buy a Liberty Bond Lest I Perish?, 1917 (Rawls #200). Miss Liberty points to the viewers to urge the purchase of bonds. Fine, 20 x 30 inches. $185–$225

Your Country's Call—Isn't This Worth Fighting For?, ca. 1915. A kilted British infantryman points to hamlet and hills. Mint, linen-mounted, 20 x 30 inches. $575–$650

❧ ARMSTRONG

Your Country Needs You, 1916. A U.S. sailor salutes the Statue of Liberty. Mint, 14 x 19 inches. $185–$250

❧ ASHE

Lend the Way They Fight, 1918 (Rawls #264). A tattered doughboy pitches a grenade into German trench. Mint, linen-mounted, 28 x 40 inches. $295–$350

❧ BAKER

For Every Fighter a Woman Worker, ca. 1918 (Rawls #164). Woman power on parade as workers are lugging tools of their trade. Fine, linen-mounted, 28 x 42 inches. $225–$275

❧ BALDRIDGE

Private Trepow's Pledge, 1918 (Rawls #95). A reminder of the bravery of a soldier killed while carrying a message to the front. Fine, linen-mounted, 20 x 30 inches. $135–$175

❧ BATTERMANN

Altona's Day of Giving, 1916. German soldier holds his rifle tight while imagining his family. Mint, 8 x 12 inches. $375–$425

❧ WLADYSLAW T. BENDA (1873–1948)

Give or We Perish. Haunting image of a girl wrapped in a shawl, appealing for aid. Fine, linen-mounted, 20 x 30 inches. $350–$400

Polish Army in France, ca. 1916 (Rawls #64). Aimed at Polish-Americans, a color bearer carries a flag toward the German lines. Very good, linen-mounted, 28 x 35 inches. $450–$500

❧ GERRIT BENEKER (1882–1934)

Sure! We'll Finish the Job, 1918 (Rawls #229). Owner of a fuel barge digs into his overall pockets, asking citizens to buy loans. Fine, 26 x 38 inches. $145–$175

❧ LUCIAN BERNHARD (1883–1973)

War Loan Bonds. Master typographer designed this war loan poster using striking black letter type. Fine, linen-mounted, 22 x 15 inches. $135–$175

✦ FRANK BRANGWYN (1867–1956)

Neuve Chapelle, 1918 (Rawls #89). A recruiting poster citing the bravery of the Allied victory at Neuve Chapelle. Mint, linen-mounted, 20 x 30 inches. $385–$450

The Zeppelin Raids. A soldier shakes his fist at the zeppelin above while a woman lies at his feet. Mint, 20 x 30 inches. $385–$450

✦ L. N. BRITTON

Eat More Corn, Oats and Rye, 1917 (Rawls #121). The government's request to reduce wheat consumption by citizens. Fine, linen-mounted, 21 x 29 inches. $425–$475

Ten Million New Members by Christmas. A Red Cross flag is seen through a snowcapped window. Fine, 20 x 30 inches. $125–$150

They Are Looking To Us for Help. Under a Red Cross moon, wounded Allied soldiers look across the sea to the United States. Fine, linen-mounted, 56 x 35 inches. $275–$325

✦ BUCHEL

Belgian Red Cross. Angel of mercy dresses head wound of Belgian soldier with a backdrop of the national colors. Fine, linen-mounted, 20 x 30 inches. $235–$300

Poster by Frank Brangwyn. Courtesy of Meehan Military Posters.

Poster by Charles Livingston Bull. Courtesy of Meehan Military Posters.

❧ CHARLES LIVINGSTON BULL (1874–1932)

Keep Him Free, 1918 (Rawls #218). American eagle guards her brood while a squadron takes off. Mint, linen-mounted, 20 x 30 inches. $325–$375

Save the Products of the Land. (Rawls #10). The Food Administration promoting fish consumption so meat could be sent overseas. Fine, 20 x 30 inches. $365–$425

❧ BURKE

Share—Jewish Relief Campaign, ca. 1915. Personification of America brings food to the Jewish war refugees. Fine, linen-mounted, 30 x 40 inches. $2,250–$2,500

❧ BUTLER

At the Sign of the Red Triangle, 1918. Poster describes the need for contributions for the Y. Mint, 24 x 38 inches. $125–$150

The Last Evidence That Anybody Cares, 1918. Another poster describing the Y as a "big brother." Mint, 24 x 38 inches. $125–$150

❧ CARLSON

The Motor Transport Corps, 1919. A soldier is repairing an engine, promising training in new technology. Fine, linen-mounted, 19 x 25 inches. $225–$275

Say! Young Fellow, 1919. With his enlistment papers, a recruit eyes the Motor Transport Corps as high-tech education. Fine, linen-mounted, 19 x 25 inches. $175–$200

❧ CHAMBERS

Food Will Win the War (Rawls #113). Immigrants entering the harbor are reminded of the need to save food. Mint, linen-mounted, 20 x 30 inches. $350–$400

❧ CHAPIN

Help Your Red Cross. Christ image stands protectively over a nurse assisting victims on the battlefield. Fine, 14 x 22 inches. $125–$150

❧ B. CHAVANNAZ

Liberation Loan, 1918 (Paillard #231). Marianne stands before a map of France pleading for help while throttling Prussian eagle. Mint, linen-mounted, 32 x 47 inches. $325–$375

To Help Right Triumph, 1918 (Paillard #240). Cavalry, like modern knights, carry their flags into the battle. Fine, linen-mounted, 32 x 44 inches. $285–$350

❦ HOWARD CHANDLER CHRISTY (1873–1952)

Americans All!, 1918 (Rawls #222). Columbia affixes a laurel wreath above an honor roll of ethnic names. Fine, linen-mounted, 30 x 40 inches. $265–$325

Clear the Way, 1918 (Rawls #223). A muse, wrapped in a billowing flag, directs fire on a gun deck. Fine, linen-mounted, 20 x 30 inches. $275–$325

Fight or Buy Bonds, 1917 (Rawls #209). Columbia waving a flag leads the infantry charge. Mint, linen-mounted, 20 x 30 inches. $300–$375

As above, 30 x 40 inches. $375–$425

GEE! I Wish I Were a Man–I'd Join the Navy!, 1918 (Rawls #80). Christy girl smiles as she snaps imaginary suspenders over her sailor uniform. Fine, linen-mounted, 27 x 41 inches. $2,500–$2,750

I Want You for the Navy, 1917 (Rawls #78). Windblown blond woman in a navy outfit tries to recruit. Fine, linen-mounted, 28 x 40 inches. $975–$1,000

If You Want to Fight, 1915 (Rawls #249). A girl playfully modeling a marine's dress blues. Fine, linen-mounted, 30 x 40 inches. $1,000–$1,100

Patriotic League, 1918 (Rawls #149). Young woman poses with the U.S. flag on behalf of the YMCA. Fine, linen-mounted, 20 x 30 inches. $325–$375

The Spirit of America, 1919. Nurse holds the U.S. flag and a poppy over her heart. Mint, linen-mounted, 20 x 28 inches. $425–$475

❦ W. HASKELL COFFIN (1878–1941)

Joan of Arc Saved France, 1918 (Rawls #217). A radiant Joan of Arc with sword raised to defend her country. Mint, 20 x 30 inches. $225–$275

Poster by Howard Chandler Christy. Courtesy of Meehan Military Posters.

Poster by Haskell Coffin.
Courtesy of Meehan
Military Posters.

Poster by Austin Cooper. Courtesy
of Meehan Military Posters.

❦ CONSTANTINI

Where Yes Resounds. Classically dressed maiden extends an olive branch under the eye of Dante. Very good, linen-mounted, 28 x 39 inches. $245–$300

❦ AUSTIN COOPER (1890–1964)

America's Tribute to Britain (Rawls #23). American eagle positions a laurel wreath on the British lion. Mint, linen-mounted, 20 x 30 inches. $395–450

❦ COUGHLIN

Go Over the Top. Gung ho marine advances with machine gun into no-man's-land. Mint, 21 x 28 inches. $275–$325

❦ ARTHUR CRISP (1881-?)

Motherless, Fatherless, Starving: How Much to Save These Little Lives? Red Cross nurse shelters war orphans. Fine, linen-mounted, 20 x 30 inches. $100–$125

❦ JAMES DAUGHERTY (1889–1974)

Follow the Flag, 1917. Powerful blond sailor plants the flag on beachhead. Fine, linen-mounted, 28 x 40 inches. $450–$500

The Ships Are Coming (Rawls #77). A brilliant American eagle flies over a steamship heading to the front. Fine, 20 x 30 inches. $350–$400

Shove Off, 1919. U.S. recruiting poster showing sailors enjoying a ride on an Indian elephant. Fine, linen-mounted, 30 x 40 inches. $750–$800

❦ DE LA LAING

Americans! Join and Fight, 1918. Two doughboys assault the German lines, one with his rifle, the other with a Colt 45. Very good, linen-mounted, 28 x 42 inches. $950–$1,000

❦ DE LAND

Before Sunset, Buy a U.S. Government Bond, 1917. Silhouetted Statue of Liberty against a patriotic sunset. Fine, linen-mounted, 20 x 30 inches. $235–$300

❦ DELASPRE

The French Infantry in Battle. French soldier stands prepared while a map of war-torn Europe provides the background. Very good, linen-mounted, 32 x 47 inches. $425–$475

❦ DEWEY

Our Daddy is Fighting, 1917. Smiling children ask for support. Fine, 20 x 30 inches. $95–$125

❦ DITZ

Der Frias. German soldier uses the butt of his rifle to fend off bayonets. Fine, 17 x 25 inches. $475–$525

❦ JAMES DONAHEY (1875–?)

Be a Dad To Him. A doughboy holds his hand out to recruit support for the YMCA. Fine, linen-mounted, 28 x 50 inches. $195–$250

❦ GEORGES DORIVAL (1879–?)

After the Battle, 1919 (Paillard #375). War-weary French soldier trudges back to the barracks in the rain. Fine, linen-mounted, 30 x 46 inches. $285–$350

❦ JEAN DROIT (1884–1961)

4th National War Loan, 1918 (Paillard #163). French soldier frozen as he goes up over the top. Very good, linen-mounted, 31 x 46 inches. $200–$250

Standing in the Trench . . . Dreams of Victory and His Home, 1917 (Paillard #253). French vet stands rugged as he faces the new day. Very good, linen-mounted, 31 x 44 inches. $285–$350

❧ DUNN

They Are Giving All, 1918. Doughboys weighed down by heavy gear sprint across snowy no-man's-land. Very good, linen-mounted, 54 x 36 inches. $275–$325

Victory Is a Question of Stamina, 1917 (Rawls #168). Doughboys sprint across a snowy no-man's-land. Mint, linen-mounted, 20 x 30 inches. $150–$175

❧ E.K. (MONOGRAM)

Follow Me!, 1914. A rugged trooper sets a patriotic example for the British as he marches. Fine, linen-mounted, 20 x 30 inches. $200–$250

❧ EDWARDS

At the Front!, 1917. Frantic team of horses lurches to avoid a shell burst. Very good, linen-mounted, 20 x 30 inches. $285–$350

❧ EMBU

Help Us to Help Them. Woman doctor kneels before a little girl with a baby who died of starvation. Mint, 22 x 28 inches. $175–$200

❧ WALTER ENRIGHT (1879–?)

Follow The Pied Piper (Rawls #123). Uncle Sam plays the flute, leading children to help out with chores. Very good, linen-mounted, 23 x 29 inches. $325–$375

❧ HANS RUDI ERDT (1883–1918)

Heroism on the Somme, 1916. Stylized design with a German throwing a grenade, celebrating a German victory. Fine, 37 x 55 inches. *See color insert, photo 20.* $8,500–$9,000

❧ FRITZ ERLER (1868–1940)

And You?, ca. 1917. A wounded German aviator standing by his craft stares out at the viewer. Mint, linen-mounted, 37 x 54 inches. $950–$1,000

Help Us Win!, 1917 (Rawls #38). A stark view of a veteran of the trenches staring vacantly. Fine, linen-mounted, 16 x 22 inches. $825–$875

❧ ABEL FAIVRE (1867–1945)

French Land, 1920. Farmer tilling the land doffs his hat to a grave marker. Fine, linen-mounted, 23 x 31 inches. $750–$800

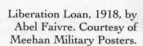

Help Us Win!, 1917, by Fritz Erler. Courtesy of Meehan Military Posters.

Liberation Loan, 1918, by Abel Faivre. Courtesy of Meehan Military Posters.

Give Your Gold to France—Gold Means Victory, 1915 (Paillard #30). An enlarged coin strikes and crushes a German soldier. Fine, linen-mounted, 31 x 42 inches. $245–$300

Liberation Loan, 1918 (Rawls #243, Paillard #245). A humbled kaiser slumps under the weight of the Allied forces. A very good example of the artist's style. Fine, linen-mounted, 42 x 31 inches. $375–$425

🌾 CHARLES BUCKLES FALLS (1874–?)

E-e-e-Yah-Yip. Marine with fixed bayonet gives the cry for attack. Mint, 20 x 30 inches. $125–$150

Earn and Learn, 1919. Welder constructs a new tank, showing trade and education. Mint, linen-mounted, 19 x 25 inches. $325–$375

Now for Some Music, 1917. U.S. soldier holds up a record by a phonograph to encourage viewers to send their disks. Fine, linen-mounted, 18 x 29 inches. $300–$350

Ten Million Members by Christmas. Gleaming Christmas candle with Red Cross and stars against window. Fine, 20 x 30 inches. $75–$100

This Device on Hat or Helmet. A marine emblem with eagle atop the globe with an anchor against a green background. Fine, linen-mounted, 30 x 40 inches. $275–$325

❦ LOUIS FANCHER (1884–1944)

Over There!, 1918 (Rawls #176). Ground crew signaling support to a Curtiss Jenny flying into the sun. Fine, linen-mounted, 30 x 38 inches. $750–$800

❦ FINOZZI

Consolidated Loan. Italian sharpshooter snipes at the enemy line. Very good, linen-mounted, 32 x 55 inches. $325–$375

❦ HARRISON FISHER (1875–1934)

Have You Answered the Call? (Rawls #127). A Red Cross nurse appears in front of marching doughboys, imploring us to join. Fine, linen-mounted, 26 x 28 inches. $125–$150

I Summon You, 1918 (Rawls #126). Nurse wrapped in U.S. flag delivers Woodrow Wilson's message. Mint, linen-mounted, 28 x 40 inches. $225–$275

❦ JAMES MONTGOMERY FLAGG (1877–1960)

Hold on To Uncle Sam's Insurance, 1919 (Rawls #279). Representatives from the army, navy, and marines show their enlistment insurance certificates. Fine, 20 x 30 inches. $150–$175

I Am Telling You, 1918 (Rawls #215). Uncle Sam with his hands on hips demanding the purchase of savings stamps. Fine, linen-mounted, 20 x 30 inches. $150–$200

I Want You for U.S. Army, 1917 (Rawls #13). America's most famous war poster, with the artist portraying himself as Uncle Sam. Fine, linen-mounted, 30 x 40 inches. $2,000–$2,500

Our Regular Divisions, ca. 1918 (Rawls #235). Army vet holds a U.S. flag and laurel-draped rifle while civilians show admiration. Mint, linen-mounted, 21 x 28 inches. $575–$625

Say, Folks!, Soldier and sailor suggest it would be shameful if you didn't invest in Liberty Loans. Fine, 12 x 17 inches. $145–$175

The Seeds of Victory Insure the Fruits of Peace, 1918 (Rawls #60). Columbia broadcasts seed in the freshly plowed field. Fine, linen-mounted, 22 x 33 inches. $375–$425

Tell That To the Marines (Rawls #166). Forceful redheaded man removing suit with newspaper at his feet. Fine, linen-mounted, 30 x 40 inches. $375–$425

Poster by James
Montgomery Flagg. Courtesy
of Meehan Military Posters.

Poster by James Montgomery
Flagg. Courtesy of Meehan
Military Posters.

Travel? Adventure? Answer—Join the Marines!, 1912. A marine rides a jaguar backwards as a master of danger. Mint, linen-mounted, 30 x 40 inches.
$2,750–$3,000

❦ ALONSO FORINGER (1878–?)

The Greatest Mother in the World, 1918 (Rawls #124). A nurse plays the role of the Virgin in a reinterpretation of Michelangelo's Pietá. Fine, linen-mounted. 30 x 40 inches.
$150–$175

❦ CLYDE FORSYTHYE (1885–1962)

And They Thought We Couldn't Fight. Doughboy ignores his wounds to display his captured German helmets. Fine, 20 x 30 inches.
$125–$150

As above, very good, linen-mounted, 30 x 40 inches.
$145–$175

❦ CHARLES FOUQUERAY (1872–1956)

Day in Honor of the African Army, 1917. North African soldiers charge the enemy. Fine, linen-mounted, 31 x 48 inches.
$650–$700

❦ FRY

There's Room for You, Enlist To-Day, ca. 1915 (Rawls #33). British soldiers wave to civilians while departing on a train. Fine, linen-mounted, 20 x 30 inches.
$275–$325

❦ ERNEST FUHR (1874–1933)

Sugar Means Ships. Girl sips on ice cream soda, oblivious to the fact that ships are needed for troops, not goods. Fine, 29 x 16 inches. $55–$100

❦ ARNOLD GENTHE (1869–1942)

The Roll Call, a Masque of the Red Cross, 1918. Photo features a statuesque dancer hailing the symbol of the Red Cross. Fine, 19 x 32 inches. $135–$175

❦ CHARLES DANA GIBSON (1867–1944)

Can You Drive a Car? Will You Drive One in France? Woman shown fending off death for wounded soldiers rescued by ambulance. Very good, 14 x 22 inches.
$250–$300

❦ MALCOLM GIBSON

Canada's Grain Cannot Be Sold Unless You Buy Victory Bonds. A field of grain illustrates a prosperous economy's dependence on an Allied victory. Fine, 24 x 36 inches. $275–$325

Nothing Doing Without Victory Bonds. Idle snowcapped factory emphasizes the link between finances and victory. Mint, linen-mounted, 24 x 36 inches. $345–$400

❦ HOWARD GILES (1876–1955)

Nothing Stops These Men. Doughboys surge forward in a sensational battlefield poster. Fine, linen-mounted, 56 x 38 inches. $375–$425

❦ JULIUS GIPKENS (1883–?)

German War Evenings, ca. 1917. German rifleman with a large shield on which specific evening's program would be listed. Fine, linen-mounted, 18 x 28 inches. $975–$1,025

❦ GRANT

The Regular Is Ready! He Was—He is—He Will Be. A wreath encircles the head of an army soldier gripping his rifle. Fine, 20 x 30 inches. $175–$200

What are YOU Doing to Help? A nurse escorts a severely wounded soldier as she appeals for civilian aid. Very good, linen-mounted, 25 x 38 inches.
$150–$175

❦ GROESBECK

Shall We Be More Tender with our Dollars?, 1917 (Rawls #204). Uncle Sam reaches out with one hand while he points to a juggernaut behind him. Mint, 20 x 30 inches. $165–$200

🕊 GROSSE

Help Crush the Menace of the Seas. A bloody arm waving a dagger in the sea, seeking U.S. transport in the background. Fine, linen-mounted, 18 x 28 inches. $225–$275

🕊 HALSTED and ADERENTE

Columbia Calls, 1916 (Rawls #52). Flag-waving Columbia with sword of justice. Fine, 30 x 40 inches. $250–$300

🕊 HANSI—aka JEAN-JACQUES WALTZ (1873–1951)

Lorraine and Alsace Are Ours. French soldiers imagine the Strasbourg Cathedral flying a French flag. Fine, linen-mounted, 23 x 30 inches. $250–$300

🕊 HENDEE

Eat Less and Let Us Be Thankful that We Have Enough to Share, 1918 (Rawls #120). Fruits and vegetables frame message to save food. Fine, linen-mounted, 21 x 29 inches. $245–$300

🕊 FREDERICK HOERTZ

Your Work Means Victory. Workers finishing a smokestack in the dockyards. Fine, linen-mounted, 28 x 38 inches. $325–$375

🕊 HOFFMAN

Join the Black Toms, They Treat 'Em Rough. A Black tomcat leaps toward the enemy with the tanks rumbling below. Very good, linen-mounted, 19 x 25 inches. $225–$275

🕊 LUDWIG HOHLWEIN (1874–1949)

Exhibition of the Work of German Prisoners of War, 1918. A disconsolate POW rests his hand on a crosscut saw. Fine, 16 x 23 inches. $1,250–$1,350

Volkspende (People's Charity Fund for German Prisioners of War), 1918 (Rawls #42). German POW remains in jail although the war is over, with a red heart behind. Fine, linen-mounted, 23 x 33 inches. $3,000–$3,250

🕊 HORMEYER

And Your Duty?, 1918 (Rawls #43). A wounded German in bloody bandages stares with one eye at viewer. Mint, 16 x 23 inches. $285–$350

Poster by Ludwig
Hohlwein. Courtesy of
Meehan Military Posters.

Poster by Argiet Hutaf. Courtesy
of Meehan Military Posters.

❦ ARGIET HUTAF (1879–1942)

Treat 'Em Rough! Join the Tanks, ca. 1918 (Rawls #254). Above the flames of
battle, a black cat lunges into action. Very good, linen-mounted, 19 x 25 inches.
$650–$700

❦ MAURICE INGRES

Let's End It—Quick, 1917 (Rawls #202). Columbia appeals to the viewer
to buy bonds while Europe lies in flames. Fine, linen-mounted, 28 x 42 inches.
$250–$300

❦ LUCIEN JONAS (1880–1947)

Association of French Women, 1918 (Paillard #65). Red Cross volunteers assist
the wounded after the battle. Fine, linen-mounted, 31 x 47 inches. $295–$350

Four Years in the Fight (Rawls 164). Women carrying molten shells to blast furnace. Fine, linen-mounted, 28 x 42 inches. $375–$425

National Loan, 1920 (Paillard #371). Worn-out soldier offers the olive branch
to a grateful Marianne. Very good, linen-mounted, 32 x 47 inches. $285–$350

🌢 KEELOR

Buy Victory Bonds for Industrial Expansion. Burly workers transform the Canadian landscape into an industrial economy. Fine, 24 x 36 inches.

$325–$375

🌢 KEITH

Join the Air Service, 1918 (Rawls #176). Airships circle as fighter revs up for takeoff. Fine, linen-mounted, 20 x 30 inches. $1,250–$1,350

🌢 W. B. KING

Hold Up Your End!, 1918 (Rawls #127). A nurse picks up a stretcher with shell exploding nearby. Fine, 20 x 28 inches. $150–$175

🌢 KLEIN

Day of Giving. Two German soldiers use a rifle as support for wounded soldier with a Red Cross behind them. Fine, linen-mounted, 23 x 32 inches. $350–$400

🌢 ROLAND KRAFTER

War Album, 1917. German infantry in camouflage march off for Christmas leave. Very good, 25 x 37 inches. $285–$350

🌢 KUHN

7th Austrian War Loan, 1917. A trooper cocks his arm to hurl a grenade while from a kneeling position. Fine, linen-mounted, 27 x 42 inches. $300–$400

🌢 LANTOINE

Enlist in the French Navy, 1924. Sailors turn a powerful searchlight at a battle-ship. Mint, linen-mounted, 22 x 31 inches. $650–$700

🌢 LEBASQUE

The Peace Loan, 1920 (Paillard #339). A family scene shown as an allegory to regeneration for France. Fine, linen-mounted, 32 x 42 inches. $425–$475

🌢 LEITZ

8th War Loan, 1918. German tocsin takes flight on wings of victory. Mint, 17 x 23 inches.
$365–$425

🌢 LENZ

6th War Loan, 1916. The Central Powers shown as the crusading saint against the beast of British imperialism. Fine, linen- mounted, 20 x 27 inches. $750–$800

7th War Loan, 1917. Austrian workers, students, and landowners rally around the flag to contribute to the war. Fine, linen-mounted, 20 x 37 inches.

$475–$525

The Tanks Are Coming! A rare woodblock poster showing tanks on their way to the front. Very good, linen-mounted, 25 x 38 inches. $325–$375

❧ AUGUSTE LEROUX (1871–?)

Third Loan for Fighting France!, 1917 (Paillard #164). French soldier kisses his daughter good-bye while his wife nurses her baby. Good, linen-mounted, 31 x 45 inches. $195–$250

❧ JOSEPH CHRISTIAN LEYENDECKER (1874–1951)

America Calls—Enlist in the Navy. Recruiting poster with the Statue of Liberty clasping the hand of a sailor. Round image on rich blue field. Extremely rare, fine condition, linen-mounted, 30 x 40 inches. $1,500–$1,600

These Men Have Come Across (Rawls #72–73). Muscular men are seen preparing to fire a deck gun. Very good, 21 x 11 inches. $475–$525

U.S.A. Bonds, 1918 (Rawls #211). Well-known image of Boy Scout on bended knee, offering a sword inscribed "Be Prepared" to Miss Liberty. Fine, linen-mounted, 20 x 30 inches. $275–$325

❧ JONAS LIE (1880–1940)

On the Job for Victory (Rawls #186–187). A bustling shipyard shows the vigor of the U.S. shipbuilding industry. Fine, linen-mounted, 40 x 30 inches. $475–$525

Poster by J. C. Leyendecker. Courtesy of Meehan Military Posters.

❧ LIPSCOMBE

Britishers Enlist Today, ca. 1916 (Rawls #59). Sumptuous Union Jack draped against a green frame. Fine, linen-mounted, 28 x 40 inches. $325–$375

❧ LOVE

If You Can't Go Across with a Gun. Wounded soldiers with woman and child reach up to the Red Cross. Fine, linen-mounted, 28 x 41 inches. $185–$225

❧ LOW

Everyone Should Do His Bit, 1915. Boy Scout poses near wall plastered with recruiting posters that he put up. Fine, linen-mounted, 20 x 30 inches.
$285–$325

❧ LURIA-FOWLER

Save Sugar. A scale holds up a bowl of sugar and a container of molasses syrup to persuade consumers to reduce sugar consumption. Fine, 20 x 30 inches.
$135–$175

❧ LYNCH

Ammunition, 1918. A gunner reaches out for more ammo with empty boxes at his feet. Fine, 20 x 30 inches. $350–$400

❧ CHARLES MACAULEY

YOU Buy a Liberty Bond Lest I Perish, 1917 (Rawls #199). Close-up of Statue of Liberty pointing out at viewer. Fine, linen-mounted, 30 x 40 inches.
$275–$325

❧ DONALD MCKEE

Food, 1918 (Rawls #122). Farmers as fife and drum players show support for home gardening. Fine, linen-mounted, 20 x 30 inches. $150–$175

❧ BURKHARD MANGOLD (1873–1950)

Storming of Spicherer Heights, 1910. An officer with sword leads the Prussian charge in the Franco-Prussian War 1870–71. A theme revived for WWI. Mint, 30 x 41 inches. $2,250–$2,500

❧ MATANIA

Help the Horse to Save the Soldier, ca. 1917 (Rawls #238). Poignant scene of a British soldier saying good-bye to his wounded horse. Mint, linen-mounted, 20 x 30 inches. $1,500–$1,600

❦ MOLLER

The U-Boat War, 1918. A scale over the view of a German sub sinking an Allied ship is tipped in favor of the attacker. Fine, 26 x 20 inches.　　$650–$700

❦ MORA

Free Milk for France, ca. 1918 (Rawls #45). U.S. soldier ladles out milk to hungry children. Mint, linen-mounted, 24 x 34 inches.　　$325–$375

❦ MORGAN

Keep This Hand of Mercy at Work. The arm of Red Cross nurse is wrapping refugees in a warm glow. Fine, linen-mounted, 20 x 28 inches.　　$85–$125

❦ MYERS

Enlist—Plow—Buy Bonds. Highlighted doughboy gives pride to AEF volunteer. Very good, 22 x 28 inches.　　$95–$125

❦ HANS NEUMANN (1888–?)

The Final Blow, 1918. A helmeted German swings a red-hot sword in a storm. Very good, linen-mounted, 9 x 14 inches.　　$135–$175

❦ MAURICE NEUMONT (1868–1930)

Day of the Poilu, 1915. Embattled French soldier tosses a grenade from a trench. Fine, linen-mounted, 31 x 47 inches.　　$325–$375

Galerie Brunner, 1918. Advertisement of war exposition within a window taped against bomb blasts. Fine, linen-mounted, 23 x 31 inches.　　$195–$250

On Ne Passe Pas (They Shall Not Pass), 1918 (Rawls #87). A weary soldier bars the way to the fortress burning in the background. Fine, linen-mounted, 31 x 47 inches.　　$650–$700

❦ JOHN WARNER NORTON (1876–1934)

Keep These Off the U.S.A., 1918 (Rawls #214). Pair of bloodstained German boots. Very good, linen-mounted, 30 x 40 inches.　　$325–$375

❦ LOUIS OPPENHEIM (1879–?)

The Best Savings Bank. Money falls into a hand-held German helmet. Very good, linen-mounted, 9 x 14 inches.　　$135–$175

As above, mint, 17 x 23 inches.　　$375–$425

On Ne Passe Pas (They
Shall Not Pass), 1918,
Maurice Neumont.
Courtesy of Meehan
Military Posters.

🌾 ALFRED EVERETT ORR (1866–?)

For Home and Country. A U.S. soldier with decorations is reunited with his family. Fine, linen-mounted, 20 x 30 inches. $100–$125

As above, 30 x 40 inches. $125–$150

🌾 HERBERT PAUS (1890–1946)

America, the Hope of All Who Suffer—the Dread of All Who Do Wrong (Rawls #114). Victims tied to iron cross point to the title. Fine, linen-mounted, 54 x 36 inches. $375–$425

Help Deliver the Goods. Sailor uses rope to hoist shells for shipping. Very good, linen-mounted, 28 x 40 inches. $225–$275

I Shall Expect Every Man Who Is Not a Slacker to Be at My Side. Poster asks American workers to extend themselves for the war effort. Very good, linen-mounted, 30 x 43 inches. $475–$525

Save Your Child from Autocracy and Poverty, 1918 (Rawls #11). A blond child holds on to the hand of Miss Liberty. Fine, linen-mounted, 20 x 30 inches. $115–$150

As above, very good, linen-mounted, 30 x 40 inches. $135–$175

To Make the World a Decent Place to Live In (Rawls #212–213). A wave of infantrymen go over the top with their flag. Very good, linen-mounted, 56 x 38 inches. $375–$425

❧ WILLIAM PAXTON (1869–1941) AND FREDERICK HALL (1879–1946)

Enlist in the Army, Navy, Marines, 1917. A powerful Columbia with U.S. flag leads an American armada. Magnificent panorama. Extremely scarce, issued by the Boston Public Safety Committee. Very good, linen-mounted, 7 x 9 feet. *See color insert, photo 19.* $3,500–$3,750

❧ JOSEPH PENNELL (1866–1925)

Provide the Sinews of War, 1918. Loading cranes and smoky atmosphere add to a rich nautical scene. Fine, 21 x 20 inches. $275–$325

That Liberty Shall Not Perish, 1918. An outstanding image: New York under aerial attack with flames all around a destroyed Statue of Liberty. Fine, linen-mounted, 20 x 30 inches. $300–$350

❧ EMIL PIRCHAN (1884–1957)

Lottery. A German soldier grabs his head as a shell explodes nearby in a highly stylized poster. Mint, linen-mounted, 16 x 24 inches. $1,200–$1,300

❧ PLONTKE

For the War Loan. Cherub wearing the German colors and holding a helmet full of gold coins. Mint, 17 x 23 inches. $275–$325

❧ PORTER

Hurray for the Boys in the Shop at Home. Doughboys raise their helmets and rifles to toast munitions workers. Very good, 12 x 18 inches. $85–$125

❧ PORTEUS

WOMEN! Help America's Sons Win the War, 1917 (Rawls #206). A grandmother backed by a patriotic banner pleads for help. Fine, linen-mounted, 20 x 30 inches. $165–$200

❧ FRANCISQUE POULBOT (1879–1946)

Day of the Vendee, 1916. A boy leads a mutilated war victim along the beach. A day set aside for the suffering in Vendee. Fine, linen-mounted, 32 x 47 inches. $285–$350

The Poilu's Day, 1915 (Paillard #47). French children dressed as soldier and nurse awaiting their father's return. Very good, linen-mounted, 32 x 47 inches. $325–$375

❦ GERALD SPENCER PRYSE (1881–1956)

The Only Road for an Englishman. British column marching through the ruins of a darkened city. Rare. Very good, linen-mounted, 25 x 40 inches.

$1,750–$2,000

❦ LOUIS RAEMAEKERS (1869–1956)

Enlist in the Navy. Heroic Uncle Sam dressed as a doughboy is seen overcoming evil. Very good, linen-mounted, 40 x 30 inches. $175–$200

In Belgium, Help, 1916. Mother and baby in rags appeal desperately for aid relief. Very good, linen-mounted, 24 x 39 inches. $225–$275

Will You Be Ready Tomorrow to Make Munitions for Germany?, 1917. Cartoon of German aiming a gun point-blank at an elderly man. Fine, 12 x 19 inches. $115–$150

❦ HENRY RALEIGH (1880–?)

Blood or Bread. Graphic depiction of one soldier holding a dead one reminds citizens to support war bonds. Fine, 20 x 30 inches. $85–$125

Halt the Hun, 1918 (Rawls #210). An American soldier arrives just in time to save the children from the German. Fine, linen-mounted, 20 x 30 inches.

$125–$150

Hunger. Woman cradling her child pleas for funds for those starving from the war. Fine, 20 x 30 inches. $75–$100

Courtesy of Meehan Military Posters.

❧ HENRY REUTERDAHL (1871–1925)

All Together (Rawls #154–155). Sailors from Japan, France, United States, England, Russia, and Italy are pictured as one big happy family. Mint, linen-mounted, 40 x 30 inches. $500–$550

The Navy Put 'Em Across, 1918. A smiling sailor splashes through the waves carrying a doughboy on his back. Very good, linen-mounted, 20 x 45 inches. $325–$350

❧ SIDNEY RIESENBERG (1885–?)

Civilians, 1918 (Rawls #162). Doughboy steps up to appeal to the support of the Jewish Welfare Board. Fine, linen-mounted, 20 x 30 inches. $175–$200

First to Fight, 1917. Marines charging in from the shoreline to join the fight. Very good, linen-mounted, 30 x 40 inches. $275–$325

For Active Service, 1913. A marine unfurls a flag above the barracks in a tropical setting. Fine, linen-mounted, 18 x 25 inches. $325–$375

Lend as They Fight. Rifleman fires from behind sandbags while his wounded buddy fights on. Fine, 20 x 30 inches. $235–$300

Over the Top, 1918 (Rawls #248). Soldier wrapped in U.S. flag going "over the top." Title is from the book by Sgt. Guy Empey. Mint, 20 x 30 inches. $150–$175

U.S. Marines, 1917. "Walking John" recruiting sergeant walks along docks with battleship in background. Fine, linen-mounted, 28 x 42 inches. $375–$425

Poster by Sheridan.
Courtesy of Meehan
Military Posters.

U.S. Marines—Interesting Duty, 1916. Marines with U.S. flag storm a tropical beach. Very good, 30 x 40 inches. $275–$325

❧ NORMAN ROCKWELL (1894–1978)

> Note: See additional listings for Norman Rockwell under World War II posters.

And NOW the Fighting Fourth, 1918. Cute Boy Scout displays his awards for selling war bonds. Mint, linen-mounted, 10 x 14 inches. $225–$275

❧ ROGERS

Only the Navy Can Stop This, ca. 1917. Kaiser with bloody sword gloating while standing over the bodies of drowned children. Fine, 20 x 26 inches. $500–$550

❧ ST. JOHN

Blot It Out, 1917 (Rawls #207). A bloody handprint to illustrate German atrocities. Fine, 20 x 30 inches. $125–$150
As above, 30 x 40 inches. $175–$225

❧ SALTZMAN

Navy Offering, 1916. Sailors on top of a battleship unpack the money necessary for the fleet. Fine, linen-mounted, 21 x 27 inches. $575–$625

❧ SAUNIER

Here They Are—the Americans! A German soldier tries to open the eastern front before the shadow of the Americans is upon him. Very good, linen-mounted, 20 x 15 inches. $125–$150

❧ SEM—aka SERGE GOURSAT (1863–1934)

For the Last Quarter of an Hour, Help Me!, 1918 (Paillard #247). The general stands on a hillock viewing the troops. Fine, linen-mounted, 47 x 32 inches. $485–$550

For the Liberty of the World, 1918 (Rawls #85, Paillard #157). A red Statue of Liberty looms over the ocean as a beacon. An outstanding example. Fine, linen-mounted, 31 x 46 inches. $925–$975

❧ SHEERES

Keep the Stars Shining for Uncle Sam—Join the Quartermaster Corps, 1919. Smiling Uncle Sam as a doughboy points his thumb to the poster's message. Fine, linen-mounted, 17 x 26 inches. $195–$250

🌿 SHERIDAN

Food Is Ammunition, ca. 1918 (Rawls #115). A basket of food is highlighted against a cavalry troop at sunset. Very good, linen-mounted, 20 x 28 inches.
$385–$425

Hey Fellows!, 1918 (Rawls #159). Soldier holds up books shipped from home while another sits reading. Fine, 20 x 30 inches.
$125–$150

Rivets Are Bayonets, ca. 1918 (Rawls #76). A riveter bends to his work under the shadow of a doughboy. Fine, linen-mounted, 25 x 38 inches.
$375–$425

🌿 SIGRIST

Subscribe To the War Loan (Rawls #37). A hawk and dove soar over the mountains. Mint, 17 x 23 inches.
$385–$450

🌿 SIMAY

Subscribe to the Liberation Loan, 1918 (Rawls #183, Paillard #262). A British tank crawls over the lip of a trench. Fine, linen-mounted, 31 x 44 inches.
$500–$550

🌿 SINDELAR

Uncle Sam Needs That Extra Shovelful. Uncle Sam restraining a worker from shoveling unnecessary fuel into a roaring furnace. Fine, linen-mounted, 20 x 28 inches.
$185–$225

Poster by Sheridan.
Courtesy of Meehan
Military Posters.

❧ JESSE WILCOX SMITH (1863–1935)

He Can Win. A soldier with a crutch is working late with the Red Cross symbol above. Fine, linen-mounted, 20 x 30 inches. $245–$300

Knowledge Wins, 1918 (Rawls #157). Doughboy sheds field kit to climb the ladder of success formed by books. Fine, linen-mounted, 20 x 30 inches. $225–$275

❧ SOUTARY

Be Honest With Yourself. A British recruiting poster with an artillery crew in silhouette. Fine, 20 x 30 inches. $250–$300

❧ SPEAR

Workers Lend Your Strength, 1918. A laborer and soldier are shown as partners against the Central Powers. Fine, 20 x 30 inches. $95–$125

❧ PAUL STAHR (1883–?)

Be Patriotic. Columbia recommends a pledge to save food for overseas. Fine, linen-mounted, 20 x 30 inches. $145–$175

❧ STEELE

Defeat the Kaiser and His U-Boats, Save Wheat, 1917. The kaiser looks on as U-Boats sink merchantmen. Mint, 14 x 22 inches. $225–$275

❧ THEOPHILE-ALEXANDRE STEINLEN (1859–1923)

Day of the Poilu, 1915 (Paillard #44). Portrait of two French soldiers smoking pipes. Fine, linen-mounted, 32 x 47 inches. $600–$650

Journée Serbe, 1916. Printed by I. Lapina, published in *La Guerre*, Paris. Good condition, linen-mounted, 30½ x 47 inches. $1,200

Save Serbia, 1918 (Rawls #39). Powerful image shows stunned survivors of Austrian attack to solicit funds for relief. Fine, linen-mounted, 24 x 36 inches. $750–$800

❧ STERN

Are You 100% American? Prove It!, 1918 (Rawls #144). Challenge to the viewer to purchase bonds. Fine, 20 x 30 inches. $75–$100

❧ ALBERT STERNER (1863–1946)

Over There, 1917 (Rawls #80). Columbia stands directing a sailor to his overseas duty. Fine, linen-mounted, 40 x 60 inches. $750–$800

Courtesy of
Butterfield &
Butterfield.

We Need You. A Red Cross nurse points out a nurse tending the wounded to a young woman as a possible recruit. Very good, 30 x 40 inches. $175–$200

🌿 STROTHMAN

Beat Back the Hun, 1918 (Rawls #194). A German with bloodstained fingers is creeping up on the viewer. Mint, linen-mounted, 18 x 27 inches. $250–$300

🌿 ADOLPH TREIDLER (1886–1981)

Another Notch Chateau Thierry, 1918 (Rawls #247). A marine carves another notch in the stock of his rifle. Fine, linen-mounted, 30 x 40 inches.

$285–$325

Buy a Liberty Bond, 1917 (Rawls #201). The first bond poster, featuring the Statue of Liberty. Fine, 20 x 30 inches. $195–$225

For Every Fighter a Woman Worker, 1918 (Rawls #164). A woman in overalls holds up a shell and a miniature airplane. Fine, linen-mounted, 30 x 40 inches.

$250–$300

Make Every Minute Count for Pershing, ca. 1917. Riveter is shown readying another ship for duty. Fine, 20 x 30 inches. $135–$175

Our Flags Beat Germany . . . Eat Less of the Food Fighters Need. Colorful waving Allied flags remind viewers of their duty. Very good, linen-mounted, 20 x 30 inches. $75–$100

Shoot Ships To Germany. A cruiser with a reminder that building ships can help win the war. Very good, 18 x 24 inches. $75–$100

❦ UNDERWOOD

Back Our Girls Over There, 1918 (Rawls #260). Telephone operator works the switchboard near the front lines. Mint, linen-mounted, 22 x 28 inches.

$135–$175

❦ UPJOHN

Happy Childhood the World Over. Red Cross poster with refugee children dancing while one flies a kite. Fine, linen-mounted, 25 x 38 inches. $285–$350

❦ J. PAUL VERREES

Join the Air Service, 1917 (Rawls #179). A Curtiss Jenny swoops low in richly colored scene. Very good, linen-mounted, 25 x 37 inches. $1,800–$1,900

Can Vegetables, Fruit, and the Kaiser Too, 1918 (Rawls #119). Image of the kaiser dunked in a mason jar. Fine, linen-mounted, 22 x 33 inches. $475–$525

❦ WEIL

Hamburg's Day of Giving, 1915. A bearded sentry walks his post in biting cold to urge donations. Fine, linen-mounted, 18 x 31 inches. $550–$600

❦ HORACE WELSH (1888–1942)

Pro Patria, 1917 (Rawls #240). Color guard on horseback trotting across field. Fine, linen-mounted, 28 x 40 inches. $450–$500

U.S. Army Signal Corps, ca. 1916 (Rawls #55). A spotter relays info to a dough-boy, who telegraphs it to Command. Fine, linen-mounted, 27 x 39 inches.

$550–$600

❦ WHELAN

Men Wanted for the Army, 1908 (Rawls #54). Prewar cavalry poster with a bugler on horseback in the American Southwest. Fine, linen-mounted, 30 x 40 inches. $1,250–$1,350

❦ WILBUR

Join! A Red Cross nurse towers protectively over a globe to heal it. Mint, linen-mounted, 21 x 31 inches. $225–$275

❦ WILCOX

We'll Help You to Win the War (Rawls #216). Young Scout shows his savings stamp book to his uniformed dad. Fine, 18 x 28 inches. $175–$200

🖋 ADOLPHE LEON WILLETTE (1857–1926)

Day in Honor of the Poilu, 1915 (Paillard #48). A wife embraces her husband after his first leave as a dog begs nearby. Fine, linen-mounted, 32 x 47 inches.

$250–$300

🖋 WRIGHT

Follow the Boys in Blue. Mass population shown assisting the U.S. sailors with supplies onto their ship. Mint, linen-mounted, 29 x 21 inches. $175–$200

Hip-Hip (Rawls #184). Elated shipbuilder waving cap while clinging to the mast-head with U.S. flag waving. Fine, linen-mounted, 30 x 40 inches. $475–$525

🖋 ELLSWORTH YOUNG (1866–?)

Remember Belgium, (Rawls #28). A rallying cry for recruiters with a German dragging off a defenseless girl while village burns. Mint, 20 x 30 inches.

$135–$175

WORLD WAR II

🖋 ANONYMOUS

America Has Plenty If It Is Used Wisely. A U.S. flag spreads out with symbols of American resources. Fine, linen-mounted, 24 x 36 inches. $285–$350

Another Tanker Torpedoed Off the Atlantic Coast!, 1942. A photo of a sinking tanker illustrates the need for caution in America. Fine, 28 x 20 inches.

$75–$100

Are You Doing All You Can?, 1942. Uncle Sam thrusts his finger through a flag. Fine, linen-mounted, 22 x 28 inches. $225–$275

Back 'Em Up!, 1944. A close-up photo of Ike with binoculars. Fine, 20 x 28 inches.

$85–$125

Be a Seabee, Join the "Can Do" Boys of the Navy, ca. 1942. U.S. recruiting poster aimed at construction workers. Fine, linen-mounted, 16 x 8 inches.

$145–$175

Beat "Firebomb Fritz." A caricature of a Nazi bomb heading down on the British. Fine, linen-mounted, 20 x 30 inches. $475–$525

Become a Nurse—Your Country Needs You. Uncle Sam caps an attractive young nurse himself. In patriotic Kodacolor. Fine condition, 20 x 28 inches.

$75–$100

Belgium—Our Friends in Need, 1945. Three generations of a Belgian family shown battered by the war. Mint, 14 x 22 inches. $95–$125

The Black Corps, 1940. Photo of Sepp Dietrich assuming command of an SS division from Hitler. Fine, linen-mounted, 12 x 24 inches. $450–$500

Britain's Air Offensive, 1940. Red markers representing bombing raids are shown on a map of Germany. Fine, linen-mounted, 22 x 32 inches. $200–$250

British Aeroplanes Guard African Skies. A formation of Hurricanes roars above an African market town. Mint, 14 x 19 inches. $165–$200

Bundle Waste Paper for War. Consumers asked to bundle waste paper, magazines, newspapers, and boxes. Good, on cardboard, 28 x 11 inches. $145–$175

Buy a Share in America, 1941. Uncle Sam's hand shakes the hand of a worker. Fine, 28 x 40 inches. $250–$300

Campaign in Poland, 1939. Poster for a documentary showing German bombers and tanks moving in on Poland. Very good, linen-mounted, 38 x 54 inches. $1,250–$1,350

Defend Him!, 1944. Arms marked with Star of David, hammer and sickle, and Masonic emblem claw at child symbolizing Italy. Fine, linen-mounted, 28 x 41 inches. $3,500–$3,750

Defend Your Country, 1941. Coast guard big guns shown ready to fire, with "Remember Pearl Harbor." Fine, 21 x 11 inches. $135–$175

Defense Needs Rubber. American tractor tows a 155-mm gun, showing the enormous tires needed for the move to the front. Fine, linen-mounted, 38 x 38 inches. $225–$275

Deliver Us from Evil, 1943. A child is shown amidst a swastika surrounded by smoke. Fine, 22 x 28 inches. $65–$100

Dig for Victory Now. A basket of vegetables points out the urgency for British citizens to grow gardens. Fine, 20 x 30 inches. $165–$200

Do with Less So They'll Have Enough, 1943. Smiling GI looks out, holding his cup. Fine, 22 x 28 inches. $85–$125

Don't Give the Japs a Single Break. A broken gear shows that mistakes in the factory help the enemy. Very good, linen-mounted, 28 x 40 inches. $175–$200

Either Can Do the Enemy's Work. A lighted match carelessly tossed is equated with a Nazi bomb. Fine, 21 x 26 inches. $75–$100

Enlist in the Auxiliary Service of the X Fleet, 1944. A woman bowed over gently kisses the Italian flag. Mint, linen-mounted, 20 x 30 inches. $1,500–$1,600

Enlist in a Proud Profession, 1942. A proud woman has joined the Cadet Nurse Corps. Fine, 20 x 28 inches. $65–$100

Every Mother's Son Is Counting on You!, 1944 (Nelson #138). Photos and painting combined to show the sea war and factory support in America. Fine, 30 x 40 inches. $135–$175

Fall in with the Fire-bomb Fighters. British poster of flaming letters with a hand holding a fire hose. Very good, 20 x 30 inches. $150–$175

Fighters of the Allies! Countrymen Are Hitting Back. The British war production, shown as a wrench, stops the gears of the Nazis. Mint, 15 x 17 inches.
$75–$100

The Five Sullivan Brothers, 1942. Smiling photo of five brothers who were killed off at Guadalcanal. Fine, 22 x 28 inches. $95–$125

Flying Corps. A German recruitment poster for the SS Air Corps shows a young man in uniform. Mint, 32 x 33 inches. $1,750–$1,850

Food Is a Weapon, 1943. An empty glass and plate with used napkin alert Americans to avoid waste. Fine, 16 x 23 inches. $75–$100

For Defense Buy United States Savings Bonds. A bronze statue of a colonial with rifle and plowshare stands alert. Mint, 19 x 26 inches. $65–$100

For Gunpowder—Save Waste Fats. A huge gun barrel frames the conservation message to Americans. Fine, 22 x 42 inches. $145–$200

For the Future, 1943. The Statue of Liberty holds her torch like a beacon. Polish. Fine, linen-mounted, 20 x 28 inches. $175–$200

As above, Hungarian, fine, 20 x 28 inches. $125–$150

For Victory, 1942. Cartoon satire of Hitler, Goering, and Goebbels. Fine, 16 x 22 inches. $75–$100

For Victory, ca. 1944. U.S. factory worker points with his thumb to war bonds. Fine, 20 x 28 inches. $75–$100

Get in the Scrap, 1942. U.S. conservation shows a bomb, tank, battleship, and antiaircraft gun emerging from scrap metal. Fine, 20 x 28 inches. $125–$150

Get in the Scrap, 1943. A bold graphic spells out the need for war industries. Fine. 20 x 27 inches. $90–$125

Get Your Farm into the Fight, 1942. A farmer displays the produce from his land as planes fly overhead. Fine, 19 x 28 inches. $165–$200

Go Places with the U.S. Army!, 1939. Ship heads to the viewer surrounded by photos of exotic duty stations. Fine, linen-mounted, 25 x 38 inches. $275–$325

Good Soldier, 1944. WAC smiles out at potential recruits. Fine, 25 x 38 inches.
$185–$225

Guard Our Shores, 1940. U.S. artillery guns search the night air for planes. Fine, 25 x 38 inches. $165–$200

Help Britain Buy American Supplies, Buy Something British!, 1941. An American hand and British hand shake at the center of this poster. Fine, 14 x 20 inches. $75–$100

Hit Hard and Often, 1942. American plane shoots down Japanese fighters over a Japanese village. Fine, linen-mounted, 28 x 40 inches. $350–$400

Hit the Beach. U.S. civilians are allowed to inspect LST-512 to see how their money was spent. Fine, 13 x 19 inches. $75–$125

How Do You Like 'Em, Mr. Hitler?, 1941. A formation of B-24D liberators fills up the sky. Fine, linen-mounted, 25 x 22 inches. $225–$275

I Keep the Home Front Pledge. A homemaker holds her hand up, ready to pledge. Fine, 20 x 28 inches. $75–$100

As above, fine, 28 x 40 inches. $90–$125

I'm Out to Lick Runaway Prices. Young woman in ruffled apron makes a stand against black marketeers. Very good, 20 x 28 inches. $75–$100

It Must Never Happen Here!, ca. 1943. An American engine crew is hijacked by Nazis. Printed by Brotherhood of Firemen and Enginemen. Fine, 21 x 27 inches. $345–$400

It's a Long Way To Rome. German propagandist shows how far the Allies had to go on the map. Very good, linen-mounted, 31 x 46 inches. $1,250–$1,350

It's Here, Tojo. A picture of a B-29 dominates this poster in which the Hudson Motor Car Company boasts of its achievements. Fine, 38 x 49 inches. $295–$350

Join the WAC Now!, 1944. Wacs are pictured performing a variety of vital tasks for the air force, ground force, and service force. Fine, 25 x 38 inches. $135–$175

Jugoslavia—Hitler's Traffic Jam. A red hand stops an oncoming tank, symbolizing the delays the Nazis experienced there. Mint, 17 x 22 inches. $65–$100

Keep 'Em Rolling!, 1944. U.S. worker lifts his wrench in triumph. Fine, 10 x 14 inches. $65–$100

Keep Us Flying!, 1943. American squadron hero Robert Diez is featured on this bond drive poster. Fine, linen-mounted, 20 x 28 inches. $425–$475

Knock Off a Japanazi. A machine gunner blasts away at a shooting gallery of Axis targets. Fine, 18 x 23 inches. $95–$125

Leaders of the R.A.F., 1941. Photographic portraits are shown against a cloudy sky. Fine, 30 x 20 inches. $135–$175

Let's Go!, 1941. Pre-Pearl Harbor recruiting poster shows cadets headed to their planes. Fine, 25 x 38 inches. $225–$275

Lick Them Over There! Come On, Canada! Gigantic Canadian trooper steps over the Atlantic to help the English. Fine, 24 x 36 inches. $275–$325

Lock Up These Papers, 1943. Warning to government employees about security. Very good, 14 x 20 inches. $95–$150

Marines Find Adventure Everywhere, 1939. Marines are shown in exciting and glamorous photos for travel, training, and education. Very good, 21 x 11 inches.
$225–$275

The Men Are Ready. A line of RCAF pilots awaits the production of planes. Fine, linen-mounted, 20 x 30 inches.
$200–$250

Men Working Together!, 1942. Trio of soldier, rigger, and sailor stand side by side, united to win for America. Fine, 40 x 28 inches.
$90–$125

Modern Barracks—Modern Ships, 1939. Sleek marine quarters and ship to match with modern lettering style. Very good, 21 x 11 inches.
$225–$275

More Production, 1942. Prizewinning MoMA poster shows a bomb headed to a composite of the Japanese rising sun and German swastika. Fine, linen-mounted, 28 x 40 inches.
$275–$300

Never Was So Much Owed by So Many To So Few, 1940. Churchill's quote is used over a photo of RAF pilots. Mint, 20 x 30 inches.
$475–$525

Now We'll Talk Their Language. Promotional poster for U.S. bonds shows a streaking fighter firing in on its prey. Fine, 22 x 32 inches.
$75–$100

One People, One Nation, One Leader, 1938. A portrait of Hitler in uniform as military commander. Mint, linen-mounted, 32 x 33 inches.
$1,350–$1,450

Our Boys Are Giving Their All, 1942. U.S. sergeant with his gun drawn leads the men into battle. Fine, 30 x 40 inches.
$150–$175

Our Fight Is Right Here—Work to Win. A plane wing flies over a factory, emphasizing the need for worker support. Fine, linen-mounted, 15 x 22 inches.
$185–$225

Our Wounded Need Help! A broadside lists ten ways nurses could be released for military service. Fine, 21 x 28 inches.
$75–$100

Plant a Victory Garden, 1943 (Nelson #36). A family bends over a garden to pick their own food so surplus can be sent to the front. Fine, linen-mounted, 22 x 28 inches.
$135–$175

Poland First to Fight. Polish pilot jumps out of his cockpit after completing his mission. Mint, 12 x 16 inches.
$125–$150

The R.A.F., ca. 1943. Photo of British fighters bombing Hamburg. Mint, 18 x 25 inches.
$125–$150

Rationing Means a Fair Share for All of Us, 1943. Illustration showing the difference between rationing and not in a grocery store. Fine, 22 x 28 inches.
$145–$175

Reich Lottery, 1935. A German eagle is proudly perched on a swastika. Fine, linen-mounted, 23 x 33 inches.
$450–$500

Save Containers, 1943. American poster gives details on how scrap becomes military containers. Fine, 14 x 20 inches. $65–$100

Save His Life and Find Your Own, 1943. Nurse keeps a careful watch over a wounded soldier in this recruitment poster. Fine, 14 x 20 inches. $95–$125

Sew, Serve and Save. An appeal for war bonds by showing a woman sewing. Fine, 20 x 30 inches. $185–$225

So Long, Gang—Don't Forget to Write! A Texaco white-collar worker marches off to war carrying his new gear. Fine, linen-mounted, 11 x 24 inches.
                    $285–$325

Sorry, Canada Got It First! A housewife rifles through her husband's pockets only to hear he's given it all to the war. Fine, 36 x 48 inches. $145–$175

Stamp Out Black Markets, 1943. Massive thumb and ration stamp crush a black marketeer. Fine, 22 x 28 inches. $95–$125

Stay on the Job Until Every Murdering Jap Is Wiped Out!, 1944. Newspaper illustration of Japanese soldier butting a prisioner with a rifle. Fine, 17 x 23 inches.
                    $135–$175

Still More Production. Raring to go, a worker rolls up his red, white, and blue sleeves. 9 x 13 inches. $50–$75

The Storm Troops Call. Filmstrip shows German SA training in the early thirties. Very good, linen-mounted, 21 x 33 inches. $325–$375

Think, 1942. Silhouettes of marines on patrol at dawn in the Pacific. Fine, linen-mounted, 20 x 27 inches. $165–$200

This Is My Fight Too!, 1942. A photo of woman factory worker using her pay to buy U.S. bonds. Fine, 22 x 28 inches. $85–$125

Triumph Over Tyranny!, 1942. The head of a woman is surrounded by artillery shells. Fine, linen-mounted, 40 x 60 inches. $425–$475

U.S. Marines Travel . . . the World, 1929. A deco design of marines circumnavigating the globe. Fine, 21 x 11 inches. $245–$275

U.S. Marines Want You, 1942. Officer demands attention with the U.S. flag behind him. Fine, linen-mounted, 28 x 40 inches. $245–$300

Victory Comes High!, 1944. Photos of wounded marines show the realities of combat. Fine, 28 x 40 inches. $145–$200

Victory Still Comes High!, 1945. Marines help carry a wounded buddy, along with photos of wounded soldiers on the beachheads. Fine, 28 x 40 inches.
                    $145–$200

Voices of Freedom Live. British photomontage of Allied nationals in uniforms reading their native newspapers. Fine, 15 x 20 inches. $65–$100

1. Posters can make a stunning interior design statement. Courtesy of Linda Tarasuk, La Belle Epoque, NY.

SFER-20 Radiola, 1925, by Leonetto ppiello (French). Courtesy of Pasquale netti, Art Galleries, CA.

3. *Phebus*, ca. 1898, by PAL (French). Courtesy of Laura Gold, Park South Gallery, NY.

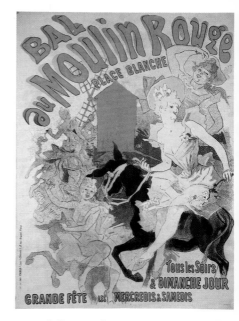

4. *La Samaritaine*, 1897, by Alphonse Mucha (French). Courtesy of Christie's, NY.

5. *Bal du Moulin Rouge*, 1889, Jules Chéret (French). Courtesy of a private collector.

6. *Normandie/New York*, 1935, by A. M. Cassandre (French). Courtesy of Christie's, NY.

7. *Camden Town, Chalk Farm or Regents Park*, 1933, by Jean Dupas for London Underground (English). Courtesy of Christie's, NY.

Compagnia d'Opere Comiche, 1910,
Leopoldo Metlicovitz (Italian).
urtesy of Bernice Jackson Fine
ts, MA.

9. *Prelittoriali Del Lavoro XXI*, 1492, by
Franco Chelini (Italian). Courtesy of
Bernice Jackson Fine Arts, MA.

. *Les Cigarettes Mekka*, 1919, by
harles Loupot (Swiss). Courtesy of The
llenberger Collection, Blonay,
vitzerland.

11. *PKZ*, 1923. by Otto Baumberger
(Swiss). Courtesy of Bernice Jackson
Fine Arts, MA.

12. *Chaliapine/Boris Godounov*, 1932, by Joop
Sjollema (Dutch). Courtesy of Bernice Jackson
Fine Arts, MA.

13. *Polska*, ca. 1928, by Stefan Norblin
(Polish). From the collection of Al Hoch,
Lexington, MA.

14. *Mozart/Don Giovanni,* by Jan Leni
(Polish). Courtesy of the Fox Collection.

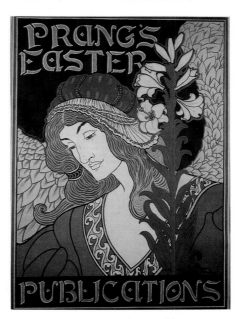

Harper's June, 1896, by Edward
nfield (American). Courtesy of a pri-
e collector.

16. *Prang's Easter Publications*,
1895, by Louis Rhead (American).
Courtesy of a private collector.

18. *The Perfect Finish*, 1929, Mather
Work Incentive Poster (American).
Courtesy of Heller & Heller/Posters at
Work, NY.

7. *Pan American Exposition*,
901, by Evelyn Rumsey Cary
American). From the collection of
l Hoch, Lexington, MA.

19. *Enlist in the Army/Navy/Marines*, 1917, by Paxton and Hall (World War Posters). Courtesy of Meehan Military Posters, NY.

20. *Helden a'∂ Somme* (Heroism on the Somme), 1916, by Hans Rudi Erdt (World War Posters). Courtesy of Meehan Military Posters, NY.

21. *Olympic Games, Helsinki*, 1940, by Ilmari Sysimetsä. Courtesy of Harvey Abrams Books, PA.

22. *Cycles Jules DuBois*, ca. 1900, Anonymous (Bicycles). Courtesy of Swann Galleries, NY.

23. *Le Nouveau Train Bleu*, 1928, by Pierre Zenobel (Trains). Courtesy of Harris Gallery, CA.

24. *Air France/Amérique Du Nord*, 1946, by Guy Arnoux (Aviation and Air Travel). Courtesy of Harris Gallery, CA.

25. *Thurston/Million Dollar Mystery*, ca. 1920s, Anonymous (Magic). Courtesy of Ken Trombly, Washington, D.C.

26. *Life and Adventures of Buffalo Bill*, Anonymous (Circus). Courtesy of Swann Galleries, NY.

27. *Frankenstein*, 1931, Anonymo (Cinema). Courtesy of Odyssey Auctions, C

28. *Atom Man vs. Superman*, 1950, Anonymous. Courtesy of Camden House, CA.

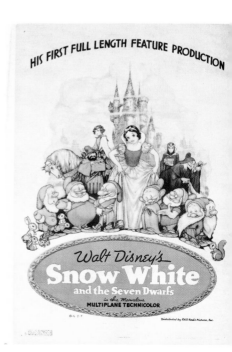

29. *Snow White and the Seven Dwarfs*, 19 Anonymous. Courtesy of Christie's, NY.

Volunteer for the SS Mountain Troops. A trooper wearing SS camouflage confronts the viewer to join the elite troops. Fine, 23 x 33 inches.　$950–$1,000

Wanted!, 1943. Graphic poster promotes bonds via payroll savings. Fine, 22 x 28 inches.　$55–$100

War Bonds Will Shield Her, ca. 1942. A young girl asleep with her teddy is unaware that a German bomber is flying overhead. Fine, 48 x 35 inches.

$185–$225

War Offering. A Nazi assault badge is shown to solicit funds. Mint, linen-mounted, 19 x 28 inches.　$450–$500

War Shipments Mean Less Fuel, 1943. Long johns are displayed as a solution to oil shortages. Fine, linen-mounted, 22 x 28 inches.　$95–$125

War-Stricken Children in Britain Still Need Our Help! Photo of British child who looks dazed and disheveled after a raid. Fine, 14 x 22 inches.　$85–$125

We Have Just Begun to Fight!, 1943 (Nelson #134). GI with rifle rallies those behind him. Fine, 16 x 22 inches.　$75–$100

As above, fine, 22 x 28 inches.　$95–$125

As above, fine, 28 x 40 inches.　$125–$175

We Will Have to Fight Our Way Ashore, 1944. Admiral King with his quote illustrated in painting and photo. Fine, 40 x 30 inches.　$200–$250

We're Helping Strike 'Em Out. A GI prepares to hurl grenade as a train rushes by underneath. Mint, 16 x 23 inches.　$75–$100

West Point of the Air, 1940. Photo of a pilot surrounded by other photos of life as a cadet. Fine, 25 x 38 inches.　$325–$375

When VE Day Comes Bridgeport Will Work . . . Attractive woman worker prays for her man to return home. Fine, 18 x 24 inches.　$125–$150

You Bet I'm Going Back To Sea!, 1942, Merchant sailor with his duffel bag faces the viewer. Fine, 14 x 20 inches.　$200–$250

As above, fine, 30 x 40 inches.　$245–$300

YOU Can Help to Build Me a Plane. A British pilot in flight suit points to the viewer to be productive. Very good, 10 x 15 inches.　$50–$75

Young Men, 1940. U.S. Navy prewar recruiting poster depicts a battleship surrounded by stars. Mint, linen-mounted, 28 x 40 inches.　$195–$225

❦ ADAMS

That's Why I Buy Victory Bonds. A smiling black porter points to a white Canadian soldier returning home to his girl. Fine, 24 x 36 inches.　$650–$700

❧ ALDWINCKLE

Canada's New Army. A dispatch rider rearing his motorcycle is echoed by a vision of a knight on horseback. Fine, 24 x 36 inches. $285–$350

❧ ALLEN

The Sky's the Limit!, 1944 (Nelson #70). Woman worker and co-workers assemble a B-17 engine. Fine, linen-mounted, 20 x 27 inches. $175–$200

❧ OTTO ANTON (1895–1976)

Leibstandarte SS Adolph Hitler. SS recruiting poster featuring two soldiers with their machine guns. Mint, 23 x 33 inches. $1,250–$1,350

Waffen, SS! Teenage volunteer wears his Nazi uniform. Fine, linen-mounted, 12 x 17 inches. $485–$550

As above, very good, linen-mounted, 17 x 23 inches. $925–$975

❧ EGMONT ARENS (1887–?)

Don't Shiver Next Winter, 1944. Cartoon image of a penguin bundled up, holding his shovel. Fine, 18 x 26 inches. $175–$200

❧ JOHN ATHERTON (1900–1952)

A Careless Word . . . Another Cross, 1943. Grave maker draped with ammo belt and helmet illustrates the danger of careless talk. Fine, linen-mounted, 22 x 28 inches. $125–$150

As above, fine, 28 x 40 inches. $150–$175

❧ BAKER

Back Up Eisenhower, 1942. Portrait of Eisenhower is used to encourage production. Fine, linen-mounted, 22 x 30 inches. $245–$300

❧ BALL

For Peace and Security, 1945. Bond poster using the three Wise Men crossing the desert following the Star of Bethlehem. Fine, 26 x 37 inches. $85–$125

❧ MCCLELLAND BARCLAY (1891–MIA 1943)

Dish It Out with the Navy, 1942. Forceful sailors fire at enemy aircraft. Mint, 28 x 42 inches. $250–$300

Save Your Cans—Help Pass the Ammunition, ca. 1942. (Nelson #45). A housewife's tomato cans are transformed into ammo for a machine gunner. Fine, linen-mounted, 25 x 33 inches. $245–$300

Poster by Otto Anton.
Courtesy of Meehan
Military Posters.

Poster by Cecil Beal. Courtesy
of Meehan Military Posters.

🌿 BAUMGARTEN

Skilled Mechanics Wanted, ca. 1935. An RAF workman leans on his saw and smiles out to the viewer. Fine, 20 x 30 inches. $375–$425

🌿 CECIL CALVERT BEALL (1892–?)

And If Your Lines Should Form, Then Break. Inspirational quote above a wounded marine still fighting. Fine, 27 x 35 inches. $185–$225

Bombs Away! AAF, the Greatest Team in the World, 1944. A bombardier is pictured releasing his stick of bombs. Fine, linen-mounted, 25 x 38 inches.
$385–$450

Do It Right, Make It Bite, 1942. Worker does his job while a German fighter is shown plunging into the sea. Fine, 28 x 40 inches. $200–$250

Loose Talk Can Cost Lives, 1942. Two workers talking at a bar are unaware of the image of Hitler listening in. Mint, 14 x 20 inches. $125–$150

Now All Together, 1945 (Nelson #122). Poster based on the famous photo of the marines raising the U.S. flag over Iwo Jima. Fine, 9 x 12 inches. $50–$75

As above, fine, 26 x 37 inches. $200–$225

As above, fine, coated stock, 20 x 28 inches. $150–$175

❦ LESTER BEALL (1903–1969)

Don't Let Him Down!, 1942. Arrow points out the pun as an aircraft fighter fires away. Fine, linen-mounted, 30 x 40 inches. $450–$500

❦ WLADYSLAW T. BENDA (1873–1948)

Polish War Relief. A fearful woman with children is threatened by bayonets. Fine, linen-mounted, 30 x 43 inches. $550–$600

❦ BINGHAM

Next!, 1945 (Nelson #124). GI grits his teeth as he peers down on a map of Japan. Fine, 20 x 28 inches. $90–$125

As above, linen-mounted, 28 x 40 inches. $145–$175

❦ GINO BOCCASILE (1901–1952)

Don't Betray My Son, 1942. A grieving Italian mother with her son's medal shining on her dress. Fine, linen-mounted, 28 x 40 inches. $3,000–$3,250

London, 1940. An Italian gives a "thumbs down" gesture above the city of London in flames. Fine, linen-mounted, 28 x 39 inches. $3,500–$3,750

Untitled, 1944. Italian poster showing a black American sergeant with his arm around a looted Roman statue, with a $2 price tag. Mint, linen-mounted, 28 x 40 inches. $5,000–$5,500

Vostro Amico? (Your Friend?). A grisly skeleton wearing a British helmet grips a ruined wall as it advances through the rubble. Mint, linen-mounted, 28 x 40 inches. $3,750–$4,250

Poster by Wladyslaw T. Benda. Courtesy of Meehan Military Posters.

Poster by Gino Boccasile.
Courtesy of Meehan
Military Posters.

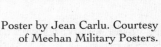

Poster by Jean Carlu. Courtesy
of Meehan Military Posters.

❦ BRAILE

The Downfall of the Dictators. British soldiers in glowing light pursue the fleeing enemy. Mint, 20 x 30 inches. $225–$275

As above, mint, 25 x 40 inches. $250–$300

❦ BRODER

Your Scrap . . . Brought It Down, 1942. A German plane in flames heads
straight down. Fine, 20 x 28 inches. $165–$200

❦ BURBANK

Old Salts, 1933. "Old salts" are shown on board a square rigger to promote the
tradition of the navy. Fine, 28 x 42 inches. $275–$325

❦ CFM (MONGRAM)

Help Greece Now! Anitiquities of Greece persevere in the battle as the mother and child do in the foreground. Fine, 15 x 20 inches. $95–$125

❦ JEAN CARLU (b. 1900)

America's Answer! Production, 1942. Strong hand tightens the screws on production. Fine, linen-mounted, 40 x 30 inches. $1,500–$1,600

Between the Hammer and the Anvil, ca. 1942. An Allied hammer comes down and shatters a swastika on an anvil. Fine, 17 x 22 inches. $275–$325

Give 'Em Both Barrels, 1941 (Nelson #65). GI fires his machine gun while a riveter performs his duty above. Fine, linen-mounted, 40 x 30 inches.
$1,250–$1,350

As above, but 20 x 15 inches. $350–$400

❧ CHANCE

War Traffic Must Come First. A close-up of the train's wheels as it speeds on by. Fine, linen-mounted, 14 x 18 inches. $175–$200

❧ COGGINS

Aircraft Insignia, 1943. American and British aircraft square off against Japanese and German planes, to help people identify aircraft insignias. Fine, 24 x 18 inches. $245–$300

❧ COOPER

Woman's Place in War, 1944. A recruiting poster for WACs with a private keeping an eye on the stormy skies. Fine, 25 x 39 inches. $125–$150

❧ BRADSHAW CRANDELL (1896–1966)

Are You a Girl with a Star Spangled Heart?, 1943. A proud WAC stands in front of the flag. Fine, linen-mounted, 25 x 39 inches. $235–$275

❧ DANIEL

Remember Greece. The faces of starving children stare out as a priest rings bells to remind the world. Mint, 14 x 22 inches. $75–$100

❧ DIMITRI

Keep 'Em Flying!, 1941. U.S. aircrew checks out a map as B-17s fly overhead. Fine, 25 x 38 inches. $325–$375

❧ WALT DISNEY (1901–1966)

Buy a Bond, 1945 (Nelson #81). Donald Duck, Pinocchio, Bambi, and three dwarfs urge kids to buy bonds. Fine, 17 x 22 inches. $285–$325

❧ STEVAN DOHANOS (b. 1907)

Award for Careless Talk, 1944. A hand with a Nazi ring awards the Iron Cross to those who carelessly aided Germany. Fine, 20 x 28 inches. $185–$250

As above, fine, 28 x 37 inches. $225–$275

Poster by Bradshaw Crandell. Courtesy of Poster Plus Posters.

Poster by Bradshaw Crandell. Courtesy of Meehan Military Posters.

Bits of Careless Talk, 1943. A hand with a Nazi ring moves the final piece into the puzzle pointing to England. Fine, 20 x 28 inches. $145–$175

As above, fine, 28 x 40 inches. $200–$225

Fill It!, 1945. Arms holding an empty basket in front of a harvest. Fine, 22 x 28 inches. $85–$125

Loose Talk Can Cost Lives, 1942. Merchant ship is shown sinking, with lifeboats trying to escape. Fine, 14 x 20 inches. $125–$150

❦ ALBERT DORNE (b. 1904)

All Fuel Is Scarce, 1945. A man looks out of his frosty windows at the thermometer. Fine, 20 x 28 inches. $75–$100

❦ DOUGLASS

Serve Those Who Served, 1945 (Nelson #74). Wounded soldier in a wheelchair reminds nurses that they are needed in VA hospitals. Fine, linen-mounted, 20 x 28 inches. $200–$250

Work on a Farm This Summer (Nelson #114). A farming couple holding their basket of vegetables. Fine, 22 x 28 inches. $85–$125

🕊 EDMUNDSEN

U.S. Cadet Nurse Corps. Recruiting poster shows a blond woman in full uniform with faraway gaze. Fine, 20 x 28 inches. $65–$100

🕊 ELLGAARD

The Police—Your Friend, Your Helper, 1938. One of a series of posters honoring German police. Here he helps an old woman cross the street. Fine, 23 x 33 inches. $295–$350

🕊 ENLEIGH

Let's Go, CANADA! A Gung ho trooper prepares for action with a Canadian flag behind him. Fine, 24 x 36 inches. $225–$275

🕊 JOHN FALTER (b. 1910)

Can I Tell 'Em You're Still With Us?, 1945. Young sailor uses a semaphone to signal to workers. Fine, 28 x 40 inches. $165–$200

Don't Slow up the Ship. A split image of a shipyard worker loafing while American POWs are being abused by a Nazi. Fine, 30 x 40 inches. $245–$300

If you Tell Where He's Going . . ., 1943 (Nelson #95). A sailor with a smile prepares to ship out, unaware that careless talk might take his life. Fine, 20 x 28 inches. $125–$150

As above, fine, 28 x 40 inches. $165–$200

Your Navy Spearhead of Victory, 1943. Overhead view of planes flying over a carrier. Fine, linen-mounted, 28 x 40 inches. $375–$425

🕊 ERNEST FIENE (1894–1965)

If You Can't Go Across . . . Come Across! Smiling sailor gives the victory sign as he boards ship. Fine, 11 x 16 inches. $65–$100

🕊 ANTON FISCHER (1882–1962)

A Careless World . . . a Needless Sinking, 1942 (Nelson #137). Merchants rowing to distance themselves from their burning ship. Fine, 22 x 28 inches.
                                                                              $145–$175

As above, fine, linen-mounted, 28 x 40 inches. $175–$200

🕊 JAMES MONTGOMERY FLAGG (1877–1960)

China Looks To Us! Chinese child looks out with bleakness. Signed in Chinese characters as well. Mint, 11 x 14 inches. $125–$150

Help China! Uncle Sam helps a fleeing Chinese family amidst flames. Mint, 14 x 22 inches. $145–$175

I Want You for the U.S. Army, 1941. A reissue of Flagg's famous poster from WWI, with Uncle Sam pointing to the viewer. Fine, linen-mounted, 25 x 39 inches. $975–$1,025

Jap, You're Next!, 1945. Uncle Sam rolls up his sleeves while holding a big wrench. Fine, linen-mounted, 14 x 20 inches. $175–$225

As above, restored, linen-mounted, 30 x 40 inches. $300–$350

The Marines Have Landed, 1942. Marines hold rifles above as they storm the beachhead. Fine, linen-mounted, 30 x 40 inches. $325–$375

Want Action?, 1942. A GI reaches out to the viewer to join the fight. Fine, linen-mounted, 30 x 40 inches. $375–$425

You Can Lick Runaway Prices (Nelson #135). Uncle Sam gives seven ways to keep prices down. Fine, 20 x 28 inches. $165–$200

❦ FREESE

Guilty, 1946. Postwar poster shows a skull with Hitler's image in hellish glow. Mint, 32 x 33 inches. $1,750–$1,850

❦ FRISSELL

Volunteer for Victory, ca. 1943. A Red Cross volunteer struts across as the flags flap in the breeze. Fine, 21 x 33 inches. $75–$100

❦ ABRAM GAMES (b. 1914)

A.T.S. Golden sculpturesque head of a volunteer in the Auxilary Territorial Service. A different poster than the rarer *Join the A.T.S.* poster described in the chapter, but still highly desirable. Mint, 20 x 30 inches. $1,200–$1,300

Radio Location. A German plane is caught like a fly in British radar. Fine, linen-mounted, 20 x 30 inches. $975–$1,025

❦ GERARD

Next!, 1943. A GI consigns Tojo and Hitler to an oblivion peopled with Herod, Pilate, Nero, and Attila the Hun. Mint, 18 x 12 inches. $65–$100

❦ S. R. GOFF

> NOTE: Goff signed his posters with a psyeudonym of his initials: "Es-Arr-Gee." His posters were privately issued by Seagrams Liquors to bars along the coast that served seamen.

Free Speech Doesn't Mean Careless Talk!, ca. 1942. A green parrot conveys the message. Fine, linen-mounted, 22 x 28 inches. $235–$300

Loose Lips Might Sink Ships, ca. 1942. U.S. ship in smoke against red sky sinks into the blue sea. One of the most famous and rarest WWII posters, the title of which forms the basis for the most misquoted saying of the war. Mint, linen-mounted, 22 x 28 inches. $1,250–$1,350

Starve Him with Silence, 1942 (Nelson #100). A rat representing Tojo with a swastika on his side feasts on war secrets. Fine, 22 x 28 inches. $135–$175

Stop Loose Talk To Strangers, ca. 1942. Graphic poster with a white hand raised as a reminder to prevent espionage. Very good, 20 x 28 inches.
$165–$200

❧ GRAVES

Right Is Might, 1942. At ground level a tank tread appears enormous. Fine, 25 x 38 inches. $185–$225

❧ GREENSHAW

Buy More War Bonds and Stamps, 1942. A fist blasts through a swastika. Fine, linen-mounted, 20 x 28 inches. $375–$425

❧ GLENN GROHE (b. 1912)

He's Watching You, 1942. Eerie figure in German helmet peers out from the shadows. Fine, 10 x 14 inches. $285–$350

❧ GUINNESS

Let's Go Get 'Em! U.S. Marines. Marines advance through the Pacific island jungle. Fine, linen-mounted, 28 x 40 inches. $500–$550

Poster by Glenn Grohe.
Courtesy of Meehan
Military Posters.

❦ **HAGEL**

Produce for Victory!, 1942. A photo of an immigrant is featured above a quote for freedom. Fine, 24 x 36 inches. $125–$150

❦ **HALLAM**

Fighting Comrades of the Skies. Canadian gunner, bomber, navigator, pilot, and operator gather before a mission. Fine, 26 x 43 inches. $485–$550

I'll Be With You, Boys. A RCAF pilot watches the sky as his comrades depart. Fine, 20 x 27 inches. $285–$325

❦ **HARRIS**

Blood Will Tell. A rugged fur trader stands behind his counterpart, a Canadian air force trooper. Fine, 24 x 36 inches. $475–$525

Join the Team! Royal Canadian Air Force. A heroic young aviator suited up and ready to go. Fine, 20 x 27 inches. $285–$325

❦ **HAYDEN**

USO Until They're Home, ca. 1943. A happy vet and pretty WAVE appreciate the USO. Mint, 14 x 22 inches. $75–$100

❦ **LEON HELGUERA**

I'm Counting on You!, 1943. Uncle Sam holds his finger to his lips to caution the viewer not to talk carelessly. Fine, 22 x 28 inches. $100–$125

As above, fine, 28 x 40 inches. $145–$175

❦ **HILL**

Fly with the Marines, 1944 (Nelson #103). A marine eagle smashes a Japanese bomber. Fine, linen-mounted, 28 x 40 inches. $375–$425

❦ **HIRSCH**

Carry Your Share, 1943. GI helps another soldier with his weighty duffel bag to demonstrate the need for civilians to buy bonds. Fine, 11 x 16 inches. $65–$100

❦ **JOHN HIX (1908–1944)**

Can't Hide There Any More, Boys, 1943. U.S. radar uncovers cowering Hitler, Tojo, and Mussolini. Mint, 18 x 12 inches. $65–$100

❦ **HOFFMANN**

Yes! Hitler!, 1933. A photo of Hitler in a confident pose with supporters cheering behind. Very good, linen-mounted, 24 x 34 inches. $650–$700

🍂 LUDWIG HOHLWEIN (1874–1949)

Come With Me, 1930. A German trooper adjusts his gear and coaxes the viewer to join. Fine, linen-mounted, 24 x 33 inches. $1,250–$1,350

Competition for German Youth, 1934. A young German in front of Nazi flags promotes vocational training. Fine, linen-mounted, 24 x 33 inches. $1,250–$1,350

Reichs-Kreigerbund, ca. 1937. An officer in shadows proud of the Nazi regime. Fine, linen-mounted, 17 x 25 inches. $975–$1,025

Second Lottery, 1940. A German soldier with shield and spear looks to the sky. Fine, linen-mounted, 16 x 19 inches. $1,100–$1,200

Scharnhorst, 1933. Scharnhorst, a great Prussian military leader, is shown in uniform. Mint, linen-mounted, 19 x 26 inches. $525–$575

🍂 HOTCHKISS

Your Enemy the JAP, 1944. A cartoon illustration of Japanese soldier with descriptions of his methods. Fine, 18 x 25 inches. $185–$225

🍂 HOTCHKISS AND LOVELL

Think of Them Before You Take a Day Off! Three stories of near-death experience by U.S. soldiers urge workers to stay on the job. Fine, 40 x 30 inches. $285–$350

🍂 JOBSON

Back Them Up!, ca. 1942. British de Havilland raids official quarters in Berlin. Fine, linen-mounted, 20 x 30 inches. $385–$450

🍂 GEORGE KANELOUS

Dig Down Deep!, 1945. Tanks and planes advance while a worker digs into his apron to help with funds. Fine, 18 x 26 inches. $65–$100

🍂 E. MCKNIGHT KAUFFER (1890–1970)

For the Conquered. A Nazi dagger pierces a hand in the shadows. Fine, linen-mounted, 9 x 12 inches. $135–$175

Freedom of Religion, 1942. A cross with a bayonet is used to drive through a swastika. Fine, linen-mounted, 14 x 20 inches. $750–$800

Greece Fights On, 1942. A silhouette of a classical head looks out while a Greek flag waves in front. Fine, 24 x 36 inches. $250–$300

Greek War Relief, 1943. Classical figure stands proudly before a waving Greek flag. A strong Deco design. Mint, 11 x 16 inches. $75–$100

Courtesy of Meehan
Military Posters.

Courtesy of Meehan
Military Posters.

The New Order, 1942. A mad Mussolini with a swastika around his neck is caricatured. Fine, linen-mounted, 14 x 20 inches. $975–$1,025

Norway Fights On, 1943. A Norwegian flag flies while a ship passes in the distance. Mint, 16 x 23 inches. $175–$200

We Fight for the Liberty of All, ca. 1942. Sleek design of helmeted warrior sweeping into patriotic colors. Fine, 14 x 20 inches. $650–$700

You Can Set Their Spirit Free. Barbed wire contrasts with a black classical figure of a POW. Fine, linen-mounted, 19 x 25 inches. $350–$400

❧ PAT KEELY (d. 1970)

Beware of Mushroomed Tools, 1941. A British poster of a bandaged worker looking out to warn for caution with tools. Fine, 20 x 30 inches. $500–$550

The Factory and Fight Line Are One, 1943. A British naval cruiser cuts through the sea, which turns into a blueprint. Fine, 20 x 30 inches. $850–$900

❧ KENNEY

Accuracy Will Build Better Corsairs. U.S. poster celebrates the prowess of the Corsair. Very good, 17 x 22 inches. $100–$125

❦ **KEPPLER**

Every Bomb Load Counts, 1943. Smiling bombardier in flight suit poses proudly over bombs. Fine, 30 x 40 inches. $275–$325

❦ **KING**

We've Made a Monkey Out of You!, 1943. In a cartoon, Hitler is Uncle Sam's monkey dancing to amuse the Allies. Fine, 15 x 20 inches. $75–$100

❦ **DANIEL KOERNER (b. 1910)**

America's Fighting Fleet and Men, 1943. Fishermen on deck pull up their nets filled with fish. Fine, 20 x 28 inches. $195–$225

Fish Is a Fighting Food, 1943. A barrel full of fish is brought into the docks, Fine, 20 x 28 inches. $195–$225

❦ **KOLADA**

Remember Me?, 1944. An evil Japanese captain tests his sword, readying for future battles. Fine, 40 x 30 inches. $385–$450

❦ **KOLNBERGER**

Munich's Artist Covers the War. German grenadiers shown rushing into action. Fine, 17 x 24 inches. $365–$425

❦ **LAMBERT**

Buy War Bonds, 1942. A GI gets a grip on Axis leaders and war finances under an American eagle. Fine, linen-mounted, 13 x 17 inches. $75–$100

❦ **LETZOLD**

Save Gas for Armaments. A gas burner is used to show a tank and bomber. Mint, 17 x 24 inches. $325–$375

❦ **LEO LIONNI (b. 1910)**

Keep 'Em Rolling, 1941. Photomontage of workman and fighters superimposed over a U.S. flag. Fine, linen-mounted, 30 x 40 inches. $1,500–$1,600

Keep 'Em Rolling, 1941. Photomontage of workman and tanks superimposed over a U.S. flag. Fine, linen-mounted, 30 x 40 inches. $1,500–$1,600

Keep 'Em Rolling, 1941. Photomontage of workman and PT boats superimposed over a U.S. flag. Fine, linen-mounted, 30 x 40 inches. $1,500–$1,600

Keep 'Em Rolling, 1941. Photomontage of workman and antiaircraft gun and crews superimposed over a U.S. flag. Fine, linen-mounted, 30 x 40 inches.
                              $1,500–$1,600

◈ FRED LUDEKENS (b. 1900)

He's a Fighting Fool. Antiaircraft gunner aims his gun at fighters above. Fine, 28 x 40 inches. $65–$100

◈ MARKS

This Is the Enemy, 1943. A Nazi hand plunges a bayonet through the Bible. Fine, linen-mounted, 20 x 28 inches. $175–$200

As above, fine, 28 x 40 inches. $200–$250

◈ MARTIN

To Have and to Hold! (Nelson #115). A tattered GI unfurls an enormous flag. Fine, 22 x 28 inches. $175–$200

◈ HERBERT MATTER (1907–1984)

America Calling, 1941. Swiss artist's call to civilian defense with the use of an eagle soaring across. Fine, 30 x 40 inches. $325–$375

◈ MCCABE

Our Street Corners Must Not Be Next! A Nazi stands guard on a French corner, unaware a victory sign is on the wall behind him. Fine, 22 x 28 inches.
$225–$275

◈ MCKIM

Greasing the Skids, 1943. Cartoon of U.S. war production causing Hitler, Mussolini, and Tojo to fall into hell. Mint, 18 x 12 inches. $65–$100

◈ MELBOURNE

Millions of Troops Are on the Move, 1943. Millions of troops pour off a train. Fine, 22 x 28 inches. $125–$150

◈ MERTE

Fourth German Cavalry Day, 1943. Saxon calvary are shown in dashing color. Fine, linen-mounted, 26 x 39 inches. $1,200–$1,300

◈ MEYER-LAHUSEN

Winter Help Week, 1939. Profile of a bronzed Nazi trooper. Fine, 16 x 24 inches. $250–$300

◈ MILLER

If the Temperature Tempts You to Take Off, 1943. A lone American gunner fires away despite flames all around. Very good, 20 x 27 inches. $95–$125

We Can't Win This War Without Teamwork on the Battlefield—and on the Home Front Too!, 1944. U.S. artillery crew zeros in on a stronghold. Fine, 20 x 27 inches. $100–$125

🕊 MJOLNIR

Crush the Enemy in One Blow. A Nazi first comes down to pummel Pétain, Churchill, and a Jew. Fine, 33 x 46 inches. $950–$1,000

Our Flags To Victory. A German eagles soars across a row of Nazi flags. Fine, linen-mounted, 36 x 47 inches. $1,250–$1,350

🕊 MOLDENHAUER

School Savings Bank. An alpine scene with Nazi tent encampment. Very good, linen-mounted, 24 x 33 inches. $185–$225

🕊 MURPHEY

Navy Training Courses, 1939. Sailor with books and tools prepares for training class. Fine, 28 x 42 inches. $125–$150

Take the Wheel . . . Steer a Course for Future Success, 1941. Recruiting poster with a destroyer. Fine, 28 x 42 inches. $235–$300

🕊 MYERS

Don't Get Hurt, 1943 (Nelson #63). GI looks up from his submachine gun to warn workers. Fine, 30 x 40 inches. $200–$250

🕊 NIMI

Italy Against the Italians, ca. 1944. A poster showing Stalin holding a baby in a bloodied room. Fine, linen-mounted, 28 x 40 inches. $1,750–$1,850

🕊 NOCKHOLDS

Back Them Up!, 1942. British bombers attack the German port of Lübeck. Fine, linen-mounted, 20 x 30 inches. $365–$425

🕊 ODELL

Buy Victory Bonds. The eyes of a concerned woman are shown over the horizon filled with tanks and men. Fine, 24 x 36 inches. $385–$450

🕊 OLIPHANT

Back Them Up!, 1943. Redcaps of the British Airborne Army land in heavy fighting. Fine, 20 x 30 inches. $275–$325

❦ PARKER

American Junior Red Cross. Young people bring donations to an American Red Cross officer. Fine, 15 x 22 inches. $135–$175

❦ PEEL

Czechoslovaks Carry On, 1942. A Czech soldier rallies Czech and Polish patriots for freedom. Winning entry from MoMA contest. Fine, 24 x 32 inches.
$135–$175

Luxembourg Resists. Workers carrying their flag, determined to prevail. Fine, 24 x 32 inches. $100–$125

❦ BERNARD PERLIN (b. 1918)

Let 'Em Have It, 1944 (Nelson #156). GI lobs a grenade toward a smoky cloud. fine, 22 x 28 inches. $125–$150

As above, fine, linen-mounted, 28 x 40 inches. $150–$175

❦ PERLIN AND MARTIN

Americans Will Always Fight for Liberty, 1943 (Nelson #10). Ranks of GIs pass by the ghostly veterans of Valley Forge. Fine, 22 x 28 inches. $165–$200

As above, fine, 28 x 40 inches. $200–$250

❦ WEIMAR PURSELL (1906–1974)

When You Ride Alone, You Ride with Hitler, 1942. Conservation call showing a housewife with her groceries. Fine, 22 x 28 inches. $185–$225

❦ R.E.Z. (MONOGRAM)

The Mediterranean, the Decisive Theater. A German tank crunches into the battlefield with German fighters above. Mint, linen-mounted, 16 x 24 inches.
$600–$650

❦ RABKIN

Don't Burn Waste Paper. Trash can with garbage in flames. Fine, 17 x 22 inches.
$175–$200

❦ LESLIE RAGAN (1897–?)

United, 1943. A fantasy of Allied flags rippling over mighty battleships. Fine, 22 x 28 inches. $75–$100

❧ RAPP

I've Found the Job Where I Fit Best, 1943. Split view in blue and red of a worker and artillery crew. Fine, linen-mounted, 28 x 40 inches. $375–$425

❧ GRANT REYNARD (1887–1967)

Lend a Hand. Pilot in his seat parachute and life vest gives the victory sign. Fine, 11 x 16 inches. $135–$175

❧ RICHARDS

Housewives! Save Waste Fat for Explosive!, ca. 1942. Frying pan drips down into an artillery gun. Fine, 16 x 20 inches. $75–$100

They've Got More Important Places to Go Than You!, 1942 (Nelson #32). GIs are flying along in their jeep as a reminder to conserve rubber. Fine, 28 x 40 inches. $175–$200

❧ NORMAN ROCKWELL (1894–1978)

Hasten the Homecoming, 1945 (Nelson #120). Willie Gillis's homecoming to the delight of his tenement neighborhood. Fine, 20 x 30 inches. $425–$475

Let's Give Him Enough and on Time, 1942. A gunner squats behind his machine gun. Fine, linen-mounted, 40 x 28 inches. $1,250–$1,350

Mine America's Coal, 1944. A weathered miner in his gear looks to the viewer sympathetically. Fine, linen-mounted, 20 x 28 inches. $475–$525

Ours to Fight For, 1943. A series of four posters to reinforce the four freedoms from Roosevelt's speech. Freedom from Fear and Want, and freedom of Speech and Worship. Fine, linen-mounted, 20 x 28 inches, each. $165–$200

As above, fine, 28 x 40 inches, each. $185–$225

❧ ROMAY

Help Holland. Grief-stricken girl in bonnet grieves over a victim of the German occupation. Mint, 14 x 20 inches. $65–$100

They Can Take Only Our Bodies. A Dutchman blindfolded against the wall faces a firing squad. Fine, 14 x 22 inches. $95–$125

❧ ROSENTHAL

Marines on Mt. Suribachi, Iwo Jima, 1945. Famous photo of marines trying to raise the flag on the mountaintop. Fine, 19 x 28 inches. $200–$250

❧ ROSS

U.S. Cadet Nurse Corps, 1945. Coeds stop to admire a uniformed cadet nurse. Fine, linen-mounted, 18 x 26 inches. $135–$175

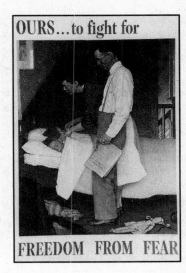

Poster by Norman Rockwell. Courtesy of Meehan Military Posters.

Poster by Norman Rockwell. Courtesy of Meehan Military Posters.

❦ ROTTER

Belgium Fights On. Belgian and Congolese soldiers pose side by side. Mint, linen-mounted, 21 x 30 inches. $250–$300

❦ ROZEN

Won't You Give My Boy a Chance to Get Home?, 1944. A mother looks out, asking civilians to reduce travel. Fine, 20 x 27 inches. $85–$125

As above, fine, 29 x 40 inches. $125–$150

❦ ALLEN R. SAALBURG (1899–?)

Get the Jap and Get It Over With, 1945. Bullet-riddled Japanese flag flies over a shredded Nazi flag. Fine, linen-mounted, 20 x 28 inches. $175–$200

❦ SALAW

The Army Calls Youth. German trainees fire at targets with the image of a suited veteran above. Mint, linen-mounted, 11 x 17 inches. $485–$550

❦ SAMPSON

All for One—One for All. A Canadian soldier, sailor, and aviator stand side by side. Mint, 24 x 36 inches. $200–$250

How About You? A dirty, worn Canadian soldier looks out pleading for support through bonds. Fine, linen-mounted, 36 x 48 inches. $325–$375

A New Generation of Fighting Canadians. Commander awards wings to a new pilot. Fine, 26 x 43 inches. $325–$375

There's a Place for You in the R.C.A.F. A woman private salutes above vignettes of air force slots for women. Fine, 26 x 43 inches. $325–$375

₩ SARRA

This Man May Die, 1943. A sailor in a porthole looks out appealing to others to keep secrets. Fine, 14 x 22 inches. $65–$100

₩ SAUTER

Be Ready for Battle with the SA, 1941. A German officer points to the para-military SA behind. Mint, linen-mounted, 24 x 18 inches. $750–$800

₩ SAVAGE

For Your Country's Sake, 1944. A women's recruiting poster with a WAC blonde, WAVE brunette, marine redhead, and black-haired Spar in alignment. Fine, 17 x 25 inches. $90–$125

₩ MARTHA SAWYERS

You Can't Afford to Miss Either!, 1944 (Nelson #155). Burning plane heads down as the machine gunner looks for new target. Mint, 10 x 14 inches.
$50–$75
Fine, linen-mounted, 20 x 28 inches. $150–$175

₩ SCHAEFFER

He Gave His Blood, ca. 1942. A medic under intense fire is shown saving a life with donated blood. Fine, linen-mounted, 28 x 42 inches. $225–$275

₩ JES WILLIAM SCHLAIJKER (1897–?)

The Battle-wise Infantryman, 1944. Rugged U.S. veteran warns the viewer to be careful with secrets. Fine, 28 x 40 inches. $165–$200

Courage and Gallantry in Action, 1943. A proud infantryman stands tall while ghosts from past U.S. wars loom from behind. Fine, linen-mounted, 19 x 25 inches. $425–$475

Let's Back Them Up!, ca. 1942. Soldier and sailor side by side approach the front. Very good, linen-mounted, 19 x 30 inches. $485–$550

In the Face of Obstacles—Courage, 1943. A machine-gun crew fire away amidst heavy fire. Fine, linen-mounted, 33 x 33 inches. $500–$550

Mine Eyes Have Seen the Glory, 1944. A spotlit woman soldier with shadows of men and planes in combat behind her. Fine, linen-mounted, 19 x 25 inches.
$300–$350

O'er the Ramparts We Watch, 1944. With a faraway gaze, a young American pilot stands in the clouds holding a bomb. An excellent example of the artist's work. Mint, linen-mounted, 19 x 25 inches.
$750–$800

Of the Troops and For the Troops—Military Police, 1943. A calm MP over-shadows the jumble of traffic he directs. A very good example of the artist's work. Mint, linen-mounted, 19 x 25 inches.
$500–$550

Service Above Self Medical Department, 1942. A medic assists a wounded solider amidst flames and chaos. An excellent example of the artist's work. Fine, linen-mounted, 18 x 25 inches.
$950–$1,000

Silence Means Security, 1943. A U.S. naval captain stands and ponders as his ship leaves port. Fine, 20 x 28 inches.
$325–$375

V-Mail to be Sure!, 1943. Grinning GI reads news from home. Fine, linen-mounted, 22 x 28 inches.
$145–$175

As above, mint, 9 x 13 inches.
$125–$150

Where Skill and Courage Count—Signal Corps, 1942. An artillery spotter relays coordinates to the batteries behind the line. Mint, linen-mounted, 17 x 25 inches.
$500–$550

Poster by George Schreiber.
Courtesy of Poster Plus Posters.

Poster by Jes William Schlaijker.
Courtesy of Meehan Military Posters.

Your Metal Is Their Might. Intense scene with two machine gunners in heavy action. Fine, linen-mounted, 40 x 28 inches. $500–$550

❦ GEORGE SCHREIBER (1904–1977)

Back the Attack, 1943 (Nelson #154). Paratrooper is shown covering with his machine guns as his buddies drop in. Fine, 10 x 14 inches. $50–$75

As above, fine, 20 x 28 inches. $150–$175

As above, cardboard placard, mint, 18 x 24 inches. $165–$200

Keep Him Flying, 1943 (Nelson #117). Young U.S. pilot climbs into his fighter at dawn, with his kills listed on the cockpit. Fine, 22 x 28 inches. $265–$325

❦ SCOTT

Closed for the Duration. Civilian with his mouth taped shut. Fine, 14 x 20 inches. $90–$125

Couldn't Have Done It Without You!, 1943 (Nelson #67). Jubilant sailor points to another painting a Japanese flag, signifying another kill. Fine, 28 x 40 inches. $195–$225

Let's Go! Where's That Landing Boat?, 1944. The soldier descends looking for his transportation. Fine, 29 x 40 inches. $200–$250

Pass the Ammunition. A sailor slams another shell into his deck gun, with an ordnance worker's image behind him. Fine, 30 x 40 inches. $245–$300

We've Still Got a Big Job to Do!, 1943. A legless veteran looks out to remind workers to keep producing. Fine, 28 x 40 inches. $125–$150

❦ SEWELL

Ready for Anything, 1943 (Nelson #57). GI storms the beach while other troops are unloaded. Fine, 22 x 28 inches. $185–$225

As above, fine, linen-mounted, 28 x 40 inches. $225–$275

❦ BEHN SHAHN (1898–1969)

This is Nazi Brutality, 1942. An abductee from the Czech village of Lidice, near Prague, stands manacled and hooded against a wall, awaiting execution. See the chapter on Ben Shahn for other posters by this artist. Mint, 28 x 40 inches. $700–$800

We French Workers Warn You, 1942. A German gang rounds up Frenchmen for forced labor in the Reich. Fine, 40 x 28 inches. $345–$400

❦ SYMEON SHIMIN (b. 1902)

Buy War Bonds. A GI embraces his girl. Mint, 11 x 16 inches. $65–$100

❦ **FRED SIEBEL**

Someone Talked!, 1942. A drowning sailor reaches out for help. Fine, 22 x 28 inches. $185–$225

As above, fine, 28 x 40 inches. $250–$300

❦ **SINGLETON**

The Netherlands Must Rebuild, 1944. A young Dutch family faces the destruction with hope for the future. Fine, 14 x 22 inches. $125–$150

❦ **SLOAN**

Doing All You Can, Brother?, 1943 (Nelson #5). A wounded GI with head bandaged looks out to encourage purchasing bonds. Fine, 22 x 28 inches. $85–$125

❦ **DAN SMITH AND DOWNE**

Keep 'Em Flying, 1942. With the U.S. flag above them, B-17–Es fly into battle. Fine, linen-mounted, 25 x 38 inches. $365–$400

❦ **SPEZIO**

Be an Aviation Mechanic, 1939. Mechanics servicing a new Douglas B-18. Fine, 26 x 38 inches. $225–$275

❦ **STANLEY**

O.K., Soldier, That's Our Job. GI carries a crate of ammo while guns boom in the distance. Fine, 28 x 40 inches. $175–$200

❦ **HERBERT M. STOOPS (1887–1848)**

Careless Talk . . . Got There First, 1944 (Nelson #92). Paratrooper slumps in his harness from wounds received by an enemy in wait. Fine, 20 x 28 inches. $165–$200

❦ **HADDON SUNDBLOM**

Ready—Join the U.S. Marines! A marine in dress blues commands attention. Fine, 28 x 40 inches. $235–$300

❦ **SAUL TEPPER (1899–?)**

I'll Give 'Em Hell, 1942. A GI skewers Hitler, Tojo, and Mussolini with his bayonet. Fine, 28 x 40 inches. $325–$375

We Caught Hell!, 1944 (Nelson #99). A GI carries wounded buddy out of inferno, obviously set by the enemy thanks to careless talk. Fine, 10 x 14 inches. $75–$100

As above, fine, 28 x 40 inches. $200–$250

❦ THOMASON

Let's Go Get 'Em, 1942. Combat-ready marine heads to the front while reaching his hand out to recruits. Fine, linen-mounted, 28 x 40 inches. $325–$375

❦ TOMASON

Supply Lines Are Life Lines, 1944 (Nelson #90). GIs and Pacific island natives unload supplies under enemy fire. Fine, 28 x 40 inches. $225–$275

❦ ADOLPH TREIDLER (1886–1981)

Loose Talk Can Cause This, 1942 (Nelson #93). A Nazi guard faces an American POW behind barbed wire. Mint, 14 x 20 inches. $185–$225

Telephones Saved Here Help the War Over There, ca. 1943. "Miss Bell" advises customers to clear the lines as bombers appear overhead. Fine, 19 x 25 inches. $245–$300

❦ VICKERY

God Help Me If This Is a Dud., 1942 (Nelson #61). A GI exposes himself in order to hurl a grenade. Fine, 28 x 40 inches. $285–$350

❦ HAROLD VON SCHMIDT (1893–?)

Have You Really Tried to Save Gas?, 1944 (Nelson #28). Close-up of a wounded GI with a grim stare at the viewer. Fine, 20 x 28 inches. $85–$125

❦ WARREN

Attack, Attack, Attack, 1942 (Nelson #82). Marines storm a Pacific beach with planes flying above for support. Fine, 22 x 28 inches. $75–$100

As above, fine, 28 x 40 inches. $95–$125

❦ WEBER

Hard Times, Hard Duties, Hard Hearts, 1944. German soldier, worker, and home guard stand under a Nazi flag. Very good, linen-mounted, 23 x 33 inches. $485–$550

❦ WEICHECKI

Poles Fight On, 1944. Powerful composition with a bayonet piercing across a red and white Polish flag. Mint, 20 x 27 inches. $225–$275

❦ JUPP WEIRTZ (1881–1939)

Nazi Flying Corps, 1937. Sport flying clubs trained future pilots. Here a biplane flies into the sky. Mint, on Japan paper, 12 x 17 inches. $425–$475

❧ HEINZ WEVER

Produce Weapons and Munitions, 1943. At the front, a German soldier reaches out for more ammo. Fine, 17 x 23 inches.　　　　$575–$625

❧ JON WHITCOMB

Be a Cadet Nurse, 1944. Two nurses in dress and hospital uniforms encourage recruitment for education and service. Fine, 20 x 28 inches.　　　$100–$125

Death on Subs!, 1944. A destroyer moves through, making waves, coming in for the kill. Fine, 30 x 40 inches.　　　　$225–$275

Join the Navy Nurse Corps. Smiling nurse in dress uniform beckons recruits. Fine, linen-mounted, 20 x 28 inches.　　　　$265–$325

The Freedom of the Seas Is in Your Hands. Golden rays shine on the Statue of Liberty as she watches over the destroyers going out. Fine, 30 x 40 inches.
　　　　$175–$200

They're Needed Everywhere, 1944. Under enemy fire, the soldiers storm the beach as ships let out more men. Fine, 40 x 28 inches.　　　$285–$350

You Deliver the Ships. Naval officer lowers his binoculars during rough seas. Fine, linen-mounted, 30 x 40 inches.　　　　$375–$425

❧ WHITMAN

Volunteer for Red Cross Motor Corps. A pilot rendezvous with a Red Cross staffer in a jeep. Fine, 9 x 14 inches.　　　　$85–$125

❧ WILBUR

The Greatest Mother in the World, 1943. Statuesque Red Cross nurse pleads for help for all the refugees behind her. Fine, 22 x 28 inches.　　$145–$175

The World . . . Can Never Forget, 1943. While civilian ponders the percentages of workers who purchased bonds, GIs fight on. Mint, 11 x 16 inches.　$55–$75

❧ NORMAN WILKINSON (1882–?)

You Buy 'Em, We'll Fly 'Em!, 1942 (Nelson #145). Young pilot gives the thumbs-up from his cockpit. Fine, linen-mounted, 20 x 28 inches.　$375–$425

❧ WILLIAMS

Of Course I Can!, 1944. A homemaker carries her jars of rations, cooperating with conservation. Fine, 19 x 25 inches.　　　　$85–$125

❧ THOMAS WOODBURN

Enlist Now, 1940. An enraged Uncle Sam rolls up his sleeves, ready for action. Fine, linen-mounted, 28 x 40 inches.　　　　$450–$500

U.S. Army Guardians of the Colors, 1940. A parade of the army with flags. Fine, 25 x 38 inches. $275–$325

U.S. Army Then—Now—Forever, 1940. Columbia with U.S. flag holds a laurel over the marching army. Fine, linen-mounted, 25 x 39 inches. $275–$325

Wings Over America. Eagle and fighters soar together for Air Corps recruitment. Fine, linen-mounted, 25 x 38 inches. $975–$1,025

❦ WOYSHNER

Always on the Alert, 1940. Machine gunner takes on the planes under a searchlight. Fine, linen-mounted, 30 x 40 inches. $325–$375

❦ N. C. WYETH (1882–1945)

The American Red Cross Carries On. A parade of Red Cross flags fly amidst billowing smoke. Fine, 15 x 19 inches. $150–$175

Buy War Bonds, 1942. Uncle Sam with billowing flag orders the viewer to buy bonds as troops march on planes fly overhead. Fine, 14 x 20 inches. $200–$250

❦ ZULAWSKI

Poland First to Fight, 1939. Polish flag torn and tattered still flies. Fine, 20 x 29 inches. $285–$350

❦ CHAPTER 23 ❦
Travel and Transportation Posters

Travel and Transportation posters are a major poster-collecting field with global impact and numerous specializations: exotic ports of call, great cities of the world, ski resorts in the Alps, World's Fairs, and adventurous journeys to new destinations. In this chapter we include a selection of posters for bicycles, train travel, ocean liners, automobiles, aviation and air travel, and some of the multitude of posters for resorts, sporting vacations, and other destinations and resorts produced by numerous countries and hundreds of artists.

Some of these posters are by well-known artists who command high prices: A. M. Cassandre, Leopoldo Metlicovitz, Alphonse Mucha, Edward Penfield, Otto Baumberger, and others. However, well- designed lithographic and even some photo-offset travel and transportation posters by lesser-known artists have earned recognition in the market over the past five years, although many still remain affordable and within the reach of beginning collectors.

Bicycle posters have long held a special place in the poster-collecting field. Happily, the bicycle craze of the late 1800s coincided with the Art Nouveau and Belle Epoque period poster craze, producing colorful, interesting lithographic posters. Bicycle posters can be serious, comical, coy, and sometimes even bizarre. A few examples feature bicycles held aloft by goddesses and gladiators.

In France there was keen competition among bicycle companies such as Jules DuBois, Solieil, Liberator, George Richard, Stella, Clement, Perfecta, and several others. Some, such as Peugeot, went on to manufacture automobiles. English and American companies included Stearns, Raleigh, Victor, and Columbia. Some of the best poster artists of the day created bicycle posters, including Alphonse Mucha, PAL, Jules Chéret, Eugene Grasset, Manuel Robbe, Will Bradley, Edward Penfield, and a host of lesser-known artists.

The popularity of bicycle posters isn't simply nostalgia for quieter times before the advent of cars. The increasing popularity of bicycles today, both as a sport and as a means of urban transportation, has added to price increases in recent years as avid cyclists became poster collectors.

The great European state-run railways were major patrons of poster art, commissioning perhaps more artists than any other type of poster patron. Starting in the late 1800s, with the rise of the urban middle class, leisure travel by train became popular. No doubt the posters themselves played a vital role in stimulating this burgeoning tourist industry.

The French state railways, or Chemins de Fer (literally: roads of iron), were the first to seize upon this new form of advertising to attract travelers. The first examples of these posters by Hugo d'Alesi (1849–1906) date from about 1890. From that point on, the history of train posters in France reads like the history of posters itself, with almost every major artist represented.

Before World War I, the Chemins de Fer had commissioned Alphonse Mucha, Jules Chéret, Georges Meunier, Jules Alexandre Grün, Alfred Choubrac, Adolphe Willette, René Pean, PAL, Henri Gray, Eugene Grasset, Misti, George Rochegrosse, and others.

People don't often think of these posters as "train" posters since the train itself is usually nowhere to be seen. Rather the posters of this period, and most of the train posters thereafter, were scenes of the colorful destinations that awaited the traveler at the end of the line.

After World War I and into the 1930s, the French railways commissioned artists such as Jean-Gabirel Domergue, Leonetto Cappiello, and Paul Colin. A true design innovator also received commissions: A. M. Cassandre. Cassandre's work epitomized the Art Deco ideal of marrying art and industry. For the first time, the emphasis of the poster was on the train itself: the very symbol of streamlined progress. Cassandre's train posters are masterpieces of avant-garde design and today sell for thousands of dollars. A few other artists, such as Pierre Fix-Masseau, are also known for putting the train back into train posters.

Roger Broders (1883–1953) is second in popularity only to Cassandre for his Art Deco-style Chemins de Fer posters. Broders's style uses the bold colors and simplified forms of Art Deco styling, and his posters for Monte Carlo and other Riviera resorts are highly sought after, easily fetching $1,500 to $3,000.

A more naturalistic, painterly style in French train posters also enjoyed popularity in the 1920s and 1930s, and is being rediscovered by collectors today. Celebrating the natural and man-made beauty of France, these lithographic posters are elegant glimpses of small towns, rural landscapes, châteaux, and rugged terrains. Like most Chemins de Fer posters, these are about 28 x 40 inches, to fit the panels created for their display in the train stations throughout France.

The most outstanding artist in this vein, though little is known about his life, is Constant-Duval. A prolific train poster artist, he created some of his best works for the many châteaux of the Loire River Valley. Constant-Duval used some of the best lithographic printers, such as Chéret's publisher, Chaix, Mucha's printer, Champenois, and Lucien Serre. Numerous other artists worked in this painterly style of lithography, and their names are becoming more familiar today: Georges Dorival, E. Paul Champseix, Charles Hallo, Louis Houpin, André Milaire, Roger Soubie, and others.

A few years ago, most of these posters could still be purchased for under $300, and while some still fall in that price range, others are now commanding up to $1,000 as exposure brings differentiation.

Unfortunately, after World War II, the quality of French Chemins de Fer posters diminished greatly. In the late 1940s and 1950s, a series of posters was issued based on artists' paintings that were not originally intended as posters. While the paintings of many famous artists were chosen—Claude Monet, Bernard Buffet, Raoul Dufy, and others—these posters have far less value because they are not original works of poster art. Rather, an artist's painting was simply reproduced within a white border that carried the text.

In addition, as France sought to dramatically increase tourism to boost its postwar economy, these posters were printed in multiple formats and languages. Prior to the war, perhaps as many as five thousand to six thousand copies of a single lithographic poster might be printed, but after the war, as many as sixty thousand copies would be printed, usually using photo-offset methods.

The story of French Chemins de Fer posters does have a happy ending, however, for in the 1960s, 1970s, and beyond, true poster artists were once again commissioned to create original designs. These pieces are not old enough or rare enough to command very high prices, but happily they are great works of graphic design from artists such as Bernard Villemot, Raymond Savignac, Phillipe Fure, and even Salvador Dali, who created six original posters for six different regions of the country.

The Swiss Chemins de Fer also played a major role in commissioning artists, as Switzerland has long depended on tourism as a major source of revenue. Among the many outstanding Swiss artists commissioned were Otto Baumberger (1889–1961), Eric Hermes (1881–1971), Albert Muret (1874–1955), and more recently Hans Falk (b. 1918). Other European countries such as Poland, Belgium, Germany, Austria, Italy, Holland, and the Scandinavian countries also produced numerous and strong examples of these specialty posters.

As travel by train peaked in the late 1920s and early 1930s, British Railways became one of the biggest patrons of the poster in that country. There were four major rail lines in England at the time: the LNER (London and North Eastern Railway); the LMS (London Midland and Scottish Railway); Great Western Railways; and Southern Railways. Again, few of these posters actually depict the trains themselves, but rather beach resorts, landscapes, and other colorful scenes.

Almost all British Rail posters were produced in two standard sizes, a vertical one-sheet 25 inches wide x 40 inches high (sometimes called a "double royal") and a large horizontal format 50 inches wide by 40 inches high (sometimes called a "quad royal").

This larger size is very popular with collectors and interior designers today. As little as five years ago most of these posters sold for under $1,000. While some can still be purchased in the range of $400 to $600, today many have reached the $2,000–$3,000 range, and some go as high as $5,000. The smaller-format British Rail posters are more affordable, but some are reaching towards the $1,000 mark.

There are numerous British Rail artists to watch for: Tom Purvis (1888–1959), who is known for his outstanding Art Deco designs using flat colors and simplified lines; Frank Newbould (1887–1950), a master of landscapes who worked directly on the lithographic stone; Fred Taylor (1875–1963), perhaps best-known for his architectural posters of cathedrals and cities; Austin Cooper (1890–1964); Norman Wilkinson; and Charles Pears (1873–1958), among others. E. McKnight Kauffer (1890–1954), who is famous for his posters for the London Underground, also designed posters for the British Rail companies. Lesser-known artists to look for are W. Smithson Broadhead, Claude Buckle, Norman Hepple, Littlejohns, and John Mace.

In the United States, travel by car quickly became a more popular means of transportation than the railroad. This, coupled with the fact that the railroads were not state-run or state-promoted, meant that fewer American train posters were created.

American train travel posters from the 1920s through the 1940s are hard to find, but some of the best posters were produced for the New York Central Railroad, the New Haven Railroad, the Boston-Maine Railroad, and Northern Pacific Railways. Artists to watch for include Dorothy Waugh, Leslie Ragan, Sascha Maurer, and Ben Nason.

After World War I, there was a rapid increase in overseas travel, and the ocean liner was the only commercial means of getting overseas. Many of the great ocean liners were deluxe floating palaces of Art Deco design, and the liner companies appealed to a sophisticated clientele with their advertising, often executed in the sleek, modern Art Deco style.

Among the ocean liner companies to look for are American Line, Compagnie Général Transatlantique (most often abbreviated Cie. Gle.

Transatlantique), Cunard, Hamburg America, the Red Star Line, Holland-America Line, and Rotterdam-Lloyd Lines. Many of the same artists who were commissioned by the railway companies also designed ocean liner posters.

Automobile posters have truly surged ahead in recent years, fueled (pun intended) by a crossover of car collectors. When a focused group of automobile posters comes up at auction, there is often a battle among collectors, sometimes sending prices skyrocketing past retail levels.

Among the top prices for automobile posters are for those by Robert Falucci (French, 1900–1989) and Géo Ham (aka George Hammel, French, 1900–1972). Both designed breathtaking posters for the races at Monaco in the 1930s, and works of both artists can bring $6,000 to $8,000 and more at auction.

Even higher prices are paid for very early, pre-World War I automobile posters, some of which were designed by famous artists such as Alphonse Mucha and Leopoldo Metlicovitz. However, many automobile and automotive posters are still affordable, and these will no doubt surface on the market in increasing numbers in the years ahead.

Aviation and air travel posters have seen an appreciable gain in popularity in the last few years. While early aviation posters featuring hot-air balloons and biplanes have always had a historical interest, it wasn't until recently that commercial air travel posters began to find an audience with younger collectors, especially those who never vacationed by train or by ocean liner.

Early airline companies to watch for include the Dutch KLM and Air France. Intercontinental commercial air travel really boomed after World War II, and some of the best posters from the 1940s are for Pan Am. In the late 1940s, American Airlines commissioned E. McKnight Kauffer (1891–1951), who produced a series of notable posters for both American and European destinations. While these are still fairly affordable, mainly in the range of $300 to $400, a few have really taken off at auction because of McKnight Kauffer's reputation.

There has also been increased interest in United Airlines posters from the 1950s, especially those for air travel to Hawaii by Frederick Lawler. Other posters to watch for include Stan Galli's designs for United Airlines, and Weimar Pursell's works for American Airlines. Unfortunately, in more recent posters, photography replaced original poster illustration almost entirely. These posters are less desirable and will doubtless remain so for some time to come.

Sports-related travel posters are enjoying great popularity today, especially those for golf, skiing, and tennis. Outstanding German travel posterists to look for include Ludwig Hohlwein (1874–1949) and Jupp

Wiertz (1881–1939). One Austrian-American, Joseph Binder (1898–1972), also produced outstanding sports-related travel posters such as his famous ski poster for Austria. Binder was also the winner of the poster competition for the 1939 New York World's Fair.

World's Fairs, festivals, and other special events are among the most popular "destination" travel posters. The 1933 Chicago Century of Progress, for instance, had posters designed by at least three artists, including Weimar Pursell.

As with the other travel poster fields above, the best destination travel posters to collect are those from before World War II, most of which were lithographically printed.

There are literally thousands and thousands of good destination poster designs available on the market. Due to the fact that many were produced anonymously or by lesser-known artists, and in large quantities both for posting and distribution to travel agencies, prices can still be in the low range of $200–$400.

The growing popularity of early travel posters also means that new research will be done to uncover more about the artists who created them. These fine decorative works help us recall places we have been, or dream of places we would like to see. Others appeal to our interests, sports, and hobbies. Since this is very unlikely to change, travel posters will undoubtedly continue to be a highly popular collecting field.

BICYCLE POSTERS—PRICE LISTINGS

NOTE: See the chapter Important Notes on the Price Listings for more information on the prices given. Some of the artists also have listings in the chapters on different countries.

❦ ANONYMOUS

Cycles Clement, ca. 1905. Lithograph. Man in green suit holds aloft the company banner as he leads a countryside parade of cyclists. Good condition, on linen, 46 x 62 inches. $750–$850

Cycles Jules du Bois, ca. 1900. Lithograph. Printed by Dupuy & Fils, Paris. Cyclist in black clothing, with green and yellow road in background. Very good condition, 40½ x 88¼ inches. *See color insert, photo 22.* $2,090 (Auc. #19)

Cycles George Richard, ca. 1898. Lithograph. Art Nouveau design in muted tones of red, tan, brown, and green on a mottled brown background, with the four-leaf clover Richard logo. Very good condition, 39 x 54 inches. $350–$400

Cycles Stella, ca. 1900. Lithograph. A witch pedals across the sky on her Stella bicycle. In yellow, green, and blue. Good condition, 23 x 31 inches. $400–$500

Courtesy of Swann
Galleries, Inc.

L'Excursionniste. Lithograph. Printed by Edw. Ancourt, Paris (printer of many Toulouse-Lautrec posters). French poster. Yellow, black, purple, and orange tricycle with white background. Very good condition, 35 x 47 inches.

$2,750 (Auc. #19)

Pneu Velo Michelin/Le Meilleur Le Moins Cher, ca. 1925. Lithograph. Printed by Chaix. "Bib," the Michelin man, rides away on a bicycle. Fine condition, on linen, 30 x 47 inches. $275 (Auc. #18)

❦ ADRIEN BARRÈRE (FRENCH, 1877–1931)

Manege Petit/Grand Magasins de Cycles, ca. 1900. Lithograph. Printed by Ch. Wall & Compagnie, Paris. Woman gives a flirting look over her shoulder while riding away on her bicycle. Very good condition, 40 x 55 inches. $2,000–$2,250

❦ P. BELLENGER (FRENCH)

Cycles Favor, 1957. Photo-offset. Printed by Chateaudun, Paris. Large male figure in red holding up a bicycle and a motorcycle. Very good condition, 62 x 46½ inches. $770 (Auc. #19)

❦ WILLIAM H. BRADLEY (AMERICAN, 1868–1962)

Victor Bicycles/Overman Wheel Company, 1896. Lithograph. Published by Overman Wheel Company. Unsigned. A rare and important poster. Fine condition, 36¾ x 57⁷⁄₁₆ inches. $20,000–$25,000

Courtesy of Swann
Galleries, Inc.

🌿 E. CELOS

Canadian Cycles—Massey Harris, ca. 1895. Lithograph. Printed by Camille Sohet & Compagnie, Paris. With text in English. Woman with long flowing hair holds a maple leaf between the handlebars. Fine condition, 36½ x 51 inches.

$2,750 (Auc. #19)

🌿 F. FABIANO (FRENCH)

Envellope Velo Michelin, 1905. "Bib," the Michelin man, shown smoking a cigar and protecting a young woman. Good condition, 31¾ x 39 inches. $350–$400

🌿 FRAIKIN (FRENCH)

Ce Michelin Est Indechirable, 1908. Lithograph. Printed by Ch. Verneau, Paris. An American Indian is shown biting into a tire to show its strength. Very good condition, on linen, 31 x 40 inches. $350 (Auc. #18)

🌿 PAOLO HENRI (FRENCH)

Cycles Gladiator. Lithograph. Printed by Kossuth, Paris. Well-dressed crowd of people in black and gray, but no bicycle in the scene. Good condition, 54½ x 34½ inches. $1,100 (Auc. #19)

🌿 F. LAGHENY (FRENCH)

Cycles Omnium, 1895. Lithograph. Printed by Des Gachons, Paris. A woman poses with her bicycle. Good condition, 30 x 45 inches. $715 (Auc. #19)

🌿 MISTI—aka FERDINAND MIFLIEZ (FRENCH, 1865–1923)

Triumph Cycles—Coventry, 1907. Lithograph. For an English client. Woman in large hat stands beside her bicycle. Very good condition, this example framed, 30 x 46 inches. $770 (Auc. #23)

Poster by Misti.
Courtesy of Oliver's.

❦ ALPHONSE MUCHA (FRENCH, 1860–1939)

Cycles Perfecta, 1897. Lithograph. Printed by Champenois. Woman with flowing hair leans over the handlebars of her bicycle. A fine example of both the artist and bicycle posters. In very good condition, on linen, 41½ x 59 inches.

$10,000–$12,000

❦ EDWARD PENFIELD (AMERICAN, 1866–1925)

The Northampton/the Northampton Cycle Co., ca. 1899. Lithograph. Published by the Northampton Cycle Company. Fine condition, 26⁵⁄₁₆ x 39¾ inches.

$10,000–$14,000

TRAIN POSTERS—PRICE LISTINGS

NOTE: See the chapter Important Notes on the Price Listings for more information on the prices given. Many of the artists are also represented under their countries.

❦ ANONYMOUS

Canadian Rockies via Canadian Pacific. Lithograph. A snow-covered mountain with three skiers, one about to rush out of the poster. Good condition, 24 x 36 inches.

$350–$400

Dungeness/the World's Smallest Railway (English), ca. 1935. Lithograph. In sunset colors showing lighthouse and steamship. Fine condition, 25 x 40 inches.

$400–$425

Durham, ca. 1935. Lithograph. For the LNER. View of the bridge and castle. Very good condition, 25 x 40 inches. $200–$225

Southport, ca. 1955. Lithograph. Printed by Jordison & Company, for British Railways. Very good condition, on linen, 25 x 40 inches. $175 (Auc. #18)

❦ HUGO D'ALESI (FRENCH, 1849–1906)

Tunisie, ca. 1900. Lithograph. Printed by Imp. Hugo. For the French Chemins de Fer. Exotic scene of a camel caravan. Very good condition, 31 x 42½ inches.
$350 (Auc. #20)

❦ HERVE BAILLE (FRENCH)

Lourdes, 1947. Lithograph. For the Chemins de Fer. Depicts the Pyrenees mountains, with a stream of light from the sky beaming on the shrine. Very good condition, 24 x 39 inches. $350–$400

❦ OTTO BAUMBERGER (SWISS, 1889–1961)

Switzerland/the Brunig Line, ca. 1930. Lithograph. Printed by Sauberlin & Pfeiffer, Vevey. For the Swiss Railways. A stunning landscape painting by this talented Swiss artist. Fine condition, 24 x 39 inches. $1,000–$1,200

❦ ROGER BRODERS (1883–1953)

L'Été Sur La Côte D'Azur, 1930. Lithograph. For the Chemins de Fer/PLM. A grand view of the beach at Juan les Pins. Very good condition, on linen, 25 x 39½ inches. $1,800–$2,200

Golf de la Soukra Tunis, 1932. Lithograph. Printed by Imp. Vaugirard. For the Chemins de Fer/PLM. Young caddy looks down from the hill on a colorful scene of golfers and distant town and ocean. Fair condition, tape stains and tears in the image, 24 x 39 inches. $600–$700

As above, in fine condition. $1,900–$2,300

Marseille, Porte de l'Afrique du Nord, 1929. Lithograph. Printed by Lucien Serre, Paris. For the Chemins de Fer/PLM. Colorful view of steamships in the harbor of Marseilles. Very good condition, 25 x 40 inches. $1,550 (Auc. #25)

La Plage de Calvi/Corse, 1928. Lithograph. Printed by Lucien Serre. For the Chemins de Fer/PLM. An excellent example of the artist's Art Deco train travel posters. Fine condition, 24⅞ x 40 inches. $3,000–$4,000

Sports d'Hiver, ca. 1930. Lithograph. For the Chemins de Fer/PLM. A group of skiers in colorful costume descend from the tourist train at Mont Blanc. Good condition, on linen, 25 x 40 inches. $1,500–$1,800

❦ P. IRWIN BROWN (ENGLISH)

Grasmere/English Lakes for the Holidays, 1932. Lithograph. For the London and North Eastern Railway. Autumn in the mountains. Very good condition, on linen, 25 x 40 inches. $300–$350

The Peak District for Holidays, 1932. Lithograph. For the London and North Eastern Railway. Bold, rich colors. Very good condition, on linen, 25 x 40 inches.

$275–$325

❦ LEONETTO CAPPIELLO (ITALIAN, WORKED IN FRANCE, 1875–1942)

Superbagnères-Luchon, 1929. Lithograph. For the Chemins de Fer du Midi. Three stylized skiers going downhill with the resort hotel in the background. A good example of the artist's style. Fine condition, 25½ x 40 inches.

$2,000–$2,200

❦ A. M. CASSANDRE (FRENCH, 1901–1968)

Étoile du Nord, 1927. Lithograph. Printed by Hachard & Compagnie. For the Chemins de Fer du Nord. Famous design of train rails plunging into the horizon, converging at the North Star. A very good example of the artist's style. Good condition, 30 x 41½ inches.

$5,950 (Auc. #18)

As above, fine condition, on linen.

$10,000–$12,000

Dunkerque Folkestone Londres, 1932. Lithograph. Printed by L. Daniel, Lille. For the Chemins de Fer du Nord. Bright beam from a lighthouse illuminates an ocean liner on the horizon. Very good condition, 24½ x 40 inches.

$5,500 (Auc. #25)

Poster by Otto Baumberger.
From the collection of Al Hoch.
Photo by Robert Four.

Poster by Roger Broders.
Courtesy of Park South Gallery.

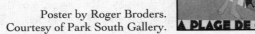

Nord Express, 1927. Lithograph. Printed by Hachard & Compagnie. For the Chemins de Fer du Nord. Powerful image of a stylized train speeding off toward the horizon. Good condition, 29½ x 41½ inches. $4,450 (Auc. #18)

As above, fine condition, on linen. $9,000–$12,000

L'Oiseau Bleu, 1929. Lithograph. Printed by L. Daniel, Lille. For the Chemins de Fer du Nord. The train is conveyed by a purple martin flying along at top speed. A good example of the artist's style. Very good condition, on linen, 24⅜ x 39¼ inches. $7,000–$8,000

Paris, 1935. Lithograph. Printed by Draeger, Paris. For the Chemins de Fer. View of the Place de la Concorde and Arch of Triumph. Fine condition, on linen, 24½ x 39½ inches. $3,000–$4,000

La Route Bleue, 1929. Lithograph. Printed by L. Daniel, Lille. For the Chemins de Fer. Stylized silhouetted and outlined trees line the road, which disappears to the horizon. An outstanding example of the artist's posters for the French railways. Fine condition, on linen, 24½ x 39 inches. $17,000–$20,000

❦ E. PAUL CHAMPSEIX (FRENCH)

Carcassonne, ca. 1930. Lithograph. Printed by Lucien Serre. For the Chemins de Fer. Colorful view of the walled city/fortress, with unusual use of gold metallic ink on the sky. An excellent example of a painterly Chemins de Fer poster. Very good condition, on linen, 24 x 39 inches. $750–$800

Cheverny/Châteaux de la Loire, ca. 1925. Lithograph. For the Chemins de Fer. The château through richly colored autumn trees. Very good condition, on linen, 24 x 39 inches. $450–$500

❦ CHRISTOPHER CLARK (ENGLISH)

London By LMS, ca. 1935. Lithograph. Printed by Benrose & Sons. For LMS. Scene with color guard outside Whitehall. Good condition, horizontal, 50 x 40 inches. $425 (Auc. #18)

❦ PAUL COLIN (FRENCH, 1892–1986)

Paris, 1946. Lithograph. For the Chemins de Fer. Blue background with yellow birds and famous monuments. A very good example of a post-World War II Chemins de Fer poster. Fine condition, 25 x 39 inches. $500–$600

❦ CONSTANT–DUVAL (FRENCH)

Azay le Rideau, 1925. Lithograph. Printed by Champenois. For the Chemins de Fer. A painterly aspect of the Loire Valley château. One of a series of château posters designed by Constant-Duval. Good condition, on linen, 31 x 42 inches. $400–$450

Château of Amboise, 1922. Lithograph. Printed by Champenois. For the Chemins de Fer. With text in English. Fine condition, on linen, 27 x 40 inches. $400–$450

From the author's collection. Photo by Robert Four.

Chenonceaux, 1926. Lithograph. Printed by Chaix. For the Chemins de Fer, advertising *circuits automobiles* (auto tours) of the Loire Valley. A very good example of Constant-Duval's château posters. Very good condition, on linen, 29 x 41 inches. $550–$600

Le Mont St. Michel, ca. 1925. Lithograph. Printed by Champenois. For the Chemins de Fer. An evening view of the rugged monastery, with rich colors. An excellent example of the artist's style. Very good condition, on linen, 30 x 40 inches. $700–$750

❦ AUSTIN COOPER (ENGLISH, 1890–1964)

Italy for Your Holidays, 1934. Lithograph. Printed by McCorquodale & Company. For Southern Railway. A striking Art Deco collage of images with strong colors. Very good condition, 25 x 40 inches. $1,125 (Auc. #20)

Paris for the Weekend, 1934. Lithograph. Printed by Waterlow & Sons. For Southern Railway. A striking Art Deco collage of images with strong colors. Very good condition, 25 x 40 inches. $975 (Auc. #20)

❦ WALTER DEXTER (ENGLISH)

Cromer, ca. 1940. Lithograph. Printed by London Lithographic Company. For LNER. View of the town on the Norfolk coast. Very good condition, horizontal, 50 x 40 inches. $400 (Auc. #17)

❦ GEO. S. DIXON (ENGLISH)

New Brighton, Wallasey, Cheshire Coast, ca. 1950. Lithograph. Printed by London Lithographic Company. For British Railway. Scene with people enjoying the beach. Good condition, horizontal, 50 x 40 inches. $550 (Auc. #18)

❧ L. F. DOMINIQUE (FRENCH)

Ile de France, 1945. Lithograph. For the Chemins de Fer. Two hunters return to the estate. With text on white banner at bottom. Good condition, 24 x 39 inches. $100–$150

❧ HANS FALK (SWISS, b. 1918)

50 ans Tunnel du Simplon, 1956. Photo-offset. For the Swiss Railways. Modern painterly view of this Swiss tunnel. Fine condition, on linen, 25 x 39 inches. $300–$350

❧ PIERRE FIX-MASSEAU (FRENCH, b. 1905)

Exactitude, 1932. Lithograph. Printed by Edita, Paris. For the Chemins de Fer. Strong image of the train in close-up traveling at the viewer. A highly sought-after poster. Fine condition, on linen, 24 x 39 inches. $10,000–$12,000

❧ GUSTAVE FRAIPONT (FRENCH, 1849–1923)

Excursions en Touraine et aux Châteaux des Bords de La Loire, 1894. Lithograph. Printed by Fraipont & Moreau. For the French Chemins de Fer. An early poster, with inset vignettes of various châteaux. Good condition, on Japan paper, 39 x 54½ inches. $450–$500

❧ RENE GENIS (FRENCH)

Discover France by Train, 1957. Photo-offset. View of a bay in Brittany. One of a series of posters using land/cityscape paintings by French artists, with text in white banner below. Fine condition, 24 x 39 inches. $125–$150

Normandie, ca. 1955. Photo-offset. For the Chemins de Fer. Painting of beach houses, text on white bottom banner. Very good condition, 25 x 39 inches. $100–$125

❧ TOM GILFILLAN (SCOTTISH)

Scotland/Its Highlands and Islands, ca. 1930. Lithograph. Printed by John Horn, Glasgow. For the LNER. Tourists and Scottish boys in kilts sightsee at a ship's rail. A very striking image. Good condition, horizontal, 50 x 40 inches. $1,125 (Auc. #18)

Scotland/Its Highlands and Islands, ca. 1935. Lithograph. For the LNER. Painterly view of sunset over the "Cullins of Skye." Very good condition, 25 x 40 inches. $300–$350

❧ GOTTHARD GUSTAFFSON (SWEDISH)

Vagen Car till Skansen, 1932. Lithograph. For the train to Skansen. Bold colors and geometric shapes. Very good condition, on linen, 27 x 36 inches. $350–$400

❦ HANSI—aka J. J. WALTZ (FRENCH, 1873-1951)

Rosheim au Mont. St. Odile, 1930. Lithograph. For the Chemins de Fer. The village square full of activity in Hansi's children's book illustrative style. Good condition, 24 x 39 inches. $250–$350

❦ PAUL HENRY (ENGLISH)

Come to Ulster for a Better Holiday, ca. 1935. Lithograph. For the LNER. Painterly view of the cliffs and bay. Very good condition, on linen, horizontal, 50 x 40 inches. $425–$475

❦ ERIC HERMES (SWISS, 1881–1971)

Montreux-Oberland-Bernois, 1929. Lithograph. Printed by Sauberlin & Pfeiffer, Vevey. For the Swiss Chemins de Fer. Skiers shown on the lift with the slopes behind them. Fine condition, on linen, 25 x 40 inches. $675 (Auc. #17)

As above, fine condition. $600 (Auc. #18)

❦ ERNST HODEL (SWISS, 1881–1955)

Schynige Platte/Interlaken, ca. 1930. Lithograph. For the Swiss Chemins de Fer. Very good condition, 25 x 40 inches. $250–$300

Wegnernalp Railway, ca. 1935. Lithograph. For the Swiss Chemins de Fer. Good condition, on linen, 25 x 40 inches. $200–$300

❦ LUDWIG HOHLWEIN (GERMAN, 1874-1949)

Engleder und Finkenzeller, ca. 1913. Lithograph. Printed by Dr. C. Wolf V. Sohn, Munich. Silhouettes of people boarding a train. Very good condition, 49 x 35 inches. $1,650 (Auc. #17)

❦ EDWARD MCKNIGHT KAUFFER (AMERICAN, LIVED IN ENGLAND 1890–1954)

Kentucky Derby/via Chesapeake & Ohio, ca. 1949. Photo-offset. Green-clad jockey on brown background. McKnight Kauffer worked primarily in England. Very good condition, 27½ x 37½ inches. $550 (Auc. #19)

❦ A. LAMBOURG (FRENCH)

Discover France by Train, 1958. Photo-offset. Painting of the Ile de France, with text in white banner below. Very good condition, 24 x 39 inches. $100–$125

❦ PRIVAT LIVEMONT (BELGIAN, 1861–1936)

Cabourg/A 5 Heures de Paris, 1896. Lithograph. Printed by P. Leminil, Asnieres. For the French Chemins de Fer, to lure Parisians to the Belgian seaside resort. Very good condition, horizontal, 43 x 29½ inches. $3,500–$4,000

Poster by Privat Livemont.
Courtesy of Butterfield &
Butterfield.

Poster by Maurice Lovan.
Courtesy of Nancy Steinbock
Posters and Prints.

🌿 MAURICE LOVAN (AMERICAN)

Carriso Gorge/Southern Pacific, ca. 1950. Photo-offset. Executed in a painterly style. Very good condition, on linen, small format, 16 x 23 inches. $250–$350

🌿 G.M. (MONOGRAM, FRENCH)

Brunnen, Suisse, ca. 1910. Lithograph. Printed by Chaix. For the French
Chemins de Fer. With vignettes showing activities in the area. Fine condition, on
linen, 29 x 42 inches. $675 (Auc. #18)

🌿 PAUL MARTIAL (FRENCH)

French Railways/Now Getting Ready to Welcome You, 1946. Lithograph. For
the Chemins de Fer. Fine illustration shows postwar construction on a trestle
with the cathedral of Chartres in the background. Fine condition, 24 x 39 inches.
                                                                $150–$250

Auvernge, 1930. Lithograph. For the Chemins de Fer. Painterly view of mountains, a castle and small village below. Finely executed, dramatic colors. Fine condition, 24 x 39 inches. $350–$400

🌿 FRANK MASON (ENGLISH)

Richmond, Yorkshire, ca. 1935. Lithograph. Printed by Vincent Brooks, Day &
Son. For the LNER. Good condition, 25 x 40 inches. $450 (Auc. #20)

❧ ALPHONSE MUCHA (FRENCH, 1860–1939)

Monaco—Monte-Carlo, 1897. Lithograph. Printed by Chamenois. For the Chemins de Fer/PLM. Stunning design of a woman encircled by a myriad of exotic flowers, with the blue sea in the background. Train information overprinted on the design in the bottom corner. A very good example of the artist's work. Very good condition, 29½ x 43 inches. $13,000–$15,000

❧ S. MULLER (FRENCH)

Alpes Mancelles, 1932. Lithograph. For the Chemins de Fer, advertising tourist circuits by automobile. A painterly scene. Very good condition, 24 x 37 inches.
$300–$350

❧ CLAUDE MUNCASTER (ENGLISH)

Norwich/It's Quicker by Rail, ca. 1935. Lithograph. Printed by Golmore & Dean. For the LNER and LMS. Very good condition, 25 x 40 inches. $475 (Auc. #20)

❧ ALBERT MURET (SWISS, 1874–1955)

Chemin de Fer Martigny-Orsiers, 1913. Lithograph. Printed by Sonor, Genève. Skiers follow one another down the hill. Fine condition, 27½ x 39 inches.
$1,125 (Auc. #18)

❧ BEN NASON (AMERICAN)

Nantucket/the New Haven Railroad, ca. 1938. Photo-offset. Aerial view of the Meeting House in a romantic, painterly style. Nason created several posters in this series for the New Haven Railroad, others featuring Cape Cod, Boston, the Berkshires, Connecticut, and Rhode Island. Fine condition, 28 x 42 inches.
$400–$450

❧ FRANK NEWBOULD (ENGLISH, 1887–1950)

East Coast Frolics. Lithograph. Printed by Chorley & Pickersgill, London. For the LNER. Black dolphin and red fish on blue background. Good condition, 25 x 39½ inches. $770 (Auc. #19)

Holland Via Harwich, ca. 1930. Lithograph. For British Railways. A colorful view of a Dutch city. Very good condition, on linen, 25 x 40 inches. $400–$450

North Berwick, ca. 1925. Lithograph. For the LNER. Beautiful, bright beach scene in Art Deco style. An excellent example of both the artist and an LNER poster. Fine condition, horizontal, 50 x 40 inches. $3,000–$3,500

❧ CHARLES PEARS (ENGLISH, 1873–1958)

Brighton and Hove, ca. 1935. Lithograph. For the LNER. View of the port from the sea. Very good condition, on linen, horizontal, 50 x 40 inches. $525–$600

Poster by Frank
Newbould. Courtesy of
Swann Galleries, Inc.

The Isle of Man, ca. 1949. Lithograph. Printed by Stafford & Company, London. For British Railways. Good condition, horizontal, 50 x 40 inches. $300 (Auc. #17)

🌿 GERALD SPENSER PRYSE (ENGLISH, 1881–1956)

British Empire Exhibition, 1924, 1924. Lithograph. Printed by Vincent Brooks, Day & Son. For the LNER. A desert caravan. One of a series depicting various exotic peoples from the empire. Very good condition, on linen, horizontal, 50 x 40 inches. $350 (Auc. #20)

🌿 SASCHA MAURER (AMERICAN, 1887–1961)

Ski/the New Haven R.R., ca. 1940. Lithograph. Close-up of a smiling man with skis thrown over his shoulder. Very good condition, on linen, 25 x 42 inches.
   $650–$900

🌿 C. NORWICH (ENGLISH)

Canadian National Railways, 1924. Lithograph. Printed by Johnson, Riddle & Company, London. Steam train speeds through the forest. Very good condition, 25 x 40 inches. $357 (Auc. #19)

🌿 AAGE RASMUSSEN (DANISH, 1913–1975)

DSB/Danische Staatsbahnen, 1937. Lithograph. For Danish Railways. Red train coming at the viewer with superimposed speedometer. Rasmussen is recognized for posters for Danish Railways. Fine condition, on linen, 24¼ x 39½ inches.
   $800–$1,200

🌿 GWEN RAVERAT (ENGLISH)

Ely Cathedral, ca. 1935. Lithograph. Printed by Vincent Brooks, Day & Sons. For the LNER. Good condition, 25 x 40 inches. $375 (Auc. #20)

❦ LESLIE RAGAN (AMERICAN, 1897–?)

New York—the Upper Bay from Lower Manhattan, ca. 1935. Photo-offset. For the New York Central. View of the skyscrapers and the Statue of Liberty. A very good example of an American train poster. In very good condition, on linen, 25 x 40 inches. $1,800–$2,200

❦ HENRI DE RENAUCOURT (FRENCH)

Le Vallée de Munster, 1930. Lithograph. For the Chemins de Fer. Dramatic view of the deep valley. Excellent color. Mint condition, 24 x 39 inches. $450–$500

❦ JAMES C. RICHARD (FRENCH)

Menton/La Perle de la France, 1926. Lithograph. For the Chemins de Fer. A sunny view of the bay with exotic foliage in bright colors. Fine condition, on linen, 24 x 40 inches. $500–$600

❦ SCHNEIDER (GERMAN)

German Railways/Safety, Speed, Comfort/60% Reduction, ca. 1950. Photo-offset. Probably for distribution in England. Shows four different trains speeding at angles across the poster. Fine condition, 25 x 40 inches. $275–$325

❦ SEPTIMUS EDWIN SCOTT (ENGLISH, 1879–?)

Blackpool, 1949. Lithograph. Printed by London Lithographic Company. For British Railways. Mother, father, and child hold hands walking along the beach. Good condition, horizontal, 50 x 40 inches. $425 (Auc. #18)

❦ HENRI SIMON (FRENCH)

Les Belles Plages de Vendée, ca. 1930. Lithograph. For the Chemins de Fer. A woman in a bright red swimsuit holds a ball aloft above a crowded beach. Very good condition, 24 x 40 inches. $350–$400

❦ W. SMITHSON BROADHEAD (ENGLISH)

Lytham St. Annes, ca. 1930. Lithograph. For LMS. Woman in swimsuit raises her arms and smiles. Very good condition, horizontal, 50 x 38½ inches.
$625 (Auc. #18)

❦ ROGER SOUBIE (FRENCH, 1898–1984)

Le Haut-Barr, ca. 1930. Lithograph. Printed by Cornille & Serre, Paris. For the Chemins de Fer. Colorful view and high cliffs of the lower Rhine Valley. Mint condition, 29½ x 41 inches. $450–$500

Thames Valley, 1946. Lithograph. Printed by Baynard Press, London. For British Railways. Pastoral setting at the river valley. Good condition, horizontal, 50 x 40 inches. $575 (Auc. #18)

❧ ANDRE STRAUSS (FRENCH)

La Corse, 1927. Lithograph. For the Chemins de Fer. Advertising the *Pacqebots Fraissinet,* which cross from France to Corsica. Painterly scene of a Corsican village in gorgeous dusty tones. Mint condition, 31 x 42 inches. $400–$450

❧ FRED TAYLOR (ENGLISH, 1875–1963)

Dresden Via Harwich, ca. 1930. Lithograph. Printed by John Waddington Ltd. For LNER. A colorful view. In very good condition, horizontal, 50 x 40 inches.
                                                                $300 (Auc. #20)

Frankfort Via Harwich, ca. 1935. Lithograph. Printed by Vincent Brooks, Day & Son. For the LNER. Depicting a café in front of a German building. Very good condition, 25 x 40 inches. $300 (Auc. #20)

Liverpool Cathedral, ca. 1939. Lithograph. For the LNER. Interior view in rich warm colors. Fine condition, on linen, horizontal, 50 x 40 inches. $625–$675

London, ca. 1930. Lithograph. For the LNER. Exquisite, rich nighttime view of the city with its neon glow and bustling traffic in the streets. An outstanding example of the artist's style and of a British Railways poster. Very good condition, on linen, horizontal, 50 x 40 inches. $4,000–$4,500

York, ca. 1930. Lithograph. For the London and North Eastern Railway. Depicting part of the old village. Very good condition, 25 x 40 inches. $300–$325

Poster by André Strauss.
From the author's collection.
Photo by Robert Four.

Poster by Fred Taylor. Courtesy of
Bloomsbury Book Auctions.

❦ TESTI (ITALIAN)

Facilités Extraordinaires pour les Voyages en Italie, ca. 1935. Lithograph. Published by ENIT, the Italian government agency. For Italian Railways. With text in French. Fine condition, on linen, 26 x 39 inches. $450–$550

❦ VECOUX (FRENCH)

Côte Basque, 1946. Lithograph. For Chemins de Fer. Painting of a beautiful coast-line view, text in white banner below. Fine condition, 24 x 39 inches. $125–$175

Winter Sports in France, 1947. Lithograph. For the French national railroads, with text in English. Ski poles mark the five mountain ranges of France. Fine condition, on linen, 24 x 39 inches. $400–$450

❦ NORMAN WILKINSON (ENGLISH, 1882–?)

Bedford School, ca. 1935. Lithograph. For the LNER. View of the private school. Very good condition, on linen, horizontal, 50 x 40 inches. $300–$350

Come to Ulster, ca. 1935. Lithograph. For the LNER. A view of the lighthouse and sailboats. Fine condition, on linen, horizontal, 50 x 40 inches. $450–$550

Dunkeld Cathedral/River Tay, ca. 1935. Lithograph. For the LNER. View across the bridge leading to the Scottish town. Very good condition, on linen, horizontal, 50 x 40 inches. $450–$550

Isle of Man, ca. 1923. Lithograph. Printed by Waterlow & Sons. Beach scene with a castle in the background. Good condition, horizontal, 50 x 40 inches.
$300 (Auc. #18)

London by LMS, ca. 1935. Lithograph. For LMS. Fine, stylized view of St. Paul's Cathedral and the river. An excellent example of the artist's work. Very good condition, horizontal, 50 x 40 inches. $1,500–$1,800

Morecambe Bay, ca. 1935. Lithograph. Printed by Jordison & Company. For LMS. Steamship puffs along in the bay. Very good condition, horizontal, 50 x 40 inches. $575 (Auc. #18)

❦ WUNSCHEIM (AUSTRIAN)

Autriche, ca. 1938. Lithograph. For the Austrian Railways. Streamlined train speeds over a trestle through the mountains. Fine condition, 25 x 38 inches.
$350–$450

❦ PIERRE ZENOBEL (FRENCH)

Le Nouveau Train Bleu Vers La Côte d'Azur, 1928. Lithograph. For the Chemins de Fer. A stunning Art Deco stylized image and very good example of Chemins de Fer posters of the period. Fine condition, this example framed, 25 x 39 inches. *See color insert, photo 23.* $2,100–$2,200

OCEAN LINER POSTERS—PRICE LISTINGS

NOTE: See the chapter Important Notes on the Price Listings for more information on the prices given. Many of the artists are also represented under their countries.

❦ ANONYMOUS

Chesapeake Steamship Company, ca. 1910. Lithograph. Printed by A. Horn & Company, Baltimore. Central image of a steamship. Fine condition, 30 x 38 inches. $500–$750

Scotland & Ireland/Burns Laird Line. Lithograph. Multicolored cruise ship with blue and green background. Good condition, 25 x 40 inches. $330 (Auc. #19)

Swedish American Line, ca. 1935. Lithograph. Ocean liner looming over gold and orange lettering. Very good condition, 25 x 39 inches. $600–$650

❦ OTTO ANTON (GERMAN, 1895–1976)

Hamburg-Amerika Line. Lithograph. Printed by Muhlmeister & Johler, Hamburg. Three North African women prepare a dish with ship in background. Fine condition, on linen, 23 x 33 inches. $450 (Auc. #18)

❦ GINO BOCCASILE (ITALIAN, 1901–1952)

Lloyd Triestino/Africa, ca. 1935. Photo-offset. Showing two stylized African women crossing a bridge. Very good condition, 24½ x 38 inches. $700–$800

Lloyd Triestino/Australia, ca. 1935. Photo-offset. Showing a huge sheep. Very good condition, 24½ x 38 inches. $250–$300

❦ WIM TEN BROEK (DUTCH, b. 1905)

Holland-Amerika Lijn, 1936. Photo-offset. Printed by Joh. Enschede, Haarlem. An outstanding design for this Dutch company, and a sought-after poster. Fine condition, 25¼ x 38½ inches. $2,500–$2,800

❦ A. M. CASSANDRE (FRENCH, 1901–1968)

L'Atlantique, 1931. Lithograph. Printed by Alliance Graphique. View of steamship appears massive when compared to tugboat at its side. Very good condition, 24½ x 40 inches. $8,350 (Auc. #25)

Normandie/New York via Le Havre et Southampton, 1935. Lithograph. Printed by Cassandre's agency, Alliance Graphique. Rare version of this poster with "New York" in bold white letters. Fine condition, on linen, 28 x 43 inches. *See color insert, photo 6.* $11,550 (Auc. #13)

As above, but a more common version, with the text "Normandie" and "French Line" in white, "Le Havre-Southampton-New York/Service Regulier" below in black. Fine condition. $7,000–$9,000

Poster by Wim Ten Broek.
Courtesy of Bernice Jackson
Fine Arts.

Poster by A. M. Cassandre.
Courtesy of Van Sabben
Poster Auctions.

Statendam/Holland-America Line, 1928. Lithograph. Printed by Nijgh & van Ditmar, Rotterdam. For the Dutch ocean liner company. A stunning design of the smokestacks, printed with a brown border. (*Note:* At this same auction, the original gouache design for this poster sold for $34,825.) Very good condition, 25½ x 35 inches.   **$5,575 (Auc. #25)**

United States Lines: London, Paris, Bremen, 1928. Lithograph. Printed by Hachard & Compagnie, Paris. Red, white, and blue smokestacks dominate the poster. Very good condition, 24½ x 40 inches.   **$4,825 (Auc. #25)**

💐 HENRI CASSIERS (BELGIAN, 1858–1944)

Red Star Line/Antwerpen—New York, ca. 1900. Lithograph. Woman and child in traditional Flemish costume watch the ocean liner sailing away. Very good condition, on linen, horizontal, 60 x 44 inches.   **$3,200–$3,400**

💐 PAUL COLIN (FRENCH, 1892–1985)

Cie. Gle. Transatlantique/Atlantique-Pacifique-Méditerranée, ca. 1937. Lithograph. Signed in plate. Stylized steamship, with French flag as backdrop. 15¾ x 23½ inches.   **$1,093 (Auc. #15)**

As above, fine condition, on linen, 25 x 30 inches.   **$700–$750**

Poster by Paul Colin. Courtesy of Christie's East.

Poster by G. H. Davis.
Courtesy of Harris Gallery.

❦ G. H. DAVIS (DUTCH)

Holland America Line/Southampton to New York, ca. 1935. Lithograph. In fine condition, this example framed, 25 x 40 inches. $1,525–$1,625

❦ REYN DIRKSEN (DUTCH, b. 1924)

Holland America Line/SS Maasdam, SS Ryndam, 1953. Photo-offset. Printed by Enschede & Sons, Haarlem. Close-up precisionist view of the stack. Very good condition, 24½ x 39 inches. $500 (Auc. #25)

❦ ALBERT FUSS (GERMAN, 1889–?)

Hamburg-American Line, Southampton to New York, ca. 1930. Lithograph. Printed in Germany. Steamship shown as enormous from below. Fine condition, 25 x 40 inches. $600 (Auc. #17)

Hamburg-American Line, Central America, Cuba & Mexico, Winter Tours to the Tropics. Lithograph. Printed in Germany. Fine condition, 25 x 39½ inches. $600 (Auc. #17)

❦ EMILE GAILLARD (DUTCH)

Batavier Line, London-Rotterdam, ca. 1935. Lithograph. Printed by Van Leer, Amsterdam. London bridge opens to let a cruise ship through. Fine condition, 24 x 39½ inches. $350 (Auc. #17)

❦ FREDERICH CHARLES HERRICK (ENGLISH, 1887–1970)

R.M.S.P., South American Service, 1921. Lithograph. Printed by the Baynard Press, London. Very good condition, on linen, 25 x 39½ inches. $975 (Auc. #18)

❦ KUCK (NORWEGIAN)

Schottland-Norwegen-Lloyd Bremen, 1938. Lithograph. Scottish Highland dancer against a plaid background. Fine condition, 23 x 34 inches. $350–$400

❦ KEES VAN DER LANN (DUTCH 1903–1983)

Engeland & Schottland (England and Scotland), ca. 1939. Lithograph. For cruises from Holland via Harwich. Large, stylized mermaid between two ocean liners. Very good condition, 25½ x 41 inches. $500 (Auc. #25)

❦ WILLIAM MCDOWELL

Cunard White Star/Queen Mary, ca. 1950. Photo-offset. For the Cunard Line. Mammoth *Queen Mary* surrounded by small ships. Very good condition, 31½ x 18½ inches. $495 (Auc. #19)

❦ MOUM

Norge/Danmark—5 Times a Day, ca. 1935. Lithograph. Ship shows the short distance between the two countries. Very good condition, on linen, 24 x 38 inches. $400–$450

❦ JOHANNES (JAN) SLUYTERS (DUTCH, 1881–1957)

Zuid-Amerika/Koninklijke-Hollandische Lloyd, ca. 1920. Lithograph. Printed by van Leer, Amsterdam. Exotic flowers in a painterly style frame a distant liner. Very good condition, 29 x 44 inches. $625 (Auc. #25)

❦ JOHANN VON STEIN (DUTCH, 1896–1965)

Rotterdamsche Lloyd, ca. 1930. Rotogravure. Printed by Nederlandische Rotogravure, Leiden. Ocean liner poster advertising Sumatra and Java. Stunning white steamship with long reflection in water echoes elongated typeface. Very good condition, 18 x 28½ inches. $4,000–$4,500

❦ BERND STEINER (GERMAN)

Norddeutscher Lloyd Bremen nach Ostasien, ca. 1930. A seaside Japanese pagoda, house, bridge, and woman in a kimono. Good condition, 24 x 48 inches. $325–$400

✹ VOH (GERMAN, MONOGRAM)

Skandinavien—Lloyd Breman, 1938. Lithograph. Beautiful design with geese flying above the ship in orange backdrop. Very good condition, on linen, 25 x 40 inches. $650–$750

AUTOMOBILE POSTERS—PRICE LISTINGS

NOTE: See the chapter Important Notes on the Price Listings for more information on the prices given. Some of the artists also have listings in the chapters on different countries.

✹ ANONYMOUS

Le Camion 6 Cyl Chevrolet, ca. 1930. Lithograph. Printed by Office d'Edition d'Art, Paris. Very good condition, on linen, 46 x 62 inches. $475 (Auc. #18)

Kansas City Automobile Show, ca. 1908. Lithograph. Printed by Tingle-Titus Company, Kansas City. An angel presents the auto show. Very good condition, 15 x 22 inches. $550 (Auc. #19)

✹ FRANCO CODOGNATO (ITALIAN, b. 1911)

20 Gran Premio Dell 'Autoromo, 1949. Photo-offset. Printed by Matelli, Milan. Franco is the son of posterist Plinio Codognato. A very good example of Italian auto sports posters. Fine condition, on linen, 39½ x 54¾ inches. $4,500–$5,000

Courtesy of Bernice Jackson Fine Arts.

Courtesy of Swann Galleries, Inc.

❦ DE BAY (FRENCH)

Renault, ca. 1925. Lithograph. Printed by J. Minot. Very good condition, on Japan paper, 46½ x 62 inches. $425 (Auc. #18)

❦ ALFRED CARDINAUX (FRENCH, b. 1905)

Chevrolet, 6 Cyl, ca. 1930. Lithograph. Printed by Office d'Edition d'Art, Paris. Glimmering Chevy is shown under spotlight and the GM sign. Very good condition, on linen, 46 x 62 inches. $1,125 (Auc. #18)

❦ DELPY (FRENCH)

36eme Salon de l'Automobile, 1949. Yellow car against a midnight blue background. Fine condition, 15¼ x 23 inches. $440 (Auc. #19)

❦ FRANCOIS GOS (SWISS, 1880–?)

Genf. 2te Schweizer/Automobil & Fahrrad-Austelling, 1906. Lithograph. Printed by Sauberlin & Pfeiffer, Vevey. For an exposition. Good condition, two sheets, 36 x 49 inches. $1,350 (Auc. #20)

❦ GEROLD (FRENCH)

Bugatti, 1932. Lithograph. Printed in France. For the Italian manufacturer. A strong visual. Fine condition, on linen, 35⅜ x 50½ inches. $7,500–$8,000

Courtesy of Bernice
Jackson Fine Arts.

❧ LEOPOLDO METLICOVITZ (ITALIAN, 1868–1944)

Mostra del Ciclo e dell Automobile, 1907. Lithograph. Printed by Ricordi. Rare design shows a winged allegorical figure racing beside the open-air touring car and motorcycle. An outstanding example of Metlicovitz's style and of an early auto poster. In fine condition, monumental size, 55 x 79 inches. $16,000–$18,000

❧ GEORGES MEUNIER (FRENCH, 1869–1942)

Automobiles Ader, ca. 1905. Lithograph. Printed by Chaix, Paris. Early comic auto poster shows a car head to head with a donkey and wagon on a narrow bridge as their owners argue. In fine condition, horizontal, 63 x 42 inches. $2,000–$2,200

❧ ROGER PEROT (FRENCH, 1908–1962)

Delahaye, 1932. Lithograph. Printed by Les Ateliers ABC, Paris. No other text than the name of the car, which is sweeping over the horizon towards the viewer. This poster comes in two different color schemes, one predominantly blue, the other red. In fine condition, on linen, 47 x 63 inches. $5,000–$6,000

❧ R.E.D. (FRENCH, MONOGRAM)

Accumulateurs Dinin, ca. 1930. Lithograph. Printed by Bedos. A striking image for Dinin car batteries. In fine condition, 46 x 61 inches. $1,200–$1,300

❧ GEORGES ROCHGROSSE (FRENCH, 1859–1938)

Automobile-Club de France/3eme Exposition Internationale, 1900. Lithograph. Printed by Barreau, Paris. Stunning Art Nouveau-style woman sits on a throne whose back is fashioned from a huge gear. In very good condition, on Japan paper, 51 x 75 inches. $4,500–$5,000

Poster by R.E.D.
Courtesy of Harris
Gallery.

❧ RENÉ VINCENT (FRENCH, 1879–1936)

Les Automobiles Georges Irat, ca. 1922. Lithograph. Fashionable Art Deco lady in high heels and plumed hat kisses the driver, who wears a checked suit. An outstanding example of Vincent's auto posters. In fine condition, on linen, 42 x 60 inches. $16,000–$18,000

❧ JAN WIJGA (DUTCH, 1902–1978)

Ford/25 Jaar in Nederland, 1949. Photo-offset. Printed by Ameets Weert. To celebrate twenty-five years of Ford in Holland. Very good condition, 31 x 43 inches. $150 (Auc. #25)

AVIATION AND AIR TRAVEL POSTERS— PRICE LISTINGS

NOTE: See the chapter Important Notes on the Price Listings for more information on the prices given. Some of the artists also have listings in the chapters on different countries.

❧ ANONYMOUS

Avia, 1937. Lithograph. Art Deco design, with close-up of the plane. Good condition, linen-mounted, 22 x 28 inches. $800–$1,000

Fly BOAC/Italy, ca. 1950. Silk screen. A colorful gondolier in the center of the poster. Fine condition, 21 x 30 inches. $225–$250

Grand Meeting d'Aviation de Chambery, 1928. Lithograph. Printed by Risacher & Compagnie, Paris. Prop plane takes off above the landscape. Good condition, on linen, 46½ x 61 inches. $750–$900

Imperial Airways Map of Air Routes, 1936. Lithograph. Poster designed as a map to show air routes. Good condition, 40 x 25 inches. $250–$350

KLM—Bénélux Map, ca. 1935. Lithograph. Designed as a map showing detailed attractions of Belgium, Holland, and Luxembourg. Fine condition, 23 x 39 inches. $200–$300

New England via Mainliner—United Airlines, ca. 1950. Photo-offset. Shadow of a plane crosses over a church steeple. Very good condition, 20 x 30 inches. $250–$300

❧ GUY ARNOUX (FRENCH)

Air France—Amerique du Nord, 1946. Lithograph. An excellent example of a postwar Air France poster, with striking imagery. In fine condition, this example framed, 24 x 39 inches. *See color insert, photo 24.* $1,750–$1,850

🐚 C. BASKERVILLE

PanAm—Siam by Clipper, 1950. Photo-offset. Exotic scene emphasizes the mystery of the people and land. Fair condition, 28 x 42 inches. $125–$175

🐚 BAUDOUIN

Air France—Paris, 1947. Lithograph. The Arc de Triomphe lights up like a star at the center of the imagery. Good condition, on linen, 24 x 39 inches.

$300–$350

🐚 L. BOUCHER (FRENCH)

Air France Map, ca. 1935. Lithograph. World map shows the routes of the airline, along with detailed illustrations in many countries. Fine condition, horizontal, 39 x 24 inches. $300–$400

Air France—Near East—Far East, 1947. Lithograph. Bird in Oriental fashion swoops over the Chinese mainland. Good condition, on linen, 25 x 40 inches.

$600–$650

🐚 A. BRENET (FRENCH)

Imperial Airways, 1937. Lithograph. Fleet of planes flies overhead. Very good condition, on linen, 25 x 40 inches. $700–$900

🐚 JEAN CARLU (FRENCH, b. 1900)

PanAm—Fly To France, ca. 1950. Photo-offset. Woman with flower basket surrounded by Parisian sites. Very good condition, 28 x 42 inches. $250–$325

PanAm—Marseilles, 1949. Photo-offset. Archway view of the Mediterranean. Fair condition, 28 x 42 inches. $150–$250

🐚 A. M. CASSANDRE (FRENCH, 1901–1968)

Fleche d'Argent, par Avion Aeropostale, 1930. Lithograph. Printed by S. A. Courbet, Paris. Abstraction of the "Silver Arrow" plane through the clouds. A rare image by Cassandre. In very good condition, 25 x 40 inches. $6,275 (Auc. #25)

🐚 DAMSLETH (NORWEGIAN)

Det Norske Luftfartselskap, 1937. Lithograph. Plane flies by with chart of destinations. Very good condition, on linen, 25 x 39 inches. $600–$750

🐚 ERIC (FRENCH)

Air France—Corse, 1952. Lithograph. Dramatic oceanside cliff view in rich colors. Good condition, 24 x 39 inches. $250–$300

❦ ERKELENS (DUTCH)

KLM—Royal Dutch Airlines, 1945. Photo-offset. Overhead view of people circling a windmill. Very good condition, 24 x 40 inches. $175–$225

KLM—Royal Dutch Airlines, 1947. Photo-offset. Humorous view of people flying in a wooden shoe. Very good condition, 24 x 39 inches. $175–$225

❦ STAN GALLI (AMERICAN)

Hawaii/United Air Lines, ca. 1960. Photo-offset. Beautiful Hawaiian woman welcoming the viewer with flower leis, standing in front of rich tropical foliage. Fine condition, 25 x 39¾ inches. $150–$250

❦ GUERRA (FRENCH)

Air France—Afrique Occidentale/Equatoriale, 1946. Lithograph. An outstanding image that uses the grains of fine woods to create its effect. This example framed, in fine condition, 24 x 39 inches. $1,600–$1,700

❦ HEUSDEN

KLM—on Their Way to Europe, ca. 1950. Photo-offset. Passengers board the plane with map of Europe above. Very good condition, 24 x 39 inches. $200–$250

Poster by Guerra.
Courtesy of Harris
Gallery.

❧ HOLLEUSDEN

KLM—New York, Far East, ca. 1935. Lithograph. Woman performs a ceremonial dance in blue field. Very good condition, 24 x 40 inches. $200–$300

❧ EDWARD MCKNIGHT KAUFFER (AMERICAN, LIVED IN ENGLAND, 1890–1954)

American Airlines/All Europe, 1948. Photo-offset. Crisp design of the globe with a Stars and Stripes banner. One of a series by McKnight Kauffer in the 1940s for American Airlines. Fine condition, 30 x 40 inches. $400–$425

American Airlines/Mexico, 1949. Photo-offset. Stylized rendering of straw-hatted Mexican carrying large birdcage in ocher, tan, blue, and black. Fine condition, 30 x 40 inches. $250–$300

❧ EDMUND MAURUS (FRENCH)

Air France—Afrique Française, ca. 1935. Lithograph. Plane comes out of the sun over the blazing sand. Fine condition, on linen, 25 x 40 inches. $500–$550

Cidna, Paris-Stamboul in the Same Day, ca. 1929. Lithograph. Large arrow points the way for the plane with a map of routes below. A very good example of the artist's style. Very good condition, on linen, 25 x 40 inches. $850 (Auc. #25)

❧ WEIMAR PURSELL (AMERICAN, 1906–1974)

American Airlines to New York, ca. 1955. Photo-offset. Colorful, stylized modernist skyline of the city. Very good condition, on linen, 30 x 39 inches.
$250–$275

Poster by Edmund Maurus.
From a private collection.
Photo by Robert Four.

❦ ALBERT SOLON (FRENCH, 1897–1973)

Air France—Marseille, ca. 1935. Lithograph. A bright sun with a plane and palm tree. Good condition, on linen, 25 x 40 inches. $550–$600

Lignes Farman, Paris, ca. 1930. Lithograph. Printed by Ch. Egler, Paris. The letter A in "Farman" produces a light beam revealing the airplane. Very good condition, on linen, 25 x 39 inches. $1,050 (Auc. #25)

❦ EDMUND SCHELL (BELGIAN)

PanAm—Fly to Belgium by Clipper, ca. 1935. Lithograph. Medieval city with land and sea bordering frame. Very good condition, 20 x 30 inches. $250–$400

❦ BERNARD VILLEMOT (FRENCH 1911–1989)

Air France—Afrique du Nord, ca. 1950. Lithograph. Modern painted view of North African cityscape. Fine condition, 24 x 39 inches. $350–$400

Air France—Afrique du Nord, ca. 1950. Lithograph. Another painted view of North African cityscape. Good condition, 24 x 39 inches. $350–$400

❦ JAN WIJGA (DUTCH, 1902–1978)

Royal Dutch Airlines, 1933. Photo-offset. Printed by Kunstdruk Luii, Amsterdam. Cleverly subtitled *The Flying Dutchman—Fiction Becomes Fact*. Depicts a four-propeller plane flying over the Dutch countryside while in the background a ghostly galleon sails. In purples, blues, and greens. A sought-after poster. Very good condition, 24¾ x 39 inches. $1,800–$2,200

Courtesy of Bernice
Jackson Fine Arts.

DESTINATION POSTERS—PRICE LISTINGS

NOTE: See the chapter Important Notes on the Price Listings for more information on the prices given. Included here are sports-related posters advertising skiing, golfing, and other resort activities. Some of the artists also have listings in the chapters on different countries.

❦ ANONYMOUS

Brides Les Bains (French), ca. 1890. Lithograph. Early scenic travel poster for the Savoie region. Good condition, linen-mounted, 30 x 40 inches. $300–$350

Brioni (Italian), 1937. Lithograph. Published by ENIT. Polo player prepares his shot. Very good condition, on linen, 25 x 39 inches. $550–$650

Championnat International Du Ski Club (Swiss), 1938. Lithograph. Printed by Wasserman & Company, Bale. Close-up of a skier in action. Fine condition, 35½ x 50 inches. $700 (Auc. #18)

Exposition—Barcelona 1929. Lithograph. Printed by Rieusset, Barcelona. For the World's Fair, showing the central plaza and buildings at the fair. Fine condition, on linen, 27½ x 20½ inches. $220 (Auc. #22)

Fano Esbjerg/Danmark, ca. 1935. Lithograph. Showing a woman in silhouette. Fair condition, 24 x 39 inches. $125–$175

Gleneagles for Golf (Scottish), ca. 1935. Lithograph. Printed by Dobson, Mole & Company, Edinburgh. Fine condition, 49 x 39 inches. $300 (Auc. #18)

Hungary. Lithograph. A couple embraces in front of a stylized architectural background. Good condition, 24 x 37 inches. $150–$250

Lac Des IV Cantons, ca. 1935. Lithograph. Ship's mast with Swiss flag. Fine condition, 27 x 39 inches. $150–$225

Rochers de Naye (Swiss), ca. 1935. Lithograph. Close-up of a redheaded skier about to go downhill. Fine condition, on linen, 25 x 40 inches. $500–$550

Soviet Armenia, ca. 1930. Lithograph. Printed in the USSR. Two tourists in an open car drive under a trestle with a train speeding overhead. Very good condition, 24 x 34 inches. $650–700

Suisse, ca. 1950. Lithograph. Printed by Fretz Freres, Zurich. Skiers are shown going down the slopes. Very good condition, 24 x 40 inches. $450 (Auc. #18)

Taormina, 1930. Lithograph. Published by ENIT, the Italian government travel agency. Colorful view with a close-up of a cactus and cliff-top. Very good condition, 24 x 39 inches. $400–$500

As above, fine condition, on linen. $700–$750

Utrecht, 51st Royal Netherlands Fair, 1948. Photo-offset. Flags as arrows hit the target. Good condition, 23 x 37 inches. $75–$125

La Vallée d'Aosta, ca. 1935. Lithograph. With seal of ENIT, the Italian government tourist agency. Fir trees create a cleft in the snow-covered mountains. Very good condition, 24 x 40 inches. $250–$300

As above, fine condition, on linen. $500–$600

❦ L. ALEXANDRE (FRENCH)

Foire de Lyon, 1949. Lithograph. Flag flies high over the expo site. Good condition, on linen, 24 x 39 inches. $150–$250

❦ ROBERT ALEXANDRE (FRENCH)

Chartres—Cathédrales de France, ca. 1935. Lithograph. Composite of the cathedral with rose window and statue. Good condition, 25 x 39 inches. $150–$250

❦ VON AXSTER HEUDTLASS (GERMAN)

Deutscher Winter, ca. 1925. Lithograph. Printed by RDV. Beautiful mountain valley filled with snow for skiing. Fine condition, 25 x 40 inches. $375 (Auc. #18)

Summer in Germany, ca. 1935. Photo-offset. Two kayakers head downstream. Fine condition, 25 x 40 inches. $300–$350

❦ UAN BALCERA (SPANISH)

Sevilla: Fiestas de Primavera 1932 Semana Santa y Feria. 1932. Lithograph. Woman at a balcony with a crucifix being carried toward a church. Good condition, 10 x 15 inches. $200–$300

❦ BARRAL (SPANISH)

Exposition International Barcelona 1929. Lithograph. Printed by Seix & Barral. For the World's Fair. An interpretation of Velasquez's painting of the infant king on horseback. Fine condition, on linen, 18 x 25½ inches. $302 (Auc. #22)

Exposition International Barcelona 1929/El Arte en Espagna. Lithograph. Printed by Seix & Barral. For the World's Fair. Woman with flowers and two gentlemen in the style of Velasquez. Fine condition, on linen, 14 x 21 inches. $330 (Auc. #22)

❦ BARTNER (GERMAN)

Berlin, 1955. Photo-offset. View of the bustle of the city at night. Very good condition, 23 x 33 inches. $100–$150

❦ BERANN (AUSTRIAN)

Austria, ca. 1950. Photo-offset. Dancers waltz in a gazebo near the edge of a lake. Good condition, 24 x 38 inches. $125–$175

🦋 JOSEPH BINDER (AUSTRIAN-AMERICAN, 1898–1972)

Austria, ca. 1930. Lithograph. Stunning ski poster, which was printed with the word "Austria" in several languages. Fine condition, 24½ x 37½ inches.

$1,600–$1,800

New York World's Fair, 1939. Lithograph. Winner of the first prize in the poster competition for the fair. Strong Art Deco design as a small squadron of red planes zooms skyward. Fine condition, 23 x 32 inches. $1,250–$1,750

🦋 BEN BLESSUM (NORWEGIAN-AMERICAN, 1877–?)

Norway, the Land of the Midnight Sun, 1950. Lithograph. Puffins overlook a lingering sunset. Very good condition, 24 x 37 inches. $250–$400

Norway Summer Season, ca. 1950. Lithograph. Beautiful fjord scene with steamship. Good condition, 24 x 39 inches. $200–$300

🦋 DPA BOTHAS (GERMAN)

International Exhibition, Paris 1937—German Pavilion, 1937. Lithograph. (DPA Bothas may be an agency or a publisher rather than the artist.) German monumental pavilion with Eiffel Tower behind. Fine condition, 25 x 39 inches.

$400–$600

Poster by Joseph Binder.
From a private collection.
Photo by Robert Four.

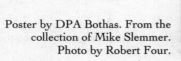

Poster by DPA Bothas. From the
collection of Mike Slemmer.
Photo by Robert Four.

❧ WILHELM FRIEDRICH BURGER (SWISS, 1882–1964)

Jungfraubahn, 1914. Lithograph. Printed by Hoper & Company, Zurich. Dogsled, mountains, great color. Fine condition, 39 x 27½ inches.
$1,500–$2,200

❧ LEONETTO CAPPIELLO (FRENCH, 1875–1942)

France, 1937. Lithograph. Statuelike woman entices tourists above France. Fair condition, 24 x 39 inches.
$600–$700

❧ JEAN CARLU (b. 1900)

Exposition—Paris 1937. Lithograph. Printed by Jules Simon. Woman's head in profile against a background made up of international flags. Fine condition, on linen, 15½ x 23½ inches.
$330 (Auc. #22)

As above, fine condition, larger size, 24 x 39 inches.
$500–$600

❧ ANTONIO CASERO (SPANISH)

The Fiesta de Toros in Spain, ca. 1950. Photo-offset. Toreador waves a bull on. Very good condition, 24 x 39 inches.
$200–$225

❧ A. M. CASSANDRE (FRENCH, 1901–1968)

Italia, 1936. Lithograph. Poster for sports equipment showing golf clubs, skis, tennis racket, etc. Fine condition, 24 x 39 inches.
$2,500–$2,750

Poster by W. F. Burger. From the collection of Al Hoch. Photo by Robert Four.

Poster by Jean Carlu.
From a private collection.

Italia, 1938. Lithograph. Outline of Madonna and child against Roman ruins. Fine condition, 24 x 39 inches. $2,000–$2,250

Venezia, 1951. Photo-offset. Printed by Clacografia & Cartevaloni, Milan. A gondolier in red and blue reflected in the canal. A good example of a later Cassandre poster. Very good condition, 25 x 39½ inches. $1,540 (Auc. #19)

As above, very good condition. $850 (Auc. #25)

🌿 CENNI (ITALIAN)

Centro America—Italia, 1936. Lithograph. Young man in a hat against a vivid blue ocean. Good condition, on linen, 27 x 39 inches. $650–$750

🌿 CHATELAIN (SWISS)

Neuchatel, ca. 1930. Lithograph. Poster showing the city as a composite with cathedral, dove, and opened book. Good condition, 26 x 41 inches. $250–$350

🌿 PAUL COLIN (1892–1985)

Paris 1937. Lithograph. Printed by Imp. Bedos, Paris. A woman's head and a globe with various colors. Fine condition, on linen, 45 x 62 inches. $770 (Auc. #22)

🌿 NEMHARD B. CULIN (AMERICAN, 1908–1990)

In 1939—The New York World's Fair, 1937. Lithograph. Printed by the New York World's Fair Corporation as an advance publicity poster for the Fair. A stunning aerial view of people entering the Perisphere from the Trylon. Very good condition, 28 x 39¾ inches. $3,500–$4,000

🌿 CURI (GERMAN)

Hospitable Germany, ca. 1950. Lithograph. View of a pub sign. Very good condition, 25 x 40 inches. $150–$250

🌿 DONNER (SWEDISH)

Stockholm, 1936. Lithograph. Harbor view with the cityscape in bright primary colors. Fine condition, 24 x 39 inches. $350–$450

🌿 TEODORO DELGADO (SPANISH)

Visit Spain, ca. 1950. Lithograph. Woman with flowers in her hair. Very good condition, 24 x 39 inches. $150–$225

🌿 FRIEDEL DZUBAS (GERMAN)

Germany, the Land of Legends, ca. 1935. Lithograph. Statue of a crusader on a cathedral facade. Good condition, 24½ x 39½ inches. $300–$350

❧ EHRENBERGER (GERMAN)

Summer in Germany, ca. 1930. Lithograph. Showing a woman with wildflowers standing before a scene with a castle. Good condition, on linen, 25 x 40 inches.
$300–$350

❧ ERICKSSONS (SWEDISH)

Lapplandia—Sweden, ca. 1950. Photo-offset. Skier in reclining chair enjoys the midnight sun. Fine condition, 24 x 39 inches.
$125–$175

❧ JEGES ERNO (HUNGARIAN)

Budapest, ca. 1935. Lithograph. Printed by the National Council of Tourist Traffic. Colorful costumed parade in front of the cathedral. Fine condition, on linen, 25 x 37 inches.
$400–$450

❧ ESOPOT (MEXICAN)

Tasco—Mexico, ca. 1950. Photo-offset. Richly colored view of a valley town with its red rooftops and old mission church. Fine condition, 18 x 26 inches.
$250–$300

❧ HENRI FEVRIER (FRENCH)

Vichy—Centre Musical d'ete, ca. 1930. Lithograph. Musical scores fill up a map of France. Very good condition, on linen, 24 x 39 inches.
$400–$450

❧ J. FILLACIER (FRENCH)

Chamonix, ca. 1940. Lithograph. Printed by Gaston Gorde, Paris. Sporting equipment is shown for all seasons. Fine condition, on linen, 23 x 38 inches.
$525 (Auc. #17)

❧ HUGO GELLERT (HUNGARIAN)

See the Soviet Union in the Making, ca. 1930. Lithograph. The onion domes of the Kremlin are seen behind the new factories. Good condition, 25 x 37 inches.
$500–$550

❧ MALLASZ GITA (HUNGARIAN)

Hungary, ca. 1935. Lithograph. Smiling boy in traditional clothing. Fine condition, 24 x 37 inches.
$200–$300

❧ G. GLORIA (FRENCH)

Vray Mistere de la Passion, ca. 1935. Lithograph. Glowing view of the crucifixion with Notre Dame above. Very good condition, 24 x 39 inches.
$225–$325

🌿 IVAR GULL (SWEDISH)

Sweden—Visby—the Town of Ruins and Roses, 1937. Lithograph. Castle view surrounded by roses. Good condition, 24 x 39 inches. $250–$350

🌿 L. HEINEMANN (GERMAN)

Germany, the Land of Music, ca. 1935. Photo-offset. German eagle is transformed into organ pipes. Fine condition, 25 x 40 inches. $275–$300

Springs and Saps in Germany, ca. 1935. Photomontage. Outlines of leaves frame a spring. Fine condition, 25 x 40 inches. $200–$250

🌿 R. HILDER (ENGLISH)

Come to Britain for Golf, ca. 1935. Lithograph. View of a golfer in a beautiful valley. Very good condition, on linen, 25 x 39 inches. $550–$600

🌿 LUDWIG HOHLWEIN (GERMAN, 1874–1949)

Berijdt Duitschlands Schoone Wegen (Motoring in Germany), 1935. A touring car sits in front of a German mountain scene. Very good condition, 25 x 39 inches. $500 (Auc. #17)

As above, legend in English, fine condition, on linen. $800–$1,000

Zoologischer Garten, 1912. Lithograph. Printed by G. Schuh, Munich. For the Munich Zoo. An outstanding design by the leading German posterist. Good condition, 36 x 49½ inches. $4,025 (Auc. #17)

Courtesy of Nancy
Steinbock Posters
and Prints.

❧ ERNEST IBBETSON (ENGLISH)

Coronation Tattoo Aldershot, 1937. Lithograph. Knight in armor stands overlooking the town. Fine condition, 20 x 30 inches. $225–$275

❧ LUDWIG KOCH (AUSTRIAN)

Semmering, 1928. Lithograph. Printed by Paul Gerin, Vienna. Skiers are pulled along by galloping horses. Fine condition, on Japan paper, 24 x 39 inches.
                                                                   $625 (Auc. #18)

❧ WALTHER KOCH (SWISS, 1875–1915)

Wintersport in Graubunden, 1906. Lithograph. Printed by Fretz, Zurich. A skier gazes down into the valley. Very good condition, 27 x 39 inches.
                                                                 $1,050 (Auc. #18)

❧ KRAMER (SWISS)

Zermatt, 1931. Lithograph. Stylized view of a ski jumper against the mountaintop. Good condition, on linen, 25 x 40 inches. $550–$600

❧ CARL KUNST (GERMAN, 1884–1912)

Heinr. Schwaiger, 1905. Lithograph. Printed by Reichold & Lang, Munich. Cross-country skier is shown in profile with mountainous background. Very good condition, on Japan paper, 48 x 36 inches. $1,050 (Auc. #17)

❧ LAMMLE (GERMAN)

Spring in Germany, ca. 1950. Photo-offset. Flowers bloom with frog down below. Good condition, 25 x 40 inches. $125–$175

❧ R. LATASTE (FRENCH)

Foire de Bordeaux, 1928. Lithograph. Printed by Deteil Fils Freres, Bordeaux. Large ship in foreground with three profiles above. Good condition, 39¼ x 56 inches. $220 (Auc. #19)

❧ JEAN LEGER (FRENCH)

Winter Sports in France, ca. 1950. Photo-offset. A bird outside its house sings while skiers pass by. Very good condition, 24 x 39 inches. $150–$175

❧ FRANZ LENHART (ITALIAN, 1898–1992)

Cortina, ca. 1920. Lithograph. Printed by Bozzetto F. Lenhart. Stylized view of skier soaring through the air, high above a village. Fine condition, on Japan paper, 27½ x 39 inches. $900 (Auc. #18)

Les Sports d'Hiver en Italie, ca. 1935. Lithograph. Skier speeds down the hill. Fine condition, on linen, 24 x 39 inches. $600–$650

🐚 G. LEROUX (FRENCH)

Universal Exposition—Paris 1900/Cartes à Jouer (Playing Cards), 1900. Lithograph. Showing king, queen, and joker from a deck of cards in various colors. Fine condition, on linen, 16 x 23½ inches. $385 (Auc. #22)

Universal Exposition—Paris 1900/Palais de l'Optique, 1900. Lithograph. Printed by Charles Verneau, Paris. Art Nouveau-style woman holding a luminous globe with pavilions in background. A very good example of the artist's style. Fine condition, on linen, 37 x 50 inches. $1,500–$2,500

🐚 LORZETH (ITALIAN)

All Roads Lead To Rome, ca. 1935. Lithograph. Arrow-shaped flags move in on the target of Rome. Fine condition, 24 x 39 inches. $450–$500

🐚 JOHN MACKILLOP (CANADIAN)

VANCOUVER, 1960. Photo-offset. Poster for the 1960 Figure Skating Championships. Very good condition, 25 x 40 inches. $150–$200

🐚 J. MASIA (SPANISH)

Exposition—Valencia 1944. Lithograph. Printed by Ortega, Valencia. A multicolored stylized boat at sea. Fine condition, on linen, 17 x 25½ inches. $275 (Auc. #22)

🐚 HERBERT MATTER (SWISS, 1907–1984)

Engelberg/Trubsee, 1936. Photomontage. Printed by Bucher, Zurich. For the ski resort. Photo of woman's face combined with illustration. A fine example of Matter's photomontage posters. In very good condition, 35 x 50 inches. $2,500–$2,750

Poster by G. Leroux.
Courtesy of Swann
Galleries, Inc.

Poster by Herbert Matter.
Courtesy of Bernice
Jackson Fine Arts.

Poster by IVG. Osswald. From
the collection of Al Hoch. Photo
by Robert Four.

❦ METHER-BORGSTROM (FINNISH)

Finland—Land of Romance, 1950. Photo-offset. Outline of Finland contains
beautiful lakes with a ship steaming through. Good condition, 24 x 39 inches.
$150–$225

❦ P. MOUNERAT (SWISS)

Davos Parsenn, 1947. Lithograph. Printed by Fretz, Zurich. Lift-car carries skiers
up the mountain. Fine condition, on linen, 25½ x 40 inches. $900 (Auc. #17)

❦ NIX (GERMAN, MONOGRAM)

Germany, the Land of Art, ca. 1950. Photo-offset. A wood carving of an angel
with lute. Good condition, 25 x 40 inches. $125–$175

❦ D. NYMAN (SWEDISH)

Skansen, 1935. Lithograph. Swedish flags fly over a garden scene with umbrellas.
Very good condition, 27 x 37 inches. $250–$300

❦ IVG. OSSWALD (GERMAN)

Stay Young Playing Golf in Germany, 1927. Lithograph. Young boy holds up a
golf club. Very good condition, 24 x 39 inches. $1,200–$1,500

Courtesy of Swann
Galleries, Inc.

🌿 T. POILPOT (FRENCH)

Universal Exposition—Paris 1889. Lithograph. Printed by Chaix, Paris. Panorama de la Compagnie Générale Transatlantique. The entire fleet of large steam-driven vessels in a harbor in blue, red, and white. Fine condition, on linen, 34 x 48 inches.　　　　　　　　　　　　　　　　　　　　$935 (Auc. #22)

🌿 PUPPO (ITALIAN)

Winter Sports in Val d'Aosta, ca. 1935. Lithograph. A smiling blond skier looks up the mountain. Very good condition, 27 x 29 inches.　　　　$800–$1,000

🌿 WIEMAR PURSELL (AMERICAN, 1906–1974)

Chicago World's Fair, 1933. Lithograph. Printed by the Neely Printing Company. A striking design in bright colors. Note that this poster has been reproduced on heavy paper, and the original paper was quite thin. Fine condition, 27 x 39 inches.　　　　　　　　　　　　　　　　　　　　$850–$1,000

🌿 RENAU (SPANISH)

Valencia Jardin d'Espagne . . . Visite l'Espagne, 1930. Lithograph. A church under hot sunlight in a grove of orange trees. Fine condition, 25 x 38 inches.　$650–$700

🌿 RANKE SANDGREN (SWEDISH)

Norrbotten, ca. 1935. Lithograph. A moose in pure white. Fine condition, 24 x 39 inches.　　　　　　　　　　　　　　　　　　　　　　　　　　$200–$225

🌿 SCHWARZ (AUSTRIAN)

Vienna, ca. 1930. Lithograph. Printed by A. Luigrad, Vienna. Beautiful view in front of the opera house. Fine condition, 24 x 37 inches.　　$1,250–$1,500

From a private collection.
Photo by Robert Four.

Courtesy of Swann
Galleries, Inc.

❦ SEGRELLEL (SPANISH)

Exposition—Barcelona 1929. Lithograph. Printed by Manen, Barcelona. Obeisant American Indians before a church with an image of Christ in background. Fine condition, on linen, 27 x 39 inches. $440 (Auc. #22)

❦ CRUANO SLOJAS (MEXICAN)

Mexico, ca. 1950. Photo-offset. Painterly view of a bullfight. Fine condition, 18 x 27 inches. $150–$175

❦ LUDWIG SUTTERLIN (GERMAN, 1865–1917)

Berlin, Exposition Industrielle, 1896. Lithograph. Printed by Otto von Holten, Berlin. Very good condition, 25½ x 36 inches. $825 (Auc. #17)

❦ TROMPF (AUSTRALIAN)

Brisbane—River City of the North, ca. 1935. Lithograph. Printed by the Queensland Government Tourist Bureau. View of the city from the hill above the lighthouse. Good condition, 25 x 39 inches. $300–$450

❦ JUPP WEIRTZ (GERMAN, 1881–1939)

Bayreuth, ca. 1935. Photo-offset. Poster celebrating the town of Wagner. Good condition, 24 x 40 inches. $350–$400

Bayreuth Stagione Wagneriana, 1937. Photo-offset. Silhouette of conductor and orchestra with a golden image of Wagner above. Very good condition, 25 x 40 inches. $400–$450

Germany/Berlin/Evening Near the Memorial Church, ca. 1930. Lithograph. Printed in Germany. With text in English. Very good condition, 25 x 40 inches. $300 (Auc. #17)

Nuremberg Festivals, ca. 1935. Photo-offset. Musician plays his harp looking at the city below. Good condition, 25 x 40 inches. $250–$350

❦ XIMA (FRENCH)

Casablanca, ca. 1935. Lithograph. Two natives transport their baskets through an Islamic archway. Very good condition, 24 x 39 inches. $550–$700

❦ YRAN (NORWEGIAN)

Norway, There Is a Fjord in Your Future, 1957. Photo-offset. Viking bow rises from the water. Good condition, 24 x 39 inches. $150–$175

❦ CHAPTER 24 ❦

Posters from the Olympic Games

BY HARVEY ABRAMS

Harvey Abrams is an Olympic historian who deals in original poster art, books, medals, and Olympic memorabilia. You can contact him at Harvey Abrams Books, P.O. Box 732, State College, Pennsylvania 16804, (814) 237-8331, fax (814) 237-8332, by appointment only.

The Modern Olympic Games began in 1896 in Athens, Greece, attended by 311 athletes from thirteen countries. The centennial celebration will be held in Atlanta, Georgia, in 1996, and ten thousand athletes from at least 170 nations will take part. The phenomenal growth and popularity of the Olympic Games make this event more than just a sports spectacle; it is a social, economic, political, and artistic phenomenon as well.

The poster collector will find that a wide variety of posters have been produced over the past century to advertise and promote the Olympic Games. Wherever the Games have been held, the local artistic community has had an influence on the posters produced. In studying the history of the Olympic Games, one finds that it is frequently the image of a particular poster that leaves a lasting impression. Today these posters are very collectible, increasing in value, and difficult to obtain in good condition.

It is best to set some guidelines about collecting Olympic posters before setting out on a buying spree. It would take many thousands of dollars to put together a "complete" set of official Olympic posters today. There are posters from the summer Olympic Games as well as from the winter Olympic Games, which started in 1924. The "official" posters are produced by the Organizing Committee for that particular Olympic Celebration, not by the International Olympic Committee, which awards the Games to host cities.

For example, the Organizing Committee for the 1936 Berlin Olympic Games commissioned one artist, Frantz Wurbel, to produce a single publicity poster, but printed it in several different languages. This memorable poster is one of the most famous images of the Olympic Games and shows the head and torso of a male athlete with an ancient victory crown upon his head. The five colored Olympic rings are above, and the quadriga atop the Brandenberg Gate occupies the lower half of the poster. Nobody knows if the athlete is raising his arm to the cheering crowds or giving the Nazi salute to Hitler, but the image itself is unforgettable either way. Other posters were produced, and some bring high prices, but this is the only official poster produced for the Berlin Games.

There are numerous "unofficial" posters that have been produced by businesses, sponsors, individuals, and organizations. Some of these posters have the Olympic rings in the design, but most do not because the rings are copyrighted by the International Olympic Committee and the various National Olympic Committees of participating countries. For example, Leroy Nieman, a noted artist, has made some very beautiful Olympic posters and serigraphs. These can sell for substantial amounts. However, Nieman has not made an official Olympic poster yet.

In 1896, 1900, 1904, 1906, and 1908 there were no specific posters made to promote the Olympic Games. However, a set of Olympic posters printed in Holland in 1972 commemorating those Games included a design for each of these years (except 1906).

The 1896 "poster" shows the goddess Athena holding the victory branch and crown with the stadium and Acropolis in the background. This design is actually the front cover of the Official Report of the 1896 Games.

Some posters were produced for specific events at the 1900 Paris Games, such as fencing, rowing, gymnastics, cycling, and athletics, but none used the words "Olympic Games" or the French version "Jeux Olympiques." The design created for the 1972 Dutch poster set filled the void. The Paris 1900 "poster" in this set is actually a collage of old photos and postcards arranged by the printer himself. The 1904 St. Louis "poster" and the 1908 London "poster" were actually the covers of the daily programs.

No poster was ever created for the 1906 Olympic Games held in Athens. Unknown to most sports fans, these were official Olympic Games that were held out of the four-year sequence because the Greeks insisted that they had the right to hold the Games when they wanted. Years later the International Olympic Committee declared these "Games" to be unofficial. In 1991 I was commissioned by the editor of a sports almanac to create a poster that could be used to represent the 1906 Games. The resulting design showed a Greek goddess holding out a victory crown with the text in Greek and French, the languages in use at the 1906 Games.

The first Olympic poster created in anticipation of the Games came in 1912 when the Swedish artist Olle Hjortzberg designed a daring poster showing naked male athletes twirling their national flags. Printed in large quantity, more than 118,000 copies were made in three sizes and printed in sixteen languages. The posters were then distributed worldwide, mostly to travel agencies, consulates, railroad stations, and other transportation locations.

Obtaining one of these beautiful posters is not very difficult, and prices range from $500 to $1,200, depending on the size and the language of the text. I have always wanted to obtain all the versions—a very difficult and expensive challenge. The same image was used as a postal sticker or "poster stamp." These are also easily available for under $30. For some collectors these miniature versions of the poster might be the only affordable copies. It is an interesting sidenote that the design was too provocative for some countries, such as China, where the mail was returned because the design of the stamp was considered obscene.

In 1916 the Olympic Games were scheduled to take place in Berlin, but World War I was raging in Europe and the Games were canceled. After the war ended, the Olympic Games resumed in Antwerp in 1920. A lovely poster was created by Martha van Kuyck and illustrated by Walter von der Ven. It showed a naked male athlete in the pose of a discus thrower, the flags of the various nations winding around him. In the rear is the city of Antwerp, and its coat of arms occupies the top right corner. At least 130,000 copies were printed in two sizes. It must be noted that at least three different versions are known to have been printed by three different printers.

The 1924 summer Olympics in Paris produced two posters, both rather difficult to obtain today. Jean Droit created the image of several male athletes standing and saluting, the red, white, and blue French flag fluttering in the rear. In my opinion this is one of the most beautiful Olympic posters ever made. The second poster, by Orsi, shows an athlete preparing to release his javelin, the city of Paris in the rear with a partial globe. Each of these lovely posters was produced in one size and limited in production to ten thousand copies. The posters were produced for advertising purposes and distributed worldwide to travel agencies, consulates, and other promoting organizations. They were not sold to the public as souvenirs. How many survived is unknown, but certainly many were glued to kiosks and later pasted over or ripped down.

It was in this year that the winter Olympics began, and one of the most striking posters for the Games, summer or winter, was produced for the event. Auguste Matisse designed a poster with an eagle carrying the crown of victory and laurel branches, the Alps hovering in the background as five bobsledders come down the track in the lower right corner. This poster is very tough to get, as only about five thousand were printed. Three other posters were also produced for the winter Games, but note that all were produced by the French state-run Paris-Lyon-Méditerranée Railroad, which sponsored the construction of the facilities. Technically, then, one might argue that these winter Games posters are "unofficial."

The 1928 summer Games were in Amsterdam, and J. J. Rovers won a competition held by the Dutch Organizing Committee with his depiction of a male runner, the stadium and tower in the background, and the white Olympic flag with five interlocking rings. This was the first poster design to incorporate the Olympic rings. Printed in two sizes, only fifty-five thousand copies were made. The winter Games, held in Saint Moritz, had a very simple but colorful poster showing the white Olympic flag and the flag of Switzerland flying above the Alps. Only twelve thousand copies were made in one size.

The 1932 summer Games were held in Los Angeles. The Depression had drained American spirits for the preceding three years, but the Games were still very successful. A poster designed by Hungarian-born Julio Kilenyl showed a male athlete holding a laurel branch, announcing the next Olympic Games. Printed in one size, there were two hundred thousand copies made, yet this poster remains difficult to obtain. The 1932 winter Olympics were held in Lake Placid, and two posters were produced. Witold Gordon produced a poster that shows a ski-jumper superimposed on a globe with the Olympic rings below. It has been described by one author as being one of the best posters ever made for the winter Games. I personally disagree and think it is among the ugliest, but then again, I have voted for only one winning president in the past twenty-two years. In a tie for the ugliest poster was the other Lake Placid poster, showing bobsledders in one large panel and four other scenes running along the left side of the poster. Though not my favorites, both are hard to find and can command high prices.

The 1936 summer Olympic Games are probably the most famous Games of the first hundred years. These Games were embroiled in the international politics of the period and had strong political interference from Hitler's governing National Socialist (Nazi) Party. Images that come to mind are those of the great runner Jesse Owens, Hitler in the stadium, and the poster by Frantz Wurbel described earlier.

There were three other posters produced for the 1936 summer Games that are less familiar to collectors. The first illustrates the course of the first ever torch run between Olympia, Greece, and Berlin. It shows a map of Europe, a hand holding the torch, and a blue line linking the cities through which the runners traveled. Printed in five languages, there were thirty-five thousand copies made.

The second poster, illustrating the quadriga atop the Brandenberg Gate, was intended to arouse enthusiasm within Germany for the Games. I also know of French and English language editions, but am not certain of print runs.

The last poster, a very attractive sailing scene by Otto Anton, was used to promote the Olympic sailing events in Kiel. Only seventy-three hundred copies were printed, and this work is very tough to get. It has sold for several thousand dollars at auction.

One of the most famous winter Olympic posters is the one designed by Ludwig Hohlwein for the 1936 winter Games held in Garmisch-Partenkirchen. Since 106,150 copies were printed in two sizes, this design is one of the easier posters to find, but is still expensive due to the reputation of the artist. There are thirteen different language editions of the larger poster, which is about 25 x 39 inches. The small edition posters were all printed in German.

In 1940 the Games were scheduled for Tokyo (summer) and Sapporo (winter). But in 1937 the Sino-Japanese war broke out. In 1938 the Japanese relinquished both the summer and winter Games, but Finland and Germany were quick to fill the role of host countries. The summer Games were rescheduled to take place in Helsinki, and the winter Games in Garmisch-Partenkirchen. But in 1939 the Soviet Union invaded Finland, Germany invaded Poland, and once again the Games were canceled when the world went to war.

The Finns had made tremendous plans to hold the 1940 Olympics and went ahead and printed posters, produced pins and badges, held a fund-raising lottery, and created a number of souvenirs that today's collectors can enjoy. The poster designed by Ilmari Sysimetsä (1912–1955) showed the great Finn runner Paavo Nurmi with a globe in the rear, the Olympic rings at the top right corner, and the dates below. This poster is highly collectible today because these Games were never held.

The same poster design was used twelve years later when the Games of 1952 were held in Helsinki. The design changed very little. Of course, the dates were changed, and closer inspection reveals that the map of Finland on the globe is also different — it's smaller, reflecting the territory it lost in the war.

The summer Games were scheduled to take place in London in 1944, but the war was still in progress and the Games did not resume until 1948. The single poster produced for the 1948 Games in London shows the statue of a discus thrower superimposed over the Parliament building, large Olympic rings below, and the dates. Printed in three sizes, there were 175,000 copies made. Four extremely lovely posters were made for the winter Games that year in Saint Moritz, all in small quantities. They are difficult to find today.

Two posters were made for the 1952 winter Olympics in Oslo, both designed by Knut Yran. The larger poster featured the Norwegian and Olympic flags fluttering from ski poles. The smaller poster, printed in eight languages, showed an athlete raising the Olympic flag up a pole.

Artistically speaking, the Olympic posters changed after 1952. Radio, television, films, and the growth of the other media changed the purpose of the poster. The 1956 Melbourne poster, designed by Richard Beck, made a dramatic departure from ancient Greek symbolism to more modern symbolism, depicting a partially unfolded invitation to the Games. The poster for the equestrian events, held in Sweden, stayed with ancient Greek symbolism and showed a Greek rider atop a horse. The 1956 winter Games poster showed the official symbol of Cortina D'Ampezzo.

The poster for the 1960 summer Games in Rome, designed by Armando Testa (b. 1917), incorporated Romulus and Remus with the she-wolf as a symbol. This appeared atop the capital of a column, with ancient Romans below. The poster for Squaw Valley, site of the winter Games, was again the official emblem of the Games.

Symbolism then took over, and the Olympic rings emblem became the central identifying mark. For the 1964 Tokyo Games the red rising sun atop Olympic rings adorned four different posters, three of which utilized photographs of athletes for the first time. For the winter Games in Innsbruck, the poster featured a close-up of a snowflake crystal.

The Mexico City Games of 1968 as well as the Grenoble winter Games that year created a whole series of posters, seventeen for Mexico City and nine for Grenoble. The Olympic poster took on a whole new meaning. One image didn't do the job; now every sport had to be illustrated.

In 1972 the summer Games were held in Munich. Most people's memory is dominated by images of slain Israeli athletes, flags at half-mast, and terrorists peeking from doorways. My own memory is much different because this was the first time I qualified for the Olympic Games in wrestling. Although I did not make the final team, I attended the games and loved the pastel colors of those posters—more than twenty of them! At the time I could not afford to buy more than a single poster. Years later, when I could afford it, I bought the remaining inventory of the company that sold them in Germany. Talk about a collector getting carried away! In all there were fifty different posters issued for the Munich Games. I recently bought up the entire inventory of the American distributor of these posters, so I confidently believe I own the largest stockpile in the world of the Munich posters. Unfortunately, my wife won't let me hang them all up.

Sapporo finally hosted the winter Games for 1972, after a wait of thirty-two years, but created only five posters supporting the event.

Posters promoting the summer Olympic Games now far outnumber those created for the winter Games. The Montreal Games of 1976 inspired thirty different posters, but only three were created for the winter events in Innsbruck. The 1980 Moscow Games generated 250 different posters with a total print run of over eighteen million copies. The designs were culled from more than twenty-six thousand sketches submitted by eighty-five hundred artists. Few of these posters have made their way to the United States because of the boycott to the 1980 Olympics. At least fifteen posters were produced for the 1980 winter Lake Placid Games. The Games of 1984, 1988, and 1992 also produced series of posters, many of which are very inexpensive to obtain.

There are few, if any, complete collections of Olympic posters in the world today. Probably the best collection is in Lausanne, Switzerland, at the newly opened museum of the International Olympic Committee. Most National Olympic Committees also have collections, but few have museums or display facilities. For years the U.S. Olympic Committee has considered opening a museum, but plans have been repeatedly delayed. Some of the best collections are in private hands, including the marvelous collection owned by Juan Antonio Samaranch, the current president of the International Olympic Committee.

Keep in mind that reproductions of many posters have been on the market for years. If you can't afford the originals and don't mind the reproductions, you should be able to get these at very low prices. However, bear in mind that these have decorative or interest value only, and will probably never see much appreciation in terms of collectibility.

OLYMPIC POSTERS—PRICE LISTINGS

NOTE: The following listings are a selection of both official Olympics posters and unofficial posters, in chronological order.

❦ **1912**

Stockholm, June 29–July 22. Lithograph. Official poster, German edition. Artist: Olle Hjortzberg (1872–1959). A naked athlete standing and facing front, waving a Swedish flag with a banner trailing and hiding his groin. Behind are several naked male figures waving national flags. Printed in three formats; largest size 29½ x 40 inches. $1,500–$2,500

🦋 1920

Antwerp, Aug.-Sept. Lithograph. Official poster. Illustration: Walter von der Ven (1884–1923). Naked male athlete facing right holding a discus in his right hand, preparing to throw. Flowing flags from all the participating nations are behind the athlete. Four firms printed the 90,000 posters in eighteen editions (seventeen languages). Printers were Stockmans et Compagnie, Van Dieran et Cie, both of Antwerp, and J. Colassin & Compagnie, Bruxelles. Good condition, 24¾ x 36 inches. $1,200–$1,800

🦋 1932

Lake Placid, Feb. 4–13. Lithograph. Official poster. Four men in bobsled in the center. Four illustrations show a ski-jumper, speed skater, figure skater, and downhill skier. At top, five Olympic rings. Good condition, 25 x 40 inches.
$1,800–$2,200

🦋 1932

Los Angeles. Lithograph for the Chicago & Northwestern Railways/Union Pacific train from Chicago to Los Angeles. A discus thrower facing right on black and red background. Rare. Very good condition, 27 x 41 inches. $3,000–$4,000

🦋 1936

Berlin, Aug. 1–16. Photo-offset. Official poster, German edition. Artist: Frantz Wurbel (1896–?). A male athlete with a crown of olive behind the quadriga atop the Brandenberg Gate. At top are the Olympic rings. Fine condition, 24⅝ x 39½ inches. $2,000–$3,000

🦋 1936

Berlin. Allemagne XIe Olympiad Berlin, 1936. Artists: Krauss & Dzubas. Illustrating the quadriga atop the Brandenberg Gate, was intended to arouse enthusiasm inside Germany for the Games. Also printed in English and French. Good condition, 25 x 39⅝ inches. $2,000–3,000

🦋 1936

Berlin. Olympia film poster, German. An advertising poster for Leni Riefenstahl's famous film of the Berlin Games. After the war the film was not permitted to be shown in occupied Germany. This poster is dated 1958, when the film was rereleased. A naked male athlete posing as the classical discus thrower. Red Olympic rings and arc showing the path of the discus. Fine condition, 23½ x 33 inches.
$800–$1,200

🦋 1940

Helsinki. Photo-offset. Official poster, English edition. Artist: Ilmari Sysimetsä (1912–1955). A statue of naked male athlete, actually Paavo Nurmi, running to

Courtesy of Harvey
Abrams Books.

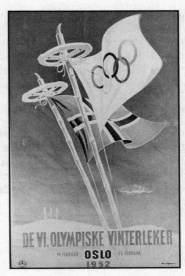

Courtesy of Harvey
Abrams Books.

the right. Behind is a globe showing Europe with Finland outlined. The 1940 Games were canceled due to the war between the Soviet Union and Finland, and then the onset of WWII. Posters were designed and issued before the cancellation and are very scarce in some languages; 25 x 38¼ inches. *See color insert, photo 21.* $1,800–$2,200

❦ **1948**

London, July 29–Aug. 14. Lithograph. Official poster. Artist: Walter Herz, b. 1909. The ancient statue of the discus thrower is superimposed on the British Parliament building. Only 25,000 posters were produced in this size. This poster remains one of the most difficult Olympic posters to find, although it is not the most expensive; 20 x 30 inches. $900–$1,400

❦ **1952**

Helsinki, July 19–Aug. 3. Photo-offset. Official poster, German edition. Artist: Ilmari Sysimetsä (1912–1955). A statue of naked male athlete, actually Paavo Nurmi, running to the right. Behind is a globe showing Europe with Finland outlined. Reissue of original 1940 poster (see 1940 entry and preceding chapter for more information); 82,000 copies in nine languages were made in the large size, 25 x 38¼ inches. $1,800–$2,000

❦ **1952**

Oslo, Feb. 14–25. Lithograph. Official poster, Norwegian edition. Artist: Knut Yran. Thirty thousand copies were printed in seven languages. The Olympic and Norwegian flags fly from bamboo ski poles; 36¾ x 40 inches. $1,500–$2,000

❦ **1972**

Munich. Twenty-eight posters from the Munich Olympic Art Series, illustrating the work of numerous artists. All measure 25 x 40 inches. Mint condition, prices range from $50–$100, depending on the artist/image, with only one valued at $400, by Allen Jones, because it features the Olympic rings.

❦ **1972**

Munich. Official posters, illustrating various sports competitions. All measure 33 x 47 inches. While probably all but one of the twenty-four posters in this series were made available to the public in a smaller size, they were never sold to the public in this size, making them more valuable. Mint condition, prices range from $200 to $400, depending on the event/artist.

PART FIVE

A World of Entertainment

❦ CHAPTER 25 ❦
Magic Posters

BY KEN TROMBLY

Since the fateful day in 1956 when his grandmother bought him "the ball and vase trick" in a Boston joke shop, Ken Trombly, a member of the Magic Collectors Association, has been a lifelong magic enthusiast. His love of magic developed into a fascination with the history of magic, and Ken was drawn to vintage magicians' posters. For the past twenty years he has focused much energy in tracking down original specimens. You can contact him at Suite 901, 1825 K Street NW, Washington, D.C. 20006, (202) 887–5000.

If time machines were available for magic collectors to travel to any period in history, some might opt to return to the days of Merlin. However, most would turn back the calendar a mere hundred years or so, to the turn of the century, a time known as the "Golden Age of Magic." How fortunate, therefore, that this period coincided with the advent of full-color stone lithography—printing's own "Golden Age." Lithography blended with magical themes in an artistic alchemy. The results were posters of creativity and wonderment that advertised magicians, both famous and obscure, during this special era.

In this chapter, when we use the term *magic poster*, we refer to those stone lithographs (sometimes sepia or two- or three-color, but mostly full-color) that were used by professional magicians to advertise their performances. While earlier letterpress posters and broadsides are technically "magic posters," these pieces of advertising have become very scarce, and are mostly of interest to magic historians only. Similarly, later photo-offset and laser-printed posters are not covered in this chapter.

Given that magic posters were, simply stated, product advertising solely intended to promote a show or a run of shows in a town, what is truly magical is that so many of the posters have survived. Referred to simple as "paper" by magic collectors, these ephemeral items were apparently pulled down and kept for posterity in a drawer or trunk by many a fledging conjurer.

Today's collectors usually are drawn to magic posters via one of two avenues. Some are nonmagicians who fall under the spell of the mystery and occasional quirkiness of the poster images. More typically, however-er, the collector is a life-long magic buff who finds these posters an adjunct to a broader appreciation of the magic art and its history. More than any other form of magic collectible (e.g., antique apparatus, magic books and magazines, autographed photos, old magic catalogs, magician's tokens), vintage magic posters convey a sense of mystery and wonderment—and that, indeed, was their purpose.

Perhaps the best way to cover this topic is to discuss the specifics of magic posters you are likely to see. So let us set our time machine back, revisit the Golden Age, and identify some performers whose posters have survived.

THE PERFORMERS

Alexander

Claude Conlin (1880–1954), aka Alexander, "The Man Who Knows," cloaked himself in an air of mystery that belied his birthplace of Alexandria, South Dakota (not Egypt). His posters typically depicted a turbaned Alexander—sometimes only a bust portrait—who occasionally held a crystal ball. The most common version is a red, black, and gray one-sheet portrait (about 28 x 42 inches), with eyes that follow the viewer around the room. Although his posters bear the words "av yaga Bombay" in the corner, this author agrees with the opinion expressed in *100 Years of Magic Posters* (hereinafter *100 Years*), by Charles and Regina Reynolds, that it is doubtful the posters were actually printed in India (see Bibliography).

The most dramatic and pleasing of the Alexander posters is a three-sheet (about 42 x 83 inches), full-color version showing Alexander's head before a green and yellow striped background, his hand extended and holding a crystal ball. For anyone interested in opening a theme bar or simply making an unusual design statement in a living room, a twenty-four-sheet billboard version in full color is also available.

From all accounts, Alexander was a colorful character who knew how to market himself. He left a legacy of striking and original poster images, through which he will be long remembered by collectors.

Blackstone

Harry Blackstone, born Henri Bouton (1885–1965), was a popular American stage magician whose lengthy career spanned the days of the full evening magic shows right up to the 1950s. He played all over the U.S.—in towns both big and small. In 1934 Harry Blackstone was crowned "King of Magicians" at the Magician's Convention in Detroit, a fact noted on some of his posters.

While the more recent Blackstone posters are produced by means of a photo-offset process, and are fairly available, his early posters are increasingly difficult to obtain. Most common is the one-sheet horizontal *Arabian Nights* poster—a busy, magical feast of dancing girls, elephants, and, of course, Blackstone himself. Be aware that this poster is one of several reproduced by Pomeroy, Ohio, magic dealer Lee Jacobs. To differentiate the original from copies, note that the reproduction usually bears Lee's rubber stamp on the back, and more important, at 21 x 29 inches, it is somewhat smaller than the one-sheet original. Fortunately, most magic poster reproductions are smaller than the standard half-sheet or full one-sheet sizes.

Many of Blackstone's signature routines, including the vanishing birdcage and the floating light bulb, can still be seen today. His son, Harry Blackstone, Jr., continues his father's magical legacy—and will undoubtedly carry the family name into the twenty-first century.

Carter the Great

On any weekend it is a safe bet that there is an antique fair somewhere in the United States with at least one booth selling a poster of Carter the Great. Charles Carter (1874–1936), a lawyer by training, was a globe-trotting stage magician in the 1920s and 1930s. In 1933 he was a featured act at the Chicago World's Fair, though his act was somewhat less than successful. However, he made several world tours and, by any measure, was a successful performer. He met his demise in India months after being crushed by an elephant.

Carter has been well-known to magic historians for years, but it was not until the 1960s that his posters became readily available, when a huge supply of his paper and equipment was found in a San Francisco warehouse. The now defunct bar of that fair city known as Merlin McFly's was the showcase and eventually the distribution site of Carter paper.

Carter's posters, printed by the Otis Lithograph Company, feature bold colors and imaginatively detailed images. They are a tribute to the artists at Otis.

Chung Ling Soo

If there ever was a figure in magic history whose memory is shrouded in an air of mystery, it is Chung Ling Soo. Known as "the Marvelous Chinese Conjurer," Soo was in reality an American by the name of William Ellsworth Robinson (1861–1918). He adopted the guise of an inscrutable visitor from the East, spoke through "interpreters" offstage, and was a very popular act in London from the early years of this century until his untimely death. His passing in no small way contributed to his exotic image: He was sticken on a London stage by an errant round of ammunition in the midst of performing a bullet-catching trick. Whether it was suicide, murder, or accident was never determined by Scotland Yard.

What is known is that his posters, printed in great variety in England, are prized by magic poster collectors, and can rarely be found in this country at prices below $1,000. While the $1,200–$1,500 range is probably closer to the norm, a fine copy of one of his more desirable posters, *A Gift from the Gods*, sold at auction in 1993 for $3,960, considerably more than the $1,000–$1,500 price estimated in the catalog.

Fak Hong

If one were to write a history of magic simply based on magicians whose posters are available today, the Fak Hong Troupe would probably be Chapter One, although they otherwise fill a minor niche in magic history. Chang (1889–1972), a Panamanian illusionist and entrepreneur, apparently produced and/or sponsored one or more groups that went by the name "the Fak Hongs," "Fak Hong," or "Fak Hong's United Magicians." Given the variety of images and the extensive use of stock posters, it is conceivable that other performers or groups of performers, with no relation to Chang, also may have used this same name.

Grover George

While Carter posters have been widely available for the last decade or so, the posters of Grover George (1887–1958), known as "George the Magician," have become more accessible within the last five years. George was a competitor of Carter and Howard Thurston. Thurston managed to keep George tied up in lawsuits to such an extent that few of George's posters saw the light of day in the United States. He was more active as a performer in South America. Ironically, George is probably now better-known to younger generations of nonmagicians in this country than Thurston was in his time simply because of his posters.

In the late 1980s, a substantial cache of George posters was uncovered in a barn in Wisconsin. As the lucky discoverer of this mother lode of lithographs wisely began to sell it off, George posters have surfaced on numerous dealers' lists and have become widely available. The posters, printed by Otis, bear striking similarity to Carter's, and are generally available in half-sheets and superb one-sheets, as well as an eight-sheet and a twenty-sheet.

Houdini

Not surprisingly, Houdini posters are among the most desired, undoubtedly due to the fact that Houdini is as much a part of American cultural history as magic history. Houdini was born Erich Weisz, in Budapest, Hungary, in 1874, and adopted his name after the French magician Robert-Houdin.

Interestingly, in this author's experience, the most commonly available Houdini posters are his first and his last. It's the ones in between that escape the clutches of poster collectors! The earliest known Houdini lithograph is his *King of Cards* poster. It depicts Houdini as a young man at such an early stage in his career that the poster does not feature what was to become his world-famous escape act. The poster was printed around 1900 by National Printing & Engraving Company of Chicago, Illinois, and is a two-color half-sheet. Although it bears the number 1838 in the right-hand corner, this obviously is not the issue date, as the performer was born in 1874.

This poster was reproduced by magician Tommy Windsor in the 1960s, and since then has been reproduced again by Lee Jacobs. Unlike most magic poster reproductions , it is only a wee bit smaller than the original. The quality of the earlier reproduction, as well as the choice of heavier paper, make it one of the finest magic poster reproductions ever printed. In fact, without carefully studying them side by side, you may have considerable difficulty confirming that you have purchased an original copy of this lithograph. Some clues to look for are: (a) the original is likely to have more white space at the top (the "header") above the image than the reproduction; (b) earlier copies did not include the

Courtesy of
Ken Trombly.

name of the National Printing & Engraving Company in the bottom right corner; and (c) many of the newer copies bear the name of the publisher "Lee Jacobs" on the back (a dead giveaway that the piece is not an original as Lee was not around in the 1890s).

The eight-sheet full-color *Buried Alive* poster (Otis, ca. 1925) shows a more mature Harry Houdini superimposed on a tableau of the Sphinx, which overlooks a mummy case that holds the "master mystifier" himself. Because of its unwieldy size, it is best purchased properly mounted. If not, it should be mounted forthwith before its pieces begin to crumble. Inasmuch as it is an eight-sheet poster, it is easy to distinguish the original from the full-color copy, printed by laser technology, which is only 21 x 29 inches.

Putting a value on Houdini posters is difficult as the sale prices you generally hear about were established at auction, and auction prices can be misleading. *King of Cards* last sold at auction a decade ago for $880, but could now fetch $2,500 to $3,000 or more.

Kar-Mi

Until the sudden availability of Carter and George posters, Kar-Mi tied with Alexander as the most common of magic posters. Printed by the National and Donaldson Lithography companies, his posters are usually available in one-sheet and three-sheet versions.

The three one-sheet versions are *Kar-Mi Shoots a Cracker Off a Man's Head, Kar-Mi Performing the Most Startling Mystery of All India—Selma*, and a vertical image depicting members of Kar-Mi's troupe swallowing swords. The sword poster actually bears the name *Victoriana Troupe*, which is then typically covered with a header bearing the name "Kar-Mi." Of the three Kar-Mi one-sheets, the latter has become increasingly desirable and hard to find.

Kellar

Kellar's name conveys a special sense of mystery to the magic collector. Harry Kellar (1849–1922) was born Heinrich Keller in Erie, Pennsylvania. As a youngster, he was an assistant to an Englishman performing in the States as "The Faker of Ava." Kellar later went out on his own, altering the spelling of his last name, it is said, so that he would not be confused with the popular magician Robert Heller. A dapper and skilled showman, from the 1890s until his retirement in 1908, Kellar was one of the foremost magicians appearing on the American stage.

Except for some early, extremely rare examples, Kellar's posters were largely printed by the Strobridge Lithography Company of Cincinnati. The most familiar of his posters, the so-called *Imps Portrait*, is a bust of

Kellar with a red devilish imp poised on each shoulder. These creatures are apparently sharing some mystical secret with him. The poster was printed in half-sheet and one-sheet versions, but is also available in three-sheet and even larger sizes. The half-sheet is most commonly available—but has become increasingly difficult to find.

Although Kellar was not the first to use devil themes in his posters, his use of imps established a trend among magicians—or at least their poster designers—that continued with other performers that followed. One such performer was Howard Thurston.

Thurston

Born 1869 in Columbus, Ohio, Howard Thurston held a variety of jobs and studied for the ministry before he turned to magic. By 1900 he found success as a card manipulator and stage magician. In 1908, in a theater in Baltimore, Maryland, Thurston received the "Mantle of Magic" from Harry Kellar, succeeding the older magician. This event was memorialized in a full-color Strobridge poster. It is a poster that is rather hard to find. Early Thurston imps portraits—similar to Kellar's version and also printed by Strobridge—sell in the same range as Kellar's imps portrait.

As Thurston matured, he regrettably took his lithography business to the Otis Lithography Company. While Otis was by no means a second-rate printer, its Thurston posters just don't convey the detail and artistry of the richer Strobridge paper.

Stock Posters

Magicians who did not have the budget of a Thurston or Kellar were still able to advertise their performances with stone lithograph posters by purchasing stock posters. Such posters, printed by a number of companies (Donaldson, National, Friedlander, Great Western, Strobridge, Russell-Morgan, and others), usually depicted a magician performing some mystery or other, and left a large blank space on the poster for the performer to insert his name and, in some cases, the place and/or date of the performance.

While some stock posters were designed as such, others were probably intended for a specific performer and later adapted into stock posters. A good example is a 1911 Nicola poster of a floating lady wrapped in the American flag. Compare this poster with the Jansen poster of the same year found in *100 Years*, page 74. In comparing the header in the Nicola to the Jansen, it becomes apparent which was the original design and which was a later stock poster, as Jansen's name is more integrated into the original design.

Courtesy of
Ken Trombly.

Stock posters can be outstanding examples of color lithography. Early Donaldson and National stock posters have a real period American look, while Friedlander stock posters generally have a touch of European elegance (see additional information on the printing companies that produced stock posters in the price listings).

TO FIND OUT MORE ABOUT MAGIC POSTERS

Three notable collections that include magic posters are those belonging to the Museum of the City of New York, The New York Historical Society, and the Billy Rose Theater Collection at the New York Public Library. In Washington, D.C., the Library of Congress Poster Division houses some fine magic posters—although prior arrangements to view them should be made.

Some other collections of varying sizes, presently open to the public, are located at the American Museum of Magic, Marshall, Michigan; the Magic Art Book Company, Watertown, Massachusetts; and the Magic Castle, Hollywood, California. Several Houdini posters are part of the permanent exhibit at the Houdini Historical Research Center, Outagamie County Museum, Appleton, Wisconsin.

Several reference books exist on magic posters, most of which include fine pictorial sections; *100 Years of Magic Posters*, already referred to in this section, is a must-read. Some of the price listings that follow this chapter have been keyed to that text. Also recommended are: *Magic: A Pictorial History of Conjurers in the Theater*, by David Price, and *Magic: A Picture History; The Illustrated History of Magic*, by Milbourne Christopher. See the Bibliography for details of these and other books on magic posters.

NOTES ON MAGIC POSTER PRICES

Unlike most other posters, magic posters have traditionally appealed to a small group of collectors. Accordingly, although they continue to become costlier, magic posters are likely to see a slower increase in prices. Additionally, although there have been recent examples of occasional auction highs—at magic conventions and other places where magic posters are likely to be for sale—there have also been some lows.

When this author began collecting magic posters in the early 1970s, you could buy a Thurston one-sheet poster printed by the Otis Lithography Company, such as the familiar *Do the Spirits Come Back?*, for $75. The price of this and comparable vintage magic posters slowly increased in the 1970s and 1980s so that a dealer catalog from 1989 offered *Do the Spirits Come Back?* for $650, mounted on linen.

Just months later, in May 1990, a New York City auction house, Swann Galleries, held a one- day auction of the magic collection of the late Neil See. A handful of collectors ran up some record high bids not just on magic posters, but the entire collection, including books and magazines, with nearly every item fetching a price in excess of the catalog estimates.

Do the Spirits Come Back? was offered in the 1990 Swann sale. Amidst an apparent bidding frenzy, it sold for a whopping $5,500 (including buyer's premium), an expenditure of nearly ten times the actual market value of the poster. This was simply a case of two uninformed buyers at the same auction, a recipe for record prices. Six months after the auction, at a magic convention, several dealers offered *Do the Spirits Come Back?* in the four-figure range, but most remained unsold. Since that time, the poster has, in fact, routinely sold in the $800–$1,200 range. With the preceding as a caveat, on to the price guide.

The list of posters set out below includes those you are most likely to see on dealer lists, in trade publications, or at antique and paper shows—posters that are fairly well established in the marketplace. Remember, however, these prices are only *estimates*. They should not be considered hard facts. They are based on this author's experience and observations. The condition of the item is an important factor that can affect its value, and the prices below assume a poster that is at least in good condition.

MAGIC POSTERS—PRICE LISTINGS

NOTE: See the preceding chapter for additional information on pricing magic posters. References following some of the titles of posters refer to 100 Years of Magic Posters, by Charles and Regina Reynolds, and Panorama of Magic, by Milbourne Christopher (see Bibliography). All posters listed below are lithographs. Sizes given as one-sheet, three-sheet, window card, etc. are approximately the same dimensions as cinema posters of the same size. See Standard Cinema Poster Sizes and Formats.

❧ ALEXANDER

Alexander—billboard size! Full-color, 109 x 205 inches. Still a bargain for the size, but the cost of mounting and framing would easily be many times the market price. $250–$350

Alexander—The Man Who Knows, ca. 1915. Dramatic two-color portrait. Still fairly common, one-sheet, 28 x 42 inches. $75–$125

As above, three-sheet, 42 x 83 inches. $175–$275

As above, 81 x 111 inches. $150–$200

Alexander—"The Man Who Knows," ca. 1915. Alexander holds a crystal ball in front of striped background. A very good example of an Alexander poster. Full-color, three-sheet. $650–$800

Alexander "Crystal Seer—Knows Sees Tells All," ca. 1915. Black, red, and white. One-sheet, about 14 x 40 inches. $250–$325

Alexander "Crystal Seer—World's Greatest Master Mental Mystic." Similar to above, but image is of multiple skulls. Very eerie. One-sheet. $250–$325

From a private collection.
Photo by Robert Four.

Ask Alexander, ca. 1915 (*100 Years*, p. 89). Alexander's turbaned head in a question mark. Full color, one-sheet. $100–$150

❦ BLACKSTONE

Baffling! World's Greatest Magician, ca. 1930. Three color, one-sheet. $300–$500

Big Combination, ca. 1930. Printed by the National Printing & Engraving Company. Two- color, with newspaper cartoon-type illustrations of Blackstone doing his tricks. A delightful poster. One-sheet. $350–$600

As above, with other cartoon vignettes, half-sheet, 20 x 30 inches. $300–$550

Blackstone, World's Greatest Magician (crowned King of Magicians at Detroit, 1934), ca. 1934. This large three-color poster features a great portrait in the upper left corner. $550– $750

Oriental Nights, ca. 1920 (*100 Years*, p. 99). Printed by Erie Litho. Depicting the Enchanted Camel, Indian Rope Trick, Burning at the Stake, and "Nautch Girls." Full-color, one-sheet. $650–$850

❦ CARTER

Carter, ca. 1920s. Printed by Otis. Billboard size! Includes portraits of Carter and other magic "Greats," sixteen-sheet. $450–$600

Carter Beats the Devil, ca. 1920. Printed by Otis. Quite common. Full-color, window card, cardboard stock, 14 x 22 inches. $50–$100

Carter Sweeps the Secrets of the Sphinx and Marvels of the Tomb of Old King Tut To the Modern World, ca. 1920. Printed by Otis. Known to collectors as *Carter on the Camel*, this spectacular image has become one of the least available Carter/Otis posters. Full color, one-sheet. $450–$550

Carter the Great, Do the Dead Materialize? Modern Princess of Delphi, ca. 1936 (*100 Years*, p. 71). Printed by Otis. Slightly more common than its "sawing" mate. One-sheet. $450– $600

Carter the Great, a Night in China—Sawing a Live Woman in Halves, ca. 1936 (*100 Years* p. 71). Printed by Otis. An increasingly scarce full-color one-sheet, 18 x 40 inches. $500– $650

Catching a Bullet, ca. 1920s. Printed by Otis. Full-color, eight-sheet. $250–$500

Cheating the Gallows, ca. 1920s. Printed by Otis. Full-color, eight-sheet. $250–$500

Delphic Oracle, ca. 1920s. Printed by Otis. An exceptional portrait poster of Carter. This poster is slightly less available than the other three-sheets. $450–$600

From a private collection.
Photo by Robert Four.

Courtesy of Poster Mail
Auction Co.

Do the Dead Materialize?, ca. 1920s. Printed by Otis. Spectacular colors, eight-sheet, 40 x 90 inches. $300–$600

The Elongated Maiden, ca. 1920s. Printed by Otis. Spectacular colors, beautifully rendered image. Full-color, three-sheet, 40 x 90 inches. $400–$550

Sawing a Lady in Half, ca. 1920s. Printed by Eagle Litho, Calcutta, India. Two-color poster that utilizes much of the image of the Otis "sawing" panel. $200–$300

Vanishing Elephant, ca. 1920s. Printed by Otis. This one is a bit harder to find than other full-color Carter eight-sheets. Sold in New York at auction for $1,100 in 1993. $500–$750

World's Weird Wonderful Wizard, ca. 1920. Printed by Otis. Quite common. Full-color, window card, 14 x 22 inches. $50–$100

As above, three-sheet. $400–$500

🌾 CHUNG LING SOO

Cauldron, ca. 1910. Printed by James Upton. Full-color of magician producing a woman and livestock from a burning cauldron. Sold at auction for $1,100 in New York in 1993. Half- sheet. $850–$950

Fans, ca. 1910. Printed by Horrocks & Company. Elegant portrait of Soo surrounded by fans. This sold at auction in 1989 for $770. Full-color, half-sheet. $950–$1,200

Courtesy of Swann
Galleries, Inc.

Courtesy of Poster Mail
Auction Co.

Ribbons, ca. 1910. Printed by James Upton. Poster showing various phases of a routine involving a production of ribbons and fire. Sold at auction in New York in 1989 for $1,210 and in 1993 for $1,760. Full-color, half-sheet. $1,200–$1,500

❦ (THE) FAK HONGS

The Bhuda [sic], ca. 1940. Printed by Mirabet, Spain. Geese, flying devils, a skeleton, a green ghoul, and a snake adorn this bizarre poster. Full-color, half-sheet.
$75–$150

Elle, ca. 1940. Printed by Mirabet, Spain. Full-color, half-sheet. $75–$150

Fak Hong/The Great Chang and Fak-Hong's United Magicians "Oriental Review," ca. 1940. Printed by Mirabet, Spain. Geisha girl-type figure with parasol, rabbit, and fiery urn in foreground. $75–$150

The Fak Hongs, ca. 1915. Printed by Friedlander, Germany. Full-color, one-sheet. $275– $425

Hara-kiri, ca. 1940. Printed by Mirabet, Spain. Blue-robed figure in front of smoking urn from which nude nymphs appear. Full-color, half-sheet. $75–$150

The Invisible Man, ca. 1940. Printed by Mirabet, Spain. Full-color, half-sheet.
$75–$150

A Night in Tokio [sic], ca. 1940. Printed by Mirabet, Spain. Full-color, one-sheet.
$100– $150

The Noe Ark [sic], ca. 1940. Printed by Mirabet, Spain. Full-color, one-sheet.
$125–$175

Numero d'Illusion: Le Plus Grand du Monde, ca. 1920s. Printed by Mirabet, Spain. A mishmash of animals, severed heads, devils, playing cards, and ghoulish creatures overseen by two portraits of the performers in this bizarre image. Full-color, 52½ x 74 inches.
$375– $550

Presented by Great Ghang [sic], ca. 1940. Printed by Mirabet, Spain. Robed, Oriental magician with skull bleeding from mouth. Full-color, half-sheet.
$75–$150

❧ GEORGE

George, ca. 1920s. Printed by Otis. Billboard features an enormous portrait of George, twenty-sheet.
$250–$500

George the Supreme Master of Magic, ca. 1920s. Printed by Otis. George scales playing cards over a Buddha as minions of devilish creatures march around. A winner, common but desirable. Sold at auction in New York in 1993 for $330. Full-color, half-sheet.
$100– $150

George—the Supreme Master of Magic, 1920s. Printed by Otis. George scales cards amid smiling geishas, the pyramids, etc. Sold at auction in New York for $357 in 1993. Full-color, one-sheet.
$150–$250

As above, eight-sheet.
$300–$400

George—the Supreme Master of Magic, 1920s. Printed by Otis. George in moonlight as owls look on. Sold at auction in New York for $220 in 1993. Full color, one-sheet.
$100–$150

Courtesy of Poster Mail
Auction Co.

George the Supreme Master of Magic, Oriental Mysteries, ca. 1920s (*Panorama of Magic,* p. 194). Printed by Otis. George and assistants in Oriental garb chasing ducks as smiling Buddha looks on. Much less common than the other half-sheet above. Full-color, half-sheet. $150– $225

❦ KAR-MI

Buried Alive, ca. 1940. Printed by National. Full-color, three-sheet. $400–$550

Kar-Mi Performing the Most Startling Mystery of All India—Selma, ca. 1914. Printed by National. Full-color, one-sheet. $200–$250

Kar-Mi Swallows a Loaded Gun Barrel and Shoots a Cracker Off a Man's Head, 1914 (*100 Years,* p. 29). Printed by National. Full-color, one-sheet.
$200–$300

Prince Kar-Mi, 1914. Printed by National. Full-color, three-sheet. $450–$600

Sword Swallowing, ca. 1910. Printed by Donaldson. Full-color, one-sheet.
$250–$450

❦ KELLAR

Imps Portrait, 1894. Printed by Strobridge. Full-color, half-sheet. $1,000–$1,200
As above, one-sheet. $1,100–$1,500

Courtesy of Poster Mail
Auction Co.

From a private collection.
Photo by Robert Four.

❦ LES MAGIQUE LEONS

Les Magique Leons, ca. 1910. Printed by Horrocks, London. Devilish character. Actually a stock poster, not a poster of The Great Leon (Leon Levy), fairly available. Full-color, half- sheet. $150–$250

❦ SOLANIS

Le Magicien Moderne, ca. 1945. Printed by Geo. Conte. Full-color, one-sheet. $175–$300

❦ STOCK POSTERS—*alphabetically by printing company*

Donaldson Lithography Company (Newport, Kentucky)

> NOTE: Donaldson's early lithographs have a simple All-American quality. The following full-color half-sheets are just some of the many stock posters they produced. In later years, Donaldson printed strikes of some of these same images utilizing newer printing techniques inferior to the earlier stone lithos.

[Cigarettes and cards]. Magician doing manipulation act onstage. A copy of this poster, which often bears the header "Elmore," sold at auction in New York City in 1993 for $412. Half- sheet. $225–$375

[Escape], ca. 1920. Generic escape artist in a number of Houdini-like poses. Quite rare and desirable because of its Houdini association. Half-sheet. $500–$750

[Levitation], ca. 1910–1915. This poster is frequently found with the name "The Great Dayton." Half-sheet. $300–$400

Courtesy of
Ken Trombly.

[Livestock—Dove pan trick], ca. 1910–1915. Smiling magician producing rabbit and birds. Half-sheet. $250–$350

[Production from Spectator], ca. 1915. Magician produces ribbon and coins from befuddled man. Sold at auction in New York in 1993 for $357. Half-sheet. $250–$300

[Spirit Cabinet], ca. 1900. Magician in front of cabinet where lady is seated and various spirit manifestations occur. Half-sheet. $300–$500

Friedlander (Hamburg, Germany)

> NOTE: Known as the Strobridge of Germany, Friedlander produced an astounding array of circus and other entertainment posters. While the Friedlander family escaped the Nazis in the 1930s, few of their posters did. Their lithographs offer fine detail and dazzling colors. Because each of their poster images bore a different number, it is possible to ascertain approximate years of printing. All posters below are full-color lithographs.

[Dr. Ormande's Coterie], ca. 1907 (No. 4061). Decapitation of a female assistant is featured in this finely detailed lithograph. $400–$500

[Levitation], ca. 1913 (No. 6157). Comely female floats in the air at an angle under Moorish arch in spectacular poster that exudes the mystery of the East. $650–$800

[Rainbow of Illusions], ca. 1885 (No. 655). A beautiful example of Friedlander's finely detailed lithography in a one-sheet used by Roca. $550–$700

[Stock stage setting], ca. 1919 (No. 6754). This looks like a later, cruder version of No. 4061. $300–$400

[Stock stage setting], ca. 1915 (No. 6393). Magician produces flowers, flags, and animals in this classic one-sheet. $400–$600

[Stock panel], ca. 1920s (No. 6970). Hourglass-shaped image includes a skeleton with a fiddle, the devil with cards, and a magician with flowers. Full-color panel, ca. 14 x 40 inches. $250–$375

National Lithograph Company (Chicago and St. Louis)

> NOTE: Another popular American lithography house, National, like Donaldson, also produced a large variety of stock posters for other forms of entertainment. The lithos listed below are all full-color half-sheets.

[Escape artist], ca. 1910. Houdini-like pose in this fanciful jail cell scene. Half-sheet. $225– $375

[Levitation], ca. 1910. Mostly yellow and blue in this imaginative poster that offers a larger header area to be filled in by the performer. Half-sheet. $250–$450

[Mind-reading], ca. 1910. This stock litho frequently bears the name "Gordon the Master Magician" on the header. Half-sheet. $275–$375

Courtesy of
Ken Trombly.

Courtesy of Swann
Galleries, Inc.

The Throne Mystery, ca. 1910. Similar to the levitation poster, a larger header nicely worked into the design. Half-sheet.　　　　　　　$300–$450

[Lady in a Cage] A bust sculpture seems to take delight in the vanish of a lady under a cloth. Half-sheet.　　　　　　　　　　　　　　　$275–$450

Russell Morgan Lithograph Company (Cincinnati and New York)

> NOTE: *This lithography house produced images of a superior quality, similar to Strobridge.*

[El Verdadero Diablo], 1903. Devil seems to pull magician "out of a hat" as magician produces rabbit. An exquisite stock poster. Full-color, one-sheet.
　　　　　　　　　　　　　　　　　　　　　　　　　　$650–$850

[The Great Jester], 1906. Similar image to the *El Verdadero Diablo* above, but with a birdcage instead of a rabbit trick. Full color, one-sheet.　$650–$850

[The Great Jester], 1903. Although not technically a magic poster, this depicts hypnosis (an "allied art") with both mock drama and elegance. Full color, one-sheet.　　　　　　　　　　　　　　　　　　　　　　$450–$600

🌡 MISCELLANEOUS

[Escher], ca. 1935. Printed by Kunstanstalt, Augsburg. Magician-type figure standing in front of a very large Buddha. Fairly common, 27 x 35 inches.
　　　　　　　　　　　　　　　　　　　　　　　　　　$150–$300

❦ THURSTON

All Out of a Hat, ca. 1925. Printed by Otis. Thurston produces show girls, umbrellas, and livestock from large hat. Full-color, one-sheet. $750–$850

Do the Spirits Come Back? ca. 1915. Printed by Strobridge. There are several versions of Thurston posters that have this title. The Strobridge versions, as opposed to the Otis versions, are far less available. $1,200–$1,500

Do the Spirits Come Back?, ca. 1925. Printed by Otis. Full-color, one-sheet.
$850–$1,200

Iasia, ca. 1929 (*100 Years*, p. 78). Printed by Otis. One-sheet panel, 13½ x 41 inches. $600–$700

As above, one-sheet. $700–$800

Imps Portrait, ca. 1914. Printed by Strobridge. This is one of a series of imps portraits that were printed over the years. Full-color, one-sheet. $1,200–$1,400

Imps Portrait, ca. 1925. Printed by Otis. One of Thurston's last posters, also available as a window card. This one-sheet sold at the 1990 See auction for $880, and another sold at auction in 1993 in New York for $1,045. $600–$750

Indian Rope Trick, ca. 1927 (*100 Years*, p. 79). Printed by Otis. One-sheet panel. $700–$800

The Million Dollar Mystery, ca. 1920s. Printed by Otis. Dazzling poster in subtle colors. Printed in both horizontal and vertical versions. Full-color, one-sheet. See *color insert, photo 25.* $1,100–$1,300

Thurston's Pets, ca. 1920s. Printed by Otis. Portraits of a horse, lion, dog, monkey, and other animals are seen on this unusual full-color, one-sheet panel.
$500–$600

Courtesy of
Ken Trombly.

Courtesy of Ken
Trombly.

The Vanishing Whippet, ca. 1929. Printed by Otis. Next to *The Million Dollar Mystery*, this rates, in this author's opinion, as the most artistically pleasing of Thurston's Otis paper. Full-color, one-sheet. $750–$950

As above, two-color, smaller. $200–$300

She Floats All Over the Stage, 1935. Printed by Otis. Thurston's head is just too big in this depiction of the floating lady illusion. A window card version sold at auction in New York in 1993 for $385. Full-color, one-sheet. $600–$750

❦ CHAPTER 26 ❦
Circus Posters

Inventive, colorful, and most of all fun with their depictions of wild beasts, clowns, elephants, and death-defying acts, circus posters are an especially appealing area of poster collecting. Luckily, because there were and still are so many circuses in this country and abroad, and because many of the fine posters were printed in the tens of thousands, many good images can still be bought—you guessed it—for peanuts.

That's not to say that all circus posters are inexpensive or easily obtained. Certainly some of the earliest and best, from Sells Bros., Barnum & Bailey, Ringling Brothers, Buffalo Bill's Wild West, and others, now command "big top" prices. Specialized collectors compete in the auction arena whenever a rare or early circus poster goes on the block. Swann Galleries in New York frequently features circus posters in its sales (see resource guide).

Circus posters were designed to emphasize the spectacular feats, great performers, and amazing clowns audiences would see in the ring. In many cases, they stretched the imagination—and the truth. But as P. T. Barnum is famed to have said, "There's a sucker born every minute," and circus fans wanted to believe what they saw advertised.

The circus was a very early form of entertainment, tracing its roots back to the days of Imperial Rome. Today's advertising and publicity professionals trace the roots of their field back to the "front man" who came to town to publicize the arrival of the circus, plastering posters to every available wall space.

It should therefore come as no surprise that the earliest illustrated poster in the collection of the Library of Congress is a circus poster. An 1856 colored woodcut poster, measuring eleven feet in width, it advertises "Five Celebrated Clowns Attached To Sands, Nathan Co's Circus," a traveling company.

By the mid-1800s, posters were already being widely used in the United States, even in billboard size. However, the vast majority of these were large-format black-and-white woodcuts, sometimes printed in as many as twenty-six sheets.

Smaller black-and-white posters were created using steel engraving, much like early newspaper illustrations. Many of the earliest posted bills weren't pictorial advertising posters as we know them, but "broadsides" or "broadsheets," which had more text than illustration. Slowly the illustration began to dominate the design of the poster.

For example, the rare ca. 1885 poster pictured here for the "Lemen Brothers/World's Best Shows" is about 13 x 17 inches, and was printed by the United States Printing Company of Cincinnati, Ohio. Apart from the other animals, it stars "Rajah," billed as "the largest elephant that walks the earth — 2 inches taller than Jumbo." The reference is to Jumbo the elephant introduced in 1881 by Barnum when he became partners with Bailey. The battle over which circus had the largest elephant raged for several years.

By the late 1880s, early major color lithographic printers such as Strobridge in Cincinnati, Ohio, and Courier in Buffalo, New York, were being commissioned to produce advertising posters. The circus was the first "industry" to truly capitalize on the advent of color lithography for posters.

As early as 1891, Strobridge was creating spectacular color posters for the Sells Bros. Circus and for Barnum & Bailey. One highly prized Barnum & Bailey series of posters from that time features the two showmen's portraits in black and white lithography next to colorful scenes such as "Bronze-Hued Performing Stallions" and the bareback-riding "Native Mexican Vacqueros." In recent years, examples from this early series have brought between $1,300 and $4,000 at auction. Early Buffalo Bill posters can also sell at the high end of this range.

Courtesy of The Antique Poster Collection.

Virtually all of the early American circus posters, like many magic posters, were printed by the great lithography company of Strobridge in Ohio. They even produced posters for American circus tours in Europe. Their masterful work meant vivid colors, exciting imagery, and startling effects. After about 1910, other printers also came to specialize in circus and entertainment posters. They include Erie Litho, Illinois Litho, Morgan Litho in Cleveland (which became famous for cinema posters), and several others, almost all in the Midwest. Unfortunately, the individual designers who created the circus posters were rarely recognized or allowed to sign their work.

Early circuses in this country included Sells Bros. Shows, which operated from about 1872 to 1895; Adam Forepaugh Circus, which operated from 1867 to 1894; and the combined Adam Forepaugh & Sells Bros. Circus, owned by James A. Bailey (later of Barnum & Bailey), which operated from 1896 to 1907.

Sells Bros., which used the subtitle "Enormous United Shows," produced outstanding posters similar to early Barnum & Bailey posters, and also printed by Strobridge. These posters can easily sell for over $1,000.

Rivalry between circuses was common, and P. T. Barnum of Bridgeport, Connecticut, who had made his fame and fortune as a promoter for Tom Thumb and opera star Jenny Lind, created his own circus in 1872. In 1881 he became partners with Bailey, and in 1888 they started operating as the Barnum & Bailey Circus. Called "the Greatest Show on Earth," they reigned supreme until challenged by a new venture started by a family of brothers from Baraboo, Wisconsin: the Ringlings.

The Ringling Brothers Circus, which operated from 1884 to 1918, bought out Barnum & Bailey in 1908, and also acquired the Forepaugh and Sells Bros. circuses. However, the actual performances and the names Ringling Brothers and Barnum & Bailey were not merged until 1919. Posters from the Ringling Brothers Circus before it merged with Barnum & Bailey appear less frequently on the market and are especially prized by circus collectors, though their posters are generally less expensive than those of Barnum & Bailey.

In the general poster market in the United States today, collectors are more likely to find posters for Ringling Brothers and Barnum & Bailey (RBB&B) "Combined Shows" than any of those mentioned above. In the 1930s their name became "Combined Circus," and in the 1940s the word "Combined" was dropped. These differences offer a way of roughly dating the posters. RBB&B used lithography to create their posters into the mid-1940s. The earlier lithographic posters will always be the most valuable, and range in price today from a few hundred dollars up to about $1,000. However, well-executed RBB&B posters from the 1940s and 1950s are surfacing more and more on the market, and often these can be purchased for under $200.

In 1956 RBB&B stopped performing under a tent, and has changed ownership several times since then, but it still retains the advertising slogan "the Greatest Show on Earth."

As is apparent from the preceding examples, circuses often merged, changed hands, and changed names. The Cole Bros. Circus started in 1906, but most of the posters on today's market are from a larger version of the show under new ownership, which toured the country by train from about 1935 to 1950. One of the featured acts was Clyde Beatty, a wild-animal trainer who also operated his own circus. After about 1950, the circus was renamed the Clyde Beatty and Cole Bros. Circus.

Other earlier American circuses to watch for are the Christy Bros. Circus, in operation from 1920 to 1930; the Downie Bros. Circus, which traveled primarily on the East Coast from 1926 to 1939; and the Hagenbeck-Wallace Circus, which performed from 1906 to 1938.

Post-World War II circuses to watch for are the Cristiani Bros. Circus; the Kelly-Morris and Kelly and Miller Bros. Circuses; and the Wallace Bros. Circus. Contemporary smaller one-ring circuses, which emphasize the artistry of circus acts, are today's circus collectibles. They include the Big Apple Circus from New York and the French Cirque de Soleil and Cirque de Demain. In addition, one can often find exciting vintage and modern posters from many short-lived and lesser-known circuses. In starting out, you might want to focus on a particular circus or on a particular theme, such as animals, clowns, or high-wire acts.

European circuses had their own favorite printers, but head and shoulders above the rest is the German firm of Adolph Friedlander (1851–1904), who until recently was practically unknown and uncollected in this country. From the years 1872 to 1938, Friedlander and his sons designed and printed nearly ten thousand different exciting posters for the Carl Hagenbeck Circus (no relation to the American circus that borrowed his name), the Max Schumann Circus, the Circus Busch, and other legendary European companies.

More than nine thousand posters of this great printer were destroyed when the Nazis forced the closure of the printing firm in the late 1930s. Their scarcity, coupled with their fantastic designs, mean Friedlander posters in most instances command higher prices than other circus posters. Friedlander also created striking lithographic posters for magicians and other entertainers.

Another factor that contributes to their limited market presence is that Friedlander often issued posters in small editions, with a minimum order of twenty-five to a maximum of probably no more than three thousand. In comparison, Strobridge littered cities and towns across the United States, sometimes with as many as thirty thousand copies of a given poster.

The circus poster market has not experienced the steep price climbs and rapid changes of many other poster fields in the last ten years. Generally speaking, circus poster collectors are not looking to speculate on an "investment" in the poster market, but rather have a love of the circus and are pursuing a rewarding hobby.

This means that a collector can generally look to acquire very good to outstanding examples of circus poster art for under $1,000. For those with even smaller budgets, numerous good examples can be purchased for under $200.

TO FIND OUT MORE ABOUT CIRCUS POSTERS

Museums mentioned at the end of the chapter on Magic Posters also have collections of circus posters; another place to see circus posters is the Bridgeport Public Library in Bridgeport, Connecticut, the home of P. T. Barnum. The Barnum Museum, also in Bridgeport, doesn't specialize in posters, but you can have fun seeing memorabilia. On display are specially designed carriages that carried Tom Thumb, costumes, cannons, and more. The Ringling Museum in Sarasota, Florida, also has some posters, but not as many as you might expect. The museum's main attraction is really the Venetian palace home of John and Mable Ringling and their extensive art collection, housed in a separate art museum (see resource guide for museum listings).

There are numerous good references on circus posters (not to mention books on circuses themselves). One author, Charles Philip Fox, has written two large pictoral works on circus posters (see Bibliography).

CIRCUS POSTERS - PRICE LISTINGS

NOTE: See the chapter Important Notes on the Price Listings for more information on prices given. The listings below are alphabetical by the name of the circus.

❧ ANONYMOUS—STOCK POSTERS

[Unlettered] Crowds assembled around the Ferris wheel, "the Whip," and the merry-go-round. Very good condition, 27 x 41 inches. $220 (Auc. #22)

[Wild West Show], ca. 1910. Frontiersmen fighting a band of Indians. Fine condition, 41 x 28 inches. $125 (Auc. #22)

❧ BARNUM & BAILEY

> NOTE: P. T. Barnum went into partnership with James Bailey in 1881, but the name Barnum & Bailey Circus was not used until 1888. It was bought out by Ringling Brothers in 1908, and in 1919 the two names were combined into "Ringling Brothers and Barnum & Bailey" (see also Ringling Brothers price listings).

Barnum & Bailey Greatest Show on Earth. Lithograph. Five herds of performing elephants in a conga line. Good condition, on linen, 38½ x 26 inches.
$440 (Auc. #21)

Barnum & Bailey Greatest Show on Earth/the Konyot Family, ca. 1901. Acrobatic performers on horseback together with family portrait. Very good condition, horizontal, 36½ x 26½ inches. $1,100 (Auc. #23)

Barnum & Bailey Greatest Show on Earth/Oriental India, 1896. Lithograph. Printed by Strobridge. Vibrant scene shows exotic people. A very good example of an early Barnum & Bailey poster. Fine condition, 37½ x 30 inches. $605 (Auc. #19)

Barnum & Bailey Greatest Show on Earth/Rare Zoological Features, ca. 1909. Lithograph. Printed by Strobridge. Four giraffes against an African grassland. Note that a later Ringling Brothers and Barnum & Bailey poster used a very similar image (see below). Very good condition, 26½ x 36½ inches. $675 (Auc. #23)

Barnum & Bailey Greatest Show on Earth/Les Rowlandes, 1906. Lithograph. Printed by Strobridge. Various scenes of the equestrian spectacle involving carriages. A very good example. In very good condition, on linen, horizontal, 37 x 27 inches. $715 (Auc. #21)

Barnum and Bailey Greatest Show on Earth/Scene Excitante Dans Le Cirque des Enfants, ca. 1898. Lithograph. Printed by Strobridge. With text in French for European tour. Monkeys riding ponies around track under the big top. Very good condition, horizontal, 39¾ x 30 inches. $525 (Auc. #23)

Courtesy of Swann
Galleries, Inc.

Courtesy of Swann
Galleries, Inc.

Courtesy of
Oliver's.

Madison Square Garden/Barnum & Bailey Greatest Show on Earth, ca. 1908. Lithograph. Printed by Strobridge. Illustration of "the Sisters LaRague" and "Wotan, the Horse Balloonist." A rare example in which the location gets top billing. Very good condition, 36½ x 26½ inches. $1,600 (Auc. #23)

❦ BUFFALO BILL

Life and Adventures of Buffalo Bill. Buffalo Bill lassoing and wrestling bulls. A very good example of a Buffalo Bill poster. Very good condition, 28 x 42 inches. *See color insert, photo 26.* $1,870 (Auc. #19)

❦ CHRISTIANI BROTHERS

Christiani Brothers/Wild Animal Circus, 1950s. Beautiful woman rides a gigantic elephant. With date banner attached. Very good condition, 21 x 36 inches. $60–$80

Christiani Brothers/Wild Animal Circus, 1950s. Two bears, one riding a motorcycle. With date banner attached. Very good condition, 28 x 49 inches. $100–$125

❦ CLYDE BEATTY CIRCUS

Clyde Beatty Circus/Clyde Beatty in Person, ca. 1950. Art by Roland Butler. Good image of the famous lion tamer at work. Red, yellow, blue, black, and brown. With date tag. Very good condition, 21 x 36 inches. $90–$125

❦ CLYDE BEATTY—COLE BROS.

Clyde Beatty—Cole Bros./the Greatest Circus on Earth, ca. 1950. Expertly drawn tiger by Roland Butler growls with anger. Fine condition, horizontal, 28 x 21 inches. $125–$150

❦ COLE BROS.

NOTE: *The name Cole Bros. Circus goes back to 1906, but most of the posters on today's market are from a larger versions of the circus under new owner-*

Courtesy of Poster Mail Auction Co.

Courtesy of Swann
Galleries, Inc.

*ship that operated as the Cole Bros. Circus from 1935 to 1950. The animal
trainer Clyde Beatty was one of the featured acts, and also had his own circus.
After 1950, the names were combined (see also preceding entries).*

Cole Bros. Circus/Boxing Horses. Lithograph. Printed "Litho in USA." Two
horses in boxing shorts engaged in a bout. Very good condition, on linen, 28 x 41
inches. $715 (Auc. #21)

Cole Bros. Circus. Lithograph. Printed by Erie Litho. Large laughing clown head.
Very good condition, on linen, 26 x 39 inches. $220 (Auc. #21)

💚 DOWNIE BROS.

Downie Bros. Big 3 Ring Circus, ca. 1925. Lithograph. Printed by Erie Litho.
Smiling clown center, with other scenes, including one where he is being chased
by a skeleton. Very good condition, horizontal, 41 x 27 inches. $250–$300

Downie Bros. Big 3 Ring Circus, ca. 1934. Lithograph. Printed by Erie Litho. A
series of equestrian feats performed by women, with a rearing black stallion in
the center. Very good condition, horizontal, 41 x 28 inches. $200–$225

💚 HAGENBECK-WALLACE

> *NOTE: The Great Wallace Shows were founded in 1884, and purchased
> the Carl Hagenbeck Circus in 1906. The combined Hagenbeck-Wallace
> Circus operated under various ownerships through 1938.*

Carl Hagenbeck-Wallace Circus. Lithograph. Printed by Erie Litho. Brown
bears perform and wrestle. Very good condition, this example framed, 25½ x 39½
inches. $412 (Auc. #19)

The Great Hagenbeck-Wallace Circus, 1933. Lithograph. Printed by Central Printing and Illinois Litho, Ohio. Orange and black tiger shows its teeth. Very good condition, horizontal, 41½ x 28 inches. $495 (Auc. #19)

❦ HAMID-MORTON

Clyde Beatty: Greatest Wild Animal Trainer. Lithograph. Clyde fights back a ring of growling lions and tigers. Very good condition, on linen, 27 x 18½ inches. $330 (Auc. #21)

❦ KING BROS. & CHRISTIANI COMBINED CIRCUS

King Bros. & Christiani Combined Circus, ca. 1960. Performing bears in red, brown, blue, yellow, and black. Very good condition, horizontal, 48 x 28 inches. $75–$125

❦ MILLER BROS.

Miller Bros. Shows/Miss Bonno, Only Girl in the World Shot from a Cannon. Lithograph. Printed by Temple Litho. Miss Bonno flying over a Ferris wheel. Very good condition, 41 x 28 inches. $247 (Auc. #22)

❦ PINDER (CIRQUE PINDER—FRENCH)

Les Éléphants Savants (The Intelligent Elephants). Lithograph. Printed by Imp. Bedos. Trainer in uniform with elephants behind him. Good condition, horizontal, 62½ x 48 inches. $357 (Auc. #19)

❦ RINGLING BROS. AND BARNUM & BAILEY

> NOTE: Ringling Brothers bought out Barnum & Bailey in 1908 but operated it separately through 1918. In 1919 the circuses were combined, and began advertising as "Ringling Brothers and Barnum & Bailey Combined Shows." In the 1930s the title became "Combined Circus," and in the 1940s the word

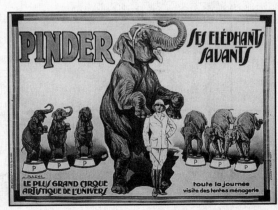

Courtesy of Swann
Galleries, Inc.

"Combined" was dropped. These differences offer a way of roughly dating the posters. The name below has been abbreviated to "RBB&B."

RBB&B. Art by Kannely. Close-up of a clown with small hat. Very good condition, 27½ x 41½ inches. $165 (Auc. #19)

RBB&B, 1943. Lithograph by Lawson Wood. A family of monkeys enters the big top as they pay "Admission 2 Nuts" to an elephant. In red, yellow, blue, green, brown, and black. Good condition, horizontal, 28 x 21 inches. $125–$150

RBB&B, 1945. Lithograph, marked "Litho in USA." Art by Bill Bailey. Tiger growls above, and lion growls below, the name. Very good condition, 21 x 27¾ inches. $440 (Auc. #19)

RBB&B, 1945. Art by Bill Bailey. White and red clown rides the trunk of an elephant. Very good condition, horizontal, 41 x 28 inches. $250–$350

RBB&B Circus, ca. 1945. Photomontage. Photo of a white-faced clown, with red and blue lettering on white background. Very good condition, horizontal, 48 x 28 inches. $100–$125

RBB&B Circus/the Great Yacopi Troupe; Argentine Acrobatic Marvels Without Equal. Lithograph. The eight-member troupe in action. Very good condition, horizontal, 42 x 28 inches. $125 (Auc. #22)

RBB&B Combined Shows. Lithograph. Printed by Strobridge. Lion stalks above, and tiger stalks below, the name. Bright blue background with gold and black lion and tiger. Earlier than the preceding poster. Very good condition, 28½ x 42 inches. $605 (Auc. #19)

RBB&B Combined Shows, 1932. Lithograph. Printed by Morgan Litho, Cleveland. Art by Benjamin Wells. A herd of multicolored animals charge the viewer. Very good condition, horizontal, 41½ x 28 inches. $990 (Auc. #19)

Courtesy of Swann Galleries, Inc.

RBB&B Combined Shows/Biggest and Most Magnificent Dressage Display Ever Presented. Lithograph. Printed by Strobridge. Showing a three-ring display. Very good condition, on linen, horizontal, 28 x 20 inches. $412 (Auc. #21)

RBB&B Combined Shows/Exclusive Rare Zoological Features. Lithograph. Printed by Strobridge. Eight giraffes on view. Note that an earlier Barnum & Bailey poster used a very similar image, and another RBB&B "Combined Circus" poster, about 1935, added elephants to the scene. Very good condition, 28 x 41½ inches.
$1,430 (Auc. #19)

RBB&B Combined Shows/Quarter Million Pound Act. Lithograph. Printed by Strobridge. A dizzying number of elephants performing in outdoor rings. Very good condition, 39 x 26 inches. $1,000 (Auc. #23)

RBB&B Combined Shows/World Famous Equestriennes in Daring Feats of Horsemanship. Lithograph. Printed by Strobridge. Six daring women on galloping horses. Fine condition, 28 x 39 inches. $990 (Auc. #21)

❦ JOHN ROBINSON

John Robinson's Circus. Lithograph. Printed by Erie Litho. Four clowns point up at the circus name. Very good condition, horizontal, 40½ x 26 inches.
$440 (Auc. #19)

❦ SELLS BROTHERS

> NOTE: Though founded earlier, by 1878 this company was operating under the title Sells Bros. Circus, and were considered the foremost circus through the 1880s. Sells Bros. combined with Adam Forepaugh Shows, and by 1910 both were bought by Ringling Brothers.

Sells Brothers' Enormous United Shows/Grand Spectacular Pageant, 1893. Lithograph. Printed by Strobridge. Rare, early color lithograph, featuring brightly colored pageantry of a procession. Very good condition, horizontal, 40 x 29½ inches. $660 (Auc. #19)

Sells Brothers' Enormous United Shows/4 Horse Chariot Race, 1893. Lithograph. Printed by Strobridge. Rare, early color lithograph, featuring a scene of Roman pageantry under the big top. Very good condition, horizontal, 40 x 30 inches. $1,200–$1,400

❦ WALLACE BROS. CIRCUS

Wallace Bros./World's Largest Circus, ca. 1950. Three elephants with their trunks raised and a clown. In red, yellow, blue, brown, and green. Fine condition, 28 x 41 inches. $75–$100

Wallace Bros. Circus. The word "CIRCUS" in giant letters, on and around which dozens of performers are leaping, dancing, and lion-taming. Good condition, horizontal, 41 x 28 inches. $125–$150

❦ CHAPTER 27 ❦
Cinema Posters

WHERE IS THE CINEMA POSTER MARKET HEADING?

Most of the chapters in this book start with a history of the collecting field, but in the case of cinema posters, we thought it was important to talk about the market right up front, because it is by far the most active and the most volatile of all poster-collecting fields today.

While many long-term indications point to a continuing rise in prices, the short-term escalation has been dramatic. Those who have been around long enough know that this kind of rapid upsurge may at some point, sooner or later, be followed by a cooling off—or even a radical drop.

The amount of material coming onto the market today is enormous. Everywhere one hears people talking about "investment in movie posters" rather than "collecting." Specialized price indexes now appear every six months, and monthly trade publications are filled with full-page ads of movie poster prices.

The number of focused auctions has increased dramatically. Formerly the domain of a few auction houses such as the well-established Camden House in Los Angeles, auctions of movie posters and other Hollywood memorabilia are spreading like wildfire.

Christie's East entered the market in December 1990, and immediately started breaking records. Hollywood Poster Art in Hackensack, New Jersey, established itself as the first East Coast specialized house in 1991. Sotheby's hosted its first Hollywood poster auction in September 1992, featuring the collection of Stanley Caidin.

Odyssey Auctions held its first event in November 1992 in Beverly Hills. In England, Christie's South Kensington jumped in on December 17 of the same year. Geurnsey's held an overwhelming sixteen-hundred-lot three-day combination auction of comic, film, fantasy, and animation art at New York's Puck Building in February 1993. Butterfield & Butterfield offered both Hollywood and rock and roll memorabilia on March 14 and 15, 1993. Swann Galleries in New York rolled out its first Hollywood poster auction on March 18, 1993.

Between December of 1992 and June of 1993, we tracked no fewer than eight Hollywood auctions that were held in this country at locations from coast to coast. While two of these also included memorabilia, the main attraction at all of them was posters. Is the material recirculating at an unbelievable pace from auction to auction, or are those long-held images finally coming out from under the beds, behind closet doors, and out of "investment portfolios"? Already we see some indications that collectors are holding back just a little, sensing that if they don't buy that special poster at one auction, they may get it for less at the next.

Movie posters have taken their place with animation art, dolls, toys, and other collectibles—even Pez candy dispensers—as big business. The collectibles departments at both Christie's and Sotheby's have become valuable assets to the auction houses, which have sagged through the recession in other areas. Sotheby's has also added baseball memorabilia and comic books to its regular schedule.

What has been emerging in the last few years is a market that is fully American, baby-boomer-fueled, and nostalgia-driven.

In the movie poster world, it's no secret that since the late 1980s, both individuals and consortiums of investors have been buying vintage material in large quantities, waiting for this moment to arrive. General antique trade and Hollywood collector publications such as *Big Reel, Movie Collector's World,* and *Classic Images* abound with "wanted" ads. One such ad proudly proclaims that the buyer has spent more than $3.5 million on pre-1945 movie posters since May of 1989.

Further market differentiation and segmentation are sure to follow in a field as broad as Hollywood memorabilia. However, what star watchers always fear when a field gets this hot is the supernova sure to explode when the big investors and major collectors bail out.

All that said, we thought it best to offer strictly auction prices in the listings that follow this chapter, rather than a combination of auction and reported retail prices as in other chapters. We invite you to draw your own conclusions.

Auction prices can vary enormously in the movie poster arena, apparently from week to week, as you will see by comparing some of the listings. Indeed, more and more collectors of cinema material—both high rollers and bargain hunters—are buying at auction.

If you are a beginning collector of cinema material, you may want to compare the auction price listings here with retail prices at dealer showrooms. Because auction prices always depend on who is bidding, sometimes prices at an energy-charged auction may exceed general retail values.

TOULOUSE-LAUTREC MEETS FRANKENSTEIN

In December 1990, before Christie's hosted its first Hollywood poster auction, the auction record for a movie poster was $17,600 for a six-sheet *Casablanca*. Bogey would say, "Here's lookin' at you, kid," as movie poster prices have flown off beyond that horizon. The 1990 Christie's auction broke the previous record four times, with a one-sheet from the 1919 *The Cabinet of Dr. Caligari* taking top honors at $37,500.

Even that price didn't hold the record for long. In December 1991, an original three-sheet *King Kong* poster at the same auction house realized $57,200. This sale also broke a psychological barrier that had previously accorded movie posters only a bit part in a saga starring Henri de Toulouse-Lautrec, Alphonse Mucha, A. M. Cassandre, and others.

Sotheby's September 1992 auction grossed $600,000, buoyed by a 1916 one-sheet from *Birth of a Nation*, that thundered in at $49,500. Three other posters at Sotheby's surpassed $20,000: an insert for the 1926 *Metropolis* at $33,000; the original 1929 German poster for *The Blue Angel* at $27,500; and a one-sheet for Charlie Chaplin's 1921 *The Kid* also at $27,500.

Christie's third blockbuster auction was held December 14, 1992, selling all 318 lots and grossing $1.2 million, led by one-sheet posters for Marlene Dietrich's 1935 *The Devil Is a Woman* at $46,200; Douglas Fairbanks's 1924 *The Thief of Bagdad* at $30,800; and the 1918 *Tarzan of the Apes*, also at $30,800. The next six top lots, though not all one-sheets, sold for more than $20,000, and four others came in at $19,800. In all, twenty-five lots sold for more than $10,000 each.

In May 1993, at the first annual Vintage Poster Art Convention and Auction held in Cleveland, Ohio, the record was broken again. One of only two known examples of a 1931 one-sheet for *Dracula* starring Bela Lugosi brought $77,000.

Organizers Marty Davis and Morris Everett, Jr., of The Last Moving Picture Company in Cleveland, had highlighted the *Dracula* poster in their advertising for the auction. The second highlighted poster—a 1933 one-sheet for *King Kong*—sold for $52,250, about double its estimate. However, over 85 percent of the posters sold at the Cleveland auction brought less than $1,000.

In June of 1993, at Christie's fourth big event, again 100 percent of the lots sold, but things seemed to cool off a bit. Only seven posters broke the $10,000 mark, with the three top prices going to a 1930 one-sheet Mickey Mouse poster for *The Cactus Kid* at $29,900; the 1925 one-sheet for *Phantom of the Opera* at $24,150; and the 1939 one-sheet for *Son of Frankenstein* at $20,125.

In September 1993, history was again made at Odyssey Auctions in California where a 1931 one-sheet for *Frankenstein* starring Boris Karloff sold for an unbelievable $198,000, *(See color insert, photo 27).*

Courtesy of
Illustration
House, Inc.

This record-breaking price almost equals the all-time poster auction record of $220,000 for Henri de Toulouse-Lautrec's three-sheet *Moulin Rouge*. Is it a portent of things to come? Or is it, as some are saying, "an aberration in the market," or "the result of two stubborn people with too much money to spend"? Only time will tell.

Even the original art for movie posters, which can rarely be found, is bringing high prices. Illustration House, a New York auction house that specializes in illustration art, broke the record for an original movie poster illustration in May 1993 with a realized price of $16,500 for the painting featured in the twenty-four-sheet *Revenge of the Creature* (1955) by Reynold Brown (1917–1991). At the same auction the painting for the 1937 Shirley Temple poster for *Heidi* by Joseph Maturo (1867–1938) sold for $10,000 plus buyer's premium.

WHERE CAN A BEGINNING COLLECTOR START?

Although prices for rare vintage cinema posters may seem staggering, the vast majority of the thousands and thousands of movie poster titles available still sell for much less. The publicity and high prices of the auctions at Christie's and Sotheby's have brought many buyers into the market who were not previously Hollywood collectors, which is exactly what the investment consortiums hoped for. However, the legions of devoted cinema collectors do not spend their time speculating at the top of the market.

If you just love movies and the images of the posters, you can still pursue a rewarding collecting hobby without being discouraged by the volatility of the market or the emphasis on investment. All collectors want to feel that what they purchase will hold its value or even increase in value, but it need not be the prime motivation for collecting.

Dealer catalogs and lists are chock-full of good examples of cinema posters, even lithographic posters, that sell for $100 to $500.

Interestingly, many silent movie posters from the teens, 1920s, and early 1930s (with the exception of those for movie classics and stars such as Charlie Chaplin, Mary Pickford, and Lilian Gish) can sell for much less than those from the mid to late 1930s and 1940s. Featuring forgotten actors and actresses, they don't have the "star" value of a poster image of John Wayne, the Marx Brothers, Marlene Dietrich, or Humphrey Bogart—icons of baby boom popular culture. Whether these stars will hold their appeal with the "X generation" or generations to come is yet to be determined.

New material will always be inexpensive. We received a catalog from Cinema City in Muskegon, Michigan, listing hundreds of titles from the 1970s to 1990s for under $20. Moviemaking is highly competitive, and posters created over the last few decades are stunning evidence that the finest artists are being recruited to help draw in the crowds.

A CINEMA POSTER PRIMER

The field of cinema poster collecting is so broad and complex that it is impossible to cover it in a single volume, let alone in the single chapter we have here. Collectors specialize in many different areas: specific studios, movie stars, directors, or genres such as westerns, film noir, sci fi, horror, cartoons, and other areas. The following is some basic information to help get you started. It's important to understand some of the terminology used in the cinema poster field if you plan to pursue collecting in this specialty.

Printers and Printing Techniques

As in other poster-collecting fields, the very earliest cinema posters were broadsides that used text more than illustration. Early American color lithographic printers include some of those already mentioned for magic and circus posters, such as Otis and Morgan. Other early lithographic printers to look for are Continental, A.B.C., Tooker, and H. C. Miner. Later posters are generally photo-offset. One of the reasons that vintage cinema posters are so rare is that the theater owner was required to return the poster to the distributor with the film at the end of the run.

Sometimes unauthorized companies produced posters for film releases. In some instances, these so-called other-company posters were produced more cheaply, and are not as desirable as the studio's own poster. However, some, such as posters from the Oklahoma City printer Leader Press, have found a place in the collecting market.

Leader Press artwork is graphically stunning, and the posters were offered to theater owners as an alternative to the studio posters as a means of increasing attendance. Leader Press posters are generally brilliant-color woodblocks in three to eight different colors. In June

1992, Camden House offered an outstanding selection of Leader Press posters from the 1930s, and sales prices ranged up to $2,250 for the 1933 *Queen Christina*, starring Greta Garbo.

Artists

Most of the artists who created images for early movie posters are unknown. Some of the earliest were designed by staff artists at the printing companies. Mostly they were designed at the film studios, sometimes by a team of staff artists: One created the human figures, another the scenery, another the lettering, etc.

Some artists' names are recognized, and an individual's reputation can enhance a cinema poster's value. However, a recognizable name in this specialty is not usually as important as age and scarcity, condition, film title, stars, and other factors in determining demand in the market.

Recognized movie poster artists from the 1930s and 1940s tend to be those who had built careers as illustrators outside of Hollywood: John Held, Jr. (1889–1958), known for his caricatures of flappers and top-hatted dandies in magazines like *The New Yorker;* Norman Rockwell (1894–1978); and Joseph Maturo (1867–1938), mentioned in the preceding market section, who was the artist of choice for Shirley Temple and Will Rogers films of the 1930s.

More recently, Hollywood has commissioned many notable nonstudio artists to produce posters. While the posters themselves may not be as valuable, a strong market has certainly been created for the original artwork when it is available. Examples include the work of Joe Smith, who created the artwork for *Gorgo* (1961), *Kiss of the Vampire* (1963), and other sci- fi and horror films of the 1960s; and Bob Peak (1928–1992), who created the artwork for *Modesty Blaise* (1966), *Star Trek* (1979), and several other films.

Styles

Some movies issued several different posters for their promotion. These are called *styles*, and are identified by the letters *A*, *B*, *C*, or *D* in the lower margin.

Different styles can bring vastly different prices, as some are rarer or more desirable than others. For example, a rare *Snow White and the Seven Dwarfs* style B one-sheet poster sold for $12,650 at auction in 1993. This poster is sought after because is actually shows Snow White. Another one-sheet for the same film, style A, showing only the dwarfs, sold the same year for only $1,870.

Release Dates, Rereleases, and Foreign Releases

Usually the last two digits of a cinema poster's year of release are printed in its lower right-hand corner. The letter *R* before the date indicates a reissue, as do the statements "A 20th Century Fox Encore Presentation," "An MGM Family Classic," etc. Reissues for notable films have gained in value over the past several years as the original posters have gone beyond reach. Also growing in popularity are posters for foreign releases of American films from many countries such as Belgium, France, Argentina, and others.

Standard Cinema Poster Sizes and Formats

American cinema posters and advertising materials were generally produced in a number of standard sizes. Foreign releases come in a myriad of styles, shapes, and sizes. Each country has its own standards. For a complete description of the varieties among European, Asian, and Central and South American paper, see Gregory J. Edward's *The International Film Poster* (see Bibliography).

One-Sheet	The most popular size for collectors, a single sheet of paper, generally 27 x 41 inches.
Insert	Long and narrow, measuring 14 x 36 inches.
Half-Sheet	The name describes this size relative to the one-sheet, horizontal, 28 x 22 inches.
Three-Sheet	The name describes this size relative to the one-sheet, 41 x 81 inches, but usually printed in two sections.
Six-Sheet	The name describes this size relative to the one-sheet, 81 x 81 inches, but usually printed in four sections.

Other posters were printed in "billboard sizes" of twelve, twenty-four, and ninety-six sheets.

Lobby Cards	Lobby cards are horizontal, 14 x 11 inches, and were usually printed in sets of eight, which included one "title card" and seven "scene cards." The title card is usually the most coveted. In the auction prices listed below, we report only full sets, single title cards, or particularly sought-after or well-known individual scene cards. A few lobby card sets, such as those for Disney films, have nine or ten cards. Today lobby card sets have no title card,

only eight scene cards. Jumbo lobby cards are horizontal, 17 x 14 inches, and usually have no white
border. Jumbo lobby cards are no longer printed.

Window Cards   Generally 14 x 22 inches, and as the name implies,
these were used in windows to advertise coming
attractions. They usually have a blank banner
above the design where the theater could overprint
its name and date information. Jumbo window
cards measure 22 x 28 inches, and mini window
cards are 8 x 14 inches. Mini window cards are no
longer printed.

Pressbooks   While we don't report prices on pressbooks in the
listings that follow, they are collected in their own
right and also serve as primary research for serious
collectors, as they can help identify poster styles
and other information. Ranging from as few as four
to as many as eighty pages, a pressbook or "campaign book" was sent to theater owners to assist
them in promoting the film. Pressbooks include
illustrations of the available posters, newspaper ads
that could be cut out for use in local papers, and
other promotional ideas.

TO FIND OUT MORE ABOUT CINEMA POSTERS

Numerous good reference books on cinema posters have been pub-
lished and more appear each year. Some good books to start with
include *The International Film Poster,* by Gregory J. Edwards, and *Reel
Art: Great Movie Posters from the Golden Age of the Silver Screen,* by Stephen
Rebello and Richard Allen. A few good specialized books include *Lobby
Cards, the Classic Films,* and *Lobby Cards, the Classic Comedies,* both by
Kathryn Leigh Scott, illustrating the outstanding Michael Hawks
Collection, and the recent *Graven Images: The Best of Horror, Fantasy, and
Science Fiction Film Art,* by Ron Borst (see Bibliography).

In addition, cinema collectors have the advantage of several specialized
trade and hobbyist publications, including *Movie Collector's World, Big Reel,*
and *Classic Images,* as well as numerous shows and events sponsored by
organizations such as the National Society for Cinephiles.

Several museums have outstanding collections of cinema posters,
including the Library of Congress and the Margaret Herrick Library at
the Academy of Motion Picture Arts and Sciences in Beverly Hills. In

New York, the Billy Rose Theatre Collection at the New York Public Library is huge, featuring not only cinema, but also stage and other popular entertainment posters (see the Resource Guide).

CINEMA POSTERS—PRICE LISTINGS
IN ALPHABETICAL ORDER BY FILM TITLE:

NOTE: Prices in this section include buyer's premiums unless otherwise noted, and some auction houses have raised their premiums to 15 percent. See list of Auction Catalogs Cited and Sale Dates in the resource guide. See the chapter Important Notes on the Price Listings for more information on prices given. For an explanation of sizes (half-sheet, one-sheet, window card, etc.) and for certain terms used in the listings, see the preceding chapter. Of all the fields of poster collecting, cinema posters are the most volatile and changing most rapidly in terms of price. Check with a reputable dealer for the latest price on the posters that interest you the most.

❦ **A**

Abbott and Costello Go To Mars, 1953 (Universal). Very good, on linen, one-sheet. $200 (Auc. #07)

Abbott and Costello Meet Dr. Jekyll and Mr. Hyde, 1953 (Universal). Good, on linen, one-sheet. $250 (Auc. #01)
As above, very good, on linen, one-sheet. $450 (Auc. #02)
As above, fine, one-sheet. $275 (Auc. #08)
As above, fine, unfolded, half-sheet. $225 (Auc. #01)

Abbott and Costello Meet the Killer, 1949 (Universal). Very good, on linen, three-sheet. $467.50 (Auc. #06)

Adventure's End, 1937 (Universal). Fine, one-sheet. $400 (Auc. #01)

Adventures of Captain Marvel, 1941 (Republic). Fine, on linen, six-sheet.
                                                               $4,620 (Auc. #04)

Adventures of Captain Marvel/Chapter 11, Valley of Death, 1941 (Republic). Good, on linen, one-sheet. $1,300 (Auc. #01)

Adventures of Robin Hood, 1938 (Warner Bros.). Errol Flynn. Fine, on linen, three-sheet. $14,950 (Auc. #09)
As above, fine, window card. $3,575 (Auc. #06)

The Adventures of Robinson Crusoe, 1922 (Universal). Fine, on linen, one-sheet. $518 (Auc. #09)

The Adventures of Sherlock Holmes, 1939 (20th Century Fox). Basil Rathbone. Fine, on linen, one-sheet. $3,850 (Auc. #06)
As above, fine, on linen, insert. $2,640 (Auc. #08)

The Adventures of Superman, Spanish, 1948 (Columbia). On linen, one-sheet.
                                                                 $250 (Auc. #02)

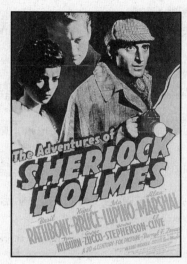

Courtesy of Christie's East.

Courtesy of Odyssey
Auctions.

Adventures of Tarzan, 1921 (Weiss Bros./Numa Pictures). Very good, on linen, window card. $1,400 (Auc. #02)

Affair in Trinidad, 1952 (Columbia). Rita Hayworth. Fine, on linen, three-sheet.
$900 (Auc. #02)
As above, good, one-sheet. $225 (Auc. #07)

The Affairs of Annabel, 1938 (RKO). Lucille Ball. Very good, one-sheet.
$250 (Auc. #02)

Africa Screams, 1949. Abbott and Costello, one-sheet. $357.50 (Auc. #06)

The African Queen, 1952 (United Artists). Humphrey Bogart and Katharine Hepburn. Very good, on linen, six-sheet. $900 (Auc. #02)
As above, good, on linen, three-sheet. $500 (Auc. #01)
As above, fine, on linen, three-sheet. $1,725 (Auc. #09)
As above, very good, on linen, three-sheet. $770 (Auc. #06)
As above, fine, one-sheet. $550 (Auc. #08)
As above, fine, complete set of eight lobby cards. $600 (Auc. #02)

After Office Hours, 1935 (MGM). Clark Gable. Fine, one-sheet. $1,320 (Auc. #04)

After the Ball, 1933. Esther Ralston and Basil Rathbone. Fine, one-sheet.
$770 (Auc. #03)

After Your Own Heart, 1921. Tim Mix. Fine, on linen, one-sheet.
$1,100 (Auc. #03)

Aggie Appleby, Maker of Men, 1933 (RKO). Charles Farrell and Wynne Gibson. Fine, one-sheet. $403 (Auc. #09)

A-Haunting We Will Go, 1942 (20th Century Fox). Laurel and Hardy. Very good, one- sheet. $700 (Auc. #07)

The Alamo, 1961 (United Artists). John Wayne. Fine, on linen, three-sheet.
$300 (Auc. #01)
As above, fine, three-sheet. $200 (Auc. #07)
As above, very good, one-sheet. $330 (Auc. #05)

The Alaskan, 1924 (Paramount). Thomas Meighan. Fine, one-sheet.
$633 (Auc. #09)

Algiers, 1938 (United Artists). Charles Boyer. Good, on linen, one-sheet.
$300 (Auc. #02)

Ali Baba Goes To Town, 1937 (20th Century Fox). Eddie Cantor. Fine, one-sheet. $300 (Auc. #07)

Alias the Night Wind, 1923 (Fox). William Russell. Fine, on linen, one-sheet.
$462 (Auc. #04)

Alice in Wonderland, 1933. Charlotte Henry. Fine, on linen, one-sheet.
$1,100 (Auc. #03)

Alkali Ike's Misfortunes, 1913 (Essanay). Fine, on linen, one-sheet.
$605 (Auc. #04)

All About Eve, 1950 (Fox). Bette Davis. Fine, on linen, three-sheet.
$475 (Auc. #01)
As above, very good, one-sheet. $375 (Auc. #07)
As above, fine, one-sheet. $330 (Auc. #08)
As above, fair, insert. $330 (Auc. #06)

All that Money Can Buy, 1941 (RKO). Edward Arnold. Fine, on linen, three-sheet. $805 (Auc. #09)

All Through the Night, 1942 (Warner Bros.). Humphrey Bogart. Very good, on linen, three-sheet. $950 (Auc. #02)
As above, fine, on linen, one-sheet. $650 (Auc. #01)
As above, fine, window card. $275 (Auc. #03)

Along Came Auntie, 1926 (Pathe). Hal Roach. Fine, on linen, three-sheet.
$800 (Auc. #01)

America, 1924. D. W. Griffith. Very good, on linen, one-sheet. $1,045 (Auc. #06)

An American in Paris, 1951 (MGM). Gene Kelly. Very good, one-sheet.
$250 (Auc. #02)
As above, fine, one-sheet. $660 (Auc. #03)
As above, French, very good, on linen, 47 x 63 inches. $825 (Auc. #05)

Anatomy of a Murder, 1959 (Columbia). Very good, on linen, one-sheet.
$192 (Auc. #03)

Anchors Aweigh, 1945 (MGM). Frank Sinatra and Gene Kelly. Good, complete set of eight lobby cards. $325 (Auc. #02)

And Then There Were None, 1945 (Fox). Good, insert. $100 (Auc. #02)
As above, very good, on linen, one-sheet. $495 (Auc. #03)

Andy Hardy Meets Debutante, 1940 (MGM). Mickey Rooney and Judy Garland. Good, one- sheet. $200 (Auc. #02)

Angel Face, 1952 (RKO). Robert Mitchum. Fine, on linen, three-sheet.
$400 (Auc. #02)

Angels Wash Their Faces, 1939 (Warner Bros.). Ronald Reagan. Good, one-sheet. $650 (Auc. #02)

Angels with Dirty Faces, 1938 (Warner Bros.). James Cagney. Fine, lobby card (Cagney goes to the electric chair). $950 (Auc. #02)

Annie Hall, 1977 (United Artists). Woody Allen. Fine, 40 x 60 inches.
$55 (Auc. #06)

Annie Oakley, 1935 (RKO). Barbara Stanwyck. Fine, half-sheet. $275 (Auc. #08)

Another Thin Man, 1939 (MGM). William Powell and Myrna Loy. Very good, on linen, one-sheet. $850 (Auc. #02)

Arch of Triumph, 1948 (Enterprise). Charles Boyer and Ingrid Bergman. Good, on linen, one-sheet. $220 (Auc. #06)

Arrowsmith, 1932 (United Artists). Ronald Colman and Helen Hayes. Fine, on linen, one-sheet. $3,300 (Auc. #04)

Artists and Models, 1937 (Paramount). Jack Benny. Very good, one-sheet.
$300 (Auc. #02)

The Aryan, 1916 (Triangle). William Hart. Fine, on linen, one-sheet.
$2,090 (Auc. #040)

As You Desire Me, 1931 (MGM). Greta Garbo. Fine, on linen, one-sheet.
$5,500 (Auc. #02)
As above, fine, title lobby card. $2,000 (Auc. #01)
As above, fine, scene lobby card. $425 (Auc. #01)

The Asphalt Jungle, 1950 (MGM). John Huston. Good, on linen, half-sheet.
$375 (Auc. #02)
As above, good, half-sheet. $247.50 (Auc. #06)
As above, fine, title card. $275 (Auc. #03)

At the Circus, 1939 (MGM). Marx Bros. Fine, window card. $650 (Auc. #02)

Courtesy of Camden
House Auctioneers.

Courtesy of Odyssey
Auctions.

At the End of the World, 1921 (Paramount). Fine, on linen, one-sheet.
$800 (Auc. #02)

Atom Man Vs. Superman, 1950 (Columbia). Very good, on linen, six-sheet. *See color insert, photo 28.* $7,000 (Auc. #07)

Attack of the Crab Monsters, 1957 (Allied Artists). Very good, one-sheet.
$600 (Auc. #01)
As above, very good, on linen, insert. $500 (Auc. #07)

Attack of the 50ft. Woman, 1958 (Allied Artists). Fine, one-sheet.
$1,600 (Auc. #02)
As above, fine, on linen, one-sheet. $2,090 (Auc. #04)
As above, very good, on linen, one-sheet. $1,300 (Auc. #07)
As above, fine, on linen, insert. $1,600 (Auc. #07)
As above, very good, half-sheet. $900 (Auc. #01)
As above, very good, half-sheet. $900 (Auc. #07)

Attack of the Puppet People, 1958 (A.I.P.). Very good, on linen, half-sheet.
$250 (Auc. #07)

The Awful Truth, 1937 (Columbia). Cary Grant. Very good, on linen, one-sheet.
$1,700 (Auc. #01)
As above, fine, one-sheet. $2,640 (Auc. #06)

🌿 **B**

Babes on Broadway, 1941 (MGM). Mickey Rooney and Judy Garland. Fine, on linen, one-sheet. $275 (Auc. #08)

Baby Take a Bow, 1934 (Fox). Shirley Temple. Fine, on linen, one-sheet. $4,950 (Auc. #06)

Back Home and Broke, 1922 (Paramount). Thomas Meighan. Fine, on linen, one-sheet. $275 (Auc. #08)

Back Street, 1932 (Universal). Irene Dunne. Fine, on linen, one-sheet. $3,520 (Auc. #04)

The Bad and the Beautiful, 1953 (MGM). Kirk Douglas and Lana Turner. Very good, on linen, three-sheet. $495 (Auc. #06)
As above, fine, one-sheet. $200 (Auc. #02)

Bad Girl, 1931 (Fox). Fine, on linen, one-sheet. $2,420 (Auc. #04)

Ball of Fire, 1941. Gary Cooper and Barbara Stanwyck. Fine, on linen, one-sheet. $605 (Auc. #03)

The Bank, 1915 (Essanay). Charlie Chaplin. Very good, one-sheet. $16,675 (Auc. #09)

The Bank Dick, 1940 (Universal). W. C. Fields. Fine, one-sheet. $863 (Auc. #09)
As above, fine, on linen, one-sheet. $700 (Auc. #07)

Courtesy of
Christie's East.

Courtesy of Odyssey
Auctions.

Bar 20, 1943 (United Artists). William Boyd. Very good, on linen, one-sheet.
$385 (Auc. #06)

The Barkleys of Broadway, 1949 (MGM). Fred Astaire and Ginger Rogers. Very good, on linen, three-sheet. $700 (Auc. #07)
As above, very good, half-sheet. $192.50 (Auc. #06)

The Baroness and the Butler, 1938 (20th Century Fox). William Powell. Very good, on linen, one-sheet. $225 (Auc. #02)

The Barretts of Wimpole Street, 1934 (MGM). Charles Laughton and Frederic March. Fine, on linen, one-sheet. $950 (Auc. #02)

The Bat Whispers, 1930 (Atlantic). Chester Morris. Very good, on linen, three-sheet. $660 (Auc. #06)

Batman, 1966 (Fox). Fine, on linen, six-sheet. $1,500 (Auc. #01)
As above, on linen, six-sheet. $350 (Auc. #07)
As above, fine, three-sheet. $275 (Auc. #01)
As above, fine, one-sheet. $125 (Auc. #07)

Battle of the Sexes, French, 1928 (United Artists). Very good, on linen, 47 x 63 inches. $375 (Auc. #01)

Beast from Haunted Cave, 1959 (Film Group). Very good, one-sheet.
$150 (Auc. #02)

The Beast from 20,000 Fathoms, 1953 (Warner Bros.). Very good, one-sheet.
$550 (Auc. #01)
As above, Australian, good, on linen, three-sheet. $475 (Auc. #01)

The Beast with 1,000,000 Eyes, 1955 (American Releasing). Fine, one-sheet.
$600 (Auc. #02)

Beau Geste, 1939 (Paramount). Gary Cooper. Fine, on linen, one-sheet.
$3,190 (Auc. #03)
As above, fine, window card. $400 (Auc. #01)

Beauty and the Beast, original French, 1946 (Discina). Fine, on linen, 47 x 63 inches. $4,000 (Auc. #07)

Becket, Italian, 1965 (Paramount). Richard Burton and Peter O'Toole. Fine, on linen, 39 x 55 inches. $330 (Auc. #06)

Bedlam, 1946. Boris Karloff. Fine, insert. $220 (Auc. #08)

Before I Hang, 1940 (Columbia). Boris Karloff. Very good, on linen, three-sheet. $550 (Auc. #06)

Beggars of Life, 1928 (Paramount). Very good, lobby card. $1,100 (Auc. #02)

Behave Yourself!, 1951 (RKO). Shelley Winters. Very good, on linen, one-sheet.
$192 (Auc. #05)

Courtesy of Hollywood
Poster Art.

The Belle of New York, 1951 (MGM). Fred Astaire. Fine, on linen, three-sheet.
$357 (Auc. #05)

Belle of the Nineties, 1934 (Paramount). Mae West. Very good, on linen, window card. $225 (Auc. #07)

Best Bad Man, 1925 (Wm. Fox). Tom Mix. Very good, one-sheet.
$825 (Auc. #06)

Betsy's Burglar, 1917 (Hamilton). Constance Talmadge. Fine, on linen, one-sheet. $248 (Auc. #08)

Beware of Bachelors, 1928 (Warner Bros.). Fine, on linen, one-sheet.
$990 (Auc. #04)

The Big Broadcast of 1938, 1933 (Paramount). W. C. Fields. Fine, on linen, three-sheet. $3,220 (Auc. #09)

Big Fella, British, 1937 (British Lion). Paul Robeson. Fine, on linen, 38 x 88 inches. $3,450 (Auc. #09)

The Big Fight, 1930 (Worldwide). Guinn Williams. Fine, on linen, one-sheet.
$633 (Auc. #09)

The Big Game, 1936 (RKO). Fine, on linen, one-sheet. $2,420 (Auc. #04)

The Big Hop, 1928. Buck Jones. Very good, on linen, one-sheet.$1,045 (Auc. #06)

The Big Noise, 1944 (Fox). Laurel and Hardy. Fine, on linen, three-sheet.
$850 (Auc. #01)
As above, very good, on linen, one-sheet. $605 (Auc. #06)
As above, title card. $100 (Auc. #02)

The Big Pond, 1930 (Paramount). Maurice Chevalier. Fine, on linen, one-sheet.
$770 (Auc. #04)

The Big Sleep, 1946 (Warner Bros.). Humphrey Bogart and Lauren Bacall. Very good, on linen, six-sheet. $2,000 (Auc. #01)
As above, good, on linen, one-sheet. $330 (Auc. #06)
As above, French, very good, on linen, 24 x 33 inches. $660 (Auc. #06)

The Big Store, 1941 (MGM). Marx Bros. Very good, on linen, one-sheet.
$1,035 (Auc. #09)
As above, very good, insert. $650 (Auc. #01)
As above, fine, insert. $495 (Auc. #03)
As above, very good, insert. $385 (Auc. #06)

The Big Street, 1942 (RKO). Henry Fonda and Lucille Ball. Fine, on linen, one-sheet. $325 (Auc. #07)
As above, good, one-sheet. $150 (Auc. #07)

The Birds, 1963 (Universal). Alfred Hitchcock. Fine, on linen, six-sheet.
$600 (Auc. #02)
As above, fine, one-sheet. $330 (Auc. #04)

Birth of a Nation, 1915. D. W. Griffith. Very good, on linen, one-sheet.
$14,300 (Auc. #06)
As above, 1921 reissue, fine, on linen, one-sheet. $7,130 (Auc. #09)

Bitter Sweet, 1940 (MGM). Jeanette MacDonald. Very good, three-sheet.
$400 (Auc. #01)

The Black Camel, 1931 (Fox). Charlie Chan. Fine, on linen, one-sheet.
$2,420 (Auc. #04)

The Black Cat, 1941 (Universal). Basil Rathbone and Bela Lugosi. Very good, on linen, one-sheet. $500 (Auc. #02)

The Black Diamond Express, 1927 (Warner Bros.). Monte Blue. Fine, one-sheet. $460 (Auc. #09)

Black Friday, 1940 (Universal). Boris Karloff and Bela Lugosi. Fine, on linen, one-sheet. $4,400 (Auc. #04)

Black Legion, 1936 (Warner Bros.). Humphrey Bogart. Good, one-sheet.
$440 (Auc. #06)

The Black Swan, French, 1942 (20th Century Fox). Tyrone Power and Maureen O'Hara. Very good, on linen, 47 x 63 inches. $357.50 (Auc. #06)

Blonde Bombshell, 1933 (MGM). Jean Harlow and Lee Tracy. Fine, title card.
$715 (Auc. #08)
As above, very good, window card. $275 (Auc. #08)

Blonde Venus, 1932. Marlene Dietrich. Very good, lobby card. $1,650 (Auc. #03)
As above, German, fine, on linen, 9 x 13 inches. $3,450 (Auc. #09)

Courtesy of Odyssey Auctions.

Courtesy of Hollywood
Poster Art.

Blondie, 1938 (Columbia). Fine, on linen, three-sheet. $1,500 (Auc. #02)

Blondie of the Follies, 1932 (MGM). Fine, on linen, one-sheet. $863 (Auc. #09)

Blood and Sand, 1922 (Paramount). Rudolph Valentino. Fine, on linen, one-sheet. $5,750 (Auc. #09)

Blood and Sand, 1941 (Fox). Rita Hayworth. Very good, on linen, one-sheet.
                                                                                                                    $375 (Auc. #02)

Blue Dahlia, 1946 (Paramount). Alan Ladd and Veronica Lake. Fine, on linen, one-sheet. $2,420 (Auc. #03)
As above, very good, on linen, half-sheet trimmed. $300 (Auc. #01)
As above, Italian, very good, three lobby cards, 13½ x 9½ inches. $100 (Auc. #07)

The Blues Brothers, 1980 (Universal). John Belushi and Dan Aykroyd. Fine, one-sheet. $75 (Auc. #07)

Body and Soul, 1947 (MGM). Very good, on linen, three-sheet. $700 (Auc. #02)
As above, good, complete set of eight lobby cards. $225 (Auc. #07)

The Body Snatcher, 1945 (RKO). Boris Karloff and Bela Lugosi. Fine, one-sheet.
                                                                                                                  $1,610 (Auc. #09)
As above, good, on linen, title card. $275 (Auc. #06)

Bohemian Girl, 1937 (MGM). Laurel and Hardy. Fine, half-sheet. $385 (Auc. #08)

Bolero, 1934 (Paramount). George Raft and Carole Lombard. Fine, one-sheet.
                                                                                                                  $6,600 (Auc. #04)

The Bonded Woman, 1922 (Paramount). Betty Compson. Fine, one-sheet.
$220 (Auc. #08)

Boomerang, 1947 (20th Century Fox). Dana Andrews. Fine, on linen, one-sheet.
$193 (Auc. #08)

The Border Wireless, 1918 (Artcraft). William Hart. Fine, on linen, one-sheet.
$3,740 (Auc. #04)

Bordertown, 1934 (Warner Bros.). Bette Davis. Very good, one-sheet.
$8,800 (Auc. #04)
As above, reissue, good, on linen, one-sheet.
$275 (Auc. #06)

Born to Kill, 1947 (RKO). Fine, on linen, three-sheet.
$400 (Auc. #01)
As above, very good, one-sheet.
$200 (Auc. #07)

Boys Town, 1938 (MGM). Spencer Tracy and Mickey Rooney. Fine, on linen, one-sheet.
$748 (Auc. #09)

The Branded Woman, 1921 (First National). Norma Talmadge. Fine, on linen, one-sheet.
$863 (Auc. #09)

The Brasher Doubloon, 1946. George Montgomery. Fine, on linen, one-sheet.
$440 (Auc. #03)

The Brat, 1931 (Fox). Sally O'Neill. Fine, on linen, one-sheet. $550 (Auc. #04)

Break of Hearts, 1934 (RKO). Katharine Hepburn and Charles Boyer. Very good, complete set of eight lobby cards.
$650 (Auc. #01)
As above, very good, window card.
$950 (Auc. #07)

Break the News, 1938 (Trio Films). Maurice Chevalier. Fine, one-sheet.
$325 (Auc. #02)

Breakfast at Tiffany's, 1961. Audrey Hepburn. Fine, one-sheet. $495 (Auc. #03)
As above, fine, on linen, one-sheet.
$805 (Auc. #09)
As above, Italian, fine, on linen, 55 x 78 inches.
$1,265 (Auc. #09)

Bride and Gloom, ca. 1922 reissue (Pathe). Harold Lloyd. Fine, on linen, one-sheet.
$1,093 (Auc. #09)

The Bride of Frankenstein, 1935 (Universal). Boris Karloff. Fine, lobby card (creation scene).
$3,300 (Auc. #06)
As above, 1953 reissue (Realart), very good, one-sheet.
$225 (Auc. #07)
As above, French, 1946 reissue, very good, on linen, 47 x 63 inches.
$1,540 (Auc. #06)

Bride 13, 1920 (Wm. Fox). Very good, on linen, one-sheet. $275 (Auc. #02)

The Bridge on the River Kwai, 1958 (Columbia). William Holden and Alec Guinness. Fine, one-sheet.
$75 (Auc. #02)

Bright Eyes, 1934 (Fox). Shirley Temple. Fair, on linen, one-sheet.
$1,430 (Auc. #06)
As above, fine, half-sheet. $660 (Auc. #08)

Bringing Up Father, ca. 1920 (George McManus). Very good, window card.
$250 (Auc. #02)

Broadway, 1929 (Universal). Complete set of eight lobby cards plus one pho-
tolobby. $3,000 (Auc. #01)

Broadway Bill, 1934 (Columbia). William Baxter and Myrna Loy. Very good, on
linen, one-sheet. $750 (Auc. #02)
As above, fine, on linen, one-sheet. $1,000 (Auc. #07)
As above, fine, insert. $275 (Auc. #08)

Broadway Rose, 1922 (Metro). Mae Murray. Very good, on linen, three-sheet.
$748 (Auc. #09)

The Broken Wing, 1932 (Paramount). Very good, on linen, one-sheet.
$500 (Auc. #02)

The Bronze Venus, (Toddy Pictures). Lena Horne. Very good, on linen, three-
sheet. $1,320 (Auc. #06)

Brother Rat, 1938 (Warner Bros.). Good, on linen, one-sheet. $175 (Auc. #06)

Brothers, 1930 (Columbia). Bert Lytell. Fine, on linen, one-sheet. $550 (Auc. #04)

Brute Force, 1947 (Universal). Burt Lancaster. Very good, on linen, three-sheet.
$350 (Auc. #02)

The Buccaneer, 1938 (Paramount). Fredric March. Fine, one-sheet.
$805 (Auc. #09)

Buck Rogers/Chapter 11, a Prince in Bondage, 1939 (Universal). Larry
Crabbe. Fine, on linen, one-sheet. $1,100 (Auc. #01)

The Bull Dogger, 1923 (Norman Film Co.). Bill Pickett. Fine, one-sheet.
$2,200 (Auc. #05)

Bus Stop, 1956 (Fox). Marilyn Monroe. Good, on linen, three-sheet.
$800 (Auc. #01)
As above, fine, on linen, one-sheet. $475 (Auc. #01)
As above, fine, one-sheet. $385 (Auc. #03)
As above, very good, on linen, one-sheet. $935 (Auc. #06)
As above, fine, one-sheet. $550 (Auc. #08)
As above, good, insert. $225 (Auc. #07)
As above, very good, complete set of eight lobby cards. $400 (Auc. #02)

Butterfly, 1924 (Universal). Fine, on linen, one-sheet. $700 (Auc. #02)

By Whose Hand, 1927 (Columbia). Fine, on linen, one-sheet. $575 (Auc. #09)

❧ C

Cabaret, 1972 (Allied Artists). Liza Minnelli. Fine, 40 x 60 inches. $220 (Auc. #06)

Cabin in the Sky, 1943 (MGM). Lena Horne and Louis Armstrong. Very good, on linen, three-sheet. $1,300 (Auc. #01)
As above, fine, on linen, one-sheet (art by Hirshfeld). $3,250 (Auc. #02)
As above, very good, on linen, one-sheet (other). $350 (Auc. #02)
As above, fine, on linen, one-sheet (art by Hirshfeld). $2,760 (Auc. #09)
As above, very good, insert. $550 (Auc. #08)
As above, very good, half-sheet. $1,800 (Auc. #01)
As above, very good, complete set of eight lobby cards. $1,600 (Auc. #01)
As above, good, complete set of eight lobby cards. $1,300 (Auc. #02)

Cafe Society, 1939 (Paramount). Fred MacMurray. Fine, on linen, six-sheet.
                                                            $330 (Auc. #08)

The Caine Mutiny, 1954 (Columbia). Humphrey Bogart. Fine, on linen, three-sheet. $247 (Auc. #05)

Call Her Savage, 1932 (Fox). Clara Bow. Fine, on linen, one-sheet.
                                                          $1,210 (Auc. #04)

The Call of the Wild, 1923 (Pathe). Hal Roach. Fine, on linen, one-sheet.
                                                          $3,850 (Auc. #04)

Camille, 1936 (MGM). Greta Garbo and Lionel Barrymore. Fine, on linen, one-sheet. $2,750 (Auc. #04)

Camille of the Yukon, 1920 (Wm. Fox). Fine, on linen, one-sheet.
                                                          $1,320 (Auc. #08)

The Canary Murder Case, 1929 (Paramount). William Powell. Fine, one-sheet.
                                                         $28,600 (Auc. #04)

Cape Fear, 1962 (Universal). Gregory Peck and Robert Mitchum. Fine, one-sheet. $325 (Auc. #07)

Captain Blood, 1935 (Warner Bros.). Errol Flynn and Olivia De Havilland. Fine, one-sheet. $6,820 (Auc. #04)
As above, good, half-sheet. $700 (Auc. #02)

Captain January, 1936 (Fox). Shirley Temple. Fine, on linen, three-sheet.
                                                          $2,500 (Auc. #02)

Captain Kidd's Kids, 1920 (Pathe). Harold Lloyd. Very good, on linen, one-sheet. $1,000 (Auc. #07)

The Captive God, 1916 (Triangle). William Hart. Very good, on linen, one-sheet. $1,870 (Auc. #04)

Carmen, 1913 (Monopol). Very good, on linen, one-sheet. $450 (Auc. #01)

Carmen, German, 1918. Artwork by Fenneker. Fine, 23 x 35½ inches.
$1,500 (Auc. #07)

Casablanca, 1942 (Warner Bros.). Humphrey Bogart and Ingrid Bergman.
Good, on linen, one-sheet. $3,250 (Auc. #01)
As above, fine, on linen, one-sheet. $4,400 (Auc. #03)
As above, good, on linen, one-sheet. $2,860 (Auc. #05)
As above, very good, on linen, one-sheet. $2,750 (Auc. #06)
As above, fine, on linen, one-sheet. $5,500 (Auc. #07)
As above, very good, folded, insert. $7,700 (Auc. #04)
Very good, lobby card (Bogart-Bergman). $1,800 (Auc. #01)
As above, fine, lobby card (letters of transit). $1,500 (Auc. #01)
As above, very good, lobby card (final scene). $950 (Auc. #01)
As above, Austrian, good, on linen, 23 x 34 inches. $400 (Auc. #01)
As above, Belgian, fine, 11 x 16½ inches. $850 (Auc. #01)
As above, Danish, fine, on linen, 24 x 34 inches. $863 (Auc. #09)
As above, French, fine, on linen, 47 x 63 inches. $19,800 (Auc. #04)
As above, French, on linen, 94 x 63 inches. $18,700 (Auc. #05)

The Case of Sergeant Grischa, 1930 (RKO). Herbert Brenon. Fine, on linen, six-sheet. $1,150 (Auc. #09)

Case of the Black Cat, 1936 (Warner Bros.). Ricardo Cortez and June Travis. Fine, one-sheet. $385 (Auc. #08)

The Cat and the Canary, 1939 (Paramount). Bob Hope. Very good, on linen, one-sheet. $1,210 (Auc. #04)

The Cat Creeps, 1946. Fine, on linen, one-sheet. $220 (Auc. #05)

Courtesy of Hollywood
Poster Art.

Courtesy of Swann Galleries, Inc.

Cat People, 1952 reissue. Simone Simon. Fine, on linen, one-sheet.
$880 (Auc. #03)
As above, very good, one-sheet. $375 (Auc. #07)

Cat Women of the Moon, 1953 (Astor). Fine, one-sheet. $500 (Auc. #01)

The Catman of Paris, 1946 (Republic). Carl Esmond. Very good, on linen, one-sheet. $440 (Auc. #08)

The Cattle Thief's Escape, 1913 (Selig). Fine, on linen, one-sheet. $660 (Auc. #04)

The Champeen, 1922 (Pathe). Our Gang. Very good, on linen, one-sheet.
$1,800 (Auc. #07)

Chandu the Magician, 1932 (Fox). Fine, complete set of eight lobby cards.
$4,370 (Auc. #09)

Chang, 1927 (Paramount). Fine, complete set of eight lobby cards.
$660 (Auc. #08)

The Charge of the Light Brigade, 1936 (Warner Bros.). Errol Flynn and Olivia De Havilland. Good, half-sheet. $650 (Auc. #02)

Charlie Chan at Monte Carlo, 1937 (20th Century Fox). Fine, on linen, one-sheet. $1,100 (Auc. #04)

Charlie Chan at the Circus, 1936 (20th Century Fox). Fine, one-sheet.
$3,080 (Auc. #04)

Courtesy of Camden House Auctioneers.

Courtesy of Odyssey Auctions.

Charlie Chan in Egypt, 1935 (Fox). Good, title and six scene cards.
$500 (Auc. #01)

Charlie Chan in the Red Dragon, 1945 (Monogram). Very good, unfolded, insert. $200 (Auc. #02)

Charlie Chan's Greatest Case, 1933 (Fox). Fine, on linen, one-sheet.
$2,300 (Auc. #09)

The Chimp, 1932 (MGM). Laurel and Hardy. Fine, on linen, one-sheet.
$2,000 (Auc. #02)

China, 1943 (Paramount). Loretta Young and Alan Ladd. Fine, on linen, one-sheet. $575 (Auc. #09)

Chinatown, 1974 (Paramount). Jack Nicholson and Faye Dunaway. Fine, one-sheet. $150 (Auc. #02)

Christmas in July, 1940 (Paramount). Dick Powell. Very good, on linen, one-sheet. $660 (Auc. #04)

A Chump at Oxford, Belgian, 1940 (United Artists). Laurel and Hardy. Fine, on linen, 24 x 33 inches. $250 (Auc. #01)

Cimarron, 1931 (RKO). Richard Dix. Very good, on linen, one-sheet.
$16,500 (Auc. #04)
As above, fine, window card. $220 (Auc. #08)
As above, Swedish, fine, unfolded, one-sheet. $3,220 (Auc. #09)

The Circus, 1928 (United Artists). Charlie Chaplin. Fine, on linen, one-sheet.
$18,700 (Auc. #04)
As above, fine, one-sheet. $11,000 (Auc. #06)

The Circus Queen Murder, 1933 (Columbia). Fine, on linen, one-sheet.
$1,035 (Auc. #09)

Citizen Kane, 1941 (RKO). Orson Welles. Very good, on linen, six-sheet.
$22,000 (Auc. #04)

As above, very good, on linen, one-sheet. $8,250 (Auc. #04)

As above, 1956 reissue, fine, complete set of eight lobby cards. $225 (Auc. #02)

City for Conquest, 1940. James Cagney and Ann Sheridan. Fine, on linen, insert. $770 (Auc. #03)

City Lights, 1931 (United Artists). Charlie Chaplin. Fine, on linen, one-sheet.
$28,000 (Auc. #02)

As above, British, very good, on linen, 12½ x 20 inches. $1,700 (Auc. #01)

Cleopatra, 1917 (Wm. Fox). Theda Bara. Very good, window card.
$825 (Auc. #08)

Cleopatra, Danish, 1934 (Paramount). Claudette Colbert. Fine, on linen, 24 x 34 inches. $1,725 (Auc. #09)

Clive of India, 1935 (20th Century Fox). Ronald Colman. Fine, on linen, one-sheet. $2,640 (Auc. #04)

The Clock, 1945 (MGM). Judy Garland. Fine, on linen, one-sheet. $440 (Auc. #03)

As above, fine, on linen, one-sheet. $518 (Auc. #09)

As above, fine, insert. $225 (Auc. #02)

Clockwork Orange, 1971 (Warner Bros.). Stanley Kubrick. Very good, on linen, one-sheet. $220 (Auc. #06)

College Swing, 1938 (Paramount). George Burns and Bob Hope. Fine, on linen, one-sheet. $403 (Auc. #09)

Colorado Pluck, 1921 (Wm. Fox). William Russell. Fine, on linen, one-sheet. $440 (Auc. #08)

Come Live with Me, 1941 (MGM). James Stewart and Hedy Lamarr. Very good, one-sheet. $425 (Auc. #01)

Come on Over, 1922 (Goldwyn). Very good, on linen, one-sheet. $200 (Auc. #07)

Coming Out Party, 1934. Frances Dee and Gene Raymond. Fine, one-sheet. $1,045 (Auc. #03)

Confidential Agent, 1945 (Warner Bros.). Charles Boyer and Lauren Bacall. Very good, complete set of eight lobby cards. $125 (Auc. #02)

A Connecticut Yankee in King Arthur's Court, 1920 (Wm. Fox). Very good, on linen, one-sheet. $800 (Auc. #02)

The Conquerors, 1932. Richard Dix and Ann Harding. Fine, one-sheet. $1,980 (Auc. #03)

Cornered, 1932 (Columbia). Tim McCoy. Very good, on linen, three-sheet. $1,650 (Auc. #06)

As above, very good, on linen, one-sheet. $650 (Auc. #02)

A Cottage Garden, ca. 1924 (Kelley). Fine, on linen, one-sheet. $550 (Auc. #04)

Cousin Wilbur, 1939 (MGM). Our Gang. Fine, on linen, one-sheet. $1,610 (Auc. #09)

The Covered Wagon, 1923 (Paramount). Fine, on linen, one-sheet. $2,500 (Auc. #02)

As above, very good, window card. $350 (Auc. #07)

The Count, 1916 (Mutual/Chaplin). Charlie Chaplin. Fine, window card. $3,000 (Auc. #01)

The Covered Wagon, 1923 (Paramount). Style B, very good, on linen, one-sheet. $990 (Auc. #06)

The Cowboy and the Kid, 1936 (Universal). Fine, on linen, one-sheet.
$350 (Auc. #02)

Crack Up, 1937 (Fox). Peter Lorre. Good, on linen, one-sheet.
$1,200 (Auc. #01)
As above, fine, one-sheet. $920 (Auc. #09)

Crack Up, 1946 (RKO). Pat O'Brien. Very good, one-sheet. $175 (Auc. #02)

Creature from the Black Lagoon, 1954 (Universal). Richard Carlson and Julia Adams. Fine, on linen, three-sheet. $8,625 (Auc. #09)
As above, fair, on linen, one-sheet. $3,500 (Auc. #01)
As above, good, on linen, one-sheet. $2,090 (Auc. #05)
As above, fine, insert. $2,250 (Auc. #01)
As above, insert. $1,210 (Auc. #05)
As above, very good, half-sheet. $1,500 (Auc. #01)
As above fine, unfolded, half-sheet. $1,950 (Auc. #04)
As above, style B, very good, half-sheet. $1,980 (Auc. #06)
As above, very good, trimmed, window card. $440 (Auc. #03)
As above, Argentine, good, one-sheet. $200 (Auc. #01)
As above, British, fine, on linen, 40 x 30 inches. $650 (Auc. #02)
As above, French, fine, 24 x 31 inches. $100 (Auc. #02)

The Creature Walks Among Us, 1956 (Universal). Good, one-sheet.
$550 (Auc. #01)
As above, fine, on linen, one-sheet. $550 (Auc. #06)
As above, fine, one-sheet. $440 (Auc. #08)
As above, very good, insert. $425 (Auc. #01)
As above, very good, half-sheet. $475 (Auc. #01)
As above, very good, half-sheet (other). $325 (Auc. #01)

Crime School, 1938 (Warner Bros.). Humphrey Bogart. Fine, on linen, one-sheet. $4,180 (Auc. #08)

Crossfire, 1947 (Paramount). Robert Mitchum. Very good, on linen, three-sheet. $375 (Auc. #01)
As above, very good, one-sheet. $550 (Auc. #07)

The Crusaders, 1948 reissue (Paramount). Cecil B. De Mille. Good, three-sheet. $100 (Auc. #07)

Cuckoo on a Choo Choo, 1952 (Columbia). The Three Stooges. Good, one-sheet. $700 (Auc. #02)

Curly Top, 1935 (Fox). Shirley Temple. Very good, on linen, one-sheet.
$1,430 (Auc. #04)

The Curse of the Cat People, 1944 (RKO). Simone Simon. Fine, on linen, one-sheet. $863 (Auc. #09)

Curtain at Eight, 1934 (Majestic). Fine, on linen, one-sheet. $300 (Auc. #07)

🦋 **D**

Dance Fools Dance, 1931 (MGM). Joan Crawford. Very good, on linen, one-sheet. $3,575 (Auc. #06)

Dance Team, 1931 (Fox). James Dunn and Sally Eilers. Very good, on linen, one-sheet. $450 (Auc. #07)

Dancing Daisies, 1924 (Universal). Fine, on linen, one-sheet. $425 (Auc. #02)

Dancing Lady, 1933 (MGM). Joan Crawford and Clark Gable. Fine, one-sheet. $2,090 (Auc. #04)

Dancing Pirate, 1936 (RKO). Fine, on linen, three-sheet. $400 (Auc. #02)

Dancing Romeo, 1944 (MGM). Our Gang. Very good, one-sheet. $325 (Auc. #02)

The Dangerous Coward, 1924 (Monogram). Fred Thomson. Good, on linen, one-sheet. $275 (Auc. #06)

Dangerous Curve Ahead, 1921 (Goldwyn). Rupert Hughes. Very good, on linen, one-sheet. $250 (Auc. #07)

Dangerously Yours, 1933 (Fox). Warner Baxter. Very good, on linen, one-sheet. $425 (Auc. #07)

Dante's Inferno, 1921. Fine, on linen, one-sheet. $4,180 (Auc. #04)

The Daredevil, 1920 (Wm. Fox). Tom Mix. Very good, on linen, three-sheet. $750 (Auc. #02)

Daring Danger, 1932 (Columbia). Tim McCoy. Fine, on linen, one-sheet. $690 (Auc. #09)

Daring Days, 1925. Josie Sedgwick. Fine, one-sheet. $275 (Auc. #08)

Dark Passage, 1947 (Warner Bros.). Humphrey Bogart and Lauren Bacall. Good, one-sheet. $325 (Auc. #01)

Dark Victory, 1938. Bette Davis. Fine, lobby card. $1,650 (Auc. #03)

Darkest Africa, 1936 (Republic). Clyde Beatty. Fine, on linen, one-sheet. $500 (Auc. #02)
As above, fine, on linen, one-sheet. $518 (Auc. #09)

Davy Crockett, King of the Wild Frontier, 1955 (Disney). Very good, on linen, three-sheet. $605 (Auc. #06)

The Dawn Patrol, 1938 (Warner Bros.). Errol Flynn. Fine, on linen, one-sheet.
$2,420 (Auc. #04)

A Day at the Races, 1937 (MGM). Marx Bros. Fine, on linen, one-sheet.
$5,000 (Auc. #02)

The Day of the Triffids, 1962 (Allied Artists). Fine, three-sheet.
$275 (Auc. #07)
As above, very good, one-sheet. $475 (Auc. #02)

The Day the Earth Stood Still, 1951 (Fox). Michael Rennie and Patricia Neal.
Fine, on linen, three-sheet. $6,000 (Auc. #01)
As above, three-sheet. $4,400 (Auc. #05)
As above, one-sheet. $1,320 (Auc. #05)
As above, fine, insert. $1,600 (Auc. #01)
As above, fine, lobby standee. $3,520 (Auc. #04)
As above, jumbo lobby card. $605 (Auc. #05)
As above, Argentine, fine, on linen, three-sheet. $900 (Auc. #01)
As above, French, very good, on linen, 47 x 63 inches. $1,045 (Auc. #05)

The Day the World Ended, 1955 (American Releasing). Fine, one-sheet.
$425 (Auc. #02)
As above, Italian, very good, 38 x 55 inches. $250 (Auc. #07)

Dead of Night, 1946. Michael Redgrave. Fine, on linen, one-sheet.
$935 (Auc. #03)

Dead Reckoning, 1947 (Columbia). Humphrey Bogart. Fine, on linen, one-sheet. $950 (Auc. #02)
As above, fine, one-sheet (other). $500 (Auc. #02)
As above, good, on linen, insert. $220 (Auc. #06)
As above, very good, complete set of eight lobby cards. $225 (Auc. #02)

Deadline U.S.A., 1952 (20th Century Fox). Humphrey Bogart. Very good, on linen, one-sheet. $220 (Auc. #06)

The Deadly Mantis, 1957 (Universal). Very good, on linen, three-sheet.
$440 (Auc. #06)

Death from a Distance, 1935 (Invincible). Fine, one-sheet. $220 (Auc. #08)

Deception, 1946 (Columbia). Good, on linen, one-sheet. $330 (Auc. #06)

Desert Fury, 1947 (Paramount). Burt Lancaster. Fine, one-sheet. $175 (Auc. #02)

Desert Valley, 1927 (Wm. Fox). Buck Jones. Fine, on linen, one-sheet.
$550 (Auc. #08)

Desperate Hours, 1955 (Paramount). Humphrey Bogart. Fair, one-sheet.
$121 (Auc. #05)

Desperate Journey, 1942 (Warner Bros.). Errol Flynn and Ronald Reagan. Fine, one-sheet. $330 (Auc. #08)

Destination Moon, 1950 (Universal). Very good, on linen, six-sheet.
$1,320 (Auc. #06)
As above, good, one-sheet. $300 (Auc. #01)
As above, good, on linen, one-sheet. $467 (Auc. #05)

Destry Rides Again, 1939. James Stewart and Marlene Dietrich. Fine, insert.
$330 (Auc. #08)

Detour, 1945 (PRC). Fine, on linen, one-sheet. $2,750 (Auc. #04)

Devil Dogs of the Air, 1935 (Warner Bros.). James Cagney and Pat O'Brien.
Fine, on linen, three-sheet. $4,600 (Auc. #09)
As above, very good, window card. $357.50 (Auc. #06)

Devil Girl from Mars, original English, 1954 (London Films). Very good, on
linen, 25½ x 38½ inches. $650 (Auc. #07)

Devil Girl from Mars, 1955 (Spartan). Fine, on linen, one-sheet.
$1,210 (Auc. #04)
As above, very good, insert. $550 (Auc. #01)
As above, very good, half-sheet. $550 (Auc. #01)

The Devil Is a Woman, 1935 (Paramount). Marlene Dietrich. Fine, unfolded,
one-sheet. $46,200 (Auc. #04)
As above, fine, unfolded, one-sheet, style B. $13,800 (Auc. #09)
As above, fine, title card. $440 (Auc. #06)
As above, fine, restored, window card. $770 (Auc. #03)
As above, good, window card. $1,000 (Auc. #07)

The Devil is Driving, 1937 (Columbia). Richard Dix. Very good, three-sheet.
$1,045 (Auc. #06)
As above, fine, on linen, one-sheet. $500 (Auc. #02)

Courtesy of
Christie's East.

Devil on Horseback, 1936 (Grand National). Very good, on linen, one-sheet.
$250 (Auc. #02)

The Devil's Brother, 1933 (MGM). Laurel and Hardy. Fine, one-sheet.
$5,290 (Auc. #09)

The Devil's Double, 1916 (Triangle). William Hart. Fine, on linen, one-sheet.
$2,640 (Auc. #04)

Devil's Island, 1938 (Warner Bros.). Boris Karloff. Fine, on linen, one-sheet.
$275 (Auc. #08)

The Devil's Mask, 1946 (Columbia). Very good, on linen, one-sheet.
$200 (Auc. #02)

Diamond Horseshoe, 1945 (Fox). Betty Grable and Dick Haymes. Fair, one-sheet.
$125 (Auc. #01)

Dick Tracy, 1945 (RKO). Morgan Conway. Fine, on linen, one-sheet.
$495 (Auc. #06)

Dick Tracy, Episode 7/The Ghost Town Mystery, 1937 (Republic). Fine, on linen, one-sheet.
$920 (Auc. #09)

Dick Tracy Vs. Crime Inc., Chapter 1/The Fatal Hour, 1938 (Republic). Fine, on linen, one-sheet.
$425 (Auc. #07)

Dirty Harry, 1971 (Warner Bros.). Clint Eastwood. Very good, one-sheet.
$150 (Auc. #07)

Dixiana, 1930 (RKO). Bebe Daniels and Everett Marshall. Fine, one-sheet.
$863 (Auc. #09)

Doctor Bull, 1936 (Fox). Will Rogers. Fine, one-sheet. $350 (Auc. #01)

Doctor Cyclops, 1940 (Paramount). Fine, on linen, one-sheet.
$1,540 (Auc. #03)
As above, fine, complete set of eight lobby cards. $425 (Auc. #02)

Dr. Jekyll and Mr. Hyde, Swedish, 1932. Fredric March. Fine, 27 x 39 inches.
$2,420 (Auc. #05)

Dr. No, 1962 (United Artists). Sean Connery. Fine, on linen, three-sheet.
$400 (Auc. #02)
As above, good, half-sheet. $200 (Auc. #07)

Dodge City, 1939 (Warner Bros.). Errol Flynn. Style A, fine, on linen, one-sheet.
$4,840 (Auc. #08)
As above, very good, on linen, insert. $1,700 (Auc. #01)

Dodsworth, 1936 (United Artists). Fine, complete set of eight lobby cards.
$2,300 (Auc. #09)

A Dog's Life, ca. 1920s reissue (Pathe). Charlie Chaplin. Very good, half-sheet.
$500 (Auc. #07)

Doin' Their Bit, 1942 (MGM). Our Gang. Fine, on linen, one-sheet.
$770 (Auc. #04)

Don Q Son of Zorro, 1925 (United Artists). Douglas Fairbanks. Very good, on linen, one-sheet. $2,300 (Auc. #09)
As above, good, half-sheet (movie still). $300 (Auc. #07)
As above, good, half-sheet (with whip). $300 (Auc. #07)

Don't Bother to Knock, 1952 (Fox). Marilyn Monroe. Good, on foamcore, three-sheet. $1,000 (Auc. #07)
As above, good, on linen, one-sheet. $800 (Auc. #01)
As above, fine, on linen, one-sheet. $1,100 (Auc. #04)
As above, good, on linen, one-sheet. $650 (Auc. #07)
As above, very good, unfolded, half-sheet. $325 (Auc. #01)
As above, very good, half-sheet. $357.50 (Auc. #06)
As above, British, good, 40 x 30 inches. $325 (Auc. #01)

Dorothy Vernon of Haddon Hall, 1924 (United Artists). Mary Pickford. Fine, one-sheet. $3,850 (Auc. #02)

Double Indemnity, 1944 (Paramount). Fred MacMurray and Barbara Stanwyck. Fine, on linen, six-sheet. $4,000 (Auc. #01)
As above, fine, on linen, one-sheet. $1,760 (Auc. #03)
As above, very good, on linen, one-sheet. $950 (Auc. #02)
As above, very good, on linen, one-sheet. $1,900 (Auc. #01)
As above, fine, on linen, insert. $715 (Auc. #08)
As above, very good, half-sheet. $660 (Auc. #06)
As above, good, complete set of eight lobby cards. $300 (Auc. #02)
As above, very good, title card. $192.50 (Auc. #06)
As above, Spanish, fine, on linen, 39 x 27 inches. $375 (Auc. #01)

Doubling for Romeo, 1921 (Goldwyn). Will Rogers. Very good, on linen, one-sheet. $900 (Auc. #07)

Down Argentine Way, 1938 (Fox). Betty Grable and Don Ameche. Fine, on linen, one-sheet. $935 (Auc. #04)
As above, very good, insert. $450 (Auc. #01)
As above, fine, unfolded, insert. $150 (Auc. #02)

Down To Earth, 1947 (Columbia). Rita Hayworth. Good, on linen, three-sheet. $400 (Auc. #02)
As above, very good, one-sheet. $325 (Auc. #07)

The Dragnet, 1928 (Paramount). George Bancroft. Fine, title card.
$330 (Auc. #08)

Dragonwyck, 1945 (Fox). Gene Tierney. Good, complete set of eight lobby cards. $200 (Auc. #07)

Dressed to Kill, 1946 (Universal). Sherlock Holmes. Good, one-sheet.
$475 (Auc. #07)

Drums of Love, 1928 (United Artists). Mary Philbin. Fine, on linen, six-sheet.
$2,300 (Auc. #09)

Duck Soup, 1933. Marx Bros. Very good, window card. $1,980 (Auc. #03)
As above, fine, lobby card. $1,100 (Auc. #08)

Duel in the Sun, French, 1947 (Selznick). Joseph Cotten, Gregory Peck, and Jennifer Jones. Very good, on linen, 47 x 63 inches. $110 (Auc. #06)

Dumb-bells in Ermine, 1930 (Warner Bros.). Robert Armstrong and Barbara Kent. Fine, on linen, one-sheet. $460 (Auc. #09)

❦ **E**

Earl Carroll Vanities, 1945 (Republic). Fine, on linen, one-sheet. $350 (Auc. #02)

Earth vs. the Flying Saucers, 1956 (Columbia). Fine, one-sheet. $750 (Auc. #07)

East Is West, 1930 (Universal). Fine, complete set of eight lobby cards.
$400 (Auc. #01)

East of Eden, 1955 (Warner Bros.). James Dean. Fine, one-sheet. $275 (Auc. #03)
As above, fine, one-sheet. $220 (Auc. #08)
As above, good, complete set of eight lobby cards. $600 (Auc. #02)
As above, good, complete set of eight lobby cards. $350 (Auc. #07)

East of the River, 1940 (Warner Bros.). John Garfield. Good, complete set of eight lobby cards. $100 (Auc. #02)

Easter Parade, 1948 (MGM). Fred Astaire and Judy Garland. Very good, on linen, three-sheet. $1,100 (Auc. #02)
As above, fine, one-sheet. $375 (Auc. #02)
As above, fine, one-sheet. $660 (Auc. #03)
As above, very good, half-sheet. $200 (Auc. #02)

Eat and Run, 1924 (Universal). Al Alt. Fine, on linen, one-sheet. $440 (Auc. #08)

The Eleventh Hour, 1923 (Wm. Fox). Very good, on linen, one-sheet.
$633 (Auc. #09)

Enter the Dragon, 1973 (Warner Bros.). Bruce Lee. Fine, three-sheet.
$100 (Auc. #07)

Every Day's a Holiday, 1938 (Paramount). Mae West. Fine, on linen, three-sheet. $1,150 (Auc. #09)
As above, fine, on linen, one-sheet. $2,200 (Auc. #04)
As above, very good, on linen, half-sheet. $2,000 (Auc. #07)

Exodus, 1966 (United Artists). Paul Newman. Very good, on linen, one-sheet.
$192 (Auc. #05)

Eye for Eye, 1918 (Metro). Nazimova. Very good, on linen, one-sheet.
$770 (Auc. #04)

❧ **F**

Fahrenheit 451, French, 1967 (Universal). Julie Christie. Very good, on linen, 47 x 63 inches. $495 (Auc. #06)

The Fair Cheat, 1923. Burton King. Good, on linen, one-sheet. $302.50 (Auc. #06)

The Fallen Idol, 1949. Ralph Richardson. Fine, one-sheet. $275 (Auc. #03)

Fashions of 1934, 1934 (Warner Bros.). Fine, title card. $715 (Auc. #08)

Fast Company, 1929 (Paramount). Very good, on linen, one-sheet.
                                                                    $275 (Auc. #02)

Faust, 1926 (MGM). Fine, unfolded, insert. $1,900 (Auc. #07)

The Fearless Vampire Killers, 1967 (MGM). Jack MacGowran and Sharon Tate. Very good, on linen, three-sheet. $275 (Auc. #06)

Fifth Avenue Girl, 1939 (RKO). Ginger Rogers. Fine, on linen, one-sheet.
                                                                    $600 (Auc. #02)
As above, fine, on linen, one-sheet. $825 (Auc. #04)

Fighting Caravans, 1931 (Paramount). Gary Cooper. Fine, one-sheet.
                                                                    $1,265 (Auc. #09)

The Fighting Code, 1933. Buck Jones. Fine, on linen, three-sheet.
                                                                    $600 (Auc. #02)
As above, very good, one-sheet. $275 (Auc. #02)

The Fighting Fool, 1931. Tim McCoy. Fine, on linen, one-sheet. $990 (Auc. #03)

The Fighting Marine, 1926 (Pathe). Gene Tunney. Fine, on linen, one-sheet.
                                                                    $715 (Auc. #04)

The Fighting 69th, 1940. James Cagney and Pat O'Brien. Fine, on linen, one-sheet. $220 (Auc. #03)

The Fighting Streak, 1922 (Wm. Fox). Tom Mix. Good, on linen, one-sheet.
                                                                    $750 (Auc. #01)

Fire Over England, British, 1937. Laurence Olivier and Vivien Leigh. Very good, 40 x 60 inches. $1,430 (Auc. #06)

First National Pictures, 1924 (First National). N. Talmadge, C. Talmadge, T. Ince, and others. Fine, one-sheet. $385 (Auc. #03)

Five and Ten, 1931 (MGM). Marion Davies. Very good, on linen, one-sheet.
                                                                    $2,200 (Auc. #04)

Five Graves To Cairo, 1943 (Paramount). Franchot Tone and Anne Baxter. Good, on linen, one-sheet. $165 (Auc. #06)

The 5,000 Fingers of Dr. T, 1953 (Columbia). Very good, on linen, three-sheet.
$220 (Auc. #06)
As above, fine, one-sheet.
$375 (Auc. #07)

Flagpole Jitters, 1956 (Columbia). Three Stooges. Very good, one-sheet.
$250 (Auc. #07)

The Flame of New Orleans, 1941 (Universal). Marlene Dietrich. Very good, half-sheet.
$2,500 (Auc. #01)

Flames of the Flesh, 1920 (Wm. Fox). Very good, on linen, three-sheet.
$275 (Auc. #06)

Flash Gordon Conquers the Universe, 1940 (Universal). Buster Crabbe. Fine, on linen, one-sheet.
$8,250 (Auc. #04)

Flash Gordon's Trip to Mars, 1938 (Universal). Buster Crabbe. Fine, on linen, one-sheet (autographed by Crabbe).
$7,820 (Auc. #09)

The Fleet's In, 1942 (Paramount). Dorothy Lamour and William Holden. Very good, on linen, 27 x 41 inches.
$150 (Auc. #07)

Flesh and the Devil, French, reissue ca. 1929 (MGM). Greta Garbo. Very good, on linen, 47 x 63 inches.
$900 (Auc. #01)

Flirting with Love, 1924 (First National). Colleen Moore and Conway Tearle. Very good, on linen, one-sheet.
$1,600 (Auc. #07)

The Fly, 1958 (Fox). Fine, on linen, three-sheet.
$300 (Auc. #02)
As above, very good, one-sheet.
$125 (Auc. #02)

The Flying Deuces, 1939 (MGM). Laurel and Hardy. Fine, on linen, six-sheet.
$4,370 (Auc. #09)

Courtesy of Camden House Auctioneers.

Courtesy of Christie's East.

Flying Discman from Mars, 1950 (Republic). Fair, on linen, one-sheet.
$700 (Auc. #01)

Flying Down To Rio, 1933. Fred Astaire and Ginger Rogers. Very good, title card. $3,740 (Auc. #03)

Flying Tigers, 1942 (Republic). John Wayne. Fine, one-sheet. $2,530 (Auc. #09)

Fog Over Frisco, 1934 (First National). Bette Davis. Very good, window card.
$300 (Auc. #07)

Follow the Fleet, 1936 (RKO). Fred Astaire and Ginger Rogers. Fine, on linen, one-sheet. $7,590 (Auc. #09)

Fool Coverage, 1939. Edgar Kennedy. Very good, on linen, one-sheet.
$165 (Auc. #06)

Fool's First, 1922 (First National). Very good, on linen, one-sheet.
$300 (Auc. #07)

Footlight Serenade, 1942 (Fox). John Payne and Betty Grable. Fine, insert.
$175 (Auc. #02)

For Me and My Gal, 1942 (MGM). Judy Garland. Very good, on linen, one-sheet. $450 (Auc. #02)

For Whom the Bell Tolls, 1943 (Paramount). Gary Cooper and Ingrid Bergman. Fine, on linen, one-sheet. $4,600 (Auc. #09)

Forbidden Planet, 1956 (MGM). Walter Pidgeon. Very good, on linen, three-sheet. $4,400 (Auc. #06)
As above, fine, on linen, one-sheet. $5,500 (Auc. #01)
As above, very good, on linen, one-sheet. $3,250 (Auc. #01)
As above, very good, on linen, one-sheet. $2,420 (Auc. #05)
As above, fine, unfolded, 30 x 40 inches. $2,750 (Auc. #04)
As above, fine, insert. $1,045 (Auc. #08)
As above, fine, unfolded, half-sheet. $1,100 (Auc. #02)
As above, very good, half-sheet. $1,200 (Auc. #07)
As above, very good, complete set of eight lobby cards. $1,500 (Auc. #01)
As above, good, complete set of eight lobby cards. $550 (Auc. #02)
As above, complete set of eight lobby cards. $1,540 (Auc. #05)
As above, Australian, fine, 30 x 13 inches. $400 (Auc. #02)
As above, Argentine, very good, 29 x 43 inches. $325 (Auc. #02)
As above, English, very good, on linen, 40 x 30 inches. $1,320 (Auc. #05)
As above, French, fine, on linen, 47 x 63 inches. $3,080 (Auc. #03)
As above, French, very good, on linen, 47 x 63 inches. $1,650 (Auc. #05)
As above, Italian, very good, fotobusta, 26½ x 19 inches. $175 (Auc. #07)

Forbidden Trails, 1941. Buck Jones. Fine, on linen, one-sheet. $715 (Auc. #03)

A Foreign Affair, 1948 (Paramount). Marlene Dietrich. Very good, one-sheet.
$300 (Auc. #07)
As above, very good, complete set of eight lobby cards. $200 (Auc. #07)

Forever Darling, 1956 (MGM). Lucille Ball and Desi Arnaz. Very good, on linen, three-sheet. $275 (Auc. #06)

Forsaking All Others, 1934 (MGM). Joan Crawford and Clark Gable. Fine, one-sheet. $1,760 (Auc. #04)

Fort Apache, 1948 (RKO). John Wayne and Henry Fonda. Very good, on linen, three-sheet. $450 (Auc. #02)

Found Alive, 1934 (Olympic). Fine, on linen, six-sheet. $935 (Auc. #06)

Four Feathers, 1939 (United Artists). Very good, one-sheet. $900 (Auc. #02)

Four's a Crowd, 1938 (Warner Bros.). Errol Flynn. Very good, on linen, one-sheet. $325 (Auc. #01)

Frankenstein, 1931 (Universal). Boris Karloff. Very good, lobby card (Karloff tortured by fire). $3,250 (Auc. #02)
As above, very good, lobby card (Karloff and the bride). $3,750 (Auc. #02)
As above, very good, lobby card (in the laboratory). $2,500 (Auc. #02)
As above, Argentine, fine, 29 x 44 inches. $8,250 (Auc. #05)
As above, Spanish, fine, unfolded, 27 x 41 inches. $11,000 (Auc. #04)
As above, 1947 reissue, on linen, one-sheet. $7,700 (Auc. #06)

Frankenstein Meets the Wolfman, 1943 (Universal). Lon Chaney. Fine, on linen, three-sheet. $5,500 (Auc. #04)
As above, fine, complete set of eight lobby cards. $3,250 (Auc. #01)

Freaks, ca. 1940s reissue (Dwain Esper/Excelsior). Fine, on linen, three-sheet.
$425 (Auc. #02)
As above, good, three-sheet. $225 (Auc. #07)
As above, good, complete set of eight lobby cards. $225 (Auc. #07)

Friends and Lovers, Swedish, 1931 (RKO). Laurence Olivier. Fine, unfolded, one-sheet. $1,093 (Auc. #09)

From Hand To Mouth, ca. 1920s reissue (Pathe). Harold Lloyd. Good, one-sheet. $400 (Auc. #07)

From Here To Eternity, 1953 (Columbia). Burt Lancaster, Frank Sinatra, and Donna Reed. Very good, insert. $577.50 (Auc. #06)

Fugitives, 1929 (Wm. Fox). Madge Bellamy. Very good, on linen, one-sheet.
$1,093 (Auc. #09)

Funny Face, 1957 (Paramount). Audrey Hepburn and Fred Astaire. Very good, on linen, three-sheet. $550 (Auc. #06)

🕯 G

G Men, 1935 (First National). James Cagney. Fine, on linen, three-sheet.
$18,700 (Auc. #04)
As above, fine, window card. $350 (Auc. #08)

The Galloping Ace, 1924 (Universal). Jack Hoxie. Fine, on linen, one-sheet.
$440 (Auc. #08)

Galloping Gallagher, 1924 (Monogram). Good, on linen, one-sheet.
$330 (Auc. #06)

The Galloping Kid, 1922 (Universal). Hoot Gibson. Good, on linen, one-sheet.
$275 (Auc. #07)

The Gang's All Here, 1943 (Fox). Very good, on linen, three-sheet.
$550 (Auc. #01)

Garden of Allah, 1936. Marlene Dietrich and Charles Boyer. Fine, lobby card.
$220 (Auc. #03)

Gaslight, 1944 (MGM). Charles Boyer, Ingrid Bergman, and Joseph Cotten. Fine, on linen, six-sheet. $2,500 (Auc. #02)
As above, fine, one-sheet. $750 (Auc. #02)
As above, very good, on linen, one-sheet. $500 (Auc. #07)
As above, fine, complete set of eight lobby cards. $450 (Auc. #01)
As above, fine, complete set of eight lobby cards. $300 (Auc. #02)

Gateway, 1938 (20th Century Fox). Don Ameche. Fine, on linen, one-sheet.
$175 (Auc. #02)

The Gay Bride, 1934 (MGM). Carole Lombard. Very good, on linen, one-sheet.
$750 (Auc. #01)

A Gem of a Jam, 1943 (Columbia). Three Stooges. Fine, on linen, one-sheet.
$3,300 (Auc. #04)

The General, 1926 (United Artists). Buster Keaton. Fine, unfolded, half-sheet.
$13,200 (Auc. #04)

General Crack, 1929 (Warner Bros.). John Barrymore. Fine, one-sheet.
$1,540 (Auc. #04)

The General Died at Dawn, 1936 (Paramount). Gary Cooper. Very good, one-sheet. $4,600 (Auc. #09)

Gentleman Jim, 1942 (Warner Bros.). Errol Flynn. Fine, complete set of eight lobby cards. $425 (Auc. #02)

Gentlemen Prefer Blondes, 1953 (Fox). Marilyn Monroe. Fine, unfolded, 40 x 60 inches. $5,500 (Auc. #04)
As above, fine, one-sheet. $700 (Auc. #07)

As above, fine, on linen, one-sheet. $863 (Auc. #09)
As above, very good, insert. $325 (Auc. #02)

The Ghost Breaker, 1922 (Paramount). Wallace Reid. Fine, on linen, one-sheet.
$650 (Auc. #02)
As above, fine, on linen, one-sheet. $1,980 (Auc. #04)

The Ghost City, 1922 (Morgan). Pete Morrison. Fine, one-sheet.
$220 (Auc. #08)

The Ghost of Frankenstein, 1942 (Universal). Lon Chaney and Bela Lugosi.
Good, three-sheet. $7,150 (Auc. #06)
As above, fine, on linen, three-sheet. $5,520 (Auc. #09)
As above, fine, on linen, one-sheet. $10,450 (Auc. #04)

The Ghost of Slumber Mountain, 1919 (World Pictures). Fine, on linen, six-sheet. $5,500 (Auc. #06)

The Ghost Walks, 1934 (Invincible). Fine, on linen, one-sheet. $330 (Auc. #08)

Giant, 1956 (Warner Bros.). James Dean. Very good, on linen, three-sheet.
$475 (Auc. #02)
As above, fine, one-sheet. $220 (Auc. #08)
As above, very good, complete set of eight lobby cards. $600 (Auc. #02)
As above, good, complete set of eight lobby cards. $325 (Auc. #07)

Gigi, 1958 (MGM). Leslie Caron and Maurice Chevalier. Fine, one-sheet.
$100 (Auc. #07)

Gilda, 1946 (Columbia). Rita Hayworth. Fine, on linen, one-sheet.
$7,700 (Auc. #04)
As above, autographed by Glenn Ford, fine, on linen, one-sheet.
$805 (Auc. #09)
As above, French, very good, on linen, 63 x 93 inches. $3,500 (Auc. #01)

The Gilded Lily, 1935 (Paramount). Claudette Colbert. Good, window card.
$440 (Auc. #06)

Girl Crazy, 1943 (MGM). Mickey Rooney and Judy Garland. Al Hirschfeld, artist.
Very good, on linen, one-sheet. $330 (Auc. #06)
As above, fine, one-sheet (other). $275 (Auc. #08)

The Girl from Missouri, 1934 (MGM). Jean Harlow and Lionel Barrymore. Fine,
one-sheet. $6,600 (Auc. #04)
As above, good, window card. $450 (Auc. #07)

The Girl from 10th Avenue, 1935 (First National). Bette Davis. Fine, unfolded,
half-sheet. $17,600 (Auc. #04)
As above, good, on linen, window card. $2,500 (Auc. #07)

The Girl Who Had Everything, 1953 (MGM). Elizabeth Taylor. Very good, on
linen, one-sheet. $165 (Auc. #06)

Girls on Probation, 1937 (other company). Ronald Reagan. Very good, one-sheet. $425 (Auc. #02)

Give Me Your Heart, 1936 (Warner Bros.). Fine, one-sheet. $175 (Auc. #02)

The Glass Key, 1942 (Paramount). Alan Ladd and Veronica Lake. Fine, one-sheet. $2,530 (Auc. #06)
As above, fine, window card. $700 (Auc. #01)
As above, very good, window card. $220 (Auc. #08)
As above, French, fine, on linen, 47 x 63 inches. $325 (Auc. #07)

The Glorious Fool, 1921 (Goldwyn). Very good, on linen, one-sheet.
                                                                $350 (Auc. #07)

Go West, French, 1926. Buster Keaton. Very good, on linen, 47 x 63 inches.
                                                                $2,640 (Auc. #03)

Godless Men, 1920 (Goldwyn). Very good, on linen, one-sheet. $350 (Auc. #07)

Godzilla, 1956 (Toho). Raymond Burr. Fine, three-sheet. $3,300 (Auc. #08)
As above, fine, one-sheet. $1,300 (Auc. #01)
As above, fine, on linen, one-sheet. $1,045 (Auc. #06)
As above, fine, one-sheet. $1,210 (Auc. #08)
As above, very good, inset. $1,000 (Auc. #07)
As above, German, 1955 (Atrium-Film), good, 23 x 33 inches. $550 (Auc. #01)

Going! Going! Gone!, 1918 (Pathe). Harold Lloyd. Very good, on linen, one-sheet. $1,430 (Auc. #04)

Going My Way, 1944 (Paramount). Bing Crosby. Very good, on linen, one-sheet. $225 (Auc. #02)
As above, very good, on linen, one-sheet. $143 (Auc. #05)

Going Up, 1923 (Encore). Fine, on linen, one-sheet. $375 (Auc. #02)

Gold Diggers of 1933, 1933 (Warner Bros.). Fine, one-sheet. $6,600 (Auc. #04)

Golden Boy, 1939 (Columbia). Barbara Stanwyck and William Holden. Fine, window card. $200 (Auc. #02)

Goldfinger, 1964 (United Artists). Sean Connery. Fine, on linen, three-sheet.
                                                                $400 (Auc. #02)
As above, very good, on linen, one-sheet. $275 (Auc. #06)
As above, fine, complete set of eight lobby cards. $330 (Auc. #06)

Gone With the Wind, 1939 (Selznick/MGM). Good, insert. $3,500 (Auc. #02)
As above, mint, complete set of eight lobby cards. $4,180 (Auc. #03)
As above, fine, lobby card (De Havilland). $425 (Auc. #01)
As above, fine, window card. $1,610 (Auc. #09)
As above, French, 1947 reissue, fine, on linen, 47 x 63 inches. $863 (Auc. #09)
As above, 1954 reissue, fine, one-sheet. $375 (Auc. #02)
As above, 1954 reissue, fine, one-sheet. $400 (Auc. #07)

Good Bad Boys, (MGM). Our Gang. Fine, on linen, one-sheet. $880 (Auc. #06)

The Good Old Summer Time, 1913 (Kalem). Fine, on linen, one-sheet.
$460 (Auc. #09)

The Good, the Bad, and the Ugly, French, 1967 (United Artists). Clint Eastwood. Fine, on linen, 47 x 63 inches. $550 (Auc. #06)

Goodbye Mr. Chips, 1939 (MGM). Robert Donat and Greer Garson. Good, one-sheet. $350 (Auc. #07)

The Goose Woman, 1925 (Morgan). Constance Bennett. Fine, on linen, one-sheet. $385 (Auc. #08)

The Gorilla, 1929 (First National). Fine, on linen, one-sheet. $748 (Auc. #09)

The Gossipy Plumber, 1931 (RKO-Pathe). Fine, on linen, one-sheet.
$518 (Auc. #09)

Grand Slam, 1933. Loretta Young and Paul Lukas. Fine, on linen, one-sheet.
$715 (Auc. #03)
As above, fine, one-sheet. $748 (Auc. #09)

Grandma's Boy, ca. 1920s reissue (Pathe). Harold Lloyd. Very good, one-sheet.
$600 (Auc. #07)
As above, good, one-sheet (other). $1,000 (Auc. #07)

The Grapes of Wrath, 1950s reissue (Fox). Henry Fonda. Good, half-sheet.
$175 (Auc. #02)

The Great Dictator, 1940 (United Artists). Charlie Chaplin. Good, on linen, half-sheet. $400 (Auc. #07)

The Great Gamble, 1919 (Pathe). Charles Hutchison. Very good, on linen, one-sheet. $605 (Auc. #04)

Great Guy, 1936 (Grand National). James Gagney. Fine, one-sheet.
$200 (Auc. #02)
As above, very good, on linen, one-sheet. $522.50 (Auc. #06)

The Great K & A Train Robbery, 1926 (Wm. Fox). Tim Mix. Fine, complete set of eight lobby cards. $220 (Auc. #08)

The Great Lie, 1941 (Warner Bros.). Bette Davis. Fair, on linen, one-sheet.
$425 (Auc. #01)

The Great Love, 1918 (Artcraft). D. W. Griffith. Fine, on linen, one-sheet.
$1,320 (Auc. #04)

Great Ocean Catastrophe of Fire at Sea, 1913 (Great Northern Film Co.). Good, on linen, one-sheet. $425 (Auc. #01)

The Great Waltz, 1938 (MGM). Luise Rainer and Fernand Gravet. Fine, one-sheet. $300 (Auc. #07)

The Great Ziegfeld, 1936 (MGM). William Powell and Myrna Loy. Good, one-sheet. $2,500 (Auc. #01)
As above, very good, on linen, title card. $300 (Auc. #07)

The Greatest Show on Earth, 1952 (Paramount). Cecil B. De Mille. Very good, on linen, one-sheet. $175 (Auc. #07)

The Green Eyed Monster, ca. 1920s (Norman). Fine, on linen, one-sheet. $2,000 (Auc. #02)

The Green Hornet, 1974 (Fox). Bruce Lee. Fine, one-sheet. $200 (Auc. #02)

Guilty as Hell, 1932 (Paramount). Edmund Lowe. Fine, one-sheet. $920 (Auc. #09)

Gun Crazy, 1950 (United Artists). Peggy Cummins and John Dall. Good, on linen, one-sheet. $2,500 (Auc. #01)
As above, fine, one-sheet. $2,640 (Auc. #03)
As above, fine, on linen, one-sheet. $3,080 (Auc. #04)
As above, fine, title card. $400 (Auc. #02)

Gunga Din, Italian, 1939 (RKO). Cary Grant and Douglas Fairbanks, Jr. Fine, on linen, 39 x 55 inches. $1,100 (Auc. #06)
As above, 1942 reissue, good, complete set of eight lobby cards. $300 (Auc. #07)

🌿 **H**

Half Marriage, 1929 (RKO). Fine, on linen, one-sheet. $690 (Auc. #09)

Hamlet, German, 1948 (Eagle-Lion). Laurence Olivier. Very good, on linen, 23 x 32 inches. $300 (Auc. #01)

The Hands of Nara, 1922 (Metro). Clara Kimball Young. Fine, on linen, one-sheet. $440 (Auc. #04)

Hangover Square, 1944 (20th Century Fox). Very good, on linen, one-sheet. $275 (Auc. #02)
As above, good, complete set of eight lobby cards. $100 (Auc. #02)

A Hard Day's Night, 1964 (United Artists). The Beatles. Very good, one-sheet. $150 (Auc. #07)
As above, fine, one-sheet. $330 (Auc. #08)
As above, Spanish, very good, 27 x 38 inches. $150 (Auc. #07)

Harvey, 1950. James Stewart. Very good, one-sheet. $660 (Auc. #03)
As above, very good, on linen, one-sheet. $605 (Auc. #06)
As above, very good, window card. $250 (Auc. #07)

The Harvey Girls, 1946 (MGM). Judy Garland. Fine, insert. $175 (Auc. #02)
As above, Italian, very good, on linen, 54 x 77 inches. $275 (Auc. #07)

Haunted Spooks, ca. 1920s reissue (Pathe). Harold Lloyd. Very good, one-sheet. $600 (Auc. #07)

The Hayseed, Danish, 1922 (Wm. Fox). Buster Keaton. Fine, on linen, 22 x 36 inches. $575 (Auc. #09)

Hazards of Helen, 1914 (Kalem). Helen Holmes. Very good, on linen, one-sheet. $920 (Auc. #09)

The Headline Shooter, 1933 (RKO). Fine, on linen, one-sheet. $325 (Auc. #02)

The Headline Woman, 1935 (Mascot). Fine, on linen, one-sheet. $660 (Auc. #04)

The Heart Specialist, 1922 (Realart). Fine, on linen, one-sheet. $715 (Auc. #04)

Heartbreak, 1931 (Fox). Fine, on linen, one-sheet. $225 (Auc. #02)
As above, fine, on linen, one-sheet. $575 (Auc. #09)

Hearts and Spurs, 1925 (Wm. Fox). Buck Jones. Fine, on linen, one-sheet. $2,185 (Auc. #09)

The Heavenly Body, 1943 (MGM). William Powell and Hedy Lamarr. Very good, on linen, three-sheet. $522.50 (Auc. #06)

Hell Bent for Love, 1934 (Columbia). Tim McCoy. Fine, on linen, one-sheet. $800 (Auc. #07)

Hell Harbor, ca. 1937 reissue (Inspirational Pictures). Lupe Velez. Fine, on linen, one-sheet. $575 (Auc. #09)

Hell's Angels, 1930 (United Artists). Jean Harlow. Fine, window card. $2,750 (Auc. #08)
As above, 1937 reissue, fine, on linen, one-sheet. $2,300 (Auc. #09)

Hell's Kitchen, 1939. Ronald Reagan. Very good, on linen, one-sheet. $440 (Auc. #03)

Hello, Frisco, Hello, 1943 (Fox). Fine, unfolded, insert. $150 (Auc. #02)

Her Wild Oat, (First National). Colleen Moore. Fine, on linen, three-sheet. $3,025 (Auc. #06)

Heroes for Sale, 1933 (First National). Richard Barthelmess. Fine, one-sheet. $825 (Auc. #04)

Hi De Ho, 1947. Cab Calloway. Fine, one-sheet. $1,760 (Auc. #03)

High Noon, 1952 (United Artists). Gary Cooper. Fine, one-sheet. $385 (Auc. #03)
As above, very good, insert. $125 (Auc. #07)

High Pressure, 1932 (Warner Bros.). William Powell. Fine, on linen, one-sheet. $690 (Auc. #09)

High Sierra, Spanish, 1941 (Warner Bros.). Humphrey Bogart and Ida Lupino. Good, on linen, 39 x 27 inches. $600 (Auc. #01)

High Society, 1956 (MGM). Bing Crosby, Grace Kelly, and Frank Sinatra. Fine, unfolded, half-sheet. $425 (Auc. #07)

Highlights and Shadows, 1916 (Mutual). Margaret Gibson and William Clifford. Fine, on linen, three-sheet. $550 (Auc. #08)

His Girl Friday, 1939 (Columbia). Cary Grant. Very good, on linen, one-sheet. $1,100 (Auc. #02)

His People, 1925 (Universal). Fine, on linen, one-sheet. $275 (Auc. #08)

Hollywood Party, 1934 (MGM). Laurel and Hardy and others. Good, window card. $550 (Auc. #07)

Hollywood Speaks, 1932 (Columbia). Pat O'Brien. Fine, on linen, one-sheet. $275 (Auc. #08)

The Home Stretch, 1921 (Paramount). Douglas MacLean. Very good, on linen, one-sheet. $150 (Auc. #07)

Hometown Story, 1951 (MGM). Marilyn Monroe. Fine, one-sheet. $150 (Auc. #02)

Hondo, Australian, 1959 (Warner Bros.). John Wayne. Very good, on linen, three-sheet. $250 (Auc. #01)

Honeymoon Limited, 1935 (Monogram). Fine, one-sheet. $748 (Auc. #09)

Hong Kong Nights, 1935. Tom Keene. Very good, on linen, one-sheet. $165 (Auc. #08)

The Honor of His House, 1918 (Paramount). Sessue Hayakawa. Fine, on linen, one-sheet. $990 (Auc. #04)

Hopalong Cassidy, 1935 (Paramount). Fine, on linen, three-sheet. $5,280 (Auc. #04)

Hot Pepper, 1933 (Fox). Fine, on linen, three-sheet. $880 (Auc. #06)

Hot Spot, 1941 (Fox). Betty Grable. Very good, insert. $850 (Auc. #01)

Hotel Imperial, 1939. Isa Miranda and Ray Milland. Fine, on linen, one-sheet. $770 (Auc. #03)

Houdini, 1953 (Paramount). Tony Curtis and Janet Leigh. Good, on linen, three-sheet. $330 (Auc. #06)

The Hound of the Baskervilles, 1959 reissue. Sherlock Holmes. Very good, on linen, one-sheet. $110 (Auc. #06)

The Hour Before the Dawn, 1944 (Paramount). Veronica Lake. Very good, one-sheet. $425 (Auc. #02)

House of Dracula, 1945 (Universal). Lon Chaney. Very good, on linen, one-sheet. $2,090 (Auc. #06)
As above, French, good, on linen, 63 x 47 inches. $600 (Auc. #01)
As above, 1950 reissue (Realart), good, unfolded, half-sheet. $350 (Auc. #02)

The House of Fear, 1945 (Universal). Sherlock Holmes. Fine, on linen, one-sheet. $700 (Auc. #02)

The House of Frankenstein, 1944 (Universal). Boris Karloff. Fine, one-sheet.
$2,530 (Auc. #09)
As above, fair, title lobby card. $650 (Auc. #01)
As above, good, lobby card (the casket). $220 (Auc. #06)

House of Horrors, 1946 (Universal). Good, unfolded, half-sheet.
$325 (Auc. #02)

House of Wax, 1953 (Warner Bros.). Veronica Lake and Fredric March. Very good, on linen, three-sheet. $412 (Auc. #05)
As above, Australian, fine, on linen, three-sheet. $275 (Auc. #01)

House on Haunted Hill, 1958 (Allied Artists). Very good, one-sheet.
$550 (Auc. #07)

How Green Was My Valley, 1941 (Fox). Walter Pidgeon and Maureen O'Hara. Fine, on linen, one-sheet. $550 (Auc. #02)

How to Marry a Millionaire, 1953 (Fox). Marilyn Monroe and Lauren Bacall. Good, on linen, three-sheet. $300 (Auc. #02)
As above, very good, one-sheet. $850 (Auc. #07)
As above, good, insert. $75 (Auc. #07)

Humoresque, 1920 (Paramount). Alma Rubens. Fine, on linen, one-sheet.
$220 (Auc. #08)

The Hunchback of Notre Dame, 1939 (RKO). Charles Laughton. Fine, on linen, three-sheet. $5,280 (Auc. #04)
As above, fine, one-sheet. $2,000 (Auc. #01)

The Hurricane Express. 1932 (Mascot). Fine, on linen, one-sheet.
$2,000 (Auc. #02)

Hurricane Hutch/Episode #5, One Against Many, 1921 (Pathe). Charles Hutchison. Very good, on linen, one-sheet. $325 (Auc. #07)

Hurricane Hutch/Episode #6, At the Risk of His Neck, 1921 (Pathe). Charles Hutchison. Good, on linen, one-sheet. $200 (Auc. #07)

Hurricane Hutch/Episode #7, On a Dangerous Coast, 1921 (Pathe). Charles Hutchison. Very good, on linen, one-sheet. $325 (Auc. #07)

Hurricane Hutch/Episode #11, Hare and Hounds, 1921 (Pathe). Charles Hutchison. Very good, on linen, one-sheet. $250 (Auc. #07)

❦ **I**

I Confess, Australian, 1953 (Warner Bros.). Alfred Hitchcock. Fine, on linen, three-sheet. $250 (Auc. #01)
As above, on linen, one-sheet. $330 (Auc. #05)

I Cover the War, 1937 (Universal). John Wayne. Fine, on linen, one-sheet.
$518 (Auc. #09)

I Love You Again, 1940 (MGM). William Powell and Myrna Loy. Fine, insert.
$250 (Auc. #02)

I Married a Witch, 1942 (United Artists). Fredric March and Veronica Lake.
Very good, on linen, three-sheet. $1,200 (Auc. #02)
As above, fine, half-sheet. $440 (Auc. #08)

I Walked with a Zombie, 1943 (RKO). Very good, on linen, one-sheet.
$715 (Auc. #08)

I Wanted Wings, 1941 (Paramount). William Holden and Veronica Lake. Very
good, on linen, insert. $475 (Auc. #07)

Igloo, 1932 (Universal). Very good, on linen, three-sheet. $1,540 (Auc. #06)

I'll Take Romance, 1938 (Columbia). Grace Moore and Melvyn Douglas. Very
good, on linen, three-sheet. $800 (Auc. #07)

In Love with Love, 1924 (Fox). Fine, on linen, one-sheet. $1,320 (Auc. #04)

In Old Kentucky, 1935 (Fox). Will Rogers. Good, one-sheet. $400 (Auc. #07)

In Old Oklahoma, 1943 (Republic). John Wayne. Good, insert. $150 (Auc. #07)

In the Days of Buffalo Bill/Chapter 5, 1922 (Universal). Very good, on linen,
one-sheet. $805 (Auc. #09)

In the Days of Buffalo Bill/Chapter 9, 1922 (Universal). Fine, on linen, one-
sheet. $805 (Auc. #09)

In the Good Old Summertime, 1949 (MGM). Judy Garland. Very good, complete set of eight lobby cards. $150 (Auc. #02)

The Incredible Shrinking Man, 1957 (Universal). Very good, on linen, one-
sheet. $600 (Auc. #01)
As above, fine, one-sheet. $425 (Auc. #02)
As above, very good, insert. $192.50 (Auc. #06)
As above, fine, complete set of eight lobby cards. $175 (Auc. #01)

The Informer, 1935 (RKO). John Ford. Fine, on linen, three-sheet.
$14,300 (Auc. #04)

Intermezzo, 1939 (United Artists). Leslie Howard and Ingrid Bergman. Very
good, on linen, one-sheet. $935 (Auc. #04)
As above, good, on linen, one-sheet. $385 (Auc. #06)

Invaders from Mars, 1953 (Fox). Very good, on linen, three-sheet.
$950 (Auc. #02)
As above, very good, on linen, one-sheet. $1,500 (Auc. #02)
As above, very good, one-sheet. $1,210 (Auc. #06)
As above, very good, one-sheet with censor stamp. $1,200 (Auc. #07)
As above, fine, on linen, one-sheet. $1,430 (Auc. #08)

The Invasion of the Body Snatchers, 1956 (Allied Artists). Six-sheet.
$880 (Auc. #05)
As above, fine, on linen, three-sheet. $550 (Auc. #01)
As above, fine, on linen, three-sheet. $750 (Auc. #07)
As above, very good, on linen, one-sheet. $935 (Auc. #05)
As above, fine, half-sheet. $2,500 (Auc. #07)

Invasion of the Saucer Men, 1957 (AIP). Fine, on linen, three-sheet.
$2,250 (Auc. #01)
As above, fine, on linen, three-sheet. $3,850 (Auc. #04)
As above, very good, on linen, three-sheet. $1,650 (Auc. #06)
As above, fine, on linen, one-sheet. $2,750 (Auc. #01)
As above, fine, on linen, one-sheet. $1,300 (Auc. #02)
As above, fine, insert. $1,000 (Auc. #07)
As above, fine, half-sheet. $770 (Auc. #05)
As above, very good, unfolded, half-sheet. $1,300 (Auc. #01)
As above, very good, on linen, half-sheet. $750 (Auc. #07)

Invisible Agent, 1942 (Universal). H. G. Wells. Very good, one-sheet.
$375 (Auc. #07)

The Invisible Boy, 1957 (MGM). Fine, on linen, three-sheet. $385 (Auc. #05)

The Invisible Man, 1933 (Universal). H. G. Wells. Fine, folded, window card.
$5,060 (Auc. #04)
As above, very good, window card. $3,520 (Auc. #08)

The Invisible Man Returns, 1940 (Universal). H. G. Wells. Fine, on linen, one-sheet. $4,620 (Auc. #05)
As above, good, complete set of eight lobby cards. $800 (Auc. #01)
As above, French, good, on linen, 31 x 41 inches. $600 (Auc. #01)

The Invisible Ray, 1935 (Universal). Boris Karloff and Bela Lugosi. Good, half-sheet. $14,000 (Auc. #01)

The Invisible Woman, 1940 (Universal). Good, complete set of eight lobby cards. $500 (Auc. #01)

Courtesy of Swann
Galleries, Inc.

Invitation To Happiness, 1939 (Paramount). Irene Dunne and Fred MacMurray. Very good, one-sheet. $150 (Auc. #07)

The Iron Horse, 1924 (Wm. Fox). John Ford. Fine, on linen, one-sheet.
$2,070 (Auc. #09)

Iron Man, 1931 (Universal). Lew Ayres. Fine, on linen, one-sheet.
$1,100 (Auc. #06)

The Iron Mask, 1929. Douglas Fairbanks. Very good, on linen, one-sheet.
$3,450 (Auc. #09)
As above, good, on linen, one-sheet. $2,500 (Auc. #07)
As above, fine, window card. $330 (Auc. #03)

It, 1927 (Paramount). Clara Bow. Fine, title card. $500 (Auc. #07)

It Came from Beneath the Sea, 1955 (Columbia). Very good, on linen, three-sheet. $350 (Auc. #07)
As above, very good, one-sheet. $475 (Auc. #01)
As above, fine, one-sheet. $325 (Auc. #02)
As above, very good, insert. $150 (Auc. #02)
As above, Italian, very good, on linen, 39 x 55 inches. $715 (Auc. #06)

It Came from Outer Space, 1953 (Universal). Fine, on linen, three-sheet.
$800 (Auc. #02)
As above, good, unfolded, half-sheet. $175 (Auc. #02)

It's a Wonderful Life, 1946 (RKO). James Stewart. Fine, on linen, one-sheet.
$8,800 (Auc. #04)
As above, fine, on linen, one-sheet. $6,000 (Auc. #07)
As above, style B, fine, half-sheet. $2,750 (Auc. #06)
As above, fine, complete set of eight lobby cards. $6,000 (Auc. #01)
As above, fine, complete set of eight lobby cards. $1,700 (Auc. #02)
As above, fine, complete set of eight lobby cards. $2,250 (Auc. #07)
As above, fine, title card. $330 (Auc. #03)
As above, British, very good, unfolded, on linen, 28 x 22½ inches. $275 (Auc. #02)
As above, French, very good, on linen, 47 x 63 inches. $2,860 (Auc. #05)

🌿 J

Jailhouse Rock, 1957 (MGM). Elvis Presley. Very good, on linen, three-sheet.
$1,200 (Auc. #07)
As above, fine, one-sheet. $2,000 (Auc. #01)
As above, fine, one-sheet. $950 (Auc. #02)
As above, fine, one-sheet. $1,045 (Auc. #03)
As above, fine, on linen, one-sheet. $1,320 (Auc. #04)
As above, very good, on linen, unfolded, half-sheet. $450 (Auc. #02)
As above, French, very good, 47 x 63 inches. $375 (Auc. #01)
As above, Italian, fine, on linen, 39 x 55 inches. $175 (Auc. #07)

The James Dean Story, 1957 (Warner Bros.). Fine, one-sheet. $110 (Auc. #08)

Jaws of the Jungle, 1936. Fine, on linen, one-sheet. $495 (Auc. #08)

Jezebel, 1938 (Warner Bros.). Bette Davis. Fine, on linen, one-sheet.
$3,300 (Auc. #04)
As above, very good, half-sheet. $6,000 (Auc. #01)

Jimmy the Gent, 1934. James Cagney. Very good, window card.
$1,045 (Auc. #08)
As above, very good, window card. $800 (Auc. #07)

Joan of Arc, 1948 (RKO). Ingrid Bergman. Fine, on linen, one-sheet.
$770 (Auc. #04)
As above, fine, complete set of eight lobby cards. $100 (Auc. #07)

Joe Palooka, Champ, 1946 (Monogram). Joe Louis. Fine, one-sheet.
$440 (Auc. #08)

Johanna Enlists, 1918 (Artcraft). Mary Pickford. Very good, on linen, one-sheet.
$4,180 (Auc. #04)

John Petticoats, 1919. William S. Hart. Fine, half-sheet. $330 (Auc. #08)

Johnny Guitar, 1954 (Republic). Joan Crawford. Very good, on linen, one-sheet.
$220 (Auc. #06)

Juarez, 1939 (Warner Bros.). Paul Muni and Bette Davis. Fine, half-sheet.
$495 (Auc. #08)
As above, fine, title lobby card. $425 (Auc. #01)

Judgment at Nuremberg, 1961 (United Artists). Spencer Tracy, Burt Lancaster, and others. Fine, one-sheet. $100 (Auc. #07)

Juggernaut, 1936. Boris Karloff. Fine, on linen, three-sheet. $550 (Auc. #06)

Juke Girl, 1942 (Warner Bros.). Ann Sheridan and Ronald Reagan. Fine, on linen, three-sheet. $1,210 (Auc. #04)

Julius Caesar, 1953 (MGM). Marlon Brando. Fine, on linen, three-sheet.
$200 (Auc. #07)

Jungle Jim/Chapter 5, The Bridge of Terror, 1936 (Universal). Good, on linen, one-sheet. $1,100 (Auc. #01)

Just Around the Corner, 1938 (Fox). Shirley Temple. Very good, on linen, one-sheet. $550 (Auc. #01)

❦ K

Kelly the Second, 1936 (MGM). Hal Roach. Fine, one-sheet. $1,265 (Auc. #09)

The Key, 1934 (Warner Bros.). William Powell. Fine, window card.
$880 (Auc. #08)

Key Largo, 1948 (Warner Bros.). Humphrey Bogart, Lauren Bacall, and Edward G. Robinson. Very good, on linen, three-sheet.　　　　　$522.50 (Auc. #06)

As above, fair, complete set of eight lobby cards.　　　　　$300 (Auc. #02)

The Kid, 1921 (First National). Charlie Chaplin. Fine, on linen, three-sheet.
　　　　　$6,600 (Auc. #04)

As above, fine, on linen, title card.　　　　　$175 (Auc. #07)

Kill or Cure, 1923 (Pathe). Stan Laurel. Very good, on linen, one-sheet.
　　　　　$4,250 (Auc. #07)

King Creole, 1958 (Paramount). Elvis Presley. Good, three-sheet.
　　　　　$325 (Auc. #07)

King Kong, French, 1933 (RKO). Fay Wray. Fine, on linen, 47 x 63 inches.
　　　　　$7,700 (Auc. #03)
As above, French, fine, on linen, 47 x 63 inches.　　　　　$14,300 (Auc. #04)
As above, French, good, on linen, 47 x 63 inches.　　　　　$7,700 (Auc. #05)
As above, French, fair, on linen, 47 x 63 inches.　　　　　$5,280 (Auc. #05)
As above, Spanish, good, on linen, 29 x 43 inches.　　　　　$715 (Auc. #05)
As above, Argentine, 1940s, very good, on linen, 29 x 44 inches.　$1,500 (Auc. #02)
As above, Belgian, ca. 1950s reissue (Cine-Vog Films), fine,
　on linen, 14 x 19 inches.　　　　　$100 (Auc. #02)
As above, 1952 reissue, good, on linen, one-sheet.　　　　　$247 (Auc. #05)

King of Kings, 1927 (Pathe). Cecil B. De Mille. Very good, on linen, three-sheet.
　　　　　$1,000 (Auc. #01)

King of the Rocket Men, 1949 (Republic). Fine, on linen, one-sheet.
　　　　　$1,400 (Auc. #02)

Courtesy of Hollywood
Poster Art.

Courtesy of Christie's East.

Kings Row, 1942 (Warner Bros.). Ronald Reagan. Good, on linen, one-sheet.
$247.50 (Auc. #06)

Kiss Me Deadly, 1955 (United Artists). Mickey Spillane. Fine, on linen, three-sheet. $400 (Auc. #02)
As above, very good, on linen, three-sheet. $750 (Auc. #07)

Klondike Annie, 1936 (Paramount). Mae West. Very good, jumbo window card.
$550 (Auc. #08)
As above, very good, on linen, window card. $300 (Auc. #07)

The Knickerbocker Buckaroo, 1919. Douglas Fairbanks. Fine, on linen, one-sheet. $770 (Auc. #03)

❦ **L**

La Belle et La Bete, French, 1946 (Paulve). Jean Cocteau. Fine, on linen, 94 x 63 inches. $9,200 (Auc. #09)
As above, French, very good, on linen, 23 x 32 inches. $1,093 (Auc. #09)

La Belle Russe, 1919 (Fox). Theda Bara. Very good, on linen, one-sheet.
$4,620 (Auc. #04)

La Dolce Vita, original Italian, 1960 (Cineriz). Federico Fellini. Fine, on linen, 55 x 78 inches. $4,250 (Auc. #07)

Ladies of the Chorus, 1948 (Columbia). Marilyn Monroe. Very good, one-sheet.
$250 (Auc. #07)
As above, very good, half-sheet. $150 (Auc. #02)

The Lady Eve, 1941 (Paramount). Barbara Stanwyck and Henry Fonda. Fine, on linen, one-sheet. $3,080 (Auc. #04)
As above, fine, on linen, one-sheet. $1,045 (Auc. #06)
As above, French; Boris Grinsson, artist; very good, on linen, 47 x 63 inches.
$1,045 (Auc. #06)

Lady for a Night, 1942 (Republic). John Wayne. Very good, on linen, one-sheet.
$150 (Auc. #07)

Lady from Louisiana, 1941 (Republic). John Wayne. Good, insert.
$100 (Auc. #07)

Lady from Nowhere, 1936 (Columbia). Mary Astor. Fine, on linen, one-sheet.
$403 (Auc. #09)

Lady from Shanghai, 1947 (Columbia). Rita Hayworth and Orson Wells. Fine, on linen, three-sheet. $3,575 (Auc. #06)
As above, fine, on linen, one-sheet. $1,900 (Auc. #02)
As above, very good, on linen, one-sheet. $1,725 (Auc. #09)
As above, good, insert. $425 (Auc. #01)
As above, Spanish, good, on linen, one-sheet. $450 (Auc. #01)

Lady in the Dark, 1943 (Paramount). Ginger Rogers. Fine, on linen, one-sheet. $275 (Auc. #02)

Lady in the Lake, 1947 (MGM). Fine, on linen, one-sheet. $225 (Auc. #02)

Lady of the Pavements, 1929 (United Artists). Very good, on linen, three-sheet. $1,000 (Auc. #01)

The Lady Vanishes, 1938 (Gaumont British). Alfred Hitchcock. Fine, on linen, one-sheet. $9,350 (Auc. #04)

A Lady Without Passport, 1950 (MGM). Hedy Lamarr. Fine, on linen, three-sheet. $150 (Auc. #02)

Lancer Spy, 1937 (Fox). George Sanders and Peter Lorre. Very good, one-sheet. $250 (Auc. #02)

The Last Flight, 1931 (First National). Richard Barthelmess. Fine, on linen, one-sheet. $660 (Auc. #04)

The Last Man, 1932 (Columbia). Charles Bickford. Fine, on linen, one-sheet. $460 (Auc. #09)

The Last of the Mohicans, 1936. Randolph Scott. Very good, on linen, one-sheet. $500 (Auc. #07)
As above, very good, one-sheet. $440 (Auc. #08)

The Last Trail, 1927 (Fox). George O'Brien. Fine, on linen, one-sheet.
$350 (Auc. #02)
As above, fine, on linen, one-sheet. $1,265 (Auc. #09)

Laugh, Clown, Laugh, 1928. Lon Chaney. Fine, window card. $495 (Auc. #08)

Laughing Sinners, 1931 (MGM). Joan Crawford. Fine, on linen, one-sheet.
$1,320 (Auc. #04)

Laura, 1944 (Fox). Very good, on linen, one-sheet. $2,250 (Auc. #02)
As above, fine, half-sheet. $1,210 (Auc. #08)

Let's Fall in Love, 1933 (Columbia). Fine, one-sheet. $605 (Auc. #04)

Let's Go!, 1920s (Truart). Richard Talmadge. Good, on linen, one-sheet.
$247.50 (Auc. #06)

Let's Make Love, 1960 (Fox). Marilyn Monroe. Fine, one-sheet. $125 (Auc. #02)
As above, fine, one-sheet. $225 (Auc. #07)
As above, British, very good, 40 x 30 inches. $325 (Auc. #07)

Life Begins for Andy Hardy, 1941 (MGM). Mickey Rooney and Judy Garland. Fine, on linen, one-sheet. $220 (Auc. #08)
As above, fine, complete set of eight lobby cards. $275 (Auc. #08)

Life in the Raw, 1933 (Fox). George O'Brien. Fine, on linen, one-sheet.
$375 (Auc. #02)

The Life of Emile Zola, 1937 (Warner Bros.). Very good, on linen, one-sheet.
$650 (Auc. #02)

Lifeboat, 1944 (Fox). Alfred Hitchcock. Very good, one-sheet. $1,600 (Auc. #02)
As above, very good, on linen, one-sheet. $1,980 (Auc. #04)
As above, very good, one-sheet. $1,500 (Auc. #07)
As above, fine, insert. $600 (Auc. #02)
As above, fine, insert. $935 (Auc. #03)
As above, very good, half-sheet. $600 (Auc. #02)
As above, good, complete set of eight lobby cards. $550 (Auc. #01)

The Light in the Dark, 1922 (First National). Hope Hampton. Fine, on linen, one-sheet. $715 (Auc. #04)

The Light That Failed, 1939 (Paramount). Ronald Colman. Fine, half-sheet.
$220 (Auc. #08)

Lights of Old Broadway, 1925 (MGM). Marion Davies. Fine, on linen, one-sheet. $1,045 (Auc. #04)

Lillian Russell, 1940 (20th Century Fox). Alice Faye and Henry Fonda. Fine, on linen, three-sheet. $2,070 (Auc. #09)

The Line Up, 1934 (Columbia). William Gargan. Fine, on linen, one-sheet.
$518 (Auc. #09)

The Lion and the Mouse, 1926 (Pathe). Mack Sennett. Fine, on linen, three-sheet. $500 (Auc. #01)

Little Annie Rooney, 1925 (United Artists). Mary Pickford. Very good, on linen, three-sheet. $5,060 (Auc. #09)

The Little Colonel, 1935 (Fox). Shirley Temple and Lionel Barrymore. Fine, on linen, one-sheet. $1,265 (Auc. #09)
As above, fine, half-sheet. $660 (Auc. #08)
As above, French, good, on linen, 47 x 63 inches. $880 (Auc. #06)

Little Foxes, 1941 (RKO). Bette Davis. Fine, on linen, three-sheet.
$3,750 (Auc. #02)

Little Lord Fauntleroy, 1936 (United Artists). Freddie Bartholomew. Fine, on linen, one-sheet. $825 (Auc. #04)

Little Miss Broadway, 1938 (Fox). Shirley Temple. Very good, on linen, one-sheet. $500 (Auc. #02)
As above, fine, on linen, one-sheet. $550 (Auc. #03)
As above, good, on linen, one-sheet. $440 (Auc. #06)

Little Old New York, 1940 (20th Century Fox). Alice Faye and Fred MacMurray. Fine, on linen, one-sheet. $1,610 (Auc. #09)

The Little Princess, 1939 (20th Century Fox). Shirley Temple. Good, on linen, one-sheet. $357.50 (Auc. #06)

Little Women, 1933 (RKO). Katharine Hepburn. Fine, complete set of eight lobby cards. $950 (Auc. #01)

As above, fine, title card. $385 (Auc. #03)

The Littlest Rebel, 1935 (20th Century Fox). Shirley Temple. Fine, unfolded, one-sheet. $1,430 (Auc. #02)

The Lives of a Bengal Lancer, 1934 (Paramount). Gary Cooper. Fine, on linen, one-sheet. $3,500 (Auc. #07)

The Living Dead, 1934 (Alliance). Very good, one-sheet. $375 (Auc. #375)

Lloyd's of London, 1936 (20th Century Fox). Freddie Bartholomew and Madeleine Carroll. Fine, on linen, six-sheet. $7,590 (Auc. #09)

The Loaded Door, 1922 (Universal). Hoot Gibson. Very good, on linen, one-sheet. $375 (Auc. #07)

The Lodger, 1943 (Fox). Fine, three-sheet. $375 (Auc. #01)
As above, fine, on linen, three-sheet. $300 (Auc. #02)

Lolita, 1962 (MGM). James Mason, Shelley Winters, and Peter Sellers. Fine, on linen, six-sheet. $900 (Auc. #01)
As above, fine, one-sheet. $175 (Auc. #02)
As above, fine, one-sheet. $193 (Auc. #08)
As above, French, fine, on linen, 47 x 63 inches. $935 (Auc. #05)

London After Midnight, 1927 (MGM). Lon Chaney. Very good, window card.
                                                        $2,750 (Auc. #06)

The Lone Chance, 1924 (Wm. Fox). John Gilbert. Fine, on linen, one-sheet.
                                                        $1,300 (Auc. #02)
As above, very good, on linen, one-sheet. $475 (Auc. #07)

The Lone Ranger/Episode #13, The Fatal Plunge, 1938 (Republic). Very good, on linen, one-sheet. $1,210 (Auc. #04)

The Lone Ranger Rides Again, 1939 (Republic). Fine, on linen, one-sheet.
                                                        $1,200 (Auc. #02)

The Lonely Trail, 1936 (Republic). John Wayne. Very good, on linen, one-sheet.
                                                        $2,000 (Auc. #01)

The Lost City, 1935 (Krellberg). Very good, on linen, one-sheet. $400 (Auc. #07)
As above, fine, complete set of eight lobby cards. $200 (Auc. #02)
As above, complete set of lobby cards. $200 (Auc. #07)

Lost Horizon, 1936. Ronald Colman. Art by Flagg. Fine, one-sheet.
                                                        $9,900 (Auc. #03)

The Lost Jungle, 1934. Clyde Beatty. Fine, on linen, one-sheet. $275 (Auc. #03)

The Lost Patrol, 1934 (RKO). Boris Karloff. Fine, half-sheet. $385 (Auc. #08)

Courtesy of Hollywood
Poster Art.

The Lost Planet, Conqueror of Space, 1953 (Columbia). Judd Holdren. Good, on linen, three-sheet. $175 (Auc. #01)

The Lost Squadron, 1932 (RKO). Richard Dix. Fine, on linen, one-sheet.
$2,860 (Auc. #04)
As above, very good, on linen, one-sheet. $1,650 (Auc. #06)

The Lottery Man, 1919 (Artcraft). Wallace Reid. Fine, on linen, three-sheet.
$1,045 (Auc. #04)

Love Before Breakfast, 1936 (Universal). Carole Lombard. Fine, on linen, one-sheet. $5,500 (Auc. #04)

Love Letters, 1945 (Paramount). Joseph Cotten. Fine, on linen, one-sheet.
$225 (Auc. #07)

Love Me Tender, 1956 (20th Century Fox). Elvis Presley. Fine, one-sheet.
$400 (Auc. #02)

Love Nest, 1951 (Fox). Marilyn Monroe. Very good, one-sheet. $250 (Auc. #02)

Love or Hate, Norma Talmadge. Fine, on linen, one-sheet. $440 (Auc. #03)

The Loves of Carmen, 1948 (Columbia). Rita Hayworth and Glenn Ford. Very good, one-sheet. $150 (Auc. #07)

The Luck of Jane, 1916 (Vitagraph). Very good, on linen, one-sheet.
$1,035 (Auc. #09)

🌿 **M**

Macao, 1952 (RKO). Robert Mitchum and Jane Russell. Fine, on linen, three-sheet. $700 (Auc. #02)

The Mad Game, 1933 (Fox). Spencer Tracy. Fine, on linen, one-sheet.
$250 (Auc. #02)

Mad Love, 1935 (MGM). Peter Lorre. Very good, window card.
$4,400 (Auc. #08)

The Mad Miss Manton, 1938 (RKO). Barbara Stanwyck and Henry Fonda. Very good, one-sheet. $325 (Auc. #02)

Madison Square Garden, 1932 (Paramount). Very good, on linen, one-sheet.
$350 (Auc. #07)

Magnificent Obsession, 1935 (Universal). Fine, miniwindow card.
$100 (Auc. #02)

Maid of Salem, 1936 (Paramount). Claudette Colbert and Fred MacMurray. Fine, one-sheet. $440 (Auc. #06)

The Maltese Falcon, 1941 (Warner Bros.). Humphrey Bogart. Fine, on linen, three-sheet. $4,950 (Auc. #04)
As above, fine, on linen, one-sheet. $3,750 (Auc. #02)
As above, fine, on linen, one-sheet. $3,430 (Auc. #09)
As above, insert. $2,860 (Auc. #05)
As above, fine, lobby card (Bogart—Astor). $1,600 (Auc. #01)

Mammy, 1930 (Warner Bros.). Al Jolson. Good, unfolded, window card.
$770 (Auc. #04)

Man About Town, 1940 (Paramount). Jack Benny, Dorothy Lamour, and Edward Arnold. Fine, on linen, one-sheet. $1,265 (Auc. #09)

The Man from Arizona, 1932 (Monogram). Rex Bell. Fine, on linen, three-sheet. $1,200 (Auc. #07)

The Man from Monterey, 1933 (Vitagraph). John Wayne. Fine, on linen, one-sheet. $3,680 (Auc. #09)

The Man from Planet X, 1951 (United Artists). Good, on linen, one-sheet.
$2,640 (Auc. #05)
As above, very good, on linen, one-sheet. $2,000 (Auc. #07)
As above, very good, on linen, door panel, 20 x 60 inches. $770 (Auc. #06)
As above, insert. $990 (Auc. #05)

The Man Who Knew Too Much, 1956 (Paramount). James Stewart and Doris Day. Fine, complete set of eight lobby cards. $150 (Auc. #02)

The Man Who Lived Again, 1936 (Gaumont British). Boris Karloff. Fine, one-sheet. $935 (Auc. #04)

The Man Who Married His Own Wife, 1922 (Universal). Frank Mayo. Fine, on linen, one-sheet. $460 (Auc. #09)

The Man Who Reclaimed His Head, 1934 (Universal). Claude Rains. Fine, complete set of eight lobby cards. $900 (Auc. #01)

Courtesy of Hollywood
Poster Art.

Courtesy of Odyssey
Auctions.

The Man Who Won, 1923 (Wm. Fox). Dustin Farnum. Fine, on linen, one-sheet. $750 (Auc. #02)

The Man with Nine Lives, 1940. Boris Karloff. Fine, one-sheet. $440 (Auc. #03)

Man's Castle, 1933 (Columbia). Spencer Tracy and Loretta Young. Very good, on linen, half-sheet. $500 (Auc. #07)

Mandrake, the Magician, 1939 (Columbia). Fine, on linen, one-sheet.
$1,320 (Auc. #04)

Manhattan Melodrama, 1934 (MGM). Clark Gable, William Powell, and Myrna Loy. Fine, unfolded, insert. $2,420 (Auc. #04)
As above, fine, title card. $715 (Auc. #03)
As above, good, window card. $500 (Auc. #07)

Mantrap, 1926 (Paramount). Clara Bow. Fine, one-sheet. $800 (Auc. #01)

Marihuana, 1936. Fine, window card. $440 (Auc. #08)

The Mark of Zorro, 1940 (Fox). Tyrone Power. Very good, window card.
$800 (Auc. #01)

Mary of Scotland, 1936 (RKO). Katharine Hepburn. Very good, on linen, 24 x 30 inches. $400 (Auc. #01)

The Mask of Fu Manchu, Belgian, 1932 (MGM). Boris Karloff. Very good, on linen, 24 x 33 inches. $3,190 (Auc. #06)

The Mask of Lopez, 1924 (Monogram). Fred Thomson. Good, on linen, one-sheet. $935 (Auc. #06)

Masked Emotions, 1929 (Fox). George O'Brien. Fine, on linen, one-sheet.
$605 (Auc. #04)

The Maze, 1953 (Allied Artists). Very good, three-sheet. $200 (Auc. #07)

Meet John Doe, 1941 (Warner Bros.). Gary Cooper and Barbara Stanwyck. Very good, on linen, one-sheet. $800 (Auc. #02)

Melodies of Spring, 1934. Fine, on linen, one-sheet. $330 (Auc. #08)

Men in White, 1934. Clark Gable and Myrna Loy. Fine, one-sheet.
$880 (Auc. #03)
As above, very good, insert. $550 (Auc. #06)

Merry Go Round, 1922. Mary Philbin. Fine, one-sheet. $1,430 (Auc. #03)

The Merry Widow, 1925 (Metro-Goldwyn). Very good, on linen, three-sheet.
$3,910 (Auc. #09)

Merry Xmas and a Happy New Year, 1934 (Fox). Promotional. Fine, unfolded, one-sheet. $3,300 (Auc. #04)

Metropolis, 1927 (Paramount). Fritz Lang. Fine, unfolded, window card.
$26,400 (Auc. #04)

Mickey's Stampede, 1931 (RKO). Mickey McGuire. Fine, on linen, one-sheet.
$935 (Auc. #04)

Midnight, 1934 (Universal). Humphrey Bogart. Very good, window card.
$825 (Auc. #08)

Midnight, 1939 (Paramount). Claudette Colbert and Don Ameche. Very good, one-sheet. $660 (Auc. #08)

The Midnight Man/9th Episode, A Society Hold-Up, 1919 (Universal). James Corbett. Very good, on linen, three-sheet. $1,650 (Auc. #04)

The Midshipman, 1925 (MGM). Ramon Novarro. Very good, on linen, one-sheet. $805 (Auc. #09)

Mighty Joe Young, 1949 (RKO). Very good, on linen, one-sheet. $770 (Auc. #06)
As above, fine, on linen, one-sheet. $825 (Auc. #08)

Mighty Like a Rose, 1923 (First National). Edwin Carewe. Fine, on linen, one-sheet. $250 (Auc. #01)

Mighty Like a Moose, 1926 (Pathe). Hal Roach. Fine, on linen, three-sheet.
$650 (Auc. #01)
As above, fine, on linen, three-sheet. $475 (Auc. #02)

Mildred Pierce, 1945 (Warner Bros.). Joan Crawford. Very good, on linen, three-sheet. $880 (Auc. #06)

The Million Dollar Legs, 1932 (Paramount). W. C. Fields, Fine, on linen, one-sheet. $1,035 (Auc. #05)

Ministry of Fear, 1944 (Paramount). Very good, on linen, one-sheet.
$357 (Auc. #05)

The Miracle Man, 1919 (Paramount). Very good, on linen, window card.
$325 (Auc. #07)

The Miracle Man, 1932 (Paramount). Sylvia Sidney and Chester Morris. Fine, one-sheet. $2,750 (Auc. #04)

The Miracle of Manhattan, 1921 (Selznick). Elaine Hammerstein. Very good, on linen, one-sheet. $770 (Auc. #04)

The Miracle of Morgan's Creek, 1943. Betty Hutton and Eddie Bracken. Fine, on linen, one-sheet. $550 (Auc. #03)

Miracle on 34th Street, 1947 (Fox). Maureen O'Hara and John Payne. Fine, on linen, six-sheet. $1,725 (Auc. #09)
As above, fine, on linen, three-sheet. $1,650 (Auc. #04)
As above, very good, on linen, one-sheet. $700 (Auc. #02)
As above, very good, insert. $200 (Auc. #07)
As above, fine, title card. $248 (Auc. #03)

The Miracle Rider, 1935 (Mascot). Tom Mix. Fair, on linen, one-sheet.
$300 (Auc. #01)
As above, same copy, different image, good, one-sheet. $300 (Auc. #01)

The Misfits, 1961 (United Artists). Clark Gable and Marilyn Monroe. Very good, on linen, three-sheet. $385 (Auc. #06)

Mrs. Miniver, 1942 (MGM). Greer Garson and Walter Pidgeon. Very good, complete set of eight lobby cards. $300 (Auc. #02)

Mississippi, 1935 (Paramount). W. C. Fields and Bing Crosby. Fine, window card. $220 (Auc. #08)

Mistaken Identity, 1919 (Triangle). Anita King. Fine, on linen, one-sheet.
$375 (Auc. #02)

Mr. and Mrs. North, 1941 (MGM). Gracie Allen. Good, one-sheet.
$275 (Auc. #07)

Mr. and Mrs. Smith, 1940 (RKO). Alfred Hitchcock. Very good, one-sheet.
$250 (Auc. #02)

Mr. Deeds Goes To Town, 1936 (Columbia). Gary Cooper. Very good, on linen, six-sheet. $2,000 (Auc. #02)
As above, good, half-sheet. $550 (Auc. #02)

Mr. District Attorney, 1941 (Republic). Peter Lorre. Very good, one-sheet.
$250 (Auc. #07)

Mr. Lucky, 1943 (RKO). Cary Grant. Fine, one-sheet. $660 (Auc. #04)
As above, very good, on linen, one-sheet. $660 (Auc. #06)

Mr. Moto's Gamble, 1938 (Fox). Peter Lorre. Good, one-sheet. $550 (Auc. #07)

Mr. Robinson Crusoe, 1932 (United Artists). Very good, on linen, one-sheet.
$247.50 (Auc. #06)

Mr. Skitch, 1933 (Fox). Will Rogers. Very good, on linen, three-sheet.
$500 (Auc. #02)

Mr. Smith Goes To Washington, 1939 (Columbia). James Stewart. Good, on
linen, three-sheet. $3,250 (Auc. #07)
As above, good, one-sheet. $2,000 (Auc. #01)
As above, very good, on linen, one-sheet. $6,050 (Auc. #04)
As above, very good, insert. $950 (Auc. #01)
As above, fine, title card. $990 (Auc. #03)
As above, fine, restored, window card. $605 (Auc. #03)

Mr. Wong, Detective, 1938 (Monogram). Very good, on linen, one-sheet.
$500 (Auc. #01)
As above, fine, on linen, one-sheet. $1,265 (Auc. #09)

The Mole People, 1956 (Universal). Very good, on linen, one-sheet.
$400 (Auc. #02)

Monsieur Beaucaire, 1924 (Paramount). Rudolph Valentino. Fine, on linen,
one-sheet. $4,620 (Auc. #04)
As above, fine, title card. $880 (Auc. #03)

Monsieur Verdoux, 1947 (United Artists). Charlie Chaplin. Fine, on linen, one-
sheet. $250 (Auc. #01)

Moon Over Miami, 1941 (Fox). Betty Grable. Fine, one-sheet. $6,440 (Auc. #09)
As above, very good, insert. $4,000 (Auc. #01)
As above, fine, jumbo window card. $1,100 (Auc. #04)

Moonlight and Noses, 1920s (Pathe). Hal Roach. Very good, on linen, three-
sheet. $385 (Auc. #06)

Morocco, 1930 (Paramount). Fine, jumbo lobby card. $3,520 (Auc. #04)

Mothra, 1962 (Columbia). Fine, one-sheet. $325 (Auc. #07)

Moulin Rouge, Danish, 1933 (20th Century Fox). Constance Bennett. Fine, on
linen, 24 x 33 inches. $1,540 (Auc. #06)

The Mountain Woman, 1921 (Fox). Pearl White. Fine, on linen, one-sheet.
$1,045 (Auc. #04)

The Mummy's Curse, 1944 (Universal). Lon Chaney. Very good, on linen, one-
sheet. $1,800 (Auc. #07)

The Mummy's Ghost, 1944 (Universal). Lon Chaney. Fine, one-sheet.
$2,760 (Auc. #09)
As above, fair, half-sheet. $1,100 (Auc. #05)

The Mummy's Tomb, 1942 (Universal). Lon Chaney. Fine, complete set of eight lobby cards. $3,000 (Auc. #01)
As above, very good, window card. $450 (Auc. #01)

Murder by Television, 1935 (Cameo). Bela Lugosi. Fine, on linen, one-sheet.
$5,280 (Auc. #04)

Murder, My Sweet, 1944 (RKO). Dick Powell. Fine, on linen, one-sheet.
$1,760 (Auc. #04)
As above, very good, on linen, half-sheet. $400 (Auc. #02)

Murder Over New York, 1940 (20th Century Fox). Charlie Chan. Very good, one-sheet. $350 (Auc. #02)

Mutiny on the Bounty, 1935 (MGM). Charles Laughton and Clark Gable. Fine, on linen, one-sheet. $1,600 (Auc. #01)

My Baby, 1912 (Biograph). Mary Pickford and Lionel Barrymore. Fine, on linen, three-sheet. $3,300 (Auc. #08)

My Darling Clementine, 1946 (20th Century Fox). Henry Fonda. Very good, on linen, one-sheet. $1,210 (Auc. #04)
As above, fine, on linen, one-sheet. $935 (Auc. #08)

My Fair Lady, Italian, 1964 (Warner Bros.). Audrey Hepburn and Rex Harrison. Bob Peak, artist. Very good, on linen, 39 x 55 inches. $385 (Auc. #06)

Courtesy of
Hollywood Poster
Art.

My Favorite Wife, 1940 (RKO). Cary Grant and Irene Dunne. Fine, one-sheet.
$748 (Auc. #09)

My Gal Sal, 1942 (Fox). Rita Hayworth. Fine, unfolded, insert. $225 (Auc. #02)

My Little Chickadee, 1940 (Universal). Mae West and W. C. Fields. Very good,
on linen, three-sheet. $2,750 (Auc. #02)
Fine, on linen, one-sheet. $5,500 (Auc. #01)

My Man Godfrey, 1936 (Universal). William Powell and Carole Lombard. Fine,
one-sheet. $7,150 (Auc. #02)
As above, mint, lobby card. $2,200 (Auc. #03)
As above, Swedish, fine, unfolded, on linen, one-sheet. $2,760 (Auc. #09)

My Weakness, 1933 (Fox). Lillian Harvey and Lew Ayres. Fine, on linen, one-
sheet. $1,610 (Auc. #09)

My Woman, 1933 (Columbia). Helen Twelvetrees. Fine, on linen, three-sheet.
$1,100 (Auc.. #09)

The Mysterious Dr. Fu Manchu, 1929 (Paramount). Fine, one-sheet.
$1,320 (Auc. #09)

Mysterious Mr. Wong, 1935 (Monogram). Bela Lugosi. Fine, on linen, three-
sheet. $1,800 (Auc. #01)

The Mysterious Pilot, 1937 (Columbia). Very good, one-sheet. $250 (Auc. #07)

❦ **N**

Nancy Drew . . . Detective, 1938 (Warner Bros.). Very good, one-sheet.
$400 (Auc. #02)

National Velvet, 1944 (MGM). Mickey Rooney and Elizabeth Taylor. Fine, one-
sheet. $300 (Auc. #07)

Navy Blues, 1930. William Haines. Fine, one-sheet. $1,980 (Auc. #03)

Nevada, 1935 (Paramount). Buster Crabbe. Fine, on linen, one-sheet.
$770 (Auc. #04)

Never Too Late, 1935 (Reliable Pictures). Richard Talmadge. Very good, on
linen, one-sheet. $125 (Auc. #07)

New Adventures of Batman and Robin, 1949 (Columbia). Fine, one-sheet.
$600 (Auc. #02)

The New Frontier, 1934 (Republic). John Wayne. Fine, on linen, three-sheet.
$4,125 (Auc. #06)
As above, fine, on linen, one-sheet. $4,600 (Auc. #09)

New York, New York, 1976 (United Artists). Liza Minnelli and Robert De Niro.
Very good, on linen, one-sheet. $110 (Auc. #05)

Courtesy of Christie's East.

Courtesy of Hollywood
Poster Art.

Next Aisle Over, ca. 1922 (Pathe). Harold Lloyd. Fine, on linen, one-sheet.
$863 (Auc. #09)

Niagara, 1953 (Fox). Marilyn Monroe. Good, on linen, three-sheet.
$1,600 (Auc. #01)
As above, very good, on linen, one-sheet. $800 (Auc. #01)
As above, very good, on linen, one-sheet. $825 (Auc. #06)
As above, fine, on linen, one-sheet. $880 (Auc. #08)
As above, very good, on linen, one-sheet. $748 (Auc. #09)
As above, fine, insert. $440 (Auc. #03)
As above, fine and good, complete set of eight lobby cards. $650 (Auc. #01)
As above, very good, window card. $200 (Auc. #07)

A Night at the Opera, 1935 (MGM). Marx Brothers. Very good, on linen, one-sheet. $7,700 (Auc. #04)
As above, Spanish, 1935 (MGM), good, on linen, three-sheet. $700 (Auc. #01)
As above, 1948 reissue (MGM), fine, one-sheet. $300 (Auc. #02)
As above, Danish, 1954–55 reissue, fine, on linen, 24 x 33 inches. $150 (Auc. #02)

Night Has 1000 Eyes, 1948 (Paramount). Edward G. Robinson. Good, on linen, one-sheet. $632.50 (Auc. #06)

Night Monster, 1942 (Universal). Bela Lugosi. Fine, one-sheet. $1,210 (Auc. #04)

A Night to Remember, British, 1958 (Rank). Very good, on linen, three-sheet. $600 (Auc. #01)
As above, fine, on linen, three-sheet. $495 (Auc. #08)

1984, 1956 (Columbia). Fine, one-sheet. $200 (Auc. #07)

Ninotchka, 1939 (MGM). Greta Garbo. Fine, on linen, three-sheet.
                                                             $1,610 (Auc. #09)
As above, Australian, good, 27 x 40 inches. $300 (Auc. #07)

North by Northwest, 1959 (MGM). Cary Grant. Very good, on linen, one-sheet.
                                                             $220 (Auc. #06)

Not of This Earth, 1957 (Allied Artists). Very good, one-sheet. $900 (Auc. #02)
As above, fine, on linen, one-sheet. $460 (Auc. #09)

Nothing But the Truth, 1941 (Paramount). Bob Hope. Very good, one-sheet.
                                                             $200 (Auc. #07)

Nothing Sacred, 1937 (United Artists). Carole Lombard and Fredric March.
Fine, title card. $165 (Auc. #08)
As above, fine, window card. $275 (Auc. #02)

Notorious, 1946 (RKO). Cary Grant and Ingrid Bergman. Very good, on linen,
one-sheet. $1,800 (Auc. #02)
As above, fine, on linen, one-sheet. $1,980 (Auc. #04)

Now and Forever, 1934 (Paramount). Gary Cooper, Carole Lombard, and
Shirley Temple. Fine, one-sheet. $3,080 (Auc. #08)

Now We're in the Air, 1927 (Paramount). Wallace Beery and Raymond Hatton.
Fine, complete set of eight lobby cards. $550 (Auc. #08)

Now, Voyager, 1942 (Warner Bros.). Bette Davis. Fine, complete set of eight
lobby cards. $1,100 (Auc. #01)
As above, fine, complete set of eight lobby cards. $650 (Auc. #02)

Nursing a Viper, 1909 (Biograph). Fine, on linen, one-sheet. $1,100 (Auc. #04)

❦ O

Of Mice and Men, 1940 (United Artists). Burgess Meredith. Fine, on linen, one-
sheet. $518 (Auc. #09)
As above, fine, window card. $500 (Auc. #02)
As above, French, very good, 47 x 63 inches. $150 (Auc. #07)

Officer 666, 1920 (Goldwyn). Tom Moore. Very good, on linen, one-sheet.
                                                             $200 (Auc. #07)

Oh, For a Man!, 1930 (Fox). Jeanette MacDonald. Fine, on linen, one-sheet.
                                                             $1,760 (Auc. #04)

The Oklahoma Kid, 1939 (Warner Bros.). James Cagney. Fine, on linen, one-
sheet. $1,980 (Auc. #04)
As above, fine, title lobby card. $550 (Auc. #01)
As above, very good, on linen, window card. $300 (Auc. #07)

Old Acquaintance, 1943 (Warner Bros.). Bette Davis. Very good, one-sheet.
$125 (Auc. #02)

The Old Dark House, 1932 (Universal.) Fine, complete set of eight lobby cards.
$12,100 (Auc. #04)

The Old Fashioned Way, 1934 (Paramount). W. C. Fields. Fine, window card.
$550 (Auc. #08)

The Old Maid, 1939 (Warner Bros.). Bette Davis. Fine, on linen, one-sheet.
$650 (Auc. #01)

Oliver, 1968 (Columbia). Very good, one-sheet. $50 (Auc. #07)

Olsen's Big Moment, 1933 (Fox). Fine, on linen, one-sheet. $633 (Auc. #09)

On a Match, 1932 (First National). Bette Davis. Fine, one-sheet.
$3,080 (Auc. #04)

On the High Seas, 1922 (Paramount). Dorothy Dalton and Jack Holt. Fine, on linen, one-sheet. $220 (Auc. #08)

On the Waterfront, 1954 (Columbia). Marlon Brando. Fine, on linen, three-sheet. $700 (Auc. #02)
As above, very good, on linen, three-sheet. $660 (Auc. #06)
As above, on linen, one-sheet. $495 (Auc. #05)
As above, good, one-sheet. $275 (Auc. #07)
As above, very good, one-sheet. $385 (Auc. #08)

One Good Turn, 1931 (MGM). Laurel and Hardy. Very good, on linen, one-sheet. $2,500 (Auc. #02)

Courtesy of Swann
Galleries, Inc.

One Mile from Heaven, 1937 (20th Century Fox). Claire Trevor. Fine, on linen, one-sheet. $403 (Auc. #09)

One Million B.C., 1940 (United Artists). Hal Roach. Fine, on linen, three-sheet. $2,090 (Auc. #06)

One Night in Lisbon, 1949 (Paramount). Fred MacMurray. Very good, on linen, three-sheet. $325 (Auc. #02)

One Touch of Venus, 1948 (Universal). Ava Gardner. Good, one-sheet. $200 (Auc. #07)

Only Yesterday, 1933 (Universal). Margaret Sullivan. Fine, on linen, one-sheet. $1,100 (Auc. #04)

Operator 13, 1934 (MGM). Gary Cooper and Marion Davies. Very good, window card. $440 (Auc. #08)

Our American Boys in the European War, 1916 (Triangle). Fine, on linen, three-sheet. $2,530 (Auc. #09)

Our Blushing Brides, 1930 (MGM). Joan Crawford. Fine, on linen, one-sheet. $990 (Auc. #04)

Our Daily Bread, 1934 (United Artists). Good, one-sheet. $550 (Auc. #02)
As above, fine, on linen, one-sheet. $1,035 (Auc. #09)

Our Dancing Daughters, 1928 (MGM). Joan Crawford. Fine, title card. $440 (Auc. #08)

Our Gang, 1922 (Pathe). The Rascals. Very good, on linen, one-sheet. $3,250 (Auc. #02)

Courtesy of Odyssey Auctions.

Our Little Girl, 1935 (Fox). Shirley Temple. Fine, one-sheet. $990 (Auc. #08)

Out of the Past, 1947 (RKO). Robert Mitchum. Fine, one-sheet.
$2,250 (Auc. #02)
As above, fine, one-sheet. $3,300 (Auc. #04)
As above, good, on linen, half-sheet. $900 (Auc. #02)
As above, 1953 reissue, autographed by four stars, fine,
on linen, one-sheet. $978 (Auc. #09)

The Outlaw, 1943 (RKO). Jane Russell. Good, one-sheet. $400 (Auc. #07)
As above, Australian, fine, on linen, 13 x 30 inches. $880 (Auc. #06)

Over the Top, 1918 (Vitagraph). Fine, on linen, one-sheet. $825 (Auc. #04)

The Ox-Bow Incident, 1942 (20th Century Fox). Fine, on linen, one-sheet.
$385 (Auc. #08)

❦ P

Pack Up Your Troubles, Swedish, 1932 (MGM). Laurel and Hardy. Fine, rolled,
one-sheet. $880 (Auc. #08)

Paddy O'Day, 1936 (20th Century Fox). Jane Withers. Fine, one-sheet.
$403 (Auc. #09)

The Painted Lady, 1924 (Fox). George O'Brien. Fine, on linen, one-sheet.
$5,720 (Auc. #04)

The Painted Veil, 1934 (MGM). Greta Garbo. Fine, on linen, six-sheet.
$11,000 (Auc. #04)
As above, fine, window card. $550 (Auc. #08)

The Palm Beach Story, 1942 (Paramount). Claudette Colbert. Fine, on linen,
insert. $440 (Auc. #08)

Paradise Canyon, 1935 (Monogram). John Wayne. Fine, on linen, one-sheet.
$1,870 (Auc. #04)
As above, fine, one-sheet (other). $4,400 (Auc. #04)

Parnell, 1937 (MGM). Clark Gable. Fine, insert. $325 (Auc. #01)

A Passport To Hell, 1932 (Fox). Paul Lukas and Elissa Landi. Fine, on linen, one-
sheet. $518 (Auc. #09)

The Patriot, 1928 (Paramount). Emil Jannings. Fine, on linen, one-sheet.
$660 (Auc. #08)

Peacock Alley, 1922 (Metro). Mae Murray. Very good, one-sheet.
$750 (Auc. #07)

The Pearl of Death, 1944 (Universal). Sherlock Holmes. Very good, half-sheet.
$375 (Auc. #02)

The Penguin Pool Murder, 1932 (RKO). Edna May Oliver. Fine, on linen, one-sheet. $1,610 (Auc. #09)

Penny Serenade, 1941 (Columbia). Cary Grant. Fine, on linen, one-sheet.
    $600 (Auc. #02)
As above, fine, on linen, one-sheet. $440 (Auc. #03)
As above, fine, complete set of eight lobby cards. $450 (Auc. #01)

The Perils of Pauline, 1914 (Eclectic). Fine, on linen, one-sheet.
    $6,600 (Auc. #04)

Personal Property, 1937. Jean Harlow and Robert Taylor. Very good, on linen, one-sheet. $748 (Auc. #09)
As above, fine, insert. $550 (Auc. #08)
As above, fine, title card. $715 (Auc. #03)

The Phantom Creeps, 1939 (Universal). Bela Lugosi. Very good, on linen, one-sheet. $1,840 (Auc. #09)

The Phantom Empire, 1935 (Mascot). Gene Autry. Very good, three-sheet.
    $1,870 (Auc. #04)

Phantom Lady, 1943 (Universal). Franchot Tone. Fine, one-sheet.
    $275 (Auc. #08)

Phantom of the Opera, 1925 (Universal). Lon Chaney. Fine, on linen, one-sheet. $24,150 (Auc. #09)
As above, very good, lobby card. $3,500 (Auc. #02)

Phantom of the Opera, 1943 (Universal). Nelson Eddy. Good, one-sheet.
    $250 (Auc. #01)
As above, fine, complete set of eight lobby cards. $750 (Auc. #01)

The Philadelphia Story, 1940 (MGM). Cary Grant, Katharine Hepburn, and James Stewart. Very good, on linen, three-sheet. $2,000 (Auc. #01)
As above, very good, title card. $750 (Auc. #02)
As above, 1955 reissue, very good, insert. $247.50 (Auc. #06)

Pick and Shovel, 1923 (Pathe). Stan Laurel. Very good, on linen, one-sheet.
    $700 (Auc. #07)

Picking on George, 1927 (Stern Bros.). Fine, on linen, three-sheet.
    $250 (Auc. #02)

Picking Peaches, 1924 (Pathe). Mack Sennett. Fine, on linen, one-sheet.
    $1,760 (Auc. #04)

The Pied Piper, 1942 (20th Century Fox). Very good, on linen, one-sheet.
    $300 (Auc. #07)

Pillow Talk, 1959 (Universal). Rock Hudson and Doris Day. Fine, three-sheet.
    $175 (Auc. #07)

The Pirate, 1948 (MGM). Judy Garland and Gene Kelly. Very good, on linen, three-sheet. $330 (Auc. #06)

Courtesy of
Christie's East.

The Pittsburgh Kid, 1941 (Republic). Fine, on linen, one-sheet. $345 (Auc. #09)

A Place in the Sun, 1951 (Paramount). Montgomery Clift, Elizabeth Taylor, and
Shelley Winters. Very good, on linen, one-sheet. $425 (Auc. #02)
As above, very good, on linen, one-sheet. $300 (Auc. #07)

Plan 9 from Outer Space, 1958 (DCA). Bela Lugosi. Fine, on linen, one-sheet.
$1,500 (Auc. #02)

Pleasure Cruise, 1933 (Fox). Fine, on linen, one-sheet. $518 (Auc. #09)

The Plumber, 1923 (Pathe). Mack Sennett. Good, one-sheet. $275 (Auc. #01)

Poppy, 1936 (Paramount). W. C. Fields. Good, one-sheet. $1,100 (Auc. #05)

Possessed, Belgian. Joan Crawford and Clark Gable. Fine, on linen, 24 x 32 inches.
$1,320 (Auc. #03)

The Postman Always Rings Twice, 1946 (MGM). Lana Turner and John
Garfield. Fine, on linen, one-sheet. $2,750 (Auc. #04)
As above, fine, on linen, one-sheet. $1,980 (Auc. #03)
As above, fine, insert. $550 (Auc. #01)

The Power and the Glory, 1933 (Fox). Spencer Tracy and Colleen Moore. Fine,
window card. $605 (Auc. #08)

The Prescott Kid, 1934 (Columbia). Tim McCoy. Very good, on linen, one-
sheet. $863 (Auc. #09)

Presenting Lily Mars, 1943 (MGM). Judy Garland and Van Heflin. Good, one-
sheet. $200 (Auc. #01)

Pride and Prejudice, 1940 (MGM). Laurence Olivier. Fine, complete set of eight
lobby cards. $450 (Auc. #01)

The Pride of New York, 1917 (Fox). George Walsh. Fine, on linen, one-sheet.
$660 (Auc. #04)

The Pride of the Yankees, 1949 reissue (RKO). Gary Cooper. Fine, on linen, one-sheet.
$690 (Auc. #09)

The Primal Law, 1921 (Wm. Fox). Dustin Farnum. Fine, on linen, one-sheet.
$1,150 (Auc. #09)

Primrose Path, 1940 (RKO). Ginger Rogers. Fine, on linen, one-sheet.
$175 (Auc. #07)

The Prince and the Pauper, 1937 (Warner Bros.). Errol Flynn. Good, on linen, three-sheet.
$750 (Auc. #01)
As above, good, on linen, one-sheet.
$440 (Auc. #06)
As above, Italian, 1952 reissue, fine, on linen, 39 x 55 inches. $1,300 (Auc. #07)

The Prince and the Showgirl, 1957 (Warner Bros.). Marilyn Monroe and Laurence Olivier. Fine, on linen, three-sheet.
$2,200 (Auc. #04)
As above, fine, one-sheet.
$385 (Auc. #03)
As above, very good, on linen, one-sheet.
$825 (Auc. #06)
As above, fine, insert.
$200 (Auc. #02)

The Prisoner of Zenda, 1937 (United Artists). Ronald Colman. Fine, on linen, one-sheet.
$5,500 (Auc. #04)
As above, fine, unfolded, insert.
$450 (Auc. #02)
As above, fine, insert.
$302.50 (Auc. #06)

The Private Life of Henry VIII, 1933 (United Artists). Charles Laughton. Fine, three-sheet.
$3,910 (Auc. #09)
As above, fine, on linen, one-sheet.
$4,600 (Auc. #09)

Professional Sweetheart, 1933 (RKO). Ginger Rogers. Fine, on linen, one-sheet.
$880 (Auc. #04)

Psycho, 1960 (Paramount). Alfred Hitchcock. Fine, on linen, three-sheet.
$650 (Auc. #02)
As above, very good, on linen, three-sheet.
$550 (Auc. #06)
As above, good, on linen, one-sheet.
$275 (Auc. #02)
As above, fine, one-sheet.
$385 (Auc. #03)
As above, very good, insert.
$225 (Auc. #02)
As above, good, insert.
$150 (Auc. #07)

 Q

Queen Christina, 1934 (MGM). Greta Garbo. Fine, on linen, one-sheet.
$5,280 (Auc. #04)
As above, very good, on linen, one-sheet.
$5,750 (Auc. #09)

The Queen of Outer Space, 1958 (Allied Artists). Zsa Zsa Gabor. Fine, three-sheet.
$550 (Auc. #02)

Courtesy of
Christie's East.

As above, very good, on linen, one-sheet. $495 (Auc. #06)
As above, good, one-sheet. $250 (Auc. #07)

The Quiet Man, 1951 (Republic). John Wayne and Maureen O'Hara. Good,
complete set of eight lobby cards. $225 (Auc. #07)

❧ **R**

Racketeers in Exile, 1937 (Columbia). George Bancroft. Fair, on linen, one-
sheet. $475 (Auc. #01)

Raffles, 1940. David Niven and Olivia De Havilland. Fine, on linen, one-sheet.
    $220 (Auc. #08)

The Rag Man, 1925 (Metro-Goldwyn). Jackie Coogan. Fine, on linen, one-sheet.
    $633 (Auc. #09)

Rainbow Trail, 1931. George O'Brien. Fine, on linen, one-sheet. $605 (Auc. #03)

The Raven, 1935 (Universal). Boris Karloff and Bela Lugosi. Very good, lobby
card (Samuel Hind's torture). $4,750 (Auc. #02)
As above, very good, lobby card (close-up of Lugosi). $3,250 (Auc. #02)

The Razor's Edge, 1946 (Fox). Tyrone Power. Very good, on linen, three-sheet.
    $350 (Auc. #01)

Reap the Wild Wind, 1942 (Paramount). John Wayne. Very good, insert.
    $220 (Auc. #06)

Rear Window, 1954 (Paramount). James Stewart and Grace Kelly. Very good,
three-sheet. $800 (Auc. #07)

Rebecca, 1939 (United Artist). Laurence Olivier and Joan Fontaine. Very good, one-sheet. $3,000 (Auc. #02)
As above, very good, unfolded, half-sheet. $1,200 (Auc. #07)
As above, 1946 reissue, fine, complete set of eight lobby cards. $275 (Auc. #02)

Rebecca of Sunnybrook Farm, 1917 (Artcraft). Mary Pickford. Fine, on linen, one-sheet. $1,955 (Auc. #09)

Rebel Without a Cause, 1955 (Warner Bros.). James Dean. Very good, on linen, one-sheet. $1,000 (Auc. #02)
As above, fine, on linen, one-sheet. $1,430 (Auc. #04)
As above, Australian, fine, on linen, three-sheet. $800 (Auc. #01)
As above, 1957 reissue, very good, half-sheet. $225 (Auc. #02)

Rebound, 1931 (RKO). Ina Claire. Fine, on linen, one-sheet. $1,955 (Auc. #09)

Reckless, 1935 (MGM). Jean Harlow and William Powell. Very good, on linen, one-sheet. $4,400 (Auc. #06)

Red Hair, 1928 (Paramount). Clara Bow. Fine, title card. $700 (Auc. #02)

Red River Valley, 1941 (Republic). Roy Rogers. Fine, on linen, one-sheet. $700 (Auc. #07)

Rembrandt, 1936 (United Artists). Charles Laughton. Fine, one-sheet. $4,620 (Auc. #04)

The Return of Chandu the Magician/Episode 7, The Mysterious Island, 1934 (Sol Lesser). Bela Lugosi. Good, on linen, one-sheet. $550 (Auc. #01)
As above, fine, on linen, one-sheet. $748 (Auc. #09)

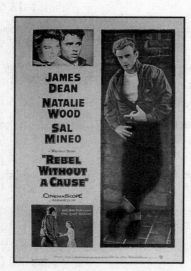

Courtesy of Hollywood
Poster Art.

The Return of Frank James, 1940 (20th Century Fox). Henry Fonda. Fine, on linen, one-sheet. $1,035 (Auc. #09)

Revenge, 1928 (United Artists). Very good, on linen, one-sheet. $1,540 (Auc. #04)
As above, fine, window card. $440 (Auc. #06)

Revenge of the Creature, 1955 (Universal). Fine, on linen, three-sheet. $1,980 (Auc. #04)
As above, very good, insert. $425 (Auc. #01)
As above, very good, insert. $450 (Auc. #02)
As above, very good, half-sheet. $800 (Auc. #01)
As above, very good, complete set of eight lobby cards. $450 (Auc. #01)

The Revenge Rider, 1935 (Columbia). Tim McCoy. Fine, on linen, one-sheet. $750 (Auc. #07)

Rhythm in the Clouds, 1937 (Republic). Patricia Ellis and Warren Hull. Fine, on linen, one-sheet. $165 (Auc. #08)

Richard III, British, 1956 (London Films). Laurence Olivier. Very good, one-sheet. $600 (Auc. #07)

Ridin' for Justice, 1932 (Columbia). Buck Jones. Good, on linen, three-sheet. $550 (Auc. #01)
As above, fine, on linen, one-sheet. $3,220 (Auc. #09)

Road House, 1948. Richard Widmark and Ida Lupino. Fine, one-sheet. $220 (Auc. #03)

The Roaring Twenties, 1939 (Warner Bros.). James Cagney and Humphrey Bogart. Fine, one-sheet. $3,910 (Auc. #09)
As above, very good, title lobby card. $1,200 (Auc. #01)

Robber's Roost, 1932 (Fox). George O'Brien. Fine, on linen, one-sheet. $425 (Auc. #02)

Roberta, 1935. Fred Astaire and Ginger Rogers. Very good, restored, window card. $440 (Auc. #03)

Robot Monster, 1953 (Astor Pictures). Fine, on linen, one-sheet. $1,600 (Auc. #07)

Rock Around the Clock, 1956. Bill Haley and the Comets. Fine, one-sheet. $275 (Auc. #08)

Rockabye, 1932 (RKO). Constance Bennett. Fine, one-sheet. $1,320 (Auc. #04)

Rocketship X-M, 1950 (Lippert). Lloyd Bridges. Fine, one-sheet. $330 (Auc. #08)
As above, fine, complete set of eight lobby cards. $275 (Auc. #01)

Rocky, 1977 (United Artists). Sylvester Stallone. Very good, one-sheet. $50 (Auc. #07)

Roman Holiday, 1953 (Paramount). Gregory Peck and Audrey Hepburn. Very good, on linen, one-sheet. $605 (Auc. #06)

Roman Scandals, 1933 (United Artists). Eddie Cantor. Fine, on linen, one-sheet. $950 (Auc. #02)

Romance in Manhattan, 1934 (RKO). Ginger Rogers. Fine, on linen, one-sheet. $2,420 (Auc. #04)

Romeo and Juliet, 1936 (MGM). Leslie Howard and Norma Shearer. Fine, on linen, one-sheet. $900 (Auc. #01)
As above, fine, on linen, one-sheet. $1,540 (Auc. #04)

Roogie's Bump, 1954 (Republic). Very good, on linen, three-sheet.
$375 (Auc. #07)

Room Service, 1938 (RKO). Marx Bros. Very good, on linen, one-sheet.
$1,100 (Auc. #04)
As above, fine, on linen, one-sheet (Hirschfeld art). $1,100 (Auc. #04)

Rose o' the Sea, 1922 (First National). Anita Stewart. Very good, one-sheet.
$400 (Auc. #07)

The Rough Riders, 1927 (Paramount). Fine, complete set of eight lobby cards.
$193 (Auc. #08)

The Roughneck, 1925. George O'Brien. Mint, on linen, one-sheet.
$1,045 (Auc. #03)

Roxie Hart, 1942 (Fox). Ginger Rogers. Very good, one-sheet. $175 (Auc. #02)

Rudyard Kipling's Jungle Book, 1942 (United Artists). Very good, on linen, one-sheet. $400 (Auc. #01)

Ruggles of Red Gap, 1935 (Paramount). Charles Laughton. Fine, complete set of eight lobby cards. $660 (Auc. #08)

Rulers of the Sea, 1939 (Paramount). Douglas Fairbanks, Jr. Fine, on linen, three-sheet. $425 (Auc. #07)

Rusty Rides Alone, 1933 (Columbia). Tim McCoy. Very good, on linen, one-sheet. $605 (Auc. #04)

🌾 **S**

Saboteur, 1942 (Universal). Alfred Hitchcock. Very good, restored, on linen, one-sheet. $400 (Auc. #07)
As above, fine, unfolded, insert. $300 (Auc. #02)

Sabrina, 1954 (Paramount). Humphrey Bogart, Audrey Hepburn, and William Holden. Very good, on linen, three-sheet. $467.50 (Auc. #06)

Sadie McKee, 1934 (MGM). Joan Crawford. Fine, half-sheet. $330 (Auc. #06)

Sadie Thompson, 1928 (United Artists). Gloria Swanson. Fine, on linen, one-sheet. $5,280 (Auc. #04)

The St. Louis Kid, 1934 (Warner Bros.). James Cagney. Fine, on linen, one-sheet. $3,080 (Auc. #04)

The Saint Strikes Back, 1939 (RKO). George Sanders. Fine, one-sheet. $325 (Auc. #02)

Sally, 1925 (First National). Colleen Moore. Fine, on linen, one-sheet. $1,540 (Auc. #04)

Salome, French, ca. 1918 (Wm. Fox). Very good, on linen, 63 x 47 inches. $3,000 (Auc. #01)

Salome, 1922 (Allied). Fine, on linen, one-sheet. $4,400 (Auc. #04)

Salome, Danish, 1956 (Columbia). Rita Hayworth. Fine, on linen, 24 x 33 inches. $1,320 (Auc. #06)

San Francisco, Spanish, 1936 (MGM). Clark Gable, Spencer Tracy, and Jeanette MacDonald. Very good, on linen, 27 x 39 inches. $400 (Auc. #01)
As above, French, by Roger Soubie, fine, 47 x 63 inches. $1,870 (Auc. #06)

Sands of Iwo Jima, 1950 (Republic). John Wayne. Fine, on linen, three-sheet. $800 (Auc. #01)
As above, fine, one-sheet. $770 (Auc. #02)
As above, very good, one-sheet. $275 (Auc. #08)
As above, French, very good, on linen, 30 x 46 inches. $330 (Auc. #06)

Santa Fe Trail, 1940 (Warner Bros.). Errol Flynn and Olivia De Havilland. Good, on linen, one-sheet. $475 (Auc. #01)
As above, very good, on linen, one-sheet. $1,017.50 (Auc. #06)

Saratoga, 1937 (MGM). Clark Gable and Jean Harlow. Fine, on linen, one-sheet. $750 (Auc. #01)
As above, very good, on linen, one-sheet. $500 (Auc. #07)

Scaramouche, 1923 (Metro). Very good, on linen, one-sheet. $805 (Auc. #09)

Scarface, Argentine, ca. late 1930s (Guaranteed Pictures). Paul Muni. Fine, on linen, 43 x 29 inches. $325 (Auc. #01)

The Scarlet Claw, 1944 (Universal). Basil Rathbone. Good, on linen, one-sheet. $450 (Auc. #01)

The Scarlet Empress, 1934 (Paramount). Marlene Dietrich. Very good, unfolded, jumbo window card. $3,850 (Auc. #04)
As above, French, fine, on linen, 47 x 63 inches. $7,700 (Auc. #04)

Scarlet Seas, 1928 (First National). Richard Barthelmess. Fine, on linen, three-sheet. $1,093 (Auc. #09)

Scarlet Street, 1945. Edward G. Robinson. Fine, on linen, one-sheet.
$385 (Auc. #03)

Scars of Jealousy, 1923 (First National). Fine, one-sheet. $460 (Auc. #09)

The Scoundrel, 1935 (Paramount). Noel Coward. Fine, window card.
$495 (Auc. #08)

The Sea Hawk, 1940 (Warner Bros.). Errol Flynn. Very good, on linen, three-sheet. $4,400 (Auc. #04)
As above, fine, one-sheet. $3,520 (Auc. #03)
As above, very good, title card. $700 (Auc. #02)

The Sea of Grass, 1947 (MGM). Spencer Tracy and Katharine Hepburn. Fine, on linen, three-sheet. $350 (Auc. #02)

The Sea Wolf, 1941 (Warner Bros.). Edward G. Robinson. Fine, on linen, three-sheet. $400 (Auc. #01)
As above, very good, on linen, one-sheet. $165 (Auc. #06)
As above, good, one-sheet. $300 (Auc. #07)

Searchers, 1956 (Warner Bros.). John Wayne. Very good, on linen, three-sheet.
$650 (Auc. #01)
As above, fine, insert. $550 (Auc. #03)

Second Fiddle, 1923 (Hodkinson). Glenn Hunter. Fine, on linen, one-sheet.
$575 (Auc. #09)

Secret Beyond the Door, 1947 (Universal). Very good, unfolded, insert.
$125 (Auc. #02)

Secret Service of the Air, 1938 (Warner Bros.). Ronald Reagan. Fine, on linen, one-sheet. $225 (Auc. #02)

Secrets, 1933 (United Artists). Mary Pickford. Very good, on linen, one-sheet.
$475 (Auc. #07)

Secrets of Paris, 1922 (Mastodon Films). Very good, on linen, one-sheet.
$850 (Auc. #07)

Sergeant York, 1941 (Warner Bros.). Gary Cooper. Very good, one-sheet.
$400 (Auc. #07)
As above, very good, complete set of eight lobby cards. $425 (Auc. #01)

Seven Brides for Seven Brothers, 1954 (MGM). Jane Powell and Howard Keel.
Very good, on linen, one-sheet. $220 (Auc. #06)

The Seven Year Itch, 1955 (Fox). Marilyn Monroe. Fine, on linen, three-sheet.
$2,750 (Auc. #04)
As above, fine, on linen, one-sheet. $605 (Auc. #03)
As above, fine, on linen, one-sheet. $1,265 (Auc. #09)
As above, fine, has censor stamp, insert. $450 (Auc. #02)
As above, very good, insert. $770 (Auc. #06)

Courtesy of Hollywood
Poster Art.

As above, very good, crease, insert.	$330 (Auc. #08)
As above, fine, complete set of eight lobby cards.	$400 (Auc. #02)
As above, fine, title card.	$330 (Auc. #08)
As above, Danish, very good, with censor stamp, 24 x 33 inches.	$100 (Auc. #02)
As above, Italian, fine, on linen, 48 x 65 inches.	$1,540 (Auc. #03)
As above, Italian, very good, 39 x 55 inches.	$300 (Auc. #07)
As above, Italian, good, five fotobustas, 28 x 20 inches.	$200 (Auc. #07)

Seventh Heaven, 1937 (20th Century Fox). James Stewart and Simone Simon. Very good, insert. $522.50 (Auc. #06)

Shadow of Chinatown, 1936 (Victory). Bela Lugosi. Fine, on linen, three-sheet. $467.50 (Auc. #06)

As above, good, on linen, one-sheet.	$650 (Auc. #01)
As above, very good, on linen, one-sheet.	$950 (Auc. #02)
As above, fine, complete set of eight lobby cards.	$600 (Auc. #01)

Shadow of the Thin Man, 1941 (MGM). William Powell and Myrna Loy. Very good, on linen, one-sheet. $522.50 (Auc. #06)
As above, fine, complete set of eight lobby cards, with censor stamp. $300 (Auc. #02)

Shadow Ranch, 1930 (Columbia). Buck Jones. Fine, on linen, three-sheet. $978 (Auc. #09)

The Shadow Returns, 1946 (Monogram). Good, unfolded, half-sheet. $100 (Auc. #02)

The Shadow Strikes, 1937 (Grand National). Very good, on linen, one-sheet.
$600 (Auc. #02)

Shadows of Paris, 1924 (Paramount). Pola Negri. Fine, on linen, one-sheet.
$825 (Auc. #04)

Shanghai Express, 1931. Marlene Dietrich. Very good, resotred, window card.
$770 (Auc. #03)

Shanghai Madness, 1933 (Fox). Spencer Tracy and Fay Wray. Fine, on linen, one-sheet.
$1,093 (Auc. #09)

Shanghaied Lovers, 1920s (Morgan). Mack Sennett. Very good, on linen, one-sheet.
$357.50 (Auc. #06)

She Devil Island, 1936 (First Division). Fine, on linen, six-sheet. $3,500 (Auc. #01)
As above, fine, on linen, one-sheet.
$550 (Auc. #06)

She Done Him Wrong, 1933 (Paramount). Mae West. Fine, on linen, three-sheet.
$4,620 (Auc. #04)
As above, fine, on linen, one-sheet.
$5,775 (Auc. #03)

She Made Her Bed, 1934 (Paramount). Richard Arlen. Fine, on linen, one-sheet.
$605 (Auc. #04)

She Wore a Yellow Ribbon, 1949 (RKO). John Wayne. Fine, one-sheet.
$1,320 (Auc. #04)

The Sheik, 1922. Rudolph Valentino. Fine, title card. $3,080 (Auc. #03)
As above, fine, lobby card (full-length scene). $1,320 (Auc. #03)
As above, fine, lobby card (close-up). $825 (Auc. #03)
As above, Australian, 1928 reissue, good, 27 x 40 inches. $550 (Auc. #07)

The Shepherd King, 1923 (Fox). Fine, on linen, one-sheet. $935 (Auc. #04)

Sherlock Holmes, 1922. John Barrymore. Fine, title card. $605 (Auc. #03)

Sherlock Holmes, French, 1939. Basil Rathbone. Good, on linen, 47 x 63 inches.
$3,300 (Auc. #05)

Sherlock Holmes and the Voice of Terror, 1942 (Universal). Basil Rathbone. Very good, on linen, three-sheet. $1,500 (Auc. #07)
As above, good, half-sheet. $425 (Auc. #07)

Sherlock Holmes in Washington, 1942 (Universal). Basil Rathbone. Good, on linen, one-sheet.
$500 (Auc. #01)

The Shooting of Dan McGrew, 1924 (Metro). Fine, one-sheet. $863 (Auc. #09)

A Short Life and a Merry One, 1913 (Edison). Fine, on linen, one-sheet.
$605 (Auc. #04)

Side Show, 1931 (Warner Bros.). Winnie Lightner. Very good, on linen, three-sheet.
$770 (Auc. #06)

Side Street, 1950 (MGM). Farley Granger. Very good, on linen, three-sheet.
$220 (Auc. #06)

The Silent Witness, 1931 (Fox). Fine, on linen, one-sheet. $715 (Auc. #04)

Silver River, 1948 (Warner Bros.). Errol Flynn. Very good, one-sheet.
$200 (Auc. #07)

Silver Wings, 1922 (Wm. Fox). Mary Carr. Fine, one-sheet. $330 (Auc. #08)

The Sin of Nora Moran, 1933 (Majestic). Fine, on linen, three-sheet.
$5,500 (Auc. #06)
As above, very good, on linen, one-sheet. $19,800 (Auc. #04)

Sing, Baby, Sing, 1936 (20th Century Fox). Good, on linen, one-sheet.
$137.50 (Auc. #06)

Singin' in the Rain, 1952 (MGM). Gene Kelly, Donald O'Connor, and Debbie
Reynolds. Very good, on linen, three-sheet. $1,300 (Auc. #02)
As above, fine, on linen, three-sheet. $1,035 (Auc. #09)
As above, fine, on linen, one-sheet. $950 (Auc. #01)
As above, fine, on linen, one-sheet. $1,320 (Auc. #04)
As above, very good, one-sheet. $550 (Auc. #06)
As above, fine, one-sheet. $1,045 (Auc. #08)
As above, fine, complete set of eight lobby cards. $700 (Auc. #01)
As above, fine, complete set of eight lobby cards. $400 (Auc. #02)
As above, Danish, fine, on linen, with censor stamp,
24 x 33 inches. $150 (Auc. #01)

The Singing Vagabond, 1935 (Republic). Gene Autry. Fine, one-sheet.
$633 (Auc. #09)

The Sisters, 1938 (Warner Bros.). Errol Flynn and Bette Davis. Fine, on linen,
one-sheet. $4,500 (Auc. #01)
As above, fine, title card. $1,100 (Auc. #08)

6 Cylinder Love, 1923 (Wm. Fox). Very good, on linen, one-sheet.
$450 (Auc. #02)

Skirt Sky, 1929 (MGM). Harry Langdon. Fine, on linen, one-sheet.
$863 (Auc. #09)

Smash-Up, 1946 (Universal). Susan Hayward. Very good, on linen, three-sheet.
$750 (Auc. #01)
As above, fine, on linen, three-sheet. $1,093 (Auc. #09)
As above, fine, on linen, one-sheet. $770 (Auc. #04)
As above, fine, insert. $225 (Auc. #01)
As above, very good, half-sheet. $100 (Auc. #02)
As above, fine, complete set of eight lobby cards. $100 (Auc. #02)

Smashing the Vice Trust, 1937 (Willis Kent Prod.). Very good, three-sheet.
$200 (Auc. #07)

Snowdrift, 1923 (Wm. Fox). Charles Jones. Fine, on linen, one-sheet.
$385 (Auc. #08)

A Society Scandal, 1924 (Paramount). Gloria Swanson. Fine, insert.
$1,045 (Auc. #08)

Some Like It Hot, 1959 (United Artists). Marilyn Monroe, Tony Curtis, and Jack Lemmon. Fine, on linen, six-sheet. $2,090 (Auc. #08)
As above, fine, on linen, three-sheet. $1,495 (Auc. #09)
As above, fine, on linen, one-sheet. $750 (Auc. #01)
As above, very good, on linen, one-sheet. $450 (Auc. #02)
As above, fine, on linen, one-sheet. $550 (Auc. #03)
As above, very good, on linen, one-sheet. $1,760 (Auc. #06)
As above, fine, on linen, one-sheet. $850 (Auc. #07)
As above, very good, insert. $350 (Auc. #02)
As above, very good, half-sheet. $325 (Auc. #02)
As above, good, complete set of eight lobby cards. $600 (Auc. #01)
As above, fine, complete set of eight lobby cards. $650 (Auc. #02)
As above, fine, window card. $165 (Auc. #08)
As above, Danish, very good, with censor stamp,
24 x 33 inches. $300 (Auc. #02)
As above, Italian, fine, on linen, 39 x 55 inches. $805 (Auc. #09)
As above, Italian, fine, 13 x 27 inches. $150 (Auc. #07)
As above, Spanish, 1963 reissue, very good, 28 x 39 inches. $200 (Auc. #02)

Somewhere in the Night, 1946 (20th Century Fox). John Hodiak and Nancy Guild. Very good, on linen, one-sheet. $467.50 (Auc. #06)

Son of Dracula, 1943. Lon Chaney. Very good, window card. $495 (Auc. #08)

Son of Frankenstein, 1938 (Universal). Boris Karloff and Bela Lugosi. Fine, on linen, three-sheet. $11,000 (Auc. #04)
As above, fair, on linen, three-sheet. $4,400 (Auc. #05)
As above, fine, on linen, one-sheet. $20,125 (Auc. #09)
As above, good, window card. $3,575 (Auc. #06)
As above, 1953 reissue, fine, on linen, one-sheet. $248 (Auc. #08)
As above, 1953 reissue (Realart), very good, unfolded,
half-sheet. $225 (Auc. #02)

The Son of the Sheik, 1926. Rudolph Valentino. Fine, insert. $2,860 (Auc. #03)

The Son-Daughter, 1932 (MGM). Helen Hayes. Very good, on linen, one-sheet.
$500 (Auc. #07)

Song of Bernadette, 1943 (20th Century Fox). Jennifer Jones. Rockwell, artist. Fine, rolled, insert. $275 (Auc. #08)

Song of the Islands, 1942 (20th Century Fox). Betty Grable. Good, on linen, one-sheet. $247.50 (Auc. #06)

Song of the Thin Man, 1947 (Loews). William Powell and Myrna Loy. Fine, half-sheet. $275 (Auc. #05)

Sorry, Wrong Number, 1948 (Paramount). Burt Lancaster and Barbara Stanwyck. Fine, on linen, three-sheet. $375 (Auc. #01)

SOS Coast Guard, 1937 (Republic). Bela Lugosi. Very good, on linen, three-sheet. $1,265 (Auc. #09)

The Southerner, 1945 (United Artists). Very good, on linen, one-sheet. $150 (Auc. #07)

Speed, 1922 (Pathe). Charles Hutchison. Fine, on linen, one-sheet. $825 (Auc. #04)

Speed Devils, 1930. Very good, on linen, one-sheet. $770 (Auc. #06)

The Speed Girl, 1921 (Realart). Bebe Daniels. Fair, on linen, one-sheet. $400 (Auc. #01)

Speedy, 1928 (Paramount). Harold Lloyd. Fine, on linen, three-sheet. $3,080 (Auc. #04)

Spellbound, 1945 (United Artists). Ingrid Bergman and Gregory Peck. Very good, on linen, three-sheet. $1,650 (Auc. #06)
As above, very good, on linen, one-sheet. $1,500 (Auc. #02)
As above, very good, unfolded, half-sheet. $425 (Auc. #07)
As above, fine, title card. $193 (Auc. #03)

Spider Woman, 1943 (Universal). Basil Rathbone. Fine, complete set of eight lobby cards. $900 (Auc. #01)

Spider Woman Strikes Back, 1945 (Universal). Very good, one-sheet. $350 (Auc. #07)

Courtesy of Swann
Galleries, Inc.

The Spiral Staircase, 1946 (RKO). Very good, complete set of eight lobby cards. $175 (Auc. #07)

Spirit of Youth, 1937 (First National). Fine, on linen, one-sheet. $4,830 (Auc. #09)

The Spoilers, 1914 (Selig). William Farnum. Good, on linen, one-sheet. $495 (Auc. #06)

The Spoilers, 1930 (Paramount). Gary Cooper. Very good, on linen, one-sheet. $1,955 (Auc. #09)

Spooks Run Wild, (Monogram). Bela Lugosi. Fine, one-sheet. $1,150 (Auc. #09)

Sporting Youth, 1924 (Universal). Reginald Denny. Fine, on linen, one-sheet. $550 (Auc. #04)

Spring Parade, 1940 (Universal). Deanna Durbin. Very good, one-sheet. $225 (Auc. #07)

Springtime in the Rockies, 1942 (20th Century Fox). Betty Grable. Good, on linen, one-sheet. $550 (Auc. #06)

Spy Smasher/A Serial in 12 Chapters, 1942 (Republic). Fine, on linen, one-sheet. $1,100 (Auc. #04)

Stagecoach, French, 1939 (United Artists). John Wayne. Very good, on linen, 47 x 63 inches. $3,300 (Auc. #06)

Stand Up and Cheer, 1934. Warner Baxter and Madge Evans. Fine, on linen, one-sheet. $880 (Auc. #03)

Star of Midnight, 1935 (RKO). William Powell and Ginger Rogers. Fine, on linen, three-sheet. $13,200 (Auc. #04)

Star Wars, 1977 (Fox). Fine, on linen, six-sheet. $900 (Auc. #01)
As above, fine, on linen, three-sheet. $250 (Auc. #02)
As above, fine, on linen, three-sheet. $175 (Auc. #07)
As above, style C, very good, on linen, one-sheet. $275 (Auc. #06)
As above, fine, one sheet. $50 (Auc. #07)

State of the Union, 1948 (MGM). Spencer Tracy and Katharine Hepburn. Fine, on linen, one-sheet. $225 (Auc. #07)

State's Attorney, 1932 (RKO). John Barrymore. Very good, unfolded, insert. $460 (Auc. #09)

Stella Dallas, 1937 (United Artists). Barbara Stanwyck. Fine, on linen, one-sheet. $1,210 (Auc. #04)
As above, fine, window card. $375 (Auc. #02)

Stingaree, 1934 (RKO). Irene Dunne and Richard Dix. Fine, on linen, one-sheet. $460 (Auc. #09)

Stolen Holiday, 1937. Kay Francis. Fine, on linen, one-sheet. $495 (Auc. #03)

A Stolen Life, 1946 (Warner Bros.). Bette Davis. Fine, complete set of eight lobby cards. $100 (Auc. #02)

Stormy Weather, 1943 (20th Century Fox). Lena Horne. Fine, on linen, one-sheet. $2,300 (Auc. #09)

The Story of Dr. Wassell, 1944 (Paramount). Gary Cooper. Very good, one-sheet. $150 (Auc. #07)

The Story of Louis Pasteur, 1936 (Warner Bros.). Very good, on linen, one-sheet. $650 (Auc. #02)
As above, good, on linen, one-sheet. $660 (Auc. #06)
As above, fine, window card. $330 (Auc. #08)

Stowaway, 1938 (Fox). Shirley Temple. Fine, on linen, three-sheet. $3,450 (Auc. #09)
As above, Belgian, fine, on linen, 24 x 33 inches. $150 (Auc. #01)

The Strange Case of Clara Deane, 1932 (Paramount). Pat O'Brien. Fine, on linen, one-sheet. $220 (Auc. #08)

The Stranger, 1946 (RKO). Edward G. Robinson and Orson Welles. Very good, one-sheet. $400 (Auc. #07)

Stranger on the Third Floor, 1940 (RKO). Peter Lorre. Very good, on linen, one-sheet. $650 (Auc. #02)
As above, good, one-sheet. $450 (Auc. #07)

Street of Chance, 1942 (Paramount). Burgess Meredith. Very good, one-sheet. $247.50 (Auc. #06)

Street Scene, 1931 (United Artists). Fine, on linen, one-sheet. $1,100 (Auc. #04)

A Streetcar Named Desire, 1951 (Warner Bros.). Vivien Leigh and Marlon Brando. Good, one-sheet with censor stamp. $225 (Auc. #02)
As above, fine, one-sheet. $275 (Auc. #08)

Strike Me Pink, 1935 (United Artists). Eddie Cantor. Good, on linen, one-sheet. $250 (Auc. #07)

Strike Up the Band, 1940 (MGM). Mickey Rooney and Judy Garland. Good, one-sheet. $550 (Auc. #01)
As above, very good, one-sheet. $200 (Auc. #02)

Submarine Patrol, 1938 (Fox). Very good, one-sheet. $150 (Auc. #02)

Suddenly, Last Summer, 1959 (Columbia). Elizabeth Taylor and Katharine Hepburn. Very good, on linen, three-sheet. $385 (Auc. #05)

Sullivan's Travels, 1941 (Paramount). Veronica Lake. Very good, on linen, three-sheet. $7,000 (Auc. #01)
As above, very good, on linen, one-sheet. $2,250 (Auc. #02)

As above, fine, on linen, one-sheet. $4,025 (Auc. #09)
As above, fine, on linen, one-sheet (with illustration art). $2,300 (Auc. #09)
As above, very good, on linen, insert. $1,045 (Auc. #03)

Summer Stock, 1950 (MGM). Judy Garland and Gene Kelly. Very good, complete set of eight lobby cards. $225 (Auc. #07)

Sunkist Stars at Palm Springs, 1936 (MGM). Good, on linen, one-sheet.
       $425 (Auc. #01)

Sunnyside, 1921 reissue (Pathe). Charlie Chaplin. Fine, on linen, three-sheet.
       $2,200 (Auc. #06)
As above, ca. 1920 reissue, very good, one-sheet. $550 (Auc. #07)

Sunrise, 1927 (Wm. Fox). George O'Brien. Very good, title card.
       $2,530 (Auc. #09)
As above, fine, window card. $880 (Auc. #08)

Sunset Boulevard, 1950 (Paramount). Gloria Swanson and William Holden.
Fine, on linen, one-sheet. $3,500 (Auc. #02)
As above, fine, on linen, one-sheet. $3,575 (Auc. #06)
As above, very good, insert, incorporates a still of the body
  floating in the swimming pool. $500 (Auc. #02)
As above, good, one-sheet, text only, no stars shown. $275 (Auc. #07)
As above, fine, insert. $978 (Auc. #09)
As above, jumbo window card. $660 (Auc. #05)
As above, Danish, fine, on linen, 25 x 33 inches. $440 (Auc. #08)

Sunvalley Serenade, 1939 (20th Century Fox). Sonja Henie and Glenn Miller
Orchestra. Good, on linen, one-sheet. $330 (Auc. #06)

Superman, 1948 (Columbia). Fine, on linen, one-sheet. $1,045 (Auc. #04)

Superman and the Mole Men, 1951 (Lippert). Fine, on linen, three-sheet.
       $4,000 (Auc. #02)
As above, fine, on linen, one-sheet. $3,300 (Auc. #04)

Sure Fire Flint, 1922 (Mastodon Films).Very good, on linen, one-sheet.
       $225 (Auc. #07)

❦ **T**

Tailspin, 1938 (Fox). Fine, on linen, six-sheet. $9,000 (Auc. #02)
As above, very good, on linen, one-sheet. $192.50 (Auc. #06)

A Tale of Two Cities, 1935 (MGM). Ronald Colman. Fine, insert.
       $990 (Auc. #03)
As above, very good, title card. $400 (Auc. #02)

Tales of Manhattan, 1942 (20th Century Fox). Charles Boyer, Rita Hayworth,
Ginger Rogers, and others. Fine, on linen, one-sheet. $690 (Auc. #09)

Courtesy of
Camden
House
Auctioneers.

Courtesy of Hollywood
Poster Art.

The Talk of the Town, 1942 (Columbia). Cary Grant. Very good, on linen, one-sheet. $1,300 (Auc. #02)

Tall in the Saddle, 1944 (RKO). John Wayne. Fine, insert. $325 (Auc. #01)

The Tango Tangle, ca. 1914. Charlie Chaplin. Fine, on linen, one-sheet. $550 (Auc. #08)

Tarantula, 1955 (Universal), Very good, on linen, one-sheet. $500 (Auc. #02)

Tarzan and the Huntress, 1947 (RKO). Very good, one-sheet. $475 (Auc. #01)

Tarzan Finds a Son, 1939 (MGM). Johnny Weissmuller. Very good, insert. $605 (Auc. #08)

Tarzan of the Apes, 1918 (First National). Fine, on linen, one-sheet. $30,800 (Auc. #04)

Tarzan the Ape Man, 1932 (MGM). Fine, lobby card. $1,300 (Auc. #01)

Tarzan the Fearless, 1933. Buster Crabbe. Fine, on linen, one-sheet. $605 (Auc. #08)

Tarzan Triumphs, 1943 (RKO). Johnny Weissmuller. Good, on linen, one-sheet. $400 (Auc. #07)

Tarzan's Revenge, 1937 (Fox). Very good, on linen, one-sheet. $500 (Auc. #01)

Tempest Cody Rides Wild, 1919 (Universal). Marie Walcamp. Fine, on linen, one-sheet. $495 (Auc. #08)

The Temple of Venus, 1923 (Fox). Very good, on linen, one-sheet. $880 (Auc. #04)

Temptation, 1923 (Micheaux). Fine, on linen, one-sheet. $1,045 (Auc. #04)

The Ten Commandments, 1956 (Paramount). Charlton Heston and Yul Brynner. Very good, on linen, three-sheet. $300 (Auc. #01)
As above, very good, on linen, one-sheet. $137.50 (Auc. #06)
As above, very good, on linen, one-sheet. $138 (Auc. #08)
As above, good, unfolded, half-sheet. $1,000 (Auc. #02)

Ten Modern Commandments, 1927 (Paramount). Esther Ralston. Fine, on linen, one-sheet. $990 (Auc. #04)

The Terror of Tiny Town, 1938 (Columbia). Fine, on linen, three-sheet. $550 (Auc. #08)

Tess of the Storm Country, 1922 (United Artists). Mary Pickford. Very good, one-sheet. $1,500 (Auc. #02)
As above, very good, on linen, one-sheet $1,380 (Auc. #09)

The Texans, 1938 (Paramount). Randolph Scott and Joan Bennett. Fine, on linen, one-sheet. $1,100 (Auc. #06)
As above, fine, on linen, one-sheet. $550 (Auc. #07)

Texas Cyclone, 1932 (Columbia). Tim McCoy. Very good, on linen, one-sheet. $550 (Auc. #02)

The Texas Streak, 1926 (Morgan). Hoot Gibson. Fine, on linen, one-sheet. $385 (Auc. #08)

Texas Terror, 1935 (Monogram). John Wayne. Fine, one-sheet. $850 (Auc. #01)
As above, very good, one-sheet. $225 (Auc. #02)

Thank You, Mr. Moto, 1937 (20th Century Fox). Peter Lorre. Very good, one-sheet. $600 (Auc. #02)

That Hamilton Woman, 1941 (United Artists). Vivien Leigh and Laurence Olivier. Very good, one-sheet. $900 (Auc. #02)

That Lady in Ermine, 1948 (20th Century Fox). Betty Grable and Douglas Fairbanks, Jr. Good, on linen, one-sheet. $275 (Auc. #06)

That's My Boy, 1932 (Columbia). Richard Cromwell. Fine, on linen, one-sheet. $220 (Auc. #08)

Them, 1953 (Warner Bros.). Fine, on linen, three-sheet. $550 (Auc. #01)
As above, very good, one-sheet. $850 (Auc. #07)
As above, insert. $990 (Auc. #05)

Theodora Goes Wild, 1936 (Columbia). Irene Dunne and Melvyn Douglas. Fine, one-sheet. $990 (Auc. #04)

There's No Business Like Show Business, 1954 (Fox). Irving Berlin. Good, on linen, three-sheet. $550 (Auc. #01)
As above, very good, on linen, three-sheet. $350 (Auc. #02)
As above, very good, complete set of eighty lobby cards. $150 (Auc. #02)

They Died with Their Boots On, 1941 (Warner Bros.). Errol Flynn and Olivia De Havilland. Good, insert. $300 (Auc. #01)
As above, very good, on linen, insert. $300 (Auc. #07)
As above, fine, insert. $385 (Auc. #08)
As above, very good, half-sheet. $400 (Auc. #01)

They Drive By Night, 1940 (Warner Bros.). George Raft and Humphrey Bogart. Very good, one-sheet. $325 (Auc. #02)

They Made Me a Criminal, 1939 (Warner Bros.). Fine, on linen, one-sheet. $550 (Auc. #02)

Thicker Than Water, 1935 (MGM). Laurel and Hardy. Very good, one-sheet.

A Thief Catcher, 1914 (Keystone). Good, on linen, one-sheet. $330 (Auc. #08)

The Thief of Bagdad, 1924 (United Artists). Douglas Fairbanks. Very good, one-sheet. $30,800 (Auc. #04)
As above, fine, on linen, one-sheet. $13,200 (Auc. #08)

The Thief of Bagdad, 1940 (United Artists). Conrad Veidt and Sabu. Very good, on linen, one-sheet. $550 (Auc. #01)

The Thin Man, 1934 (MGM). William Powell and Myrna Loy. Fine, window card. $1,320 (Auc. #06)
As above, good, window card. $1,100 (Auc. #07)
As above, fine, window card. $1,100 (Auc. #08)

Things To Come, 1936 (United Artists). H. G. Wells. Fine, on linen, six-sheet. $22,000 (Auc. #04)

Think Fast, Mr. Moto, 1937. Peter Lorre. Fine, on linen, one-sheet. $660 (Auc. #03)

The 3rd Man, 1949 (London Films). Orson Welles and Joseph Cotten. Very good, one-sheet. $275 (Auc. #07)

The 39 Steps, 1935 (Gaumont British). Alfred Hitchcock. Fine, one-sheet. $14,300 (Auc. #04)
As above, 1938 reissue, fine, one-sheet. $495 (Auc. #08)
As above, 1938 reissue, fine, complete set of eight lobby cards. $700 (Auc. #01)

This Above All, 1942 (Fox). Tyrone Power and Joan Fontaine. Very good, one-sheet. $750 (Auc. #02)
As above, fine, on linen, one-sheet. $990 (Auc. #08)

This Gun for Hire, 1942 (Paramount). Alan Ladd and Veronica Lake. Very good, one-sheet. $5,500 (Auc. #07)
As above, Danish, good, with censor stamp, 24 x 33 inches. $500 (Auc. #01)
As above, French, very good, on linen, 25 x 33 inches. $225 (Auc. #07)
As above, 1947 reissue, good, half-sheet. $800 (Auc. #01)

This Island Earth, 1955 (Universal). Fine, on linen, three-sheet. $1,045 (Auc. #06)
As above, good, insert. $250 (Auc. #01)

Courtesy of Camden House Auctioneers.

Thousands Cheer, 1943 (MGM). Fair, on linen, three-sheet. $412 (Auc. #05)

3 Gold Coins, 1920 (Wm. Fox). Tom Mix. Very good, on linen, one-sheet.
$600 (Auc. #02)

The Three Musketeers, 1933 (Mascot). Fine, on linen, one-sheet.
$1,320 (Auc. #04)

The Three Musketeers, 1939 (Fox). Don Ameche and the Ritz Bros. Good, one-sheet. $300 (Auc. #07)

Three Wise Girls, 1931 (Columbia). Jean Harlow. Fine, on linen, one-sheet.
$1,430 (Auc. #04)

Thunderball, 1965 (United Artists). Sean Connery. Very good, on linen, three-sheet. $450 (Auc. #02)
As above, good, 40 x 60 inches. $100 (Auc. #07)
As above, German, fine, 23 x 33 inches. $110 (Auc. #06)

Thunderbolt, 1929 (Paramount). George Bancroft. Very good, on linen, one-sheet. $1,210 (Auc. #04)

Tiger Rose, 1923 (Warner Bros.). Lenore Ulric. Fine, one-sheet. $330 (Auc. #08)

Tiger Shark, 1932 (First National). Edward G. Robinson. Fine, on linen, one-sheet. $863 (Auc. #09)

The Tiger Woman, 1944 (Republic). Adele Mara. Fine, on linen, one-sheet.
$288 (Auc. #09)

Till the Clouds Roll By, 1946 (MGM). June Allyson, Judy Garland, and others.
Good, on linen, one-sheet. $300 (Auc. #01)
As above, very good, on linen, one-sheet. $300 (Auc. #02)
As above, fine, unfolded, insert. $250 (Auc. #02)

Times Have Changed, 1923 (Wm. Fox). William Russell. Fine, on linen, one-sheet. $550 (Auc. #08)

To Catch A Thief, 1955 (Paramount). Cary Grant and Grace Kelly. Very good, on linen, one-sheet. $330 (Auc. #06)

To Have and Have Not, 1944. Humphrey Bogart and Lauren Bacall. Very good, insert. $495 (Auc. #06)

The Toast of New York, 1937 (RKO). Cary Grant. Fine, on linen, one-sheet. $715 (Auc. #04)

Tobacco Road, 1941 (20th Century Fox). John Ford. Fine, one-sheet. $660 (Auc. #04)

Tobor the Great, 1954 (Republic). Fine, on linen, one-sheet. $750 (Auc. #02)
As above, insert. $302 (Auc. #05)
As above, very good, unfolded, half-sheet. $900 (Auc. #01)
As above, fine, unfolded, half-sheet. $550 (Auc. #07)
As above, Italian, very good, 39 x 55 inches. $150 (Auc. #07)

Too Busy to Work, 1932 (Fox). Will Rogers. Fine, on linen, one-sheet. $650 (Auc. #02)

Too Hot to Handle, 1938 (MGM). Clark Gable. Fine, on linen, one-sheet. $425 (Auc. #01)
As above, Australian, very good, 27 x 40 inches. $300 (Auc. #07)

Top Hat, 1953 reissue (RKO). Fred Astaire and Ginger Rogers. Very good, on linen, three-sheet. $357.50 (Auc. #06)

Topper, 1937. Cary Grant. Fine, on linen, one-sheet. $770 (Auc. #03)

Topsy and Eva, 1927 (United Artists). Duncan Sisters. Very good, on linen, one-sheet. $880 (Auc. #04)

Tortilla Flat, 1942. Hedy Lamarr. Fine, on linen, one-sheet. $248 (Auc. #03)

Touch of Evil, 1958 (Universal). Very good, one-sheet. $300 (Auc. #02)
As above, very good, on linen, one-sheet. $825 (Auc. #06)
As above, very good, complete set of eight lobby cards. $175 (Auc. #02)

Tower of London, 1939 (Universal). Basil Rathbone and Boris Karloff. Very good, on linen, six-sheet. $1,200 (Auc. #02)
As above, fine, on linen, one-sheet. $440 (Auc. #03)

The Trail of '98, 1929 (MGM). Fine, on linen, one-sheet. $748 (Auc. #09)

A Trap for Santa Claus, 1909 (Biograph). Fine, one-sheet. $3,520 (Auc. #04)

Treason, 1933 (Columbia). Buck Jones. Very good, one-sheet. $425 (Auc. #07)

The Treasure of the Sierra Madre, 1948 (Warner Bros.). Humphrey Bogart. Fine, one-sheet. $900 (Auc. #02)

As above, fine, on linen, one-sheet. $990 (Auc. #03)

As above, very good, on linen, one-sheet. $825 (Auc. #06)

As above, fine, on linen, insert. $1,100 (Auc. #01)

As above, very good, on linen, insert. $400 (Auc. #02)

As above, very good, insert. $425 (Auc. #07)

As above, Spanish, fine, 27 x 39 inches. $325 (Auc. #01)

As above, French, 1950s, fine, on linen, 47 x 63 inches. $600 (Auc. #07)

Trouble in Morocco, 1937 (Columbia). Jack Holt. Fine, on linen, one-sheet. $425 (Auc. #07)

The Truth Juggler, 1922 (Pathe). Hal Roach. Very good, on linen, one-sheet. $325 (Auc. #07)

Twelve Crowded Hours, 1939 (RKO). Richard Dix and Lucille Ball. Fine, on linen, three-sheet. $375 (Auc. #07)

Twelve O'clock High, 1950 (20th Century Fox). Gregory Peck. Very good, on linen, one-sheet. $385 (Auc. #06)

Twentieth Century, Swedish, 1934 (Columbia). Carole Lombard. Fine, on linen, 27 x 41 inches. $3,450 (Auc. #09)

20,000 Leagues Under the Sea, 1954 (Disney/Buena Vista). Kirk Douglas. Good, three-sheet. $325 (Auc. #01)

As above, good, one-sheet. $75 (Auc. #02)

20,000 Years in Sing Sing, 1933 (First National). Spencer Tracy and Bette Davis. Very good, on linen, one-sheet. $475 (Auc. #07)

Two Arabian Nights, 1927 (United Artists). William Boyd and Mary Astor. Fine, insert. $300 (Auc. #02)

Two Faced Woman, 1941 (MGM). Greta Garbo and Melvyn Douglas. Fine, on linen, one-sheet. $748 (Auc. #09)

Two Flaming Youths, 1927 (Paramount). W. C. Fields. Fine, title card. $715 (Auc. #08)

2001: A Space Odyssey, 1968 (MGM). Very good, three-sheet. $275 (Auc. #02)

As above, very good, on linen, one-sheet. $1,000 (Auc. #02)

As above, good, one-sheet (other). $125 (Auc. #02)

As above, style B, Robert McCall, artist; fine, on linen, one-sheet. $275 (Auc. #06)

As above, fine, half-sheet. $165 (Auc. #08)

The Two Mrs. Carrolls, 1947 (Warner Bros.). Humphrey Bogart and Barbara Stanwyck. Good, complete set of eight lobby cards. $175 (Auc. #02)

❧ **U**

Uncle Tom's Cabin, 1927 (Universal). Fine, on linen, six-sheet. $4,950 (Auc. #04)
As above, fine, on linen, one-sheet. $825 (Auc. #04)

Unconquered, 1947 (Paramount). Gary Cooper. Very good, on linen, one-sheet. $440 (Auc. #06)
As above, very good, on linen, one-sheet. $600 (Auc. #07)

The Uncovered Wagon, 1923 (Pathe). Hal Roach. Good, on linen, one-sheet. $550 (Auc. #07)

The Undead, 1957. Fine, on linen, one-sheet. $220 (Auc. #08)

Under Fiesta Stars, 1941 (Republic). Gene Autry. Fine, on linen, one-sheet. $275 (Auc. #08)

Under the Red Robe, 1937 (Fox). Conrad Veidt. Fine, on linen, one-sheet. $550 (Auc. #02)

Undercover Man, 1932 (Paramount). George Raft. Fine, three-sheet. $1,100 (Auc. #06)

Underwater!, 1955 (Hughes). Jane Russell. Very good, on linen, six-sheet. $770 (Auc. #06)

Union Pacific, 1939 (Paramount). Barbara Stanwyck. Fine, one-sheet. $550 (Auc. #01)
As above, very good, on linen, one-sheet teaser. $605 (Auc. #06)

The Unknown, 1927 (MGM). Lon Chaney and Joan Crawford. Very good, folded, insert. $3,080 (Auc. #04)
As above, very good, title card. $990 (Auc. #08)

Unknown Valley, 1933 (Columbia). Buck Jones. Fine, on linen, one-sheet. $920 (Auc. #09)

The Unmarried Mother, ca. 1920s. Good, on linen, one-sheet. $325 (Auc. #07)

Upper World, 1934 (Warner Bros.). Ginger Rogers and Mary Astor. Fine, one-sheet. $748 (Auc. #09)

❧ **V**

The Vanishing American, 1926 (Paramount). Zane Grey. Fine, on linen, three-sheet. $5,280 (Auc. #04)

Vertigo, 1958 (Paramount). James Stewart. Very good, three-sheet. $450 (Auc. #01)
As above, very good, on linen, three-sheet. $1,210 (Auc. #05)

Virginia City, 1940. Errol Flynn. Fine, one-sheet. $715 (Auc. #03)

The Virginian, 1929 (Paramount). Gary Cooper. Very good, on linen, one-sheet.
$3,680 (Auc. #09)

Voodoo Man, 1944 (Monogram). Bela Lugosi. Good, one-sheet. $330 (Auc. #06)

🌿 **W**

Wabash Avenue, 1950 (Fox). Betty Grable. Good, one-sheet. $325 (Auc. #01)

The Wagons Roll at Night, 1941 (Warner Bros.). Humphrey Bogart. Good, on linen, one-sheet.
$200 (Auc. #01)

Waifs, 1914 (Biograph). Fine, on linen, one-sheet. $660 (Auc. #04)

Wake Up and Live, 1937 (20th Century Fox). Walter Winchell. Good, on linen, one-sheet.
$220 (Auc. #06)

The Walking Dead, 1936 (Warner Bros.). Boris Karloff. Fine, on linen, six-sheet.
$28,600 (Auc. #04)
As above, very good, unfolded, half-sheet. $3,520 (Auc. #04)

The Wanderer, 1926 (Paramount). Very good, on linen, one-sheet.
$1,725 (Auc. #09)

War of the Worlds, 1953 (Paramount). H. G. Wells. Fine, on linen, six-sheet.
$1,700 (Auc. #01)
As above, good, on linen, one-sheet. $825 (Auc. #05)
As above, very good, on linen, one-sheet. $1,210 (Auc. #06)
As above, insert. $495 (Auc. #05)
As above, fair, half-sheet. $3,740 (Auc. #05)

Washington Merry-Go-Round, 1932 (Columbia). Fine, on linen, one-sheet.
$1,045 (Auc. #04)

The Wasp Woman, 1959 (The Film Group). Very good, insert. $800 (Auc. #01)

The Watch Dog, 1923 (Pathe). Hal Roach. Very good, on linen, one-sheet.
$350 (Auc. #07)

Way Down East, 1935. Henry Fonda. Fine, one-sheet. $440 (Auc. #03)

Way Out West, 1937 (MGM). Laurel and Hardy. Fine, unfolded, insert.
$2,070 (Auc. #09)

The Way to Love, 1933 (Paramount). Maurice Chevalier. Fine, on linen, one-sheet.
$1,045 (Auc. #04)

We Live Again, 1934 (United Artists). Fredric March. Fine, on linen, one-sheet.
$2,200 (Auc. #04)

We Were Dancing, 1942 (MGM). Melvyn Douglas and Norma Shearer. Good, one-sheet.
$200 (Auc. #07)

The Wedding March, 1926 (Paramount). Erich von Stroheim. Fine, window card.
$495 (Auc. #08)

Weird Woman, 1944 (Universal). Lon Chaney. Fine, complete set of eight lobby cards. $300 (Auc. #02)

Werewolf of London, 1951 reissue (Realart). Good, insert. $425 (Auc. #02)

The Western Code, 1932 (Columbia). Tim McCoy. Very good, one-sheet. $250 (Auc. #02)

Westside Story, 1961 (United Artists). Natalie Wood. Good, one-sheet. $75 (Auc. #07)

What a Widow!, 1930 (United Artists). Gloria Swanson. Fine, unfolded, half-sheet. $825 (Auc. #04)

What Every Girl Should Know, 1927 (Warner Bros.). Fine, on linen, one-sheet. $825 (Auc. #04)

What's the Matador, 1942 (Columbia). Three Stooges. Fine, on linen, one-sheet. $2,750 (Auc. #04)

When Romance Rides, 1922 (Goldwyn). Zane Grey. Good, on linen, one-sheet. $550 (Auc. #07)

When Thief Meets Thief, 1937 (United Artists). Douglas Fairbanks. Fine, on linen, one-sheet. $403 (Auc. #09)

When Worlds Collide, 1951 (Paramount). Very good, on linen, one-sheet. $715 (Auc. #05)

As above, very good, on linen, one-sheet. $990 (Auc. #06)

Whispering Wires, 1926 (Wm. Fox). Anita Stewart. Fine, on linen, one-sheet. $495 (Auc. #08)

White Christmas, 1954 (Paramount). Bing Crosby and Danny Kaye. Very good, two styles, half-sheets. $375 (Auc. #02)

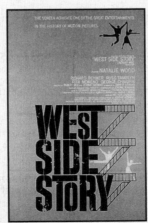

Courtesy of Camden House Auctioneers.

White Eagle, 1931. Buck Jones. Fine, on linen, three-sheet. $2,420 (Auc. #08)

White Heat, 1949 (Warner Bros.). James Cagney. Fine, insert. $495 (Auc. #03)
As above, good, complete set of eight lobby cards. $225 (Auc. #01)

White Man, 1924 (Preferred). Fine, on linen, one-sheet. $400 (Auc. #02)

The White Sister, 1923 (Metro). Lillian Gish. Very good, on linen, three-sheet.
                                                        $8,250 (Auc. #04)

The White Sister, 1933 (MGM). Helen Hayes and Clark Gable. Very good,
insert. $400 (Auc. #01)

Why Leave Home?, 1929 (Wm. Fox). Fine, on linen, one-sheet. $1,265 (Auc. #09)

Wife, Doctor and Nurse, 1937 (Fox). Very good, one-sheet. $100 (Auc. #07)

Wife Versus Secretary, 1936 (MGM). Clark Gable and Jean Harlow. Very good,
window card. $325 (Auc. #02)

Wild Cargo, 1934 (RKO). Frank Buck. Fine, on linen, one-sheet. $660 (Auc. #04)

Wild Company, 1930 (Fox). Frank Albertson. Fine, on linen, one-sheet.
                                                         $660 (Auc. #08)

The Wild One, 1954 (Columbia). Marlon Brando. Fine, on linen, one-sheet.
                                                         $460 (Auc. #09)

The Window, 1949 (RKO). Barbara Hale and Bobby Driscoll. Very good, on
linen, three-sheet. $425 (Auc. #07)

Winds of the Wasteland, 1936 (Republic). John Wayne. Fine, on linen, three-
sheet. $5,980 (Auc. #09)

Wine, Women and Horses, 1937 (other company). Very good, one-sheet.
                                                         $150 (Auc. #02)

Wings, 1927 (Paramount). Clara Bow. Fine, window card. $2,000 (Auc. #02)

Wise Guys Prefer Brunettes, 1926 (Pathe). Hal Roach. Fine, one-sheet.
                                                         $275 (Auc. #08)

The Wiser Sex, 1932 (Paramount). Melvyn Douglas and Claudette Colbert. Fine,
on linen, one-sheet. $550 (Auc. #04)

The Wizard of Oz, 1939 (MGM). Judy Garland. Very good, unfolded, half-sheet.
                                                      $11,000 (Auc. #02)
As above, fine, unfolded, half-sheet. $19,800 (Auc. #04)
As above, fine, lobby card (wiping the Lion's tears). $3,850 (Auc. #04)
As above, very good, lobby card (wiping the Lion's tears). $3,000 (Auc. #07)
As above, very good, lobby card (Tin Man). $2,000 (Auc. #01)
As above, very good, lobby card (Land of Oz). $650 (Auc. #01)
As above, very good, lobby card (on the road to Oz) $2,750 (Auc. #07)

As above, very good, lobby card (Lion, Scarecrow and
  Tin Man as soldiers). $1,100 (Auc. #07)
As above, 1955 reissue, fine, on linen, insert. $300 (Auc. #02)

The Wolf Man, 1941 (Universal). Lon Chaney. Very good, on linen, one-sheet.
                                                          $8,500 (Auc. #02)
As above, very good, on linen, one-sheet. $9,900 (Auc. #05)
As above, very good, lobby card (in the forest). $4,950 (Auc. #06)

Woman, 1918 (Maurice Tourneur). Fine, on linen, one-sheet. $863 (Auc. #09)

The Woman Accused, 1933 (Paramount). Cary Grant. Fine, insert.
                                                            $325 (Auc. #02)

The Woman Alone, 1936 (Gaumont British). Alfred Hitchcock. Very good, on
linen, three-sheet. $7,700 Auc. #06)
As above, fine, insert. $1,500 (Auc. #07)

A Woman Commands, 1932 (RKO). Pola Negri. Fine, on linen, three-sheet.
                                                          $1,100 (Auc. #06)

The Woman in Green, 1945 (Universal). Sherlock Holmes. Fine, on linen, one-
sheet. $385 (Auc. #08)
As above, fine, insert. $330 (Auc. #03)
As above, very good, half-sheet. $225 (Auc. #02)
As above, fine, complete set of eight lobby cards. $550 (Auc. #01)

Courtesy of
Swann
Galleries.

Courtesy of Odyssey Auctions.

Woman of the Year, 1942 (MGM). Spencer Tracy and Katharine Hepburn. Very good, on linen, window card. $200 (Auc. #07)

Woman Trap, 1929 (Paramount). Evelyn Brent. Fine, on linen, one-sheet. $275 (Auc. #08)

A Woman's Face, 1941 (MGM). Joan Crawford and Melvyn Douglas. Very good, on linen, one-sheet. $302 (Auc. #05)

The Women, 1939 (MGM). Joan Crawford. Fine, insert. $600 (Auc. #02)

Women in Prison, 1937 (Columbia). Very good, one-sheet. $275 (Auc. #02)

The Women on Trial, French, 1927 (Paramount). Good, on linen, 47 x 63 inches. $750 (Auc. #01)

World Without End, 1956 (Allied Artists). Fine, insert. $100 (Auc. #02)

Wuthering Heights, 1939 (United Artists). Laurence Olivier. Fine, on linen, one-sheet. $1,045 (Auc. #04)
As above, Belgian, very good, on linen, 23 x 31 inches. $600 (Auc. #07)
As above, French, good, on linen, 44 x 60 inches. $150 (Auc. #07)

Wyoming Outlaw, 1939 (Republic). John Wayne. Very good, on linen, one-sheet. $800 (Auc. #01)

❦ **Y**

A Yank in the RAF, 1941 (Fox). Tyrone Power and Betty Grable. Very good, on linen, three-sheet. $400 (Auc. #01)

The Yankee Clipper, 1927. William Boyd. Fine, one-sheet. $880 (Auc. #08)

Yankee Doodle Dandy, 1942 (Warner Bros.). James Cagney. Fine, on linen, six-sheet. $4,500 (Auc. #01)
As above, fine, one-sheet. $375 (Auc. #02)
As above, fine, half-sheet. $550 (Auc. #06)
As above, very good, complete set of eight lobby cards. $650 (Auc. #01)
As above, fine, window card. $425 (Auc. #07)

Yellow Submarine, 1968 (United Artists). The Beatles. Fine, one-sheet. $385 (Auc. #08)

Yes or No?, 1920 (First National). Norma Talmadge. Very good, on linen, one-sheet. $500 (Auc. #02)

You Can't Cheat an Honest Man, 1939 (Universal). W. C. Fields. Fine, on linen, one-sheet. $3,300 (Auc. #04)

You Can't Fool Your Wife, 1940 (RKO). Lucille Ball. Very good, one-sheet. $175 (Auc. #02)

You Can't Get Away With Murder, 1939 (Warner Bros.). Humphrey Bogart. Fine, on linen, one-sheet. $2,750 (Auc. #04)

You Can't Take It With You, 1938 (Columbia). James Stewart. Fine, on linen, one-sheet. $950 (Auc. #02)
As above, Australian, fine, on linen, one-sheet. $375 (Auc. #01)

You Only Live Twice, 1967. (United Artists). Sean Connery as James Bond. Very good, 40 x 60 inches. $125 (Auc. #07)

You Said a Mouthful, 1931 (First National). Joe E. Brown and Ginger Rogers. Fine, one-sheet. $1,430 (Auc. #06)
As above, fine, on linen, one-sheet. $1,093 (Auc. #09)

You'll Never Get Rich, 1941 (Columbia). Fred Astaire and Rita Hayworth. Fine, on linen, one-sheet. $518 (Auc. #09)
As above, good, complete set of eight lobby cards. $100 (Auc. #02)

Yukon Jake, 1924 (Pathe). Mack Sennett. Very good, on linen, one-sheet.
$1,815 (Auc. #06)

❦ **Z**

Zaza, 1938 (Paramount). Claudette Colbert. Fine, on linen, three-sheet.
$863 (Auc. #09)
As above, fine, one-sheet. $1,100 (Auc. #01)

Ziegfeld Follies, 1945 (MGM). Fred Astaire, Judy Garland, Gene Kelly, and others. George Petty, artist. Very good, on linen, six-sheet. $1,650 (Auc. #06)
As above, good, on linen, three-sheet. $1,000 (Auc. #02)
As above, good, one-sheet. $900 (Auc. #01)
As above, very good, one-sheet. $650 (Auc. #02)
As above, fine, on linen, one-sheet (Vargas art). $605 (Auc. #08)
As above, fine, unfolded, insert. $325 (Auc. #02)

❦ CHAPTER 28 ❦
Cartoon Film Posters

BY MARK WILSON

Mark Wilson is an avid collector of cartoon film posters, and a comic book dealer. You can write to him at P.O. Box 340, Castle Rock, Washington 98611.

Many of us grew up during the television era, watching those wonderful old cartoon reruns after school and on Saturdays. I am from the second generation of cartoon connoisseurs who grew up in a time when theaters no longer offered a cartoon before each movie.

I've often wondered what it would have been like to see it all from the beginning. To stand in front of an early theater house looking up at the first images of Bugs Bunny, Popeye, Mickey Mouse, Tom and Jerry, Donald Duck, and the like, proudly displayed outside, beckoning me in.

Cartoon posters are one of the most beautiful of all animation collectibles. They are pieces of history, in their words and pictures.

WHY THE RECENT POPULARITY OF CARTOON POSTERS?

Cartoons have come back to the theaters, where they belong. Thanks to recent technological advances, cartoons are becoming a profitable business once again. More full-length feature cartoons have been made in this last decade than in the previous twenty-five years. People are lining up to see cartoon stars, new and old, by the millions.

The posters made for these new features are stunning, to say the least. What was once a throwaway item is now looked upon as an art form, highly prized by many. What seems to be happening in the market today is a reshuffling of material from established to newer collectors.

As this collecting field has become increasingly "legitimized" through the attention of major auction houses such as Christie's, a recent influx of new collectors has created a demand for earlier posters like never before.

Most collectors entering the field have the same questions: What posters should I look for? How much are they worth? Where can I acquire them? Hopefully I can answer these questions well enough to get you started.

THE SILENT ERA

It all began shortly after the turn of the century. One of the earliest cartoon posters ever made was Winsor McCay's poster for *Little Nemo in Slumberland,* 1911. McCay had this poster made for his vaudeville act, which included a two-minute cartoon short. Animation was in its infancy and had not yet achieved theater status. Cartoons were considered a curiosity and fit very well into his act, which had great success in the United States and Europe. McCay made three more cartoons during the next few years, his most popular being *Gertie the Dinosaur,* 1914. The poster promoting this film is spectacular. Although McCay was not the first to make a cartoon, he is recognized by many as the creator of the animated cartoon.

The next animation studio of note was the Bray Studio, created by John R. Bray in 1913. Many beautiful posters came out of the Bray era, most notably the first KoKo the Clown, created by a couple of new animators, Max and Dave Fleischer, in 1918.

About this time Bud Fisher's Mutt & Jeff came to the screen, followed by such notables as Gorge Herriman's Krazy Kat and Otto Messmer's Felix the Cat.

The 1920s brought us Paul Terry's *Aesop's Fables,* and Walt Disney's *Alice* series and *Oswald the Luck Rabbit* series.

Collecting cartoon posters from the silent era is very difficult at best. In those days, cartoons were considered a "freebie" for the patron, and many times the posters were an unwanted expense for theater owners, who spent very little advertising the current cartoon.

Consequently, few posters were rented from the theater exchanges, leaving only a fraction of them surviving today. Acquiring a cartoon poster from the silent era for your collection is truly an accomplishment that takes a certain amount of sleuthing and patience. However, the reward of owning so valuable an early piece of animation history is well worth it.

THE GOLDEN AGE

It all began, strangely enough, with a crudely drawn mouse that talked. In 1927 Warner Bros.' *The Jazz Singer* created a sensation. This film brought a new and welcome innovation to filmmaking that would change the industry forever: sound. The public loved it.

About this same time a man by the name of Walt Disney had just lost his job and his newest cartoon creation, Oswald the Rabbit. Teaming up with his longtime friend, U. B. Iwerks, they started a new studio with a new character named Mickey Mouse.

There was nothing special about Mickey Mouse that set him above any of the other cartoon characters of the day. It was Disney's brilliance and a little luck that made Mickey great. Disney and U. B. Iwerks had finished two Mickey cartoons (not yet released) and were just completing their third, *Steamboat Willie* (1928), when Disney had an idea. Why not add sound? The rest is history.

Recently another rare early sound cartoon poster starring Mickey Mouse came on the market: *The Cactus Kid*, from 1930. This one-sheet poster, described in the listings following this chapter, sold for $29,900 including buyer's premium at Christie's East in June 1993. Recently yet another rare Mickey Mouse poster, *Ye Olden Days* (1933), was reportedly sold privately for $60,000.

Mickey's success gave Walt the money to release his creativity. Over the next several years, many familiar faces made their debut on the screen: Minnie Mouse, Donald and Daisy Duck, Goofy, Pluto, Huey, Duey, and Louey, Chip and Dale, and a multitude of lesser characters from his *Silly Symphonies* series.

Some of Disney's greatest work was achieved in his full-feature cartoons such as *Snow White* (1937), *Pinocchio* (1940), *Dumbo* (1941), *Bambi* (1942), *Fantasia* (1941), *Cinderella* (1950), *Alice in Wonderland* (1951), *Lady and the Tramp* (1955), *Sleeping Beauty* (1959), and *One Hundred and One Dalmations* (1961). These posters are extremely popular and highly sought after by collectors.

Generally speaking, the earlier Disney full-length feature posters command higher prices than those produced in the 1950s and 1960s. For example, a *Dumbo* three-sheet poster recently sold for $19,800 at auction, including buyer's premium; a *Fantasia* one-sheet poster brought $6,600; and a *Pinocchio* one-sheet also fetched $6,600.

Among the most sought after is *Snow White and the Seven Dwarfs*, Disney's first full-length feature cartoon. Recently a rare style B one-sheet poster sold for $12,650 at auction, including buyer's premium. This poster is sought after because it actually shows Snow White, whereas another one-sheet for the same film, style A, showing only the dwarfs, sold for only $1,870.

There are many less expensive Disney posters from the later years, so don't be discouraged by these prices. Many of the one-sheet posters for full-length Disney films of the 1950s and 1960s still sell for under $1,000 at auction. Bargains can also be found when buying posters for reissues.

For example, the poster for the 1943 reissue of *Snow White* recently sold at auction for only $350, and $500 can still buy you a beautiful Pluto or Goofy cartoon poster from the 1950s.

Another way to buy cartoon posters at lower prices is to look for the foreign film posters for Disney cartoons. Many were released in Spain, Argentina, France, and a host of other countries. For example, an Argentine version of *Fantasia,* in approximately the same size as a one-sheet, recently sold at auction for only $1,045, including buyer's premium. Prices on foreign cartoon posters will undoubtedly increase in the years ahead as the market generally advances.

Seeing Disney's success, other studios were formed or restructured to wage battle for their share of the market. Cartoons were finally becoming a profitable business.

Paul Terry ended his *Aesop's Fables* series and created the Terry Toons studio in 1930, showcasing the likes of Farmer Alfalfa, Kiko the Kangaroo, and Puddy the Pup. The late 1930s and early 1940s brought Gandy Goose, Sour Puss, and Dinky Duck to the screen. Very few people remember these characters, but they were well received in their day. Terry Toons' finest hour came in 1942 with the creation of Super Mouse, who was renamed Mighty Mouse the following year.

Terry Toons posters are among the most inexpensive of the period, mainly because of their lack of a dynamic cast of characters and because they relied almost exclusively on semistock posters to market their cartoons. Prices will usually range from $200 to $800, depending on age and featured character. The earlier posters from 1930 to 1932, however, can bring as much as $2,500, especially if they are not duotone graphics, but full poster art not intended for a stock sheet.

Leon Schlesinger (Warner Bros.) entered the market with his *Looney Tunes* series in 1930, and featured a character named Bosko, who was an immediate success. He later added his *Merrie Melodies* series to compete with Disney's *Silly Symphonies*. In 1935 a new star was born by the name of Porky Pig. This was the beginning of the golden years for Warner Bros.

Soon many other stars would follow from this talented studio, including Bugs Bunny, Daffy Duck, Elmer Fudd, Tweety and Sylvester, Yosemite Sam, Foghorn Leghorn, and many more. No studio, other than Disney (perhaps), created as many true cartoon stars as the Warner Bros. studio.

Like Terry Toons, the Warner Studio (unfortunately) relied almost exclusively on stock posters, so there are no posters designed specifically for any one cartoon. Even so, most are very beautiful and highly sought by collectors. Prices will range from a low of $200 for a 1950s duotone (two-color) poster to a high of $8,000 for the first Bosko poster. Many of their very best posters are still available for under $2,000. A real bargain for the collector or investor.

Big things were happening at the Fleischer Studio in the 1930s. Betty Boop made her debut in 1931, followed by Popeye in 1933. These two characters were Fleischer's biggest stars.

In 1935 Popeye was voted the nation's most popular cartoon character (even ahead of Mickey Mouse) and went on to star in three highly successful full-color featurettes. Betty Boop was more popular with the adult crowd because of the skimpy outfits she wore and the sexual innuendo present in most of her cartoons. Betty Boop's cartoons were definitely not G-rated, even by today's standards. The success of these two characters carried the studio for nearly a decade until Superman came to the rescue in 1941. Unfortunately, even Superman couldn't save the Fleischer studio from closing its doors a year later.

There were many other characters created by Fleischer Studios, including two full-feature cartoons—*Gulliver's Travels* and *Mr. Bug Goes To Town*—an achievement only Disney could top.

Posters from the Fleischer Studio are highly sought after and quite scarce. However, many of their lesser titles can still be purchased for under $1,000. The one-sheet for *Gulliver's Travels*, Fleischer's first full-feature cartoon from 1939, sells for about $3,000.

Early appearances of their main characters can command several thousand dollars. For example, the first full-color Popeye poster from 1934 has sold for as high as $25,000 due to its large size (42 x 62 inches), early vintage, and full-color graphics. Only two are known to exist.

MGM entered the market in 1934 with its *Happy Harmonies* series, which included a new-look Bosko, Little Cheezer, and other less notable characters. In 1938 they brought the *Captain and the Kids* to the screen, with mild success.

MGM may have boasted the most successful movie studios with "more stars than in the heavens," but they were new at making cartoons, and it showed.

It wasn't until the 1940s that the lion could finally roar with the birth of several new cartoon stars. The first was Barney Bear, followed by seven-time Academy Award winner Tom and Jerry (in 1941) and a load of incredibly funny Tex Avery-directed cartoons, which included Droopy, Red and the Wolf, Screwy Squirrel, Spike, and many more.

Posters from the MGM golden era are distinctive and beautiful. It wouldn't be unfair to say that this studio consistently created the best posters during the 1940s. During this decade (and for a few years into the 1950s) they used no stock posters for any of their cartoons, a feat duplicated only by Disney. But they did even more. Nearly all of their posters during this era were beautiful full-color stone lithographs, a costly expenditure for a cartoon studio. MGM went first-class.

Posters from this studio are very affordable and desirable, ranging from a low $300 for a 1950s full stock poster to more than $3,000 for a classic Tex Avery cartoon or an early Tom and Jerry. Many people don't realize that Tom and Jerry cartoons won seven Academy Awards over a ten-year period. Their posters were stone lithographs until 1952. Many of MGM's most beautiful posters can still be purchased for under $800. I'm sure this will soon change as more collectors become aware of their beauty.

Other studios that produced cartoons and cartoon posters include Columbia, Walter Lanz, Paramount (Famous), U. B. Iwerks, Van Beuren, and UPA. Space does not allow us to describe the posters of these studios here, but with a little research you can learn more about them and watch the market for examples.

HOW SCARCE IS SCARCE?

The number of posters printed for a particular cartoon short depended on the number of theaters signed up with the studio to show the cartoon. That could mean printing a few hundred (as was the case prior to 1920) or a few thousand.

The Disney and Fleischer full-feature cartoon posters had among the largest print runs, as they were a main event promoted with the same energy and budget as any big movie of their day. Still, very few posters from these early features have survived.

Unlike many of today's collectibles, original cartoon posters were never sold to the general public. They were rented to theaters by a theater exchange in their area, and had to be returned to the exchange along with the cartoon reel when the cartoon had finished its run. When the exchange received its poster back, it would either be sent on to the next theater, or destroyed if it was damaged.

Ultimately, nearly all were destroyed. Those that survived were left in theaters, where the owner simply forgot or didn't bother to return them to the theater exchange. Others have survived in old theater exchanges that went out of business but never disposed of their inventory. Very few were purposely saved.

No one knows for sure, but I would estimate that of the six thousand or so different cartoon posters that were produced from 1910 to 1950, one-sheet posters for only about 20 percent of these titles, or about twelve hundred, have survived.

For beginning collectors there is a wide variety of affordable, colorful cartoon posters from the 1960s, 1970s, and 1980s that range in price from under $25 to about $100. For example, you can still buy a beautiful *Jungle Book* poster for under $100, or a *Roger Rabbit* poster for about $20.

Because of the growing competition in Hollywood for cartoon film audiences, some of the best artwork ever has been produced in the last ten years. Most of these are too cheap for dealers or auction houses to bother with, but they can be found at paper collectible and antique shows, and in movie poster stores across the country.

HOW TO START COLLECTING CARTOON POSTERS

First and foremost, collect what you like. I cannot overemphasize this first step. Start by going to your local theater and asking the manager for any old posters. This will sometimes yield great rewards. Another good source is antique and paper collectible shows already mentioned. These shows are held many times a year in almost every state.

Subscribe to *Movie Collectors World* (see the listing in the Resource Guide), a bimonthly tabloid designed for the express purpose of movie poster collecting. They also list information about the latest poster sales conventions. Poster conventions are a treasure house for the new collector as you can establish contact with many dealers while searching for posters for your collection.

Contrary to popular belief, you will get some of your best deals at auction houses, if you are informed about the market and know what to look for in terms of subject and condition. When buying at auction, it is important to decide beforehand how much you are willing to spend on a given poster, and then do your best not to exceed your limits in the excitement of the auction process.

Contact the auction houses that hold special auctions of movie posters listed in the Resource Guide in this volume. Usually movie poster auctions include at least a few cartoon posters.

CARTOON POSTERS—PRICE LISTINGS
IN ALPHABETICAL ORDER BY FILM TITLE:

NOTE: See the chapter Important Notes on the Price Listings for more information on prices given. For an explanation of sizes (half-sheet, one-sheet, window card, etc.) and for certain terms used in the listings, see the chapter on Cinema Posters. Also note that, of all the fields of poster collecting, cinema posters are changing most rapidly in terms of price. Check with a reputable dealer for the latest price on the posters that interest you the most.

❦ **A**

Alias St. Nick, 1935 (MGM). Fair, on linen, one-sheet. $325 (Auc. #01)

Alice in Wonderland, 1951 (RKO-Disney). Fine, one-sheet. $900 (Auc. #01)
As above, fine, one-sheet. $750 (Auc. #02)
As above, very good, on linen, one-sheet. $770 (Auc. #06)
As above, fine, on linen, one-sheet. $800 (Auc. #07)
As above, very good, one-sheet. $880 (Auc. #09)
As above, insert. $325 (Auc. #02)
As above, very good, insert. $500 (Auc. #07)
As above, fine, unfolded, half-sheet. $200 (Auc. #02)
As above, very good, unfolded, half-sheet. $450 (Auc. #07)
As above, very good, complete set of eight lobby cards. $600 (Auc. #01)
As above, good, complete set of eight lobby cards. $550 (Auc. #01)

❦ **B**

Bambi, 1942 (Disney). Fine, on linen, three-sheet. $1,320 (Auc. #03)
As above, very good, insert. $550 (Auc. #02)
As above, fine, insert. $385 (Auc. #03)
As above, 1948 reissue, fine, on linen, one-sheet. $400 (Auc. #07)
As above, 1957 reissue, fine, on linen, six-sheet. $500 (Auc. #07)
As above, Spanish, ca. 1940s/50s, good, 27 x 39 inches. $400 (Auc. #01)

Barney Bear's Victory Garden, 1942 (MGM). Fine, on linen, one-sheet.
  $770 (Auc. #04)

Batty Baseball, 1943 (MGM). Fine, on linen, one-sheet. $700 (Auc. #02)

The Bear and the Beavers, 1942 (MGM). Barney Bear. Fine, on linen, one-sheet. $550 (Auc. #03)
As above, fine, on linen, one-sheet. $920 (Auc. #09)

Beezy Bear, 1955 (RKO-Disney). Donald Duck. Fine, on linen, one-sheet.
  $550 (Auc. #02)

Boston Beanie, 1947 (Rhapsody). Good, one-sheet. $220 (Auc. #06)

The Boy and the Wolf, 1943 (MGM). Very good, on linen, one-sheet.
  $475 (Auc. #01)

The Brave Tin Soldier, 1934 (Celebrity Prod.). Fair, on linen, one-sheet.
  $850 (Auc. #01)

Bugs Bunny Cartoon Revue, 1953 (Warner Bros.). Fine, on linen, one-sheet.
  $450 (Auc. #02)
As above, fine, on linen, one-sheet. $500 (Auc. #07)

🌿 **C**

The Cactus Kid, 1930 (Columbia). Mickey Mouse. A Walt Disney Comic, drawn by U. B. Iwerks. Very good, on linen, one-sheet. This outstanding, rare poster advertises, "He talks! He Sings! He Dances!" and gives credit to the original Mickey Mouse artist, U. B. Iwerks. $29,900 (Auc. #09)

Chips Ahoy, 1956 (RKO-Disney). Donald Duck. Fine, on linen, one-sheet.
$750 (Auc. #02)

Cinderella, 1950 (Disney). Very good, one-sheet. $450 (Auc. #01)
As above, fine, one-sheet. $440 (Auc. #03)
As above, good, insert. $125 (Auc. #02)
As above, very good, insert. $150 (Auc. #07)
As above, very good, unfolded, half-sheet. $175 (Auc. #02)
As above, very good, complete set of eight lobby cards. $150 (Auc. #02)

Cruise Cat, 1952 (MGM). Tom and Jerry. Fine, on linen, one-sheet.
$440 (Auc. #03)

🌿 **D**

Der Fuehrer's Face, 1943 (RKO-Disney). Donald Duck. Fine, on linen, one-sheet. $2,760 (Auc. #09)

The Dissatisfied Cobbler, 1922 (Pathe). Aesop's Film Fables. Fine, on linen, one-sheet. $3,520 (Auc. #04)

Courtesy of
Christie's East.

Courtesy of Camden House
Auctioneers.

Don Quixote, 1934 (Celebrity Prod.). Fair, on linen, one-sheet.
$1,300 (Auc. #01)

Dumbo, 1941 (RKO-Disney). Fine, on linen, three-sheet.　$19,800 (Auc. #04)
As above, very good, on linen, one-sheet.　$3,680 (Auc. #09)
As above, fine, complete set of eight lobby cards.　$3,500 (Auc. #01)
As above, fine, complete set of eight lobby cards.　$2,250 (Auc. #02)

❦ E

The Early Bird, 1928 (Pathe). Aesop's Film Fables. Good, on linen, one-sheet.
$825 (Auc. #04)

❦ F

Fall Out Fall In, Australian, ca. 1940s (RKO-Disney). Fine, on linen, 13 x 30 inches.　$200 (Auc. #02)

Falling Hare, 1941–42 (Warner Bros.). Bugs Bunny. Fine, on linen, one-sheet.
$1,320 (Auc. #04)

Fantasia, 1941 (Disney). Fine, on linen, one-sheet.　$6,600 (Auc. #04)
As above, fine, insert.　$1,650 (Auc. #03)
As above, fine, unfolded, half-sheet.　$2,645 (Auc. #09)
As above, Argentine, fine, on linen, 29 x 43 inches.　$1,000 (Auc. #01)
As above, Argentine, on linen, 29 x 44 inches.　$1,045 (Auc. #05)
As above, Australian, good, 14½ x 39½ inches.　$850 (Auc. #07)

Flip the Frog, 1933 (MGM). Fine, on linen, one-sheet.　$4,180 (Auc. #04)

The Flying Squirrel, 1955 (RKO-Disney). Donald Duck. Fine, on linen, one-sheet.　$425 (Auc. #02)

Food for Feudin', 1950 (RKO-Disney). Pluto. Very good, on linen, one-sheet.
$600 (Auc. #02)

Frankenstein's Cat, 1942 (20th Century Fox). Terry Toons. Fine, on linen, one-sheet.　$330 (Auc. #08)

Fun and Fancy Free, 1947 (Disney). Mickey, Goofy, and Donald. Very good, on linen, one-sheet.　$385 (Auc. #06)

❦ G

Get Rich Quick, 1951 (RKO-Disney). Goofy. Fine, on linen, one-sheet.
$550 (Auc. #02)

❦ H

Halloween Hilarities, 1953 (Disney). Donald Duck. Fine, one-sheet.
$330 (Auc. #03)

Happy Days, 1934 (Celebrity). P. A. Powers. Fine, on linen, one-sheet.
$1,150 (Auc. #09)

Heir Bear, 1952 (MGM). Fine, one-sheet. $225 (Auc. #02)

The Hick Chick, 1946 (MGM). Fine, on linen, one-sheet. $400 (Auc. #02)

Hollywood Graduation, 1938 (Columbia). Fine, on linen, one-sheet.
$550 (Auc. #02)

The House of Tomorrow, 1949 (MGM). Fine, on linen, one-sheet.
$500 (Auc. #02)

🌿 **J**

Joining the Tanks, ca. 1910s (Wm. Fox). Mutt & Jeff. Very good, one-sheet.
$3,500 (Auc. #02)

🌿 **K**

Krazy Kat, ca. 1930s (Columbia). Very good, on linen, one-sheet.
$1,100 (Auc. #02)

🌿 **L**

Lady and the Tramp, 1955 (Disney). Very good, on linen, three-sheet.
$1,000 (Auc. #01)
As above, very good, on linen, three-sheet. $467.50 (Auc. #06)
As above, very good, three-sheet. $750 (Auc. #07)
As above, fine, on linen, one-sheet. $900 (Auc. #01)
As above, fine, on linen, one-sheet. $900 (Auc. #02)

Courtesy of Camden
House Auctioneers.

As above, fine, on linen, one-sheet. $475 (Auc. #07)
As above, fine, on linen, one-sheet. $690 (Auc. #09)
As above, unfolded, insert. $550 (Auc. #02)
As above, very good, insert. $500 (Auc. #07)
As above, very good, unfolded, half-sheet. $500 (Auc. #07)
As above, fine, title card. $150 (Auc. #02)

Little Boy Blue, ca. early 1930s (Celebrity Prod.). Good, on linen, one-sheet.
               $475 (Auc. #01)

The Little Mole, 1941 (MGM). Very good, one-sheet. $550 (Auc. #01)

Looney Tunes Stock Poster, 1944 reissue (Warner Bros.). Daffy Duck and Porky Pig. Fine, on linen, one-sheet. $375 (Auc. #02)
As above, very good, on linen, one-sheet. $357.50 (Auc. #06)

Loopy De Loop!, 1960 (Columbia). Fine, on linen, one-sheet. $300 (Auc. #02)

❦ **M**

Magoo Breaks Par, 1957 (Columbia). Fine, on linen, one-sheet. $500 (Auc. #02)

Make Mine Music, 1946 (RKO-Disney). Very good, one-sheet. $125 (Auc. #02)

Melody Time, 1948 (RKO-Disney). Very good, unfolded, half-sheet.
               $50 (Auc. #02)

MGM Cartoons, 1955 (MGM). Tom and Jerry and others. Very good, one-sheet. $225 (Auc. #02)

Mr. Bug Goes To Town, 1941 (Paramount). Fleischer Studios. Fair, on linen, three-sheet. $1,600 (Auc. #01)
As above, fine, on linen, one-sheet. $748 (Auc. #09)
As above, very good, insert. $225 (Auc. #02)
As above, good, complete set of eight lobby cards. $375 (Auc. #01)

Mutt & Jeff in Havana. Bud Fisher. Fine, one-sheet. $385 (Auc. #08)

❦ **N**

Noveltoon, 1943 (Paramount). Very good, on linen, one-sheet. $150 (Auc. #07)

❦ **O**

Officer Duck, 1939 (Disney). Donald Duck. Good, on linen, one-sheet.
            $4,180 (Auc. #04)

One Hundred and One Dalmations, 1961 (Disney). Fine, on linen, six-sheet.
               $850 (Auc. #02)
As above, very good, one-sheet. $800 (Auc. #02)
As above, good, one-sheet. $175 (Auc. #02)
As above, fine, on linen, one-sheet. $748 (Auc. #09)

As above, fine, unfolded, insert. $300 (Auc. #02)
As above, fine, unfolded, insert. $425 (Auc. #07)
As above, very good, unfolded, half-sheet. $250 (Auc. #02)
As above, very good, on linen, half-sheet. $550 (Auc. #07)
As above, fine, complete set of nine lobby cards. $400 (Auc. #07)

🕯 **P**

Peter Pan, 1953 (Disney). Fine, on linen, one-sheet. $385 (Auc. #08)
As above, fine, on linen, one-sheet. $475 (Auc. #07)
As above, good, insert. $150 (Auc. #02)

The Pig's Curly Tail, 1926 (Bray). Fine, on linen, one-sheet. $1,650 (Auc. #04)

Pinocchio, 1940 (RKO-Disney). Fine, on linen, three-sheet. $4,675 (Auc. #08)
As above, fine, on linen, one-sheet. $6,050 (Auc. #04)
As above, fine, on linen, one-sheet. $5,280 (Auc. #05)
As above, very good, unfolded, half-sheet. $3,000 (Auc. #02)
As above, fine, unfolded, half-sheet. $6,380 (Auc. #04)
As above, fine, window card. $880 (Auc. #03)
As above, 1945 reissue, very good, half-sheet. $100 (Auc. #02)

Popeye, 1943 (Paramount). Very good, one-sheet. $425 (Auc. #01)
As above, very good, one-sheet. $200 (Auc. #02)
As above, fine, on linen, one-sheet. $200 (Auc. #07)

Popeye Cartoon, 1950 (Paramount). Fine, on linen, one-sheet. $900 (Auc. #02)

Courtesy of Swann
Galleries, Inc.

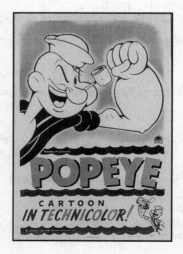

Courtesy of Camden House
Auctioneers.

Practical Pig, 1951 reissue (Disney). Good, on linen, one-sheet.
$500 (Auc. #01)

Puppetoon, 1944 (Paramount). Good, one-sheet. $225 (Auc. #01)

❦ **R**

Rock-A-Bye Bear, 1952 (MGM). Fine, one-sheet. $300 (Auc. #01)

❦ **S**

Sea Scouts, 1939 (Disney). Donald Duck. Fine, on linen, one-sheet.
$6,600 (Auc. #04)

Señor Droopy, 1948 (MGM). Droopy Dog. Fine, on linen, one-sheet.
$1,650 (Auc. #03)

Sham Battle Shenanigans, 1940 (20th Century Fox). Terry Toons. Good, on linen, one-sheet. $165 (Auc. #06)

The Shooting of Dan McGoo, 1944 (MGM). Fine, on linen, one-sheet.
$1,045 (Auc. #04)

Sleeping Beauty, 1959 (Disney). Fine, one-sheet; style B, sought-after style showing Sleeping Beauty with woodland creatures. $1,210 (Auc. #03)
As above, fine, on linen, one-sheet, style B. $690 (Auc. #09)
As above, very good, on linen, one-sheet, style B. $550 (Auc. #06)
As above, fine, one-sheet, a different style, showing castles and armies, with the headline "Wondrous to See, Glorious to Hear." $330 (Auc. #08)
As above, very good, unfolded, 30 x 40 inches, with the headline as above. $500 (Auc. #02)
As above, fine, unfolded, insert, with the headline as above. $200 (Auc. #02)
As above, fine, unfolded, half-sheet, the wedding scene, with the headline as above. $200 (Auc. #02)
As above, very good, unfolded, half-sheet, the wedding scene, with the headline as above. $500 (Auc. #07)

Sleepy Time Tom, 1950 (MGM). Tom and Jerry. Fine, on linen, one-sheet.
$440 (Auc. #03)

Smitten Kitten, 1951 (MGM). Tom and Jerry. Fine, on linen, one-sheet.
$1,000 (Auc. #02)

Snow White and the Seven Dwarfs, 1937 (RKO-Disney). Fine, on linen, one-sheet, style B. This rare style depicts Snow White and announces, "His First Full Length Feature Production." *See color insert, photo 29.* $12,650 (Auc. #09)
As above, good, on linen, one-sheet, style A. Shows the dwarfs, but not Snow White. $1,200 (Auc. #01)
As above, good, on linen, one-sheet, style A. $1,870 (Auc. #05)

As above, insert. $9,350 (Auc. #05)
As above, fine, half-sheet. $3,520 (Auc. #08)
As above, fine, complete set of eight lobby cards. $5,520 (Auc. #09)
As above, very good, title lobby card. $500 (Auc. #02)
As above, 1943 reissue, good, on linen, one-sheet. $350 (Auc. #01)
As above, 1951 reissue, fine, on linen, one-sheet. $400 (Auc. #07)

The Sultan's Birthday, 1943 (Fox). Mighty Mouse. Fine, on linen, one-sheet.
                                                  $550 (Auc. #02)

🦋 **T**

Terry-Toon Cartoons, 1950 (Fox). Mighty Mouse, Heckle & Jeckle, and others. Fine, on linen, stock one-sheet. $650 (Auc. #02)

Terry-Toon Cartoons, 1955 (Fox). Mighty Mouse. Fine, on linen, stock one-sheet. $600 (Auc. #02)
As above, fine, on linen, stock one-sheet. $500 (Auc. #07)

🦋 **U**

The Uninvited Pest, 1943 (MGM). Barney Bear. Fine, on linen, one-sheet.
                                             $1,093 (Auc. #09)

🦋 **V**

The Valiant Tailor, 1934 (Celebrity Prod.). Very good, on linen, one-sheet.
                                             $950 (Auc. #01)

Courtesy of
Mark Wilson.

❦ **W**

Warner Brothers Cartoon, 1946. Bugs Bunny, Porky Pig, Elmer Fudd, Daffy Duck, and others. Fine, on linen, one-sheet. $1,650 (Auc. #08)

When Magoo Flew, 1954 (Columbia). Very good, on linen, one-sheet.
$275 (Auc. #02)

Wild and Woolfy, 1945 (MGM). Droopy Dog. Fine, on linen, one-sheet.
$2,750 (Auc. #04)

Woody Woodpecker Cartune, 1950 (Universal). Fine, on linen, one-sheet.
$425 (Auc. #02)

❦ **Z**

The Zoot Cat, 1944 (MGM). Fine, on linen, one-sheet. $1,840 (Auc. #09)

PART SIX

Resource Guide

❦ CHAPTER 29 ❦
Resources

AUCTION CATALOGS AND SALE DATES CITED

NOTE: The auction numbers below correspond to those found in the price listings throughout this book.

#01—Camden House Auctioneers, Vintage Film Posters & Entertainment Memorabilia, June 6 & 7, 1992. (Prices do not include 10 percent buyer's premium.)

#02—Camden House Auctioneers, Vintage Film Posters & Entertainment Memorabilia, November 7 & 8 1992. (Prices do not include 10 percent buyer's premium.)

#03—Hollywood Poster Art Auction, December 12, 1992. (Prices include 10 percent buyer's premium.)

#04—Christie's East, Hollywood Posters III, December 14, 1992. (Prices include 10 percent buyer's premium.)

#05—Swann Galleries, Movie Posters, March 18, 1993. (Prices include 10 percent buyer's premium.)

#06—Odyssey Auctions, Rock-n-Roll & Hollywood Memorabilia, Autographs & Vintage Film Posters, May 16 & 17, 1993. (Prices include 10 percent buyer's premium.)

#07—Camden House Auctioneers, Vintage Film Posters & Entertainment Memorabilia, June 5 & 6, 1993. (Prices do not include 10 percent buyer's premium.)

#08—Hollywood Poster Art Auction, June 12, 1993. (Prices include 10 percent buyer's premium.)

#09—Christie's East, Hollywood Posters III, June 14, 1993. (Prices include 15 percent buyer's premium.)

#10—Butterfield & Butterfield, Fine Art Nouveau, Art Deco & Arts & Crafts, September 21 & 22, 1992. (Prices include 10 percent buyer's premium.)

#11—Butterfield & Butterfield, Fine Art Nouveau, Art Deco & Arts & Crafts, March 31, 1993. (Prices include 15 percent buyer's premium.)

#12—Butterfield & Butterfield, Fine American, European & Contemporary Prints, May 19, 1993. (Prices include 15 percent buyer's premium.)

#13—Christie's New York, Important 20th Century Decorative Arts, December 12, 1992. (Prices include 10 percent buyer's premium.)

#14—Christie's New York, Important 20th Century Decorative Arts, March 27, 1993. (Prices include 15 percent buyer's premium.)

#15—Christie's East, 20th Century Decorative Arts, March 25, 1993. (Prices include 15 percent buyer's premium.)

#16—Leslie Hindman Auctioneers, May 16, 17 & 18, 1993. (Prices do not include 10 percent buyer's premium.)

#17—Christie's South Kensington, 19th and 20th Century Posters, February 4, 1993. (Prices include 10 percent buyer's premium. An exchange rate of 1.35 U.S. dollars to the pound sterling was used to calculate results, rounded up to the nearest increment of $25.)

#18—Christie's London, 19th and 20th Century Posters, June 3, 1992. (Prices include 10 percent buyer's premium. An exchange rate of 1.35 U.S. dollars to the pound sterling was used to calculate results, rounded up to the nearest increment of $25.)

#19—Swann Galleries, Posters, August 6, 1992. (Prices include 10 percent buyer's premium.)

#20—Bloomsbury Book Auctions, England, Posters, March 12, 1992. (Prices include 10 percent buyer's premium. An exchange rate of 1.35 U.S. dollars to the pound sterling was used to calculate results, rounded up to the nearest increment of $25.)

#21—Swann Galleries, Performing Arts, February 25, 1993. (Prices include 10 percent buyer's premium.)

#22—Swann Galleries, Ephemera, April 29, 1993. (Prices include 10 percent buyer's premium.)

#23—Rivo Oliver's, Advertising & Country Store Auction, April 3-4, 1992. (Prices do not include 10 percent buyer's premium.)

#24—Van Sabben Poster Auctions, Holland, November 1, 1992. (Prices include 18 percent buyer's premium. An exchange rate of .59 U.S. dollars to the Dutch guilder was used to calculate results, rounded up to the nearest increment of $25.)

#25—Van Sabben Poster Auctions, Holland, May 16, 1993. (Prices include 18 percent buyer's premium. An exchange rate of .59 U.S. dollars to the Dutch guilder was used to calculate results, rounded up to the nearest increment of $25.)

AUCTION HOUSES

BLOOMSBURY BOOK AUCTIONS, 3 and 4 Hardwick Street, London EC1R 4RY, ENGLAND, 071-833-2636, Fax 071-833-3954. Occasional specialized poster sales (French 1880-1930, Railways and London Underground, Shell, Travel, Shipping, etc.). Posters also sometimes included in twice yearly print sales. Also, poster reference books and clients' "wants" list kept for items and subjects.

BUTTERFIELD & BUTTERFIELD, 7601 Sunset Boulevard, Los Angeles, CA 90046, (213) 850-7500, fax (213) 850-5843. Laura Horn Nagle, diretor of prints. Also: 220 San Bruno Avenue, San Francisco, California 94103, (415) 861-8951. In business since 1865, fifth largest appraisal and auction house in the world. Posters are included in print sales as well as in Art Nouveau/Art Deco sales.

CAMDEN HOUSE AUCTIONEERS, 427 North Canon Drive, Beverly Hills, CA 90210, (310) 246-1212, fax (310) 246-0416. Michael Schwartz, president. Camden House Auctioneers is the oldest auction company dealing exclusively in film and entertainment memorabilia.

CHRISTIE'S (Christie, Manson & Woods International, Inc.), 502 Park Avenue, New York, NY 10021 (212) 546-1000. Nancy McClelland, senior vice president and head, 20th Century Decorative Arts Department. Christie's includes posters in its Art Nouveau/Art Deco auctions.

CHRISTIE'S EAST, 219 East Sixty-seventh Street, New York, NY 10021, (212)

606-0543. Collectibles Department. Major auctions of Hollywood posters yearly. Christie's East also includes posters in its Art Nouveau/Art Deco auctions.

CHRISTIE'S LONDON, 85 Old Brompton Road, London, England SW7 3LD, (071) 321-3321, fax (071) 321-3206. Richard Barclay. Biannual sale of posters, with a strong specialization in British Rail, but representing the posters of numerous countries.

LESLIE HINDMAN AUCTIONEERS, 215 West Ohio Street, Chicago, IL 60610, (312) 670-0010. Maron Matz Hindman. The Midwest's leading fine art auctioneers. Monthly auctions of works of art, prints, English, American, and Continental furniture and Decorative Arts, Oriental works of art, rugs, and jewelry.

HOLLYWOOD POSTER ART, 65 Hudson Street, Hackensack, NJ 07601, (201) 488-6333, fax (201) 488-8746. Joe Burtis. The East Coast's most complete source for original movie memorabilia. Twelve years of experience buying, selling, auctioning. Consignments, free appraisals. Sample catalog $10.

ILLUSTRATION HOUSE, INC., 96 Spring Street, New York, NY 10012, (212) 966-9444, fax (212) 966-9425. Walter and Roger Reed. Dealers and auctioneers in original art created for posters, as well as illustrations for books, magazines, and advertising.

ODYSSEY AUCTIONS, 510 A South Corona Mall, Corona, CA 91720, (714) 371-7137, fax (714) 371-7139. By appointment only, Bill Miller, president. Specializing in rock and roll and movie memorabilia auctions. Each sale features hundreds of vintage posters, autographs, props, and costumes. Bidders participate from around the world.

ONSLOW'S AUCTIONEERS, Metrostore, Townmead Road, London SW6 2R2, ENGLAND, (071) 793-0240. Patrick Bogue. Specialists in European travel posters of 1900-1960, i.e., motoring, railway, shipping, airline, winter sports, World War I and II and other printed related ephemera.

POSTER MAIL AUCTION COMPANY, P.O. Box 133, Waterford, VA 22190, (703) 882-3574, fax (703) 882-4765. R. Neil Reynolds, owner. Catalog/absentee auctions of original posters conducted entirely by mail and telephone. Posters from all categories are sold. Catalog subscription $12 annually.

SKINNER, INC., 357 Main Street, Bolton, MA, 01740, (508) 779-6241. And 63 Park Plaza, Boston, MA 02116, (617) 236-1700. Colleene Fesko, director of

American and European Paintings and Prints. Posters are included in painting and print sales as well as in arts and crafts sales, among others. Active "want list."

SWANN GALLERIES, INC., 104 East Twenty-fifth Street, New York, NY 10010, (212) 979-1017. George S. Lowry, president. Swann Galleries is the oldest and largest U.S. auctioneer specializing in rare books, autographs, photographs, Judaica, and works of art on paper. Thirty-five auctions annually, including one or more devoted exclusively to posters.

VAN SABBEN POSTER AUCTIONS, Bennebroekerlaan 41, 2121 GR Bennebroek, the Netherlands, 31-2502-49871. Piet Van Sabben, owner. Biannual auctions in Holland, with a strong specialization in Dutch posters, but representing the posters of many countries.

DEALERS AND CONTRIBUTORS TO THIS VOLUME

ANTIQUE POSTER COLLECTION GALLERY, 17 Danbury Road, Ridgefield, CT 06877, (203) 438-1836, fax (203) 431-8712. George J. Goodstadt, owner. A wide range of antique posters, including American turn-of-the-century (i.e., Bradley, Rhead, and others), World Wars I and II, general advertising, European travel, British theater, American theater 1860-1910, and circus.

BAILLY GALLERY, 89 Fifth Avenue #901, New York, NY 10003, (212) 627-4398, fax (212) 932-1703. Nicolas Bailly, owner. A wide range of posters from Lautrec to Warhol, including Cassandre, Chéret, Colin, Mucha, etc. Large and decorative a specialty, such as Villemot and Razzia.

BARBARA LEIBOWITS GRAPHICS LTD., 80 Central Park West, New York, NY 10023, (212) 769-0105, fax (212) 769-0058. By appointment only, Barbara Leibowits, president. Fine prints, posters, and modern illustrated books. Specializing in Art Nouveau, Art Deco, Dada, surrealism, and Russian avant-garde.

BARCLAY—SAMSON LTD., 39 Inglethorpe Street, London, England, SW6 6NS, (071) 381-4341, fax (071) 610-0434. By appointment only, Richard Barclay. General stock of posters, specializing in British Rail.

BERNICE JACKSON FINE ARTS, P.O. Box 1188, Concord, MA 01742, (508) 369-9088. Bernice Jackson, owner. Fine arts consultant offering a wide range of posters, and specializing in posters of several countries such as Italy, Holland, Switzerland, Russia, and others.

CHISHOLM GALLERY, 89 Fifth Avenue, ninth floor, New York, NY 10003, (212) 243-8834, fax (212) 929-6398. Gail Chisholm, owner. Recently relocated after eighteen years in business. Collectors and dealers welcome. Emphasis on decorative French, British Rail, and American turn-of-the-century publishing.

CHISHOLM PRATS GALLERY, 145 Eighth Avenue, New York, NY 10011, (212) 741-1703. Robert Chisholm, owner. Vintage advertising posters from the 1890s to 1950s. Vast selection of movie, travel, product, and WWI and WWII posters.

CINEMA CITY, P.O. Box 1012. Muskegon, MI 49443, (616) 722-7760, fax (616) 722-4537. Jim Valk. Specializing in contemporary movie posters of the 1970s to 1990s. Also Hollywood photos, autographed items, scripts, and thousands of other items. Current catalog $3.00.

CIRCA 1900/EUROPEAN & AMERICAN GRAPHICS, 4 Helena Court, Morganville, NJ 07751, (908) 536-2874, fax (908) 972-6250. By appointment only, Barbara Kaplan. Specializing in turn-of-the-century original prints, posters, drawings, paintings, and illustrated books by European and American artists, with emphasis on Japonisme and the Belle Epoque.

CLUB OF AMERICAN COLLECTORS OF FINE ARTS, INC., 1 Lincoln Plaza, Suite 21 K, 20 West Sixty-fourth Street, New York, NY 10023, (212) 769-1860, fax (212) 873-1853. Jacques Athias, president. Museum-quality works of the Art Nouveau and Art Deco periods: Toulouse-Lautrec, Mucha, Chéret, Steinlen, Cassandre, as well as other artists from the Belle Epoque.

COLLETTI GALLERY, 67 East Oak Street, Chicago, IL 60611, (312) 664-6767. Russell Colletti, owner. Original American and European lithographic posters 1890-1950. Ongoing poster show with special features quarterly. Residential and corporate consulting.

CRAIG FLINNER GALLERY, 505 North Charles Street, Baltimore, MD 21201, (410) 727-1863. Craig Arthur Flinner, owner. Old print and map gallery carrying a selection of American and European posters. No catalog but will respond to "want" lists.

DWIGHT CLEVELAND, P.O. Box 10922, Chicago, IL 60610-0922, (312) 266-9152. By appointment only, Dwight Cleveland, owner. Movie posters wanted; highest prices paid for lobby cards, one-sheet, three-sheets, window cards, glass slides, etc. Guide to movie poster sizes available free with 29-cent stamp.

EASTERN EUROPEAN ART COMPANY, 0061 Arapahoe, Carbondale, CO 81623, (303) 963-8789. Judy Sullivan. Specializing in Polish posters 1945-1980s. Subject matter includes American and Foreign films, sports, music, political, circus, theater, travel, and exhibits.

FRANK FOX, 51 Merbrook Lane, Merion, PA 19066, (215) 667-4725. Frank Fox is a professor of history, specializing in Eastern Europe. His series of articles on Polish poster artists has appeared in The *World & I* magazine, *The Poster Quarterly*, and other publications. Posters from his collection have been exhibited at Philadelphia's Port of History Museum and at Lincoln Center.

FUSCO & FOUR, ASSOCIATES, 1 Murdock Terrace, Brighton, MA 02135, (617) 787-2637. Tony Fusco and Robert Four. Poster appraisal, brokering, and curatorial services for private collectors and institutions. As dealers, specializing in signed fine prints, 1900–1950, with occasional posters by artists who were also printmakers: Rockwell Kent, Robert Bonfils, Manuel Robbe, and others, with an emphasis on the Art Deco period. Also available: *The Confident Collector Art Deco Identification and Price Guide* (Avon Books, 1993), $21, postpaid.

GARY BORKAN ANTIQUES, Box 870, Melrose MA 02176, (617) 662-5757. By appointment only, Gary Borkan, owner. Wide range of antique graphics, including travel, military, and advertising posters.

GRAPHIC EXPECTATIONS, INC., 757 West Diversey, Chicago, IL 60614, (312) 871-0957, fax (312) 871-9978. Arthur Bernberg, director. A premiere gallery specializing in contemporary posters for the performing arts. More than fifty thousand titles covering film, theater, television, music, dance, "Mobil Masterpiece Theater," and other related topics.

HARRIS GALLERY, 3032 Claremont Avenue, Berkeley, CA 94705, (800) 458-6609, fax (510) 658-4851. Stephen Harris, president. Specializing n European and American posters from 1885 to 1950, in all subject areas. One of the largest selections of classic original posters.

HARVEY ABRAMS BOOKS, P.O. Box 732, State College, PA 16804, (814) 237-8331, fax (814) 237-8332. By appointment only, Harvey Abrams, owner. Specializing in the Olympic Games and history of sport. An Olympic historian who deals in original poster art, books, medals, and Olympic memorabilia.

HELLER AND HELLER/POSTERS AT WORK, 50 Webster Avenue, New Rochelle, NY 10801, (914) 235-0300, fax (914) 235-0314. By appointment only, John L. Heller, president. Specializing in American work incentive posters, particularly those produced by Mather & Company. Also, an ever-changing eclectic collection of American and European posters of outstanding graphic quality.

HIRSCHL AND ADLER GALLERIES, INC., 21 East Seventieth Street, New York, NY 10021, (212) 535-8810, fax (212) 772-7237. Joseph Goddu, director of American Prints. Emphasizing American art posters of the 1890s.

JANE MOUFFLET GALLERY, 8840 Beverly Boulevard, Los Angeles, CA 90048, (310) 275-3629, and 1 Marche Bîron, 85 Rue des Rosiers, 93400 St. Ouen, France, 40 10-84-09. Jane Moufflet, owner. Mainly French posters from 1900 to 1950s, with specializations in of Mucha, Colin, Cassandre.

KATE HENDRICKSON, 1211 North La Salle, Suite 703, Chicago, IL 60610, (312) 751-1932. By appointment only, Kate Hendrickson, owner. European advertising art with an emphasis on Italian posters, ads, magazine covers, and miscellaneous ephemera (1860s-1960s).

KELLENBERGER COLLECTION, Chemin Planaz 22, Blonay, Montreux, Switzerland CH-1807, 41-21-943-4444, fax 41-21-943-4888. By appointment only, Eric Kellenberger, owner. Specializing in fine, rare quality poster design by top artists. Permanent international display of more than seven thousand different posters of all periods. Exposition catalog "La Femme S'Affiche" (The Woman in Poster Art) available for $30. Sales catalog $10, postpaid.

KEN TROMBLY, 1825 K Street NW Suite 901, Washington, D.C., 20006, (202) 887-5000, fax (202) 457-0343. By appointment only, Ken Trombly, owner. Collector/dealer Ken Trombly—"the Sultan of Swap"—buys, trades, and sells magic posters and related memorabilia. Occasional lists are available.

KEZAR GALLERY, 4 Battery Street, Boston, MA 02109, (617) 720-2283, fax (617) 720-0076. Guild Nichols, owner. Specializing in early 20th century poster art for interior design. Offering consulting services for private and corporate collections.

KIKI WERTH POSTERS, 185 Westbourne Grove, London, England, W11 2SB, 071-229-7026, fax 071-229-4532. By appointment only, Kiki Werth, owner. Specializing in British posters, but a wide variety of other posters always in stock.

LA BELLE EPOQUE VINTAGE POSTERS, INC., 282 Columbus Avenue, New York, NY 10023, (212) 362-1770, fax (212) 362-1843. Linda Tarasuk or Elie Saporta, owners. One of the world's largest collections of Art Nouveau to Art Deco lithographic posters from as early as the turn of the century.

LARRY EDMUNDS BOOKSHOP, INC., 6644 Hollywood Boulevard, Hollywood, CA 90028, (213) 463-3273. Mike Hawks. Specializing in books on movies, theater, and television. Sells original and reproduction photographs from silent and sound films. Has many original posters, lobby cards, and fan magazines.

THE LAST MOVING PICTURE COMPANY, 2044 Euclid Avenue, Cleveland, OH 44115, (216) 781-1821, fax (216) 579-9172. Morris Everett, Jr., owner. We specialize in vintage movie memorabilia. We deal in movie posters, half-sheets, inserts, lobby cards, stills, and other sizes. Also organizers of the annual "Vintage Poster Art Convention & Auction" in Cleveland, Ohio, each spring.

THE LAST MOVING PICTURE COMPANY, 6307 Hollywood Boulevard, Hollywood, CA 90028, (213) 467-0838. Mike Nemeth, manager. We specialize in vintage movie memorabilia, concentrating on better titles from 1920s to 1950s. We buy, trade, and sell.

LUCY BROIDO GRAPHICS, LTD., (215) 527-3415. By appointment only, Lucy Broido, owner. Fine, original Art Nouveau ant Art Deco posters from the nineteenth and early twentieth centuries. Working with the trade and serious collectors.

MARIO CARRANDI COMPANY, INC., 122 Monroe Avenue, Belle Mead, NJ 08502-4608, (908) 874-0630, fax (908) 874-4892. By appointment only, Mario Carrandi, president. Vintage pre-1930 circus, magic, wild West, and entertainment posters.

MARK WILSON, P.O. Box 340, Castle Rock, WA 98611, (206) 274-9174. Mr. Wilson is an avid collector of cartoon film posters, and a dealer in comic books.

MEEHAN MILITARY POSTERS, P. O. Box 477, Gracie Station, New York, NY 10028, (212) 734-5683, fax (212) 535-4249. By appointment only, Mary Ellen Meehan, owner. Forty-eight-page catalog of World War I and World War II original posters containing descriptions and color illustrations of more than five hundred posters ($10). Prices range from $50 to $10,000, with most reasonably priced at between $100 and $200.

MOVIE ART ORIGINAL FILM POSTERS, P.O. Box 164291, Austin, TX 78716-4291, (512) 479-6680, fax (512) 480-8225. By appointment only, Kirby McDaniel, owner. Original posters and lobby cards from the international cinema from 1900 to the present. Computerized data base of inventory, and we describe and sell posters over the phone, and/or send photos for customer evaluation. We broker posters from other sources. We specialize in large posters.

MOVIE POSTER SHOP, #9 3600 Twenty-first Street NE, Calgary, Alberta, T2E 6V6, CANADA, (403) 250-7588. Robert Candel. Original movie posters and lobby cards. More than ten thousand titles in stock from the present to the 1930s. Poster reproductions and prints of nonmovie material. Mail-order catalog available for $3.

NANCY STEINBOCK POSTERS AND PRINTS, 197 Holmes Dale, Albany, NY 12208, (800) 438-1577, fax 446-1649. By appointment only, Nancy Steinbock, owner. Wide variety: Art Deco, Art Nouveau, product advertising, travel, war, sports, airplanes, ships, bicycles, literary, theatrical, etc. Always looking to purchase collections of vintage posters.

THE PAPER MAN, 8213 Scotch Bend Way, Potomac, MD 20854, (301) 299-6087, by appointment and at shows. Samuel and Ruth Rondberg, owners. An eclectic collection of antique posters, with special emphasis on travel and patriotic posters.

PARK SOUTH GALLERY, 885 Seventh Avenue, New York, NY 10019, (212) 246-5900, fax (212) 541-5716. Laura Gold, president. Original lithographic antique posters, Art Nouveau and Art Deco. We specialize in quality top-of-the-line items; largest collection of Mucha and Chéret available.

PASQUALE IANNETTI ART GALLERIES, INC., 522 Sutter Street, San Francisco, CA 94102, (415) 433-2771, fax (415) 433-4105. Steven D. Little, vice president. Dealers in fine original prints and other works of art on paper from the sixteenth through twentieth centuries.

POSNER GALLERY, Milwaukee, WI (414) 273-3097, fax (414) 273-1436. By appointment only, Judith Posner, director. Specializes in nineteenth- and twentieth-century French and American, and other posters from the turn of the century to the present. We also publish contemporary posters and have a catalog.

THE POSTER COLLECTOR, 390 West End Avenue, New York, NY 10024, (212) 873-1893, fax (212) 769-9348. By appointment only, Mark J. Weinbaum, owner. Private dealer since 1976. Fine original European/American posters— decorative and product-oriented mix— from 1890s–1930s; 1950s–1970s Swiss and French art posters. Poster reference books and ephemera stocked.

THE POSTER MASTER, 215 Main Street, Chatham, NJ 07928, (201) 635-6505, fax (201) 635-0212. George Dembo, president. Vintage posters specializing in political, propaganda, and patriotic posters.

POSTER PLUS, 210 South Michigan Avenue, Chicago, IL 60604, (312) 461-9277, fax (312) 461-9084. David Gartler, president. Offering a wide variety of vintage posters: American and French turn-of-the-century, WWI and II, circus, London Underground, British Rail, Russian revolutionary, and Russian film. Catalog is available.

POSTERGRAPHICS, 376 South County Road, Palm Beach, FL 33480, (407) 833-8448. Peter Langlykke and Robert Perrin. General collection of European and American posters produced from the 1880s to 1950s. Broad representation of styles, subjects, sizes, and artists.

REINHOLD-BROWN GALLERY, 26 East Seventy-eighth Street, New York, NY 10021, (212) 734-7999, fax (212) 734-7044. Robert Brown or Susan Reinhold. Swiss and German posters 1905-1935. Avant-garde posters of the twentieth-century design movements, Cassandre, Hohlwein, Stomberg Brothers, Bernhard, Art Deco, and scarce contemporary posters.

STEPHEN GANELES ANTIQUE POSTERS AND PRINTS, P.O. Box 91, New York, NY 10012, (212) 674-7624. Stephen Ganeles, owner. Specializing in vintage posters and prints (1890-1950), especially from the Art Deco period; travel and transportation posters; French decorative posters; Dutch posters, including the Amsterdam school. Catalogs occasionally available.

STEVE TURNER GALLERY, 7220 Beverly Boulevard, Los Angeles, CA 90036, (213) 931-1185, fax (213) 931-1187. Steve Turner, owner. Avant-garde poster design 1900-1950, including Russian film and propaganda; American WPA, travel, etc.; Danish, especially those by Sven Brasch. No common French posters.

THACKREY & ROBERTSON, 2266 Union Street, San Francisco, CA 94123, (415) 567-4842, fax (415) 567-1355. Sally Robertson. Established in 1970, Thackrey & Robertson specializes in old and rare posters in their original editions; we also handle the posters of David Lance Goines.

THOMAS G. BOSS FINE BOOKS, 355 Boylston Street, Boston, MA 02116, (617) 421-1880, fax (617) 536-7072. Tom Boss, owner. Posters from 1890–1940. Arts and Crafts, Art Nouveau, Art Deco. American, English, and Continental artists, especially those who designed book and magazine posters.

TWENTIETH CENTURY LIMITED, 89 Charles Street, Boston, MA 02114, (617) 742-1031, Wendy Rubin, owner. Dealing in European and American advertising posters 1880s-1960s. The collection is comprised of food and drink, general products, travel, exhibition, WWI and II, entertainment, and British Railway posters.

VINTAGE EUROPEAN AND AMERICAN POSTERS, 245 Ocean Drive—1019, Miami Beach, FL 33139, (305) 673-8145, and in NY, (516) 931-2787. By appointment only, Richard Rudnitsky, owner. We carry a large and varied collection of decorative and fine posters.

VINTAGE MOVIE POSTERS, 23 East Tenth Street, New York, NY 10003, (212) 477-2499. By appointment only, Sam Sarowitz. Buy, sell, trade vintage movie posters and lobby cards from 1900 to the 1970s.

VINTAGE POSTERS INTERNATIONAL, LTD., 1551 North Wells Street, Chicago, IL 60610, (312) 951-6681, fax 951-6565. Susan Cutler, president.

Specializing in European and American posters 1880-1990. We have one of the largest and most diverse collection in the Midwest, including product advertising, transportation, theater, opera, war, aviation, film, etc.

WILLIAM R. DAVIS FINE ARTS, 737 Park Avenue, Suite 2B, New York, NY 10021, (212) 988-4886, fax (212) 988-4676. By appointment only, Benno Bordiga, managing director. A private dealer specializing in works on paper from the late nineteenth and early twentieth centuries. With more than one hundred original Toulouse-Lautrec works in our inventory, our selection is unmatched.

SHOW MANAGEMENT/CONVENTIONS

LOUPRO, LTD./INTERNATIONAL VINTAGE POSTER FAIR, 138 West Eighteenth Street, New York, NY 10011, (212) 206-0499, fax (212) 727-2495. Louis Bixenman, director. Biannual fair of original vintage posters with exhibitors from Europe and throughout the United States held each spring and fall in New York and Chicago.

MOVIE IMAGES LEASING

EVERETT COLLECTION, 117 West Twenty-sixth Street, third floor, New York, NY 10001, (212) 255-8610, fax (212) 255-8612. By appointment only, Ron Harvey, manager. From a library of 2.5 million movie images, you can lease images for whatever your needs. For rates, please call.

GRAPHIC DESIGNER COLLECTION

THE PUSHPIN GROUP, 215 Park Avenue South, New York, NY 10003, (212) 674-8080, fax (212) 674-8601. Seymour Chwast, president. More than fifty posters and limited-edition prints by world-renowned artist Seymour Chwast, whose works are in museum collections all over the world. His work has been featured in galleries in Asia, Europe, and the United States. The Pushpin Group was the first graphic design group from the United States to be honored with a retrospective show at the Louvre.

MUSEUMS AND COLLECTIONS

ART INSTITUTE OF CHICAGO, Michigan Avenue at Adams Street, Chicago, IL 60603, (312) 443-3600. Anselmo Carini, associate curator, Department of Prints and Drawings. A fine group of nineteenth-century French posters, including almost all posters done by Toulouse-Lautrec, plus Theophile Steinlen and Alphonse Mucha. Hours: Monday, Wednesday-Friday, 10:30-4:30; Tuesday, 10:30-8:00; Saturday, 10:00-5:00; Sunday, 12:00-5:00. Recommended admission: adults, $6; students, $3.

THE BALTIMORE MUSEUM OF ART, 10 Art Museum Drive, Baltimore, MD 21218, (410) 396-6347, fax (410) 396-7153. Jay M. Fisher, curator of Prints, Drawings, and Photographs. An important collection of posters, a part of its world-renowned prints and drawings collection. Particular strengths include French nineteenth-century examples by Lautrec, Chéret, Steinlen, and others; turn-of-the-century Art Nouveau posters; and an extensive number of World War I and II posters. The Museum mounts occasional exhibitions utilizing this collection. Otherwise posters can be viewed by appointment in the BMA's Samuel H. Kress Foundation for Prints, Drawings, and Photographs offices. Hours: Wednesday-Friday, 10:00-4:00; Saturday-Sunday, 11:00-6:00. Admission: adults, $5.50; Ages seven to eighteen, $1.50; students and seniors, $3.50; No admission on Thursday. Free to members and age six and under.

BILLY ROSE THEATER COLLECTION, New York Public Library for the Performing Arts, 40 Lincoln Center Plaza, New York, NY 10023-7498, (212) 870-1639. Bob Taylor, curator. Documents all areas of public entertainment. We collect materials in all formats, including posters, photographs, programs, scripts, archival collections, and books. Hours: Monday-Saturday, 12:00-6:00.

BRIDGEPORT PUBLIC LIBRARY, HISTORICAL COLLECTIONS, 925 Broad Street, Bridgeport, CT 06604, (203) 576-7417. Mary K. Witkowski, head librarian. Posters and broadsides include circus posters from the nineteenth century to the present. Hours: Tuesday, 9:00-5:00; Wednesday and Thursday, 11:00-7:00; Friday and Saturday, 9:00-5:00.

COOPER-HEWITT, NATIONAL MUSEUM OF DESIGN, 2 East Ninety-first Street, New York, NY 10128, (212) 860-6893, fax (212) 860-6909. Marilyn Symms, curator of Drawings and Prints. A selection of more than one thousand American, European, and Japanese posters, mostly twentieth century, with special emphasis on the posters of E. McKnight-Kauffer (1890-1954). Hours: Tuesday, 10:00-9:00; Wednesday-Saturday, 10:00-5:00; Sunday, 12:00-5:00; closed Monday. Admission: adults, $3; students and senior citizens, $1.50; children under twelve, free.

EDISON POSTER ARCHIVE, Box 1211, Glastonbury, CT 06033, (800) 527-5633. Matthew E. Schapiro, curator. Private archive organizing the most significant collection of film-related posters in the world.

HARRY RANSOM HUMANITIES RESEARCH CENTER, The University of Texas at Austin, Box 7219, Austin, TX 78713, (512) 471-4663, fax (512) 471-9646. Sue Murphy. Poster collection of 8,000 World War I posters (American, French, German, a few British); 600 World War II posters (primarily British and American); 250 Spanish Civil War posters; 100 Japanese occupation posters. Call for appointment, no admission.

HOOVER INSTITUTION ARCHIVES, Stanford University, Stanford, CA 94305, (415) 723-1687. Carol Leadenham, assistant archivist. Political posters from 1900 to the present. Thirty thousand cataloged posters from many countries, mostly American, British, French, German, and Russian, relating to twentieth-century history, including World Wars I and II and the Russian Revolution. Color slides of the posters may be purchased for $3 each. Hours: Monday-Friday, 8:15-4:45. Open to the public.

JANE VOORHEES ZIMMERLI ART MUSEUM, Rutgers University, George and Hamilton Streets, New Brunswick, NJ 08903, (908) 932-7237, (908) 932-8201. Trudy V. Hansen, curator of Prints and Drawings. Collection includes: French posters from the mid-nineteenth century through the 1920s, with a concentration of Chéret and lesser-known artists of the 1890s; Belgian posters from the 1890s through 1910; and a sampling of American posters of the 1890s. Call for hours and admission.

JERSEY CITY MUSEUM, 472 Jersey Avenue, Jersey City, NJ 07302, (201) 547-4584. Thomas Strider, collections manager. Permanent collection of American art and design, including nineteenth- and early twentieth-century posters and broadsides. Hours: Tuesday, Thursday-Saturday, 10:30-5:00; Wednesday, 10:30-8:00. Suggested donation $1.

LIBRARY OF CONGRESS, PRINTS AND PHOTOGRAPHS DIVISION, First and Independence SE, Washington, D.C. 20540 (202) 707-8726, fax (202) 707-6647. Elena G. Millie, curator of posters. The poster collection dates between ca. 1836 and the present, and is international in scope, numbering about one hundred thousand pieces. The collection includes works by the early poster masters as well as documenting the poster as an art form and as a tool of advertising, politics, and communication. Hours: 8:30-5:00.

MARGARET HERRICK LIBRARY, ACADEMY OF MOTION PICTURE ARTS AND SCIENCES, 333 South Lacienega Boulevard, Beverly Hills, CA 90211, (310) 247-3000. Linda Harris Mehr, director. More than thirteen thousand film posters from 1911 to the present. Where reference photos available, researchers view at no charge. Charge for retrieval of posters. Hours: Monday-Friday, 10:00-6:00; closed Wednesday.

MUSEUM OF THE CITY OF NEW YORK, 1220 Fifth Avenue, New York, NY 10029, (212) 534-1672, fax (212) 534-5974. Marty Jacobs, acting curator. Comprehensive collection of posters and window cards with reference to theatrical activity in New York City from mid-nineteenth century through the twentieth century. Call for hours and admission prices. Research fee, $25 per day.

MUSEUM OF MODERN ART, 11 West Fifty-third Street, New York, NY 10019, (212) 708-9750, fax (212) 708-9691. Jessica Schwartz, acting director of public information. Begun in 1935, the Museum of Modern Art's graphic design collection now numbers more than thirty-five hundred examples of poster art dating from 1880 to the present, representing outstanding artists from around the world. A small selection of the museum's poster holdings in continuously displayed at the entrance to the fourth-floor Architecture and Design galleries. In 1988 the museum organized The Modern Poster, a survey of more than 350 examples from its collection; the accompanying catalog ($50 cloth, $25 paper) is available from the MMA bookstore or by calling the mail-order department, (212) 708-9888. Hours: Friday-Tuesday, 11:00-6:00; Thursday, 11:00-9:00; closed Wednesday. Admission: adults, $7.50; full-time students and senior citizens, $4.50; children under sixteen accompanied by an adult, free; museum members, free; Thursday 5:00-9:00, pay what you wish.

PORTHOLES INTO THE PAST MUSEUM, 4450 Poe Road, Medina, OH 44256, (216) 725-0402, fax (216) 722-2439. Mickey Mishne, managing director. Featuring motor sports, auto/aviation racing, WWI and WWII-era vehicles, plances, ships in action, Bugatti, Cuneo, DeGrineau, Dryden/Deutsch, Cassandre, Lautrec, Moran. Open weekdays. Admission free.

WAR MEMORIAL MUSEUM OF VIRGINIA, 9285 Warwick Boulevard, Newport News, VA 23607, (804) 247-8523, fax (804) 247-8627. Bill Barker, registrar. U.S. and foreign military and propaganda posters, with special emphasis on World War I and World War II. Hours: Monday-Saturday, 9:00-5:00; Sunday 1:00-5:00. Admission: adults, $2; children, seniors, military, $1.

WEST POINT MUSEUM, U.S. Military Academy, West Point, NY 10996, (914) 938-2203. David Meschutt, art curator. The museum owns an extensive collection of twentieth-century posters primarily having to do with WWI and WWII. Hours: 10:30-4:15. Admission free.

THE WOLFSONIAN, 1001 Washington Avenue, Miami Beach, FL 33139, (305) 531-1001. Lynn Lambuth, development coordinator. The Wolfsonian has a collection of nearly fifty thousand objects of art and rare books dating from the late nineteenth to the mid-twentieth centuries. Through exhibitions, a fellowship program, and other activities, the Wolfsonian promotes education and awareness of the United States and Europe in the period 1885 to 1945. Hours: weekdays 1:00-5:00. Admission: adults, $1; seniors, 50 cents; free for members.

CONTEMPORARY POSTER PUBLISHERS

GRAPHIQUE DE FRANCE, 9 State Street, Woburn, MA 01801-2050, (617) 935-3405, (617) 935-5145. Kimberly Reddick, Marketing. Graphique de France publishes and distributes a wide range of posters featuring fine art, comtemporary, and photographic images. Catalog available.

LINCOLN CENTER POSTER PROGRAM, 132 West Sixty-fifth Street, New York, NY 10023, (212) 875-5018, fax (212) 875-5011. By appointment only, Thomas Lollar, director. Original silk-screen posters and signed prints commemorating Lincoln Center programs.

SCHOOL OF VISUAL ARTS, 209 East Twenty-third Street, New York, NY 10010, (212) 679-7350, fax (212) 725-3587. Girvan Douglas. Posters do their job as recruitment advertising for the college, but more than that, they have become a form of public art in New York, brightening otherwise dismal subway stations. Catalog $32, tax-deductible.

PERIODICALS

AFFICHE, P.O. Box 60224, 6800 Arnhem, the Netherlands, 31-85-430512, fax 31-85-460081. Wilma Wabnitz, publisher. *Affiche* is published four times a year in English. Subscription rate $78 (U.S.) airmail. *Affiche* is the only international poster magazine. Every issue contains more than one hundred full-color photographic reproductions of posters.

ART BUSINESS NEWS, 19 Old Kings Highway South, Darien, CT 06820, (203) 656-3402, fax (203) 656-1976. Sarah Seamark. Monthly trade news journal covering the art and framing industry in North America. Subscriptions are free to qualified galleries and retailers; $25 a year to others.

BIG REEL, Empire Publishing, Inc., Box 717, Madison, NC 27025-0717, (919) 427-5850, fax (919) 427-7372. Rhona Lemons. Movie collectibles—posters, films, video, books, publications, autographs, and more. Free catalogs.

CLASSIC IMAGES, P.O. Box 809, Muscatine, IA 52761-0809, (319) 263-2331, (319) 262-8042. Bob King, editor. Monthly newspaper with in-depth articles on classic films and memorabilia, conventions, videos, films, laser discs, film books, etc. Subscriptions: $27.50 (U.S.) for twelve months, $38.00 foreign.

JOURNAL OF THE PRINT WORLD, 1008 Winona Road, Meredith, NH 03253-9599, (603) 279-6479. Charles S. Lane, editor. Periodical in the field of rare print collecting. Published quarterly, with articles and advertisements covering six centuries of rare prints. For sample copy, write to the address above.

MOVIE COLLECTOR'S WORLD, P.O. Box 309, Fraser, MI 48026, (313) 774-4311, fax (313) 774-5450. Brian Bukantis, publisher. World's leading publication for poster and movie memorabilia dealers and collectors, having published over 425 consecutive biweekly issues. Sample, $3 United States, $5 foreign.

PAPER AND ADVERTISING COLLECTOR, Route 230 West, Mount Joy, CA 17552, (717) 653-1833. Doris Ann Johnson, editor. Monthly newspaper of the National Association of Paper and Advertising Collectors. Carrying features and advertising of interest to ephemera collectors. First-class subscription in United States, $25. No research or appraisal service.

PRINT COLLECTOR'S NEWSLETTER, 119 East Seventy-ninth Street, New York, NY 10021, (212) 988-5959. Jacqueline Brody, editor. A bimonthly publication specializing in articles and information on works of paper of all periods. Subscriptions: $60 for a year. For sample copy contact the address above.

RESTORATION/CONSERVATION

ANDREA PITSCH, PAPER CONSERVATOR, (212) 594-9676. By appointment only. Evaluation of condition, conservation treatment of art and historical artifacts on paper, including prints, drawings, watercolors, posters, documents. Examination and condition reporting on artworks prior to purchase, evaluation and recommendations regarding storage facilities of private and public collections.

J. FIELDS, INC., 163 Varick Street, sixth floor, New York, NY 10013, (212) 989-4520. Larry Toth. Our process includes linen mounting, replacement of paper, and color restoration. J. Fields utilizes conservation techinques developed over the course of fourteen years of quality service.

KATHRYN MYATT CAREY ASSOCIATES, 24 Emery Street, Medford, MA 02155, (617) 396-9495. Kathryn Myatt Carey, conservator. Offering a full range of conservation services for works of art on paper, manuscripts, posters, historic wallpaper, and books. Facility, environmental, and conservation surveys. Disaster, grant, storage, exhibition, and project planning.

POSTER PLUS, 210 South Michigan Avenue, Chicago, IL 60604, (312) 461-9277. David Gartler, president. Fabric mounting and restoration of vintage posters. Services also include Japan paper backing, deacidification, encapsulation, and relining.

POSTER RESTORATION STUDIO, 7466 Beverly Boulevard #205, Los Angeles, CA 90036, (213) 934-4219, fax (213) 934-0929. By appointment only, Igor Edelman. Major restorer for Christie's New York. Twenty-five years of professional experience in double-mounting on Japan paper and cotton canvas, using only acid-free materials. Restoration of damaged artwork from rotten, torn, or missing sections. All work fully guaranteed.

❦ BIBLIOGRAPHY ❦

NOTE: The extensive bibliography that follows is intended to give readers numerous starting points for delving further into the world of posters. More has been written about poster art than any other form of advertising, and more good resources continue to appear every year.

EXHIBITION CATALOGS

1936. *Posters by Cassandre*. Catalog by E. M. Fantl. New York: the Museum of Modern Art, 1936.

1950. *Vingt-Cinq Ans d'Affiches Parisiennes*. Catalog by Georges Duthuit. Lucern: Kunstmuseum Luzern.

1967. *The American Poster*. Catalog by Edgar Breitenbach and Margaret Cogswell. New York: the American Federation of Arts in association with October House, 1967.

1968. *Toulouse-Lautrec and His Contemporaries*. Catalog by Ebvia Feinblatt. Los Angeles County Museum of Art in association with New York: Harry N. Abrams, 1968.

1970. *La Belle Epoque: Belgian Posters, Watercolors and Drawings*. Catalog by Yolande Oostens-Wittamer. International Exhibitions Foundation in association with New York: Grossman Publishers, Inc., 1970.

1971. *American Posters of Protest 1966-1970*. Catalog edited by David Kunzle. New York: New School Art Center, 1971.

1972. *Will Bradley: American Artist and Craftsman (1868-1962)*. New York: Metropolitan Museum of Art, 1972.

1972. *L'Affiche Anglaise: Les Années '90*. Catalog of the British poster exhibition. Paris : Musée des Arts Décoratifs.

1974. *American Posters of the Nineties.* Introduction by Roberta Wong. Boston: Boston Public Library, 1974.

1976. *San Francisco Rock Poster Art.* Catalog by Walter Medeiros. San Francisco: San Francisco Museum of Modern Art, 1976.

1976. *Les Arts du Spectacle en France—Affiches Illustrés 1850-1950.* Catalog by Nicole Wild. Paris: Bibliotheque de l'Opera, 1976.

1977. *Le Café Concert 1870-1914.* Catalog by Alain Weill. Paris: Musée des Arts Décoratifs, 1977.

1978. *Poster Art in Poland.* Catalog by Joseph S. Czestochowski. Washington, D.C.: Smithosonian Institution, 1978.

1978. *Herbert Matter: A Retrospective.* A & A Gallery, School of Art, Yale University. New Haven: Yale University, 1978.

1980. *Retrospective Jean Carlu.* Catalog edited by Alain Weill. Paris: Musée de l'Affiche, 1980.

1980. *L'Affiche en Belgique 1880-1980.* Catalog by Alain Weill. Paris: Musée de L'Affiche, 1980.

1980. *Das Pilnische Plakat (The Polish Poster).* Berlin: Hochschule der Kunst and Warsaw: Polish Poster Museum.

1981. *Cappiello.* Catalog of the exhibition. Paris: Galerie Nationale du Grand Palais, 1981.

1982. *Deutsche und Europaische Plakate 1945-1959.* Munich: Muchen Stadmuseum, 1982.

1982. *Objects-Realismes Affiches Suisses 1905-1950.* Catalog by Eric Kellenberger. Paris: Bibliotheque Fornay, 1982.

1983. *Achille Mauzan.* Catalog of the exhibition. Paris: Musée de la Publicité, 1983.

1984. *Designed to Persuade: The Graphic Art of Edward Penfield.* Catalog by David Gibson. Yonkers, NY: Hudson River Museum, 1984.

1984. *The Modern American Poster.* Catalog by J. Stewart Johnson. The National Museum of Modern Art, Kyoto, and the Museum of Modern Art, New York, in association with New York: New York Graphic Society Books, and Boston: Little, Brown Co., 1983.

1984. *The 20th-Century Poster—Design of the Avant Garde.* Catalog by Dawn Ades. Walker Art Center, in association with New York: Abbeville Press, 1984.

1984. *L'Automobile et la Publicité.* Catalog of the exhibition. Paris: Musée de la Publicité, 1984.

1984. *Burkhard Mangold.* Catalog of the exhibition. Zurich: Kunstegewerbemuseum, 1984.

1985. *Emil Cardinaux.* Catalog of the exhibition. Zurich: Kunstegewerbemuseum, 1985.

1985. *Henri de Toulouse-Lautrec: Images of the 1890s.* Catalog edited by Riva Castelman and Wolfgang Wittrock. New York: Museum of Modern Art, 1985.

1986. *The Basel School of Design and Its Philosophy: The Armin Hofmann Years, 1946-1986.* Philadelphia: Goldie Paley Gallery, Moore College of Art, 1986.

1987. *American Art Posters of the 1890s.* Catalog by David Kiehl. New York: Metropolitan Museum of Art, 1987.

1987. *Jules Chéret, Creator of the Color Lithographic Poster.* San Francisco: Pasquale Iannetti Art Galleries, Inc., 1987.

1987-1989. *The Modern Dutch Poster.* Catalog by Prokopoff, Marcel, ed., and Franciscono, Marcel. Urbana: Krannert Art Museum, and Cambridge and London: The MIT Press, 1987.

1988. *The Modern Poster.* Catalog by Stuart Wrede. Museum of Modern Art, New York. New York: Museum of Modern Art in association with Boston: Little, Brown and Company.

1988. *Otto Baumberger 1889–1961.* Catalog of the exhibition. Zurich: Museum fur Gestaltung, 1988.

1988. *I Manifesti Mele.* Catalog of the exhibition of Mele posters at the Museo Deigo Aragona Pignatelli Cortes, Naples. Milan: Arnoldo Mondadori, 1988.

1989. *American Art Posters of the 1890s.* Catalog by Joseph Goddu. New York: Hirschl & Adler Galleries, Inc., 1989.

1990. *La Femme s'Affiche (The Woman in Poster Art)*. Catalog of the Kellenberger Collection exhibition. Montreux: Eric Kellenberger, 1990.

1991. *A. M. Cassandre*. Catalog of the exhibition. Tokyo: Metropolitan Teien Art Museum, 1991.

1992. *Un Voyage Gourmand*. Catalog of the exhibition. Paris: Musée de a Seita, 1992.

1992. *Deutsches Plakate 1888-1933*. Catalog of the exhibition at the Deutsches Historiches Museum, Berlin. Heidelberg: Edition Braus, 1992.

HISTORIC REFERENCES

Periodicals

> NOTE: Listed here are magazines and periodicals with articles and infor-
> mation about the development of the poster, as well as some with tipped-in
> color plates of posters themselves. Pages or plates from some of the follow-
> ing early editions have become collector's items in their own right.

1889-1913	*La Plume*, (biweekly), Paris
1894-1897	*The Chap-Book*, Chicago
1896-1897	*Bradley: His Book*, Springfield, Massachusetts
1896	*The Poster*, New York
1896	*Poster Lore*, Kansas City
1896-1900	*Les Maîtres de L'Affiche* (monthly), Paris
1897-1899	*L'Estampe et L'Affiche* (biweekly) Paris
1898-1901	*The Poster and Art Collector*, London
1899	*Poster Collector's Circular*, London
1899	*Album d'Affiches et d'Estampes Modernes*, (quarterly), Paris
1913-1921	*Das Plakat*, Berlin, originally published from 1910 to 1912 as *Mitteilungen des Vereins des Plakatfreunde*

1910-1930	*The Poster,* Chicago
1924 to date	*Modern Publicity,* London (annual), originally from 1924 as *Posters and Their Designers;* from 1925 as *Art and Publicity;* and from 1926 to 1930 as *Posters and Publicity*
1925-1930	*Vendre,* Paris
1925-1939	*Arts et Métiers Graphiques,* Paris (quarterly)
1941 to date	*Pramierte Plakate,* Zurich and Basel
1942 to date	*Die Besten Plakate des Jahres,* Basel, which changed its title in 1976 to *Schweizer Plakate*
1949-1973	*International Poster Annual,* New York

Other Periodicals

In addition to the preceding, numerous annual and periodical publications continue to be issued by the graphic design and advertising industries, including *Biennale Plakatu Warszawa,* Warsaw, 1966 to date; *Graphis Posters,* Zurich, 1973 to date; *The Lahti Poster Biennale,* Finland, 1973 to date; *The Best in Covers and Posters,* Washington, D.C., 1975 to date; and *World Advertising Review,* Eastbourne, U.K., 1985 to date. See also the resource guide for current periodicals that cover posters and poster collecting.

Books and Catalogs

Alexandre, Arsene, et al. *The Modern Poster.* New York: Charles Scribner's Sons, 1985.

Bauwens, M., et al. *Les Affiches Etrangères Illustrées.* Paris: Boudet, 1897.

Bolton, Charles Knowles. *A Descriptive Catalogue of Posters, Chiefly American, in the collection of Charles Knowles Bolton.* Boston: W. B. Jones, 1895.

Bolton, Charles Knowles. *The Reign of the Poster.* Boston: Winthrop B. Jones, 1895.

Flood, Ned Arden. *A Catalog of an Exhibition of American, Dutch, English, French and Japanese Posters from the Collection of Mr. Ned Arden Flood.* Meadville, PA: Flood and Vincent, 1897.

Hiatt, Charles. *Picture Posters*. London: George Bell, 1895 (reprinted 1976).

Maindron, Ernest. *Les affiches illustrées*. Paris: H. Launette, 1896.

Maindron, Ernest. *Les affiches illustrées 1886-1895*. Paris: G. Boudet, 1896.

Pollard, Percival. *Posters in Miniature*. New York: R. H. Russell, 1896.

Rodgers, W. S. *A Book of the Poster*. London: Greening & Co., 1901.

Sponsel, Jean Louis. *Das Moderne Plakat*. Dresden: Gerhard Kuhtmann, 1897.

BOOKS

> NOTE: See also books that accompanied the exhibitions listed at the front
> of this Bibliography.

OVERVIEWS

Ades, Dawn. *Twentieth Century Poster—Design of the Avant Garde*. New York: Abbeville Press, 1984.

Allner, Walter H. *Posters: 50 Designers Analyze Methods and Design*. New York: Reinhold, 1952.

Appelbaum, Stanley, ed. *The Complete "Masters of the Poster—All 256 Plates from "Les Maîtres de l'Affiche."* New York: Dover, 1990.

Battersby, Martin. *The Decorative Twenties*. New York: Walker & Company, 1969.

Barnicoat, John. *A Concise History of Posters*. New York and Toronto: Oxford University Press, 1980.

Circker, Hayward. *Golden Age of the Poster*. New York: Dover Publications, 1971.

Delhaye, Jean. *Art Deco Posters and Graphics*. London: Academy Editions, London, and New York: St. Martin's Press, 1977, 1984.

Fusco, Tony. *The Official Identification and Price Guide to Posters*. New York: House of Collectibles, 1990.

Gallo, Max. *The Poster in History*. New York: American Heritage Publishing, 1974.

de Harak, Rudolph, ed. *Posters by Members of the Alliance Graphique Internationale (1960-1985)*. New York: Rizzoli International, 1986.

Hillier, Bevis. *Posters*. New York: Stein and Day, 1969.

Hillier, Bevis. *100 Years of Posters*. New York: Harper & Row, 1972.

Holme, Bryan. *Advertising: Reflections of a Century*. London: Heineman, 1982.

Hutchinson, Harold F. *The Poster—An Illustrated History from 1860*. New York: The Viking Press, 1968.

Kauffer, Edward McKnight. *The Art of the Poster: Its Origin, Evolution and Purpose*. New York: Albert & Charles Boni, 1928.

Kery, Patricia Frantz. *Art Deco Graphics*. New York: Harry N. Abrams, 1986.

Kery, Patricia Frantz. *Great Magazine Covers of the World*. New York: Abbeville Press, 1982.

Menten, Theodore. *Advertising Art in the Art Deco Style*. New York: Dover Publications, 1975.

Müller-Brockmann, Josef and Shizuko. *History of the Poster*. Zurich: ABC Verlag, 1971.

Price, Charles Matlack. *Poster Design*. New York: G. W. Bricka, 1922.

Rennert, Jack. *Posters of the Belle Epoque: The Wine Spectator Collection*. New York: The Wine Spectator Press, 1990.

Rickards, Maurice. *The Rise and Fall of the Poster*. New York: McGraw Hill, 1971.

Sainton, Roger. *Art Nouveau Posters and Graphics*. New York: Rizzoli, 1977.

Sheldon, Cyril. *A History of Poster Advertising*. London: Chapman and Hall, 1937.

Weill, Alain. *The Poster—A Worldwide Survey and History*. Boston: G. K. Hall & Co., 1985.

Weill, Alain. *Affiches Art Deco*. Paris: Inter-Livres, 1990.

Wrede, Stuart. *The Modern Poster*. New York: Museum of Modern Art in association with Boston: Little, Brown and Company, 1988.

BOOKS BY COUNTRY

AMERICAN POSTERS

Berman, Levi. *Posters U.S.A.* New York: American Heritage Publishing Co., 1957.

DeNoon, Christopher. *Posters of the WPA (Works Progress Administration).* Los Angeles: Wheatley Press in association with Seattle: University of Washington Press, 1987.

Garrigan, John (intro). *Images of an Era: The American Poster 1945-1975.* Washington, D.C.: Smithsonian Institution, 1975.

Goines, David Lance. *The David Lance Goines Poster Book.* New York: Crown Publishers, 1979.

Goines, David Lance. *Goines: Posters 1968-1973.* Berkeley, CA: Saint Heironymous Press, 1973.

Goines, David Lance. *Goines Posters.* Natick, MA: Alphabet Press, 1985.

Hornung, Clarence P., ed. *Will Bradley Posters and Graphics.* New York: Dover Publications, 1974.

Johnson, J. Stewart. *The Modern American Poster.* National Museum of Modern Art, Kyoto, and the Museum of Modern Art, New York, in association with New York: New York Graphic Society Books, and Boston: Little, Brown Co., 1983.

Keay, Carolyn. *American Posters of the Turn of the Century.* New York: St. Martin's Press, 1975.

Kiehl, David W. *American Art Posters of the 1890s in the Metropolitan Museum of Art, Including the Leonard A. Lauder Collection.* New York: Metropolitan Museum of Art in association with Harry N. Abrams, 1987.

List, Vera, and Kupferberg, Herbert. *Lincoln Center Posters.* New York: Harry N. Abrams, 1980.

Ludwig, Coy. *Maxfield Parrish.* New York: Watson Guptill Publications, 1973.

Malhorta, Ruth; Thorn, Christina; et. al. *Das Frühe Plakat in Europa und den U.S.A.,* Volume I, *British and American Posters.* Berlin: Mann Verlag, 1973.

Margolin, Victor. American *Poster Renaissance*. New York: Watson-Guptill Publications, 1975.

Prescott, Kenneth W. *Prints and Posters of Ben Shahn*. New York: Dover Publications, 1982.

Shahn, Bernarda Bryson. *Ben Shahn*. New York: Harry N. Abrams Inc., 1972.

Wong, Roberta, and Hornung, Clarence P. *Will Bradley: His Graphic Art*. New York: Dover Publications, 1974.

AUSTRIAN POSTERS

Koschatsky, Walter, and Kossatz, Horst-Herbert. *Ornamental Posters of the Vienna Secession*. London: Academy Editions, and New York: St. Martin's Press, 1974.

BELGIAN POSTERS

Berko, Patrick and Viviane, and Rey, Stephane. *Fernand Toussaint 1873-1956*. Knokke-Zoute: Collection Berko, 1986.

Bernard, Marie-Laurence. *Affiches de la Cote Belge 1980-1950*. Brugge: Uitgeverji Marc van Wiele, 1992.

Malhorta, Ruth; Thorn, Christina; et. al. *Des Frühe Plakat in Europa und den U.S.A.*, Volume II, *French and Belgian Posters*. Berlin: Mann Verlag, 1977.

Oostens-Wittamer, Yolande. *De Belgische Affiche 1900*. Brussels: Koningklijke Bibliotheek, 1975.

DUTCH POSTERS

Dooijes, Dick. *A History of the Dutch Poster 1890-1960*. Amsterdam: Schellema & Holkema, 1968.

Prokopoff, Maracel, ed., and Franciscono, Marcel. *The Modern Dutch Poster*. Urbana: Krannert Art Museum, and Cambridge and London: The MIT Press, 1987.

ENGLISH POSTERS

Bernstein, David. *The Shell Poster Book.* London: Hamish Hamilton, 1992.

Campbell, Colin. *The Beggarstaff Posters.* London: Barrie & Jenkins, 1990.

Cooper, Austin. *Making a Poster.* London: The Studio, 1938.

Green, Oliver. *Art for the London Underground.* New York: Rizzoli, 1990.

Haworth-Booth, Mark. *E. McKnight Kauffer: A Designer and His Public.* London: Gordon Fraser, 1979.

Hudson, Derek. *James Pride, 1866-1941.* London: Constable, 1949.

Hutchinson, Harold F. *London Transport Posters.* London: London Transport Board, 1963.

Levey, Michael F. *London Transport Posters.* Oxford: Phaidon Press, 1976.

Malhorta, Ruth; Thorn, Christina; et al. *Das Frühe Plakat in Europa und den U.S.A.,* Volume I, *British and American Posters.* Berlin: Mann Verlag, 1973.

McKnight Kauffer, E. *The Art of the Poster.* London: Cecil Plamer, 1924.

Purvis, Tom. *Poster Progress.* London: The Studio, 1938.

Reade, Brian. *Aubrey Beardsley.* New York: Viking Press, and London: Studio Vista, Ltd., 1967.

Sparrow, Walter Shaw. *Advertising and British Art.* London: John Lane, 1974.

Steen, Marguerite. *William Nicholson.* London: Collins, 1943.

Strong, Ray. *London Transport Posters.* London: Phaidon, 1976.

FRENCH POSTERS

Abdy, Jane. *The French Poster: Chéret to Cappiello.* London: Studio Vista, 1969.

Adhemar, Jean. *Toulouse-Lautrec: His Complete Lithographs and Drypoints.* New York: Harry N. Abrams, 1965.

Adriani, Gotz. *Toulouse-Lautrec: The Complete Graphic Works*. London: Thames and Hudson, 1988.

Arwas, Victor. *Belle Epoque Posters and Graphics*. New York: Rizzoli International Publishers, 1978.

Arwas, Victor. *Berthon & Grasset*. Paris: Denoel, 1978.

Barigel, Rejane, and Zagrodski, Christophe. *Steinlen-Affichiste, Catalogue Raisonné*. Lausanne: Editions du Grand-Pont, 1986.

Bazin, Jean-Francois. *Les Affiches de Villemot*. Paris: Editions Denoel, 1985.

Baruch, Hugo. *Toulouse-Lautrec and Steinlen*. London: Modern Art Gallery, 1946.

Bouvet, Francis. *Bonnard: The Complete Graphic Work*. New York: Rizzoli, 1981.

Bridges, Ann, ed. *Alphonse Mucha: The Complete Graphic Works*. New York: Harmony Books, 1980.

Broido, Lucy. *French Opera Posters*. New York: Dover, 1976.

Broido, Lucy. *The Posters of Jules Chéret (a catalogue raisonné)*. New York: Dover, 1980.

Broido, Lucy. *The Posters of Jules Chéret, Second Edition (a catalogue raisonné)*. New York: Dover, 1992.

Brown, Robert K., and Reinhold, Susan. *The Poster Art of A. M. Cassandre*. New York: E. P. Dutton, 1979.

Cate, Phillip, and Gill, Susan. *Theophile-Alexandre Steinlen*. Salt Lake City: Gibbs Smith, 1982.

Defert, Theirry, and Lepape, Claude. *From the Ballets Russes to Vogue: The Art of Georges Lepape*. New York: Vendome Press, 1984.

Malhorta, Ruth; Thorn, Christina; et. al. *Das Frühe Plakat in Europa und den U.S.A.*, Volume II, *French and Belgian Posters*. Berlin: Mann Verlag, 1977.

Marx, Roger; Rennert, Jack; and Weill, Alain. *Masters of the Poster 1896-1900*. A softcover reproduction of all 256 plates of the *Maîtres de L'Affiche* as originally printed by Chaix 1896-1900. New York: Images Graphiques, Inc., 1977.

Millman, Ian. *Georges De Feure: Maître du Symbolisme et de l'Art Nouveau*. Courbevoie: ACR Editions, 1992.

de Montry, Annie, and Lepeuve, Francois. *Voyages: Les Affiches de Roger Broders.* Paris: Syros-Alternatives, 1991.

Mourlot, Fernand. *Les Affiches Originales des Maîtres de L'École de Paris: Braque, Chagall, Dufy, Leger, Matisse, Miró, Picasso.* Monte Carlo: A. Sauret, 1959.

Mouron, Henri. *A. M. Cassandre.* New York: Rizzoli, 1985.

Mucha, Jiri. *Alphonse Mucha.* London: Hamlyn Publishing Group, 1967.

Rennert, Jack. *100 Posters of Paul Colin.* New York: Images Graphiques, 1979.

Rennert, Jack, and Weill, Alain, *Mucha: The Complete Posters, and Panels (a catalog raisonné).* Boston: G. K. Hall, 1984.

Rennert, Jack and Weill, Alain. *Colin Affichiste.* Paris: Editions Denoel, 1991.

Schardt, Hermann, ed. *Paris 1900: Masterworks of French Poster Art.* New York: Putnam, 1970.

Weill, Alain. *100 Years of Posters of the Folies Bergère and Music Halls of Paris.* New York: Images Graphiques, 1977.

Wittrock, Wolfgang. *Toulouse-Lautrec: The Complete Prints.* London: Sotheby's Publications, 1985 (2 vols.).

GERMAN POSTERS

Malhorta, Ruth; Thorn, Christina, et. al. *Das Frühe Plakat in Europa und den U.S.A.,* Volume III, *German Posters.* Berlin: Mann Verlag, 1980.

Rademacher, Hellmut, trans. by Rhodes, Anthony. *Masters of German Poster Art.* New York: October House, 1966.

ITALIAN POSTERS

Curci, Roberto. *Marcello Dudovich—Cartellonista.* Trieste: Edizioni Lint, 1979.

Menegazzi, Luigi. *Il Manifesto Italiano.* Milan: Electra Editrice, 1976.

Sangiorgi, Giovanni; Mascherpa, Giorgia; and Veronesu, Giulia. *Grafica Ricordi.* Rome: Ente Premi, Ricordi, 1967.

Sparti, Pepa, ed. *L'Italia Che Cambia.* Florence: Artificio, 1989.

POLISH POSTERS

Amman, Dieter. *Polnische Plakatkunst.* Dortmund: Haremberg, 1980.

Kowalski, Tadeusz. *The Polish Film Poster.* Warsaw: Filmowa Agencja Wydawnicza, 1976.

Schubert, Zdislau. *Plakat Polski 1970-1978.* Warsaw: Filmowa Agencja Wydawnicza, 1979.

SWISS POSTERS

Margadant, Bruno, ed. *The Swiss Poster: 1900-1983* (text in German, French, and English). Basel: Birkhauser Verlag, 1983.

Rotzler, Willy, and Wobmann, Karl. *Political and Social Posters of Switzerland.* Zurich: ABC Verlag, 1985.

Rotzler, Willy; Scharer, Fritz; and Wobmann, Karl. *Das Plakat in der Schweiz* (text in German). Zurich: Ex Libris AG, 1991.

Triet, Max, and Wobmann, Karl, eds. *Swiss Sport Posters.* Zurich: ABC Verlag, 1983.

Tschanen, Armin, and Bangerter, Walter, eds. *Official Graphic Art in Switzerland.* Zurich: ABC Verlag, 1964.

BOOKS BY SUBJECT

CARE AND IDENTIFICATION OF POSTERS AND PRINTS

Dolloff, Francis W., and Perkinson, Roy L. *How to Care for Works of Art on Paper.* Boston: Museum of Fine Arts, 1985.

Gascoigne, Bamber. *How to Identify Prints.* New York: Thames and Hudson, 1986.

CINEMA POSTERS

Borst, Ron. *Graven Images: The Best of Horror, Fantasy and Science Fiction Film Art.* New York: Grove Press, 1992.

Brown, Jay A., and the editors of *Consumer Guide. Rating the Movies* (alphabetical movie listing and capsule reviews, not a book on the posters themselves). Skokie, IL: Publications International, Ltd., 1987.

Edwards, Gregory J. *International Film Poster: The Role of the Poster in Cinema Art, Advertising and History.* Topsfield, MA: Salem House Ltd., 1985.

Kobal, John. *Fifty Years of Movie Posters.* London: Hamlyn, 1973.

Morella, Joe; Epstein, Edward; and Clark, Eleanor. *Those Great Movie Ads.* New Rochelle, NY: Arlington House, 1972.

Rebello, Stephen, and Allen, Richard. *Reel Art: Great Movie Posters from the Golden Age of the Silver Screen.* New York: Abbeville Press, 1988.

Schapiro, Steve, and Cierichetti, David. *The Movie Poster Book.* New York: E. P. Dutton, 1979.

Scott, Kathryn Leigh. *Lobby Cards, the Classic Films: The Michael Hawks Collection.* London and Los Angeles: The Pomegranate Press, Ltd., 1987.

Scott, Kathryn Leigh. *Lobby Cards, the Classic Comedies: The Michael Hawks Collection, Volume II.* London and Los Angeles: The Pomegranate Press, Ltd., 1988.

Shipman, David. *The Great Movie Stars: The Golden Years* (guide to movies themselves, not posters). New York: Hill and Wang, 1979.

Shipman, David. *The Great Movie Stars: The International Years* (guide to movies themselves, not posters). New York: Hill and Wang, 1980.

MAGIC, CIRCUS AND THEATER

Andrews, Val. *A Gift from the Gods* (featuring a compendium of Chung Ling Soo Posters). New York: Goodlife Publications, 1981.

Christopher, Milbourne. *Panorama of Magic.* New York: Dover Books, 1962.

Christopher, Milbourne. *Magic: A Picture History*. New York: Dover Books, 1990. Reissue of *Panorama of Magic*.

Christopher, Milbourne. *The Illustrated History of Magic*. New York: Crowell, 1973.

Davis, Paul. *Paul Davis—Posters and Paintings*. New York: E. P. Dutton, 1977.

Fox, Charles Phillips. *American Circus Posters in Full Color*. New York: Dover, 1978.

Fox, Charles Phillips. *The Great Circus Street Parade in Pictures*. New York: Dover, 1978.

Haill, Catherine. *Theatre Posters*. London: Victoria and Albert Museum, 1983.

Hearn, Michael Patrick. *The Art of the Broadway Poster*. New York: Ballantine Books, 1980.

Price, David. *Magic: A Pictorial History of Conjurers in the Theatre*. Cornwall Books, 1985.

Rennert, Jack. *100 Years of Circus Posters*. New York: Darien House, 1976.

Reynolds, Charles and Regina. *100 Years of Magic Posters*. New York: Darien House, 1975.

ROCK POSTERS

Grushkin, Paul. *The Art of Rock*. New York: Abbeville Press, 1987.

King, Eric. *A Collector's Guide To the Numbered Dance Posters Created for Bill Graham and the Family Dog, 1966-1973*. Berkeley: Svaha Press, 1980.

TRAVEL AND TRANSPORTATION

Belves, Pierre. *Cent Ans d'Affiches de Chemin de Fer*. Paris: Editions NM/La Vie du Rail, 1981.

Camard, Florence, and Zagrodski, Christophe. *Le Train à l'Affiche*. Paris: La Vie du Rail, 1989.

Choko, Marc H., and Jones, David L. *Canadian Pacific Posters, 1883-1963*. Montreal: Meridian Press, 1988.

Cole, Beverly, and Durack, Rochard. *Railway Posters 1923-1947*. New York: Rizzoli, 1992.

Dubarry, Dominique. *100 Years of Auto Posters*. Paris: Maeght Editeur, 1990.

Hiller, Bevis. *Travel Posters*. New York: E. P. Dutton, 1976.

Hillion, Daniel. *La Montagne s'Affiche*. Rennes: Editions Ouest-France, 1991.

Peignot, Jerome. *Air France: Posters 1933-1983*. Paris: Fernand Hazan, 1988.

Rennert, Jack. *100 Years of Bicycle Posters*. New York: Darien House, 1973.

Shackleton, J. T. *The Golden Age of the Railway Poster*. Paris: New English Library, 1976.

Wobmann, Karl. *Tourist Posters of Switzerland*. Aarau: AT Verlag, 1980.

SPORTS

Chevallier, Jean-Pierre. *La Tennis à L'Affiche 1895-1986*. Paris: Albin Michel, 1986.

Durry, Jean. *Le Sport à L'Affiche*. Paris: Editions Hoebeke, 1988.

International Olympics Committee. *L'Olympisme par L'Affiche/Olympism Through Posters*. Lausanne: International Olympics Committee, 1983.

Wobmann, Karl, and Triet, Max. *Swiss Sport Posters*. Zurich: ABC Verlag, 1973.

WAR AND REVOLUTION

Cantwell, John D. *Images of War—British Posters 1939-45*. London: HMSO, 1989.

Crawford, Anthony. *Posters of World War I and World War II in the George C. Marshall Research Foundation*. Charlottesville, VA: The University Press of Virginia, 1979.

Darracott, Joseph. *The First World War in Posters*. New York: Dover, 1974.

Nelson, Derek. *The Posters That Won the War—The Production, Recruitment and War Bond Posters of WWII*. Osceola, WI: Motorbooks International, 1991.

Paillard, René. *Affiches 14-18* (French posters 1914-1918). Reims: Matot-Braine, 1986.

Paret, Peter; Lewis, Beth; and Paret, Paul. *Persuasive Images—Posters of War and Revolution*. Princeton, NJ: Princeton University Press, 1992.

Rawls, Walton H. *Wake up America!* New York: Abbeville Press, 1988.

Rickards, Maurice. *Posters of Protest and Revolution*. New York: Walker, 1970.

Rickards, Maurice. *Posters of the First World War*. New York: Walker, 1968.

Stanley, Peter. *What Did You Do in the War, Daddy?* Melbourne and New York: Oxford University Press, 1983.

Theofiles, George. *American Posters of World War I*. New York: Dafran House, 1973.

Zeman, Zbynek. *Art and Propaganda in World War II*. London: Orbis, 1978.

❦ INDEX ❦